Financial Data Science with SAS®

Babatunde O. Odusami

§.sas.

sas.com/books

Contents

About This Book

What Does This Book Cover?

The use of data science techniques such as machine learning, data visualization, and optimization is widespread in the financial services industry. However, it is very hard to find books and reference materials that explain the theory behind these techniques and how to implement them using real-world examples. There are also not that many instructional and reference materials for those interested in using SAS for financial data science, although SAS is arguably one of the best applications for tackling pretty much any type of analytics problems you might encounter in the finance domain, as you will see shortly in the book.

The book will provide readers with a comprehensive coverage of the theoretical and practical implementation of the various types of analytical techniques and quantitative tools that are used in the financial services industry using SAS as the main analytics platform. It will show you how to implement data visualization, simulation, statistical predictive models, machine learning models, and financial optimizations using real-world examples in the SAS analytics environment.

You will learn how to use visualizations to measure financial performance and examine the salient characteristics of financial and economic data. You will also learn how to implement various types of simulations and how to use simulations to build models of financial data, such as stock prices and capital project outcomes. You will be introduced to advanced applications of simulations, such as using simulations for risk management and pricing of derivatives contracts.

In subsequent chapters, you will be introduced to various statistical and machine-learning models and how they are used in the financial services industry. These include credit risk models, algorithmic trading models, economic analysis models, and strategic portfolio management models. You will also enhance your analytics skills with practice exercises that apply these models to real-world data.

In the last section of the book, you will learn about the various types of optimization techniques and how they are used to solve decision problems in finance. You will review and practice the use of optimization for capital budgeting, profit maximization, risk management, performance attribution, portfolio construction, and portfolio optimization.

The book is a reference material for anyone interested in learning more about how data science is used in the financial services industry and how to develop data science competencies in finance using the SAS Analytics suite.

Is This Book for You?

If you are interested in building competencies that will prepare you for career roles such as investment analyst, quantitative analyst, or financial data scientist, or just interested in learning more about how to use data science methods to improve your financial skills, then this book is for you. This book aims to make the data science journey in finance a much easier experience for everyone, both seasoned and aspiring data scientists. It is also a great handbook for data science generalists who would like to transition into financial data science. The book can be used for a semester-long course in financial data science for graduate or advanced undergraduate students in finance, mathematics, business analytics, and computer science programs.

SAS Programming Experience

Minimal SAS experience is required. You will be introduced to the fundamentals of SAS programming and the SAS Windowing environment in the early chapters before we delve into some of the more advanced topics. Some familiarity with programming logic and general finance and economic concepts (such as stocks, bonds, stock index, returns, risk, portfolios, income, capital projects, GDP, and unemployment) will be helpful. Most of the advanced concepts are also summarized in plain language, so you can focus your attention on the practical applications of the techniques that will be discussed. The book will also point you to where you can find additional resources from the vast repository of SAS support documentation and on the internet.

What Should You Know About the Examples?

This book includes many tutorials for you to follow so that you can gain hands-on experience with using SAS for solving a wide range of analytical problems that you might come across in the financial services industry. In many cases, the links between the statistical and economic theories and the SAS code in the book are highlighted so that you can see the connections between them. You will learn about the code, but more importantly why specific code or methods are relevant from the theoretical point of view.

Software Used to Develop the Book's Content

To get the full experience of the tutorials in the chapters and to complete the practice exercises, you will need access to the SAS 9.4 environment. You can access the SAS 9.4 environment using client applications such as SAS Studio, Enterprise Guide, and Enterprise Miner. The SAS 9.4 environment includes the Base SAS software. You will also need a license for SAS Analytics 15.3, which includes:

- SAS/ETS
- SAS/STAT

- SAS/IML
- SAS/OR
- SAS Enterprise Miner

If you are a student or employee of an academic institution, you can sign up for access to SAS OnDemand for Academics at https://welcome.oda.sas.com, which will give you access to all of the features above in a cloud-enabled environment. Independent learners can also sign up for SAS OnDemand for Academics for access to SAS Studio.

Example Code and Data

You can access all the SAS code and data for this book by visiting the book's GitHub page at https://github.com/finsasdata/bookdata.

In the GitHub repository, you will find two SAS programs that will enable you to easily download the data that you need for the tutorials and practice exercises. The first program (GitDownload. sas) will download the entire repository into a SAS library called FINDATA. The second program (Datapull.sas) is a SAS macro that you can invoke to download the data files as you need them. You should note that both programs will only work in the SAS environment. You will learn more about the code for both programs in the first two chapters of the book.

SAS OnDemand for Academics

This book is compatible with SAS OnDemand for Academics. If you are using SAS OnDemand for Academics, then begin here: https://www.sas.com/en_us/software/on-demand-for-academics.html.

Where Are the Exercise Solutions?

One of the great features of this book is the practice exercises at the end of each chapter. They will enable you to hone your skills in some of the techniques that you will come across in the book. You can request the solutions to the practice exercises through the book's GitHub repository.

About The Author

Babatunde Odusami, PhD, CFA, is a professor of finance at Widener University in Chester, PA. Alongside his academic roles, he's engaged in investment management and governance, corporate governance, and consulting. He received an MBA with a concentration in management information systems, as well as an MS and PhD in financial economics from the University of New Orleans. He is also a CFA charterholder. His research interests are in statistical and machine learning models that can explain how the values and risks of financial assets and portfolios evolve. His commentaries on financial topics are periodically featured in print and TV media.

Learn more about this author by visiting his author page at https://support.sas.com/en/books/authors/tunde-odusami.html. There you can download a free book excerpt, read the latest reviews, get updates, and more.

Acknowledgments

I would not have been able to write this book without the help and support of so many incredible people that are more than I can fit onto this page. But I would like to start by expressing my deepest gratitude to my late dad and my mum for inspiring me to have a deep appreciation for knowledge. And to my brothers and sisters, especially Gbenga, who continues to inspire and support me in all of my endeavors in life. I would also like to thank my amazing wife, Toyin, who has always been there for me since I was a doctoral student and honestly without whom I would not have had the resolve to write this book. And my daughters, Michelle and Abigail, who bring so much joy and happiness to my life. I appreciate how you periodically check-in on me to ask how you can help and what I am working on.

I would also like to thank my current and past students at Widener University, who inspired some of the topics presented in this book. Special thank you to everyone at SAS who made this book a reality, especially my developmental editor Catherine Connolly, who guided the book project from its ideation to its completion. To my technical reviewers, Sharad Saxena and Chip Wells, copy editor, Suzanne Morgen, and to Rick Wicklin, whose blog is my go-to for anything on the IML procedure.

Thanks to distinguished and emeritus professors, Yvonne Antonucci and Iqbal Mansur, both of whom encouraged me to extend my financial data science expertise into something more enduring. And to Kola Akinsomi, James Nguyen, Marius Mihai, and Irfan Safdar for their constructive feedback on the book.

Chapter 1: Financial Data Science: An Overview

Introduction

The primary job of a data scientist is to create value out of data. Although organizational data is commonly accepted as an intangible asset that presently cannot be capitalized on the balance sheet, it is now one the most lucrative means to create value. Indeed, the business models of some of the most valuable companies today are built on monetizing the data that they collect from the end-users of their platforms. As these types of companies continue to emerge and as other businesses continue to seek opportunities to extract value from their own data or data acquired from other businesses, the demand for data scientists is expected to continue to grow into the future.

There are academic programs such as computer science, data science, mathematics, and statistics that have a formal curriculum for those interested in pursuing a career in data science. There are also many data scientists who are self-taught as well as domain experts who pick up the skills along the way to enhance their functional knowledge of their business domain. Therefore, it is quite possible that we might see a reversal in the future where the data scientists are the domain experts working alongside a team of citizen data scientists who use data science techniques regularly, although their primary job function is not data science. This textbook is written for such professionals. It aims to provide professionals and students in graduate and advanced undergraduate programs with a rigorous foundation on the different types of data science tools in use in the financial services industry. The book is based on the SAS Analytics Platform, which provides end-to-end solutions for data science applications across all disciplines.

In this chapter, we will conduct an overview of financial data science. We will discuss the advantages and disadvantages of some of the common data science platforms that are currently available. We will also highlight some of the features of SAS that set it apart as the preferred tool for financial data science as well as showcase some simple practical applications of SAS in financial settings. We will conclude the chapter by delving into some of the key aspects of financial data science and emerging areas of concern as societies further embrace this novel approach to solving problems.

Data Science and Financial Systems

Data science and information systems are related fields in the sense that they both work with data. However, the focus of their relationships with data is distinct. Along the same lines, financial data science and financial information systems are also interrelated because they both work with financial data. Let's attempt to outline the differences between these domains in the next subsections.

Data Science

Science is the study of events, structures, patterns, and phenomena in the real world, through observations, experiments, and testable justification and predictions about how these events and patterns occur. For example, natural sciences (such as physics, chemistry, and biology) study the natural world, while social sciences (such as economics, finance, sociology, and anthropology) study human societies and the social interactions that occur within them. Data science is a unique field of science in the sense that it also studies aspects of the real world but uses data as the primary artifact. Data scientists do not necessarily require physical observations or experiments when conducting research but rely mostly on advanced computational methods, programming, and statistics to extract insights about the real world from the data. Years of advancements in computing and Internet connectivity have led to a deluge of data. Indeed, data is arguably the most ubiquitous resources available today. However, in the same way we create value by turning raw materials into finished products through our manufacturing processes, data also needs to be processed and analyzed to extract value from it. This requirement has led to the development of advanced analytical tools to sift through these massive amounts of data for actionable knowledge that might be buried in them. These advanced analytical tools include those that are created to allow us to depict large amounts of data in visually compelling forms, as well as those that allow us to iteratively combine, transform, explore, model, simulate, and discover hidden patterns in the data.

Another unique attribute of data science is its interdisciplinary applications. Data science techniques and data scientists can be found across all other disciplines. Indeed, most data scientists do not require extensive domain expertise to work in cross-disciplinary teams, which will typically include domain experts who will possess a deeper understanding of the essential body of knowledge in the areas of inquiry. Therefore, data scientists are unencumbered in terms of the business disciplines where they can practice their craft. For example, a data scientist could be working with a team of doctors to understand how patients are responding to specific types of therapies or with the marketing team of a firm to understand what types of sales incentives are more likely to elicit desired purchase decisions from current or prospective clients. Readers are more likely to see that the same data science techniques commonly used in one business discipline often transcend that discipline. This is because regardless of the area of inquiry, the underpinning of the tasks in which data science techniques are used is the data itself.

Shown in Figure 1.1 is a typical configuration of data science teams. In financial settings, the project owner could be a portfolio manager or a risk manager. Project owners typically bear the

Figure 1.1: Data Science Team Configuration

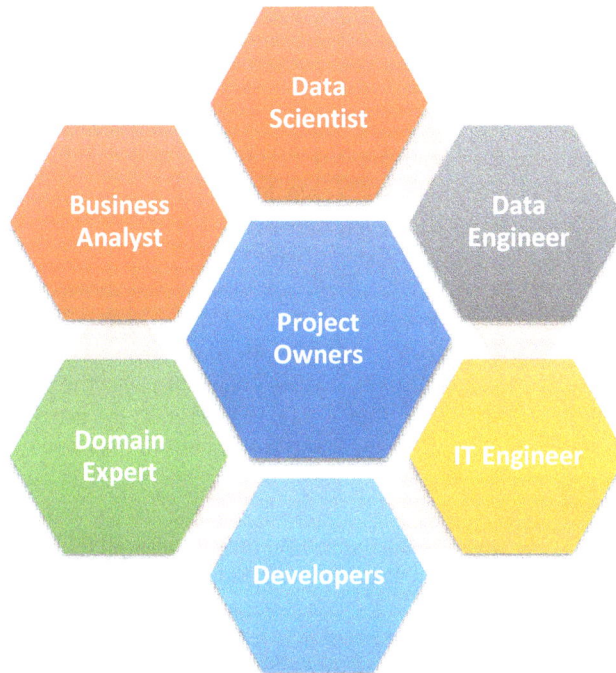

ultimate responsibility for the success or failure of the project. Data engineers are responsible for maintaining the software components of the infrastructure that are used for collecting, processing, and retrieving the business data that will be analyzed and modeled during the project. The main responsibilities of IT engineers are to design, install, and maintain the hardware component of the data infrastructure and any other systems that work in tandem with the data infrastructure to ensure that the project runs smoothly. The developers typically work with the data scientist to design and produce business applications and dashboards that incorporate the models developed by the data scientist as their building blocks. A domain expert would be someone with deep knowledge of the theory and/or practice in the area of inquiry such as a financial economist, trader, or risk officer. Business analysts are members of the team that is responsible for generating data-driven analysis for decision-makers. In finance settings, these would include investment or credit analysts. The data scientist interfaces with all of these entities to develop the algorithms and models that would solve the business problem that required the project.

Financial Data Science

Financial data science is an emerging sub-field of data science. It involves the creation of ad hoc analysis to answer specific business questions and forecast possible future financial scenarios. Finance as a sub-field of economics often uses theories to explain or predict the relationships between financial and economic variables.

Most financial theories do not work very well in the real world because they rely on assumptions that are often unrealistic or theories based on abstractions of the real world that are too limiting to function in modern societies. For example, a well-known financial theory asserts that the prices of financial assets evolve in a random manner such that it is impossible to accurately forecast their future prices by simply observing past price changes. The motivation for this theory is that rational, profit-maximizing investors will quickly arbitrage away any such predictable patterns. Thus, the only patterns that are observable in the financial markets are the unpredictable ones. This theory implies that any attempt to predict the future directions or specific attributes of financial markets using statistical or algorithmic models is essentially a futile effort. However, the conjecture of this theory is inconsistent with the reality that between 60-73% of equity trades and large proportions of fixed-income and currency trades that are executed in each of these markets are performed by applications that were developed using data science tools. It may be that these patterns are indeed predictable and that most investors lack the means or motivation to exploit them, leaving only those with the motivation and computational resources to do so. Even if they are not predictable as postulated by the theory, data science still provides many tangible benefits to the organizations that deploy them, as you will see shortly.

While theories might not provide perfect insights into how financial data behave, they still provide a solid framework to bring to bear other tools and methodologies that can further our understanding of how financial and economic variables behave in the real world. Thus, financial data science involves the application of new and established data science methods and techniques to business and financial data, to gain new insights into trends and relationships in the data that are not previously revealed in standard financial theories and models. It is important to note that financial data science is not a substitute for conventional financial and economic theories. Data science and theory are merely complementary tools that allow us to extend the scope of our understanding of how financial variables behave and consequently derive better forecasts of their future directions.

Business Applications of Financial Data Science

Finance is a business discipline that is mainly concerned with how financial resources are raised, allocated, and used to achieve an increase in the stock of wealth of individuals or organizations. There are some elements of risk entailed in each of these activities; hence, finance is also involved in risk identification, analysis, mitigation, and governance. Financial activities often generate large amounts of data, which generally have been collected and archived in a well-structured manner. For example, at the macro-level, there are publicly available and proprietary databases containing daily stock market information on all publicly listed companies in the US since the 1900s. As well as data on various economic variables, which have been systematically collected and curated for over 100 years. Organizations also possess large amounts of financial data that they typically collect for operational needs, such as revenue and cost data, which are normally collected for financial reporting or financial planning purposes. Hence, financial data are well-primed for the application of data science techniques.

Arguably, the financial services industry is one of the first industries to deploy data science techniques as tools for day-to-day business processes. These include a wide range of applications in the field of investment and risk management, as well as financial planning and forecasting. In investment settings, financial data science techniques such as predictive modeling, simulations, and optimizations are broadly used for decision-making, asset allocation, trading strategies, risk, and performance measurement purposes. In corporate finance settings, simulations and optimization are also used for capital sourcing, capital expenditure analyses, revenue and profit optimization, and risk management. In insurance and financial intermediation settings, predictive modeling, simulations, and optimizations are used for risk measurement, analysis, pricing, and governance.

More recent innovations in the applications of financial data science techniques are in the financial technology (FinTech) spaces, where all of the previously mentioned tools are used to create platforms and products that are essentially designed to disintermediate the flow of funds between lenders and borrowers, and investors and investment opportunities. In subsequent chapters of this book, we will explore various data science techniques and their common applications in finance settings.

Financial Information Systems

Information systems are organized methods for collecting, processing, archiving, reproducing, and analyzing business data. Financial information systems are perhaps the most widely used information systems since all organizations require some type of organized approach to managing their financial records and making plans for their future financial needs and investments. Modern financial information systems, which could range from a simple Microsoft Excel workbook or Access database to mid-level accounting software such as Intuit QuickBooks and Oracle NetSuite, or even more sophisticated enterprise or custom solutions, are typically computerized systems that collect, process, archive, reproduce, and provide analysis of the financial data that are stored in them.

Financial information comes in different forms depending on the needs of the entity. For a retail organization, financial information could be sales data collected through interfaces such as point-of-sales (POS) systems, or price data received as Extensible Business Reporting Language (XBRL) file from the supplier, or inventory data, which are created and tracked using radio frequency identification (RFID) tags. This information is then processed to fit a specific format and archived in the databases, for future reproduction and analysis depending on the organization's needs.

Financial information systems used in the financial services industry vary from those used in retail and manufacturing organizations because of the unique nature of the industry. The industry is highly regulated, and its operations and financial structure are usually different from other business sectors. The financial services industry is also quite broad. It is comprised of a wide range of businesses, including depository and non-depository institutions, investment companies and intermediaries, capital market makers, insurance companies, and the more recent financial technology (FinTech) companies.

Components of Information Systems

All information systems consist of elements that work together to meet the organizational objective. In general, components of financial information systems include:

- **Hardware**: This is the physical component of the information system, including computers, peripherals, and media devices. Peripheral devices include input (such as POS, barcode, and QR code readers), output devices (such as displays, printers, and speakers), and media devices, which are disks on which the information is typically stored.
- **Software**: Two types of software are used in information systems. System software is the program used to control the hardware. Application software includes sets of packaged code that are used to collect, archive, reproduce, and analyze information. System software provides the interface between the hardware and application software, while application software executes sets of tasks that are typically unrelated to the operation of the computer itself. Many readers are familiar with Microsoft Windows, which is the most popular family of operating system software in the market. The SAS software that will be introduced in more detail in subsequent sections of this book is an example of an application software that can be used for collecting, processing, archiving, reproducing, and conducting statistical analysis of the data.
- **Network**: Information systems require network communications to effectively work because their data repository often needs to be accessed by multiple users, from multiple locations, and using different devices. Hence, information systems must have a network architecture (wired or wireless connections and network topology) for the devices, system, and application software to communicate with each other. Networks could be built to allow access only within the organization (intranet) or beyond the organization (extranet) and, more recently, in the cloud, in which case all or some of the IT infrastructure of the organization is hosted in public or private platforms hosted by other organizations.
- **People**: All organizations require people to operate, and since information systems are designed for organizational use, people are critical elements of all information systems. These include end-users who use the information system to carry out their respective business tasks, developers who build applications and technologies that run the systems, as well as administrators and system specialists who ensure the systems operate as intended. Examples of end-users would be a payroll specialist who uses the human resource database to run payroll reports every month, a financial data scientist who uses the loan portfolio database to build credit scoring models for the bank, and developers who build applications such as dashboards, graphical user interfaces, program packages, and manuals that allow other users to access resources in the system.
- **Processes**: These are the methods used in the governance and operations of information systems to ensure that they achieve their intended design. For example, processes could include tasks and procedures relating to how data is collected, organized, stored, altered, retrieved, and transmitted within the system (data processing). They would also include the access level available to users and devices within the systems (controls) and procedures that are manual and those that are automatically executed in the system.

Figure 1.2: Components of Financial Information Systems

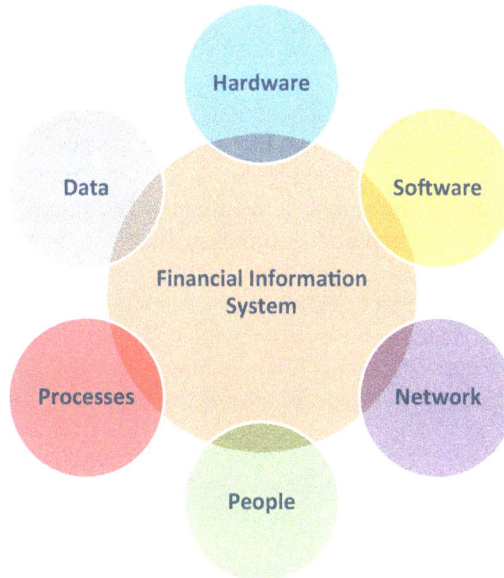

- **Data and Databases**: It is straightforward to think of data as pieces of relevant information that are collected and stored in data repositories that are popularly called databases. Within this context, financial data can then be regarded as any piece of data that has financial relevance to an entity. Financial data could exist either as structured or unstructured data in its raw form. Structured financial data are pieces of information that have been collected and archived using predefined formatting, while unstructured data are typically archived without preformatting. We will discuss these two concepts in more detail in Chapter Two. Financial data scientists mostly work with structured financial data. The three types of data structures that are commonly used for archiving structured financial data include:
  - **Cross-sectional Data** – Data on a statistical unit or items of interest that are collected at a single point in time. For example, the company names and the industry of the stocks in a portfolio at the end of the quarter.
  - **Time Series Data** – Data on the same item or statistical units that are collected over multiple periods. For example, the daily closing price of a stock in the portfolio that was collected over two years.
  - **Panel (Longitudinal) Data** – Cross-sectional data that are collected over multiple periods. For example, the daily closing prices of all the stocks in the portfolio that were collected over two years.

Regardless of the data structure or the format that you will encounter while implementing your analytics project, note that you will still end up spending a significant amount of your time preparing your data for modeling.

Financial Intelligence

Along the same line as business intelligence, which leverages the power of software and databases to draw insight from past events and outcomes, financial intelligence applies similar tools to historical financial data to draw insights about relevant key performance indicators (KPIs), scorecards, dashboards, or any other metrics that are of value to the decision maker. For example, portfolio managers use portfolio reporting tools to visualize and analyze the performances of their investment portfolios. Banks use loan dashboards to monitor and analyze applications, approvals, payments, and default trends in their loan portfolios. The primary difference between financial intelligence and financial analytics is the window of opportunity that is under consideration. With financial intelligence, the emphasis is on figuring out what happened in the past so that decision-makers can judge how well the organization or portfolio is meeting its intended objectives. Whereas in financial analytics, the emphasis is on figuring out what will happen in the future so that decision-makers can exploit those insights for business purposes.

Financial Econometrics

Financial econometrics explores financial and economic problems and theories by applying inferential statistics, as well as structural, and descriptive models, to financial and or economic data. In financial econometrics, the theory is normally the starting point, followed by the implementation of the model to prove or disprove the theory. Econometric models are abstractions of the real world that are designed to test theories, underlying assumptions, or forecast future trends. In one way, financial econometrics can be thought of as a subset of financial data science that sets out to prove or disprove financial phenomena or relationships, while financial analytics are designed to find financial phenomena and relationships. With that said, it is important to reiterate that financial and economic data often occur in time series format, which raises a range of issues that many of the advanced data science tools are not necessarily equipped to tackle. For example, financial and economic data often display a wide range of statistical characteristics such as time-varying volatilities, trends, cyclicality, seasonality, outliers, serial correlations, and endogeneity to name a few. Thus, financial data scientists must pay special attention when applying advanced data science tools such as machine learning to financial and economic data. In subsequent chapters, we will discuss in more detail how to address some of these features in the data science framework.

Data Science Toolkit

One of the privileges of being a data scientist today is the wide array of tools at our disposal. Data science tools fall into two categories: those based on open-source platforms such as Python and R and those based on proprietary platforms such as Microsoft Excel, SAS, SPSS, Tableau, and MATLAB. Each of the platforms has its benefits and disadvantages, which are discussed in the succeeding section.

Microsoft Excel

Microsoft Excel is arguably the most widely used data science application. Since its introduction in 1987, Excel has grown to become the leading spreadsheet and perhaps the easiest to learn data science application. To an average user, Excel might look like a simple spreadsheet that contains data items that are organized into rows and columns. However, behind the scenes is a wide array of powerful analytic and data science engines that users with minimal computing skills can implement for data science purposes. Indeed, many of the tasks that would require advanced Excel skills in the past now have menu options or have been automated such that minimal programming is needed to implement. For example, users can enable the Analysis ToolPak and Solver Add-in to access the statistical data analysis and optimization and equation-solving solutions in Excel.

More recent versions of Microsoft Excel also include data engines to connect to most databases, data lakes, and data files, as well as web scraping tools that can pull data directly from online data sources. It also includes powerful visualization tools and data query tools that run on an artificial intelligence (AI) platform. Together, these features allow users to access needed data relatively quickly, conduct drill-downs and basic data analyses, and produce compelling visualizations with minimal computing skills. Microsoft Excel format is also the most common format in which data is stored and accessed by the other and more sophisticated data science tools that will be discussed shortly.

IBM SPSS Statistics

Since its acquisition by IBM in 2009, IBM SPSS statistics has grown to be a major contender in the data science landscape. Despite its roots in social science research, SPSS is equipped with multiple advanced features that enable it to support the needs of both novice and seasoned data scientists. Most users will find its graphical user interface easy to navigate. Users can also execute simple and complex analytics tasks and produce visualizations using custom-built menus.

SPSS supports the use of structured query language (SQL), which allows it to connect directly to databases. It also supports data in multiple file formats such as Excel, CSV, SAS, and Stata. For more advanced users, SPSS supports three types of programming languages: its own native SPSS syntax, as well as the R and Python programming languages, which we will discuss shortly. Users with an interest in implementing more advanced and automated data science techniques can also subscribe to the IBM SPSS modeler.

The SPSS platform has some key disadvantages when compared to other data science platforms. First, SPSS does not have a robust visualization engine, so output graphics tend to be of lower quality than those produced by other platforms. SPSS was not initially designed to handle financial data, which tends to follow a time series format, so financial data scientists will find it limiting in terms of the number of prebuilt menus and functions that can analyze financial data and support the writing of programs for advanced financial data analysis. SPSS also lacks a visual programming platform that can be used to manage and automate tasks, routines, and subroutines on data science projects. The last disadvantage of SPSS is cost. Students and faculty interested in using SPSS must pay for an annual license.

Tableau

Visual exploration of data is a crucial aspect of data science. Indeed, visualizations allow data scientists to quickly observe and communicate trends, intensities, and relationships in large amounts of data. Tableau is perhaps the most widely used data visualization application. It is easy to learn, and users can quickly produce graphically compelling and interactive visualizations without advanced programming knowledge. Tableau can also automatically pre-process and post-process very large amounts of data quickly and link data in different formats together. Tableau probably has the most comprehensive list of data connectors (over 90), which allows it to connect to data stored in various file formats as well as those in open-source databases such as MySQL and PostgreSQL. It also has a webscraping tool that can pull data directly from online data sources such as Google Analytics. With some configurations, Python can be integrated into Tableau to access some of the advanced data science features that are not native to Tableau but are readily available in Python. Together, all these features allow Tableau users to quickly draw insights from data and report their findings using high-quality graphics.

However, it is important to note that Tableau, at its core, is a business intelligence application that is well-suited for reporting purposes but not for conducting advanced data science techniques, such as machine learning and deep learning. Some of the advanced features of Tableau, such as access to data on servers and integration with Python, require significantly higher levels of expertise in computing, which makes it challenging for novice users. Finally, there is also an annual cost for its license and some users might find that prohibitive.

MATLAB

Those coming to data science from the engineering and science disciplines might already be familiar with MATLAB due to its popularity in the engineering and scientific fields. It is a proprietary programming language for technical computing and modeling in the scientific fields. With a wide range of built-in functions and routines, and a robust ability to manipulate and visualize data stored in matrix format, MATLAB can be a potent tool for data science. Indeed, one of the advantages of MATLAB is the growing number of toolboxes that it has for data science applications. For example, MATLAB currently has a Statistics and Machine Learning Toolbox, Deep Learning Toolbox, and a Text Analytics Toolbox, to name a few. These toolboxes, along with its long-available Econometric, Financial, Math, and Optimization toolboxes make MATLAB a comprehensive arsenal for advanced financial data science. However, readers interested in using MATLAB and its associated toolboxes for data science might find the cost to be quite prohibitive for use as a learner. Consequently, MATLAB has a smaller ecosystem and community of users, relative to the other data science platforms.

Python

Python is a high-level and scalable open-source programming language with a wide range of applications. It is concise, easy to read, and supports an object-oriented programming approach. It is also an interpreted language, so it does not need a compiler to run. It is used for technical computing, data science, web development, and application programming. Therefore, Python also has a large user community that spans multiple professions. It is able to achieve such versatility because Python supports an extensive list of libraries that contain modules and/or packages.

Python modules and packages are collections of reusable Python code that perform related tasks. Python programmers can quickly call up these code in other programs without the need to rewrite them all over again. For example, a developer who is conducting numerical analysis in Python can call up the NumPy (Numerical Python) library within a Python program to execute mathematical operations such as linear algebra, Fourier transformation, matrix analysis, and random simulations. There are other Python libraries such as Pandas, which is used extensively for data processing and analysis; Matplotlib, which is used for data visualization; SciPy, which is used for technical computing tasks such as optimization, integration, and signal processing; and Scikit-learn, which is used for advanced data science tasks such as predictive modeling and machine learning. Python also supports cross-platform integrations. Indeed, many of the current proprietary data science applications such as SAS, SPSS, and Tableau integrate with Python. Thus, users can switch back and forth between Python and proprietary applications and essentially get the best of both worlds.

All these features make Python well-suited for data science applications. Within the data science community, it is arguably the most widely used data science application. Despite its impressive list of features, Python has some limitations that novice users might find challenging to overcome in their data science journey. Python does not have native support for data connectors to enterprise data repositories. It is also memory intensive and slower than other high-level languages such as C++. Nevertheless, it is highly recommended that aspiring data scientists acquire some functional knowledge of Python programming, irrespective of their preferred platform.

R

In contrast to the versatility of Python, R is an open-source statistical programming language that has a variety of data science functionalities. It also has a large community of users, but they are mostly in the academic and research space. It shares some similarities with Python in the sense that it is an interpreted language and supports an extensive list of R packages. Indeed, there are over 19,000 packages that have been published for R users. These include packages for executing a wide range of statistical analyses, data visualizations, advanced econometric models, mathematical operations, and optimizations, as well as packages for advanced financial data science tasks such as predictive modeling and machine learning. R can also integrate with proprietary applications such as Tableau, SAS, and SPSS. Many of the advanced data science functions and routines in some of the proprietary applications are essentially wrappers around R packages running in the background.

R can also be installed as a standalone application, in which case the user will need to rely on codes to interact with the application, or use RStudio, which adds a graphical user interface with menu functions and a syntax editor to R. Packages in R often lack the transparency and comprehensive support resource that are much easier to access for the libraries and functions of similar data science platforms.

SAS

The SAS analytic suite is possibly the best-suited platform for data science. It offers a comprehensive suite of data science tools that span every aspect of the analytic and business intelligence life cycle that a data scientist can possibly encounter. As with most data science applications, SAS is at its core a statistical programming language with a wide range of applications that transcend all business domains.

There are several appealing features of SAS for aspiring and seasoned data scientists. First, it is a versatile and powerful programming language that is easy to learn. All SAS users appreciate its robust support infrastructure, which is built on a vast repository of SAS documents, sample code, technical support, training programs, conferences, and a passionate user community. There is also a broad range of tools available to users at various levels of SAS expertise. Beginner and advanced users will find many of the menu-driven SAS applications (which still retain their programming capabilities) such as Enterprise Guide and Enterprise Miner particularly useful in their analytics journey. Others will find the flexibility and on-demand access to the SAS engine through web-based platforms such as SAS Studio and SAS Viya extremely convenient. Besides these, SAS also has a comprehensive list of data connectors that allow it to connect to data stored in various file formats, including data in open-source and proprietary data repositories, as well as powerful reporting tools that can automate the analytic life cycle for most data science projects.

SAS has robust capabilities for advanced financial data science applications in artificial intelligence and its subfields such as machine learning, deep learning, computer vision, natural language processing, and financial econometrics. It integrates seamlessly with Python and R, such that users can combine SAS code with these programs in the same analytics environment. Although it is a proprietary solution, SAS offers free software options for learners in both academic and non-academic communities through its SAS OnDemand Platform.[1]

Another appealing feature of SAS is its credentialing program. SAS users can demonstrate their competence in SAS by enrolling and passing one or more of the certification exams offered by SAS. SAS is also a market leader in the analytic space, and the demand for SAS talent remains very strong. Lastly, from a risk management point of view, users can be sure that all SAS products

---

[1] To access SAS Studio for free on the web, readers should go to https://welcome.oda.sas.com/ to create a free SAS profile. This will provide you access to SAS Studio and 5GB of free storage for your personal data files.

and procedures have been subjected to rigorous testing before their release, and there is a single point of accountability for future upgrades, a feature that is lacking in many of the open-source platforms. All of these features make SAS a compelling tool for financial data scientists and the primary application that will be highlighted in this textbook.

Working with SAS

Although the book does not assume that readers have significant SAS programming skills, many of the concepts we will discuss in succeeding sections of the text do require some foundation in finance, mathematics, statistics, and computer information systems. Hence, one of the aims of the book is to provide these readers with advanced knowledge of how these fields are interrelated in the financial services industry. Users interested in working with SAS will be delighted by the assortment of environments through which they can access the SAS analytic engine. In enterprise settings, the SAS engine (the current version of which is SAS 9.4) is usually located on a SAS server that can be accessed by client applications. On personal computers, the server is locally installed and can be accessed using the SAS Windowing Environments (Explorer, Results, Enhanced Editor, Log, and Output windows), SAS Enterprise Guide, and SAS Studio.

It is also important for you to be aware of SAS Viya, which is the newest member of the SAS Analytics Platform. SAS Viya is a full suite of cloud-based applications with artificial intelligence, data visualization, advanced analytics, and data management features that allow it to support the entire analytic life cycle. Although it shares some similarities and interoperability with SAS 9, it was built from the ground up to support processing in-memory and distributed processing. It also has its own programming language, known as the cloud analytics services (CAS) language. However, it supports the SAS programming language.

Windows in the SAS Windowing Environment

PC users can also access SAS using a powerful but menu-based desktop application such as the SAS Enterprise Guide, or web-based client applications such as SAS Studio. Advanced analytic applications such as SAS Enterprise Miner are used throughout the entire scope of the data science project. In this textbook, we will focus on three SAS environments: SAS Enterprise Guide, SAS Studio, and SAS Enterprise Miner. There are some similarities between the three environments. All three are menu-based but also have robust programming interfaces, such that users can seamlessly switch back and forth between point-and-click menu-based tasks and writing code to implement unique tasks. All three environments also support automation for repetitive tasks, as well as provide a mechanism to organize a sequence of tasks (process flow), data items, and results into a single repository called projects. Each menu-based task is usually a packaged set of code, which all three windows generate as the menu-based task are implemented. Novice users will also find these features to be very helpful for writing future code or customizing the software-generated code for their own unique tasks.

Many readers would be delighted to learn that financial data science in SAS does not always entail writing SAS programs. For many tasks, it might be more efficient to use menus than to write programs to implement them. Nevertheless, all data scientists must be highly competent in programming and be ready to apply their programming skills when there are no menu options to implement a task.

SAS Enterprise Guide

SAS Enterprise Guide is a point-and-click desktop client for working with SAS and managing analytic projects. As you click on the task menu, the SAS Enterprise Guide generates SAS code behind the scenes. The SAS code is then submitted to a local or remote SAS server for processing. Enterprise Guide also has a full programming interface that can be used to write, edit, and submit SAS programs to a SAS server for processing. The software also has other project management features such as the process flow tab, which allows you to manage and track your analytics project from end to end. You can also automate and schedule the execution of your completed project as well as share any elements of your project using process flow.

Enterprise Guide 8.3 is fully integrated with GitHub, a platform for collaborating and tracking changes on software development projects. Users can also connect to the SAS Viya platform using the SAS Enterprise Guide.

Figure 1.3: SAS Enterprise Guide 8.3 Environment

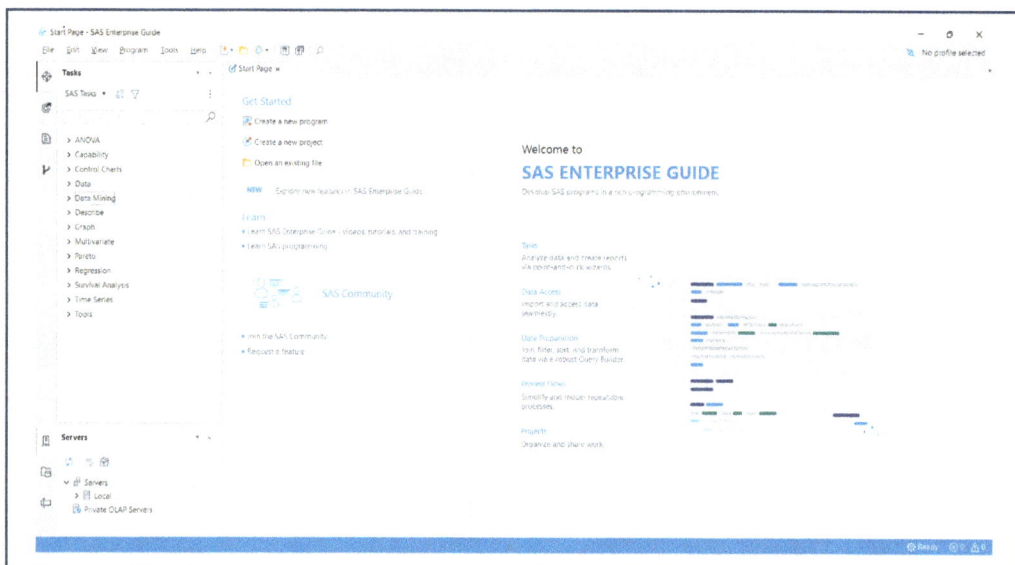

SAS Studio

SAS Studio is a web-based interface for working with SAS. In SAS Studio, SAS programs are sent to a local or cloud-based SAS server using common web browsers. The server processes the code and publishes the output in various formats, including HTML, RTF, and PDF. SAS Studio also supports a comprehensive list of point-and-click menu tasks, which can be used to implement both basic and advanced analytics procedures.

The cloud-based version of SAS Studio provides access to the SAS engine from anywhere with an Internet connection. SAS Studio also shares many of the features available in SAS Enterprise Guide, such as process flow and connection to the cloud-based SAS Viya. Although it runs on a browser, SAS Studio can be installed as a Progressive Web App (PWA). This approach provides more user-friendly features, such as placing an icon for SAS Studio on the desktop of your computer. This means you can skip multiple steps to reach the SAS environment because the steps are automatically performed once you click the SAS Studio icon. PWA also enables application persistence, which allows the user to remain logged in to the server unless the time-out feature is enabled. You can also create multiple icons for each instance of PWA.

SAS Enterprise Miner

SAS Enterprise Miner is another point-and-click SAS application that is used for building descriptive and predictive models of large data. The software supports a wide range of data management, statistical procedures, and analytics algorithms, all of which can be accessed by simple point-and-click

Figure 1.4: SAS Studio Environment

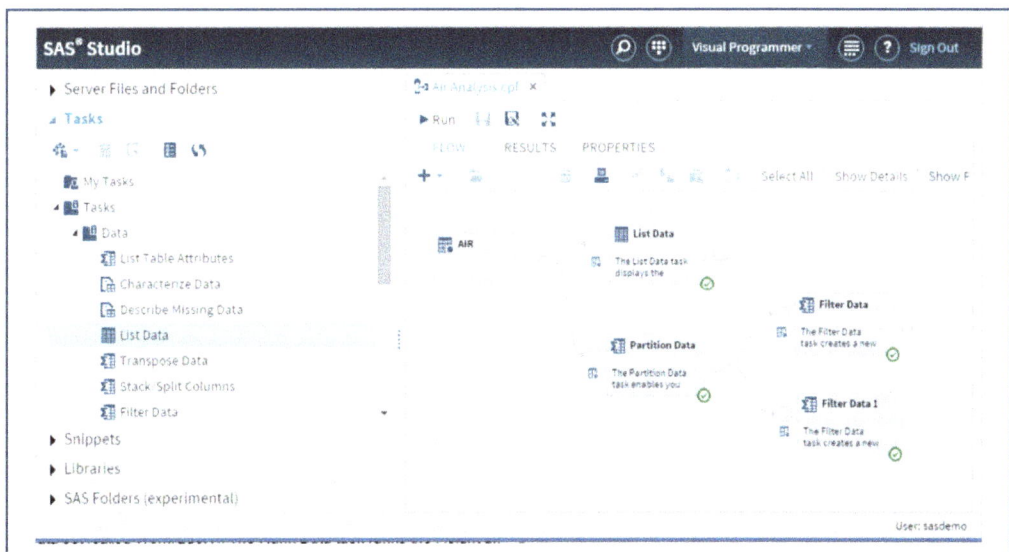

Figure 1.5: SAS Enterprise Miner 15.2 Environment

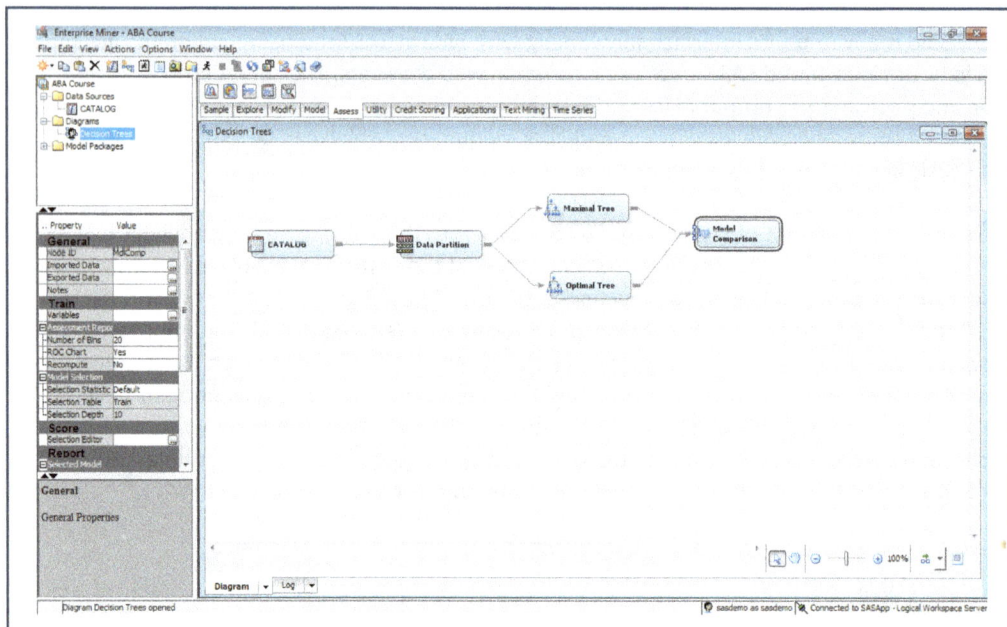

actions. Most of your analytics tasks in Enterprise Miner will be done in the process flow diagram using pre-built code packages, which are called Nodes. However, the application still supports full SAS programming capabilities as well as the ability to deploy analytics models into production within the software environment. Enterprise Miner projects can be imported into SAS Viya. Another great feature of Enterprise Miner is its integration with R and Python. With some programming, R packages and Python modules can be integrated into the Enterprise Miner process flow.

SAS Model Studio

Although you can access SAS Viya through any of the three previous platforms if you have a license to the SAS/CONNECT bridge, most users will find it more beneficial to use SAS Model Studio as the default application because it is native to the SAS Viya platform. SAS Model Studio is an integrated visual environment that provides access to a suite of analytics products and features that are built on the SAS Viya platform. The list includes data management and governance, visual data mining and machine learning, visual text analytics, visual forecasting, visual model management, optimization, and robust support for the integration of open-source platforms such as Python and R. You can also execute code written in both the SAS and CAS programming languages in SAS Model Studio. Pipelines are a key feature that SAS Model Studio shares with the previous windowing environment (pipelines are what process flows are called in SAS Model Studio). Just like SAS Studio, SAS Model Studio can also be installed as a PWA.

Figure 1.6: SAS Model Studio

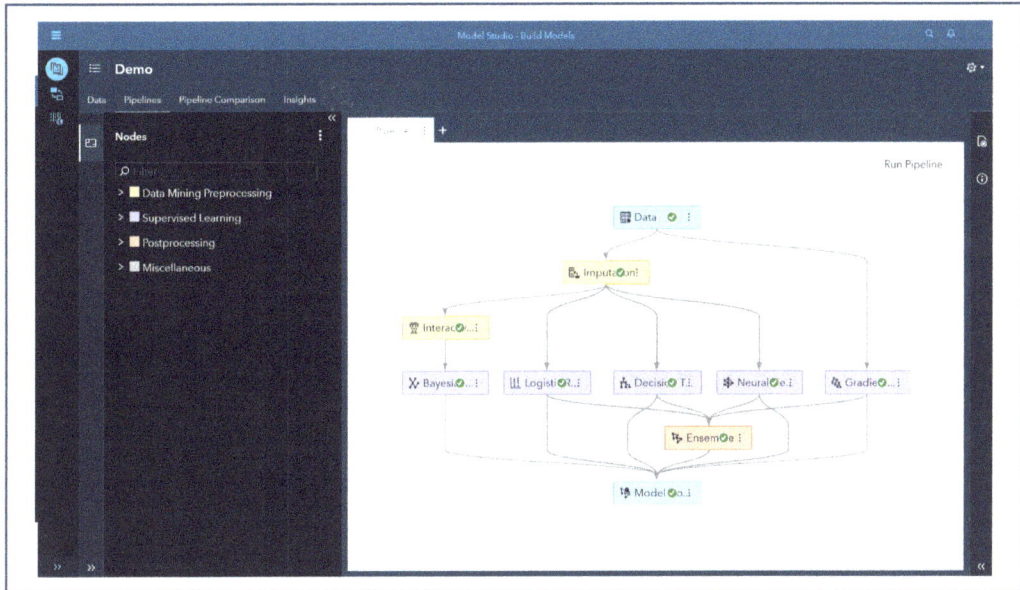

SAS Statements

SAS programming covers a wide range of steps, procedures, and functions. Unfortunately, not all can be discussed in this book. Hence, we will focus only on the code and functions that are most relevant for financial data science purposes.[2] All code written in the SAS programming language can be grouped into two broad categories: the DATA step and PROC statements (also known as SAS procedures).

DATA Step

The DATA step is a group of SAS statements that are used for importing and manipulating data in SAS. It usually begins with DATA as the initial statement, followed by blocks of code that SAS sequentially executes. The DATA step normally ends with a RUN statement. All data, regardless of their current format must first be read and stored in SAS before they can be accessed by other SAS statements. There are various ways to read your data into SAS, depending on the current format of the data. In the example below, we create a new SAS data set called SP500FIN by entering the data directly into SAS. The raw data contains the aggregate annual sales per share

---

[2] Those interested in developing a broader range of SAS competencies should visit the SAS bookstore at https://support.sas.com/en/books.html for other great books such as *The Little SAS Book: A Primer and Learning SAS By Example: A Programmer's Guide.*

(SPS), earnings per share (EPS), dividend payout (DPR) ratio, and price-to-earnings (PE) ratios for all companies listed in the S&P 500 index from 2015 to 2022.

Program 1.1: Reading Raw Data into SAS

```
data SP500FIN;
     input  Date MMDDYY10. SPS EPS DPR PE;
     format Date MMDDYY10. SPS Dollar10. EPS Dollar10.;
     label SPS = 'Sales Per Share' EPS ='Earnings Per Share' DPR= 'Dividend Payout
Ratio' PE = 'Price-to-Earnings Ratio';
     datalines;
12/31/2015 1106.96 89.73 53.38 18.73
12/30/2016 1128.45 98.90 52.35 20.44
12/29/2017 1210.13 109.99 52.11 21.48
12/31/2018 1313.58 133.01 46.10 16.64
12/31/2019 1391.09 140.42 52.45 20.86
12/31/2020 1342.44 97.00 72.10 30.37
12/31/2021 1541.77 200.35 37.18 24.71
12/30/2022 1708.91 188.41 39.34 18.61
;
run;
```

The DATA statement creates the SAS data set named SP500FIN. The INPUT statement assigns variable names to the columns. The MMDDYY10. Is an INFORMAT statement that tells SAS how to read or input data (in this case to read the date in MM/DD/YYYY format). The FORMAT statement tells SAS how to display the data. The LABEL statement assigns variable labels to the variable name and the DATALINES statement indicates the beginning of the observations of the values of each variable.

PROC Statements

The second group of SAS statements is SAS procedures or PROC statements. These are used to execute a variety of tasks in SAS. They include statistical analysis, econometrics, data management, visualizations, reporting, and advanced analytics to name a few. When implementing a PROC step in SAS, you generally need to refer to the data set on which the procedure will be executed. Hence, most PROC statements will include a "DATA=" in the code line as shown in the examples below. In the next code example, we sort the SP500FIN data set by date using the PROC SORT statement and then request a print of the sorted data using the PROC PRINT statement.

Program 1.2: Sorting Data by Date

```
proc sort data=SP500FIN;
by Date;
run;

proc print data=SP500FIN;
run;
```

Output 1.2: Printing SAS Data Set Sorted in Ascending Order

Obs	Date	SPS	EPS	DPR	PE
1	12/31/2015	$1,107	$90	53.38	18.73
2	12/30/2016	$1,128	$99	52.35	20.44
3	12/29/2017	$1,210	$110	52.11	21.48
4	12/31/2018	$1,314	$133	46.10	16.64
5	12/31/2019	$1,391	$140	52.45	20.86
6	12/31/2020	$1,342	$97	72.10	30.37
7	12/31/2021	$1,542	$200	37.18	24.71
8	12/30/2022	$1,709	$188	39.34	18.61

The default order for sorting in SAS is ascending, but you can change the order to descending. PROC SORT replaces the original data with the sorted data. However, you can also specify that the data should be sorted into a new data set by using the optional argument (OPTIONS) for PROC SORT.

> Most PROC statements have optional arguments that specify how the procedure should be executed by SAS. Tasks in Enterprise Guide and SAS Studio have options in the built-in menus for each procedure. Enterprise Guide and SAS Studio also have a recommendation engine that suggests options for you as you write your code. You can learn more about the accompanying options for each statement by consulting the SAS documents for the procedure.

Program 1.3: Sorting Data by Date Descending

```
proc sort data=SP500FIN out=Dsorted_SP500FIN;
by descending Date;
run;

proc print data=Dsorted_SP500FIN;
run;
```

Output 1.3: Printing SAS Data Set Sorted in Descending Order

Obs	Date	SPS	EPS	DPR	PE
1	12/30/2022	$1,709	$188	39.34	18.61
2	12/31/2021	$1,542	$200	37.18	24.71
3	12/31/2020	$1,342	$97	72.10	30.37
4	12/31/2019	$1,391	$140	52.45	20.86
5	12/31/2018	$1,314	$133	46.10	16.64
6	12/29/2017	$1,210	$110	52.11	21.48
7	12/30/2016	$1,128	$99	52.35	20.44
8	12/31/2015	$1,107	$90	53.38	18.73

Output

Outputs from SAS DATA steps are usually new data sets created from data that is entered into SAS (as in the previous example), read from existing data sets, or imported from the data stored in many of the data file formats (such as Text, CSV, and XLSX) that SAS supports. Outputs obtained from PROC steps can take various forms. These include those in results form, which are tables and graphs that are published in various file formats, data, and reports, which are results that are compiled into document files. In the example shown in Program 1.4, we use PROC SGPLOT to create a plot of the annual sales per share (SPS) and earnings per share (EPS) for the S&P 500 index from 2015 to 2022. For each plot, we use the SERIES statement to specify the variables to plot on the X-axis (Date) and the Y-axis (SPS and EPS). The graph shown in Output 1.4 is the result you will obtain from running the SAS code.

Program 1.4: Series Plots of Aggregate Financial Performance of S&P 500 Firms Using PROC SGPLOT

```
title 'Annual Sales Per Share and Earnings Per Share for the S&P 500 Index';
proc sgplot data= SP500FIN;
      series x=Date y=SPS ;
      series x=Date y=EPS ;
      xaxis grid;
      yaxis grid;
run;
title;
```

Output 1.4: Series Plots of Aggregate Financial Performance of S&P 500 Firms

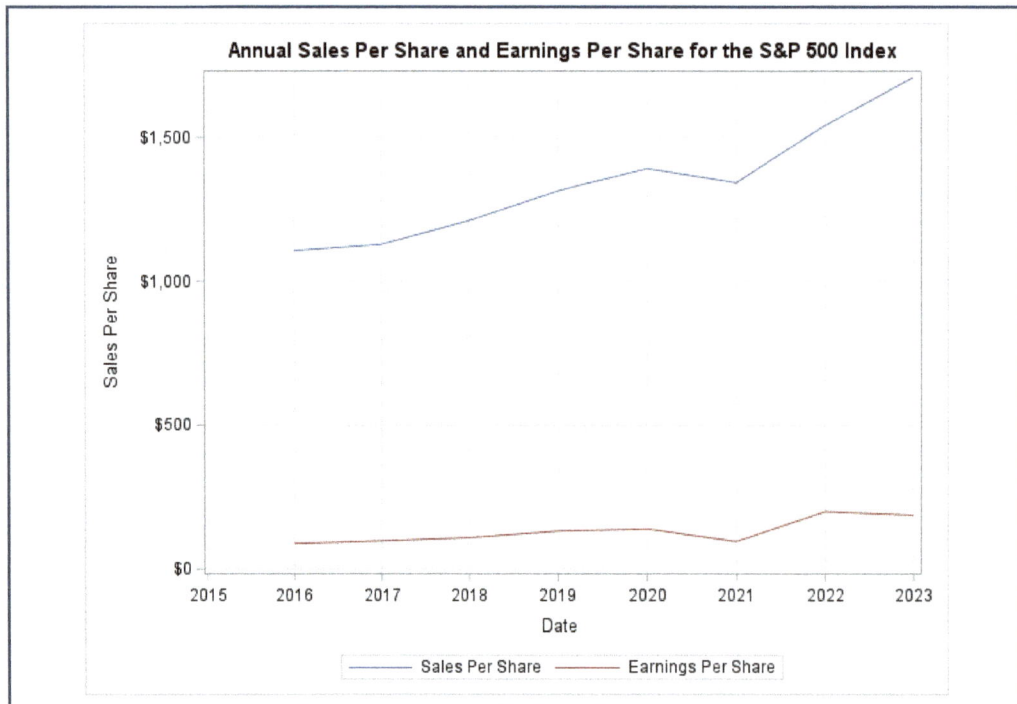

SAS Data and Library

SAS data are stored in SAS Libraries, which are collections of one or more SAS files that are recognized by SAS and can be referenced and stored as a unit in the local or cloud drive of the SAS server. Libraries are file addresses on computer drives that allow SAS to access files that SAS supports. There are two types of SAS libraries: permanent and temporary. Permanent libraries contain files that are permanently stored by SAS until deleted by the user. The files can be accessed in subsequent SAS sessions. Files in the temporary (WORK) library are only available during the current SAS session and are typically deleted once the session is ended. There are two types of permanent libraries, default SAS libraries and user-assigned libraries. Default SAS libraries are automatically created by SAS in each SAS session. They include SASDATA, SASUSER, SASHELP, and MAPS. User-assigned libraries are created using the LIBNAME statements. LIBREF is the SAS name for the library, followed by the physical address of the library on your computer drive between the quotation signs.

Although the data stored in the user-assigned library are permanent until deleted, the user will have to reassign the library in each SAS session to relink the physical address with the SAS library. Therefore, the LIBNAME statement and the accompanying LIBREF and physical address of the folder must be invoked in each SAS session to reassign the library.

> To create a SAS library, submit the following SAS command. Replace the area in italics with your preferred LIBREF and the physical address of the folder on your computer. LIBNAME *mylib 'c:\mysasdir\'*;

You can automate this process to ensure that your library persists across sessions by including an autoexec file in your Enterprise Guide project to automatically reassign your library every time you launch the project. For SAS Studio, use the GUI option to create your library. Right-click on My Libraries, include your LIBREF, and check Re-create this library at start-up.

Accessing the Data Repository for the Book

Most of the data and code used in this textbook have been made available on a GitHub repository (https://github.com/finsasdata/Bookdata). GitHub is a cloud-hosting platform for collaborative projects. SAS Enterprise Guide 8.3 and SAS Studio support full integration with GitHub.[3]

The data in the book's GitHub repository can be accessed in multiple ways. You can download the data and code into the preferred directory of your personal computer by visiting the GitHub repository for the book using a web browser. Users with SAS Enterprise Guide 8.3 and SAS Studio

---

[3] To learn more about SAS Enterprise Guide 8.3 Git integration, please review "Understanding Git Integration in SAS Enterprise Guide" in the *SAS® Enterprise Guide®* 8.3: User's Guide available at https://documentation.sas.com/doc/en/egug/8.3/titlepage.htm.

can also download all of the data and code into a SAS library named FINDATA by submitting the SAS statement in Program 1.5 below. To make it easy for readers to use the same code in both the Enterprise Guide and SAS Studio environments, all data files and programs that are pulled from the GitHub repository will be stored in the temporary SAS folder directory of your computer or the SAS OnDemand server.

Program 1.5: Access GitHub Data Repository Using SAS Git Integration

```
options dlcreatedir;
%let datapath = %sysfunc(getoption(WORK))/finsasdata;
libname findata "&datapath.";
run;

data _null_;
 rc = git_clone("https://github.com/finsasdata/Bookdata/",
   "&datapath.");
    %put rc=;
run;
```

It is also important to note that SAS Git integration can only clone the GitHub repository into an empty directory on your computer. You will get an error log if you try to copy the repository into a folder with existing files. If you encounter such an error, locate the physical address of the FINDATA library by submitting the SAS statement in Program 1.6 below, then delete or move all the files (including hidden files) into a separate folder.

Program 1.6: Identifying the Physical Address of SAS Libraries

```
proc datasets library=findata;
run;
quit;
```

SAS can also retrieve files from the Internet by using HTTP requests. We can access one of the data sets in the GitHub repository by submitting the PROC HTTP statement in Program 1.7 below. The STOCKS data set contains the monthly stock prices and trading volume for six technology stocks. The FILENAME statement uses the 'STOCKS' FILEREF to identify the name and file directory in which the requested data set will be stored (in this case the directory used by SAS for the WORK library). The %SYSFUNC(GETOPTION(WORK)) statement obtains the physical address of the location of the WORK library. In most cases, this will be the same folder that contains your temporary SAS files.

Program 1.7: Access GitHub Data Repository Using SAS HTTP Request

```
filename stocks "%sysfunc(getoption(WORK))/stocks.sas7bdat";

proc http url="https://github.com/finsasdata/Bookdata/raw/main/stocks.sas7bdat"
       out=stocks
       method ="get";
run;
```

```
proc print data=Stocks(where= (Stock='AMZN' and Date>'31Dec2021'D));
      format volume comma13.;
run;
```

Output 1.7: Daily Stock Prices and Volume of Amazon Inc.

Obs	Date	Stock	Price	Volume
244	31JAN2022	AMZN	$149.57	1,530,000,000
245	28FEB2022	AMZN	$153.56	1,690,000,000
246	31MAR2022	AMZN	$163.00	1,630,000,000
247	29APR2022	AMZN	$124.28	1,470,000,000
248	31MAY2022	AMZN	$120.21	2,260,000,000
249	30JUN2022	AMZN	$106.21	1,770,000,000
250	29JUL2022	AMZN	$134.95	1,340,000,000
251	31AUG2022	AMZN	$126.77	1,170,000,000
252	30SEP2022	AMZN	$113.00	1,210,000,000
253	31OCT2022	AMZN	$102.44	1,460,000,000
254	30NOV2022	AMZN	$96.54	2,040,000,000
255	30DEC2022	AMZN	$84.00	1,550,000,000

Data Science Concepts and Their Finance Applications

Throughout this book, you will come across various data science concepts and their applications in the finance domain. We will discuss a few of these concepts here. We will also provide basic demonstrations of their applications in SAS. In subsequent chapters, we will conduct in-depth explorations of most of these concepts and provide practical applications of their use in various finance settings.

Descriptive Analytics

Descriptive statistics are essentially the synopses of the main characteristics of the data. Such characteristics include the tally and frequency of the data, and the shape of the distributions as presented using measures of central tendencies and dispersions. In cases where more than one variable is under study, bivariate or multivariate descriptive statistics that present a summary of the relationships between variables might also be presented. Descriptive statistics highlight key attributes of the data and help the researcher formulate the appropriate methodology for executing other statistical and data science techniques. There are two categories of descriptive statistics: numerical descriptive statistics and visual descriptive statistics.

Figure 1.7: Aspects of Financial Data Science

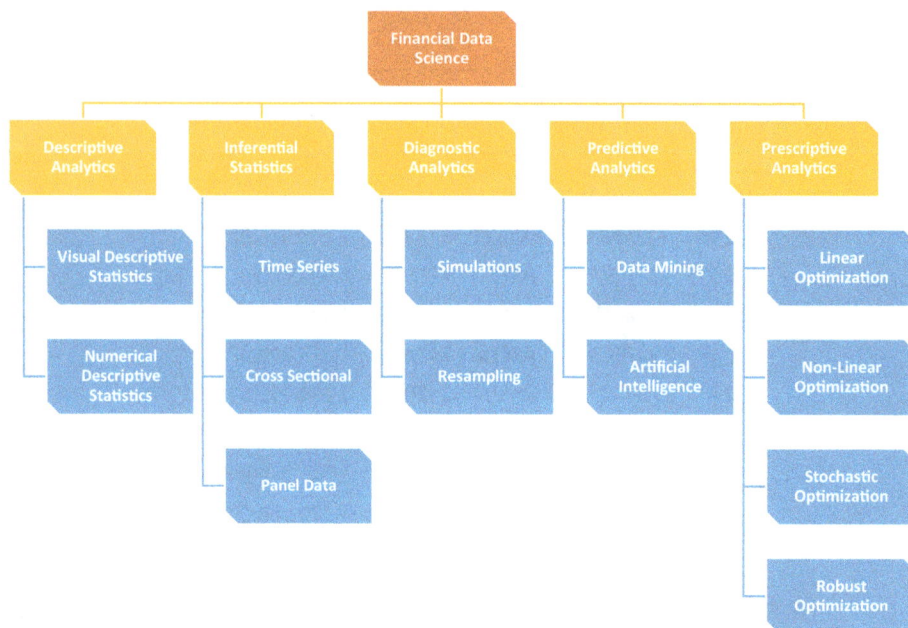

Numerical Descriptive Statistics

Numerical descriptive statistics are usually presented in tabular form and consist of measures of the variable characteristics described above. They might also include results of diagnostic tests that examine various properties of the data, such as skewness, autocorrelations, and stationarity, to name a few. We will discuss many of these statistics in more detail in subsequent chapters of the book.

Financial data are generally presented using a wide variety of numerical descriptive statistics. In the example below, we highlight the SAS program and the results showing simple descriptive statistics of the aggregate financial statement performances of the companies in the S&P 500 index. First, we use the DATA step to compute the annual growth rate in sales (SPSG), earnings per share (EPSG), and dividend payout ratio (DPRG). This is done by calculating the logarithmic return (log difference between current values and lagged values of the same variable, $LOG(\frac{X_t}{X_{t-1}})$, where $X_t = (SPS_t, EPS_t, DPR_t)$. We then calculate the trailing annual price-to-earnings growth (PEG) by dividing the PE ratio by the growth rate of earnings per share ($PEG = PE/EPSG$). The PEG ratio is a popular measure of how expensive a stock is relative to the growth rate. Higher PEG ratios (above 2) are widely seen as indicative of overvaluation, while lower PEG (below 1) is indicative of undervaluation.

Next, we display the results from our computation using the PROC PRINT statement. We conclude the code by submitting a PROC MEANS statement to compute the mean, standard deviation, minimum, median, and maximum values for each variable.

Program 1.8A: Formatting and Calculating Descriptive Statistics of Aggregate Performance of S&P 500 Companies Using DATA Step and PROC MEANS

```
data NSP500FIN;
    set SP500FIN;
    SPSG=LOG(SPS/LAG(SPS));
    EPSG=LOG(EPS/LAG(EPS));
    DPRG = LOG(DPR/LAG(DPR));
    PEG = PE/(EPSG*100);
label SPSG = 'Sales Growth Rate' EPSG ='Earnings Growth Rate' DPRG='Dividend Payout Ratio
Growth Rate'
        PEG = 'Price-to-Earning Growth Ratio';
format SPSG percent8.2 EPSG percent8.2 DPRG percent8.2 PEG bestd6.;
run;
```

```
proc print data=NSP500FIN;
run;

proc means data=NSP500FIN mean stddev min median max nolabels;
    var SPSG EPSG DPRG PEG;
run;
```

Output 1.8A: Descriptive Statistics of the Aggregate Financial Performance of S&P500 Companies

Obs	Date	SPS	EPS	DPR	PE	SPSG	EPSG	DPRG	PEG
1	12/31/2015	$1,107	$90	53.38	18.73				
2	12/30/2016	$1,128	$99	52.35	20.44	1.92%	9.73%	(1.95%)	2.101
3	12/29/2017	$1,210	$110	52.11	21.48	6.99%	10.63%	(0.46%)	2.021
4	12/31/2018	$1,314	$133	46.10	16.64	8.20%	19.00%	(12.25%)	0.876
5	12/31/2019	$1,391	$140	52.45	20.86	5.73%	5.42%	12.90%	3.848
6	12/31/2020	$1,342	$97	72.10	30.37	(3.56%)	(36.99%)	31.82%	-0.821
7	12/31/2021	$1,542	$200	37.18	24.71	13.84%	72.54%	(66.23%)	0.341
8	12/30/2022	$1,709	$188	39.34	18.61	10.29%	(6.14%)	5.65%	-3.029

Page Break

The MEANS Procedure

Variable	Mean	Std Dev	Minimum	Median	Maximum
SPSG	0.0620340	0.0568013	-0.0355988	0.0698828	0.1384423
EPSG	0.1059736	0.3286245	-0.3699270	0.0973041	0.7253549
DPRG	-0.0435992	0.3060010	-0.6622831	-0.0045951	0.3181937
PEG	0.7622938	2.2347515	-3.0287053	0.8756288	3.8477417

> There are no formatting options for PROC MEANS. To display similar results with your preferred format, use the PROC TABULATE statement.

Program 1.8B: Descriptive Statistics of the Aggregate Financial Performance of S&P 500 Companies

```
proc tabulate data = NSP500FIN;
 var SPSG EPSG DPRG PEG;
 table SPSG*F=percent8.2 EPSG*F=percent8.2 DPRG*F=percent8.2 PEG, mean stddev median max;
run;
```

Output 1.8B: Descriptive Statistics of the Aggregate Financial Performance of S&P 500 Companies

	Mean	StdDev	Median	Max
Sales Growth Rate	6.20%	5.68%	6.99%	13.84%
Earnings Growth Rate	10.60%	32.86%	9.73%	72.54%
Dividend Payout Ratio Growth Rate	(4.36%)	30.60%	(0.46%)	31.82%
Price-to-Earning Growth Ratio	0.76	2.23	0.88	3.85

Visual Descriptive Statistics

Graphical descriptive statistics or data visualization is a data science technique that uses graphical and pictorial depictions to convey stylized facts (such as patterns, trends, and correlations) about the data in a visually compelling and interactive way. Data visualization skills are crucial for financial professionals. Indeed, some financial data are generated at such high frequencies that the only way to quickly communicate and digest the information embedded in them is through visualizations. Hence, financial data is often conveyed through visualizations by the financial media (for example, stock charts, yield curves, and macroeconomic graphs). Visualizations are also used for investment and financial analyses, as well as performance analysis and financial planning.

The SAS program shown in Program 1.8C invokes the SGPLOT procedure to graph the time series of the growth rate of aggregate EPS and PEG of the S&P 500 index. In the DATA statement, we use a filter (WHERE) to specify the range of values to plot (post-December 2015). We use the XAXIS statement to specify various configurations for the rendering of the X-axis of the plot.[4]

---

[4] The SGPLOT procedure is a versatile SAS ODS graphics procedure that can be used to produce a large number of statistical and data visualization charts. We will go into more details about the procedure in Chapter Two. You can learn more about the ODS Graphics procedures by reviewing SAS® 9.4 ODS Graphics: Procedures Guide, Sixth Edition available at https://documentation.sas.com/doc/en/pgmsascdc/9.4_3.5/grstatproc/titlepage.htm.

Program 1.8C: Visualizing the Financial Performance of S&P 500 Companies Using PROC SGPLOT

```
title 'Annual EPS Growth Rate and PEG Ratios for the S&P 500 Index';
proc sgplot data= NSP500FIN (where=(date>'31Dec2015'd));
      series x=Date y=EPSG;
      series x=Date  y=PEG /Y2AXIS;
      xaxis values=('31Dec2016'd to '31Dec2022'd by year);
      yaxis grid;
run;
title;
```

Output 1.8C: Financial Performance of S&P 500 Companies

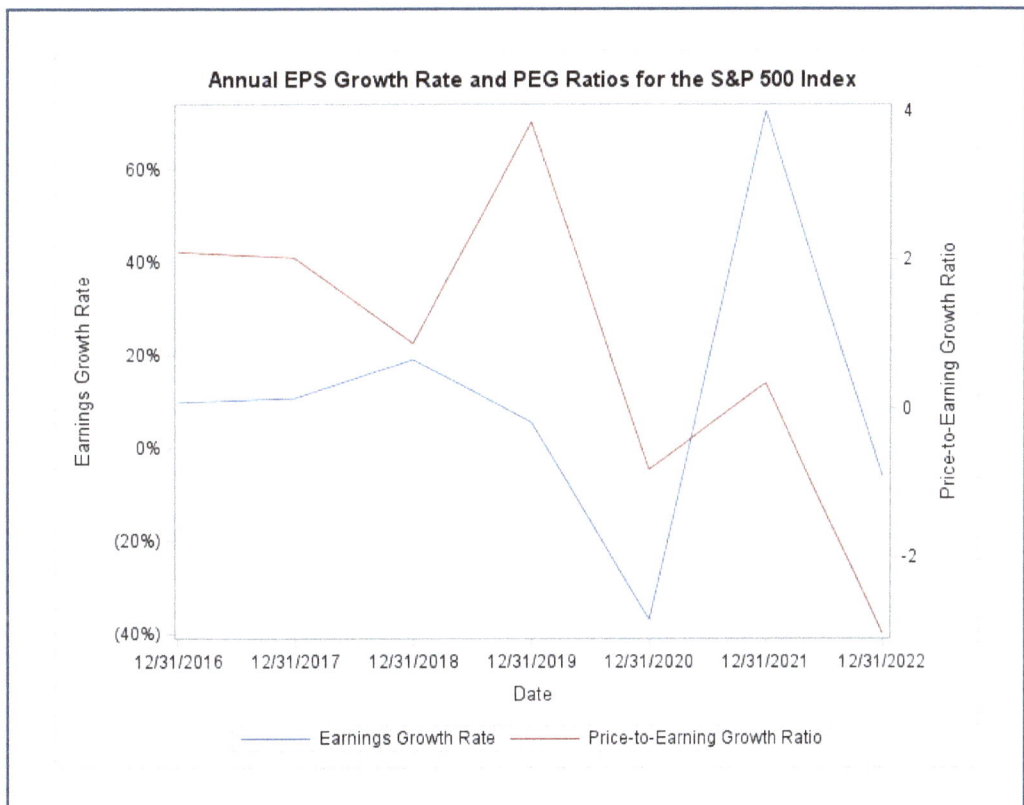

Annual EPS Growth Rate and PEG Ratios for the S&P 500 Index

The graph shown in Output 1.8C suggests that the aggregate valuation of large capitalization stocks appears to move in tandem with the growth in their aggregate earnings. Apparent in the plot are episodes of aggregate overvaluation and undervaluation relative to the growth rate of aggregate earnings.

Inferential Statistics

Most readers of this book would have encountered inferential statistical methods in prior statistics or econometric courses. Remember from the previous section of this chapter that financial econometrics also uses inferential statistical methods. Inferential statistics aim to draw conclusions about events or phenomena that occur in a large group (population) by studying a subset of that group (sample). This is achieved by estimating the value of the unknown characteristics of the population using the sample as the proxy. Hypothesis testing is then performed to validate that the statistics drawn from the sample are reliable estimates of the unknown population characteristics. Hypothesis testing normally would require accepting a set of assumptions and theorems concerning the level of measurement of the variable of interest, the method of sampling, the shape of the population distribution, and the sample size. For example, suppose an equity analyst asserts that over five years, the average growth rates of the return on assets (ROA) of large firms are the same across all sectors of the S&P 500, or a risk manager proclaims that the expected default rate in the bank's auto loan portfolio would not exceed 5% over the life of the loan. These types of assertions are claims that can be tested by inferential statistics.[5]

Let us examine the accuracy of the first claim using inferential statistics. Specifically, we will conduct an ANOVA test (using SAS) of the equality of means to judge whether the five-year average growth rate of the ROAs of firms in the S&P 500 index is the same across the sectors of the index. The Microsoft Excel file SPX_Members.xlsx contains financial data (sales growth, earnings growth, ROA growth, as well as the one-, three-, five-, and ten-year annualized returns) for the 503 firms in the S&P 500 index. Since this data is in Excel format, we will also introduce the SAS code for importing Microsoft Excel files into SAS.

First, let's request the SPX_Members.xlsx file from the GitHub repository by submitting the PROC HTTP statement below. The FILENAME statement uses the 'SPX' FILEREF to identify the name and file directory in which the requested data set will be stored (in this case the directory used by SAS for the WORK library). This will be the SAS temporary folder on your computer or server.

> Modify Program 1.7, which contains the SAS code used for requesting the STOCKS data set from the GitHub repository. SPX_Members.xlsx file might already be in the SAS temporary folder of your computer if you have cloned the entire GitHub repository using Program 1.5.

---

[5] For those who are new to statistics or need a refresher on basic statistical concepts, SAS offers "Introduction to Statistical Concepts," a free online course in statistics. You can learn more about the course at https://learn.sas.com/course/view.php?id=643.

Program 1.9A: Requesting Excel File from GitHub Data Repository Using SAS HTTP Request

```
filename SPX "%sysfunc(getoption(WORK))/SPX_Members.xlsx";
proc http
      url="https://github.com/finsasdata/Bookdata/raw/main/SPX_Members.xlsx"
      out=SPX
      method ="get";
run;
```

Program 1.9B: Importing Excel File into SAS Using PROC IMPORT

```
/*PROC IMPORT statement below is used to import files from various
systems into SAS. The set of code below imports the SPX_Members.xlsx
file from its current location on the computer into the SPX_Members SAS
datafile in the WORK library*/
proc import out=SPX_Members
      datafile= spx
      dbms= xlsx
      replace;
      getnames= YES;
      sheet= Sheet1;
run;
```

The SPX_Members.xlsx is still in Excel format and would need to be imported into SAS file format using the PROC IMPORT statement below. The DATAFILE statement specifies the name of the Excel data to import into SAS. The OUT statement specifies the SAS name for the imported data set. The DBMS statement informs SAS that the data will be imported from an Excel file format. The REPLACE statement instructs SAS to replace the current version of the SPX data set that might exist in the library with the newly imported version. The GETNAMES statement informs SAS to obtain the variable names from the first row of the Excel file, while the SHEET statement informs SAS to read the data from the specified sheet.

The ANOVA test requires some assumptions about the distribution of the data. These include:

- The five-year growth rates of returns, in general, follow a normal distribution.
- The growth rates of returns have homogenous variance.
- The growth rates of returns were independently sampled.

$$H_0: \ \mu_1 = \mu_2 = \mu_3 \ldots \ldots = \mu_6$$

$$H_{01}: \textit{The means are not equal}$$

Program 1.9C shows the SAS code for implementing the ANOVA procedure. The ANOVA statement invokes the procedure, followed by the DATA statement that specifies the name of the SAS data set we will be conducting the test on. The CLASS statement specifies the group, which in this case is a group of 11 GIC sectors of the S&P 500 index.

Program 1.9C: Using PROC ANOVA for the Test of Equality of Five-Year Growth Rates Sector ROAs

```
ods graphics on;
proc anova data= SPX_Members;
      title 'Anova Test of Equality of Industry Performance';
      class Sector;
      model ROAG5Y = SECTOR;
      /*Let's also test for equality of variance by including the code
below. If the p-value of the Levene test rejects the null of equal variance,
then the Welch Anova Test of the Equality of means will be used*/
      means SECTOR/hovtest=levene welch;
run;
title;
ods graphics off;
```

Output 1.9C: ANOVA Test for Equality of Five-Year Sector ROA Growth Rates

Anova Test of Equality of Industry Performance

The ANOVA Procedure

Dependent Variable: ROAG5Y ROAG5Y

Source	DF	Sum of Squares	Mean Square	F Value	Pr > F
Model	10	3917.38735	391.73874	11.80	<.0001
Error	481	15972.45322	33.20676		
Corrected Total	491	19889.84057			

R-Square	Coeff Var	Root MSE	ROAG5Y Mean
0.196954	82.10198	5.762531	7.018748

Source	DF	Anova SS	Mean Square	F Value	Pr > F
Sector	10	3917.387351	391.738735	11.80	<.0001

Anova Test of Equality of Industry Performance

The ANOVA Procedure

Levene's Test for Homogeneity of ROAG5Y Variance ANOVA of Squared Deviations from Group Means					
Source	DF	Sum of Squares	Mean Square	F Value	Pr > F
Sector	10	144449	14444.9	3.45	0.0002
Error	481	2013921	4186.9		

Welch's ANOVA for ROAG5Y			
Source	DF	F Value	Pr > F
Sector	10.0000	20.02	<.0001
Error	157.2		

The MODEL statement specifies the numeric dependent variable (ROAG5Y) and the independent effect (SECTORS). The MEANS statement is used to request the computation of the means of the dependent variable for the effect groups. The HOVTEST=LEVENE option is used to request the Levene (1960) test of the homogeneity of variances. While the WELCH option is used to request the Welch (1951) variance-weighted one-way ANOVA.

The p-value of the Levene's test for homogenous variance indicates that we should reject the null. Hence, the results of the Welch ANOVA test (shown below), which adjusts for unequal variances in a one-way ANOVA, will be used. From the Welch ANOVA results, the null of an equal five-year growth rate of ROA for all sectors of the index is rejected. We can then conclude from the results that the five-year average growth rates of ROA and the degrees of their dispersion are statistically not the same across all sectors of the index.

Output 1.9D shows the box plot of the five-year growth rate of ROA for all the sectors. You will notice on the plot that the averages of the growth rates of ROA are not the same across the sectors and that the degrees of dispersion of growth rates are also distinctly different within each sector. The information technology sector appears to have the highest average growth rate, while the consumer discretionary sector appears to have the highest degree of dispersion of the average growth rates. The visualization provides further corroboration for the conclusion that we derived from our inferential test that the equity analyst's assertion is most likely inaccurate.

Output 1.9D: Distribution of Five-Year Sector ROA Growth Rates

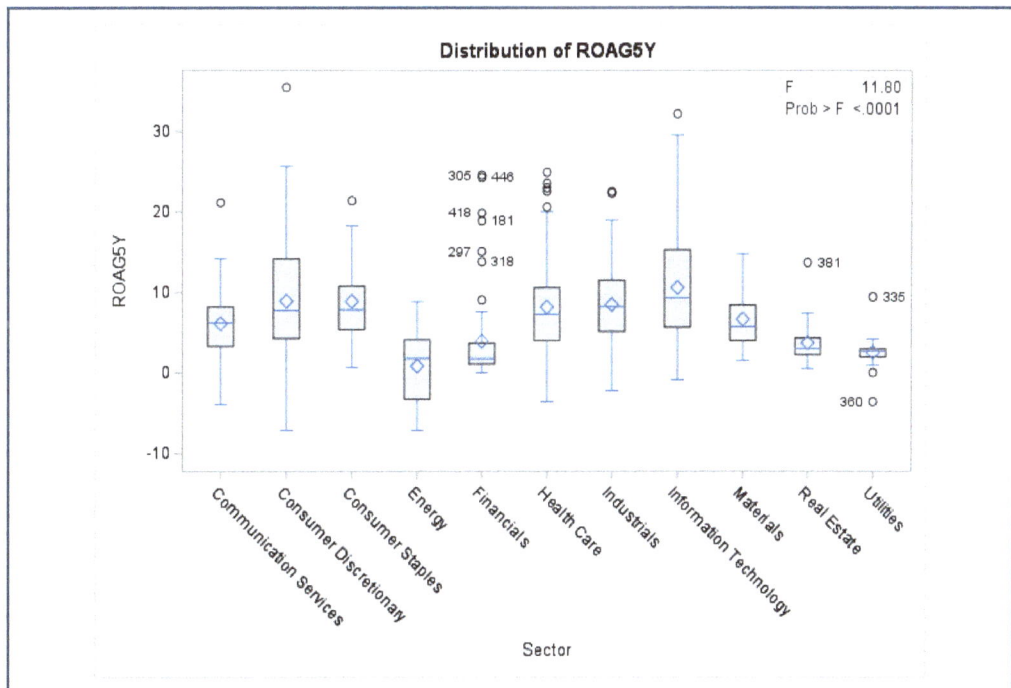

Diagnostic Analytics

Diagnostic analytics are used to understand why and how trends, events, and phenomena occur. Although they are often used in conjunction with other types of analytics approaches such as descriptive and predictive analytics, diagnostic analytics are especially useful because they allow us to study how phenomena occur in controlled environments. The insight that we obtained from such studies might establish or rule out the need to conduct further exploration of the problem with other analytics techniques. Financial data scientists use diagnostic analytics to model complex real-world problems, which often involve elements of uncertainty in controlled settings. These models are then used to examine how the system or phenomenon behaves or responds to different inputs or signals.

Simulation is a common methodology used in diagnostic analytics. Simulations are mathematical models that incorporate the essential characteristics of the real-world system or processes to be studied. For example, simulations are used in sensitivity analyses to study why and how outcomes respond to fluctuations in some variables of interest. An index portfolio manager might be interested in how the portfolio will perform over time or when significant events occur in the market. The manager might also be interested in how the portfolio would behave if the assumptions the portfolio manager has made about the distributional properties of the portfolio actually hold in the real world. Banks and other financial services organizations use stress testing (a simulation approach) to also study how their financial structure might be impacted by adverse economic or market conditions.

Simulations will be discussed in more detail in subsequent chapters of the book. For now, let us explore a simple use case of how simulations can be used to examine the assumption about the distributional properties of asset returns. From historical observation, we have determined that the average and standard deviation of the monthly returns on the index from 1985 to 2022 (approximately 457 months) are 0.677% and 4.466%, respectively. If we accept that stock index returns also follow a Gaussian random walk process, we can use simulations to study the theoretical distribution of the monthly returns on the S&P 500 index. A Gaussian random walk process is a stochastic process with a drift component. It is commonly used in simulating the patterns of price evolution for stocks. The discrete version of the equation specification is below.

$$R_t = \mu\Delta t + \sigma\varepsilon\sqrt{\Delta t} \qquad (1.1)$$

where $\mu\Delta t$ is the drift component that represents the average monthly rate of return on the index and $\sigma\sqrt{\Delta t}$ is the random or stochastic component in the return process for the index.

For now, let's focus on simulating the stochastic components of the stock return process. In subsequent chapters of the book, we will expand the scope of the simulation and incorporate the drift aspect of the process. If we assume that the stochastic component of the process follows a normal distribution with mean $\mu = 0.677\%$ and standard deviation $\sigma = 4.466\%$, then we can simulate the monthly returns on the S&P 500 using the SAS code in Program 1.10.[6]

---

[6] It is common in practice to use significantly higher number (in the thousands) of replications to ensure that your results are stable. We will use this approach in subsequent chapters of the book when we cover simulations in more detail. For now, we will use ten replications to keep things simple.

Program 1.10: Simulating Monthly Returns of the S&P 500 Index

```
%let smean=0.0067658;
%let ssd = 0.04465726;
data SSPX;
    call streaminit(123);
        do iter=1 to 10; /*number of replication*/
                do time = 1 to 457; /*Simulation window*/
                        simret =rand("normal",&smean,&ssd);
                        output;
                end;
        end;
        label Simret='Simulated Monthly Returns';
run;

/* Extracting the Descriptive Statistic for the Simulated Returns*/

proc tabulate data=SSPX;
        class iter;
        var  simret;
        table iter*simret,mean*f=percent8.2 stddev*f=percent8.2;
        table simret='Average Simulated Returns',mean*f=percent8.2 stddev*f=percent8.2;
run;
```

In the code, we stored the mean and standard deviation of the monthly returns in two macrovariables (SMEAN and SSD). The CALL STREAMINIT statement is used to specify the seed values for the subsequent random number generator function, which is invoked using the RAND function. The two DO statements iterate the random number generator over two instances. The instance (1 to 10) is the number of replications to perform, while the second instance (1 to 457) is the number of monthly returns to simulate. Specified in the RAND functions are the two parameters of the normal distributions, which are mean and standard deviation. The OUTPUT statement informs SAS to write the observation to the SAS data set named SSPX. We close each instance of the DO loops with the END statement.

To compute the descriptive statistics, we invoke the TABULATE procedure. We use the ITER variable as a classification variable so that SAS can compute the statistics for each replication of the simulation. The mean and standard deviation statistics for each replication and the entire simulated series are requested using the TABLE statement.

Output 1.10 shows the descriptive statistics produced by invoking the TABULATE statement. Notice the variation in the sample averages computed from each iteration, but a slightly more compact range of values for the standard deviation. You will also notice that the average of the simulated values is very close to the parameters of the distributions that we fed into the RAND function. We will discuss the theory of sampling distribution that supports these findings in Chapter Four.

Output 1.10: Descriptive Statistics from Simulated Monthly Returns of the S&P 500 Index

iter		Mean	StdDev
1	Simulated Monthly Returns	0.79%	4.34%
2	Simulated Monthly Returns	1.02%	4.61%
3	Simulated Monthly Returns	0.69%	4.64%
4	Simulated Monthly Returns	0.43%	4.75%
5	Simulated Monthly Returns	0.83%	4.60%
6	Simulated Monthly Returns	0.73%	4.46%
7	Simulated Monthly Returns	0.43%	4.36%
8	Simulated Monthly Returns	0.69%	4.40%
9	Simulated Monthly Returns	0.96%	4.32%
10	Simulated Monthly Returns	0.51%	4.35%

	Mean	StdDev
Average Simulated Returns	0.71%	4.48%

Predictive Analytics

Predictive analytics is one of the fundamental aspects of data science. It involves the use of data and an assortment of advanced statistical methods to predict future events, behaviors, and trends. More generally, predictive analytics aims to provide decision-makers with the best insights into what will happen in the future. With its origin in data mining, predictive analytics has grown to encompass the use of a wide range of statistical algorithms, data modeling techniques, and artificial intelligence applications such as machine learning and deep learning.

Given the substantial amount of computing power and a vast amount of readily available data to deploy, the applications of predictive analytics in the finance domain are limitless. Predictive analytics is used for algorithmic trading, high-frequency trading, portfolio construction, portfolio risk management, credit risk management, liquidity risk management, fraud prevention, regulatory compliance, and enforcement, to name a few. Indeed, right now, approximately 80 percent of the trading volume on the US stock exchanges is implemented by super-fast computers that have been trained to digest and analyze large amounts of pertinent stock market and economic information for trade signals, which are then implemented at lightning speed to maximize their investment value.[7] Many financial institutions also use predictive analytics to identify suspicious events and prevent fraudulent transactions. Another common

---

[7] See Amaro (2018).

use of predictive analytics in the financial services industry is for developing credit scoring models for making loan decisions. In subsequent sections of the book, we will showcase some implementations of the financial services applications of predictive analytics models in SAS.

Prescriptive Analytics

Prescriptive analytics involves the use of data and computational algorithms to identify critical factors and the optimal course of action for a particular scenario or business problem. Although its roots are in operations research, prescriptive analytics share similar underpinning with other analytics techniques, in the sense that it is based on unearthing statistical relationships between the choice variables and assessing the impact of the fluctuations in these variables on the decision pattern and possible outcomes under consideration. The aim of prescriptive analytics is to provide decision-makers with the best choice from a variety of possible choices. In some organizations, prescriptive analytics are implemented to extend the insights acquired from prior predictive analytics activities. In finance, prescriptive analytics is mostly used to solve optimization problems. These include linear optimization problems such as revenue and profit maximization, non-linear optimization problems such as portfolio optimization, and stochastic optimization problems, which are common in the risk management and governance domain.

Machine Intelligence and Machine Learning

Although intelligence and learning are used interchangeably, they are not the same. Intelligence is the ability to develop knowledge through cognition, while learning is the acquisition of knowledge through the application of specific methods. For example, by reading and going over the practice exercises in this book, readers will learn about the techniques used in data science. Intelligence encompasses learning as well as other cognitive functions such as perception, attention, memory, and judgment. Therefore, it is evident that learning is a subset of intelligence.

Artificial intelligence and machine learning are data science concepts that are also used interchangeably. However, drawing from the earlier distinction, we can see that they are essentially not the same. Artificial intelligence is the computational mimicry of human intelligence through the development of algorithms that can perceive and adapt to new inputs and synthesize knowledge from them, just like we humans do. Machine learning is a subset of artificial intelligence in which algorithms are trained to sift through large amounts of data and learn from them. Artificial intelligence and machine learning algorithms are used in finance for the predictive analytics cases described in the previous section. Black box trading strategies, which are widely used in finance, rely on algorithms that use machine learning to deduce trading signals from financial and economic data. These signals are often based on complicated and sometimes uninterpretable relationships which the algorithms can decipher from the data by sheer application of brute computing power and complex transformations of the input variables.

Supervised, Unsupervised, and Reinforcement Learning

Machine learning techniques fall into three broad categories: supervised, unsupervised, and reinforcement learning. The main difference between these categories is the process by which the algorithm is trained to solve the prediction or classification problem.

Supervised Learning

In supervised learning, algorithms are trained to discern the predictors of a target outcome or range of outcomes from a set of potential predictors. The algorithm iteratively learns by evaluating obvious and latent relationships between a given set of pre-classified outcomes and its potential predictors. Essentially, the algorithm learns about what variables can predict the target outcome(s) by establishing the existence of relationships between the predictors and the target variable. Although supervised learning is conceptually simple, it is nevertheless a powerful and widely used data science technique in the finance domain. Supervised learning techniques are used for investment decisions, stock prediction models, and credit risk models to name a few. Examples of these algorithms include:

- Decision tree
- Random forest
- Neural network
- Regression models
- Support vector machines

Unsupervised Learning

Unsupervised learning algorithms are fed unlabeled data and tasked with discerning whether commonalities exist between them. What distinguishes this approach from other learning techniques is the minimal level of human intervention that is needed in the iterative process. The algorithm is essentially tasked with sifting through the data to find common patterns or hidden groupings that exist in it without prior knowledge of such structures or patterns. The algorithm learns by iteratively clustering or organizing the variables such that each grouping of the data increasingly would share common attributes or distinguishing features from other groupings.

Financial data scientists use unsupervised learning for dimension reductions and data clustering. Financial and economic variables sometimes share similar underlying properties; therefore, dimension reduction and data clustering are especially useful for big data applications in finance. They help to achieve well-calibrated supervised learning models that are parametrically and non-parametrically efficient. Practical applications of unsupervised learning in finance include portfolio construction, risk governance, and asset pricing. Common types of unsupervised learning include:

- Principal component analysis
- K-means clustering
- Hierarchical clustering

Reinforcement Learning

Reinforcement learning algorithms apply the carrot and stick concept to machine learning. The algorithm learns to discern the relationships in the data through incentive functions, which penalize the algorithm for making wrong predictions and reward it for accurate predictions. The algorithm is typically not told what to predict or classify, but only rewarded or penalized for the accuracy of its predictions or classification. In the same manner as human behavior, the algorithm iteratively learns to solve the prediction or classification problems through the link that the incentive function has to the problem. Learning is fundamentally framed as an optimization problem in which the algorithm seeks to maximize rewards and minimize costs through prediction or classification accuracy. Reinforcement learning is an emerging field in finance, but it has promising future applications in areas such as automated personal financial advisory services (also known as robo-advisors), investment gamification, and trade execution. Common types of reinforcement learning algorithms include:

- Sequential decision-making algorithms
- Value-based decision algorithms
- Policy-based decision algorithms

Parametric Versus Nonparametric Algorithms

Parametric algorithms use a defined set of parameters to model the relationship between the target outcomes and the predictor variables. They typically employ a set of assumptions to define the relationships between the predictors and the target. These assumptions fundamentally then define the mapping functions that the algorithm learns to build the prediction or classification model for the target variable. For example, simple logistic regressions assume a binary target variable, independence between observations, little to no multicollinearity between the predictor variables, and a linear relationship between the predictor variables and the logit of the target variable, to list a few. Nonparametric algorithms do not make specific assumptions about the relationship between the predictor variables and the target variable. Hence, they do not require a specific mapping function and can estimate the unknown function, which could be of any form.

It is important to note that while supervised and unsupervised learning algorithms include those that are parametric and nonparametric, nonparametric algorithms tend to be more frequently seen in the category of unsupervised learning algorithms. An example of a nonparametric type of supervised algorithm is the decision tree algorithm, which we will discuss in a subsequent chapter of the book.

Limitations of Financial Data Science

Data science techniques are powerful tools for solving a myriad of societal and business problems. However, they do have some limitations. We highlight two of these below.

Performance Degradation

As highlighted earlier, the algorithm's ability to solve prediction and classification problems relies on discovering patterns and relationships in the data. In many cases, these patterns and relationships are transitory in nature. Thus, the efficacies of these algorithms in business settings are also often transitory. Performance degradation of predictive algorithms is a widely recognized problem in predictive and machine learning models. This is a particularly challenging problem because there tends to be a lot at stake (at least financially) when these models are applied in financial settings. As the functional efficacy of analytics models degrades, the economic cost of deploying them in financial settings increases. Therefore, the analytic life cycle for financial data scientists is a continuous loop predicated on the need to continuously update or develop new models as existing models lose their potency over time.

Overfitting Versus Underfitting

Figuring out the optimal accuracy of predictive models before deploying them for production continues to be at the forefront of debate in the data science domain. While it is generally agreed that models that are overfitted in the development stage will most likely perform poorly in the production stage, the same notion also applies to under-fitted models. Given the ramifications of such outcomes in financial settings, conducting an honest assessment of model performance is crucial.

Honest model assessment judges the performance of the models using different sets of data than the ones used to train the model. The training data set is used to train the algorithm and as the model is being trained, the validation data set is iteratively used to assess the desired model characteristics. In some cases, a final test data set might also be used to conduct further assessment before the model is deployed for production. We will discuss honest assessment in more detail in Chapter Seven.

You should note that concerns with model fitness in finance transcend the issues of overfitting and underfitting the data. In some finance settings such as stock trading, algorithms are in constant interaction with other algorithms and human traders. However, stock trading is inherently a pseudo-adversarial transaction, and therefore the algorithm might be susceptible to the adversarial tactics of other market actors. (See Nehemya et. al, 2020.) For example, the algorithm might inadvertently fit the model to bad inputs that are intentionally fed to it by other algorithms or market actors. Since trading algorithms learn from the data, they could also inadvertently learn unethical or illegal patterns in market data – these include market manipulation or collusive behaviors. Therefore, the scope of concern with model fit in finance extends beyond overfitting or underfitting but also includes the possibility that the model might be learning the wrong lessons from the data. And with the pervasiveness of black box trading, we might not know that this might be indeed what is happening.

Ethics, Biases, Transparency, and Economic Issues

The widespread applications of data science in virtually every scope of human activity have raised several ethical, social, and economic concerns. As you practice your data science craft, it is important to be cognizant of these issues and how they impact the utility of data science in finance applications. We present a quick summary of some of the ethical, social, and economic issues arising from the widespread use of data science techniques in modern society.

Ethical Issues in Financial Data Science

From an ethical point of view, concerns have been raised about the reliance on algorithms for decision-making. Human decision-making often requires balancing various trade-offs and nuances that algorithms are not naturally equipped to handle. Algorithms are generally designed around the concepts of efficiency and rationality, which sometimes conflict with observed human behaviors, emotions, and preferences such as altruism and fairness, to name a few.

One area of ethical concern in the use of data science in finance is the impact of algorithms on the structure and functioning of financial markets. Critics of algorithmic trading argue that the high levels of volatility that are now a common feature of the financial markets are due to the pervasiveness of algorithm-based trading strategies.[8] Others have argued that algorithmic trading provides little utility in terms of price discovery and allocative efficiency while extracting value from investors who do not have access to similar tools (Yadav, 2015). In May 2010, a self-taught stock trader operating out of his bedroom triggered a $1 trillion momentary crash in the US stock market. In May 2022, a trader at Citigroup's London office mistakenly added an extra zero to the trade order and in a split second, caused the entire stock market across Europe to crash by as much as 8% (over $300 billion) in a matter of minutes.[9] In reality, the amplifying forces that cause

---

[8] Articles in the financial news media periodically feature arguments along this line. See for example, "Volatility: How 'Algos' Changed the Rhythm of the Market" in the January 9th, 2019, edition of Financial Times and "A Down Day on the Markets? Analysts Say Blame the Machines" in the February 8th, 2018, edition of The Washington Post.

[9] On August 24th, 2015, another algorithm-related flash crash occurred in the first 15 minutes of trading. This crash is speculated to have been caused by overnight drying-up of liquidity. Algorithms responded to the dislocation in the market by halting trades, thereby further exacerbating the liquidity problem. More on the cause of this crash can be found at https://www.cnbc.com/2015/09/25/what-happened-during-the-aug-24-flash-crash.html.

the actions of these single individuals to result in such devastating financial outcomes are the innumerable number of trading algorithms that have been deployed in financial markets across the globe.

Bias

Algorithms learn from the information provided to them, and if the information is biased, the predictions or classifications made by the algorithm might also be biased as well. Along this line, some have argued that algorithms actually exacerbate social problems because they learn and then reinforce existing biases from the societal data. For example, a 2018 study by professors from the University of California Berkeley found that while algorithmic-based mortgage decisions result in less discriminatory (in terms of loan approval) outcomes for minority borrowers than face-to-face underwriting, they still result in significantly higher loan rates for minority borrower compared to white borrowers, after controlling for all other risk factors (such as income, credit scores, and loan amount) that go into loan underwriting process (Bartlett et al., 2019).

Transparency

One of the costs associated with the increasing sophistication of algorithms that are being developed is the loss of interpretability. Algorithms are essentially becoming black boxes that accept inputs and spew out output, which the end user must accept with blind faith. Interpretable models are vital in decision-making because they allow the decision-maker to link the decision outcomes to observable, repeatable, and assessable functions of the inputs. It allows the user to know why they are following the set of actions that the algorithm is recommending. Machines are not perfect, they sometimes malfunction, and without transparency, we might not know that such malfunction has occurred until it is too late. Concerning our earlier discussion of the flash crashes, it is useful to think of the actions of these traders as inputs, which eventually led all these trading algorithms to react in ways that moved the markets precipitously. However, given that we, in general, still lack the full understanding of how the black boxes of algorithmic trading work, the intervention by regulators so far has been limited to implementing circuit breakers to prevent the problems from getting worse when they do occur.

Economics

Many of the structural changes that we have seen in the global economy over the past three decades can be traced to advancements in computing. If we are to conceptualize what the future economy would look like, given our recent history, the conclusion will be that a computational economy driven by advanced data sciences is what the future portends. However, this future raises a lot of questions that data scientists and policymakers would need to grapple with. For example, What would happen to people whose jobs or industries are disrupted or replaced by algorithms? How would policymakers respond to economic inequality, which some argue has been made worse by algorithms? (Zatko, 2022) How much control and autonomy are we as a society willing to surrender to algorithms? How would the regulatory and legal landscape evolve to potentially new and disruptive technologies? These are a few of the economic dilemmas that society will need to address as we become more reliant on data science to drive our economies.

Regulatory Landscape

Financial institutions are highly regulated entities and over the years, these organizations have become more reliant on data science to drive their business process and regulatory compliance reporting, thereby creating a nexus of regulatory concerns for how data science is used in the industry. In this book, we will explore two areas where data science is used by financial institutions for regulatory reporting purposes. Specifically, we will focus on how data science is used for market and credit risk modeling.

Risk modeling is in itself a risky endeavor because it entails making forecasts about future risk outcomes. For financial institutions, such forecasts are often associated with regulatory mandates concerning capital provisioning, risk governance and budgeting, and strategic business choices. Therefore, extra care is warranted when employing data science techniques in financial services organizations. Indeed, all financial services organizations with regulatory reporting mandates are required to adhere to a framework for model risk management. This mandate was set to ensure that their modeling processes are in line with best practices and that they present accurate pictures of the financial standing of the organization for regulatory purposes.

For market risk, we will explore examples of value-at-risk (VaR) implementations in SAS. For credit risk, we will explore the implementation of various reportable measures relating to credit portfolios in SAS. These include modeling the credit exposures, default probabilities, and their determinants for portfolios of credit obligations.

Exercises

1. The text file Portfolio01.txt contains the stock tickers, number of shares, cost basis, ending beats, and the betas of nine stocks in a concentrated portfolio.

```
Ticker Shares Price TotRet Beta
AAPL 5907.17 11.85 405 1
BA 4002.46 32.48 72.92 1.14
BAC 4835.16 22.75 5.55 2.07
CAT 7115.75 21.08 90.2 2.01
GE 1707.07 29.29 17.75 1.67
IBM 820.94 109.63 183.17 0.61
LMT 2910.82 37.79 80 0.7
MSFT 5245.41 26.69 25.79 1.03
PNC 3465 43.29 57.34 1.36
```

a. Write a SAS program to create a temporary SAS data set (**Portfolio01**) using the data in Portfolio01.txt.

b. Using the created **Portfolio01** data set, create a new variable InitValue that calculates the initial dollar investment in each stock (multiply Shares by Cost) and a variable that calculates the final value (FinValue) of the dollar investment in each stock (multiply Shares by Price).

c. Create a new variable (TotRet) that calculates the ten-year return on each stock.

d. The total initial dollar amount invested in the portfolio is one million dollars. Use this information to create a new variable (InitWeight) that calculates the initial portfolio weights in each stock (InitValue/$1,000,0000).

e. Assign the following formats and labels to each variable.

Variable	Format	Label
Shares	Comma10.2	Number of Shares
Cost	Dollar10.2	Cost Basis
Price	Dollar10.2	Current Price
Beta	Bestd6.2	Beta
TotRet	Percent8.2	Holding Period Return
InitValue	Dollar13.2	Initial Investment Value
FinValue	Dollar13.2	Final Investment Value
InitWeight	Percent8.2	Initial Weight

f. Use the PROC PRINT statement to display your completed Portfolio01 data set using the format and variable labels.

   i. Which stocks had the highest and lowest initial values?

   ii. Which stocks had the highest and lowest final values?

   iii. Over the ten years, did cheaper stocks perform better than more expensive stocks?

   iv. Over the ten years, did stocks with higher initial shares (weights) perform better than those with a lower initial number of shares (weights)?

   v. Did stocks with higher betas perform better than stocks with lower betas?

2. Let's conduct a portfolio-level analysis of our Portfolio01 data set.

a. Write a SAS program to calculate the average, sum, minimum, maximum, and median number of shares, costs, prices, and holding period returns for the stocks in the portfolio. If your result is unformatted, you probably used PROC MEANS. Create the same result using PROC TABULATE and specify the correct format for each statistic as shown in the table above.

> **Hint:** Include the following modification to the TABLE statement in PROC TABULATE.
> Shares*F=comma10.2 Cost*F=dollar10.2 Price*F=dollar10.2
> Beta*F=bestd6.2 initvalue*F=dollar13.2 FinValue*F=dollar13.2
> TotRet*F=percent8.2,mean sum median min max;

      i. What is the average number of shares, costs, prices, beta, initial values, and final values of the stocks in the portfolio?

     ii. What was the ending value of the portfolio? Given the initial value of the portfolio, what were the dollar and percent holding period returns on the portfolio?

   iii. Which stocks contributed the most value to the portfolio? Which contributed the least?

  b. Now write a SAS program to calculate the holding period return and the beta of the portfolio. Compare the result to the calculations you performed in Part A.

> **Hint:** Include the following modification to the TABLE statement for PROC TABULATE.
> Shares*F=comma10.2 Cost*F=dollar10.2 Price*F=dollar10.2
> initvalue*F=dollar13.2 FinValue*F=dollar13.2 TotRet*F=percent8.2 ,mean;

3. A macro analyst at a boutique investment fund is evaluating the impact of various economic factors on the stock market performance. The analyst collects data on the monthly percent change in the following variables from the Federal Reserve Bank of St. Louis's FRED economic database[10] and compiles them into the Freddata01 SAS file. (The data set is available in the book's GitHub Repository: https://github.com/finsasdata/Bookdata/raw/main/freddata01.sas7bdat). The variable names and their labels are shown in the table below.

UNRATE	Unemployment Rate, Seasonally Adjusted
PCE	Personal Consumption Expenditures, Seasonally Adjusted Annual Rate
AAA10Y	Moody's Seasoned Aaa Corporate Bond Yield Relative to Yield on 10-Year Treasury Constant Maturity
HOUST	New Privately-Owned Housing Units Started: Total Units, Seasonally Adjusted Annual Rate
ICSA	Initial Claims, Seasonally Adjusted
T10Y3M	10-Year Treasury Constant Maturity Minus 3-Month Treasury Constant Maturity, Not Seasonally Adjusted
PPIACO	Producer Price Index by Commodity: All Commodities, (Index 1982=100), Not Seasonally Adjusted
WILLLRGCAP	Wilshire US Large-Cap Total Market Index, Not Seasonally Adjusted

---

[10] The Federal Reserve Bank of St. Louis' FRED economic database is one of the largest free databases of US and international economic and financial time series. Visit https://fred.stlouisfed.org/ to learn more about it and to request your own data for further exploration.

WILLMIDCAP	Wilshire US Mid-Cap Total Market Index, Not Seasonally Adjusted
WILLSMLCAP	Wilshire US Small-Cap Total Market Index, Not Seasonally Adjusted
WILL5000IND	Wilshire 5000 Total Market Index, Not Seasonally Adjusted
UMCSENT	University of Michigan: Consumer Sentiment, Percent Change

a. Write a SAS procedure (PROC CORR) to examine the relationships between these macroeconomic variables and the four market indices.

> **Hint:** This can also be executed using the TASK menu in both Enterprise Guide and SAS Studio.

   i. Which economic variables have statistically significant positive and negative correlations with the four market indices? Why do some variables have positive and others negative relationships with the market indices?

   ii. Are there any differences in the correlations between the economic variables and the four market indices? What could explain these differences?

   iii. Which economic variables have statistically significant positive and negative correlations with other economic variables? Why are these economic variables correlated?

b. Write a SAS Program (PROC SGPLOT) to graph the relationship between the Wilshire 5000 Total Market Index (WILL5000IND) and consumer sentiments (UMSCENT).

> **Hint:** This can also be executed using the TASK menu in both Enterprise Guide and SAS Studio.

   i. Repeat the same graph for the Wilshire Large Cap, Mid Cap, and Small Cap indices.

4. A portfolio analyst at the same investment fund wants to examine if stock index returns truly follow a normal distribution by analyzing the distributional properties of the four Wilshire market indices (WILLLRGCAP, WILLMIDCAP, WILLSMLCAP, and WILL5000IND). Using the Freddata01 SAS data file, write a SAS program that uses PROC UNIVARIATE to analyze each index return to assess whether the distribution is truly normal. Include both tables and graphs in your results.

> **Hint:** This can also be executed using the TASK menu in both Enterprise Guide and SAS Studio. Look for the DISTRIBUTION ANALYSIS Menu.

a. What are the mean, median, and standard deviation of the monthly returns for the indices?
b. Using the Moments, Quantiles, and Extreme Observations Table as references, characterize the shape of the distribution of the monthly returns (is it symmetric or asymmetric, compact or dispersed).
c. Modify your PROC UNIVARIATE statement to include a histogram. Also, superimpose the Normal (expected) and Kernel (fitted) densities of the returns on the histogram. Do these graphs support the notion that monthly returns on the Wilshire indices are normally distributed?
d. What are the investment implications (in terms of portfolio behaviors and performance measurement) of the statistical features observed in parts a, b, and c for investors who hold the Wilshire indices in their portfolios?

5. **Case Analysis**

Sally Smith graduated a year ago with a Ph.D. in financial engineering from a prestigious university. Upon graduation, she immediately landed a lucrative job as a quantitative data analyst at one of New York City's Wall Street banks. Her main responsibility is to develop machine learning models that can sift through large volumes of social media posts and macroeconomic news to draw trading signals for the bank's equity trading desk. Her annual compensation is partly tied to how much profit the trading desk can earn using her models. She spent the first six months developing various machine-learning models that can decipher which social media posts convey positive and negative sentiments about a few stocks in the technology industry. While developing the models, she noticed that specific sets of social media posts appear to consistently convey sentiments that are in line with the future movement in the price of some stocks. However, she is unable to tell if her models are incorporating the social media posts in the trading signals they yield for the equity trading desk because they are based on black box algorithms. She's worried that the persons behind the social media handles could be using insider information and trying to manipulate the market with their posts. Sally also recently discovered another algorithm that is in direct conflict with her algorithms (taking opposite trades every time Sally's algorithm trades). The adversarial algorithm does not appear to have much impact on the predictive performance of Sally's algorithm.

Discussion Questions

a. Is it ethical for the bank to tie Sally's compensation to the profitability of her algorithm?
b. What ethical responsibilities does Sally have as a data scientist regarding the social media posts?
c. What legal responsibilities does she have regarding the same issue?
d. How should Sally proceed with the development of her machine-learning models without compromising her values?
e. What should Sally do to address the issue of the adversarial algorithm?

Chapter 2: Exploring and Visualizing Financial and Economic Data

Learning and Communicating Using Visualizations

Most people learn through a combination of the four generally accepted learning styles: visual learning, auditory learning, reading and writing, and kinesthetic learning (learning by doing). Interconnecting with these learning styles are methods of communication, which are verbal, non-verbal, written, listening, and visual communication. Apparent in Figure 2.1 are the overlaps between how we learn and how we communicate. Indeed, two key objectives of communications that are related to the job of a data scientist are to use data to inform and to influence. In the data science domain, to inform implies using data to convey knowledge through the process of exploration and discovery, and to influence implies presenting the discovery in a manner that effectively conveys the value of the knowledge.

During the analytics life cycle, all data scientists will switch roles, between learning from the data and communicating their discoveries to other stakeholders. To successfully unlock the value in the data during the analytics life cycle, data scientists need to deploy both hard skills (such as programming, data analysis, and modeling) and soft skills (such as communication, creativity, critical thinking, adaptability, problem-solving, and teamwork). This is because, in most analytics projects, data scientists serve in consulting roles, in which they provide their expertise to the project owners, who might not have a data science background. Therefore, to enhance the value proposition of their expertise, data scientists must develop competencies and best practices in both the hard and soft skills that are related to data science.

Most of the chapters of this book will focus on developing your hard skills in financial data science. The topics that we will cover in this chapter will merge those hard skills with soft skills such as communication, adaptability, critical thinking, and creativity. These soft skills are the framework for good data storytelling, which is the process of translating insights obtained from the data into compelling narratives that help to inform and influence the stakeholders in the analytics project. The most common method for data storytelling is data visualization.

Figure 2.1: Learning Styles and Communication Methods

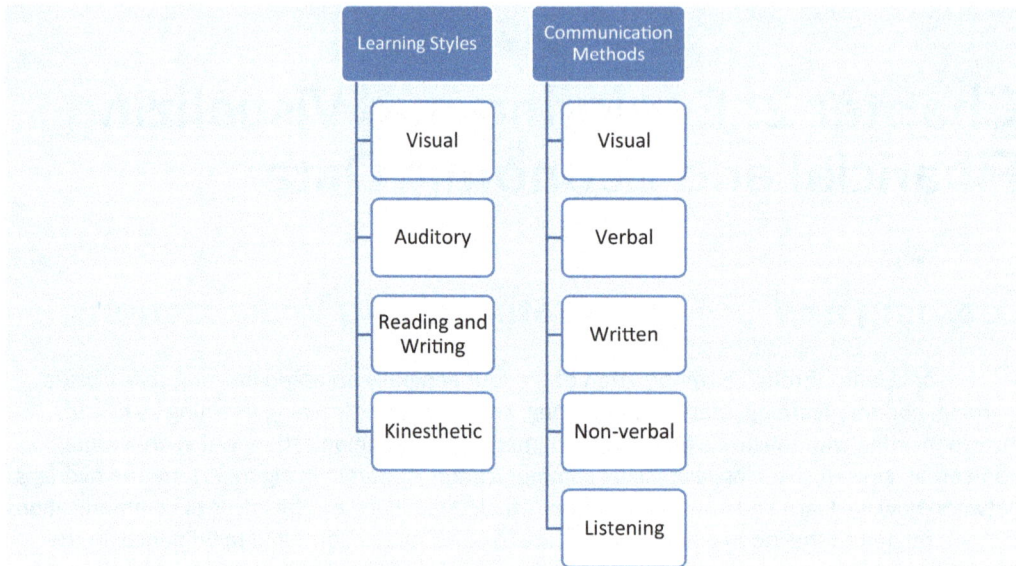

Types of Data Visualization

In Chapter One, data visualization was defined as a data science technique that uses graphical and pictorial depictions to convey stylized facts (such as patterns, trends, and correlations) about the data in a visually compelling and interactive way. Because of the unique (statistical, frequencies, completeness, size, scope, relevance) properties of financial and economic data, financial data scientists use visualization for both descriptive and diagnostic purposes.

Descriptive Data Visualization

Descriptive visualizations use graphical and pictorial depictions that highlight the synopses of trends, events, patterns, and relationships in raw data. Since they are essentially summaries of findings in the data, they are used in both the exploration and discovery phases of the analytics cycle. Descriptive visualizations are typically consumed by a broader range of stakeholders, so the emphasis tends to be on the following best practices when creating them:

- **Clarity:** Descriptive visualization should promote clarity by shedding light on the insights that are embedded in the data. It should also make it easier to understand the features of the data that are too complex to explain in words alone. Some types of financial decisions are made in real-time using visualizations that are layered over streaming financial data, such as those used by technical traders. For such purposes, the trade signal emanating from the visualizations must be obvious for it to be of value to the user.

Figure 2.2A: Example of a Bad Visualization

Figure 2.2A: S&P 500 Companies Domiciled in Each State

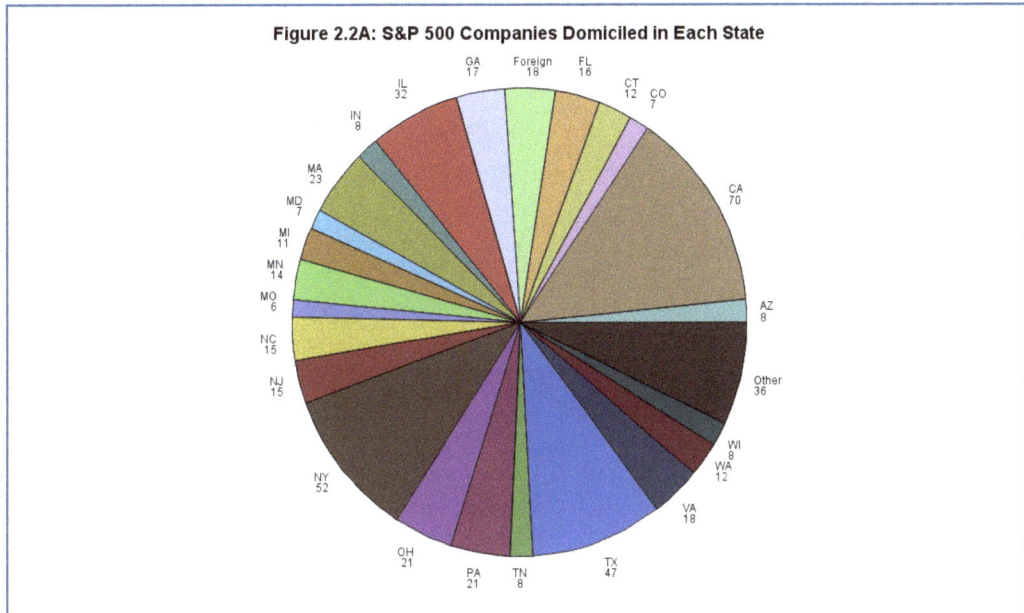

- **Simplicity:** Going by Occam's razor, the simplest and most compelling visualization is often the best. This helps to keep the audience's attention on the insight and not the visualization. For example, it is best to avoid visualizations that require the presenter to explain what the visualization is. In the venture capital space, entrepreneurs frequently have very limited time to present their pitch deck. In such instances, visualization is only of value if it is used as a time-saving tool for storytelling rather than as a fancy embellishment that would end up distracting the presenter from driving down the main points of the presentation.

  Trying to display the number of S&P 500 companies domiciled in all 50 US states on a pie chart as shown in Figure 2.2A is probably not a good idea. Not only does it appear cluttered, but viewers would also have a hard time locating a state if it is not one of the largest slices of the pie.

  The same information can be presented in a visually compelling manner using the geographic map shown in Figure 2.2B. The viewers' focus is quickly drawn to the deeply shaded states as those with a large concentration of companies, while still preserving the ability to quickly locate other states based on their familiarity with the geographic distribution of US states.

- **Relevance:** The visualization must be consistent with the type of data and the phenomenon that is being highlighted. For example, relationships in the data should be described by visualizations that have at least two dimensions such as scatter plots, while trends in the data should be described by visualizations that include a time element. Financial data analyses include cross-sectional and time-trend elements; hence, knowing the appropriate visualization for each element is essential.

Figure 2.2B: Best Practice in Visualization

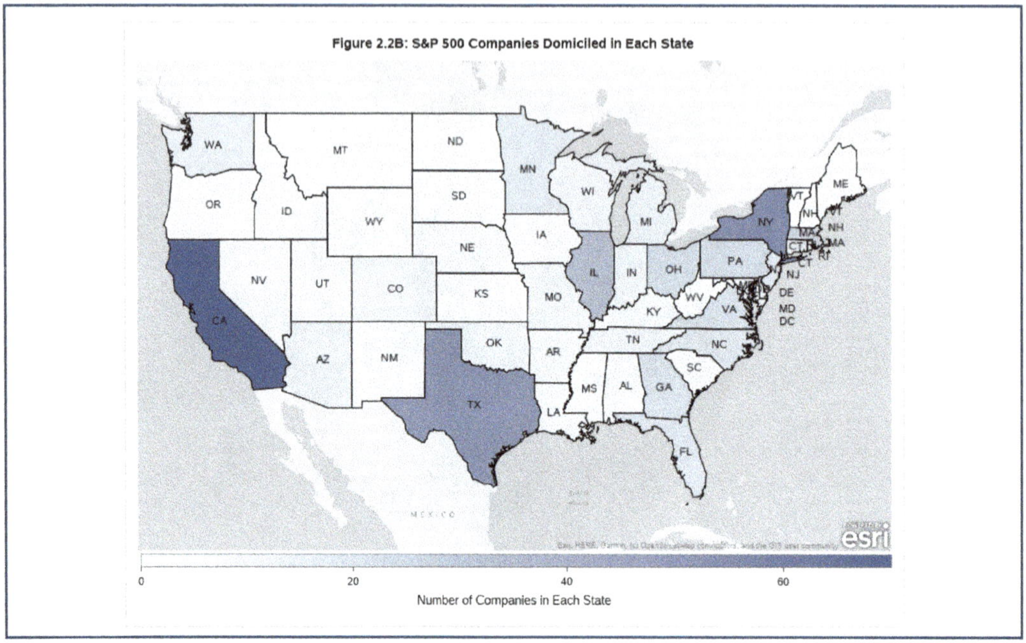

Figure 2.2B: S&P 500 Companies Domiciled in Each State

- **Consistency:** Regardless of the domain of application in business, effective visualizations require consistency in the use of graphical features. This is because these features (such as colors, chart types, legends, markers, and shapes) are parts of the essential components of good storytelling. In situations where the audience is remotely located from the preparer of the visualization (such as consumers of sell-side investment reports) or where the visualization is presented as a standalone document or a document with little synopsis, the visualization should provide the audience with a coherent depiction of the insight in the data.

Diagnostic Data Visualization

Diagnostic visualizations are mostly used to analyze statistical properties and anomalies in the data during the exploration phase. They help the data scientist to design the appropriate methodology for analyzing the data during the discovery phase. Diagnostic visualizations can also be used in the post-modeling phase to assess the appropriateness of the modeling technique used for the data. Unlike descriptive visualizations, which tend to be consumed by a wider range of stakeholders, consumers of diagnostic visualizations are often the data scientists themselves. Indeed, most diagnostic visualizations tend to be by-products of the applications of some statistical or econometric methods on the data. Besides following the same best practices as descriptive visualizations, diagnostic visualization must have statistical relevance.

Figure 2.3: Comparing Simple, Logarithmic, and Annual Holding Period Returns

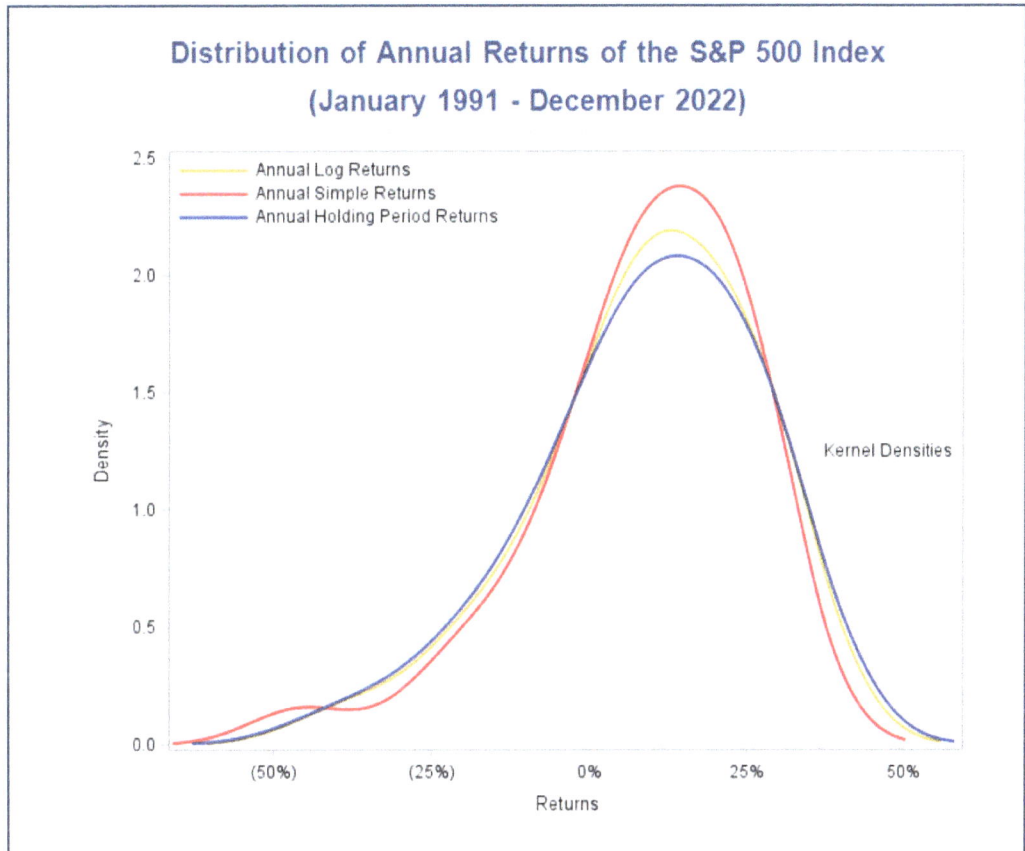

The visualization must be aligned with the statistical framework (theory and properties) of the data that is under scrutiny. Visualizations that are not grounded in the right statistical framework increase the likelihood that statistical errors might be committed in the assessment of the properties of the data and in the statistical models that are used to further explore the data.

Consider the Q-Q plot, which is a scatter plot type of visualization that is commonly used to assess whether an empirical distribution is close to a theoretical distribution. Since different types of distributions have varying statistical properties, the usefulness of the plot is contingent on matching the correct empirical distribution to the theoretical distribution. For example, take the concept of normality in stock price distribution. Since stock prices cannot be negative, therefore the distribution of stock prices has an empirical lower bound but no empirical upper bound. This implies that stock price distribution is right-skewed and hence non-normal. Considering this, it is common to apply some type of transformation (calculating returns) to the stock price series before plotting the data on the normal Q-Q plot. However, simple return (calculated as $R_t = \frac{P_t - P_{t-1}}{P_{t-1}})^1$, which most readers are familiar with, is also nonsymmetric and nonadditive, and thus inherently non-normal. Hence, the most appropriate transformation for exploring the statistical properties of stock prices when using a normal Q-Q plot is the logarithmic return series (calculated as $R_t = Log(\frac{P_t}{P_{t-1}})$, which is both symmetric and additive.[1]

Figure 2.3 displays three graphs of the kernel densities of the annual returns of the S&P 500 index from 1991 to 2022, which were calculated using cumulative simple monthly, cumulative log monthly returns, and annual holding period returns. The distribution of cumulative annual returns that were calculated from simple returns displays a remarkably different shape from the cumulative returns that were calculated from logarithmic returns and the actual holding period returns. The simple return plot shows a higher peak and fatter negative tail than the logarithmic and actual returns. The logarithmic returns also appear to track the actual holding period more accurately than the simple return.

Preprocessing Financial Data

All data in raw form would require some type of preprocessing before they can be visualized and analyzed. As a financial data scientist, you should expect to spend a significant proportion of the analytics life cycle on data preprocessing. The raw data that you will use for your analytics project exists in one of the following three data structures: structured, unstructured, or semi-structured.

Structured Data

These are data that have been collected and organized systematically, such that they can be easily read and analyzed. They consist of alphanumeric values that are stored in preformatted rows and columns. Each row or column is preformatted to accept a specific type of alphanumeric value.

In SAS, the formats fall into two broad categories of data types: NUMERIC (such as integers, float, real, date, and time, to name a few), and CHARACTERS or CHAR (which includes Boolean, fixed-length, and varying-length character strings). It is important to note that the format determines the type of visualizations, analysis, and mathematical operations that can be performed on these variables.

Examples of structured data include data stored in text files, spreadsheet applications, and relational databases. Financial data scientists are more likely to encounter data stored in a structured format

---

[1] Given the above distributional characteristics, it is common to assume that stock prices follow a log-normal distribution. This is because the probability distribution of the log-normal distribution has a lower bound of zero (with no upper bound) and is skewed to the right.

Table 2.1: Structured Data in Tabular Format

Ticker	Name	Price	Sales/Share	Profit Margin	ROA	ROE
AAPL	Apple Inc	$150.82	$24.10	25.3%	28.4%	175.5%
META	Meta Platforms Inc	$188.77	$43.43	19.9%	13.2%	18.5%
WMT	Walmart Inc	$143.62	$218.85	2.4%	3.6%	11.6%
CAT	Caterpillar Inc	$244.90	$112.89	11.3%	8.1%	41.4%
WFC	Wells Fargo & Co	$47.23	$21.78	17.9%	0.7%	7.4%

than in any other format. However, recent innovations in the data science domain have led to more prominent roles for unstructured and semi-structured data in financial data science projects.

Unstructured Data

These are data that are collected and stored without preformatting or into any specific data model. Unstructured data are typically stored in their raw form, and hence they require sophisticated techniques to process before they can be analyzed or visualized. Due to their lack of a defined data model, they are unsuitable for conventional data management systems. Therefore, they sometimes require specialized data repositories such as Non-relational (NoSQL) databases for data management purposes.

Unstructured data could be of any format, but they are mostly comprised of textual, imagery, audio, and Internet of Things (IoT) sensor data. From a financial data science perspective, unstructured data could provide qualitative richness to the insights that might be embedded in structured data. And thus, provide a compelling motivation for the increased interest in their use in the financial data science domain. For example, there has been a lot of advancement in infusing natural language processing of textual data and audio commentary into investment models. Textual data include Tweets, company disclosures, news articles, economic reports, etc. Audio commentary includes conference calls, news reports, social media posts, etc. In SAS, unstructured data types are formatted as VARBINARY.

Table 2.2: Unstructured Data in Tabular Form

Date	Ticker	Tweets	Company
11/29/21 6:58 AM	TSLA	Tesla announces new upgrades to Model3	Tesla, Inc.
11/29/21 6:59 AM	AMZN	AMZN had positive third-quarter sales	Amazon.com, Inc.
11/29/21 7:00 AM	AAPL	AAPL nearing $3T market capitalization	Apple Inc.
11/29/21 7:01 AM	MSFT	MSFT launches new platform to compete with AMZN	Microsoft Corporation

Semi-Structured Data

Semi-structured data share attributes of unstructured data in the sense that they do not have a defined data model. Unlike structured data, which are captured in tabular form, data in semi-structured form contains tags and markers (metadata) that define the structure of the data repository. The metadata specifies the characteristics and the grouping and hierarchy of the data in the repository. Together these features allow for data to be more efficiently recorded, analyzed, and visualized compared to unstructured data.

Semi-Structured data includes data in JavaScript Object Notation (JSON), eXtensible Markup Language (XML), eXtensible Business Reporting Language (XBRL), and comma-separated-value (CSV) files. It also includes data that is transmitted using certain Internet protocols, such as emails, TCP/IP packets, and HTML files.

Figures 2.4A and 2.4B display two examples of semi-structured data. Figure 2.4A displays the registration record for the Vanguard Bond Index Funds in XML format. In the angle brackets are the tags, which contain elements that are usually in a hierarchy starting with a root element such as <company>, child elements such as <reporting_file_number>, and text fields such as the name of the investment company.

Several data providers, including those in the financial data industry, now provide client interfaces that support access to data in a semi-structured format. For example, you can access all filings submitted to the Security Exchange Commission's (SEC) Electronic Data Gathering,

Figure 2.4A: Semi-Structured Data: Investment Company Registration Record in XML Format (SEC EDGAR)

```
<company>
        <reporting_file_number>811-04681</reporting_file_number>
        <cik>0000794105</cik>
        <entity_name>VANGUARD BOND INDEX FUNDS</entity_name>
        <entity_org_type>30</entity_org_type>
        <series_id>S000071399</series_id>
        <series_name>Vanguard Ultra-Short Bond ETF</series_name>
        <class_id>C000226472</class_id>
        <class_name>ETF Shares</class_name>
        <class_ticker>VUSB</class_ticker>
        <address_1>PO BOX 2600</address_1>
        <city>VALLEY FORGE</city>
        <zip_code>19482</zip_code>
        <state>PA</state>
        <address_2>V26</address_2>
</company>
```

Figure 2.4B: Semi-Structured Data: Public Company Listing Record in JSON Format (SEC EDGAR)

```
{"CIK":320193,"Name":"APPLE INC.","Ticker":"AAPL","Exchange":"Nasdaq"},
{"CIK":789019,"Name":"MICROSOFT CORP","Ticker":"MSFT","Exchange":"Nasdaq"},
{"CIK":1067983,"Name":"BERKSHIRE HATHAWAY INC","Ticker":"BRK-B",
"Exchange":"NYSE"}
```

Analysis, and Retrieval (EDGAR) system by publicly listed companies in the US using the site's application programming interface (API). All the public filings for each entity are cataloged in a JSON file and can be pulled using the Central Index Key (CIK) assigned to the entity or individual. For example, the CIK for Apple Inc. is CIK0000320193.

Working with semi-structured data in SAS is fairly easy because SAS can also parse data in all the semi-structured formats listed above into SAS readable format for analysis and visualization. Figure 2.4B displays data stored in JSON format. In double quotation are the objects that define the field name, followed by the corresponding value for the field.

Program 2.1: SAS Program to Read JSON File into SAS

```
/*Reading JSON File into SAS*/
filename compinfo "%sysfunc(getoption(WORK))/company_tickers_exchange.json";
filename myjmap "%sysfunc(getoption(WORK))/myjmap.json";
proc http
url="https://github.com/finsasdata/Bookdata/raw/main/company_tickers_exchange.json"
    out=compinfo
    method ="get";
run;
proc http
   url="https://github.com/finsasdata/Bookdata/raw/main/myjmap.json"
   out=  myjmap
   method ="get";
run;
libname compinfo JSON map="%sysfunc(getoption(WORK))/myjmap.json" automap=reuse;
/*Printing the first 5 observations*/
proc print data=COMPINFO.DATA (obs=5);
title 'Stock Listings by Exchange';
var cik Ticker Name Exchange;
run;
title;
```

Program 2.1 demonstrates how a JSON file stored at a web location can be read into SAS. The **COMPANY_TICKERS_EXCHANGE.JSON** file contains the CIK, Ticker, Company name, and primary stock exchange for the stocks. The **MYJMAP.JSON** contains the JSON map that SAS uses to understand the data structure of the JSON file when reading it into SAS. In the sample code, we pull both files from the repository using PROC HTTP. The LIBNAME statement informs SAS of the data format, and the location of the JSON map to use when reading the company data.

The two JSON files are stored in the physical location of the WORK library on your computer as noted in the **%sysfunc(getoption(WORK))** statement. However, a new library COMPINFO is created with a LIBREF that points to the physical location of the COMPANY_TICKERS_EXCHANGE. JSON file.[2]

Use the SAS DATA step or COPY statement to copy the data set to a permanent library if you prefer to keep a local copy of the file for future use. We use the PRINT procedure to print the first five observations from the newly created SAS data set. Shown on the output are the CIK, TICKER, the name of the company, and the stock exchange on which the stock is listed.

Output 2.1: Stock Listing by Exchange

Stock Listings by Exchange

Obs	CIK	Ticker	Name	Exchange
1	320193	AAPL	APPLE INC.	Nasdaq
2	789019	MSFT	MICROSOFT CORP	Nasdaq
3	1067983	BRK-B	BERKSHIRE HATHAWAY INC	NYSE
4	1045810	NVDA	NVIDIA CORP	Nasdaq
5	1046179	TSM	TAIWAN SEMICONDUCTOR MANUFACTURING CO LTD	NYSE

SAS Macros

At this point, it is probably a good idea to implement a more efficient way to pull the data we will use in subsequent examples from the book's data repository. Macro statements are used by SAS programmers to create a block of SAS code that can be easily reinvoked to repeat the same tasks (such as pulling data from the book's data repository) when needed in the future.

To define a SAS macro, start with a %MACRO statement followed by the assigned macro name and macro parameters and options (if needed). Macro parameters are macro variables that are used as inputs to the blocks of code that are executed within the SAS macro. The blocks of code that need to be executed are then included. The %MEND macro statement ends the macro definition. Defined SAS macros are stored in a SAS catalog in the WORK library as session-compiled macros, which makes them available only during the current SAS session.[3] They can

---

[2] Right-click on the library and select View properties to locate the physical location of the COMPINFO library.

[3] You would need to rerun the macro at the beginning of each SAS session. You can also include the macro in an Autoexec file, which can run at the beginning of your SAS session if properly configured for your specific SAS Windowing environment.

also be stored in other libraries using the autocall macro facility or the stored compiled macro facility.

Program 2.2 is used to create and submit the DATAPULL macro, which we will use to pull data files from the book's GitHub repository as needed. Moving forward, the macro will be invoked at the beginning of sample code programs in which data needs to be pulled from the repository. **FREF** and **PNAME** are two macro parameters that refer to the SAS file reference and physical name for the file we will pull from GitHub.

Program 2.2: SAS Macro to Pull Data from GitHub Repository

```
/*SAS Macro to pull data from GitHub Repository*/
%macro datapull(fref,pname);
filename  &fref "%sysfunc(getoption(WORK))/&pname";
proc http
   url="https://github.com/finsasdata/Bookdata/raw/main/&pname"
   out=&fref
   method ="get";
run;
%mend datapull;

%datapull('File Reference','Physical Name');
```

The macro is invoked as needed using the macro statement **%DATAPULL('File Reference', 'Physical Name')** and specifying the file reference and physical name of the data file.

Data Quality

Regardless of whether the data was internally generated or ingested from a data vendor feed, the data repositories for all organizations will consist of both human-generated data and machine- (system) generated or curated data. Human-generated data are data that are manually entered into the data repository during the course of business. For example, a customer filling out a credit application at the bank or an HR analyst entering the name of new employees into the payroll system. Machine-generated data are automatically created in the data repository without human intervention. The data is created by digital systems as they execute their design-specified business process. For example, a billing system would calculate and record the monthly bill for each customer before mailing them out to the recipients.

The extent to which a financial data scientist will work with machine-generated data versus human-generated data depends on the financial service settings in which the data scientist is employed. In investment management settings, the data scientist may mostly work with machine-generated or curated data such as stock market and economic data. For depository institutions such as banks and credit unions, the data scientist may work with a mix of both, depending on the business segment of the bank where they are employed. Those supporting the front office may work mostly with human-generated data, while those supporting the middle and back offices may work mostly with machine-generated data. If we consider the various sources of the data that the data scientist will work with, it is worthwhile to explore some of the common data quality issues that could affect the project timeline.

Dimensions of Data Quality

In general, data quality is seen across the dimensions of accuracy, consistency, completeness, timeliness, and validity.

- **Accuracy** is the extent to which the data represents the real-world thing or phenomenon that is being recorded. For example, a customer walks into a bank and deposits a $1,000 check in the customer's checking account. The data recorded in the repository should accurately reflect a credit entry to the customer of the same amount.
- **Consistency** is the extent to which the data model employed in one data repository aligns with the data in another repository. For example, the customer ID field should contain the same values and format in all the tables in which they appear.
- **Completeness** is the extent to which all the fields that are relevant to the real-world thing or phenomenon that is being recorded in the data set are populated with the required data values. For example, the sales table should at minimum include the item that is sold, the price of the item, the quantity of the item, and preferably the date and time of sale.
- **Timeliness** is the degree of lag between when the actual real-world event occurs and when the data relating to it is recorded.
- **Validity** is the extent to which data values are in line with the specified values for a field or calculation. For example, negative values appearing in the age field are probably incorrect entries.

From the five listed dimensions above, the prominent issues for financial data scientists are data consistency across data sources, data completeness, and to some extent, data validity.

Data Consistency

Financial data scientists frequently need to combine raw data from multiple sources before visualizing and analyzing the data. Most financial and economic data are in time series format; therefore, the frequency at which their values were recorded will affect how easily these types of data can be combined. The reality is that financial market data are usually recorded at higher frequencies than economic data and public filings made by companies (**frequency incompatibility**). Public filings by companies also vary in frequency and timing. Some public filings such as 10-Q are filed quarterly, some annually (such as 10-K), and some sporadically (such as 8-K). Besides these, there are also significant variations in the fiscal years and consequently the reporting period amongst publicly listed companies.

In Table 2.3, we attempt to merge daily stock market data for the S&P 500 index with the weekly initial jobless claims and mortgage applications, the monthly home sales, unemployment rate,

Table 2.3: Frequency Incompatibility Between Financial Market and Economic Data

Date	S&P 500 Index	Initial Jobless Claims	Mortgage Applications	Home Sales	Unemployment Rate	GDP	CPI
3/22/2022	4511.61						
3/23/2022	4456.24		-8.10%	772			
3/24/2022	4520.16	184					
3/25/2022	4543.06						
3/28/2022	4575.52						
3/29/2022	4631.60						
3/30/2022	4602.45		-6.80%				
3/31/2022	4530.41	202				-1.6%	8.5%
4/1/2022	4545.86				3.60%		
4/4/2022	4582.64						

and CPI, and lastly the quarterly GDP data. As seen in the table, the frequency incompatibility would first need to be addressed before further analysis can be performed on the data set.

There are also some variations in how data are recorded across financial markets due to the differences in their market structure (**time-stamp incompatibility**). Financial markets for traditional asset classes such as stocks and bonds operate within set hours of each business day Monday to Friday (for stocks – 9:30 AM to 4:00 PM; for bonds – 8:00 AM to 5:00 PM). The US futures markets open at 6:00 PM (EST) on Sundays and remain mostly open until 4:00 PM (EST) on Fridays. Other markets that are globally linked and trade in more exotic products such as cryptocurrencies and foreign currencies operate 24 hours a day and seven days a week. The fixed-income market observes all federal holidays, while the equity markets do not observe two federal holidays.

Synchronizing data from all the markets must be done carefully to avoid bias in the analyses. Table 2.4 shows the partially synchronized hourly data for six market indices: Bitcoin, S&P 500, Crude Oil, US Dollar-EURO exchange, S&P 500 E-Mini futures, and Gold. Although the prices of all six indices were recorded using the same frequency, due to the differences in the structure of each market, the prices for some markets were not recorded at every time index.

There is a high probability that you will encounter these types of variations in the structure of the financial data for your analytics project. You should note that special attention is necessary

Table 2.4: Time-Stamp Incompatibility Between Financial Markets Data

Date	Bitcoin	S&P 500 Index	Crude Oil	USD/EUR	E-Mini Futures	Gold
1/30/2022 15:00	37751.700			1.115		
1/30/2022 17:00	37913.010		87.780	1.115	4412.750	1789.630
1/30/2022 19:00	36846.200		88.030	1.116	4416.000	1790.250
1/30/2022 21:00	37046.000		87.900	1.116	4435.250	1787.150
1/30/2022 23:00	37024.860		87.830	1.117	4435.250	1789.290
1/31/2022 1:00	37142.140		87.760	1.117	4427.000	1789.280
1/31/2022 3:00	37229.860		87.470	1.118	4428.000	1789.630
1/31/2022 5:00	37286.260		87.120	1.116	4414.750	1792.390
1/31/2022 7:00	37282.660		87.440	1.119	4414.000	1797.810
1/31/2022 9:00	37737.300	4465.390	87.260	1.121	4457.000	1796.500
1/31/2022 11:00	38510.350	4487.220	87.790	1.122	4478.250	1796.920
1/31/2022 13:00	38437.200	4495.190	88.150	1.124	4485.500	1798.710
1/31/2022 15:00	38437.880	4515.550	88.150	1.124	4491.750	1797.170
1/31/2022 17:00	38496.270	4515.550	88.390	1.123	4493.000	1797.860
1/31/2022 19:00	38262.500		88.210	1.123	4481.500	1797.520
1/31/2022 21:00	38627.950		88.400	1.123	4491.250	1796.560
1/31/2022 23:00	38472.040		88.460	1.124	4493.500	1802.800
2/1/2022 1:00	38467.780		88.030	1.127	4498.750	1803.770

when combining raw data from different sources before they can be visualized and analyzed. A selection of methods to address the issue is presented below.

Dealing with Data Structure Incompatibility

Three ways to manage frequency and time-stamp incompatibilities include:

- **Data aggregation**: The first approach is to aggregate (sum or average) the higher frequency data across the period between two consecutive observations of the lower frequency data as shown in Program 2.3A. You should note that SAS also supports other types of aggregation, including total, minimum, maximum, first, last, and standard deviation.
- **End of period/time-stamp matching**: The second approach is to record the observations of the higher frequency data at the same frequency as the lower frequency data as shown in Program 2.3B.

The first two approaches would lead to a loss of granularity in the higher-frequency data. However, the tradeoff may favor being able to draw insights from the relationship between the lower and higher frequency variables than any loss in data granularity. As you will see in subsequent paragraphs, the loss in granularity could lead to better project outcomes in some instances.

In Program 2.3A, we employed the TIMEDATA procedure to aggregate all of the financial and economic data that were collected at different intervals into quarterly intervals using mean aggregation. In Program 2.3B, we used the same TIMEDATA procedure to record one observation for each variable in the data set at the same frequency, which in this case is the quarterly interval. For both programs, the OUT option in the PROC TIMEDATA statement specifies the name of the output data set. The ID statement specifies the date variable as the ID variable, the INTERVAL statement is used to specify quarterly as the requested interval, and the ACCUMULATE statement specifies the method of accumulation, which in Program 2.3A is the mean and in Program 2.3B is the last observation in each quarter. The VAR statement specifies the variables to be transformed.

Program 2.3A: Using PROC TIMEDATA to Accumulate High-Frequency Observations

```
%datapull(ecod,ecodata.sas7bdat);
/*Accumulating Data into Quarterly Frequency*/
proc timedata data=ecodata out=necodata;
 id date interval=qtr
             accumulate=mean;
  var SPX INJCJC MBAVCHNG ETSLTOTL USURTOT GDP CPI;
run;
proc print data=necodata;
run;
```

Output 2.3A: Accumulated High-Frequency Observations

Obs	Date	SPX	INJCJC	MBAVCHNG	ETSLTOTL	USURTOT	GDP	CPI
1	2022:1	4459.91	202	-2.35	6.15	3.9	6.86	7.5
2	2022:2	4104.26	206	-1.99	5.58	3.6	-1.6	8.5
3	2022:3	3977.15	232	-1.95	4.9	3.6	-.54	8.6
4	2022:4	3854.56	222	-1.47	4.39	3.6	3.2	7.6

Outputs 2.3A and 2.3B show the results of implementing the TIMEDATA procedure on the financial and economic series. The printed output shows that all series have now been aggregated into quarterly frequencies, which is the lowest frequency observed in all of the variables shown in Table 2.3. Notice the differences in the values of the variables obtained from both aggregation methods. Aggregation using the mean generates less volatile output variables than aggregation based on the last observation in each quarter. In both cases, there is some loss in granularity from aggregating the higher frequency variables such as the daily values of the S&P

500 index and the weekly initial jobless claims and mortgage applications. However, the ability to extract meaningful insights from jointly modeling these variables with the lower frequency variables such as CPI and GDP may outweigh the loss in granularity.

Program 2.3B: SAS Program to Time-Stamp Match Observations

```
%datapull(ecod,ecodata.sas7bdat);
/*Time-Stamping Data into Quarterly Frequency*/
proc timedata data=ecodata out=necodata;
    id date interval=qtr
                accumulate=last;
  var SPX INJCJC MBAVCHNG ETSLTOTL USURTOT GDP CPI;
run;
proc print data=necodata;
run;
```

Output 2.3B: Time-Stamp Matched Data

Obs	Date	SPX	INJCJC	MBAVCHNG	ETSLTOTL	USURTOT	GDP	CPI
1	2022:1	4530.41	171	-6.8	5.75	3.6	-1.6	8.5
2	2022:2	3785.38	231	0.7	5.11	3.6	-0.6	9.1
3	2022:3	3585.62	219	-14.2	4.71	3.5	3.2	8.2
4	2022:4	3839.5	206	-10.3	4.08	3.6	3.2	7.1

> PROC TIMESERIES also has similar features. However, PROC TIMEDATA enables you to import your own defined functions and subroutines using the FCMPOPT statement. PROC TIMESERIES has a lot of built-in graphics that users might find useful for performing diagnostics and model assessments. These include series and cross-series graphs, as well as autocorrelation and partial correlation, and time series decomposition plots.

- You can also keep the lower-frequency series constant during the intervening periods as shown in Table 2.5. The frequency incompatibility can then be addressed using special modeling techniques such as Mixed Data Sampling and State-Space models; however, these topics are beyond the scope of this book.

Data Completeness

Missing values are the most common type of data completeness issues. Missing data can be random or systematic occurrences in the data set. They might constitute a small subsect or large proportion of the data set. Regardless of how they occur, they pose a potential problem

Table 2.5: Data Structure Incompatibility Between Financial Markets Data

Date	S&P 500 Index	Initial Jobless Claims	Mortgage Applications	Home Sales	Unemployment Rate	GDP	CPI
3/22/2022	4511.61	166	-8.1%	5.93	3.8%	7.0%	7.9%
3/23/2022	4456.24	166	-8.1%	5.93	3.8%	7.0%	7.9%
3/24/2022	4520.16	166	-8.1%	5.93	3.8%	7.0%	7.9%
3/25/2022	4543.06	171	-6.8%	5.93	3.8%	7.0%	7.9%
3/28/2022	4575.52	171	-6.8%	5.93	3.8%	7.0%	7.9%
3/29/2022	4631.6	171	-6.8%	5.93	3.8%	7.0%	7.9%
3/30/2022	4602.45	171	-6.8%	5.93	3.8%	7.0%	7.9%
3/31/2022	4530.41	171	-6.8%	5.75	3.6%	-1.6%	8.5%
4/1/2022	4545.86	168	-6.3%	5.75	3.6%	-1.6%	8.5%
4/4/2022	4582.64	168	-6.3%	5.75	3.6%	-1.6%	8.5%

for visualizing and analyzing the data. Some algorithms also use complete case analysis, which implies that the algorithm will exclude all observations that have missing values when building the model. From a practical point of view, machine-generated and curated data are less prone to errors; therefore, they are less likely to generate incomplete data. However, if care is not employed when merging machine-generated data with different data structures, then the output data might end up with missing values as shown in Programs 2.4A, 2.4B, and 2.4C.

In Program 2.4A, we use the DATA step to create the BITCOIN and SPX data sets. The BITCOIN data set records the daily closing values of BITCOIN prices in US dollars, while the SPX data set records the daily closing values of the S&P 500 index. Because Bitcoin trades 24 hours a day, while the S&P 500 index trades only on business days, you will notice that the SPX data set is missing observations for 12/17/2022 and 12/18/2022 (weekend dates), as well as from 12/24/2022 to 12/26/2022. In Programs 2.4B and 2.4C, we show how merging these two data sets could lead to two types of data structure compatibility issues.

Program 2.4A: Using DATA Steps and PROC PRINT to Display Issues with Merging Incomplete Data

```
data bitcoin;
input date mmddyy10. bitcoin;
format date mmddyy10. bitcoin
dollar10.;
datalines;
12/16/2022   16837.95
12/17/2022   16718.5
12/18/2022   16753.05
12/19/2022   16586.82
12/20/2022   16881.54
12/21/2022   16793.1
12/22/2022   16792.25
12/23/2022   16811.33
12/24/2022   16829.82
12/25/2022   16830.25
12/26/2022   16833.01
12/27/2022   16692.55
;
run;
proc sort data=bitcoin;
by date;
run;
```

```
data spx;
input date mmddyy10. spx;
format date mmddyy10. spx
dollar10.;
datalines;
12/16/2022   3852.36
12/19/2022   3817.66
12/20/2022   3821.62
12/21/2022   3878.44
12/22/2022   3822.39
12/23/2022   3844.82
12/27/2022   3829.25
;
run;

proc sort data=spx;
by date;
run;
```

Remember that the Bitcoin and stock market data were both machine-generated with no missing values; however, the time-stamp incompatibility issues we discussed earlier led to missing values being generated when both tables were merged. The outer join performed in Program 2.4B creates missing values for the SPX variable, while the inner join performed in Program 2.4C deletes values of Bitcoin that were recorded on the 17th, 18th, 24th, 25th, and 26th of December 2022.

> There are multiple ways to merge data sets in SAS. They include Concatenating, One-to-One, One-to-Many, Many-to-One, and Match-Merging. Programs 2.4B and 2.4C use Match-Merging, which requires the data to be sorted using the BY variable before merging.

Program 2.4B: Using DATA Step and PROC PRINT to Show Outer Join Issues

```
data bitspx;
    merge bitcoin spx;
    by date;
run;

proc print data=bitspx;
run;
```

Output 2.4B: Outer Join Merge

Obs	Date	Bitcoin	SPX
1	12/16/2022	$16,838	$3,852
2	12/17/2022	$16,719	.
3	12/18/2022	$16,753	.
4	12/19/2022	$16,587	$3,818
5	12/20/2022	$16,882	$3,822
6	12/21/2022	$16,793	$3,878
7	12/22/2022	$16,792	$3,822
8	12/23/2022	$16,811	$3,845
9	12/24/2022	$16,830	.
10	12/25/2022	$16,830	.
11	12/26/2022	$16,833	.
12	12/27/2022	$16,693	$3,829

Program 2.4C: Using DATA Step and PROC PRINT to Show Inner Join Issues

```
data crypto_stock;
      merge bitcoin (in=a) spx(in=b);
      by date;
      if b and  a;
run;
proc print data=crypto_stock;
run;
```

The IN= data set option assigns binary variables A and B to the Bitcoin and SPX data sets, respectively. The values of the new variables are then used to indicate whether two data sets contribute to the current observation. In Program 2.4C, both data sets can only contribute to the current observation if the matching values of the BY variables (DATE) exist in both data sets. Since matching values of DATE do not exist in the SPX data sets on the 17th, 18th, 24th, 25th, and 26th of December 2022, observations on those dates in the Bitcoin data set are not included in the newly created data set. You should note that the IN= variables are not added to the input data sets. They are only available to the programming statement while the code is being executed.

Output 2.4C: Inner Join Merge

Obs	Date	Bitcoin	Spx
1	12/16/2022	$16,838	$3,852
2	12/19/2022	$16,587	$3,818
3	12/20/2022	$16,882	$3,822
4	12/21/2022	$16,793	$3,878
5	12/22/2022	$16,792	$3,822
6	12/23/2022	$16,811	$3,845
7	12/27/2022	$16,693	$3,829

Dealing with Missing Values

Human-generated data are more prone to errors such as missing values. When such cases arise, the data scientist must carefully decide on the best possible course of action to address the problem. The options include the following:

- If missing values are limited and random, consider replacing the missing values with a default value. This could be the previous observation if the data is a time series (as shown in Program 2.5); it could also be the mean, mode, median, highest, lowest, or an indicator for missing value. In Program 2.5, the SAS DATA step uses a temporary variable ($\_SPX\_$) to record the current values of the SPX in the PDV as it iterates through the observations. This value is then used to replace the values in the next observation if that value is missing. The result we obtained from implementing the SAS code is shown in Output 2.5.

Program 2.5: Using DATA Step to Resolve Issues with Merging Incomplete Data

```
/*Populating the missing values using lagged values*/
data nbitspx;
set bitspx;
retain _spx_;
if not missing(spx) then _spx_=spx;
else spx=_spx_; drop _spx_;
run;
```

Output 2.5: Merging Incomplete Data

Obs	Date	Bitcoin	SPX
1	12/16/2022	$16,838	$3,852
2	12/17/2022	$16,719	$3,852
3	12/18/2022	$16,753	$3,852
4	12/19/2022	$16,587	$3,818
5	12/20/2022	$16,882	$3,822
6	12/21/2022	$16,793	$3,878
7	12/22/2022	$16,792	$3,822
8	12/23/2022	$16,811	$3,845
9	12/24/2022	$16,830	$3,845
10	12/25/2022	$16,830	$3,845
11	12/26/2022	$16,833	$3,845
12	12/27/2022	$16,693	$3,829

- The data scientist could also try to infer the missing value by estimating it using the other available fields in the data set as shown in Program 2.6. In the program, we first simulated two years of monthly stock returns for four stocks. We also used the INTX function to generate the monthly dates, beginning with the initial date of January 31, 2021. In the INTX function, the END option informs SAS to use the end of the period dates in the computation. In the next DATA step, we simulated random patterns of missing values. We then attempt to infer the missing values using the multiple imputation (MI) procedure.[4] PROC MI replaces the missing values with a set of random samples of plausible values. The method creates multiple versions of the same data set, with each containing a plausible value of the missing data. The imputed data sets are then estimated and analyzed using standard procedures and their results are combined to draw statistical deductions. In the code for the MI procedure, the NIMPUTE statement specifies the number of imputations to draw for each missing observation. The minimum and maximum statements specify the minimum and maximum values for the imputed variables. MCMC specifies that the imputations should be done using the Monte Carlo Markov Chain.

Program 2.6: Using PROC MI to Impute Missing Values in Incomplete Data

```
/*Simulate monthly returns for 4 stocks*/
data simult;
    format date date.;
    array ret[4] ret1-ret4 ;
    keep date ret1-ret4;
```

---

[4] The code for the missing value simulation was adapted from Rick Wicklin's example for creating missing values. Interested readers should visit Rick Wicklin's online blog (The DO Loop) for more information: https://blogs.sas.com/content/iml/2016/10/26/patterns-of-missing-data.html.

```
    call streaminit(1);
        initdate = '31dec2020'd;
        dt=0;
    do i = 1 to 24;
        dt+1;
     do k = 1 to 4;
date= intnx('month',initdate,dt,'end');
        ret[k] = rand('normal');
        end;
        output;
     end;
run;

/*Simulate Random Missing Values*/
data Randsimul(drop=i);
        call streaminit(1234);
        set work.simult;
            array x {*} _numeric_;
            do i = 2 to dim(x);           /*Set i=2 to skip date column*/
             if rand("Bern", 0.2) then   /*Random Binary Value*/
             x[i]=.;
             end;
run;

proc print data=randsimul(obs=10);
run;


/*Inferring Missing Values using PROC MI*/
proc mi data=randsimul nimpute=25 minimum=-10 maximum=10 out=imfsimul;
        mcmc start=value    plots=all;
        var Ret1 Ret2 Ret3 Ret4  ;
run;

proc print data=imfSimul (obs=10);
run;
```

Output 2.6 shows the results obtained from implementing the code in Program 2.6. The first section of the output shows the simulated data set with randomly simulated missing values. The second section shows the same data set after inputting the missing values. Next are the tables that report the expectation maximization (EM) parameter estimates (posterior mode), the missing data patterns, and parameter estimates. The EM algorithm iterative process is used to derive the maximum likelihood estimates of models with unobservable (latent) variables. The missing data patterns show the distinct missing data patterns in the data. The parameter estimate shows the mean, standard deviations, and confidence interval of the means derived from the 25 imputations performed on the data. Notice the differences between the estimates from the EM algorithm and the parameter estimates approach.

Output 2.6: Simulated Incomplete Data

Obs	Date	Ret1	Ret2	Ret3	Ret4
1	31JAN21	0.01983	1.01202	0.15041	0.35207
2	28FEB21	0.78258	-0.02251	0.29827	0.40191
3	31MAR21	0.75946	1.88186	.	-0.30056
4	30APR21	0.97419	0.11198	-0.16299	0.32134
5	31MAY21	0.32811	1.02528	.	-0.68538
6	30JUN21	0.46069	1.40578	-0.10604	-0.78373
7	31JUL21	0.86984	0.10916	0.73612	-1.16411
8	31AUG21	.	-0.41118	-0.77766	.
9	30SEP21	1.51497	.	-1.08448	-0.36535
10	31OCT21	.	-0.51941	-0.05371	-1.05030

Obs	_Imputation_	date	ret1	ret2	ret3	ret4
1	1	31JAN21	0.01983	1.01202	0.15041	0.35207
2	1	28FEB21	0.78258	-0.02251	0.29827	0.40191
3	1	31MAR21	0.75946	1.88186	-0.46479	-0.30056
4	1	30APR21	0.97419	0.11198	-0.16299	0.32134
5	1	31MAY21	0.32811	1.02528	-1.38680	-0.68538
6	1	30JUN21	0.46069	1.40578	-0.10604	-0.78373
7	1	31JUL21	0.86984	0.10916	0.73612	-1.16411
8	1	31AUG21	1.12498	-0.41118	-0.77766	-2.15195
9	1	30SEP21	1.51497	-1.30909	-1.08448	-0.36535
10	1	31OCT21	-0.05641	-0.51941	-0.05371	-1.05030

EM (Posterior Mode) Estimates

TYPE	_NAME_	ret1	ret2	ret3	ret4
MEAN		-0.202602	0.077600	-0.042845	-0.031717
COV	ret1	1.271434	0.174515	-0.064917	-0.095824
COV	ret2	0.174515	0.955043	0.013699	-0.084606
COV	ret3	-0.064917	0.013699	0.548557	-0.155076
COV	ret4	-0.095824	-0.084606	-0.155076	0.612488

Missing Data Patterns

Group	Ret1	Ret2	Ret3	Ret4	Freq	Percent	Ret1	Ret2	Ret3	Ret4
1	X	X	X	X	12	50.00	-0.372019	0.090871	0.120783	0.232885
2	X	X		X	3	12.50	0.410470	1.607691		-0.134175
3	X	X			1	4.17	-0.250490	-1.021792		
4	X		X	X	2	8.33	-0.108701		-0.107205	-0.419919
5		X	X	X	2	8.33		-0.896704	-0.139302	-1.257675
6		X	X		1	4.17		0.411183	-0.777655	
7		X		X	2	8.33		-0.573960		-0.149234
8			X		1	4.17			-0.964412	

(columns under "Group Means": Ret1 Ret2 Ret3 Ret4)

Parameter Estimates (25 Imputations)

Variable	Mean	Std Error	95% Confidence Limits		DF
Ret1	-0.1960	0.3517	-0.9595	0.5674	12.4240
Ret2	0.0448	0.2392	-0.4554	0.5451	19.2450
Ret3	-0.0762	0.2445	-0.6102	0.4577	11.7480

- The next set of options should be employed only as a last resort as they might impair any analyses that are subsequently performed on the data. Nevertheless, they are:
  - Excluding the missing observation.
  - Deleting the missing observation.

Data Validity

The most common data validity issues in financial and economic data are outliers. Outliers might be due to incorrect data entry, sample contamination, or imprecise calculations of the data field. They might also be perfectly valid data values, although unrepresentative of the general pattern or trend of the variable. Such as a one-off event that is unlikely to repeat itself in the future. From a data science point of view, outliers are problematic because they violate some statistical assumptions and distort the precision of the statistical measures and inferences. For example, outliers skew the distribution of the data in the direction of the outlier value. This could make the characteristics of the data that were distorted by the outlier unstable for statistical analysis.

To control for outliers in your data, the data scientist should first conduct a quality check on the data in the preprocessing stage by reviewing the metadata. Metadata contains a summary of information about the data that the scientist might find helpful in assessing the validity of the data. The data can also be visualized using a histogram, box plot, or Q-Q plot, as shown in Program 2.7.

Program 2.7: Using PROC CAPABILITY to Visualize Outliers in the Data

```
/*Using Proc Capability to Visualize Outliers*/
%datapull(vol,rspx_monthly.sas7bdat);
proc capability data=rspx_monthly noprint;
    title 'Outlier Detection Plots for Monthly S&P 500 Trading Volume';
    var volume;
    qqplot/ normal(mu=est sigma=est color=blue );
    ppplot / normal (mu=est sigma=est color=blue);
    format Volume best8.;
run;
```

Program 2.7 shows the SAS program that uses the CAPABILITY procedure to graph the monthly trading volume of the S&P 500 index from January 1991 to December 2022 on normal P-P and Q-Q plots. The Q-Q plot compares the empirical quantiles of the trading volume to the theoretical quantiles of a normal distribution. The P-P plot compares the empirical cumulative probability distribution of the trading volume against the theoretical distribution. The plotted blue dots for both plots should fall on the diagonal line if the distribution of trading volume is perfectly normal. The visualizations displayed in Output 2.7 suggest that the distribution of monthly trading volume is non-normal.

Output 2.7: Outlier Detection Plots for Monthly S&P 500 Trading Volume

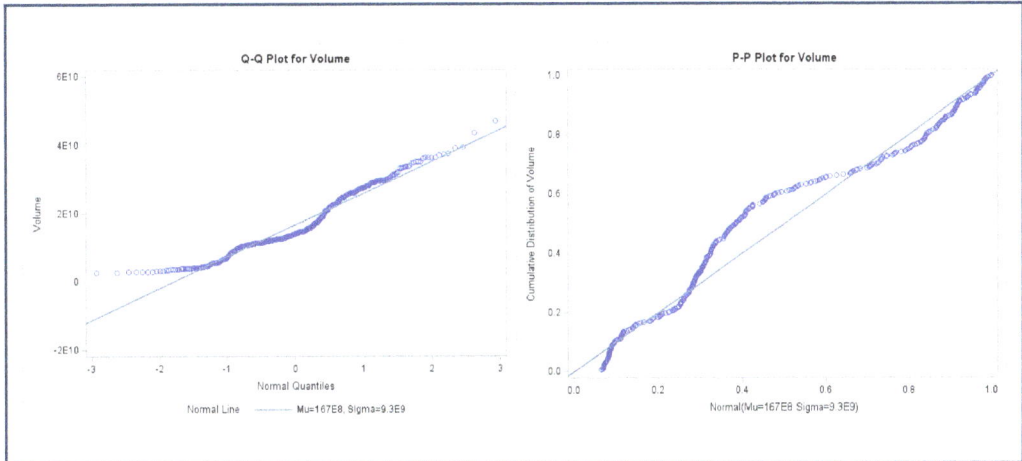

Dealing with Outliers

When outliers are found, the data scientist could:

- Replace the outlier value with a default value (mean, mode, median, highest, lowest, indicator for missing value).
- Infer a replacement value for the outlier by estimation using other available information. For time series data, the X11, X12, and X13 procedures in SAS can automatically identify and replace the outlier observations using a smoothing function (exponential) as shown in Program 2.8. In the program, we invoke the automatic outlier detection option for the procedure by specifying the OUTLIER statement. Outliers are denoted as any values that are outside the 3.6 standard deviations of the mean.
- The last two options – excluding or deleting the observation with the outlier values – should be employed only as a last resort as they might impact the analyses performed on the data in subsequent steps.

Program 2.8: Using PROC X13 to Resolve Outlier Problems in the Data

```
%datapull(vol,rspx_monthly.sas7bdat);
/*Automatic Outlier Detection and Correction Using PROC X13*/
proc x13 data=rspx_monthly  date=Date INTERVAL = month;
   var volume;
   transform function=log;
   arima model=( (0,1,1)(0,1,1) );/*ARIMA with Exponential Smoothing*/
   outlier cv=3.6 ;
   estimate; x11;
/*a1 is the preadjusted timeseries,e1 is the outlier adjusted series*/
   output out=arspx_monthly a1 e1;
run;
```

Output 2.8: Outlier Corrections Using PROC X13

			Regression Model Parameter Estimates For Variable Volume			
Type	Parameter	NoEst	Estimate	Standard Error	t Value	Pr > |t|
Automatically Identified	AO AUG2007	Est	0.37212	0.09261	4.02	<.0001
	AO AUG2008	Est	-0.34145	0.09265	-3.69	0.0003
	AO AUG2011	Est	0.55428	0.09251	5.99	<.0001
	AO MAR2020	Est	0.46323	0.09402	4.93	<.0001

The X13 procedure uses the Autoregressive Integrated Moving Average specification (which we will discuss in more detail in the visual diagnostic section) and the exponential smoothing method to process the volume series for a range of statistical anomalies, including outliers. In Output 2.8, we report the results of the regression model and the parameter estimates. Notice how remarkably well the algorithm performed at unearthing the outlier months in the data. In contrast to the popular view, the 2008–2009 financial crisis actually started in early 2007 as the default rate of subprime mortgages started to rise remarkably, leading to the collapse of two (now defunct) Bear Sterns hedge funds and other US and European funds with significant exposure to subprime mortgages. The extreme trading volume identified in August 2007 started when several quant hedge funds experienced a liquidity crunch and suffered significant losses while trying to unwind their portfolios in a market that was already unnerved by the recent collapse of several subprime-related entities. In August 2008, the market experienced another bout of extremely high trading volume following the collapse of IndyMac, which then was one of the largest mortgage lenders in the US. At that point, the collapse was the fourth largest bank failure in the US. The high levels of trading volume seen in August 2011 were due to the US debt ceiling crisis, while the March 2020 spike in trading was due to the advent of the COVID-19 pandemic.

Besides detecting outliers, the X13 procedure also automatically adjusts for them and generates an outlier-adjusted series. In Program 2.9, we graph the outlier-adjusted and unadjusted trading volumes on a series plot using the SGPLOT procedure. The red plot represents the unadjusted volume series, while the blue line plots the outlier adjusted series.

Program 2.9: Using PROC SGPLOT to Plot Raw and Adjusted Trading Volume Series

```
/*Plotting the Raw and Adjusted Trading Volume*/
proc sgplot data=arspx_monthly;
      title 'Automatic Outlier Detection and Correction ';
      series x=date y=volume_A1 / name="Preadjusted Volume" markers
      markerattrs=(color=red symbol='circle')
      lineattrs=(color=red) legendlabel="Preadjusted Volume";
      series x=date y=volume_E1 / name="Adjusted Volume" markers
      markerattrs=(color=blue symbol='asterisk')
      lineattrs=(color=blue) legendlabel= " Outlier Adjusted Volume";
      yaxis label='Original and Outlier Adjusted S&P 500 Trading Volume';
      keylegend "Preadjusted Volume" "Adjusted Volume" / across=3 noborder
      position=bottomRight location=inside;
run;
title;
```

Assigning a name to your plot statement allows you to quickly call it up in the KEYLEGEND to coordinate the color and plot design between the graph and legend.

Output 2.9: Trading Volume on S&P 500

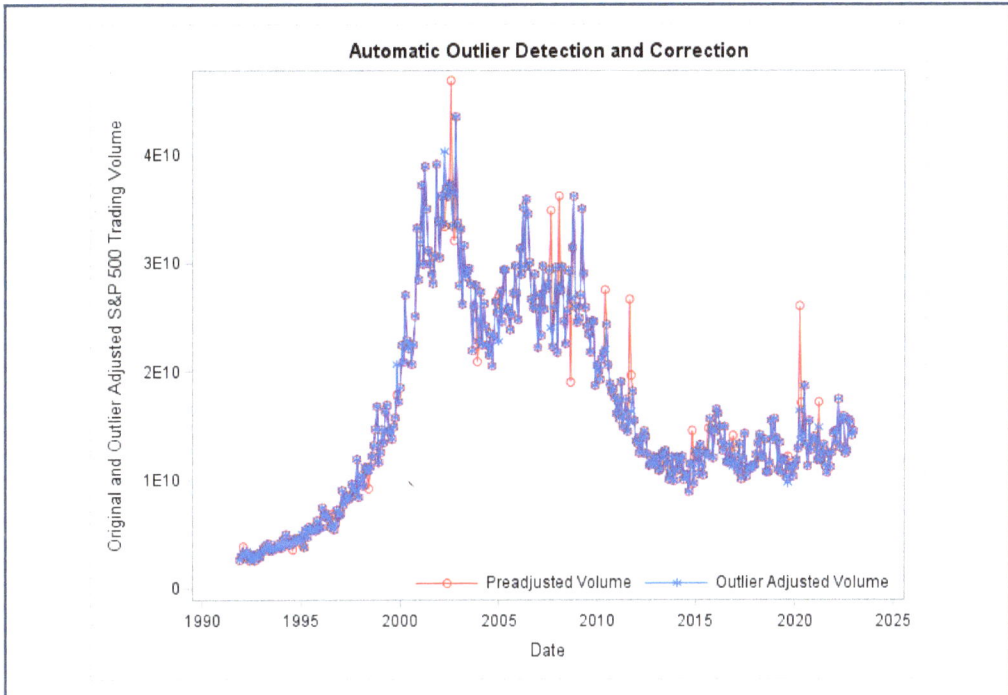

In Output 2.9, we display the time series plot generated by the SGPLOT procedure. Notice the differences between the plot of the unadjusted series and the outlier adjusted series. The plot of the former shows relatively high peaks and lower troughs in the same period as the adjusted series. The process of smoothing out the outliers ensures that the adjusted series is relatively less volatile than the unadjusted series.

Noisy Data

High-frequency financial data such as intraday stock market data are inherently noisy (in other words, display excessive random movements) and might obfuscate the underlying trends and patterns that the data scientist is trying to examine. They might also be a technical artifact of the market microstructure as proposed by some financial theories such as the Random walk model. Either way, noise makes it harder for algorithms to discern true signals from meaningless ones in market data and hence is a major interest for financial data scientists.

Figure 2.5: Sampling Frequency and Statistical Noise

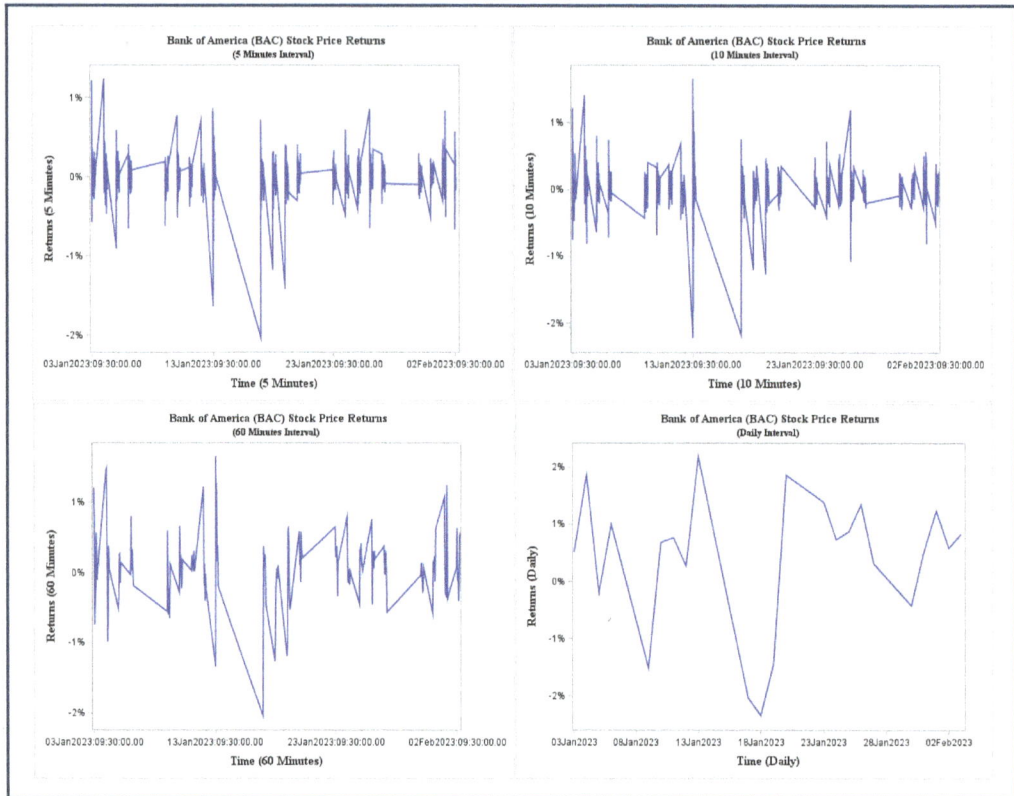

Dealing with Noisy Data

To reduce the impact of noisy data on the accuracy of your analysis, the data scientist could use one of the following two options.

- **Slower Sampling Frequency**: The data can be sampled at lower frequencies. This is because the lower the sampling frequency, the less noisy the data will be. Ideally, the optimal sampling frequency is the one that maximizes the signal-to-noise ratio in the data. While there is no predefined optimal frequency, the data scientist can use an iterative approach until the optimal sampling rate is identified. Figure 2.5 shows the stock return of Bank of America (BAC) using market prices that were sampled at different rates. Notice how the overall pattern of price movement over the sample period becomes more distinct as the sample rate reduces from five minutes to daily.

- **Data Aggregation**: Data sampled at higher frequencies can also be aggregated over a longer period. This approach provides the data scientist some flexibility to analyze and compare the signal-to-noise ratio at the different levels of aggregation.

As in the case of data consistency, higher sampling frequency and aggregation would lead to a loss in data granularity. This might not necessarily be an issue if the bulk of the details in higher granularity data is the statistical noise that the data scientist is trying to eradicate. Regardless of the approach pursued, the optimal rule should weigh granularity against the practical usefulness of the results in terms of being able to generalize it to the business needs of the project owners. Highly granular data that has no practical implementation or deployment value or that generates overfitted models are less desirable than data with lower granularity.

Program 2.10: Using PROC TIMEDATA to Resolve Issues with Noisy Data

```
/*Simulating One year of 5 minutes Returns for Bitcoin*/
data Bitcoin;
      format Date datetime.;
      length Bitcoin 8;
      call streaminit(1);
      InitDate = '1Jan2021:00:00'dt;
      dt=0;

      do I = 1 to 105120;/*Number of 5 mins Interval in ayear*/
            dt+5;
            Date=  intnx''minute'',InitDate,dt);
            Bitcoin = rand''norma'');
            output;
      end;
run;

/*Accumulating Returns into Hourly, Last Observation*/
proc timedata data=Bitcoin out=mseries plot=all;
      id date interval=hour
            /*Options include Hour,Day, Week, Month, Qtr, Year*/
      accumulate=last; /*Option include first, mean, median, last,*/
      var Bitcoin;
run;
```

In Program 2.10, we simulate one year of Bitcoin returns using the DATA step. We then apply the TIMEDATA procedure to transform the series. The TIMEDATA procedure supports a range of accumulation and sampling frequency options. In the sample code, the INTERVAL=Hour and ACCUMULATE=Last statements are used to specify that the last observation in each hour should be recorded from the five-minute series. In Output 2.10, we display the series plot of the hourly cumulated values of the simulated Bitcoin prices.

Output 2.10: Time Series Plot of Frequency Adjusted Bitcoin Prices

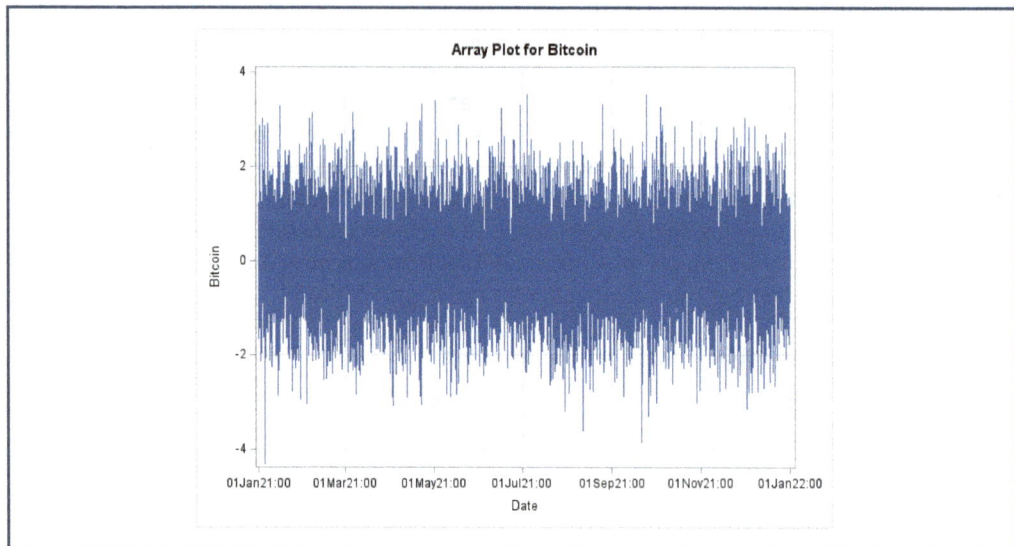

In summary, many of the built-in features and procedures in SAS make it well-suited for data wrangling and preprocessing. In Table 2.6, a catalog of common data quality issues, possible solutions, and SAS procedures that can be invoked to resolve them is provided.

Table 2.6: Summary of Data Quality Issues and SAS Solutions to Resolve Them

Data Quality Issue	Solution	SAS Procedure
Non-normality	Transformation	EXPAND TIMEDATA TIMESERIES DATA
Frequency incompatibility	Aggregation	EXPAND TIMEDATA TIMESERIES
Time-Stamp incompatibility	Synchronization Aggregation	TIMEDATA
Missing values	Replacement	TIMEDATA TIMESERIES
	Inference Complete Case Analysis	MI, SURVEYIMPUTE, MIANALYZE [5]

---

[5] PROC MIANALYZE analyzes the results obtained from the SAS procedure that was used on the imputed data to the generate statistical inferences. The MIANALYZE procedure reads parameter estimates and associated standard errors or covariance matrices that are computed by the standard statistical procedure for each imputed data set and then derives valid univariate statistical inferences for the parameters of the model.

Table 2.6: (Continued)

Data Quality Issue	Solution	SAS Procedure
Noise	Aggregation	EXPAND
		TIMEDATA
		TIMESERIES
		STATESPACE
Outlier	Replacement	ARIMA
		X13
		UCM

Other Data Wrangling Tools

Besides the DATA step, another versatile way to manipulate data in SAS is by using Structured Query Language (SQL), and the new SAS proprietary programming language for advanced data manipulation that is called DS2.

The SQL Procedure

SQL is a database programming language for managing and manipulating data stored in relational databases. Although there are many variants of the programming language in the public domain, they all share common standards that are governed by the American National Standard Institute (ANSI) and the International Standard Organization (ISO), so their core syntaxes are mostly the same. We will use the SQL procedure for some of the code examples you will see in subsequent sections of this chapter and the book.

PROC SQL is the SAS implementation of the Structured Query Language (SQL). Although SAS implementation of SQL is slightly different from other implementations, it shares many of the syntaxes that they all use, such as SELECT, JOIN, CREATE, UPDATE, ALTER, and DROP, to name a few. PROC SQL is often used by SAS programmers to execute data-wrangling tasks that are not well suited for the DATA step, such as those that are inconsistent with the way the DATA step compiles and executes commands in the Program Data Vector (PDV).[6] PROC SQL can access and manipulate data stored in tables and views, as well as the structure of the tables and views themselves. They can also be used to create SAS macro variables from data retrieved from the rows in the query result.[7]

---

[6] Interested readers can learn more about SAS PDV by visiting: https://support.sas.com/resources/papers/proceedings13/125-2013.pdf.

[7] You can learn more about all of the features of PROC SQL by reviewing the *SAS® 9.4 SQL Procedure User's Guide, Fourth Edition*, at https://documentation.sas.com/doc/en/pgmsascdc/9.4_3.5/sqlproc/titlepage.htm.

The DS2 Procedure

The DS2 programming language is an object-oriented programming language that extends the features of the DATA step to now include ANSI SQL syntaxes, programming structure elements, and user-defined methods and packages. PROC DS2 and its high-performance equivalent (PROC HPDS2) are both available in the Base SAS and SAS Viya environments.

Although you might not come across examples of DS2 procedures in this book, it is worth noting some of the main features of the procedure that you might find helpful with your data-wrangling tasks. DS2 supports a variety of data types; however, the data type must be declared as it is created in the DS2 statement. You can also create methods and packages or call up prebuilt methods and packages in your DS2 statements. Methods in DS2 statements are similar to user-defined functions. While packages are blocks of methods (similar to libraries). In reality, the DS2 language is a fairly advanced data-wrangling language to learn, and most of the examples we will explore in the book will not require such sophistication.[8]

Visual Description of the Data

Recall from Chapter One that in finance settings, data about the real world falls into the following taxonomy: cross-sectional, time series, and panel data. Given the growing role of unstructured data, we will add it to the list and provide some suggested visualizations to explore each type of data.

- **Cross-sectional data** are data on a statistical unit or items of interest that are collected at a single point in time. To draw insights from these types of data through visualizations, consideration should be given to the types of visualizations that highlight centrality and central tendencies, dispersions, symmetry, intensities, and associations.
- **Time series data** are data on the same item or statistical units that are collected over multiple periods. To draw insights from these types of data through visualizations, consideration should be given to the types of visualizations that highlight trends and serial correlations, as well as centrality and central tendencies, dispersions, symmetry, intensities, and associations.
- **Panel (longitudinal) data** are cross-sectional data that are collected over multiple periods. To draw insights from these types of data through visualizations, consideration should be given to the types of visualizations that highlight trends and serial correlations, causal relationships, as well as centrality and central tendencies, dispersions, symmetry, intensities, and associations.
- **Unstructured data** are data without a predefined framework. They require preprocessing before they can be visualized. To draw insights from these types of data through visualizations, consideration should be given to the types of visualizations that highlight intensities and associations.

---

[8] You can learn more about the DS2 programming language and its accompanying procedures by reviewing the SAS® 9.4 DS2 Programmer's Guide at https://documentation.sas.com/doc/en/pgmsascdc/9.4_3.5/pgmsaswlcm/home.htm.

Visualization Options in SAS

Visualizations are rendered in SAS using two distinct systems. The first system, which is known as the ODS Graphics uses a template-based system that is delivered with prebuilt templates in Base SAS. The second system, which is known as SAS/GRAPH, is a device-based graphics system that is licensed and installed separately from Base SAS.

ODS Graphics

Visualizations generated by ODS Graphics procedures (also known as Statistical Graphics procedures) are output created from compiled ODS graphics templates. The templates were prebuilt using the SAS Graph Template Language (GTL) and preprogrammed to allow for user customizations with very little programming effort. ODS Graphics procedures can be used to generate a wide range of visualizations including both statistical and non-statistical graphics. The SG prefix in the procedure name (such as SGPLOT, SGPIE, SGRENDER, SGMAP, SGPANEL, and SGSCATTER) is the common characteristic that the collection of ODS graphics procedures share. PROC SGPLOT, which is arguably the most popular, creates a variety of single-cell plots, chart types, and overlays. PROC SGPIE creates pie and donut charts, PROC SGMAP creates geographic maps, and PROC SGRENDER renders visualizations using graph templates that are written in GTL.[9]

SAS/GRAPH

Over the years, SAS has added several visualization statements to its already extensive array of SAS statements.[10] Many of these visualizations are included in the SAS/GRAPH package, which is a data visualization and presentation software that is a part of the SAS product family. SAS/GRAPH programming uses elements of the Base SAS programming language, the ODS statements, as well as its own SAS/GRAPH language elements. SAS/GRAPH language elements also use the PROC step (for example PROC GCHART and PROC GMAP), so users can call up the charts within a SAS file that contains other SAS statements.

Both ODS Graphics and SAS/GRAPH share common ODS statements that are used to control how the charts and graphs appear and where SAS should store them after they are generated. This could be an HTML file, or a LISTING, RTF, or PDF file. In Table 2.7, a catalog of various descriptive measures, visualization options, and SAS statements that can be invoked to render them are shown.

---

[9] You can learn more about SAS ODS Graphics Output systems in the "About the SAS ODS Graphics Procedures" section of the SAS® 9.4 ODS Graphics: Procedures Guide, Sixth Edition available at https://documentation.sas.com/doc/en/pgmsascdc/9.4_3.5/grstatproc/titlepage.htm.

[10] You can also find more information about SAS/GRAPH in *SAS/GRAPH® 9.4: Reference, Fifth Edition,* available at https://documentation.sas.com/doc/en/pgmsascdc/9.4_3.5/graphref/titlepage.htm.

Table 2.7: Descriptive Measures, Visualizations, and Related SAS Statements

Measure	Visualization	SAS Statement
Central Tendency	Histogram Box Plot	UNIVARIATE
Centrality	Cluster Plot	CLUSTER*SGPLOT FASTCLUS*SGPLOT
Dispersion	Q-Q Plot Histogram Residual Plot	UNIVARIATE CAPABILITY SGPLOT
Symmetry	Q-Q Plot Histogram	UNIVARIATE CAPABILITY SGPLOT
Intensity	Bar Chart Column Chart Donut Chart Pie Chart Word Cloud Heat Map Bubble Plot	SGPLOT GCHART
Association	Scatter Plot Area Plot Heat Map Treemap Bubble Plot Geo Map Contour Plot Surface Plot	SGPLOT GMAP, SGMAP
Trend	Line Plot Scatter Plot	SGPLOT

Using SAS to Analyze Portfolio Performance

As highlighted in the previous table, you can implement a wide range of visualizations in SAS. Let's explore some applications of these visualizations in an investment setting. Specifically, we will consider the use case for SAS in a portfolio reporting and analysis setting. Our sample portfolio consists of 63 stocks, spread over 11 GIC sectors, and all three categories of market capitalizations. The stock tickers and names of the companies are shown in Table 2.8. We will analyze the performance of the portfolio for the year 2021, beginning January 1st and ending December 31st.

Before we start our visualization, let us succinctly set up some parameters that would guide our examination of the portfolio for the reporting year. First, readers should note that performance

Table 2.8: Listing of Stocks in the Sample Portfolio

Ticker	Name	Ticker	Name	Ticker	Name
ABBV	ABBVIE INC.	RCII	RENT-A-CENTER INC.	SBNY	SIGNATURE BANK
HD	HOME DEPOT INC.	MSI	MOTOROLA SOLUTIONS INC.	HBI	HANESBRANDS INC.
WMT	WALMART INC.	IP	INTERNATIONAL PAPER CO	NVR	NVR INC.
CAT	CATERPILLAR INC	D	DOMINION ENERGY INC.	IVZ	INVESCO LTD.
AAPL	APPLE INC.	GWW	WW GRAINGER INC.	TSLA	TESLA INC.
DAL	DELTA AIR LINES INC.	ET	ENERGY TRANSFER LP	MPC	MARATHON PETROLEUM CORP.
BKNG	BOOKING HOLDINGS INC.	KFRC	KFORCE INC.	LYB	LYONDELLBASELL INDUSTRIES
CG	THE CARLYLE GROUP INC.	TSN	TYSON FOODS INC.	PII	POLARIS INC.
CVX	CHEVRON CORP.	MAR	MARRIOTT INTERNATIONAL	CNC	CENTENE CORP.
CSCO	CISCO SYSTEMS INC.	DLB	DOLBY LABORATORIES INC.	RMD	RESMED INC.
CVS	CVS HEALTH CORP.	DVA	DAVITA INC.	JNPR	JUNIPER NETWORKS INC.
DD	DUPONT DE NEMOURS INC.	ALG	ALAMO GROUP INC.	SUN	SUNOCO LP
JPM	JPMORGAN CHASE & CO	PAYC	PAYCOM SOFTWARE INC.	TOL	TOLL BROTHERS INC.
META	META PLATFORMS INC.	KMI	KINDER MORGAN INC.	VFC	VF CORP.
PFE	PFIZER INC.	CMS	CMS ENERGY CORP.	STE	STERIS PLC
SWK	STANLEY BLACK & DECKER INC.	WM	WASTE MANAGEMENT INC.	HAS	HASBRO INC.
UNH	UNITED HEALTH GROUP INC.	BXP	BOSTON PROPERTIES INC.	ALLY	ALLY FINANCIAL INC.
VTRS	VIATRIS INC.	GEN	GEN DIGITAL INC.	KO	THE COCA-COLA COMPANY
FDP	FRESH DEL MONTE PRODUCE INC.	ALK	ALASKA AIR GROUP INC.	CPT	CAMDEN PROPERTY TRUST
CMI	CUMMINS INC.	CCI	CROWN CASTLE INC.	DG	DOLLAR GENERAL CORP.
FE	FIRST ENERGY CORP.	VNO	VORNADO REALTY TRUST	TSCO	TRACTOR SUPPLY COMPANY

evaluation is a very sophisticated and comprehensive process that is governed by industry best practices (such as the Global Investment Performance Standards [GIPS]) and regulatory standards (such as the Financial Accounting Standards Board [FASB]) and the Securities Exchange Commission (SEC) rules and regulations.[11] Therefore, full coverage of the topic is beyond the scope of this book. In general, performance evaluation consists of five activities: performance measurement, performance attribution, performance appraisal, manager selection, and performance presentation. In this example, we will focus our visualizations on two of the five aspects listed above (measurement and attribution).

Performance measurement is concerned with what happened to the portfolio over the reporting period in terms of returns and risks. Be aware that risk and returns are typically evaluated in both absolute and relative terms (that is, relative to a benchmark). Since our portfolio is spread across the three categories of capitalization, the appropriate benchmark (which is usually selected before the investment period and disclosed in the investment policy statement) should also display similar characteristics. Hence, the benchmark we will use for this exercise is the Russell 3000 index, which is a market-value weighted index that tracks the performance of the 3,000 largest publicly traded companies in the US.

Performance attribution is concerned with how the portfolio achieved the measured performance. To put it another way, performance attribution is focused on identifying and quantifying the drivers of portfolio performance with regard to both portfolio risk and portfolio returns. Attribution provides deeper insights into how portfolio decisions were made during the reporting period. It also sheds light on whether the portfolio decisions or strategies are sustainable and repeatable moving forward. Thus, it is arguably one of the most value-adding aspects of performance evaluation.

We will need four data sets for this exercise. The PORTFOLIO_PRICES data set contains the monthly stock prices for all 63 stocks in the portfolio, while the PORTFOLIO_ATTRIB data set contains the attributes for each stock in the portfolio. These include the company name, the beginning and ending period prices of all 63 stocks, their portfolio weights, returns, standard deviations, beta, sector, and state of domicile to name a few. The BENCHMARK_PRICES data set contains the monthly levels of the Russell 3000 index, while the BENCHMARK_ATTRIB data set contains the sector weightings and returns for the 11 Global Industry Classification (GIC) sectors in the index. In Table 2.9, some descriptive characteristics of the portfolio and the benchmark are reported.

Numerical Performance Measurement

Program 2.11 pulls the four data sets we will use from the repository using the DATAPULL macro. The first DATA step merges the PORTFOLIO_PRICES and PORTFOLIO_ATTRIB data sets into the PORTA data set. It then uses the monthly prices and the units of each of the 63 stocks in the portfolio to calculate the monthly values of their respective portfolio holdings (MHOLDINGS).

---

[11] Interested readers can learn more about the GIPS standards by visiting https://www.cfainstitute.org/en/ethics-standards/codes/gips-standards/firms, FASB standards by visiting https://asc.fasb.org/Home, and SEC standards by visiting https://www.sec.gov/rules/rulemaking-index.shtml.

Table 2.9: Sector Components of Stocks in Sample and Benchmark Portfolio

Sector	Number of Companies		Weights		Returns	
	Portfolio	Benchmark	Portfolio	Benchmark	Portfolio	Benchmark
Communication Services	1	65	4.49%	2.91%	23.13%	2.75%
Consumer Discretionary	13	483	18.12%	16.71%	31.00%	17.47%
Consumer Staples	4	123	4.24%	5.15%	9.70%	14.75%
Energy	5	127	3.59%	3.37%	39.74%	44.24%
Financials	5	467	5.70%	10.95%	50.10%	31.89%
Health Care	9	646	14.13%	13.90%	29.54%	17.09%
Industrials	9	459	24.01%	13.47%	12.59%	15.52%
Information Technology	7	329	17.25%	26.31%	26.41%	35.62%
Materials	3	106	2.83%	1.97%	8.56%	22.80%
Real Estate	4	183	4.54%	3.41%	38.52%	33.56%
Utilities	3	80	1.11%	2.31%	13.50%	14.64%
Aggregate	63	3,068	100%	100%	25.24%	24.51%

Next, we use PROC SORT to sort the data by date, after which the PROC SQL statement is used to compute the monthly values of the portfolio (TOTALHOLDINGS) by taking the sum of the monthly holdings of each stock. The computed monthly portfolio values are saved in the TOTALHOLD data set. Notice that we also created another data set named PORTB that retains all of the information from the PORTA data set. We will merge this data set with the TOTALHOLD data in Program 2.12. The last DATA step in Program 2.11 calculates monthly portfolio returns (PRETURNS) using the logarithmic returns formula.

Program 2.11: Calculate Total Monthly Portfolio Holdings and Returns

```
/*Using DATAPULL Macro to download portfolio data from GitHub*/
%datapull(pprice,portfolio_prices.sas7bdat);
%datapull(pattrib,portfolio_attrib.sas7bdat);
%datapull(bprice,benchmark_prices.sas7bdat);
%datapull(battrib,benchmark_attrib.sas7bdat);

/*Merging attributes and price and calculating monthly returns */
data PortA;
     format Price dollar13.2 MHoldings dollar16.2
     Mcap dollar32.;
     merge Portfolio_Attrib  Portfolio_Prices;
     by Ticker;
     MHoldings = price*quantity;/*Monthly Holdings for each stock*/
run;
```

```
proc sort data= PortA ;
By Date;
run;
/*Calculating Total Monthly Portfolio Holdings and Returns*/
proc sql;
      create table portb as select * from porta;
      create table Totalhold as select date,
      sum(mholdings) as Totalholdings /*Monthly portfolio values*/
      format=dollar16.2 from porta group by date;
quit;

data Totalhold;
      set Totalhold;
      /*Calculating monthly portfolio returns-PReturns*/
      PReturns =log(Totalholdings/lag(Totalholdings));
      format PReturns Percent8.2;
      label PReturns ='Portfolio Returns';
run;
```

In Program 2.12, we create the PORTFOLIO_METRICS data set using PROC SQL to perform an inner merge of the TOTALHOLD and PORTB data sets. We then compute the monthly portfolio weights of each stock by dividing the monthly portfolio holdings in each stock (MHOLDHINGS) by the total portfolio values in each month (TOTALHOLDINGS).

Program 2.12: Using PROC SQL to Calculate Monthly Portfolio Weights

```
/*Calculating Monthly Weights for Stocks in the Portfolio by merging Totalhold and
Portb*/
proc sql;
      create table Portfolio_Metrics as select * from  Totalhold right join portb
            on totalhold.date=portb.date;

/*Monthly Weights calculated as Monthly Holdings(per stock)/Total Holdings(per month)*/

      alter table Portfolio_Metrics add Weights num label='Portfolio Weights';
      update Portfolio_Metrics set Weights= (Mholdings/TotalHoldings);
quit;
```

In Program 2.13, we create the MBMPORT data set by using the DATA step to merge the TOTALHOLD and BENCHMARK_PRICES data sets. We then use PROC MEANS to compute the average monthly returns, the standard deviations, skewness, and kurtosis for both the portfolio and the benchmark returns, and excess returns. We use the mean excess return and standard deviation of excess return to compute the Sharpe ratio in a separate step. The results of these computations are reported in Table 2.10.

Table 2.10: Average Monthly Performance of the Sample and Benchmark Portfolios

	Mean	Standard Deviation	Sharpe Ratio	Beta	Treynor	Skewness	Kurtosis
Portfolio Returns	1.88%	3.49%	0.504	0.98	0.018	-0.3515	-0.7474
Russell 3000 Returns	1.79%	3.05%	0.549	1.02	0.016	-0.7055	0.6139

Program 2.13: Using the DATA Step and PROC MEANS to Calculate Portfolio and Benchmark Statistics

```
/*Monthly Portfolio Performance Relative to Benchmark*/
data MBMPort;
    format Date monyy.;
    merge TotalHold Benchmark_Prices;
    EXPort = PReturns - TBY;
    EXRUA = RRUA -TBY;/*TBY-Monthy Yield on 10Yr Treasury Bond*/
    label EXPort ='Excess Portfolio Return';
    label EXRUA ='Excess Benchmark Return';
    by Date;
run;

proc means data=MBMPort(where=(date>'31Dec20'D)) mean stddev skew kurt;
var PReturns RRUA EXPORT EXRUA;
run;
```

The Sharpe Ratio is calculated as $S_p = \dfrac{E(R_p - R_f)}{\sigma_p}$, where $(R_p - R_f)$ is the excess return of the portfolio over the risk-free rate and σ_i is the standard deviation of excess return.

The Treynor Measure is calculated as $S_p = \dfrac{E(R_p - R_f)}{\beta_p}$, where $\beta_p = \sum_{i=1}^{N} w_i \beta_i$ is the beta of the portfolio.

From a performance measurement point of view, two things are immediately evident in Tables 2.9 and 2.10. First, the portfolio (63 stocks) is concentrated relative to its benchmark (3,068 stocks) and that might just be a distinct aspect of the strategy of the portfolio manager. Second, the portfolio slightly outperformed the benchmark during the reporting period (25.24% and 24.24%, for the portfolio and benchmark, respectively). The beginning value of the portfolio on January 1st, 2021, was $60.85 million while the year-end value was $76.2 million. The level of the Russell 3000 index was 2,248 at the beginning of the year and 2,799.13 at year-end.

The impact of the concentrated portfolio strategy employed by the manager is apparent in the total risk and total risk-adjusted measures of the portfolio performance as shown in the standard deviations and Sharpe ratios. In both measures, the portfolio underperformed the benchmark. The portfolio did perform better than the benchmark based on systematic risk-adjusted measures as captured by the betas and Treynor measures. The difference in the risk ranking is due to the portfolio attributes, which we will visualize shortly. Although the portfolio is concentrated in a relatively lower number of stocks than the index, it is mostly comprised of large capitalization stocks that have lower betas, while the index is mostly comprised of medium and small capitalization stocks that tend to have higher betas. In summary, the portfolio outperformed the benchmark on a total return and systematic risk-adjusted returns basis.

Visual Performance Measurement

In Program 2.14, we use the TEMPLATE and SGRENDER procedures to visualize the monthly values and returns of the portfolio. The portfolio values are graphed using a bar chart that is overlaid with a line chart of monthly returns. To combine different types of graphs, it is often expedient to invest some time in creating a layout that can be called up and reused with relatively minor modifications in the future. Graph templates are produced using GTL, which is an extension of SAS ODS. These templates are stored in the SAS template store. They can then be called up and rendered using the SGRENDER procedure. Although most graphs can be created directly without using a template, the template provides more control over how the visualizations are rendered in SAS. Moving forward, we will experiment with both approaches (that is, directly plotting the graphs and rendering them using custom templates).

Program 2.14: Using PROC TEMPLATE and PROC SGRENDER to Generate Bar-Line Chart of Monthly Portfolio Performance

```
/*Graphing Monthly Portfolio Returns and Value*/
proc template;
   define statgraph barline;
      begingraph;
         entrytitle "Portfolio Performance in 2021";
         layout overlay /
         xaxisopts=(label="Month" timeopts=(tickvalueformat=monname3.))
         yaxisopts=(label="Values (Millions)" offsetmin=0
         linearopts=(tickvaluesequence=(start=0 end=80 increment=20)
         tickvaluepriority=true))
         y2axisopts=(label="Returns" offsetmin=0
         linearopts=(viewmin=-.1 viewmax=.1));
         barchart category=date response=eval(Totalholdings/1000000) /
         name="bar" legendlabel="Portfolio Values"
         fillattrs=(transparency=0.6 color=bip);
            linechart category=date response=PReturns /
            legendlabel="Portfolio Returns" vertexlabel=true
            vertexlabelattrs=(color=darkblue weight=bold)
```

```
            name="line" stat=sum yaxis=y2 display=(line markers)
                markerattrs=(symbol=circlefilled color=darkblue)
                lineattrs=(color=darkblue);
            discretelegend "bar" "line";
        endlayout;
      endgraph;
    end;
run;

proc sgrender data=totalhold(where=(date>'31dec20'd))  template=barline;
    format date monname3. PReturns percent6.2;
run;
```

In the PROC TEMPLATE statement, we begin by defining the name of the template using the DEFINE STATGRAPH statement. Next, the BEGINGRAPH statement, which is required for all STATGRAPH templates is used to define the outermost block of statement for the template. We then specify the title of the graph using the ENTRYTITLE statement. The LAYOUT statement is then used to specify that the composite of GTL statements will be used (one or more 2-D plots). This statement is followed by a series of statements that specify the axis and graph options. Notice in the BARCHART statement (which we use to specify the category variable [DATE] and the response variable [TOTALHOLDINGS]) that we specify that the values of the response variable (TOTALHOLDINGS) should be divided by one million to improve the aesthetic value of the bar chart. For the line chart, the category variable is also specified as DATE, while the response variable is specified as PRETURNS. The next block of code specifies various formatting options for the line chart (which includes using the Y2 for its vertical axis) and the legend. The sequence of the END statements is used to complete each sequential block of statements. The rendering of the template is invoked using the PROC SGRENDER statement. There is no need to specify any variable or the type of graph to be plotted in the SGRENDER statement because both pieces of information have already been included in the template statement.

You will observe on the bar-line chart of the monthly portfolio values and returns that are shown in Output 2.14 that the portfolio values did not increase monotonically through the reporting period. Indeed, there were significant variations in the portfolio performance during the course of the months, with the best-performing months being March, October, and December, and the worst monthly performance occurring in September.

Output 2.14: Monthly Portfolio Performance

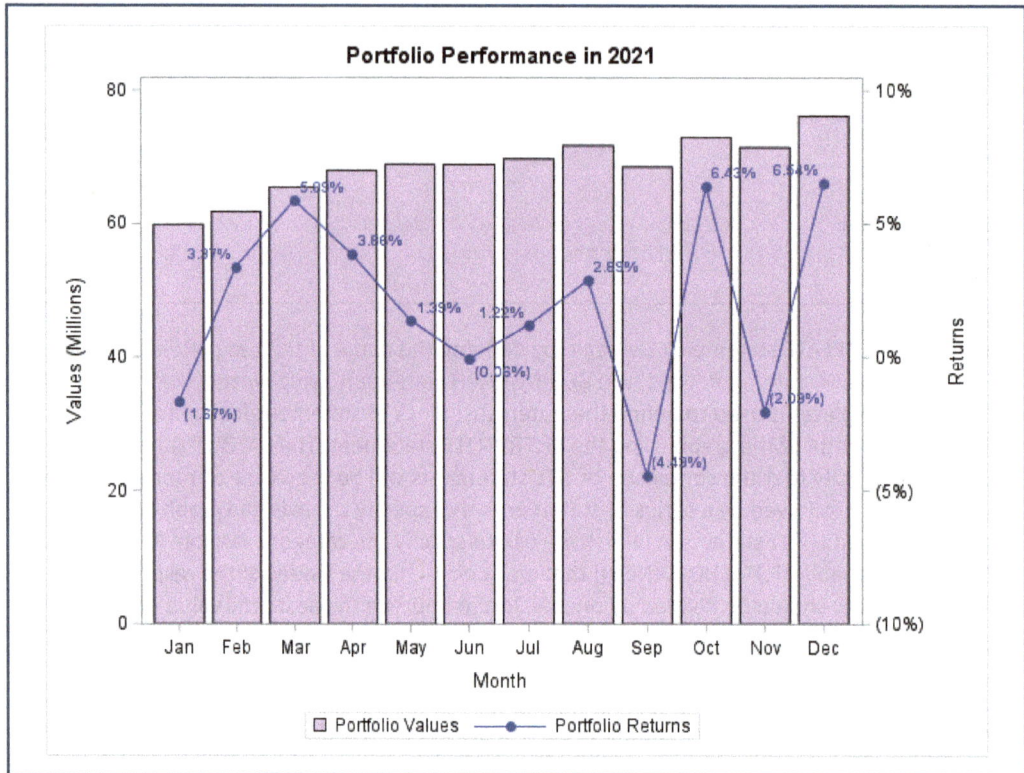

In Program 2.15, we compare the performance of the portfolio to the benchmark on a monthly basis using column charts of the monthly returns of the portfolio and benchmark. This time around, the graph is produced without using a template. It is simply called up using the SGPLOT procedure. You might have come across the SGPLOT statements in previous sections of the book. That is because the procedure is a versatile SAS ODS statement that can produce a variety of visualizations, as well as combine them using one set of SAS statements. In this visualization, its bar chart feature is invoked using the VBAR statement, which is followed by the category to aggregate (DATE) and a response variable (PRETURNS). The DISCRETEOFFSET statement is used to demarcate the monthly returns of the portfolio from those of the benchmark.

Program 2.15: Using PROC SGPLOT to Compare Monthly Portfolio and Benchmark Returns

```
/*Comparing the Monthly Performance of the Portfolio to the Benchmark*/
proc sgplot data=MBMPort(where=(date>'31dec20'd));
title "Monthly Portfolio and Bechmark Performances in 2021";
  styleattrs datacolors=(olive purple);
    vbar date/response=PReturns /*Portfolio Returns*/
```

```
            dataskin=pressed barwidth=0.6
              baselineattrs=(thickness=0)
              discreteoffset=-0.1 ;
        vbar date/response=RRUA /*Benchmark Returns*/
              dataskin=pressed barwidth=0.6
              baselineattrs=(thickness=0)
              discreteoffset= 0.1;
        xaxis label='Date' valuesrotate=vertical;
     yaxis display=(noline) grid;
  run;
  title;
```

Output 2.15: Comparing Monthly Portfolio and Benchmark Returns

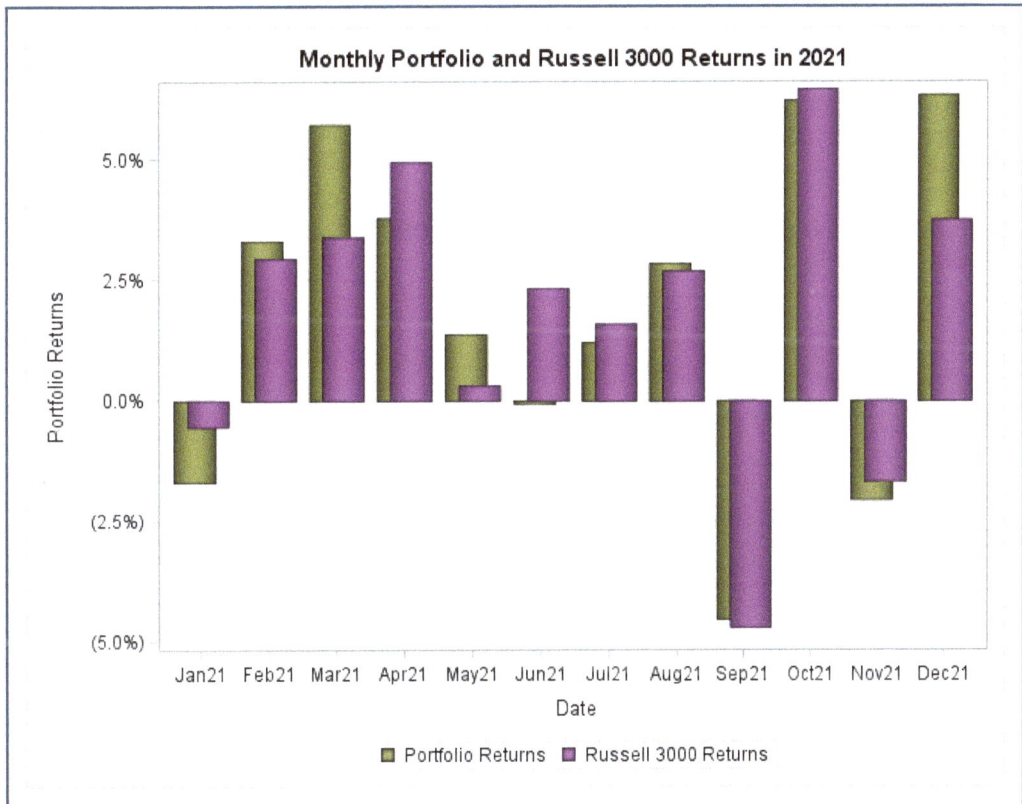

Output 2.15 shows vertical bar charts of the monthly returns on the portfolio and its benchmark, which is the Russell 300 index. From the graph, the outperformance of the portfolio relative to the benchmark appears to be concentrated in the March and December months, which is in line with the earlier identified periods of best performances for the portfolio. From a relative performance point of view, the portfolio also outperformed the benchmark in May, although the absolute returns of the portfolio and benchmark were much lower in that month, relative to the

other months. It would be worthwhile to examine what happened to the portfolio and market in these three months, as well as in January when the portfolio significantly underperformed the index, and in September, when both portfolios had substantial negative performances.

Visual Performance Attribution

Let us conduct a drill-down into our portfolio characteristics and performance using other types of visualizations. Specifically, we will use visualizations to examine the portfolio holdings, valuations, returns, risk, income, and dispersions in the returns at the sector level. We will also examine the geographic dispersion of the portfolio holdings across the 50 states in the US.

Portfolio Allocations

Program 2.16 contains the SAS code that displays the sector weights of the portfolio using a pie chart TEMPLATE and SGRENDER procedures. In this example, a pie chart template is created to define the layout of the chart. The layout is then invoked in the SGRENDER procedure to render the chart.

Program 2.16: Using PROC TEMPLATE and SGRENDER to Display Sector Weights for Portfolio Using Pie Chart

```
/*Using Pie Chart to Display Portfolio Attributes*/
proc template;
      define statgraph pietemp;
      begingraph;
      entrytitle "Portfolio Sector Weights";
      layout region;
      piechart category=Sector / stat=pct datalabellocation=outside
      othersliceopts=(percent=1.5);
      endlayout;
      endgraph;
      end;
run;

proc sgrender data=Portfolio_Attrib template=pietemp;
run;
```

Output 2.16: Portfolio Sector Weights

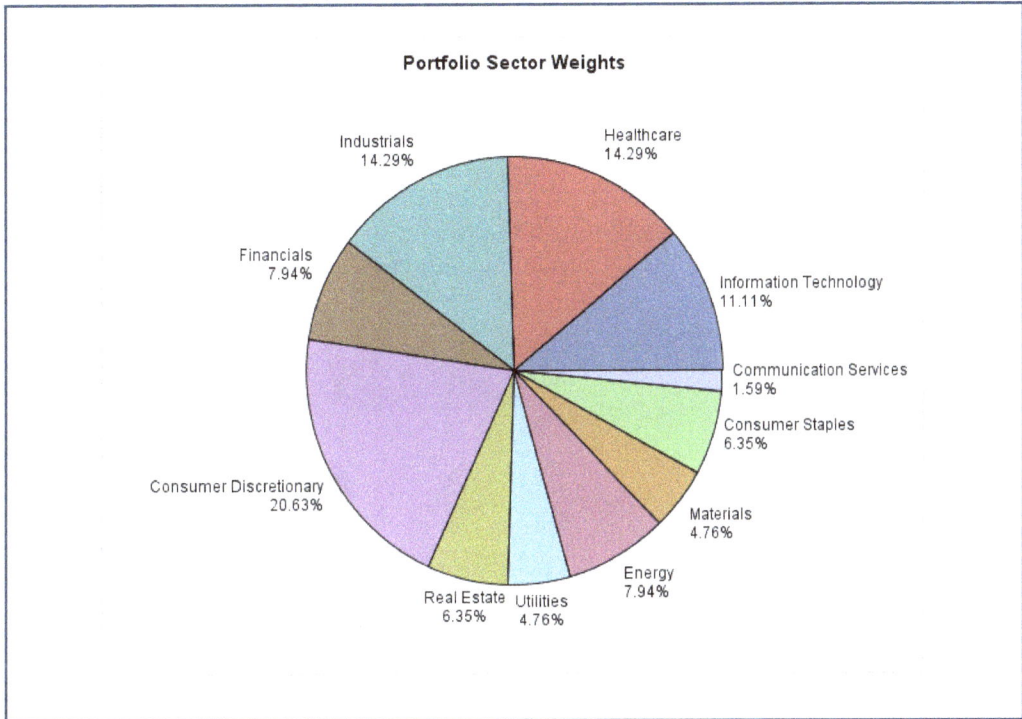

Output 2.16 shows the sector-based weights of the 63 stocks in the portfolio. From a market value point of view, about 60% of the portfolio is concentrated in four sectors: consumer discretionary, health care, industrials, and information technology.

Valuation

We can explore the interactions between three characteristics of the portfolio on a heat map, using the SGPLOT procedure as shown in Program 2.17. On the map, we graph the Sector distribution against the market capitalization distribution and their interaction with the well-known valuation multiple (price-to-earnings ratio). Average valuation appears to be high amongst large-cap stocks, particularly those in the consumer discretionary, technology, and real estate sectors. The extreme valuation in the mid-cap real estate sector is because only one stock in the portfolio falls into that box, which is Vornado Realty Trust (VNO).

Program 2.17: Using PROC SGPLOT to Display Sector Weights for Portfolio Using a Heat Map

```
/*Using a Heat Map to Display Portfolio Attribute*/
proc sgplot data=Portfolio_Attrib;
      title 'Sector-Level Portfolio Characteristics';
      heatmap x=mcapc y=sector/ colorresponse=pe colorstat=mean weight=weights;
run;
```

Output 2.17: Heat Map of Portfolio Sector Weights

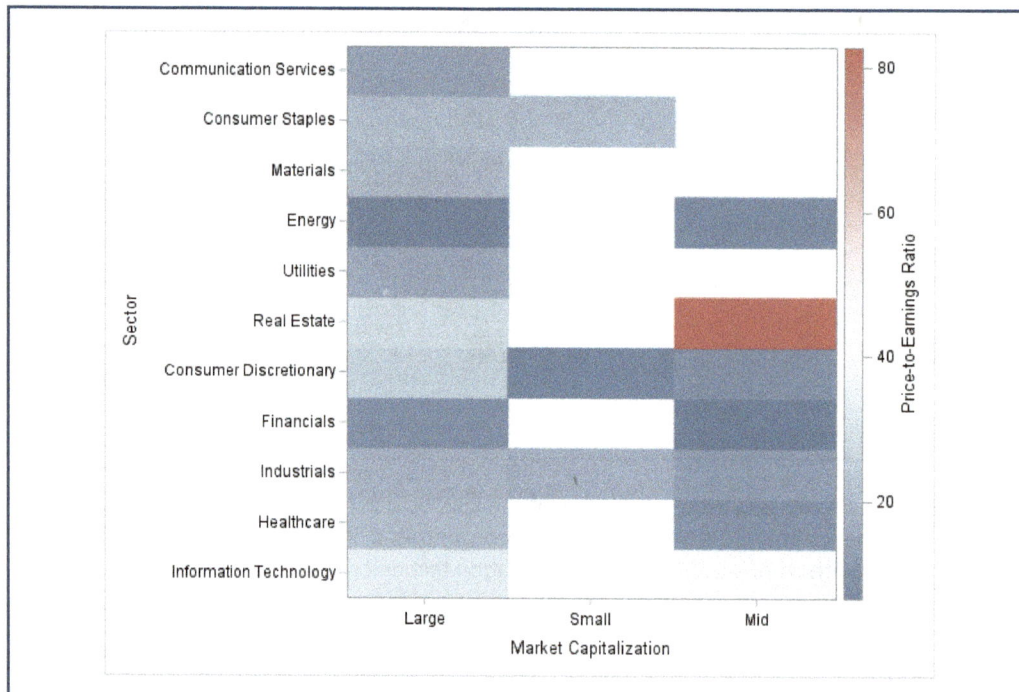

Program 2.18: Using PROC TEMPLATE and PROC SGRENDER to Display Valuation Premium for Portfolio Using Bar Chart

```
/*Using Bar Chart to Display Portfolio Attribute*/
proc template;
  define statgraph barchart;
    begingraph/border=false
              datacolors = (pink plum paleturquoise)
              datacontrastcolors = (black);
      entrytitle "Portfolio Factor Exposure By Capitalizations" ;
      layout overlay;
```

```
        barchart category=mcapc  response=pb / name="pbar"
          stat=mean orient=vertical dataskin=sheen
            colorbyfreq=true  colorstat=pct colormodel=datacolors;
        continuouslegend "pbar" /
          title="Market Capitalization Allocations";
      endlayout;
        endgraph;
    end;
proc sgrender data=Portfolio_Attrib template=barchart;
run;
```

Another valuation element we can examine is the price-to-book (market-to-book) ratio. In Program 2.18, we again draw upon the BARCHART template and SGRENDER procedure to graph the relationship between the portfolio exposure across market capitalizations and valuation premiums.

Output 2.18: Valuation Premium for Portfolio Components

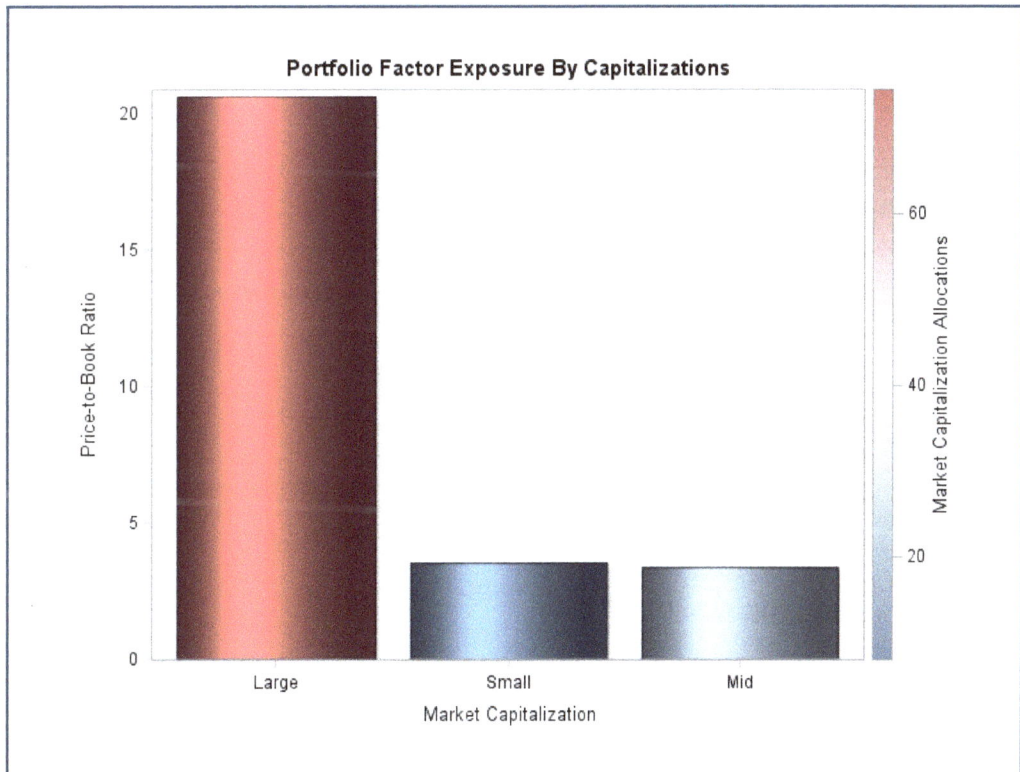

The chart shown in Output 2.18 provides further confirmation that valuation appears to be relatively higher in large-cap stocks compared to other categories of capitalization.

Returns

If large capitalization stocks in consumer discretionary, technology, and real estate sectors are so expensive relative to their earnings, it is prudent to examine their contributions to the overall performance of the portfolio. We use a stacked horizontal column chart using SECTORS as the category, RETURNS as the response variable, and market capitalization (MCAPC) as the group variable. The code and output are shown in Program 2.19 and Output 2.19.

On the stacked column chart, we can see that the large-cap stocks that made the most contribution to the portfolio were those in the financial, energy, and real estate sectors. Mid-cap stocks in the financial, energy, and consumer discretionary, as well as small-cap stocks in the industrial sector also added more value to the portfolio relative to the four expensive large-cap sectors.

Program 2.19: Using PROC SGPLOT to Display Sector Returns for Portfolio Using Stacked Column Chart

```
/*Using Stacked Column Chart to Display Portfolio Attributes*/
proc sgplot data=Portfolio_Attrib;
title 'Performance Attribution by Sectors and Market Capitalizations';
      hbar sector /
response=returns weight=weights stat=mean group=mcapc
      dataskin=pressed;
run;
title;
```

Output 2.19: Portfolio Returns by Sector Allocations

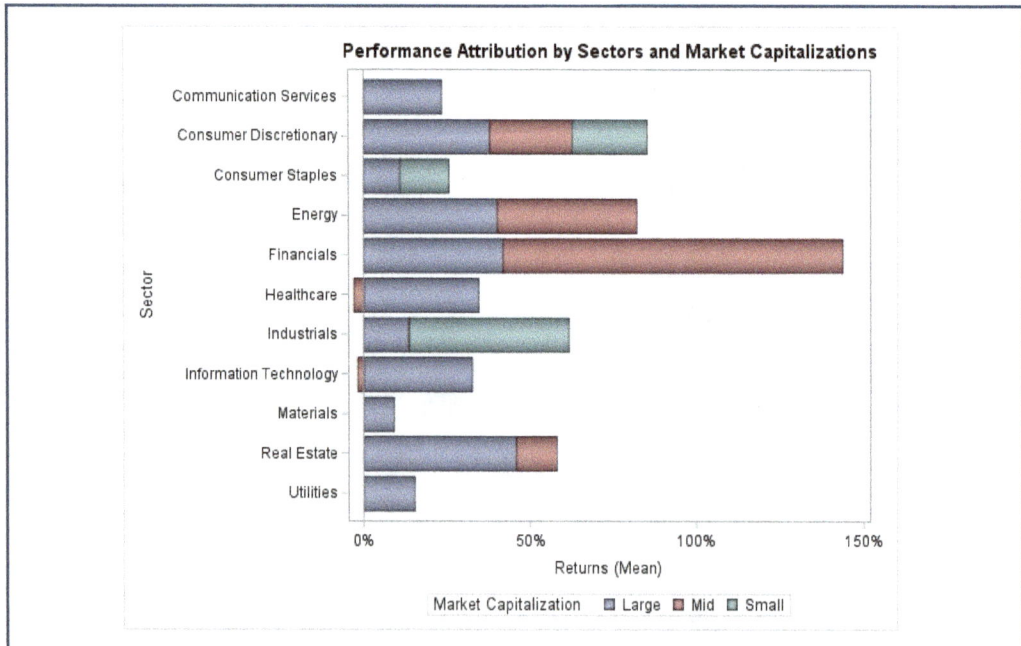

Performance Attribution by Sectors and Market Capitalizations

Income

For some portfolios, income from dividends and interest is also a major element of the portfolio objective and therefore assessed as an aspect of the overall performance. In Program 2.20, we replicate the stacked column chart to show the income contribution from each sector to the overall portfolio income. The graph shows that most of the income received by the portfolio came from large-cap stocks, particularly those in the industrial, health care, energy, financial, and real estate sectors. No income was received from the communication sector. In view that a large number of US stocks do not pay dividends, we can assess that the portfolio appears to also have an income focus.

Program 2.20 Using PROC TEMPLATE and PROC SGRENDER to Display Sector Income for Portfolio with Stacked Column Chart

```
/*Using Stacked Column Chart to Display Portfolio Income*/
proc template;
  define statgraph barchart2;
    begingraph;
      entrytitle "Portfolio Income by Sectors" ;
      layout overlay;
        barchart category=Sector  response=income / name="pdisplay"
          stat=sum display=all orient=horizontal group=mcapc;
                 discretelegend "pdisplay";
      endlayout;
        endgraph;
  end;

proc sgrender data=Portfolio_Attrib template=barchart2;
run;
```

Output 2.20: Portfolio Income by Sector Allocations

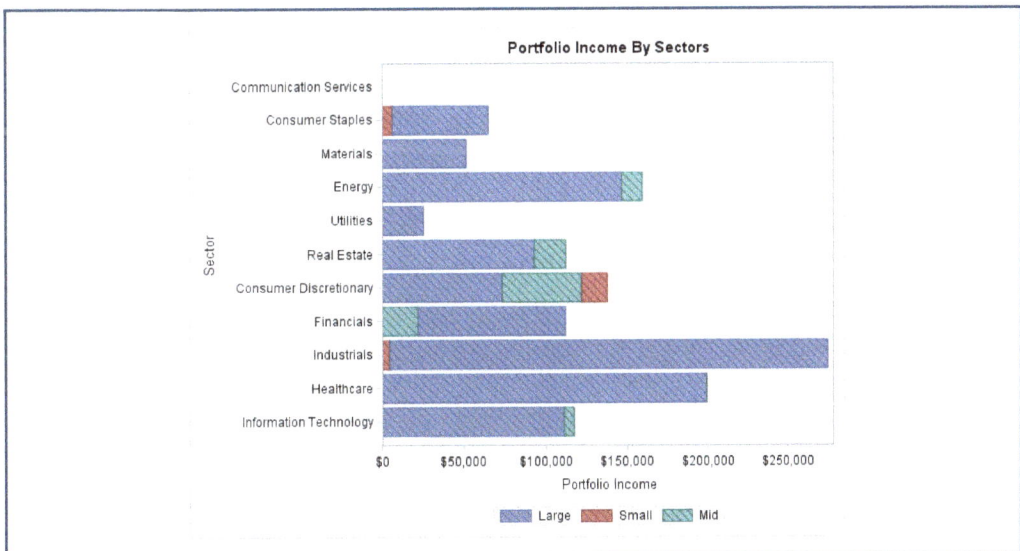

Risk

Now turning our attention to portfolio risk and return dispersion. In Program 2.21, a scatter plot, which graphs the return of each stock against its beta was created using the SGPLOT procedure. We also draw a regression line (using the REG statement) through the plot to see if the prediction of the capital asset pricing model (CAPM) also holds for this portfolio. The CLM statement is used to define the confidence limit for the prediction area for the portfolio returns.

Program 2.21: Using PROC SGPLOT to Display Portfolio Risk and Reward Relationship on Scatter Plot

```
/*Using Scatterplot to Display Reward to Risk*/
 proc sgplot data=Portfolio_Attrib;
     title ' Portfolio Reward-to-Risk';
     scatter x=beta y=returns/;
     reg x=beta y=returns/CLM  CLI='Prediction' alpha=.05;
     Xaxis label = 'Beta' values=(0 to 2 by 0.2)    ;
     yaxis label ='Returns'  valuesformat=percent12.2;
     keylegend / location=inside position=bottomright;
 run;
 title;
```

Output 2.21: Security Market Line of Portfolio Components

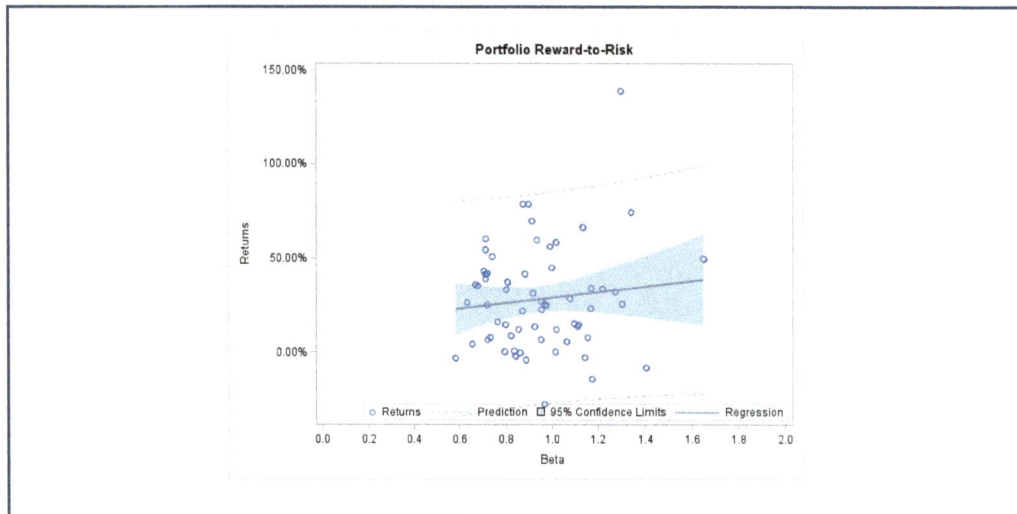

Going by the prediction line and area, the security with close to 150% return in a year appears to be an outlier. The positive slope of the regression confirms the commonly held notion that higher-risk assets should reward investors with higher returns.

Return Dispersion

Let's also examine managers' ability to select high-performing stocks within each sector by examining the dispersion of returns in each sector. Wide dispersion could be indicative of luck and not necessarily acuity in stock selection. Along the same line, a concentration of low-performing stocks within a sector might also be indicative of poor judgment in that sector. There could also be other factors at play. Nevertheless, let's examine return dispersion within each sector using the box plot option in PROC SGPLOT with the SAS code in Program 2.22.

Program 2.22: Using PROC SGPLOT to Display Sector-Level Return Dispersion Using a Box Plot

```
/*Using a Box Plot to display return dispersion*/
proc sgplot data=Portfolio_Attrib;
     title ' Performance Dispersion by Sector';
     hbox returns/category=sector dataskin=matte fillattrs=(
color='Aquamarine');
run;
title;
```

Output 2.22 shows noticeably higher degrees of return dispersions in the financials, industrials, consumer discretionary, health care, and real estate sectors, relative to other sectors. Also evident in the plot is the presence of outliers in terms of return performance in the energy, financial, and industrial sectors. The stock with the outlier performance in the financial service sector for that year was Signature Bank, which had a return of 139.1%. Interestingly, 13 months later, Signature Bank was placed into receivership by Federal and state regulators due to a bank run that was triggered by the collapse of Silicon Valley Bank and Signature Bank's exposure to the cryptocurrency industry.[12]

Output 2.22: Sector-Level Return Dispersion

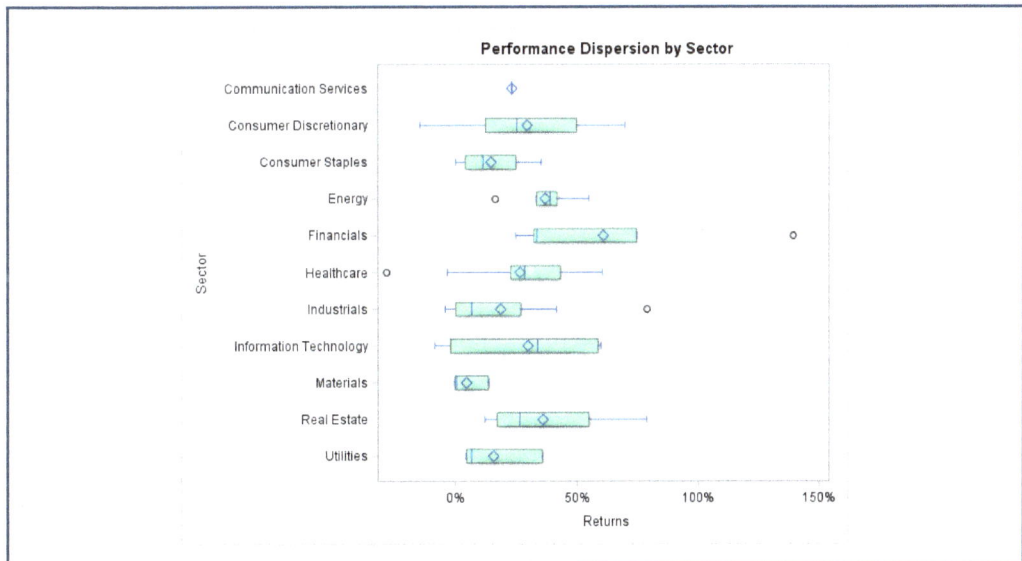

_____

[12] You can read more about the collapse of Signature Bank at https://www.nytimes.com/2023/03/12/business/signature-bank-collapse.html.

Geographic Dispersion

Geographic diversification or preferential tax treatment at the state level might be a concern for some investors. So, let's examine the geographic concentration of the portfolio across the 50 US states by using the SGMAP procedure. The procedure does require a fair amount of preparatory coding to align the geographic information (in this instance, state abbreviations) in the data with the map template that SAS uses to render the geographic maps. The SGMAP procedure works by overlaying a polygon outline area on a map template produced by third-party map providers. To create the polygon, SGMAP requires Federal Information Processing Standards (FIPS) codes for the location. For US states and territories, it is a numeric value with a range of 1 to 72.[13] This information is then translated into a map data set that consists of X (horizontal) and Y (vertical) coordinates that SAS uses to render the map. The MAPDATA statement is used to read the boundary areas into SAS. The MAPRESPDATA statement reads the data set that contains the response variable that is projected onto the map. The PLOTDATA statement reads into SAS other data sets that can be used to overlay other plots such as scatter and bubble plots onto the map. The third-party map provider used in this example is OpenStreetMap. The CHOROMAP statement specifies the set of rules that is used to render a two-dimensional map (Choropleth) of the response variable (COUNT) on the base map.

Program 2.23: Using PROC SGMAP to Display Geographic Concentration of Portfolio Holdings

```
/*Using Geomaps to Display Geographic Portfolio Concentration*/
%datapull(plot,plot_data.sas7bdat);
%datapull(states,states.sas7bdat);
proc sgmap mapdata=states      /* Map boundaries */
      maprespdata= plot_data
      plotdata=plot_data; /* location data */
       title 'Portfolio Concentration By State';
      openstreetmap;
      choromap  count / mapid=state density=2
      name='choro';
      text x=long y=lat text=statename /textattrs=(size=7pt);
      gradlegend 'choro'/title='Number of Companies in Each State'
      extractscale;
run;
```

In Program 2.23, the geographic distribution of the portfolio across the 50 US states is plotted on the US map. We first use the %DATAPULL macro to download the PLOT_DATA and STATES SAS data sets from the GitHub repository. Next, the SGMAP procedure is invoked. The MAPDATA statement instructs the procedure to use the STATES data set to define the boundaries of each US state. The actual data to be plotted are in the PLOT_DATA. The data set contains map details for 58 of the 63 companies that are domiciled in the US. The business addresses of the remaining

---

[13] Interested readers can see the listing for the FIPS codes for US states and counties at https://www.census.gov/library/reference/code-lists/ansi.html.

five stocks are not in the US. The COUNT and the PERCENT variables in the PLOT_DATA are the counts and proportions of the companies in each state. We use the CHOROMAP statement to plot the numeric counts of the number of companies in each state. The TEXT statement is used to specify the coordinates for plotting the STATENAME variable, which is the abbreviated name of each state.

Output 2.23 shows the geographic map that was obtained from invoking the SGMAP procedure. The map emphasizes a noticeable concentration of the portfolio with companies that are domiciled in Texas and California. Also evident on the map are higher numbers of companies on the eastern side of the US than on the western and central areas of the US. In reality, the concentration of the companies appears to be in line with the geographic distribution of the US population.

Output 2.23: Geographic Concentration of Portfolio Holdings

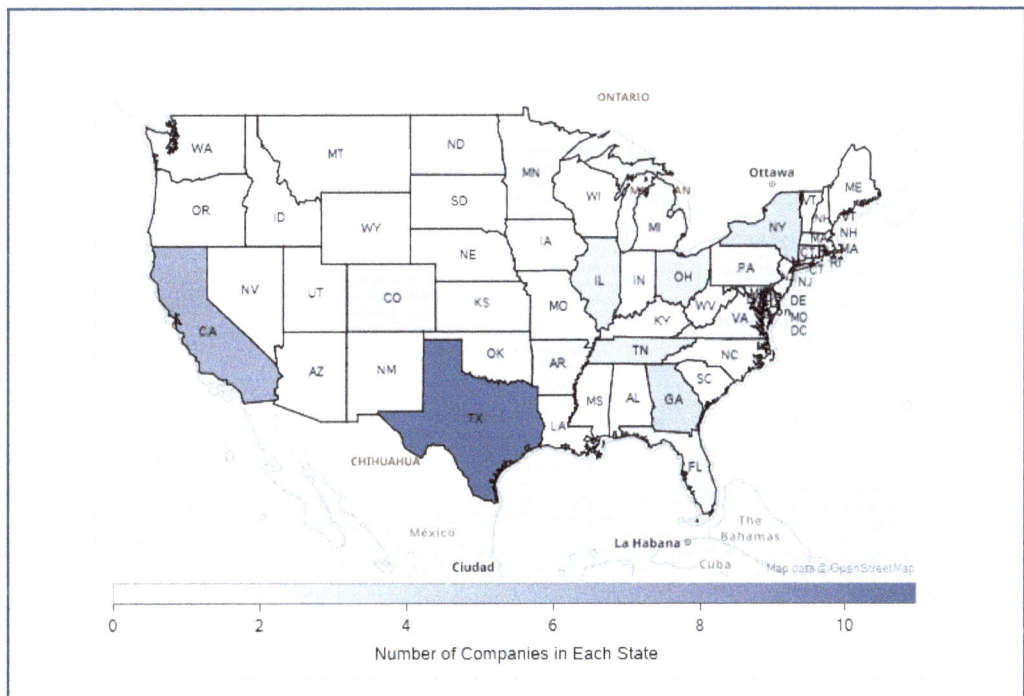

Numerical Performance Attribution in SAS

So far, we have mostly conducted a visual attribution of the portfolio performance. Let's conclude by conducting a numerical attribution of the portfolio performance. In the previous visualizations, we show that large-cap stocks in the financial, energy, and real estate sectors; mid-cap stocks in the financial, energy, and consumer discretionary; as well as small-cap stocks in the industrial sector appear to be the main drivers of the portfolio's performance. But these results could be the effect of the so-called rising tide that lifts all boats. So, let's attempt to disentangle actual managerial expertise from market effect by using the widely used Brinson model (1985, 1986) performance attribution model which decomposes overall portfolio performance into:

$$\text{Portfolio Performance} = \text{Benchmark Contribution} + \text{Managerial Selection} \qquad (2.1)$$

Let's define our portfolio and benchmark performances as follows:

$$\text{Portfolio Performance} \quad (P) = \sum_{i=1}^{N} w_i R_i,$$

$$\text{Benchmark Performance} \quad (B) = \sum_{i=1}^{N} W_i B_i, \qquad (2.2)$$

where:

$$w_i = \text{portfolio weight in sector } i$$
$$R_i = \text{portfolio return in sector } i$$
$$W_i = \text{benchmark weight in sector } i$$
$$B_i = \text{benchmark return in sector } i$$
$$N = \text{number of sectors (11)}$$

Then managerial selection (M) could be defined as:

$$M = P - B = \sum_{i=1}^{N} w_i R_i - \sum_{i=1}^{N} W_i B_i \qquad (2.3)$$

M, which is also known as "Alpha" can be further decomposed algebraically into three subcomponents:

- Allocation (A): this is the value added through selecting a different weight in each sector than the index. And expressed as: $\sum_{i=1}^{N} (w_i - W_i) B_i$

- Selection (S): this is the value added by selectively picking only the best stocks within each sector. And takes the following expression. $\sum_{i=1}^{N} W_i (R_i - B_i)$

- Interaction (I): this is the value added through the interaction of allocation and selection decisions. It is sometimes considered as the summing effect that equalizes allocation and selection to M. This amount is often trivial but could be substantial in some instances. It is defined as: $\sum_{i=1}^{N} (w_i - W_i)(R_i - B_i)$.

We can now lay out the numerical performance attribution of the portfolio as:

$$P = B + A + S + I \qquad (2.4)$$

Program 2.24: Using PROC Print to Generate Portfolio Performance Attribution Table

```
/*Generating Portfolio Performance Attribute Report*/
%datapull(attrib,performance_attrib.sas7bdat);

proc print data=Performance_Attrib noobs label
        style(header)={just=c fontsize=1.8} style(data)={just=c fontsize=1.8}
        style(grandtot)={just=c fontweight=bold fontsize=1.8} grandtot_Label='Total';
    title ' Portfolio Performance Attribution';
    variables Sector/style(data)={just=l fontweight=bold width=1.8in};
    var BGWeights Returns Sector_P Index_Weights  Index_Returns Sector_I Sector_T
        Sector_Alpha  PAllocation  PSelection  PInteraction;
    sum BGWeights Index_Weights Sector_P Sector_I PAllocation PSelection Pinteraction;
    footnote H=0.5 'Benchmark is the Russell 3000 Index | Sector tilt = Portfolio
                    overweighting(underweighting) of each sector relative to the index
                    | Sector Alpha = Portfolio Outperformance(underperformance) of each
                    sector relative to the index';
run;

title;
footnote;
```

Estimating the performance attributions measures of the portfolio using SAS is achieved using a sequence of DATA steps, PROC SQL, PROC TABULATE, and PROC PRINT statements.[14] First, the sector-level performance attributes of the portfolio are obtained using PROC TABULATE and stored in the output files DSTATSONE (sum attributes) and DSTATSTWO (weighted average attributes). The data sets were then merged with the Benchmark attribute data set (BENCHMARK_ATRRIB) and formatted to yield the MERGEDSTATS data set using PROC SQL. The performance attribution measures P, B, A, S, and I were computed using the DATA step and saved in the PERFORMANCE_ATTRIB data. The actual attribution table shown in Output 2.24 is generated by invoking the PRINT procedure and specifying the option as shown in Program 2.24.

Output 2.24: Portfolio Performance Attribution Table

Portfolio Performance Attribution

Sector	Beginning Weights	Returns	Sector Contribution (Portfolio)	Benchmark Weights	Benchmark Returns	Sector Contribution (Benchmark)	Sector Tilt	Sector Alpha	Allocations	Selection	Interaction
Communication Services	4.49%	23.13%	1.04%	2.91%	2.75%	0.08%	1.58%	20.38%	0.04%	0.59%	0.32%
Consumer Discretionary	18.12%	31.00%	5.62%	16.71%	17.47%	2.92%	1.41%	13.53%	0.25%	2.26%	0.19%
Consumer Staples	4.24%	9.70%	0.41%	5.15%	14.75%	0.76%	(0.91%)	(5.06%)	(0.13%)	(0.26%)	0.05%
Energy	3.59%	39.74%	1.43%	3.37%	44.24%	1.49%	0.22%	(4.50%)	0.10%	(0.15%)	(0.01%)
Financials	5.70%	50.10%	2.85%	10.49%	31.89%	3.35%	(4.79%)	18.21%	(1.53%)	1.91%	(0.87%)
Healthcare	14.13%	29.54%	4.17%	13.90%	17.09%	2.38%	0.23%	12.45%	0.04%	1.73%	0.03%
Industrials	24.01%	12.59%	3.02%	13.47%	15.52%	2.09%	10.54%	(2.93%)	1.63%	(0.39%)	(0.31%)
Information Technology	17.25%	26.41%	4.56%	26.31%	35.62%	9.37%	(9.08%)	(9.21%)	(3.23%)	(2.42%)	0.83%
Materials	2.83%	8.56%	0.24%	1.97%	22.80%	0.45%	0.86%	(14.23%)	0.20%	(0.28%)	(0.12%)
Real Estate	4.54%	38.52%	1.75%	3.41%	33.56%	1.14%	1.13%	4.96%	0.38%	0.17%	0.06%
Utilities	1.11%	13.50%	0.15%	2.31%	14.64%	0.34%	(1.20%)	(1.14%)	(0.18%)	(0.03%)	0.01%
	100.0%		25.24%	100.0%		24.36%			(2.43%)	3.13%	0.18%

Benchmark is the Russell 3000 Index | Sector tilt = Portfolio overweighting(underweighting) of each sector relative to the index |Sector Alpha = Portfolio Outperformance(underperformance) of each sector relative to the index

---

[14] The full code is available in the SAS program file for the chapter in the book's GitHub repository.

From the attribution table shown in Output 2.24, we can deduce that most of the portfolio performance was due to selection (in other words, the manager's selectivity in terms of stock choices within each sector), particularly in the consumer discretionary, energy, and financial sectors. The manager underweighted two sectors that did relatively better in the index (consumer staples and information technology), which led to the negative allocation. The selection (3.13%) and allocation effect (-2.43%), when combined with the interaction effect (0.18%) account for the 88-basis points outperformance of the portfolio relative to the Russell 3000 index.

From a deployment point of view, all that is needed to regenerate the same analysis, visualizations, and report in the future is a fresh set of data for the reporting period. It is also possible to build a dashboard of the portfolio visualizations that were presented using PROC TEMPLATE and PROC SGRENDER. These and many other visualizations are what make SAS a compelling tool for financial data science.

Exercises

1. An equity analyst is reviewing the financial performance of Amazon.com during the past 10 years. The analyst collects 10 years of financial statement information for the company and compiles them into the AMNZFS SAS data set. (The data set is in the book's GitHub Repository: https://github.com/finsasdata/Bookdata/raw/main/amznfs.sas7bdat). The variable names and their labels are shown in the table below.

> **Hint:** You can also use the DATAPULL macro to download the data into your work library. %datapull(amzn,amznfs.sas7bdat).

Variable	Label	Variable	Label
PRODUCT_SALES	Net Product Sales	OTGS	Other Operating Income/Expense
SERVICE_SALES	Net Service Sales	IEXPENSE	Interest Expense
TOTAL_SALEs	Total Revenues	IINCOM	Interest Income
COGS	Cost of Sales	OE	Other Income/Expense-net
SAGS	Sales and Marketing Expenses	PRGS	Provision for Income Tax
GEGS	General and Administrative Expenses	EMI	Equity-method Investment Activity, Net of Tax
FUGS	Fulfillment Expenses	TA	Total Assets
TEGS	Technology and Content Expenses	TSE	Total Shareholder Equity

a. Write a SAS program to create a SAS data set (**AMZNFR**) from the AMZNFS data set. Create the following financial statement items using the following calculations.

GROSS_PROFIT = TOTAL_SALES-COGS	**OPE** = SAGS+GEGS+FUGS+TEGS+OTGS	**EBIT** = GROSS_PROFIT-OPE
EBT = EBIT-IEXPENSE+IINCOM+OE	**NI** = EBT-PRGS+EMI;	**TAT** = TOTAL_SALES/TA
GM = GROSS_PROFIT/TOTAL_SALES	**OM** = EBIT/TOTAL_SALES	**PM** = NI/TOTAL_SALES
ROA = NI/TA	**EM** =TA/TSE	**ROE** = NI/TSE

b. Assign the following formats and labels to the newly created variables.

Variable	Label	Format
GROSS_PROFIT	Gross Profit	nlmny10.2
OPE	Operating Expense	nlmny10.2
EBIT	Operating Income	nlmny10.2
EBT	Earnings before Taxes	nlmny10.2
NI	Net Income	nlmny10.2
GM	Gross Margin	percent8.2
OM	Operating Margin	percent8.2
PM	Profit Margin	percent8.2
TAT	Total Asset Turnover	Best5.2
ROA	Return on Assets	percent8.2
ROE	Return on Equity	percent8.2
EM	Equity Multiplier	best5.2

c. Write a PROC PRINT statement to print only the income statement items and balance sheet accounts (exclude the following ratio variables: GM, OM, PM, ROA, ROE, EM). Include the title 'Amazon Inc. Ten-Year Income Statements'. Specify that the variable labels should be printed instead of the variable names in the output.

d. Write a PROC PRINT statement to print only the financial ratios (include the following ratio variables: GM, OM, PM, TAT, ROA, ROE, EM. Also, include the title 'Amazon Inc. Selected Financial Ratios'. Specify that variable labels should be printed in the output.

e. Use the SGPLOT procedure to graph Amazon's total revenue and profit margin (on the Y2AXIS) for the 10 years. Specify the values of the XAXIS from 31st December 2013 to 31st December 2022 by year.

Hint: The aim of the graph is to show trend and relationship, so select a visualization that can do both.

i. What trends are observable on the graph concerning profitability and sales?

ii. Add gross margin (GM) to the Y2AXIS. Are both measures of profitability rising with sales?

f. Use the SGPLOT procedure to create a heat map that explores the relationship between profitability (measured using ROA) and the interaction between product sales (PRODUCT_SALES) and service sales (SERVICE_SALES). Specify 10 bins for both the X (NXBINS=10) and Y (NYBINS=10) axes.

   i. Is the correlation between product and service sales positive or negative?

   ii. Which of the two sales segments is the main driver of profitability?

g. To explore if the DUPONT analysis also applies to Amazon's financial performance. Let's use the G3GRID and G3D procedures to examine the relationship between how the company generates profit per unit of equity investment **(ROE)** and how efficient the company has been at using **(ROA)** and financing **(EM multiplier, EM)** its assets.

> **Hint:** Specify OUT=PLOTGRID right after the DATA statement of the G3GRID.

   i. First, let's use the G3GRID procedure to create the data set that would be plotted using the G3D procedure by specifying **GRID ROA*EM=ROE /spline**. Also, specify that the output data set should be saved in the PLOTGRID data set. How many observations are in the PLOTGRID data set?

   ii. Invoke the PROC G3D procedure to graph the data in the PLOTGRID data set. Specify **PLOT ROA*EM=ROE statement.** Does the Dupont identity also apply to Amazon? What are the implications of the Dupont relationship for managerial decision-making in terms of improving profitability?

   iii. What other visualizations can you explore to analyze other aspects of Amazon's financial performance?

2. The SAS data set **SPX_Members** contains the financial, governance, risk, and stock price attributes for the 503 companies in the S&P 500 Index. We will use this data set to examine industry trends and patterns amongst the largest publicly listed companies in the US.

> **Hint:** Use PROC CONTENTS to review the metadata for all variables in the data set before starting your analysis.

a. Use the SGPIE procedure to create a pie chart that shows the number of stocks in each of the 11 GIC sectors of the index. Include the title 'Sector Representation in the S&P 500 Index'.

   i. Which sector had the highest and lowest number of stocks?

> **Hint:** SGPIE is a relatively straightforward procedure. Specify the title and PIE as Sector. For Part B, include RESPONSE=Weight.

b. Redo the graph including sector weight as the RESPONSE variable.

   i. Which sectors have the highest and lowest weights?

   ii. The top three sectors account for what proportion of the index weight? What are the implications of this result for investment risk and diversification?

c. Create a bar chart using the SGPLOT procedure to display the average five-year return on invested capital (ROIC5Y) for each sector. Format the XAXIS to display vertical labels. Include the title 'Sector-Level Return on Invested Capital for S&P 500 Companies'.
   i. Which sectors have the highest and lowest ROICs?
   ii. Why do some sectors have high ROIC relative to others?
d. Redo the bar chart using the five-year stock return (RET5Y).
   i. Which sectors have the highest and lowest five-year stock returns?
   ii. Are the sectors with the highest ROIC the same as those with the highest five-year stock return? What does this result say about the ability of the market to reward good financial performance with higher valuations?
e. Examine the relationship between financial performance (ROIC, ROA) and stock return (RET5Y) at the company level by creating a scatter plot with RET5Y on the YAXIS and ROA5YR on the XAXIS.
   i. Are there any issues with how the graph was rendered?
   ii. Attempt to fix the issue by specifying a range of values to plot on the YAXIS (-10 to 150 by 10).
   iii. Include a regression line in the plot to predict the direction (positive or negative) of the relationship. What is the general direction of the relationship between profitability and stock price performance?
f. Do institutional investors such as mutual funds, ETFs, and hedge funds have preferences for the types of stocks they own? Explore this question by generating a heat map using the SGPLOT procedure, with PE on the YAXIS and Beta on the XAXIS. Specify INSTSHROUT as the COLORRESPONSE and Mean as the COLORSTAT. Include the title 'Institutional Stock Preferences'.
   i. Notice that a few outliers are distorting the graph. Use the WHERE statement to filter stocks with PE of more than 400 from the plot.
   ii. Do high beta stocks have high P/E ratios?
   iii. Do institutional investors have preferences for high PE or high beta stocks?

Chapter 3: Visual Diagnostics of Financial and Economic Data

Visual Diagnostic of the Salient Properties of Financial Data

Data scientists use visualizations in the exploration phase of the analytics cycle to analyze the statistical properties of the data and to determine how those properties might impact the models under consideration for deployment. This is because most statistical models and machine learning algorithms are trained based on some assumptions about the underlying statistical properties of the data such as normality, random sampling, and homoscedasticity (constant variance). If these assumptions are violated in the data properties, then the data scientist would have to weigh that information in the choice of the models for the discovery phase. Therefore, the main benefit of diagnostic visualizations is that they help the data scientist select and properly calibrate the models that would be deployed in the discovery phase. Diagnostic visualizations are also used to assess the performances of models in the discovery phase of the analytics life cycle.

In this chapter, we will highlight some statistical properties of the data and the visualization options that can be used in SAS to diagnose and analyze them. It is important to note that although the topics that will be presented subsequently are based on well-established econometric and statistical theories, the mathematical presentations of the concepts are beyond the scope of this book. Therefore, mathematical constructs and notations will be used sparingly and only as necessary to describe aspects of the statistical properties that cannot be presented in a descriptive manner.[1]

Dealing with the Anomalous Statistical Properties of Time Series Data

Since the most common types of financial data are in time series format, we will start our discussion by analyzing the statistical properties of a time series variable Y_t that describes some real-world phenomenon that is of interest to the data scientist. Y_t can consist of the

---

[1] Mathematical presentation and proofs of these concepts can be found in *Introductory Econometrics: A Modern Approach* by Jeffery M. Wooldridge.

combination of some or all of the following features: a trend component, a cyclical component, a seasonal component, and a stochastic (random) component (that is, $Y_t = f(T_t, C_t, S_t, \varepsilon_t)$ where T_t represents the trend component, C_t represents the cyclical component, S_t represents the seasonal component, and ε_t represents the random component, which is also assumed to be stationary with mean $E(\varepsilon_t) = 0$).

$$Y_t = T_t + C_t + S_t + \varepsilon_t \qquad (3.1)$$

Equation (3.1) is an additive time series decomposition of Y_t. However, it is also possible to observe a multiplicative time series decomposition of Y_t as shown in Equation (3.2) below.

$$Y_t = T_t * C_t * S_t * \varepsilon_t \qquad (3.2)$$

Notice from the above that a time series that consists of only a trend, and random component will behave differently from a time series that consists of trend, seasonal, and random components. In the additive decomposition, each observation of the time series is assumed to be a linear accumulation of the effect of the underlying properties and does not vary with the levels of the time series. In the multiplicative decomposition shown in Equation (3.2), each observation is assumed to be a non-linear accumulation of the effects of the underlying properties that vary with the levels of the time series.

Trends

Trends are long-term changes (positive or negative) to the variable. They could be deterministic trends that cause non-permanent changes, or stochastic trends that result in permanent changes to the nature of the time series. They could also be mixed trends, which are combinations of trends and random components. The random walk model discussed in Chapter One is an example of a mixed trend model that consists of a trend and a random component. Because trends are time-related, if they are not carefully addressed in the data, they might lead the models to erroneously infer spurious relationships that are based on the inherent characteristic of each variable rather than the actual relationship between them. For example, the models might erroneously indicate that a relationship exists between two variables that are trending in the same direction, although they might be trending for different reasons.

Trends can be visualized using a series plot, in which the value of the variable is plotted on the vertical axis against a time index on the horizontal axis. The presence of a positive or negative slope on the series plot is indicative of a trend. Note that a variable could also be trend stationary, in which case the visualization will display both slope and mean reversion.

PROC X13

The X13 procedure in SAS is based on the US Bureau of the Census X-13ARIMA-SEATS seasonal adjustment program. The procedure has extensive time series modeling and model selection features. Some of these include linear regression models with ARIMA errors (regARIMA models), model diagnostics, visualizations, seasonality adjustments, and time series decomposition, to name a few. The X13 procedure is an enhancement over the X11 procedure and shares making functionality with the X12 procedure. The X11 procedure, which is also an adaptation of the U.S. Bureau of the Census X-11 Seasonal Adjustment program, seasonally adjusts monthly or quarterly time series and creates additive and multiplicatively adjusted time series. The X12 procedure incorporates the seasonal adjustment program developed from Statistics Canada's X-11-ARIMA program and automatic modeling methods.[2]

Program 3.1: Using PROC X13 and PROC SGPLOT to Visualize Trends and Cyclicality in Monthly Trading Volume

```
/*Enable ODS graphics to automatically generate accompanying plots*/
ods graphics on;
proc x13 data=rspx_monthly  date=Date INTERVAL = month;
      var volume;
      transform function=log;
      arima model=( (0,1,1)(0,1,1) );/*ARIMA with Exponential Smoothing*/
      outlier CV=3.6;
      estimate;
      x11;
      output out=arspx_monthly a1 d1 d10 d12 d13 e18;

      /* a1 =original series|d1=Modified Series| d10= Seasonal component|
         d12 = trend cycle components| d13 = irregular component*/
run;

/*Plot Time Series Component Using SGPLOT*/
proc sgplot data=arspx_monthly;
      title 'Time Series Components of S&P 500 Trading Volume ';
      series x=date y=volume_d13 / name="Volumeb" lineattrs=(color=aquamarine)
       legendlabel= " Irregular Component";
      series  x=date y=volume_d10 / name="Volumea"
      lineattrs=(color=green) legendlabel= " Seasonal Component";
      series x=date y=volume_d12 /name="Volumec" y2axis  lineattrs=(color=blue)
       legendlabel= "Trend Cycle Component ";
      yaxis label='Seasonal and Irregular Components';
      y2axis label='Trend Cycle Components';
      keylegend "Volumea" "Volumeb" "Volumec" / across=3 noborder
position=bottomleft
      location=outside;
run;
title;
```

[2] The regARIMA model, which is a regression model with ARIMA (autoregressive integrated moving average) errors is one of the improvements in the X12 procedure.

In Program 3.1, we use the X13 procedure to extract the trend cycle component of the monthly trading volume of the S&P 500 index. These values, along with seasonal and irregular components of the trading volumes, are then graphed on a series plot using the SGPLOT procedure. The TRANSFORM statement is used to transform the series (volume into log volume) before the ARIMA specification is estimated. The ARIMA statement is used to specify the seasonal and non-seasonal autoregressive (AR) and the moving average (MA) components of the model. The OUTLIER statement is used to specify the critical value (CV) for detecting outliers in the series. The X11 statement is used to request the seasonal adjustment to the series using the enhanced version of the methodology of the US Census Bureau X-11 and X-11Q programs. The OUTPUT statement is used to request the creation of the SAS data set ARSPX_MONTHLY.SAS7BDAT, which consists of the original series (A1), modified series (D1), seasonal component (D10), trend cycle components (D12), irregular component (D13), and the final adjustment ratio (E18). The final adjustment ratio is the ratio of the original series to the seasonally adjusted series.[3]

The X13 procedure generates a lot of data, tables, and graphs. We will focus on graphing the series that are relevant to trends in the data series using the SGPLOT procedure for now. Output 3.1 shows the plots of the time series components of the trading volume for the S&P 500. The trend cycle components are plotted in blue, while the seasonal and irregular components are colored in green and aquamarine, respectively.

Output 3.1: Visualizing the Time Series Components of S&P 500 Trading Volume

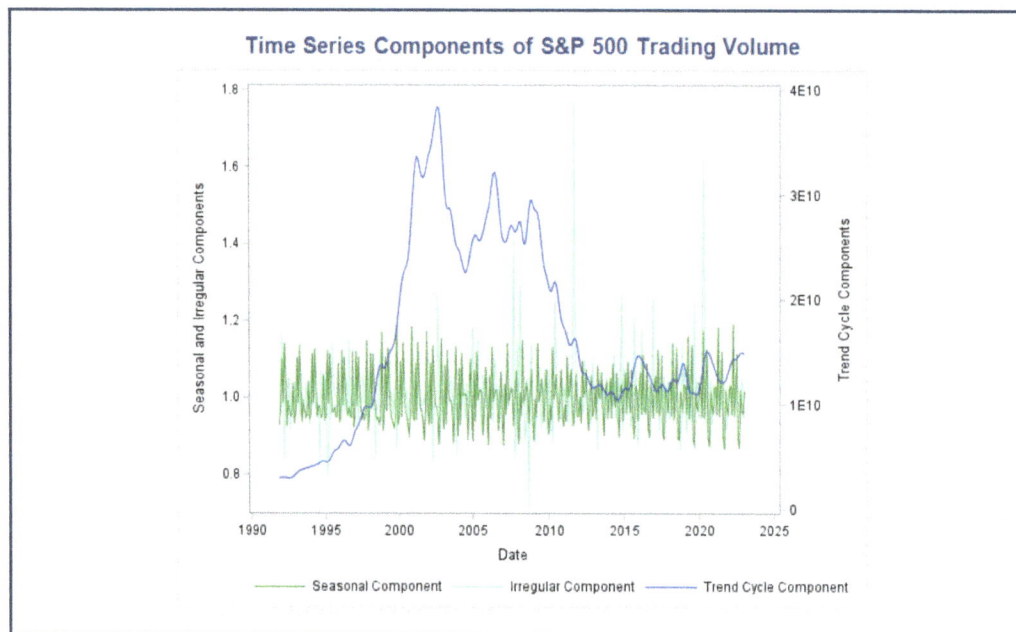

_____

[3] You can learn more about the X13 procedure by reviewing the SAS/ETS®15.2 User's Guide for the procedure at https://documentation.sas.com/doc/en/etsug/15.2/etsug_x13_toc.htm.

Cyclicality

Cyclical variations are long-term fluctuations in the variable that occur around the trend line. And because of this, they are often described as cyclical trends. However, they differ from pure trend components in the sense that they occur repeatedly, albeit over a long period, which pure trend components might not do. The frequency of occurrence is also not predetermined as in the case of seasonality, which we will highlight next. Although they are mostly observed in aggregate financial and macroeconomic data such as industry sales and gross domestic product (GDP), they are important to emphasize because they influence the behavior of these time series, particularly when the data set consists of data from a long period such as a decade or more. Cyclicality in a series can be visualized by plotting the series against time on a series plot as shown in Output 3.2.

Dealing with Trends and Cyclicality

Each type of trend component requires special treatment to remove the component from the data if that is the desired outcome. Stochastic trends can be removed by calculating the first difference of the variable. Deterministic trends can be removed by regressing the variable on a time index. The residuals obtained from the regression should be stationary. Trend and cyclical components in the data can also be isolated using the Hodrick-Prescott (1997) filter (HP filter), which is an option in the PROC EXPAND procedure.

Program 3.2: Using PROC EXPAND to Adjust for Trends and Cyclicality in the Data

```
/*Using HP Filter in PROC Expand*/
proc expand data=rspx_monthly out=frspx
      method=none;
      id date;
      convert volume=volume_t/transformout=(hp_t 14400);
      /*HP Filter for Trend component Lambda=14400*/
      convert volume=volume_c/transformout=(hp_c 14400);
      /*HP Filter for Cycle component lambda=14400*/
run;

/*Plot Time Series Component Using SGPLOT*/
proc sgplot data=frspx;
      title 'Trend and Cycle Components of S&P 500 Trading Volume ';
      series x=date y=volume_t/ name="Volumed" lineattrs=(color=black thickness=2)
      legendlabel= " Trend Component";
      Series  x=date y=volume_c / name="Volumee"
      lineattrs=(color=green) legendlabel= " Cycle Component";
      series x=date y=volume /name="Volumef"  lineattrs=(color=blue)
      legendlabel= "Volume ";
      yaxis label='Trend and Cycle Components';
      keylegend "Volumed" "Volumee" "Volumef" / across=3 noborder position=bottomleft
      location=outside;
run;
title;
```

PROC EXPAND

The EXPAND procedure is used to convert time series data from one sampling frequency or interval to another. It can also interpolate missing values, perform trend and cyclicality time series decompositions, as well as implement a wide array of data transformations, including lead, lag, differencing, moving average, moving sum, and moving product to name a few. A select number of ODS graphic plots of the transformed series can also be generated by the procedure.[4]

In Program 3.2, the EXPAND procedure was used to perform a Hodrick-Prescott filter to extract the trend and cyclical component of the S&P 500 trading volume series. The CONVERT statement is used to request the creation of the two new variables VOLUME_T (the trend component of volume) and VOLUME_C (the cyclical component of volume). The TRANSFORMOUT option is used to request the HP filter method for extracting the trend and cycle components from the unadjusted volume series.

Output 3.2 displays the plot of the extracted trend component (in black) and cyclical component (in green). The unadjusted volume series is also plotted on the same graph (in yellow). Evident on the graph is an upward trend in volume from the mid-1990s to the early 2000s. This period coincides with the dot-com boom era. The trend line then shifts downward, culminating in a precipitous drop toward the end of that decade, which is right after the global financial crisis.

Output 3.2: Trends and Cyclicality in S&P 500 Trading Volume

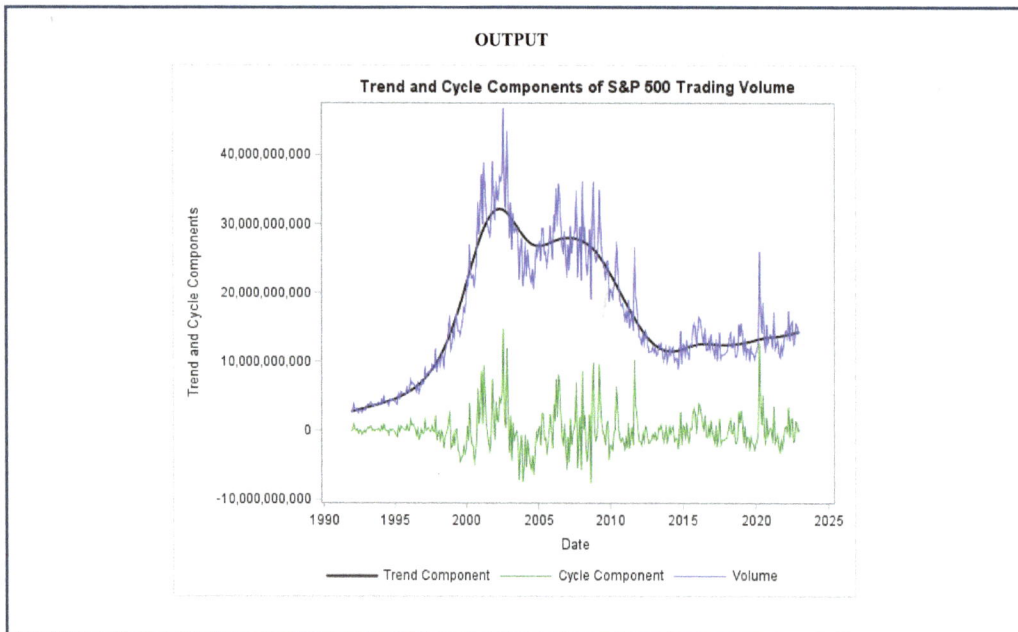

---

[4] You can learn more about the EXPAND procedure by reviewing the SAS/ETS®15.2 User's Guide for the procedure at https://documentation.sas.com/doc/en/etsug/15.2/etsug_expand_toc.htm.

Figure 3.1: Seasonality in US Retail Sales Data

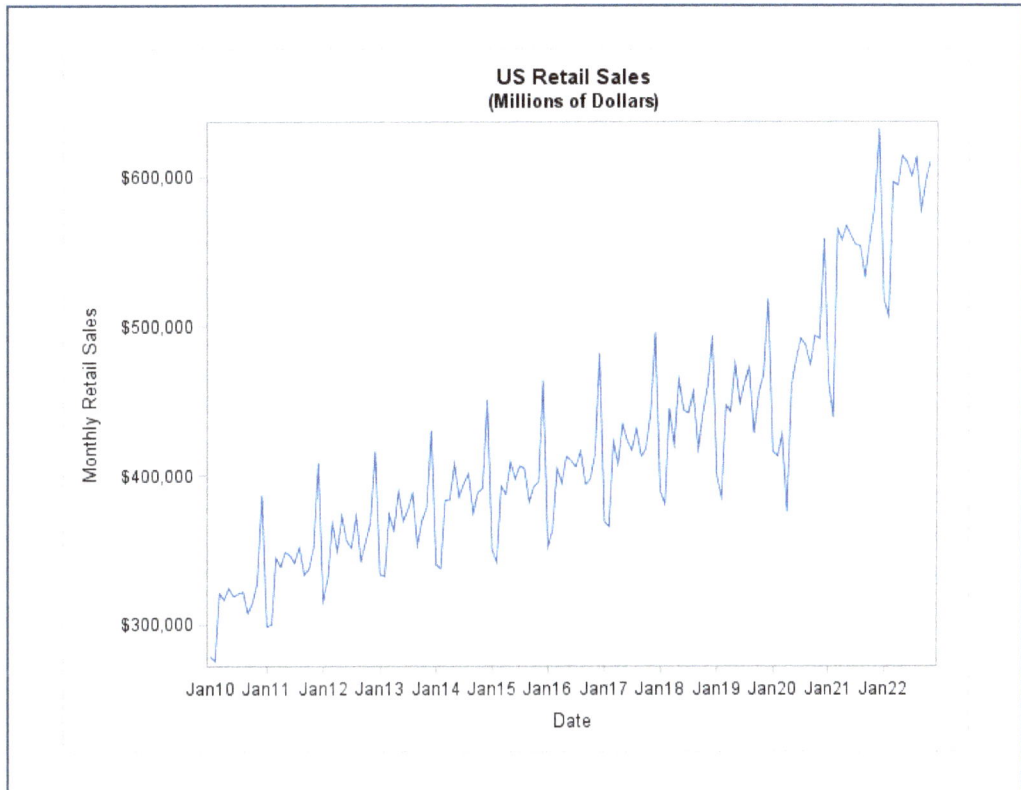

Seasonality

Seasonal variations are another common feature of financial and economic data. They are patterns of changes in the data that occur during the same period of the year. These could be monthly or quarterly.[5] For example, retail sales in general tend to rise during the fourth quarter of the year due to the holiday shopping season. Demand for natural gas would normally rise during the colder months of the year and fall during the warmer months. You should note that these are repetitive and predictable patterns of changes in the data. From a statistical point of view, seasonality also implies that the current values of the variable are influenced by time factors. They are problematic from a modeling point of view because they might mask other patterns or trends in the data if they are not properly adjusted for. Seasonality in time series data can also be visualized by plotting the series against time on a series plot as shown in Figure 3.1, which graphs aggregate monthly retail Sales (MRTSAG)

---

[5] It is also possible to encounter weekly or day-of-the-week seasonality or even more complex combinations of seasonality in high-frequency data. However, monthly and quarterly seasonality are the most frequently analyzed occurrences in the time series econometrics.

in the US on a series plot. Notice how repetitive and predictable the sharp increase in retail sales is in the last quarter of the year.

Dealing with Seasonality

Many of the publicly distributed macroeconomic data provide versions of the data that have been seasonally adjusted using the X11, X12, and X13 methods. Hence, you are less likely to encounter the need to seasonally adjust these data. In cases where the data scientist is working with proprietary data (such as firm-level transaction data), then it would be prudent to adjust for seasonality before performing further analyses on the data. A simple approach to adjust for the seasonality in the data is to compute the first difference of the series. This approach, as well as other types of transformation to the series, can be implemented by applying generalized models such as the Autoregressive Integrated Moving Average (ARIMA) model to the series. The ARIMA model is a general class of autoregressive models that are built around the Box-Jenkins method of identifying, estimating, and assessing the goodness of fit of models based on the time series properties of the data. It combines lags and differences of the series with realizations of past forecast errors (moving averages) in building the model specification. It can account for seasonality through the inclusion of seasonal lags, seasonal differences, and seasonal moving averages in the model specification.[6] The ARIMA method is also an option in the X11, X12, and X13 procedures. We highlight the ARIMA option in the X13 procedure in Program 3.3.

The SEASONS option is invoked in the ARIMA procedure to generate seasonal differences and moving averages in the order stated in the second parentheses (0,1,1). This implies zero seasonal lag, one seasonal difference, and one seasonal moving average. The first parentheses specify the options for the regular lags, differences, and moving averages.

Program 3.3: Using PROC X13 to Adjust for Seasonality

```
%datapull(trade,trade.sas7bdat);
ods graphics on;

/*Using X13 to Adjust for Seasonality in Retail Sales*/
ods output D8A=MRTSAG_D8;
ods output D10=MRTSAG_D10;

proc x13 data=trade date=date seasons=12 interval = month;
      var MRTSAG;
      transform power=0;
      arima model=((0,1,1)(0,1,1) );/*ARIMA with Exponential Smoothing*/
      estimate;
      x11;
```

---

[6] A full description of the ARIMA model is beyond the scope of this book. Interested readers should review the ARIMA procedure by checking the SAS/ETS®15.2 User's Guide for the procedure available at https://documentation.sas.com/doc/en/etsug/15.2/etsug_arima_overview.htm.

```
       output out=adjtrade a1 d8 d10 d11;
       /* a1 =original series| d8=Seasonality tests| d10=Seasonal adjustment Factor| d10d=
Seasonal Difference| d11=seasonally adjusted series */
run;

data stest;
       set MRTSAG_D8 (where=(cvalue1 ^='') keep=label1 cvalue1 firstobs=2);
       rename label1 = 'Seasonality Tests'n;
       rename cvalue1 = 'Probability Level'n;
run;

proc print data= stest noobs;
run;
```

> The input data set (ADJTRADE) for Program 3.4 is the output data set from Program 3.3. Make sure you run Program 3.3 before running Program 3.4.

Output 3.3: Statistical Tests of Time Series Components

Seasonality Tests	Probability Level
Stable Seasonality F-test	0.000
Moving Seasonality F-test	0.993
Kruskal-Wallis Chi-square Test	0.000
Combined Measures:	Value
T1 = 7/F_Stable	0.02
T2 = 3*F_Moving/F_Stable	0.00
T = (T1 + T2)/2	0.01
Combined Test of Identifiable Seasonality:	Present

Output 3.3 shows the statistical tests of the time series components of the volume series that were generated by the X13 procedure. The result of the seasonality test is saved in the ODS Table D8. The output is requested using the ODS OUTPUT D8A=MRTSAG_D8 statement, which was placed above the PROC EXPAND statement in the code. A DATA step is then used to clean up the data table containing the results before the PROC PRINT statement is used to print the results. The results of the seasonality test confirm the presence of the stable seasonality pattern we previously observed (Figure 3.1) during our earlier visualization of the data.

Program 3.4: Using PROC SGPLOT to Display Seasonally Adjusted Retail Sales Data

```
/*Using SGPLOT to Display Seasonality in Sales Data*/
ods graphics on;

proc sgplot data=adjtrade;
      title 'Seasonality Adjusted Monthly US Retail Sales ';
      title2  '(Millions of Dollars)';
      series x=date y=mrtsag_d11/ name="salesa" lineattrs=(color=blue) legendlabel= "
Seasonality Adjusted Retail Sales";
      series  x=date y=mrtsag_a1 / name="salesb"
              lineattrs=(color=Green) legendlabel= " Unadjusted Retail Sales";
      xaxis label = 'Date' values=('01jan10'd to '01nov22'd by month)
valuesformat=monyy.;
      yaxis label='US Retail Sales';
      keylegend "salesa" "salesb"/ across=3 noborder position=bottomleft
location=outside;
run;

title;
ods graphics off;
```

In Program 3.4, we use the SGPLOT procedure to graph the unadjusted and seasonally adjusted series that was obtained from the X13 procedure. In Output 3.4, notice how the seasonality-adjusted retail sales (in blue) display less volatility around the trend line, in comparison to the unadjusted retail sales (in green).

Output 3.4: Seasonally Adjusted Retail Sales Data

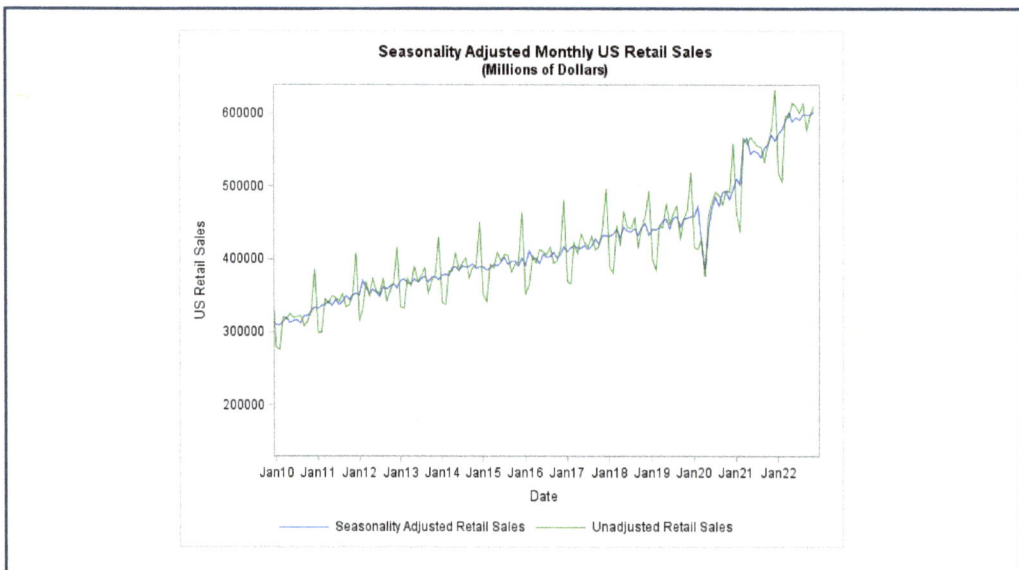

Autocorrelation

Autocorrelation (serial correlation) is a characteristic of the data in which the realizations of the variable in one period are related to realizations in past periods. This is also another fairly common feature of financial and economic time series, where the errors in one period are correlated with errors in another period. Autocorrelations that arise in the error term are caused mainly by two factors:

- Pure serial autocorrelation, which is an artifact of the lagging effect in the time series (that is, realizations of the variable in one period retain information from prior periods).
- Misspecification of the model, which could be due to variable exclusion or the use of an imprecise functional form for modeling the time series.

Statistically, autocorrelation creates biases in the standard errors of the regression and therefore leads to unreliable t-statistics, which makes those statistics also unreliable for hypothesis testing. Within the context of predictive analytics where hypothesis testing is not paramount, autocorrelations do have significant implications. Because they bias the error term, they impair the maximum likelihood estimate (MLE) of the model and thereby impact the overall performance of models that are based on the MLE approach such as logistic regression and neural network models.

Autocorrelations can be visualized by using the autocorrelation function plots (Autocorrelation, Partial Autocorrelation, and Inverse Autocorrelations). On the graph, the autocorrelation coefficients for a specified number of lags are obtained from a regression specification of the variable using AUTOREG or ARIMA procedures. The correlation coefficients are then plotted on the vertical axis against a time lag index (on the horizontal axis).

Frequently used statistical methods for testing for autocorrelations are the Durbin-Watson (DW) and White Noise (WN) tests. The Durbin-Watson test is an option included in the AUTOREG procedure, while the White Noise test is an option in the ARIMA procedure. The code for implementing the DW statistics and autocorrelation visualizations using the AUTOREG procedure are shown in Program 3.5. In the program, we test for autocorrelation in the monthly trading volumes of the S&P 500 index by regressing the volume variable on its lag (NLAG=1). The DW=1 generates the Durbin-Watson statistics for up to the first-order autocorrelation. The DWPROB requests the p-value of the test statistics.[7]

Program 3.5: Using PROC AUTOREG to Visualize Autocorrelations S&P 500 Trading Volume

```
%datapull(rspx,rspx_monthly.sas7bdat);

/*Visualizing Autocorrelations in Volume using AUTOREG*/
ods graphics on;
```

---

[7] Interested readers can learn more about the AUTOREG procedure by reviewing the SAS/ETS®15.2 User's Guide for the procedure at https://documentation.sas.com/doc/en/etsug/15.2/etsug_autoreg_toc.htm.

```
proc autoreg data= rspx_monthly  plots= all;
      model volume= / nlag=1 dw=1 dwprob;
run;

ods graphics off;
```

Output 3.5A: Autocorrelations in S&P 500 Trading Volume

The AUTOREG Procedure

Yule-Walker Estimates

SSE	4.08732E21	DFE	372
MSE	1.09874E19	Root MSE	3314728304
SBC	17470.6238	AIC	17462.7753
MAE	2239313541	AICC	17462.8076
MAPE	14.4686956	HQC	17465.8915
Durbin-Watson	2.6910	Transformed Regression R-Square	0.0000
		Total R-Square	0.8737

Durbin-Watson Statistics

Order	DW	Pr < DW	Pr > DW
1	2.6910	1.0000	<.0001

Parameter Estimates

Variable	DF	Estimate	Standard Error	t Value	Approx Pr > |t|
Intercept	1	1.6092E10	2.42592E9	6.63	<.0001

Estimates of Autoregressive Parameters

Lag	Coefficient	Standard Error	t Value
1	-0.931794	0.018820	-49.51

Output 3.5A shows the results of the parameter estimates obtained from invoking the AUTOREG procedure. The sign of the coefficient of the autoregressive lag variable and its t-value statistics suggest the presence of mean reversion in the time series of the volume variable. Pr<DW is the p-value for the test of the presence of positive autocorrelation, and Pr>DW is the p-value for the test of negative autocorrelation. The result of the tests fails to reject the null of no positive autocorrelation but rejects the null of no negative autocorrelations. Altogether, the statistics suggest that past levels of trading volume have some effect on future trading volumes and that the residuals of the regression model are also correlated over time.

Output 3.5B: Visualizing Autocorrelations in S&P 500 Trading Volume

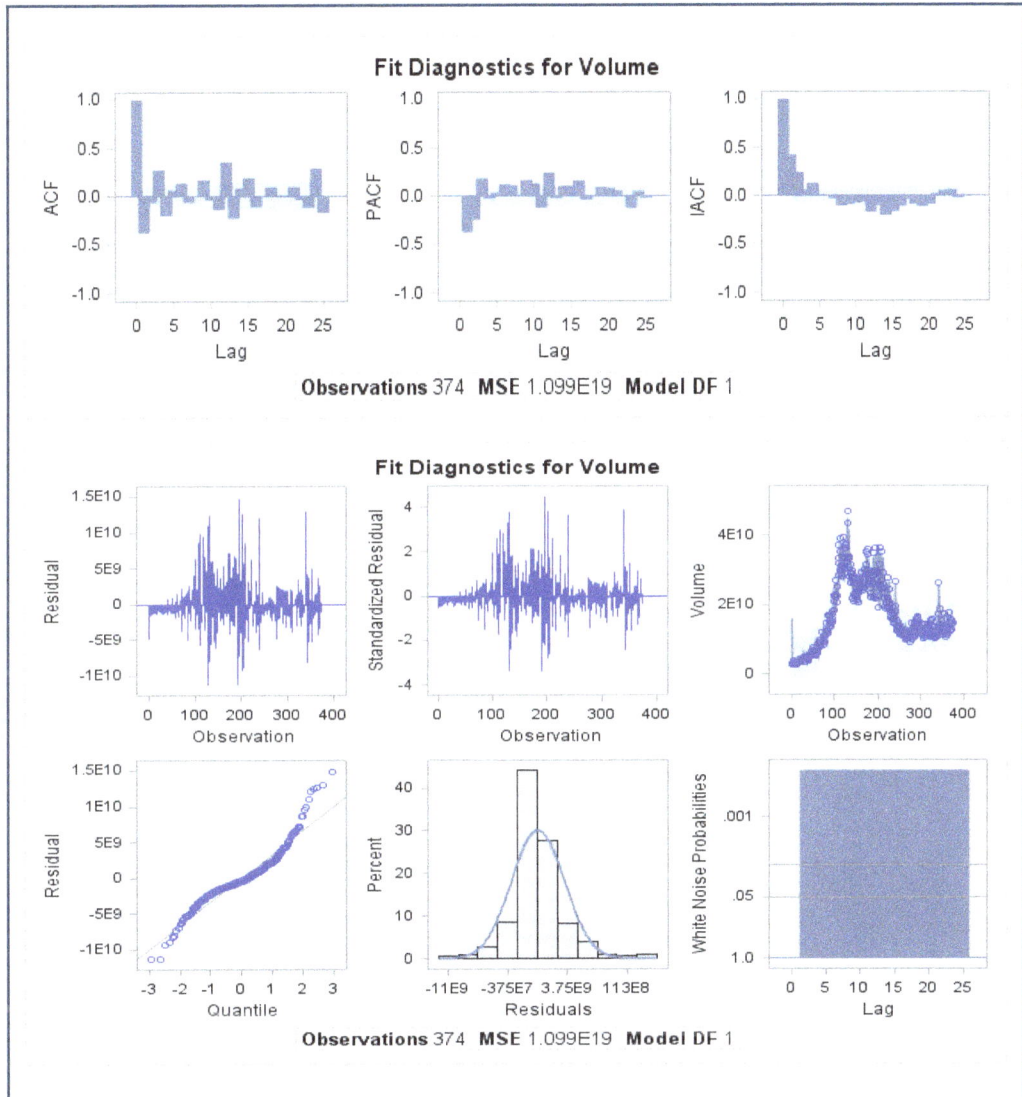

The first three graphs shown in Output 3.5B are the plots of the autocorrelation, partial autocorrelation, and integrated autocorrelation functions for up to 25 lags of the series. All three plots indicate the presence of autocorrelations in the residuals of the model. The next set of plots displays an array of fit diagnostic plots for the residual. Notice the large periodic changes in the values of the residuals in both plots. We can infer from the plots that it is unlikely that the variance of the series will be constant over time, which is a violation of the homoscedasticity assumption of linear regression models. This assertion is also supported by the White Noise

Probabilities plot, which shows statistically significant evidence of White Noise in the series for up to 25 lags. We can also observe on the quantile plot that the residuals of the volume series are not normally distributed.

Heteroscedasticity

Heteroscedasticity in time series data implies that the variance of the error term is not constant over time. Furthermore, the variance in each period might be correlated with the variance in another period (autoregressive conditional heteroscedasticity). Earlier, we highlighted that homoscedasticity (constant variance) is a requirement for stationarity. It turns out that it is possible to obtain stationarity even in the presence of time-varying (conditional) variance. This is the case as long as the process remains covariance stationary and the unconditional variance that is the expected value of the conditional variances is constant over time. Nevertheless, heteroscedasticity impacts the efficiency of some regression models such as OLS and logistic regression because it violates their homoscedasticity assumption. This is because the standard errors of the regression coefficients will no longer be constant over time, and thus can lead to misleading inferential deductions.

Heteroscedasticity can arise from factors such as model misspecification; however, with time series data, it is mostly due to the periodic occurrence of outlier observation as shown in the series plot (in Figure 3.2) for the daily returns of the ICE BofA AAA Corporate Bond Total Return index. Apparent on the graph are strings of episodic spikes in returns (both positive and negative), which are then followed by periods of relatively lower price movements.

Figure 3.2: Conditional Volatility in Corporate Bond Index Returns

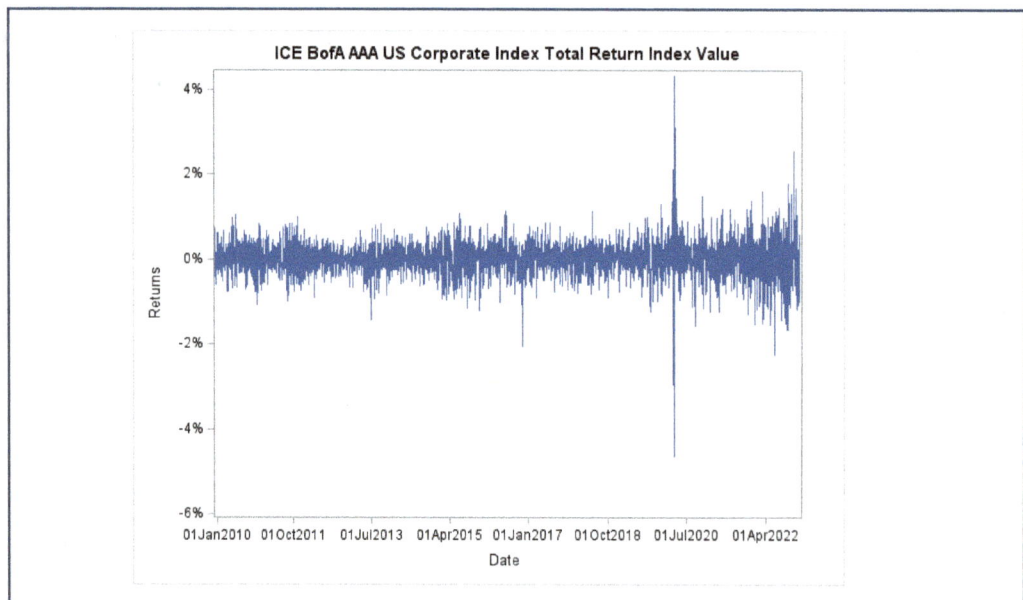

Heteroscedasticity can be visually diagnosed through a two-step process. First, the residual from a regression specification of the variable is obtained using the AUTOREG or ARIMA procedure. The residuals are then plotted on the vertical axis against the dependent variable or any variable (or time index for time series) in the regression specification (on the horizontal axis) using the SGPLOT procedure.

The AUTOREG procedure includes the ARCHTEST option, which can be used to perform the LaGrange, Q, Lee, and King (1993), and Wong and Li (1995) tests for heteroscedasticity. The codes for the implementation of the visualizations and test statistics are shown in Program 3.6.

Program 3.6: Visualizing Heteroscedasticity in Corporate Bond Index Return

```
/*Using PROC AUTOREG to Display Heteroscedasticity*/
%datapull(bonds,corporate_bonds.sas7bdat);
ods graphics on;

proc autoreg data= corporate_bonds (where=(date>'31dec12'd)) plots=all;
      model raaap= / archtest=(qlm);   /*Q&LM-Test for Heteroscedasticity*/
      model raaap= / archtest=(wl,lk);/*wl-Wong and Li |LK - Lee and King*/
      output out=pred residual=resid  predicted=rhat;
run;

quit;

ods graphics off;
```

In the program, we test for heteroscedasticity in the daily returns of the ICE BofA AAA Corporate Bond Total Return index using the AUTOREG procedure. The PLOTS=ALL statement invokes a set of diagnostic plots using the ODS. These include goodness-of-fit plots, autocorrelation plots, and outlier effects (Cook's D). The results of the tests and the ODS outputs from invoking the procedure are shown in Outputs 3.6A and 3.6B. The results obtained from both tests for heteroscedasticity that were requested from the AUTOREG procedures and shown in Output 3.6A indicate statistically significant evidence of heteroscedasticity exists in the bond return series. The plot of the White noise probabilities which is included in Output 3.6B, also shows statistically significant evidence of White Noise up to 25 lags. Furthermore, the ACF plot (also in Output 3.6B) shows strong positive first-order autocorrelation in the residuals of the series, which also suggests heteroscedasticity.

Output 3.6A: Heteroscedasticity in Corporate Bond Indices

Tests for ARCH Disturbances Based on OLS Residuals				Tests for ARCH Disturbances Based on OLS Residuals				
Order	Q	Pr > Q	LM	Pr > LM	Order	LK	Pr > |LK|	WL	Pr > WL
1	333.6945	<.0001	333.2535	<.0001	1	47.5031	<.0001	13700.7979	<.0001
2	524.7777	<.0001	394.1490	<.0001	2	50.6463	<.0001	22305.1098	<.0001
3	1100.3969	<.0001	728.7658	<.0001	3	65.4122	<.0001	39745.7207	<.0001
4	1523.0205	<.0001	799.5919	<.0001	4	69.7437	<.0001	49896.4288	<.0001

Output 3.6B: Heteroscedasticity in Corporate Bond Indices

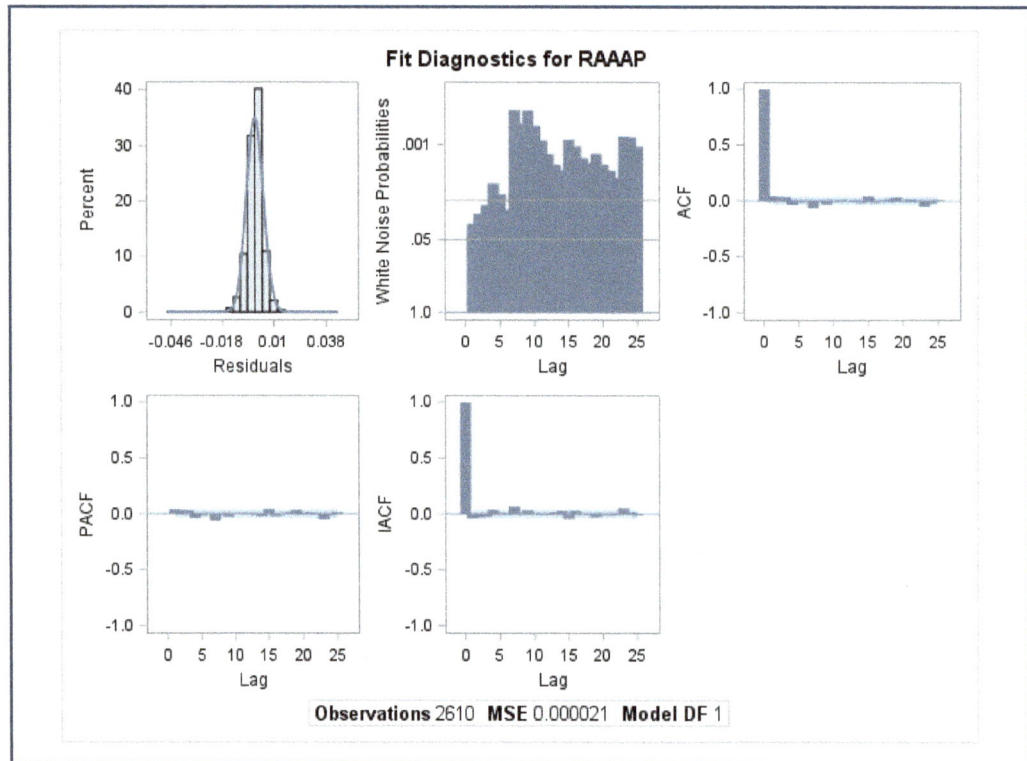

Fit Diagnostics for RAAAP

Observations 2610   MSE 0.000021   Model DF 1

Dealing with Autocorrelations and Heteroscedasticity

Two straightforward methods for fixing autocorrelation problems in the data are to locate and include the omitted variable in the model specification or to respecify the model using the correct functional form. However, these options might not be feasible in some instances.

Another approach that is used for both serial correlation and heteroscedasticity is to use serial correlation-robust standard errors (sometimes called heteroscedasticity and autocorrelation consistent [HAC] standard errors) when drawing statistical inferences from the model. Most statistical packages provide this option for linear and non-linear models by default.

Another approach is to compute a generalized least square estimator, which accounts for the information about the residual variance in the estimate of the model parameters, or a weighted least square (WLS) estimator by specifying a functional form of the variance.

Lastly, for time series data, a common approach is to model the heteroscedasticity in the errors by specifying a function for the conditional variance of the error term using the Generalized Autoregressive Conditional Heteroscedasticity (GARCH) specification. Besides controlling for heteroscedasticity, this approach also allows the data scientist to analyze the behavior of the conditional variance and make predictions for its future values.[8] Features such as HAC errors, generalized least squares, and the option to model the variance of the residual using the GARCH specification, can be found in some SAS procedures such as AUTOREG, and MODEL.

In Program 3.7, we request the HAC errors using the COVEST=NEWEYWEST statement and the Yule-Walker (YW) estimation method using METHOD=YW in the AUTOREG procedure. The YW is a type of generalized least square estimator. We also include the autoregressive lag variable of the first order in the model because we observed a first-order autocorrelation in the ACF plot. We show the results that we obtained from executing the program in Output 3.7.

Program 3.7: Adjusting for Heteroscedasticity Using HAC Errors (PROC AUTOREG)

```
/* Using Generalized Least Square and HAC Errors*/
ods graphics on;

proc autoreg data= corporate_bonds (where=(date>'31dec12'd)) plots=all;
      model raaap=/ nlag=1    /*AAA Bond Indices*/
      method=yw /*Yule-Walker is a type of Generalized Least Square estimator*/
      covest=Neweywest;/*Heteroscedasticity and Autocorrelation Robust Errors*/
      output out=pred residual=resid   predicted=rhat;
run;
quit;
ods graphics off;
```

[8] GARCH models are commonly used in time series econometrics and have a wide range of applications in the finance domains. There are also many statistical functional forms (such as ARCH, simple GARCH, exponential GARCH, threshold, hyperbolic, and integrated to name a few) and machine-learning functional forms (such as Artificial Neural Network ARCH) of GARCH models. More details about earlier GARCH specifications are summarized in "GARCH101: The Use of ARCH/GARCH Models in Econometrics" by Engle (2001) and Estimating GARCH Models at: https://communities.sas.com/t5/SAS-Code-Examples/Estimating-GARCH-Models/ta-p/905609/index.html

Output 3.7: Autoregressive Model of Corporate Bond Returns Using Yule-Walker Estimates

The AUTOREG Procedure

Yule-Walker Estimates

SSE	0.05443849	DFE	2608
MSE	0.0000209	Root MSE	0.00457
SBC	-20707.435	AIC	-20719.169
MAE	0.00318136	AICC	-20719.165
MAPE	106.315349	HQC	-20714.918
Durbin-Watson	2.0021	Transformed Regression R-Square	0.0000
		Total R-Square	0.0019

Parameter Estimates

Variable	DF	Estimate	Standard Error	t Value	Approx Pr > |t|
Intercept	1	0.0000583	0.0000925	0.63	0.5285

In the next example, we model the variance of the residuals using a simple GARCH specification. The unconditional variance term σ^2 is respecified as a conditional variance process, where future variance is a function of contemporaneous variance and squared residuals as shown in Equation (3.3).

$$Y_t = \mu + \varepsilon_t \qquad \text{| Mean equation}$$
$$\sigma_{t+1}^2 = \omega + \alpha\varepsilon_t^2 + \beta\sigma_t^2 \quad | \; \varepsilon_t \; \sim N(0,1)$$

(3.3)

The conditional variance specification above implies that current variance is influenced by both past events as well as carryover effects from past periods' variance. Indeed, it is quite reasonable to expect the impact of major shocks or events to linger on in the data for some periods, especially when the data is sampled at high frequencies such as daily or intraday.

In Program 3.8A, we reemploy PROC AUTOREG and respecify the unconditional variance of the bond index returns as a GARCH process by invoking the GARCH options.[9] The P=1 and Q=1 request one lag of the squared error term, and one lag of the conditional variance term, respectively. Also requested are forecasts of the conditional variance using the OUTPUT statement. The HT=HT statement saves the GARCH forecast to the HT data set. The forecasted conditional variances are then plotted on a series plot using the SGPLOT procedure.

---

[9] The GARCH option can be used to request other types of GARCH specifications, such as the exponential, integrated, Nelson, power, quadratic, and threshold specifications. You can also request the estimation of GARCH-In mean models, in which the conditional variance process is also included in the mean equation. These types of specifications are commonly used to estimate time-varying risk premium models.

Program 3.8A: Adjusting for Heteroscedasticity Using GARCH Models (PROC AUTOREG)

```
/* Using Modeling Conditional Variances Using GARCH Specification*/
ods graphics on;

proc autoreg data= corporate_bonds (where=(date>'31dec12'd)) plots=all;
    model raaap=/ nlag=1  /*AAA Bond Indices*/
    garch=(p=1,q=1);
    output out=pred residual=resid  ht=ht  predicted=rhat;
run;
quit;
```

Output 3.8A shows the results obtained from invoking the AUTOREG procedure and GARCH statement in the procedure. The GARCH Estimate table shows the typical model diagnostics statistics that are produced by regression models such as SSE and unconditional variance, to name a few. The Parameter Estimates table shows the coefficients of the mean components of the model (intercept and AR1) and the conditional variance components of the model. Notice that all conditional variance parameters are statistically significant. This means that past events and past variances have meaningful effects on future variances.

Output 3.8A: Conditional Autoregressive Heteroscedasticity Model of AAA Corporate Bond Returns

The AUTOREG Procedure

GARCH Estimates

SSE	0.05482302	Observations	2610
MSE	0.0000210	Uncond Var	0.00001893
Log Likelihood	10706.4998	Total R-Square	
SBC	-21373.664	AIC	-21403
MAE	0.00316968	AICC	-21402.977
MAPE	105.832316	HQC	-21392.373
		Normality Test	343.7023
		Pr > ChiSq	<.0001

Parameter Estimates

Variable	DF	Estimate	Standard Error	t Value	Approx Pr > |t|
Intercept	1	0.000136	0.0000711	1.91	0.0557
AR1	1	0.0385	0.0201	1.92	0.0550
ARCH0	1	2.7258E-7	5.9935E-8	4.55	<.0001
ARCH1	1	0.0587	0.005338	11.00	<.0001
GARCH1	1	0.9269	0.007142	129.78	<.0001

In Program 3.8B, we graph the monthly estimated conditional variance of our corporate bond index returns using the SGPLOT procedure. We request a series using the SERIES statement, which specifies that the estimated conditional variances (HT) should be plotted on the vertical axis against the DATE variable on the horizontal axis.

Program 3.8B: Plotting the Conditional Variance of AAA Corporate Bond Returns Using PROC SGPLOT

```
/*Plotting the conditional variance using SGPLOT Procedure*/
proc sgplot data=pred;
      title 'Conditional Variance Plot ';
      Series x=Date y=ht/;
      Xaxis label = 'Date';
      yaxis label='Conditional Volatility';
run;

title;
ods graphics off;
```

Output 3.8B shows the series plot of the conditional variances of the corporate bond index return. Notice on the graph the remarkable rise in conditional volatility of the bond index returns that occurred around the beginning of the COVID-19 pandemic in the US. In the following months, the volatility reverted to the historic level until 2022, during which you will also notice a slight increase in volatility due to the change in the monetary policy stance of the Federal Reserve Bank (Fed). During that year, the Fed's monetary policy stance changed from an accommodative regime to a restrictive regime to deal with the high inflationary trends in the US economy. The noticeable increase in the volatility of the bond index returns that occurred in 2022 was due in part to the series of consecutive increases in the benchmark interest rate by the Fed, in line with its restrictive monetary policy.

Output 3.8B: Conditional Autoregressive Heteroscedasticity of US AAA Corporate Bond Returns

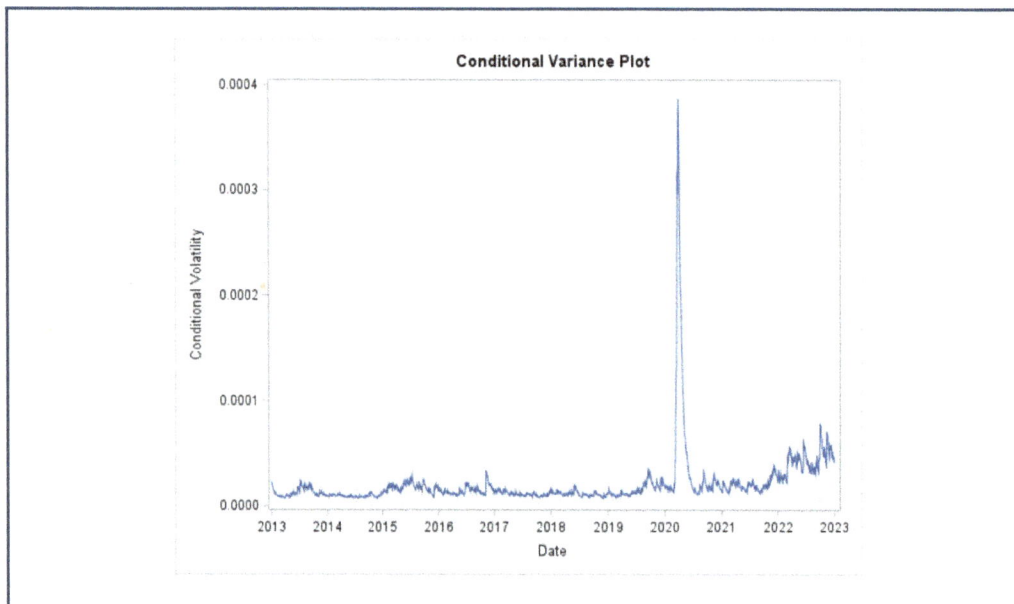

Stationarity

A time series variable is considered stationary if its statistical properties such as its mean, variance, and covariance with past values do not change over time (in other words, time-insensitive). This implies that shocks to the variable are transitory with no long-lasting impact. From a statistical point of view, this feature implies that random samples of the same variable will yield the same values of the statistical properties of the variable. The desirable qualities of this statistical feature explain why most statistical forecasting and machine-learning algorithms assume stationarity in the distribution of the values of the variable. However, many financial and economic time series are not stationary in their raw form.[10] Therefore, they require preprocessing using special techniques and transformations before they can be analyzed. Stationarity can be visualized using the series plots, in which the value of the variable is plotted on the vertical axis, against the time index on the horizontal axis.

Figure 3.3: Visualizing Non-Stationarity in US GDP Series

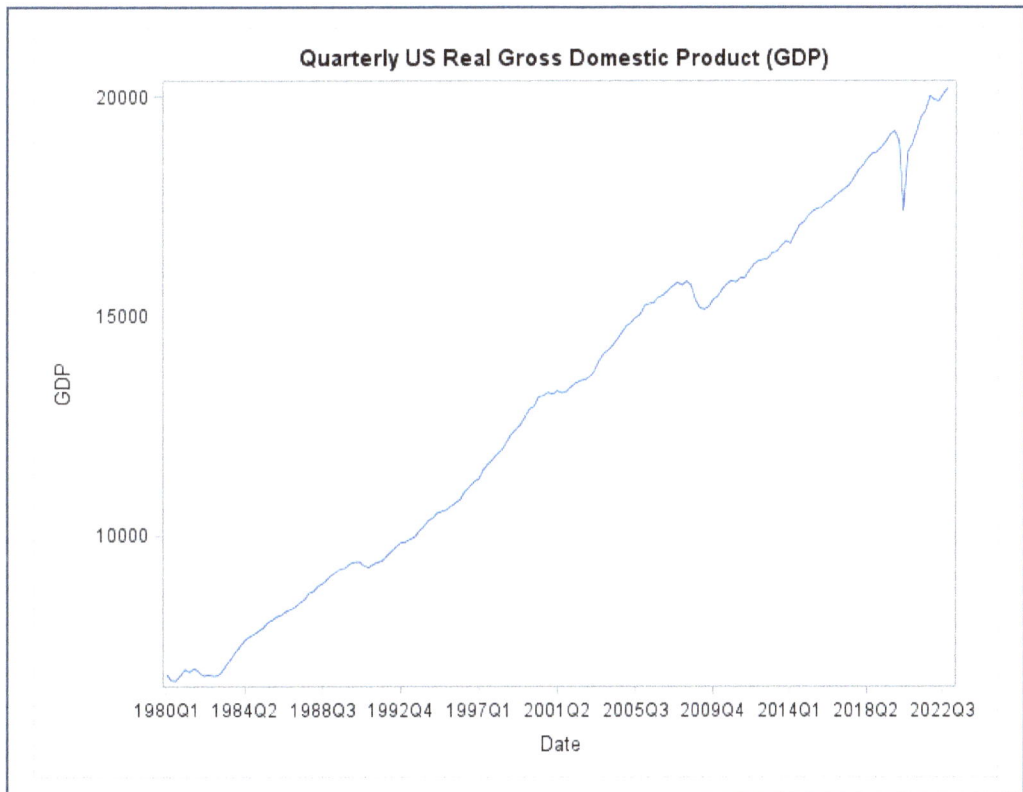

---

[10] Some financial and economic variables are stationary – for example, real interest rate and unemployment rate.

A stationary time series will display mean reversion. However, not all reverting processes are stationary. Reversions can occur around a trend. In this case, the series will be described as trend stationary. For trend stationary series, the removal of the trend component (through differencing) would result in stationarity if it is not also comprised of a unit root process. A unit root process is a special case of non-stationarity that is not caused by trend components. They are due to very high levels of persistence in the process, such that perturbations to the process do not dissipate over time. Mathematically, a unit root process is described as a stochastic process that is integrated of the order of 1 (that is, a first difference stationary process with a root of 1) as shown in the simple *AR(1)* specification in Equation (3.4).

$$Y_t = \phi_0 + \phi_1 Y_{t-1} + \varepsilon_t \qquad | \, \varepsilon \sim N(1,0)$$

(3.4)

When the parameter $\phi_0 = 1$, shocks to the processes will not dissipate over time. Indeed, perturbations to the process become a permanent component of the process, thereby making the process inherently unstable over time. This pattern is evident in the graph of the US real gross domestic product (GDP) shown in Figure 3.2. Notice how the recessionary shocks of 1990, 2001, and 2008 appear to have had an enduring impact on the trajectory of the US GDP.[11] Also apparent on the graph is the trend cycle process, which is characterized by successive periods of growth and contractions. When taken together with the diagnostic plots, which display strong autocorrelation in the residuals, the visualizations indicate that the US GDP follows a trend stationary process.

Program 3.9: Testing for Non-Stationarity in US GDP Series Using PROC AUTOREG

```
/*Transforming US Real GDP Series*/
%datapull(gdp,gdp.sas7bdat);

data GDP;
      set gdp (where=(date>'31dec1979'd));
      format date year4.;
      y= log(rgdp);
      dy = dif(y);
      Label Y='Log Real GDP';
      Label DY = 'Change in Log Real GDP';
      t=_n_;
run;

/*Testing for Stationarity in US Real GDP*/
proc autoreg data= gdp;
      model y= /                          /*Log US Real GDP*/
      stationarity=(adf=(1 2 3),pp=(1 2 ));

      /*adf-Augmented Dickey-Fuller //pp-Phillips-Perron*/
run;
quit;
```

---

[11] A noticeable exception to this pattern is the 2020 COVID-19 induced recession, which lasted for only two months according to the National Bureau of Economic Research (NBER).

Statistical tests that are commonly used to test for stationarity include the Augmented Dicky-Fuller (ADF) and Phillips-Perron (PP) tests. Both tests, as well as other newer tests, are options in the AUTOREG and ARIMA procedures. In Program 3.9, the AUTOREG procedure is invoked to test for stationarity in the US real GDP. In the model, we use log real GDP for statistical convenience. The STATIONARITY (adf=3, pp=3) statement invokes both the ADF and PPF tests for up to three autoregressive lags in the model specification. This is a reasonable specification given the high levels of persistence in the series as shown in the autocorrelation plots. Both tests estimate three regression specifications (zero mean or random walk, a random walk with drift, and a random walk with deterministic trend) shown in a generalized form in Equation (3.5).

$$Y_t = \phi_0 + \phi_1 Y_{t-1} + \delta t + \gamma_1 \Delta Y_{t-1} + \cdots + \gamma_p \Delta Y_{t-p} + \varepsilon_t$$

(3.5)

Output 3.9 shows the results that we obtained from invoking the AUTOREG procedure and STATIONARITY statement in Program 3.10. Going by the results of the Phillips-Perron (PP) and augmented Dickey-Fuller tests (ADF), we fail to reject the null of unit root (using the statistics Rho) and no trend (using the statistics Tau) in the real GDP process for all three regression specifications using both the ADF and PP tests. Indeed, the values of the ADF and PP tests indicate that real GDP might be trend-difference stationary.

Output 3.9: Statistical Test of Stationarity in US GDP Series

Phillips-Perron Unit Root Test					
Type	Lags	Rho	Pr < Rho	Tau	Pr < Tau
Zero Mean	1	0.1140	0.7084	7.4199	1.0000
	2	0.1140	0.7084	7.3627	1.0000
	3	0.1140	0.7084	7.2748	1.0000
Single Mean	1	-0.6091	0.9183	-1.3935	0.5851
	2	-0.6090	0.9183	-1.3937	0.5850
	3	-0.6099	0.9182	-1.3891	0.5873
Trend	1	-3.3033	0.9221	-1.1603	0.9145
	2	-3.3468	0.9200	-1.1693	0.9128
	3	-3.4283	0.9160	-1.1861	0.9095

Augmented Dickey-Fuller Unit Root Tests							
Type	Lags	Rho	Pr < Rho	Tau	Pr < Tau	F	Pr > F
Zero Mean	1	0.1159	0.7088	6.9207	0.9999		
	2	0.1162	0.7089	5.8858	0.9999		
	3	0.1143	0.7084	4.9509	0.9999		
Single Mean	1	-0.7511	0.9070	-1.8007	0.3791	26.5760	<.0010
	2	-0.8253	0.9007	-1.9217	0.3214	20.1012	<.0010
	3	-0.7818	0.9044	-1.7146	0.4221	14.3748	<.0010
Trend	1	-3.3685	0.9189	-1.2384	0.8986	2.0924	0.7595
	2	-3.9007	0.8903	-1.3836	0.8622	2.4509	0.6878
	3	-4.1335	0.8763	-1.3713	0.8656	2.0949	0.7590

Dealing with Non-Stationary Data

Non-stationary series can be made stationary by transforming them using appropriate mathematical operations (such as differencing, and detrending). Several procedures in SAS can be used when dealing with non-stationary data. These include the ARIMA, AUTOREG, X13, TIMEDATA, EXPAND, and TIMESERIES procedures, to mention a few. The ARIMA and X13 procedures can automatically generate differenced data using the order of differencing specified in the MODEL statement. TIMEDATA, TIMESERIES, and EXPAND can also be used to transform the time series data to the specified order of differencing. The ARIMA procedure is used in Program 3.10 to automatically generate the first difference of the log real GDP. The series is then subsequently retested for unit root using the ADF and PP tests.

Program 3.10: Adjusting for Non-Stationarity in US GDP Series

```
/*Creating Stationary Series Using PROC ARIMA*/
ods graphics on;

proc arima data=gdp
      plots=all;
      identify var=y(0,1,0) scan stationarity=(pp=3);
      identify var=y(0,1,0) scan stationarity=(adf=3);
run;
quit;
ods graphics off;
```

Output 3.10: Stationarity in US GDP Series

Phillips-Perron Unit Root Tests

Type	Lags	Rho	Pr < Rho	Tau	Pr < Tau
Zero Mean	0	-138.517	0.0001	-10.85	<.0001
	1	-134.819	0.0001	-10.81	<.0001
	2	-146.070	0.0001	-10.95	<.0001
	3	-159.674	0.0001	-11.14	<.0001
Single Mean	0	-182.179	0.0001	-14.16	<.0001
	1	-181.456	0.0001	-14.17	<.0001
	2	-184.743	0.0001	-14.15	<.0001
	3	-188.349	0.0001	-14.12	<.0001
Trend	0	-184.095	0.0001	-14.32	<.0001
	1	-182.920	0.0001	-14.33	<.0001
	2	-185.161	0.0001	-14.31	<.0001
	3	-187.705	0.0001	-14.29	<.0001

Augmented Dickey-Fuller Unit Root Tests

Type	Lags	Rho	Pr < Rho	Tau	Pr < Tau	F	Pr > F
Zero Mean	0	-138.517	0.0001	-10.85	<.0001		
	1	-81.6680	<.0001	-6.36	<.0001		
	2	-49.2739	<.0001	-4.59	<.0001		
	3	-36.6920	<.0001	-3.90	0.0001		
Single Mean	0	-182.179	0.0001	-14.16	<.0001	100.34	0.0010
	1	-167.323	0.0001	-9.21	<.0001	42.43	0.0010
	2	-144.243	0.0001	-7.05	<.0001	24.87	0.0010
	3	-148.887	0.0001	-6.22	<.0001	19.35	0.0010
Trend	0	-184.095	0.0001	-14.32	<.0001	102.62	0.0010
	1	-174.524	0.0001	-9.42	<.0001	44.41	0.0010
	2	-155.843	0.0001	-7.24	<.0001	26.21	0.0010
	3	-166.542	0.0001	-6.38	<.0001	20.35	0.0010

Output 3.10: Stationarity in US GDP Series (Continued)

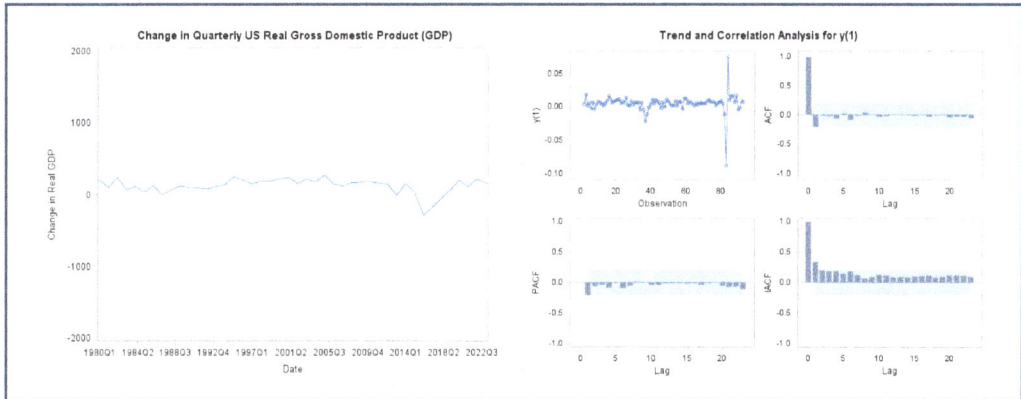

The *p*-values of statistics Rho and Tau shown in Output 3.10 provide further confirmation that the GDP process appears to be a trend-stationary process. The null hypotheses of unit root and trend effects are now rejected for all three specifications. As can be seen in the subsequent visualizations, the differenced GDP series now appears more stable and devoid of trend effect.

Non-Normality

The main characteristics of a normal distribution are symmetry, asymptotic limit, and continuous unimodal density function (one peak) in which the mean, median, and mode are equal. Together, these characteristics define the well-known bell shape of the normal distribution. There is also the empirical rule of the normal distribution, which states that 68% of the observation must be within one standard deviation of the mean, 95% will be within two standard deviations of the means, and about 99.7% will be within three standard deviations of the mean. Statistically, the normal distribution is characterized by two moment functions, the mean, and the standard deviation. The other moment functions, which are skewness and kurtosis, are assumed to have a constant value of 0 and 3, respectively. Therefore, non-normality is a catch-all for any statistical characteristics of the data that are inconsistent with the properties described above. These include:

- **Fat Tails (Leptokurtosis)** – Kurtosis values that are more than 3, which implies that more observations of the variable are clustered around the tail of the distributions relative to a normal distribution.
- **Thin Tails (Platykurtosis)** – Kurtosis values that are lower than 3, which implies that more observations are clustered closer to the center of the distribution relative to what is expected in the normal distribution.
- **Asymmetry** (*Skewness* ≠ 0) – When skewness is not equal to zero, it implies that the mean is not equal to the median. Hence, more observations are on one side of the mean relative to the other. Negative skewness implies more observations are above the mean (median is greater than the mean), while positive skewness implies more observations are below the mean (median is lesser than the mean).

A visual diagnostic of the distributional properties of the data can be implemented in SAS using histograms, Q-Q plots, box plots, and cumulative distribution (CDF) plots. Many statistical procedures in SAS will include some diagnostic plots that test normality in the residuals and in some cases in the dependent variables in the output of the procedures. For many of these procedures, the plot might need to be invoked using the ODS option as shown in Program 3.10. Statistical tests for normality are options included in the UNIVARIATE, CAPABILITY, REG, and AUTOREG procedures, to list a few.

PROC CAPABILITY

The CAPABILITY procedure was created primarily for quality control but has many features relating to data diagnostics, which we will use shortly. The procedure compares the distribution of output from a process to the specification limit of that process. The diagnostic features that the procedure supports include the creation of descriptive statistics, computation of various tests for normality, signed rank statistics, and percentiles, as well as the creation of ODS graphs such as the histogram, P-P, and Q-Q plots.

In the code example shown in Program 3.11, the NORMALTEST option is invoked in the CAPABILITY procedure to execute a test of normality on the quarterly change in the US Real GDP. Also invoked in the PROC CAPABILITY statement are the Q-Q and P-P plots for the series.

Program 3.11: Visualizing Non-Normality in Quarterly Changes to US GDP Using PROC CAPABILITY

```
/*Assessing Normality in Quarterly Changes in US Real GDP*/
proc capability data=gdp normaltest;
      Var dy;
      qqplot/ normal(mu=est sigma=est color=blue);
      ppplot / normal (mu=est sigma=est color=blue);
run;

title;
```

Output 3.11 shows the results obtained from implementing the code in Program 3.11. Notice that all of the tests of normality indicate that the US GDP series is not normally distributed. The graphs of the P-P and Q-Q plots also support this conclusion.

Output 3.11: Non-Normality in US GDP Series

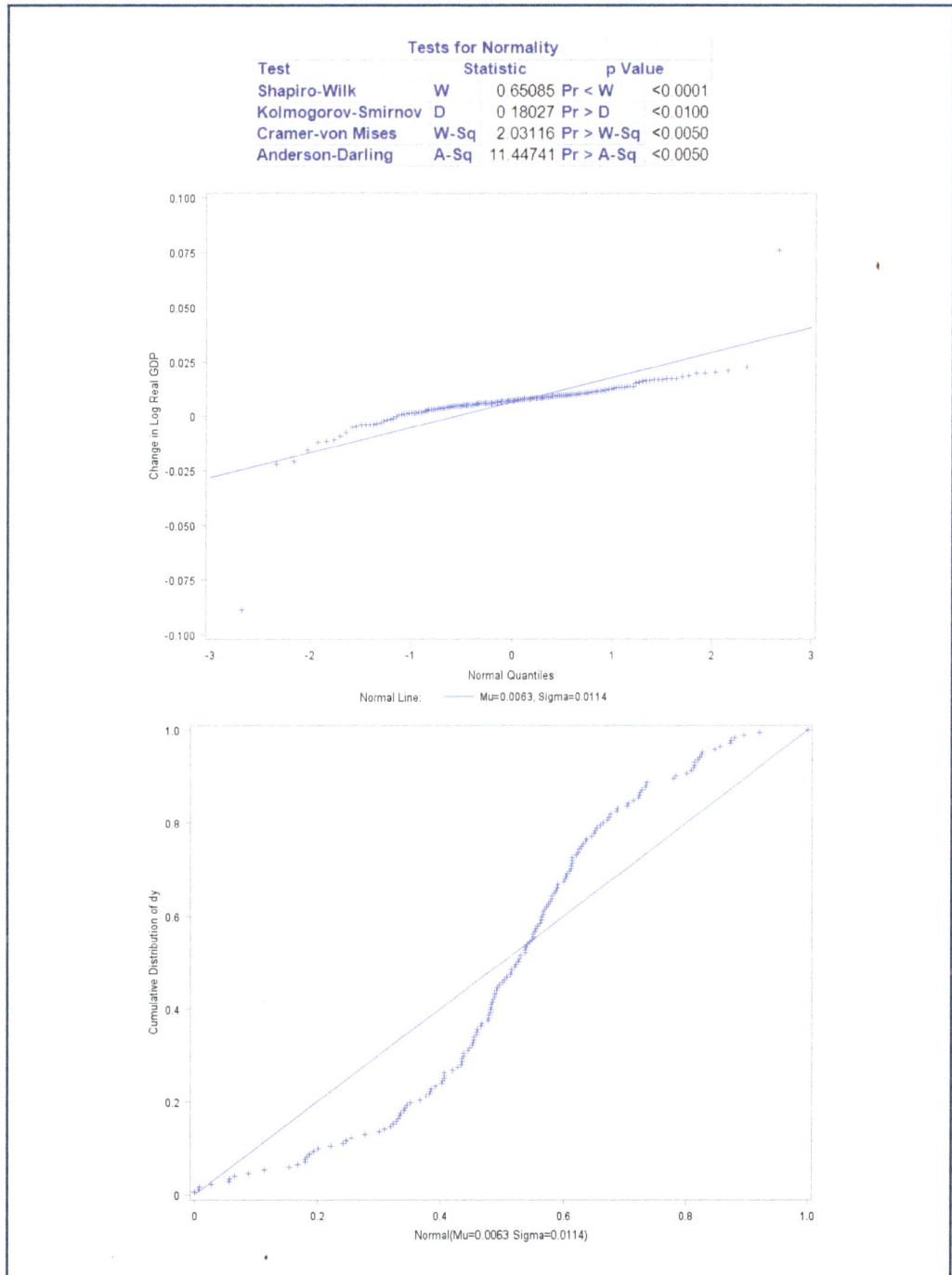

Tests for Normality

Test		Statistic		p Value	
Shapiro-Wilk	W	0.65085	Pr < W	<0.0001
Kolmogorov-Smirnov	D	0.18027	Pr > D	<0.0100
Cramer-von Mises	W-Sq	2.03116	Pr > W-Sq	<0.0050
Anderson-Darling	A-Sq	11.44741	Pr > A-Sq	<0.0050

Normal Line: Mu=0.0063, Sigma=0.0114

Figure 3.4: Visualizing 2% Jumps in S&P 500 Returns

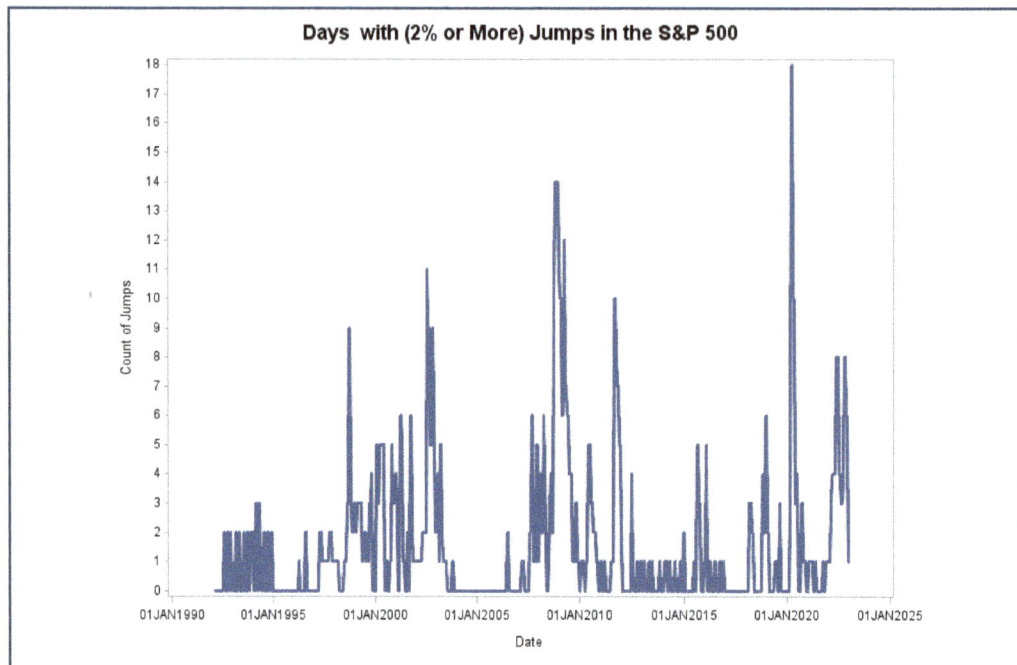

Dealing with Non-Normality

Normality (univariate or multivariate) is a highly desired data attribute because it provides the data scientist with more flexibility in terms of the range of models that can be deployed. Normality in the data also underlies many theoretical models in finance and economics. Therefore, when dealing with non-normally distributed data, the first option the data scientist should consider is to transform the non-normal data into a normally distributed one using appropriate mathematical functions (such as logarithmic) or mathematical operations (such as differencing), or statistical procedures such as Winsorizing. If these are not feasible, then the data scientist should consider using parametric models such as the generalized linear model (GLM), or nonparametric models such as the generalized additive model (GAM) that do not require normality in the series.[12]

Model for Non-Normal Data

Events with significant market-wide impact occur in a discrete manner that is not characteristic of the normal distribution. These types of events are often triggered by news release about a major

---

[12] We will discuss the GLM specification in more detail in Chapter Seven.

change in the macroeconomic fundamentals or the occurrence of a significant geopolitical event. Hence, they are typically episodic by nature.

Suppose we want to examine the pattern by which these significant market-moving events occur in the US stock market. Let's define a significant market event as one that is described by at least 2% positive or negative swings (jumps) in the daily levels of the S&P 500. Such swings are extremely rare events; they occur in about 7.5% of all trading days and tend to cluster around specific periods or events as shown in Figure 3.4. One way to model the arrival rate of these phenomena is to assume that their rate of occurrence follows a Poisson process. A Poisson process is a stochastic process that is commonly used in finance to analyze events with discrete arrival times which follows the Poisson distribution. The distribution is unique in the sense that it has only one parameter λ (lambda), which is the mean number of events that occur within a window of opportunity, which in our case is a month. If we define the stochastic process for days in the month with 2% or more jumps as a Poisson process, we can use the GAM procedure to examine whether there is seasonality in the occurrences of these extreme events in the US stock market.

PROC GAM

The GAM procedure fits a flexible form of the generalized additive model that can implement both parametric and nonparametric spline regressions of a dependent variable on a vector of regressors. The model specifies a density function for the dependent variable and a functional form (link function) for the vector of regressors as shown in Equation (3.6).

$$G\left(Y_t\right) = \beta_0 + f_1\left(X_{1,t}\right) + f_2\left(X_{2,t}\right) + \ldots\ldots f_n\left(X_{n,t}\right)$$ (3.6)

The functional form can be parametric, nonparametric (SPLINE, LOESS), semiparametric, additive, and thin-plate spline. The main advantage of PROC GAM is that it can combine various sub-model specifications into one model, which is beneficial for modeling linear and non-linear relationships between the dependent variable and its covariates. ODS graphics plots of the additive components and the confidence limit of the smoothing components can also be requested from the procedure.[13]

In Program 3.12, we invoke the GAM procedure to estimate the monthly dependencies in jump incidences in the S&P 500 index returns. We use the PLOTS option to request the CLM plot. The CLASS statement is used to specify that Month is a classification variable. The MODEL statement specifies the parametric functional form of our model, which we indicate with the PARAM(MONTH) option. The OUTPUT statement is used to request for the estimated parameters to be saved in the EST_P data set.

---

[13] You can learn more about the GAM procedure by reviewing the SAS/STAT User's Guide for the procedure at https://documentation.sas.com/doc/en/pgmsascdc/9.4_3.3/statug/statug_gam_toc.htm.

Program 3.12: Modeling Jump Seasonality in S&P 500 Returns Using PROC GAM

```
/*Examining Jumps in S&P 500 Index Returns*/
%datapull(jumps,jumps.sas7bdat);

proc gam data=jumps plots=components(clm);
        class month;
        model SPC=param(month) / dist=Poisson;
        output out=est p;
run;

proc sort data=est;
        by month;
run;

/*Plot conditional Jumps Using SGPLOT*/
proc sgplot data=est;
        title ' Days Per Month with 2% Jumps in the S&P 500 Index';
        Scatter x=month_name y=spc/ name="spca" markerattrs=(color=Green) legendlabel= "
Actual Jumps";
        Series x=month_name y=p_spc / name="spcb" lineattrs=graphfit legendlabel= "
Predicted Jumps";
        Xaxis label = 'Month';
        Yaxis label='Number of Days with Jumps';
        keylegend "spca" "spcb"/ across=3 noborder position=bottomleft location=outside;
run;
```

Output 3.12: Time-Dependent Jumps in S&P 500 Index Returns

Regression Model Analysis Parameter Estimates				
Parameter	Parameter Estimate	Standard Error	t Value	Pr > |t|
Intercept	0.22957	0.16013	1.43	0.1525
Month 1	0.07411	0.22237	0.33	0.7391
Month 2	-0.08004	0.23112	-0.35	0.7293
Month 3	0.57054	0.20033	2.85	0.0047
Month 4	0.30673	0.21097	1.45	0.1468
Month 5	-0.10821	0.23283	-0.46	0.6424
Month 6	0.05001	0.22368	0.22	0.8232
Month 7	0.12063	0.21993	0.55	0.5837
Month 8	0.16508	0.21767	0.76	0.4487
Month 9	0.54113	0.20141	2.69	0.0076
Month 10	0.54113	0.20141	2.69	0.0076
Month 11	0.36179	0.20856	1.73	0.0837
Month 12	0			

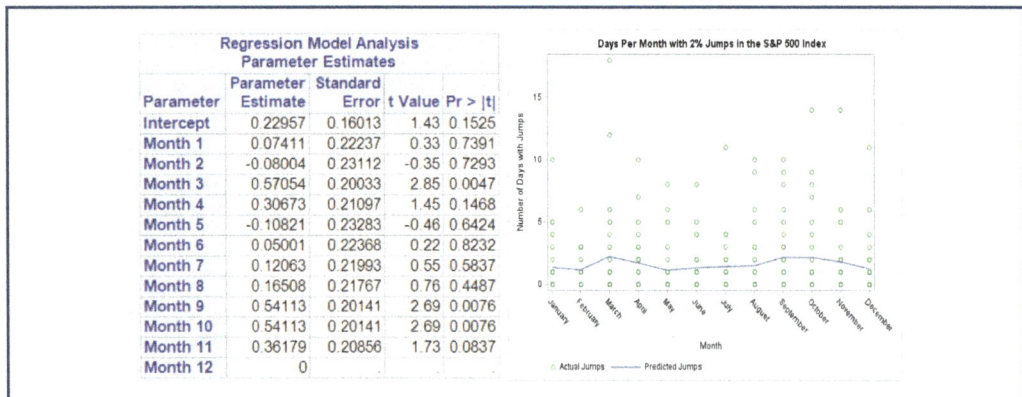

Days Per Month with 2% Jumps in the S&P 500 Index

The results shown in the parameter estimate table indicate that relative to the base month of December, March, September, and October appear to be the months with the most prevalence of extreme price movements in the S&P 500. The forecast plot for the monthly jumps was generated using the SGPLOT procedure. It shows a higher jump prediction for the months of March, September, and October, in line with the estimate from the GAM model.

Table 3.1: Summary of Statistical Properties and Potential SAS Solutions

Measure	Visualization			SAS Procedures	
	Type	Vertical Axis	Horizontal Axis	PROC	Statistical Tests
Normality	Q-Q Plot	Empirical Quantile	Theoretical Quantile	UNIVARIATE CAPABILITY	Shapiro-Wilk test Kolmogorov-Smirnov
	P-Plot	Empirical Probability	Theoretical Probability	UNIVARIATE AUTOREG REG	Anderson-Darling test Cramér–von Mises
Stationarity	Series Plot	Variable	Time	AUTOREG ARIMA REG SGPLOT	Phillips-Perron Dickey-Fuller
Trends	Series Plots	Variable	Time	ARIMA TIMESERIES UCM EXPAND X13 SGPLOT	
Cyclicality	Series Plot	Variable	Time (Qtrs. or Years)	UCM SGPLOT	
Seasonality	Series Plot	Variable	Time (Monthly)	ARIMA TIMESERIES UCM SGPLOT X13	
Autocorrelation	Autocorrelation functions (ACF, ACIF, PACF)	Autocorrelation	Lagged Index	AUTOREG ARIMA X13	Durbin-Watson
Heteroscedasticity	Residual Plots	Residual	Time Dependent Variable	AUTOREG ARIMA MODEL X13 SGPLOT	Q and LM Statistics Breusch-Pagan and White test

Table 3.1 displays a summary of the statistical properties of financial and economic data and suggests visualizations for exploring them. It also highlights SAS procedures and statistical test options in the procedures that can be used to conduct further analysis of the properties.

Exercises

1. The SAS data set GDP contains real GDP (RGDP), nominal GDP (GDP), real GDP per capita (RGNP), and nominal GDP per capita (GNP) for the US.

   > **Hint:** You can also use the DATAPULL macro to download the data into your work library: %datapull(gdp,gdp.sas7bdat).

   a. Write a SAS program to create a new SAS data set (SGDP) from the GDP data set using data from Q1-1980 to Q3-2022. Create a variable (LGNP) that calculates the log of the real GNP (RGNP). Label the variable as "Log GDP Per Capita".

   b. Use the SGPLOT procedure to graph the RGNP on the Y axis, LGNP on the Y2 axis, and Date on the horizontal axis. Include a title for your graph.

      i. Besides the unit of value, are there any differences between the plot for RGNP and LGNP?

      ii. Which time series components are evident on the graph for both series?

      iii. Which time series properties are apparent on the graph for both series?

      iv. What types of visualization would you consider to drill-down further into the statistical properties of the two series?

   c. Let's test for autocorrelation in the LGNP series by using the AUTOREG procedure. Include the PLOTS=ALL option in your statement. Also, apply NLAG=1, DW=1, and DWPROB. Save your results.

      i. What can you infer about the autocorrelation in the series, going by ACF and PACF plots?

      ii. What do the results of the test imply for bias in the coefficients of the statistical models applied to the series?

      iii. What does the result imply for statistical inferences drawn from the models applied to the series if autocorrelation is found in the series?

   d. Now let's explore if we can adjust for autocorrelation by calculating the first difference of the series and retesting for autocorrelation using the ARIMA (0,1,0) procedure. The (0,1,0) denotes zero lags, first difference, and zero moving averages. To test for autocorrelation, specify WHITENOISE=ST.

      i. Compare the ACF and PACF plots generated time with the previous result. Did the first-differencing solve the autocorrelation problem?

2. The data set TRADE contains monthly retail sales for various sub-sectors of the US retail sector.

    a. Write a SAS program to create a new SAS data set (BDC), which is a subset of TRADE. Keep the following variables.

Date	Monthly Dates
MRTS4453	Beer, Wine, and Liquor Sales
MRTSP4453	Month-over-Month Beer, Wine, and Liquor Sales
MRTS44611	Pharmacies and Drug Store Sales
MRTSP44611	Month-over-Month Pharmacies and Drug Store Sales
MRTS44112	Used Car Sales
MRTSP44112	Month-over-Month Used Car Sales

    b. Use the SGPLOT procedure to graph MRTS4453 on the Y axis, MRTS44611 on the Y2 axis, and Date on the horizontal axis. Label YAXIS as "Monthly US Beer, Wine, and Liquor Sales" and the Y2AXIS as "Monthly US Pharmacies and Drug Store Sales." Specify a date range (January 1995 to December 2021) and monthly frequency for your plot. Also, include a title for your graph.

        i. What time series components are observable in alcoholic beverages and drug store sales?
        ii. What are the directions and magnitude of those components?
        iii. Are those components correlated between the two series?
        iv. What month(s) of the year do we see spikes in sales in one or both categories?
        v. What month(s) of the year do we see drops in sales in one or both categories?
        vi. What could explain the spikes in drugstore sales in certain months?
        vii. What could explain the spikes in alcoholic beverage sales in certain months?

    c. Estimate the trend and seasonal components in the alcoholic beverage sales series using the X13 procedure. Retain the following series in your output data: a1,d10,d12, d11, and d13. Save the output in the ADJUSTED data set.

    Hint: Use Program 2.27 as reference.

        i. Examine the Summary of the Result and Combined Test for Seasonality. Do the tests confirm the pattern displayed on the graph? What type of seasonality exists in the data (Moving or Stable)?

    d. Use the SGPLOT procedure to graph your d10 series on the YAXIS and your a1 and d12 series on the Y2AXIS. These series should be graphed against the DATE variable on the horizontal (XAXIS).

        i. Compare the adjusted series to the unadjusted alcoholic beverage sales series graphed in Part B of Question 3.
        ii. Going by the graph and the results, what is your estimate of the average contribution of seasonality to the monthly alcoholic beverage sales?

Chapter 4: Simulating Financial and Economic Data

Introduction to Simulations

Many of the phenomena and events we study in the data science domain are complex and random. And sometimes we might need to study these events in a controlled environment. For example, a loan portfolio manager might want to study how many loans in the bank's portfolio will default over a certain period of time, or an equity portfolio manager might be interested in learning how the portfolio would perform over time. The uncertainty faced by both portfolio managers is how to capture the future realizations of the factors that could affect their portfolios over the study period. One way is to wait for the actual outcome to happen, but that approach is unlikely to be very helpful from a business point of view. Another approach is to build analytical models that can allow us to study these factors and their effects on the portfolios under various possible scenarios. But that could also be a very expensive proposition and in some cases, might not even be achievable due to the randomness of these factors. Another is to use mathematical models to generate artificial data that mimics the phenomenon we are trying to study and then use that data to develop our understanding of the phenomena. The process of generating artificial data from mathematical models of the real world is called simulation. Today, most simulations are done using computer systems, which allows us to execute simple to complex tasks in a timely manner.

Simulation is used across all industries, including agriculture, weather forecasting, automotive, aerospace, gaming, epidemiology, and financial services, to name a few. As highlighted in the previous chapter, many of the topics that will be presented in this chapter are based on well-established econometric and statistical theories. However, in-depth mathematical presentations of the concepts are beyond the scope of this book. Therefore, mathematical constructs and notations will be used only as needed to describe concepts that cannot be presented in a descriptive manner. Nevertheless, readers who are less proficient in mathematical statistics may find some of the math a bit daunting. In such instances, they might find it helpful to focus on the general concept and the accompanying SAS program as they go through the chapter.

Simulations are numerical solutions drawn from abstractions of complex real-world systems or phenomena. In the financial services industry, simulation is used to solve problems or find answers to questions about how patterns and events occur in the real world. We rely on simulations because other approaches such as analytical methods are unable to yield a solution or are too expensive to implement. In general, simulations can only provide estimates of what the most likely solution will be. And in a lot of cases, that approximation may suffice in terms of answering the question.

Types of Simulation Models

Simulation models generally fall under two broad categories: deterministic and stochastic. Deterministic models are generally easier to implement and provide perfectly predictable output to a given set of inputs in each run of the model. Stochastic models are probabilistic models of the system or phenomenon that is under study. Thus, their outputs may not be the same in each run of the model, unless the models are calibrated to do so.

Deterministic Models

These types of models do not have randomness built into them, so their behaviors and outcomes are entirely predictable. For example, suppose the payroll department would like to simulate the total payroll expense for its employees for a given month. Such an outcome can simply be expressed as a function of the sum of the fixed payroll cost (mostly the cost of benefits) and the product of the hourly rate for the employees and the number of hours worked, compounded by the associated payroll tax rate as shown below.

$$\left(\text{Payroll\_Expense}_t\right)=$$
$$\text{Benefit\_Cost}+(\text{Hourly Rate}*\text{Hours\_Worked}_t)*(1+\text{Payroll\_Tax\_Rate})$$

(4.1)

Figure 4.1: Types of Simulation

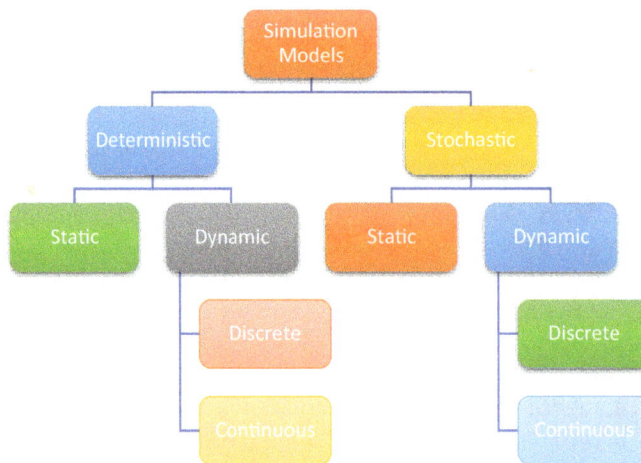

The deterministic simulation model example shown above will help the company in answering the "What if" question or in conducting a sensitivity analysis such as, "What is the largest driver of our payroll expense"?

Stochastic Models

Stochastic models incorporate randomness in the system; therefore, their outcomes are also random. The pattern of randomness is defined by the underlying probability distribution that controls the random process. The system can be constructed entirely of random variables, or as a combination of random variables and fixed values of other variables. Suppose the payroll department is uncertain about the number of hours that the company employees will complete in any given month, but on average they tend to complete about 10,000 hours. In this case, we can introduce randomness into our deterministic payroll model by specifying a law of motion for hours worked as follows.

$$\text{where Hours\_Worked}_t = 10,000 + \varepsilon_t \text{ and } \varepsilon_t \sim G(\mu, \sigma^2) \qquad (4.2)$$

ε_t is now the random component of the model. The probability distribution that governs how hours worked evolve over time is defined by $G(\mu, \sigma^2)$, which is a function of two parameters: the mean and the variance. For normally distributed variables, the distribution function is typically expressed as $N(\mu, \sigma^2)$.

Stochastic models are particularly useful for making predictions or studying how random systems behave when external shocks are applied to them, such as portfolio outcomes during periods of high stock market volatility.

Both deterministic and stochastic models can be used for static and dynamic simulations. Static simulations are representations of the real-world phenomenon at a particular point in time. Static simulations carry no memory of past occurrences of the event; therefore, they are not affected by time. The monthly payroll expense simulation is an example of a static simulation. Later on in the chapter, we will introduce a common type of static simulation that is known as the Monte Carlo simulation. Dynamic simulations represent the phenomenon as it evolves over time. An example of these will be simulating the cumulative monthly payroll expense over twelve months. Notice that in this example, the magnitude of the preceding month's payroll expense will affect the cumulative value of the payroll expense in subsequent months.

Systems that operate in discrete time and continuous time can be simulated using dynamic models. Continuous time systems have input and output values for all possible points in time within an interval, while discrete-time systems have values for only the discrete time within the interval. It is easier to think of continuous-time systems as those that yield output at every possible moment within an interval. For example, older electricity meters, which rely on spinning disks, record the amount of electricity consumed at a location at every moment in time and accumulate them over time to produce the monthly unit of energy consumed. Newer digital solid-state electricity meters use the discrete approach by taking snapshots of the electrical signal at discrete intervals and using them to calculate the total amount of energy consumed during the same period. In reality, the difference between continuous and discrete systems is the sampling frequency. With continuous systems, the sampling frequency can potentially be infinite within an interval of time, while discrete systems have finite numbers of samples or realizations within the same interval.

Stochastic Simulations

All stochastic models will require some basic information about the event or process that you are trying to simulate. This information includes the pattern of occurrence of the event or phenomena in the real world and the basic parameters that are used to describe the characteristics of that pattern. The former is called distribution, while the latter is called statistics. For example, the observable pattern that appears in a coin toss has two possible outcomes: heads or tails. For a single dice roll, there are six possible outcomes, which range from 1 to 6. The statistics that describe the characteristics of the coin toss or the dice rolls include the probability of obtaining a specific outcome or the average value of the outcomes. Notice that the patterns of occurrence between these two events are distinctly different: one has two possible outcomes, while the other has six possible outcomes. In reality, different distributions have different ranges and patterns of outcomes. Indeed, the distribution followed by a single coin toss is also different from the distribution that multiple coin tosses will follow. The same intuition applies to tossing multiple coins, multiple times, as well as rolling multiple dice multiple times. That is because each of these processes is unique, so we expect that they will have different probability distributions.

Probability Distributions

In your previous statistics course, you might have come across probability distributions. There are two common types of univariate (marginal) probability distribution: discrete and continuous distributions. The third type of probability distribution is the multivariate probability distribution (that is, the probability distribution of the collection of a pair or more random variables).

Discrete Distributions

Discrete distributions are patterns of occurrence that follow a counting process. For example, the coin toss and roll of dice examples have a finite set of countable outcomes. The types of discrete distributions that are commonly used in finance and their applications are shown in Table 4.1.

Continuous Distributions

These types of events or occurrences have a continuum range of outcomes that follows a measurement process. The range of outcomes is typically infinitesimal because each outcome might not be distinctly different from its adjacent value. Therefore, the probability for a

Table 4.1: Discrete Probability Distributions and Their Finance Applications

Discrete Distributions	Applications
Bernoulli	Discrete stock or stock market outcomes
Binomial	Option pricing, risk management
Geometric	Asset pricing, portfolio management
Poisson	Asset pricing, risk management

Table 4.2: Continuous Probability Distributions and Their Finance Applications

Continuous Distribution	Applications
Normal	Asset pricing, risk management
Log-Normal	Asset pricing, risk management
Student-t	Asset pricing, risk management
Uniform	Simulations, asset pricing, risk management
Exponential	Risk management, event modeling
Gamma	Risk management
Beta	Risk management
F	Inferential statistics
Chi	Inferential statistics
Pareto	Risk management
Logistics	Inferential statistics, risk management
Weibull	Risk management

continuous random variable is always measured over an interval. Common types of continuous distributions and their applications in finance are shown in Table 4.2.

Multivariate Probability Distribution

Multivariate distributions are the joint distribution of two or more random variables. For example, the pattern followed by rolling two or more dice will have a multivariate probability distribution. Multivariate probability distributions could be discrete or continuous. They might also consist of the marginal or conditional distributions of two or more random variables. Examples of common multivariate distributions and their applications in finance are shown in Table 4.3.

Table 4.3: Multivariate Probability Distributions and Their Finance Applications

Multivariate Distribution	Finance Applications
Multivariate Normal	Asset pricing, portfolio risk management
Multivariate Student-t	Asset pricing, portfolio risk management
Multinomial	Portfolio risk management

Simulating Random Values from Various Probability Distributions

There are multiple ways to conduct simulations in SAS:

- DATA step and RAND function: This approach works very well for simulating data from univariate distributions.
- PROC statements: Some SAS procedures such as MODEL, COPULA, and SIMNORMAL have options for simulating data for both univariate and multivariate distributions.
- SAS Interactive Matrix Language (IML): PROC IML harnesses the power of matrix algebra for complex univariate and multivariate simulations. It is also slightly more computationally efficient than the DATA step approach to simulation.
- SAS Simulation Studio: For those interested in building simulations of discrete events using a graphical user interface and drag-and-drop menus, SAS Simulation Studio is a powerful application that can interface with the SAS engine for programming integration. One of the benefits of SAS Simulation Studio is the ability to visualize and animate the model that was used to build the simulations.

In this book, we will explore the first three methods for building our simulation models with specific emphasis on their applications in the finance domain. Simulating data from discrete and continuous distributions in SAS is relatively straightforward. With the DATA statement, you will need to provide at least three sets of information – the type of distribution, the parameters of the distribution from which the simulated data will be derived, and the number of repetitions (samples to be drawn) for the simulation.[1]

Discrete Distribution

Let us start by simulating a coin toss. A fair coin should yield a 50% probability of obtaining either heads or tails over a sufficiently large number of trials. Since there are only two possibilities from a toss of a single coin, the experiment will be equivalent to simulating data from a Bernoulli

---

[1] In-depth coverage of simulations for all types of distributions is beyond the scope of this book. Readers interested in a comprehensive coverage of the topic should review another book published by SAS titled *Simulating Data with SAS®* by Rick Wicklin.

distribution. In Program 4.1, we show the SAS code that was used to simulate values from the Bernoulli distribution. Besides specifying the distribution, the two other pieces of information to provide are the parameter of the distribution (the probability of obtaining one of the two outcomes) and the number of repetitions (trials to conduct). The RAND function in SAS can simulate data from all the discrete and continuous distributions listed in the previous section of the chapters.

The CALL STREAMINIT statement sets the seed values for the random number generator. Using this statement ensures that you get the same output in every run of the simulation. SAS uses the computer clock to generate the seed values if you do not include the statement in your code. Notice that although we specified a 50% probability of success (probability of obtaining the value of 1), the frequency of success did not match that value. In reality, for discrete events, you would need to run a significantly larger number of trials to increase the chances that the empirical probability will match the theoretical probability.

Program 4.1: Simulating Data from Bernoulli Probability Distribution

```
/*Simulating Data from Bernoulli Distribution */
%let prob=0.5; /*Probability of Success*/
data simul1;
      call streaminit(4321);/*Random seed generator*/
      do i=1 to 100; /*Number of Iteration*/
            Simnum =rand("Bernoulli", &prob); /*Invoking the RAND
function*/
            output; /*To the values from each iteration*/
      end;
run;

/*Computing Simulation Statistics*/
ods graphics on;

proc freq  data=simul1;
      table Simnum/
            plots = freqplots;
run;
```

Output 4.1: Simulated Data from Bernoulli Distribution

		The FREQ Procedure		
Simnum	Frequency	Percent	Cumulative Frequency	Cumulative Percent
0	52	52.00	52	52.00
1	48	48.00	100	100.00

We can modify the code in Program 4.1 to simulate values from a binomial distribution. The binomial distribution summarizes the Bernoulli distribution for N number of trials, where each trial has an independent probability of success P.

Program 4.2: Simulating Data from Binomial Probability Distribution

```
/*Simulating Data from Binomial Distribution */
%let prob=0.5; /*Probability of Success*/
%let num = 1; /*Number of trials*/

data simul2;
      call streaminit(4321);/*Random seed generator*/

      do i=1 to 100; /*Number of Iteration*/
              Simnum =rand("Binonmial", &prob,&num); /*Invoking the RAND function*/
              output; /*To the values from each iteration*/
      end;
run;

/*Computing Simulation Statistics*/
ods graphics on;

proc freq  data=simul2;
      table Simnum/
            plots = freqplots;
run;
```

Output 4.2: Simulated Data from Binomial Probability Distribution

The FREQ Procedure

Simnum	Frequency	Percent	Cumulative Frequency	Cumulative Percent
0	48	48.00	48	48.00
1	52	52.00	100	100.00

Notice that the statistics we obtained for our variable are the same as those in the Bernoulli distribution. This is because the Bernoulli distribution represents the number of successes and failures in one trial. Since the number of trials in the binomial distribution was also set to one, the value from the simulation is essentially the same as those from the Bernoulli distribution. They would be different for the Binomial distribution if we change the number of trials to a different value than one. In Figure 4.2, we plot the frequency of the number of successes that were simulated from 10 trials and 100 repetitions.

Notice on the graph that we did not obtain any instance with zero success (or 10 failures), nine successes (or one failure), or 10 successes (or zero failures) in the 10 trials. There was one instance where we obtained one success and nine failures. The closer we get to the prior probability of 50%, the more instances of the outcome we observe in the simulated data. The probability distribution of a series of coin tosses is an example of the binomial distribution.

Figure 4.2: Frequency Plot for Number of Successes in Binomial Distribution

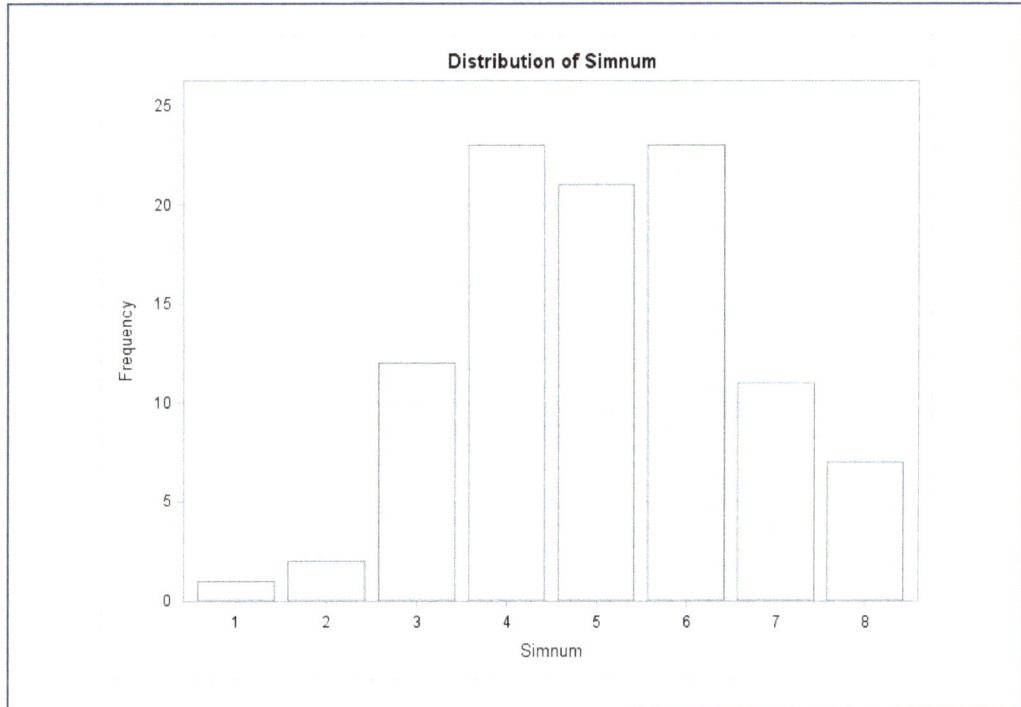

Continuous Distribution

Now let's try to simulate values from a continuous distribution such as the normal distribution. Just like in the case of discrete distribution, we will also need to specify the parameters of the distribution (which in the case of a normal distribution will be the mean and standard deviation) and the number of repetitions. In SAS, the RAND function assumes that the distribution is a standard normal distribution with a mean of 0 and a standard deviation of 1 if both parameters are not specified. Program 4.3 shows the SAS code for simulating 100 observations of a variable from the standard normal distribution using the DATA step. The statistical properties of the simulated series are computed using the UNIVARIATE procedure.

Program 4.3: Simulating Values from the Normal Distribution

```
/*Simulating Data from the Normal Distribution */
data simul3;
      call streaminit(4321);/*Random seed generator*/
```

```
        do i=1 to 100; /*Number of Iteration*/
            Simnum =rand("normal"); /*Invoking the RAND function*/
            output; /*To the values from each iteration*/
        end;
run;

/*Computing Simulation Statistics*/
proc univariate  data=simul3;
        Var  Simnum;
        histogram;
run;
```

Output 4.3: Simulated Values from the Normal Distribution

The UNIVARIATE Procedure
Variable: Simnum

Moments			
N	100	Sum Weights	100
Mean	0.06010182	Sum Observations	6.01018242
Std Deviation	1.05423595	Variance	1.11141343
Skewness	-0.1686229	Kurtosis	0.11904219
Uncorrected SS	110.391153	Corrected SS	110.02993
Coeff Variation	1754.08311	Std Error Mean	0.10542359

Similar to the results obtained from the discrete distribution, the statistics obtained from the empirical distribution are also slightly different from the theoretical distribution due to the relatively low number of repetitions. Let's modify Program 4.3 to explore some practical applications of simulations in investment settings. In the next example, we will simulate the monthly returns on the S&P 500 index. The average monthly return on the S&P 500 is 0.677%, and the standard deviation of monthly returns is 4.47%. We will modify the program by specifying these two statistics in the RAND statement. We will also increase the number of repetitions to 1,000 and compare the empirical distribution of the simulated values to the theoretical normal distribution by invoking the HISTOGRAM statement in PROC UNIVARIATE. We will superimpose the kernel density function of the simulated data on the histogram by specifying the KERNEL option. Note that smoothing the data distribution with a kernel density estimate can be more valuable than using a histogram when exploring the features of the data. This is because the choice of histogram bins or sampling variation could impact how the data is plotted on the histogram. By default, PROC UNIVARIATE uses the approximate mean integrated square error (AMISE) method to compute kernel density estimates.[2]

---

[2] Kernel density and kernel estimation methods will be discussed in more detail in Chapter Six. In the meantime, you can learn more about the kernel density estimation method that is employed in the UNIVARIATE procedure at the SAS® Viya® Platform Programming Documentation for the procedure at https://go.documentation.sas.com/doc/en/pgmsascdc/v_046/procstat/procstat_univariate_details60.htm.

Program 4.4: Simulating S&P 500 Index Returns Using the Normal Distribution

```
/*Simulating S&P 500 Returns Using the Normal Distribution */
/*Specify distribution statistics*/
%let smean=0.0067658;
%let ssd = 0.04465726;

data simul4 (keep=i simnum);
     call streaminit(4321);/*Random seed generator*/
     do i=1 to 1000; /*Number of Iteration*/
          Simnum =rand("normal",&smean,&ssd); /*Invoking the RAND function*/
          output; /*To the values from each iteration*/
     end;
run;

/*Computing Simulation Statistics*/
proc univariate  data=simul4;
     Var  Simnum;
     histogram / normal kernel;
run;
```

Output 4.4: Simulated Values of the S&P 500 Index Returns Using the Normal Distribution

The UNIVARIATE Procedure
Variable: Simnum

Moments

N	1000	Sum Weights	1000
Mean	0.00715585	Sum Observations	7.15584672
Std Deviation	0.04339341	Variance	0.00188299
Skewness	0.10141124	Kurtosis	-0.0915316
Uncorrected SS	1.9323112	Corrected SS	1.88110505
Coeff Variation	606.40497	Std Error Mean	0.00137222

The mean and standard deviation of the simulated values are very close to the mean and standard deviation of the historical monthly returns on the S&P 500. However, looking at the histogram and the plots of the normal and kernel densities, it is apparent that the simulated data is approximately normally distributed and not perfectly normal.

So, what can we learn from this simulation? First, we can see that there is a very low chance of observing absolute monthly returns above 16% in any given month. Second, we can also see that there is a higher probability of obtaining a positive return in a month than the chance of a negative return (in other words, the probability density that we will obtain a positive monthly return on the index is greater than the probability density of observing a negative return). This seemingly mundane statistical fact is actually the basic pillar of why long-term investing is a

Figure 4.3: The Distribution of Simulated S&P 500 Returns

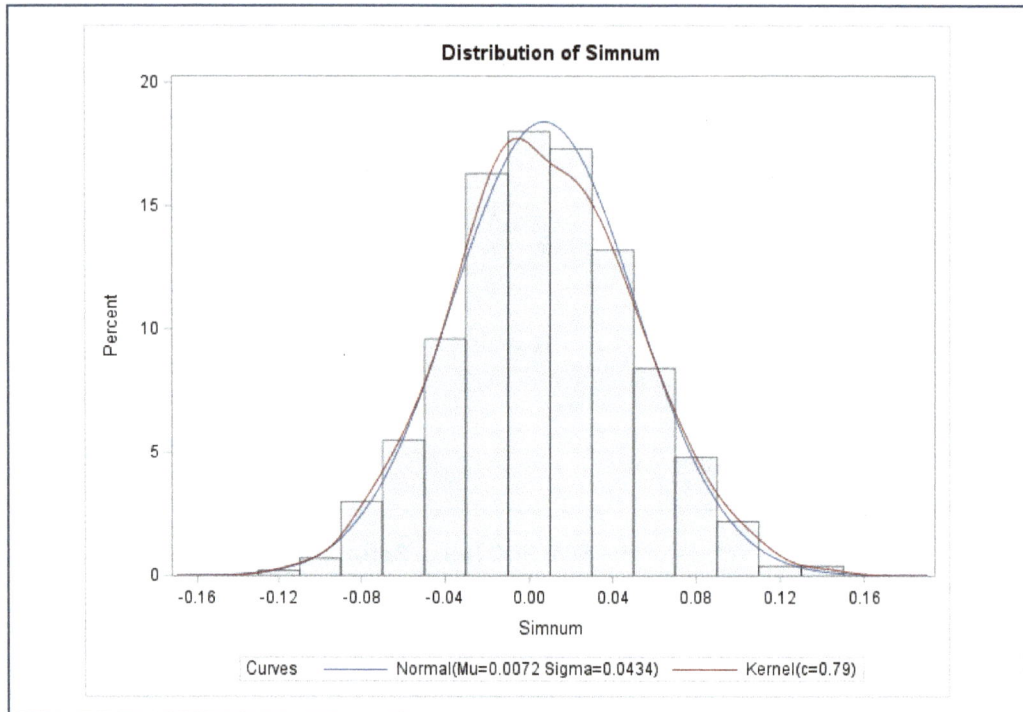

positive sum game. Because there are more positive months than negative months, investors will almost always make money in the long term by holding a broadly diversified portfolio of equities.

Multivariate Distribution

Although simulating multivariate distributions can be done using the DATA step, it is often more efficient to do so using the IML procedure. Rather than using a loop-over-loop approach to simulate the multivariate data using the DATA step, the IML procedure simulates the values for all variables at once as it iterates over successive rows or columns. It is a simpler and computationally more efficient approach to implement than the DATA step.

Let's simulate the monthly returns for two retail stocks (Amazon and Walmart). The correlation between the returns of both stocks is 0.081. Their average monthly returns, as well as their variances and covariance, are shown in Table 4.4 below.

Table 4.4: Descriptive Statistics of the Stock Returns of Amazon and Walmart

		Simple Statistics	
	Variable	**Mean**	**Std Dev**
Amazon Inc.	**AMZN**	0.022	0.111
Walmart Inc.	**WMT**	-0.004	0.051
	Covariance Matrix		
		AMZN	**WMT**
	AMZN	0.0122	0.0005
	WMT	0.0005	0.0026

Before we invoke the IML procedure, let us set the number of repetitions or sample size to 5000. We will also need to specify the vector of mean returns and covariances in matrix form as shown in the program. The RANDNORMAL statement is used by PROC IML to simulate the values from a multivariate normal distribution. The simulated values are stored in the column vector MRET. The means, covariance, and correlations of the simulated stock returns are computed and saved in the SMEAN vector and SVCV matrix, respectively. The first five observations of the MRET vector, as well as the means, covariance, and correlations, are printed using the PRINT statement. The CREATE statement is then used to store the simulated data in the SAS data set named SIMUL5. We then used the SGPLOT procedure to generate a scatter plot of the simulated returns from both stocks from the SIMUL5 data set.

Program 4.5: Simulating Stock Returns from a Multivariate Normal Distribution

```
/*Simulating Stock Returns Using the Multivariate Normal Distribution */
%let n=5000; /*number of repetitions or sample size*/

proc iml;
    mean = {0.0215,-0.0038}; /*Mean Vector*/
    vcv ={0.0122 0.000452,
          0.000452 0.00258}; /*Covariance Matrix*/
    call randseed (4321);
    MRET =RandNormal(&n,mean,vcv); /*Simulate 1000x2 vector*/
    smean =mean(MRET); /*calculate sample mean*/
    svcv = cov(MRET); /*calculate sample covariance*/
    scorr = inv(sqrt(diag(svcv)))*svcv*inv(sqrt(diag(svcv)))/* sample correlation*/
    vname ={"AMZN","WMT"}; /*specify column and row label*/
    print(MRET[1:5,])[colname=vname];
    print(smean)[colname=vname] [label='Sample Mean'];
    print(svcv)[colname=vname rowname=vname] [Label='Sample Covariance'];
    print(scorr)[colname=vname rowname=vname] [Label='Sample Correlations'];
    /*Following step creates a SAS data set
    (simul5) to store the simulated values*/
```

```
        create simul5 from MRET[colname=vname];
        append from MRET;
        close simul5;
quit;

proc sgplot data=simul5;
        inset "Amazon and Walmart"/title="Scatter Plot of Monthly Returns" position=top
        textattrs=(family="Times New Roman" color=darkblue size=12 ) valuealign=center
        titleattrs=(family="Times New Roman" color=darkblue size=12 weight=bold)
        labelalign=center;
        scatter x=amzn y=wmt;
        reg   x=amzn y=wmt/ clm;
        xaxis label= "Amazon Returns" valuesformat= percent8.2 values=(-0.4 to 0.4 by .1);
        yaxis label= "Walmart Returns" valuesformat= percent8.2 values=(-0.2 to 0.2 by .1);
run;
```

Output 4.5A: Simulated Stock Returns from a Multivariate Normal Distribution

AMZN	WMT
0.1585369	-0.025826
-0.090493	0.0269666
-0.014351	-0.092102
-0.053255	-0.117309
0.0645635	-0.017439

Sample Mean	
AMZN	WMT
0.0201859	-0.004194

Sample Covariance		
	AMZN	WMT
AMZN	0.0122789	0.0005187
WMT	0.0005187	0.0025365

Sample Correlations		
	AMZN	WMT
AMZN	1	0.0929504
WMT	0.0929504	1

Output 4.5B: Scatter Plot of Simulated Monthly Stock Returns for Amazon Inc. and Walmart Inc.

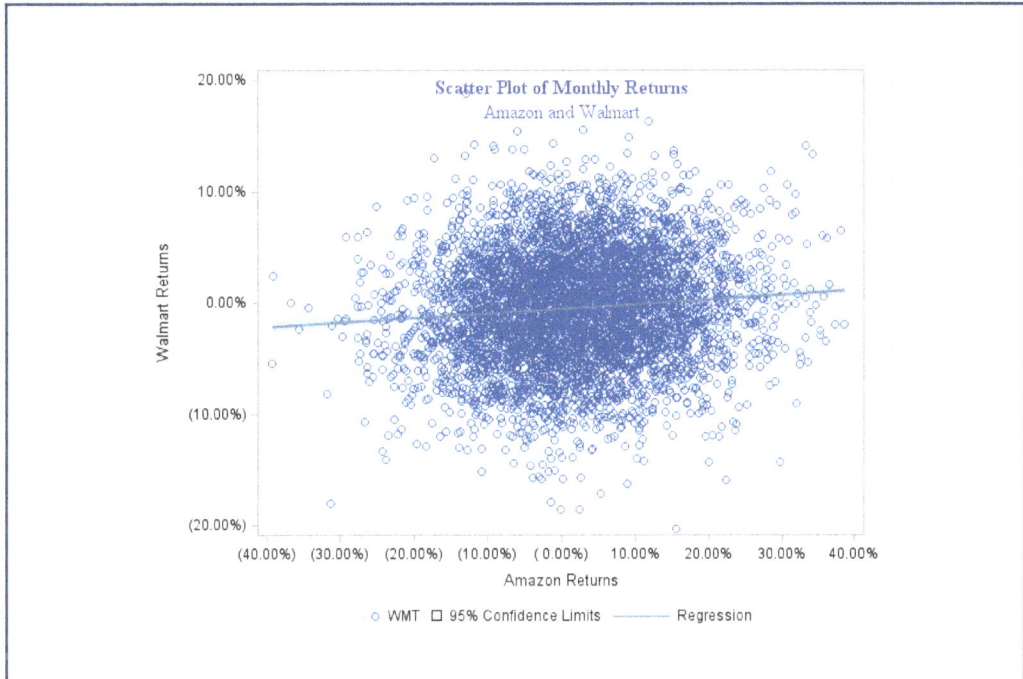

Output 4.5A shows the results from executing the IML procedure. You will observe that the means and covariance matrix of the simulated returns are close to the theoretical values that were used to generate the simulation.

Output 4.5B displays the scatterplot (that was created using PROC SGPLOT) of the simulated returns from both stocks. Although Amazon and Walmart are the two largest retailers in the US, the correlation between their simulated and actual stock returns is actually low as reported in the correlation matrix and displayed on the plot. This could somewhat reflect the differences in their business strategies. Amazon dominates the online space, while Walmart leads in the brick-and-mortar space. Over the years, Amazon has also increased its focus on growing its service sales segment and now generates more revenue from service sales (52.7%) than from product sales (47.3%). In contrast, Walmart generates about 99% of its revenue from product sales.[3]

---

[3] All data reported is based on the 2022 fiscal year ended (Source: Company 10-k).

Stochastic Processes

So far, we have explored examples of static simulation in which time is not considered. However, most financial data are in time series format, and therefore you are more likely to encounter the need to simulate time series data than any other types of data. A common application of probability distributions in finance is to define the characteristics of stochastic or random processes.

A stochastic process describes how a random variable occurs over time. The statistical properties of the common types of stochastic processes are an essential body of knowledge to acquire before proceeding to build simulation models of real-world phenomena or systems, particularly in finance. In Chapter Three, we discussed various statistical properties of time series data such as trends, cyclicality, seasonality, and autocorrelation to name a few. These properties, along with the distributional properties of the data form the basis of the different types of stochastic processes you will encounter in finance. As with distributions, stochastic processes can be in the form of continuous or discrete time processes. A continuous-time random process $X(t)$ is defined as the collection of the realizations $\left\{ X_{t_1}, X_{t_2}, \ldots\ldots X_{t_j} \right\}$ over a fixed time t, where $t \in [0,\infty)$. Here the index variable t are elements of the continuous set of real values as shown below.

$$\left\{ X_t, \ t \in [0,\infty) \right\} \tag{4.3}$$

For example, $X(t)$ can be the collection of stock prices, sampled at time t intervals, which could be in minutes, hours, or daily. Notice that within each interval, there are almost infinitesimal numbers of data points that you can collect, depending on the computational resource available. Although most are familiar with daily stock prices, in reality, stock prices are normally recorded at a much higher frequency than daily.[4]

A discrete-time stochastic process $X(t)$ is such that the realizations $\left\{ X_{t_1}, X_{t_2}, \ldots\ldots X_{t_j} \right\}$ occur over a countable set J where $J = \left\{ t_1, t_2, \ldots.. \right\}$. Here the index variable t are elements of the countable set J as shown below.

$$\left\{ X_t, \ t \in J \right\} \tag{4.4}$$

A discrete-time stochastic process is also known as a sequence of random variables that are sampled at the discrete interval t. In this case, $X(t)$, for example, could be the quantity of a product that is sold by a company during a defined period, such as daily, weekly, monthly, or quarterly. Notice that each of these intervals is a distinct unit of time. It is also possible to discretize continuous-time stochastic processes by increasing the sampling window (such as going from tick-by-tick stock prices to daily prices, which are sampled at the close of each trading day).

---

[4] High frequency stock market data can be in the form of tick-by-tick price or intraday prices that could be in seconds or minutes.

Regardless of whether the stochastic process evolves in a discrete or continuous manner, the common characteristic that these processes share is the elements of uncertainty embedded in how they evolve over time. We will explore these elements and draw upon them in the simulations that we will conduct for stock prices and capital projects in subsequent sections of this chapter. Continuous and discrete-time stochastic processes are broad generalizations of the various types of random processes that are commonly used in finance. In reality, many of these processes have unique characteristics that make them suitable for modeling specific types of phenomena in the finance domain. Examples of a more specific class of stochastic process include: Gaussian, Wiener (Brownian motion), random walk, Itô, Geometric Brownian motion, and mean reverting (Ornstein-Uhlenbeck) processes.

Gaussian Process

Generally, a Gaussian process is a continuous-time stochastic process that displays the properties of the Gaussian distribution. It is a unique process in the sense that it is completely determined by its mean and covariance matrices when sampled over a finite interval. Gaussian processes are commonly known as normal random processes because they share properties of the normal distribution. Indeed, a random process is considered Gaussian (normal) if all realizations of the process are also jointly normal. (In other words, for the interval t, the random variable

$\{X_t, t \in J\}$ follows the Gaussian [normal] process if the realizations of the random variable

$\{X_{t_1}, X_{t_2}, \ldots\ldots X_{t_j}\}$ within the interval are jointly normal.)

It is easy to think of a Gaussian process as any real-world system that evolves in continuous time and follows a normal distribution, for example, logarithmic stock returns. The Gaussian process is the basis of many of the other stochastic processes we will discuss later. They also have a wide range of applications including times series econometric and machine learning.

To simulate values of random variables that follow a Gaussian process, we need to assume that the process is stationary (in other words, the mean and covariances are unaffected by time). Therefore, the mean and covariance are invariant concerning the sampling window. For all values of t, the mean and covariance can be expressed as:

$$E(X_t) = \mu \text{ and } COV(X_t, X_{t+h}) = COV(X_{t+j}, X_{t+h+j}) = \Sigma \qquad (4.5)$$

Consider a standard Gaussian noise process, defined by:

$$X_t = \varepsilon_t \text{ where } \varepsilon_t \sim N(\mu, \sigma^2) \qquad (4.6)$$

Let us assume the mean $\mu = 0$ and variance $\sigma^2 = 1$. Notice that this specification is similar to the properties of a standard normal distribution. This implies that simulating a simple Gaussian process is equivalent to simulating data from a normal distribution with each value having a corresponding time index. The Gaussian noise has many applications in the fields of financial theory, machine learning, and cryptography. High-frequency financial data such as 10-minute intraday foreign exchange returns tend to display significantly higher levels of statistical noise. If we assume that the noise in the stochastic process of the 10-minute US dollar to Euro (USD/EUR) exchange rate is Gaussian as specified in Equation (4.6), we can simulate one week of 10-minute returns of the exchange rate using Program 4.6. From historical data, the average 10-minute return is approximately -0.00066%, while the standard deviation is 0.036%.

In the SAS program, we stored the mean and standard deviation of the exchange rate series in two macrovariables. The FORMAT statement is used to specify the format of the DATE variable that will be generated using the INTNX function. The INTNX function returns an increment of the value of the date, time, or datetime value by a given date, time, or datetime interval. In the function, we specify minutes as the interval frequency, the initial date and time as midnight of January 2nd, 2021, and the interval as 10 minutes. The 10-minute incremental interval in time is generated by the DT+10 formula. There are 1,008 10-minute intervals in a full (seven-day) week. The RAND statement is used to simulate the values of the exchange rate return variable (RETURN) using the simulation parameters. The OUTPUT statement informs SAS to retain the values of the DATE and RETURN variables from each iteration of the simulation. The KEEP statement informs SAS to save only the DATE and RETURN variables in the DATA step. We then used the SGPLOT procedure to plot the simulated data on a series plot.

Program 4.6: Simulating High-Frequency Foreign Exchange Returns

```
/*Simulating 10-minute FX Returns */
data simul6;
%let mu=-0.0000066;
%let sigma=0.003600;
    format Date datetime.;
    keep Date Returns;
    call streaminit(4321);
        InitDate = '2Jan2021:00:00'dt;
        dt=0;
    do i = 1 to 1008;/*Number of 10 mins in one week*/
                dt+10;
                Date=      intnx('minutes',InitDate,dt);
                Returns= rand('normal',&mu,&sigma);
          output;
        end;
 run;
proc sgplot data=simul6;
        inset "USD/EUR Exchange Rate"/title="Simulated Ten-Minutes FX Returns" position=top
            textattrs=(family="Times New Roman" color=darkblue size=12 ) valuealign=center
            titleattrs=(family="Times New Roman" color=darkblue size=12 weight=bold)
            labelalign=center;
        series x=date y=Return;
        xaxis label= "Date" valuesformat= datetime.;
        yaxis label= "Returns" valuesformat= percent8.2 values=(-0.02 to 0.02 by .01);
 run;
```

Output 4.6 displays the simulated values of the USD/EUR exchange returns. Although a cursory glance at the plot appears to suggest that the series is very volatile, in reality, it is more noisy than volatile. That is because a closer examination of the plot shows that 10-minute price changes above 1% are extremely rare in the simulated series.

Output 4.6: Simulated High-Frequency Foreign Exchange Returns

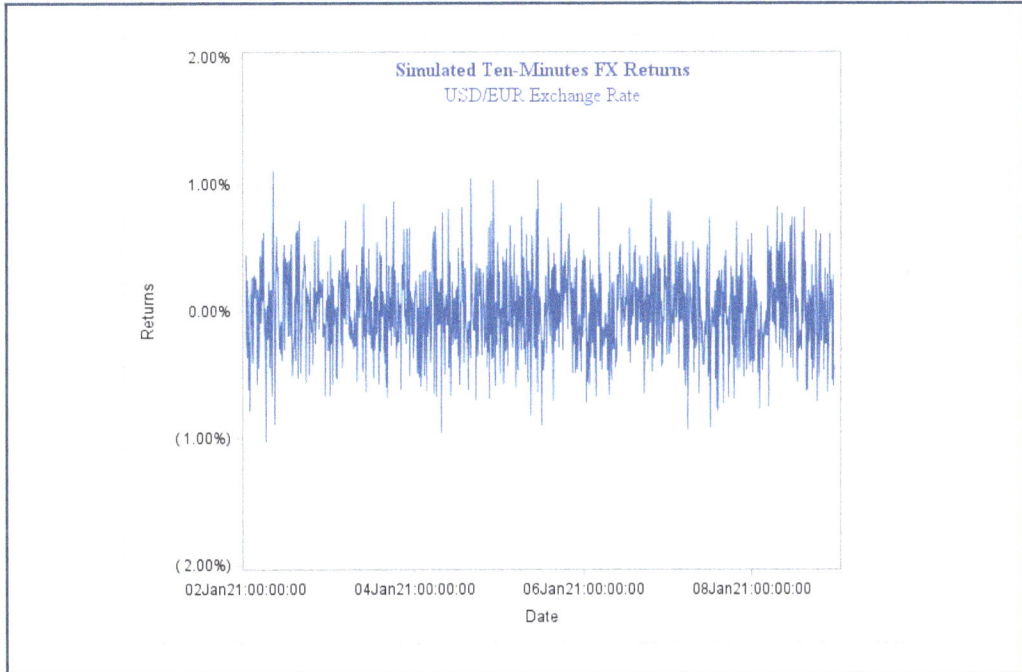

The vast majority of the price movements are very small price corrections that are typical in noisy market data.

Wiener (Brownian Motion) Process

This is a special type of Gaussian stochastic process that has an initial value $W_{t_0} = 0$ and W_t for all $t > 0$ having a stationary independent increment such that for all future realizations of W_t at $\{t_0 < t_1 < t_2 < , ... t_j\}$, the increments $\{W_{t_1} - W_{t_0}, W_{t_2} - W_{t_1}, ..., W_{t_j} - W_{t_{j-1}}\}$ are independent random variables. W_t is also continuous in time t.[5] Drawing from the central limit theorem, for any $t \in [0, \infty)$, as the $t \to \infty$ and the interval between each increment $(t_j - t_{j-s}) \to 0$, the increments $W_{t_j} - W_{t_{j-s}} \sim N(0, t)$ for all s, t ≥ 0.

---

[5] But non-differentiable because it has an infinite number of edges.

An easy way to think about the properties of Brownian motion is that it is a continuous process that consists of independent stationary increments drawn from a normal distribution. Because the increments are stationary, random samples drawn from the process at different equidistant intervals will have the same distributional properties $N(0,t)$, which implies a finite variance.

Other properties of Brownian motion include:

- Markov property: This implies that present and future realizations of the process do not depend on its past outcome. (In other words, suppose $X_t = W_{t_j} - W_{t_{j-s}}$; then X_t is independent of the information set $\Im(s)$[6] that is available at the time t_{j-s}.)
- Martingale property: Drawing from the Markov property, since past information is irrelevant for future outcomes of the process, the expectation of the future outcome is also time irrelevant. Thus, its expected future value $E\left[X_{t+s} \mid \Im(s)\right]$ given the information set available is the same as its current value X_t.

The Brownian motion process is the limit of the more commonly known random walk process. There are also other generalizations of the process such as the Brownian motion with drift and the Geometric Brownian Motion process. It is important to be familiar with this concept because it is the building block for some of the simulations that we will perform in subsequent sections of this chapter. The generalization of the Brownian motion is shown as:

$$dX_t = \mu(X_t)dt + \sigma(X_t)dW_t \tag{4.7}$$

where μ is the drift rate and σ^2 is the variance rate of the process. When $\mu = 0$, the process is generally called a simple Brownian motion process. Equation (4.7) and the other variants of it that we will encounter shortly are commonly known as stochastic differential equations (SDE).[7] You should note that Equation (4.7) describes the change in the values of X_t within a time interval, which is usually ($t-1$ to t). The actual values of X_t at each point in time can be derived by computing the integral of the SDE over a window of time.

Random Walk Process

The discrete version of the Brownian motion process is commonly known as the random walk with drift and is shown as:

$$\Delta X_t = \mu(X_t)\Delta t + \sigma(X_t)\sqrt{\Delta t} \tag{4.8}$$

Because the expected value of the Brownian motion component of the process is zero, the expected value of the process with the drift component is $E(\Delta X) = \mu \Delta t$, while the variance is $\sigma^2 \Delta t$. The main characteristic of the random walk with drift process is the presence of

---

[6] The information set is the information available from observing the process all up to time t.
[7] That is, the SDE is a differential equation that consists of one or more stochastic components.

both deterministic trend and stochastic trend components. Furthermore, the stochastic trend component is changing in magnitude irregularly. Notice that Equation (4.7) describes the rate of changes in the values of the underlying variable and not the levels of the variables, which we can infer from the changes. One way to think of the drift component is that it is the long-term effect of some underlying factor on the stochastic process. In the context of stock price movement, a random walk with a drift price process implies that the best forecast of tomorrow's stock price is today's stock price plus a drift term.

You should note that there is also a pure random walk process, in which there is no drift. In this case, the best forecast of tomorrow's price will simply be today's price as shown in Equation (4.9) below.

$$X_{t+1} = X_t + \varepsilon_{t+1} \qquad\qquad (4.9)$$

Equation (4.9) can also be written in a discretized SDE form as $\Delta X_t = \sigma\left(X_t\right)\sqrt{\Delta t}$.

Simulating Random Walk Returns

The Random Walk Hypothesis is one of the seminal theories in finance. It states that stock market prices evolve according to a random walk (no discernible pattern over time). Therefore, stock market returns or (price changes) are random in nature and consequently unpredictable. The motivation for this theory is that if market actors are rational wealth maximizers, any discernible pattern of price movement will be quickly arbitraged away, leaving only the undiscernible sequence of price movements in the dynamics of stock prices. Other seminal theories such as the Efficient Market Hypothesis and the Adaptive Market Hypothesis build upon the Random Walk Hypothesis.

Let us simulate how stock market returns will behave if it indeed follows a random walk process. We will assume that stock prices evolve according to the specification in Equation (4.8) with a drift rate $\mu = 0$ and variance rate $\sigma^2 = 0.001$. We also assume that the time interval $\Delta t = 1$. We will use both the DATA step and the IML procedure to simulate the random walk stock return data and perform some comparisons at the end of the simulations. Program 4.7A shows the code used in the DATA step approach, while Program 4.7B shows the code used in the IML approach. Concerning the DATA step approach, the difference between the Gaussian return simulation and the random walk simulation is the inclusion of the drift rate in the specification. This is because we are simulating a special case of the random walk that is called the Gaussian Random Walk. However, unlike the Gaussian process, the Gaussian Random Walk is not weakly stationary in the sense that the mean and autocovariance of the process are not constant over time.[8] The trend component of the process is evident in the graph shown in Output 4.7.

Program 4.7A: Simulating Stock Returns with Random Walk Properties (Using DATA Step)

```
/*Simulating Random Walk Returns */
/************Data Step***********/
%let n=100;
%let sigma=0.001;
%let mu=0;

data simul7A;
        format Date datetime.;
        keep Date ret Err;
        call streaminit(4321);
        InitDate = '2Jan2021:00:00'dt;
        dt=0;
        Ret=&mu;

        do i = 1 to &n;
                dt+1;
                Date=      intnx('minutes',InitDate,dt);/*Simulating Date variable*/
                Err= (rand("normal",&mu,&sigma)); /*Simulating Gaussian Errors*/
                Ret = Ret+err; /*Cumulating Values Over time*/
                output;
        end;
run;

proc sgplot data=simul7A;
        inset "DATA Step"/title="Series Plot of Random Walk with Drift" position=top
        textattrs=(family="Times New Roman" color=darkblue size=12 ) valuealign=center
        titleattrs=(family="Times New Roman" color=darkblue size=12 weight=bold)
        labelalign=center;
        series x=date y=Ret;
        xaxis label= "Date" valuesformat= datetime.;
        yaxis label= "FX Returns" valuesformat= percent8.2 values=(-0.04 to 0.04 by .01);
run;
```

---

[8] Weak stationarity implies that the mean and autocovariance of the process do not vary as we shift the window of time (i.e., both measures are time invariant such that when computed over the same intervals at the different points in time, you will obtain the same values for the mean and autocovariances of the stochastic process).

Program 4.7B: Simulating Stock Returns with Random Walk Properties (Using PROC IML)

```
/*Simulating Random Walk Returns */
/************IML Procedure************/
%let N=100;
%let sigma=0.001;
%let mu=0;

proc iml;
      Rt =j(&n,2,.);
      xj= j(&n,1,.);
      InitDate = '2Jan2021:00:00'dt; /*Initial Date*/
      call randseed(4321);
      call randgen(xj,"Normal",&mu,&sigma);
      Rt[,2]=xj;
      Rt[,2]=cusum(Rt[,2]); /*Cumulating Values over time*/
      dt=0;

      do i = 1 to &n;
            dt=dt+1;
            Rt[i,1]=intnx('minutes',InitDate,dt);/*Simulating Date variable*/
      end;

      vname ={"Date" "Ret"}; /*specify column and row label*/
      create simul7B from Rt[colname=vname];
      append from Rt;
      close simul7B;
quit;

proc sgplot data=simul7B;
      inset "PROC IML"/title="Series Plot of Random Walk with Drift" position=top
      textattrs=(family="Times New Roman" color=darkblue size=12 ) valuealign=center
      titleattrs=(family="Times New Roman" color=darkblue size=12 weight=bold)
      labelalign=center;
      series x=date y=Ret;
      xaxis label= "Date" valuesformat= datetime.;
      yaxis label= "FX Returns" valuesformat= percent8.2 values=(-0.04 to 0.04 by .01);
run;
```

In the IML approach shown in Program 4.7B, we first created two vectors (RT and XJ). RT is a $(n \times 2)$ vector, while XJ is a $(n \times 1)$ vector. We used the XJ vector to collect the simulated values of the stochastic component of the process. We then stored XJ in the second column of RT. We reserved the first column of RT for the DATE variable, which was generated using the INTNX function as shown in the subsequent lines of code. We also used the CUMSUM function to accumulate the simulated values of the return series in the RT vector. We then saved the elements of RT in the SIMUL7B SAS data set using the CREATE statement.

Output 4.7: Comparing Random Walk Returns from DATA Step and PROC IML

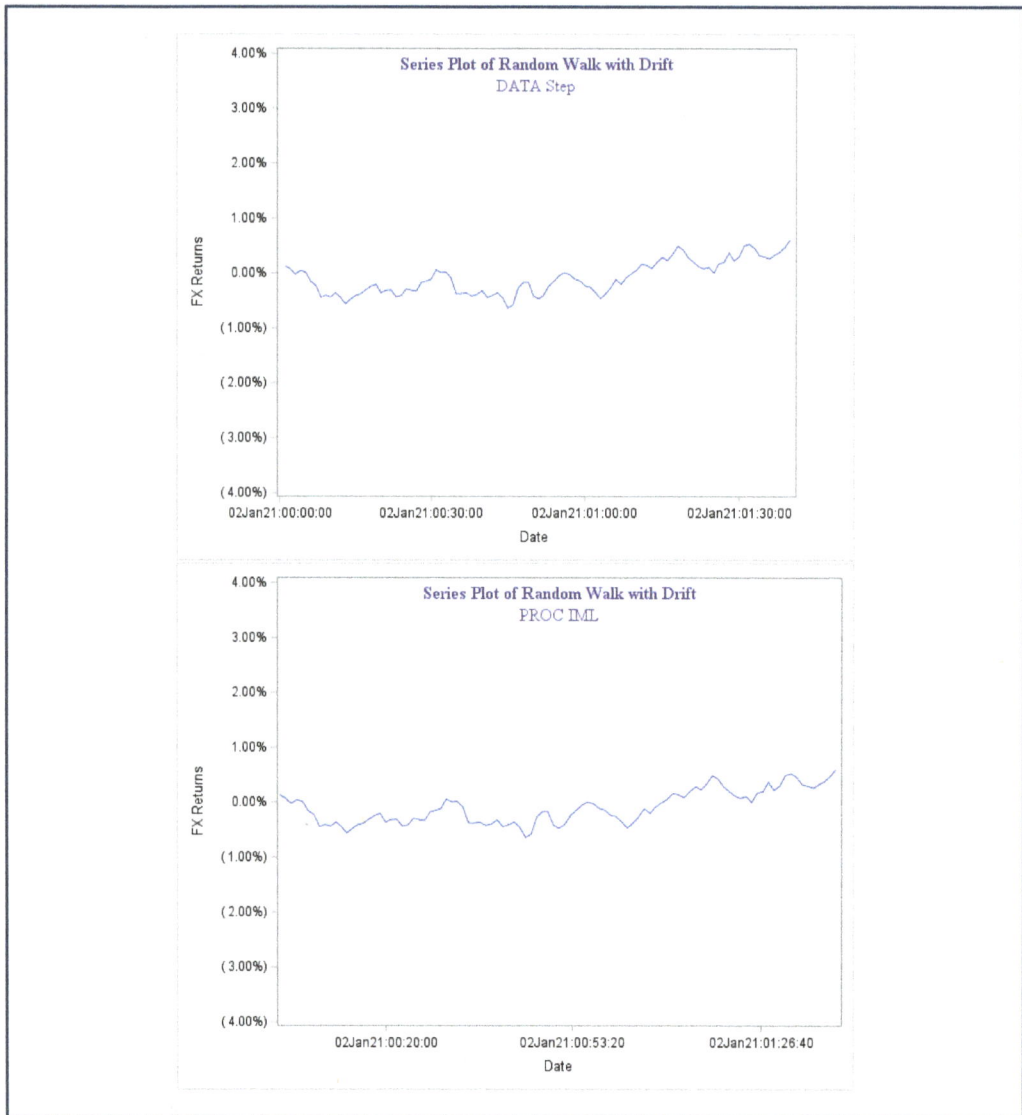

To ensure that the simulated values from both approaches are as close as possible, the same random seed values are called up in both the DATA step and IML procedure. Notice that the graphs of the simulated random walk series using both the DATA step and the IML procedure, which are shown in Output 4.7, are essentially the same.

Table 4.5: Descriptive Statistics of the Stochastic Component of Random Walk Simulations

Basic Statistical Measures			
Location		**Variability**	
Mean	0.000	Std Deviation	0.001
Median	0.000	Variance	0.000
Mode	.	Range	0.006
		Interquartile Range	0.001

Tests for Location: Mu0=0				
Test	**Statistic**		**p Value**	
Student's t	t	0.570	Pr > |t|	0.570
Sign	M	5.000	Pr >= |M|	0.368
Signed Rank	S	212.000	Pr >= |S|	0.469

In Equation (4.8), we learned that the expected value of the random walk with the drift component is $E(\Delta X_t) = \mu(X_t)\Delta t$, while the variance is $Var(\Delta X_t) = \sigma^2(X_t)\Delta t$. Since $\Delta t = 1$, then $E(\Delta X_t) = \mu(X_t)$ (drift rate) and $Var(\Delta X_t) = \sigma^2$ (variance rate). We can generate descriptive statistics from the simulated data by invoking PROC UNIVARIATE. The results from the code are shown in Table 4.5.

The mean of the simulated random component of the returns data is approximately zero, while the standard deviation is approximately 0.001. Both values are the same as the theoretical values that were used to simulate the data. Indeed, the p-values of the test that the mean is equal to zero indicate that the mean of the simulated series is statistically not different from zero. Although we obtained the same values in this run, it is important to note that simulations do not provide exact solutions – they provide approximate or best-case solutions given multiple runs of the system as shown in Programs 4.1 and 4.2. We will explore other examples of simulations with multiple trials in subsequent sections of the chapter.

Itô Process

Another generalization of the Brownian motion is the Itô process, which can be written in the SDE form[9] as:

$$dX = \mu(X,t)dt + \sigma(X,t)dW_t \tag{4.10}$$

---

[9] The Itô process can also be written in the integral form as $X_t = X_0 + \int_0^t \mu(X_t,t)dt + \int_0^t \sigma(X_t,t)dW_t$.

In this process, the drift rate $\mu(X,t)$ and variance rate $\sigma(X,t)$ are not constant. They are functions of X and t, so they require a special computational rule that is known as Itô's lemma to derive their solutions. The discrete version of the process is written as:

$$\Delta X = \mu(X,t)\Delta t + \sigma(X,t)\sqrt{\Delta t} \qquad (4.11)$$

It is easier to think of the Itô process as one in which the mean and variance are also time-dependent. Therefore, as the window of time increases, so does the mean and the variance of the process. In reality, the Itô process is a broad framework for many stochastic processes that you will come across. Notice that the Brownian motion process is a special case of the Itô process, in which the drift rate is not time-dependent.

Geometric Brownian Motion

Drawing on the Itô process, we can derive a more practical finance application of the Brownian motion process by introducing the Geometric Brownian motion (GBM) process, which is written as:

$$\frac{dS}{S} = \mu(S,t)dt + \sigma(S,t)dW_t \qquad (4.12)$$

In the GBM process, the drift rate function $\mu(S,t)$ is specified as a function of the asset price $S: \mu(S,t) = \mu S$ and the variance rate $\sigma^2(S,t)$, which takes the form: $\sigma^2(S,t) = \sigma^2 S^2$

The specification above implies that both the drift and variance rates are time-invariant but dependent on the magnitude of prices. The discrete version of the process is specified as:

$$\frac{\Delta S_t}{S_t} = \mu\Delta t + \sigma\sqrt{\Delta t}, \qquad (4.13)$$

$$\frac{\Delta S_t}{S_t} = \frac{S_t - S_t}{S_t} \qquad (4.14)$$

Equations (4.13) and (4.14) are the specifications for the well-known holding period return formula. In effect, Equations (4.12) to (4.14) are used extensively in finance for asset pricing and portfolio management. This includes the pricing of stocks and portfolios of stocks (such as index portfolios), options, futures, forwards, and swaps. In this chapter, we will explore its application for asset pricing and for studying the behavior of financial assets over time.

Stock Price and Geometric Brownian Motion

In the previous chapter, we introduced the concept of logarithmic returns for stock prices. The use of the log return of stock prices is based on the notion that stock prices are lognormally distributed. Thus, if we substitute for S with $\log(S_t)$ in Equation (4.12) and apply Itô's lemma. The GBM process for the log of stock prices can be written as:

$$d \log(S_t) = \left(\mu - \frac{\sigma^2}{2} \right) dt + \sigma dW_t \qquad (4.15)$$

The GBM process for $\log(S_t)$ follows the generalized Brownian motion process, with drift rate $\mu - \dfrac{\sigma^2}{2}$ and variance rate σ^2. The discrete version of the process is written as:

$$\Delta \log(S_t) = \left(\mu - \frac{\sigma^2}{2} \right) \Delta t + \sigma \sqrt{\Delta t} \qquad (4.16)$$

For $\Delta t = T$, $\Delta \log(S_t) = \log(S_T) - \log(S_0)$ is normally distributed and defined as:

$$\log(S_T) - \log(S_0) \sim N\left(\left(\mu - \frac{\sigma^2}{2} \right) T, \sigma\sqrt{T} \right) \qquad (4.17)$$

It also follows that.

$$\log(S_T) \sim N\left(\log(S_0) + \left(\mu - \frac{\sigma^2}{2} \right) T, \sigma\sqrt{T} \right) \qquad (4.18)$$

From all the above, we can calculate the expected value and variance of S_T at any time as follows.

$$E(S_T) = S_0 \exp\left(\mu - \frac{\sigma^2}{2} \right) T \qquad (4.19)$$

$$Var(S_T) = S_0^2 \exp\left(2\mu T + \sigma^2 T \right)\left(\exp\left(2\sigma^2 T \right) - 1 \right) \qquad (4.20)$$

Simulating Stock Prices Using Geometric Brownian Motion

In Chapter One, we presented a simulation of the monthly returns of the S&P 500 index under the assumption that the index returns follow a Gaussian random walk process. In this chapter, we will extend the scope of Program 1.10 to allow for drift in the returns and to simulate prices from the return series. We will rely on Equation (4.16) to build our index price simulation. If we assume that $\Delta t = 1$, we can write Equation (4.16) as follows:

$$S_t = S_{t-1} \exp\left(\mu - \frac{\sigma^2}{2} \right)\Delta t + \sigma\sqrt{\Delta t} \qquad (4.21)$$

where $\left(\mu - \dfrac{\sigma^2}{2} \right)\Delta t$ and $\sigma\sqrt{\Delta t}$ are the deterministic and stochastic components of returns, respectively.

From Chapter One, we know that the average monthly return μ and standard deviation σ of the returns on the S&P 500 over approximately four hundred and fifty-seven months are 0.677% and 4.466%, respectively. To simulate future prices of the index, we also need a reference price of the index to use as the initial price S_0. Let us use the price of the index (3,756.07) on December 31st, 2020, as the initial price. Using these values along with the assumptions that the sample path of stock prices follows the GBM and that stock prices are log-normally distributed, we can simulate the sample path of the index for the next 24 months by using the SAS code in Program 4.8.

Program 4.8: Simulating the Sample Path for the S&P 500 Index

```
/*Simulating the Sample Path for S&P 500 Index*/
%let smean=0.0067658;/*Mean Return*/
%let ssd = 0.04465726;/*Standard Deviation of Returns*/
%let inprice=3756.07; /*Initial Index Level*/

data simul8;
      format Date monyy.;
      keep Date Fmret Sumret Price;
      call streaminit(4321);
      InitDate = '2Jan2021'd;
      Sumret=&smean-&ssd *0.5;
      do iter=1 to 24; /*number of replication*/
            Date=intnx('month',InitDate,dt,'end');/*Simulating Dates*/
            Fmret =rand("normal",&smean,&ssd);/*Simulating Monthly Returns*/
            Sumret =sumret+fmret; /*Cumulating the returns*/
            Price =&inprice*exp(sumret);/*Continuously compounded Prices*/
            dt+1;
            output;
      end;
```

```
        label
                Fmret='Simulated Monthly Returns'
                Price = 'Simulated Monthly Index Level'
                Sumret = 'Cumulative Monthly Returns';
run;

proc sgplot data=simul8;
        inset "January 2021 to December 2022"
                /title="Simulated Values of S&P 500" position=top
        textattrs=(family="Times New Roman" color=darkblue size=12 ) valuealign=center
        titleattrs=(family="Times New Roman" color=darkblue size=12 weight=bold)
         labelalign=center;
        series x=date y=Price;
        series x=date y=fmret/ y2axis;
        xaxis label="Date" valuesformat= monyy. values=('31Jan21'D to '31Dec22'D by month);
        yaxis  valuesformat= best8.2 values=(1000 to 6500 by 500);
        y2axis valuesformat= percent8.2 values=(-0.1 to 0.4 by .1);
run;
```

In Table 4.6, we report some descriptive statistics from the simulated monthly levels and returns for the index. We also compare the statistics obtained from the simulated series with the actual values obtained for the index in the corresponding months. In Output 4.8, we show the series plot of the simulated prices and returns of the S&P 500 index.

First, the simulation suggests that the index will end lower in December 2022, which is indeed what happened. However, most of the values derived from the simulation for each of the months in the 24-month windows did not match the actual values obtained. It is important to reiterate that simulations are approximate solutions or best guesses of what will happen; they are unlikely to yield precise estimates of what will exactly happen to the phenomena that are being simulated. From a decision-making point of view, simulations are still very helpful in the sense that they are informed estimates of how the system will behave.

So far, we have simulated a single sample path for the index over the 24-month window. In a subsequent section, we will explore how to include additional robustness into our simulation by simulating multiple paths for the index and then analyzing the characteristics of the paths to predict the most likely path to be followed by the index over the 24-month period.

Table 4.6: Descriptive Statistics from S&P 500 Index Simulations

	Prices			Returns		
	Min	**Max**	**Ending**	**Min**	**Max**	**Ending**
Simulated	3,136.98	3,935.28	3,611.58	-9.09%	6.22%	1.74%
Month	**Jan-22**	**Jan-21**	**Dec-22**	**Aug-21**	**Jan-21**	**Dec-22**
Actual	4,515.55	3,714.24	3,839.50	2.86%	-1.12%	-6.08%

Output 4.8: Simulated Return and Price Path for the S&P 500 Index

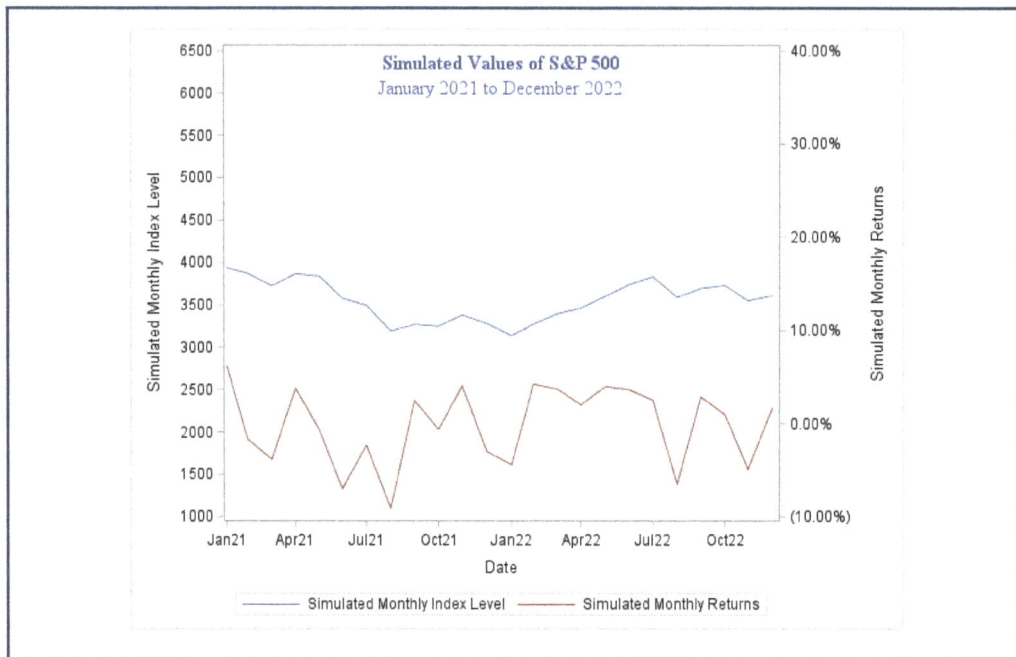

Mean Reverting (Ornstein-Uhlenbeck) Process

Ornstein-Uhlenbeck (OU) stochastic processes share similar properties with the Brownian motion process, such as stationarity, Markovian, and continuous probability. They differ from the Brownian motion process because they tend to rise when their realizations are below their mean and fall when they are above their mean. OU processes can also be considered as the continuous-time equivalent of the random walk model, in which the sample path tends to converge back to the center as more realizations deviate away from it. The farther the realizations occur from the center, the stronger the pull that exists to push future realizations back to the center. The mathematical generalization of the OU process is expressed as:

$$dX_t = \theta\left(\mu(X_t) - X_t\right)dt + \sigma(X_t)dW_t \tag{4.22}$$

where θ, $\mu(X_t)$, and $\sigma(X_t)$ are known constants. θ is the speed of the reversion, $\mu(X_t)$ and $\sigma(X_t)$ are the drift and variance rates, respectively. Removing (X_t) reference from the constants and solving the stochastic differential equation for X_t, also by applying Itô's lemma yields:

$$X_t = X_0 \exp(-\theta t) + \mu\left(1 - \exp(-\theta t)\right) + \sigma\int_0^t \exp\left(-\theta(t-s)\right)dW_s \tag{4.23}$$

The mean of the process is:

$$E[X_t] = X_0 \exp(-\theta t) + \mu(1 - \exp(-\theta t)) \tag{4.24}$$

While the variance of the process is:

$$Var(X_t) = E\left[\left(\exp(-\theta t)\int_0^t \sigma \exp(-\theta s) dW_s\right)^2\right] = \frac{\sigma^2}{2\theta}(1 - \exp(-2\theta t)) \tag{4.25}$$

Therefore $(X_t \mid X_0) \sim N\left(\mu + (X_0 - \mu)\exp(-\theta t), \frac{\sigma^2}{2\theta}(1 - \exp(-2\theta t))\right)$. The discrete version

of the process using the Euler-Maruyama Method can also be written as:

$$X_{t+1} = X_t + \theta(\mu - X_t)\Delta t + \sigma(X_t)\sqrt{\Delta t} \tag{4.26}$$

Despite the mathematically rigorous construct above, the OU process can be viewed as the continuous time limit of an *AR(1)* process for X_{t+1} as $\Delta t = 1$ and is written as:

$$X_{t+1} = \alpha + \beta X_t + \sigma \varepsilon_t \tag{4.27}$$

where $\alpha = \theta\mu$, $\beta = (1-\theta)$ and $\varepsilon_t \sim N(0,1)$. Thus, an OU process can be simulated either as a special case of an *AR(1)* process using Equation (4.27) or as a numerical solution to Equation (4.23).

There are various applications of the OU process in finance. These include interest rate and exchange rate modeling, bond pricing, volatility modeling, and pricing of interest rate contingent claims.

Simulating an Ornstein-Uhlenbeck Process

Let's use the OU process to simulate one year of daily values of the Chicago Board Options Exchange Volatility (VIX) index. The VIX index is a measure of the 30-day expected volatility of the S&P 500 Index. The VIX, which is also sometimes called the "fear index" is calculated from the near-term volatility implied by the prices of options on the S&P 500 index. Although the average level of the VIX index is 17.00%, with a standard deviation of 7.12%, since we are simulating an *AR(1)* process, we will need to derive the parameters of the simulation from an *AR(1)* model of the actual series. The SAS data set named VIX contains ten years of daily data for the VIX of various asset classes and equity indices. First, we will use the data to estimate an ARIMA(0,1,0) model of daily VIX for the S&P 500 index to derive the parameters for our simulation. The result of the ARIMA estimation is shown in Table 4.7.

Table 4.7: Estimation Results from PROC ARIMA with *AR(1)* for the VIX Index

Conditional Least Squares Estimation					
Parameter	Estimate	Standard Error	t Value	Approx Pr > |t|	Lag
MU (α)	13.8262	2.04144	6.77	<.0001	0
AR1,1 (β)	0.97559	0.0074283	131.33	<.0001	1

Constant Estimate	0.337506	
Variance Estimate	5.821609	
Std Error Estimate	2.412801	(σ)
AIC	4638.247	
SBC	4648.079	
Number of Residuals	1008	

As shown in the table, the unconditional mean of the VIX index from our sample period is 13.83%, while the autoregressive coefficient is 0.976. The standard error of the model, which is our σ, is 2.413. We will use these values, along with the RANDGEN function in PROC IML, to simulate the daily values of the VIX index as shown in Program 4.9A. We set the model parameters and the number of days to simulate to 364, using the macrovariables that we specified at the beginning of the program. Dates are simulated using the INTNX function. The CREATE statement is then used to save the simulated series in the SIMUL9A data set, which is then plotted using the SGPLOT procedure.

Program 4.9A: Simulating the Ornstein-Uhlenbeck Process for CBOE VIX Index (Numerical Approach)

```
/*Simulating Daily CBOE VIX Index Ornstein-Uhlenbeck Process*/
/*Numerical Solution*/
%let N=364;
%let sigma=2.412801;
%let alpha=13.8262;
%let beta=0.97559;
```

```
proc iml;
      X0=0;
      theta=1-&beta; /*Theta is calculated from beta*/
      mu=&alpha/theta; /*Mu is calculated from regression alpha called */
      xj= j(&n,1,.); /*vector random variables*/
      Volt=j(&n,1,0); /*Interest rate vector*/
      Vol=j(&n,2,&mu); /*Vector to merge simulate rates and date*/
      InitDate = '1jan2021'd; /*Initial Date*/
      call randseed(4321);
      call randgen(xj,"Normal");
      Volt=X0*exp(-theta)+mu*(1-exp(-theta))+&sigma*exp(-2*theta)*xj;
      Vol[,2]=Volt;
      dt=0;

      do i = 1 to &n;
            dt=dt+1;
            Vol[i,1]=intnx('day',InitDate,dt);/*Simulating Date variable*/
      end;
vname ={"Date" "VIX"}; /*specify column and row label*/
create simul9A from Vol[colname=vname];
append from Vol;
close simul9A;
quit;
proc sgplot data=simul9A;
      inset "Ornstein-Uhlenbeck Process -Numerical Approach"/title="Simulating CBOE
        Volatility (VIX) Index" position=top
      textattrs=(family="Times New Roman" color=darkblue size=12 ) valuealign=center
      titleattrs=(family="Times New Roman" color=darkblue size=12 weight=bold)
        labelalign=center;
      series x=date y=VIX;
      xaxis label= "Date" valuesformat=mmddyy10. values=('2jan21'd to '31dec21'd by
        month) interval=day;
      yaxis label= "Volatility" valuesformat= best8.2 values=(0 to 30 by 5);
run;
```

We can also show that the OU process is indeed analogous to the *AR(1)* model by simulating the same series using the *AR(1)* model of the volatility series as shown in Program 4.9B.

Program 4.9B: Simulating AR(1) Process for CBOE VIX Index

```
/*Simulating Daily CBOE Volatility (VIX) Index Using AR(1) Model*/
%let N=364;
%let sigma=2.412801;
%let mu=13.8262;
%let beta=0.97559;
```

```
proc iml;
      xj= j(&n,1,.); /*vector random variables*/
      Volt=j(&n,1,0); /*Interest rate vector*/
      Vol=j(&n,2,&mu); /*Vector to merge simulate rates and date*/
      InitDate = '1jan2021'd; /*Initial Date*/
      call randseed(4321);
      call randgen(xj,"Normal");
      Volt=&mu+&beta*lag(Volt)+&sigma*xj;
      Vol[,2]=Volt;
      dt=0;

      do i = 1 to &n;
            dt=dt+1;
            Vol[i,1]=intnx('day',InitDate,dt);/*Simulating Date variable*/
      end;

      vname ={"Date" "VIX"}; /*specify column and row label*/
      create simul9B from Vol[colname=vname];
      append from Vol;
      close simul9B;
quit;

proc sgplot data=simul9B;
      inset "Discretized OU Process - AR(1)"/title="Simulating CBOE Volatility (VIX)
      Index" position=top
      textattrs=(family="Times New Roman" color=darkblue size=12 ) valuealign=center
      titleattrs=(family="Times New Roman" color=darkblue size=12 weight=bold)
       labelalign=center;
      series x=date y=VIX;
      xaxis label= "Date" valuesformat=mmddyy10. values=('2jan21'd to '31dec21'd by
      month) interval=day;
      yaxis label= "Volatility" valuesformat= best8.2 values=(0 to 30 by 5);
   run;
```

Notice that the main difference between the code for the simulations shown in Program 4.9A and 4.9B is the formulas for computing the daily values of the VIX index. In Program 4.9A, the volatility variable (VOLT) was computed using the specification shown in Equation (4.24), while in Program 4.9B, the same variable was computed using the much simpler *AR(1)* expression shown in Equation (4.27). Nevertheless, the graphs of both series, which are shown in Output 4.9, show a remarkable equivalence between the values of the variables that were obtained from both methods. You can also observe the mean reversion pattern in the simulated VIX index series on both graphs. Periods with higher-than-normal volatility (which are more prevalent in the series) are followed by a downward trend to the mean, while periods with lower-than-normal volatility are followed by an upward trend to the mean.

Output 4.9: Comparing the Simulated Ornstein-Uhlenbeck Process for CBOE VIX Index (Numerical and Discrete Approaches)

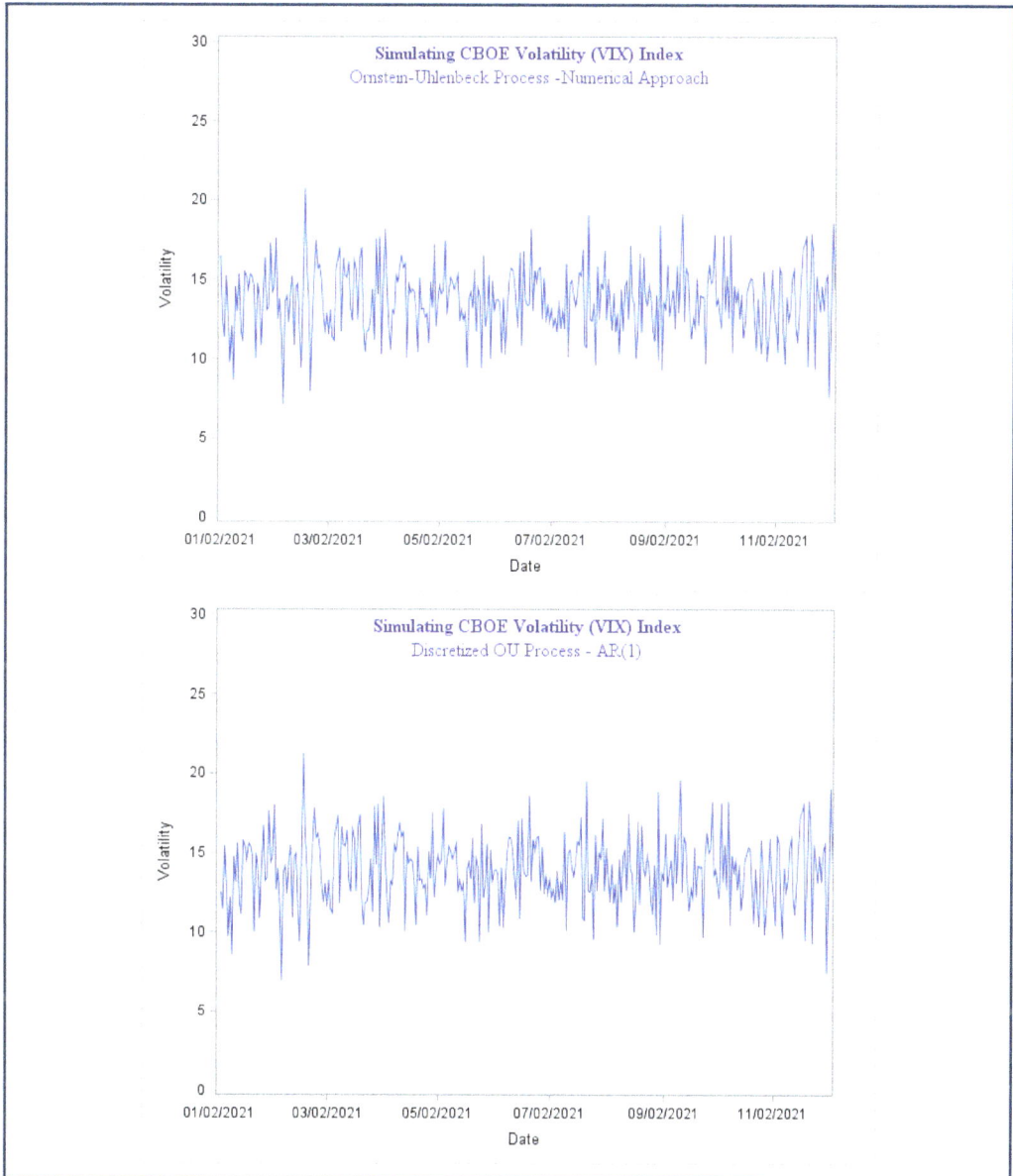

Monte Carlo Simulation

The term Monte Carlo Simulation applies to a general class of computational methods for solving probabilistic problems using numerical approximations. The general idea behind the approach is to use repeated samples of the population to approximate some distributional properties of the population.

Making deductions about the future sample path for the S&P 500 using the simulation of a single path alone is probably not a prudent idea. A better approach is to rely on the application of the law of large numbers (LLN), which states that the distribution of large samples that are independent and identically distributed tends to converge to the distribution of the underlying population. Thus, the average results that are drawn from the collections of large samples of random variables should be approximately the same as those of the underlying distribution. In Programs 4.1 and 4.2, we present the SAS code that was used to simulate values from the Bernoulli and binomial (with one trial) distributions, which are analogous to a coin flip. Notice that in both simulations, we did not obtain 50-50 percent outcomes for both 1 and 0 in 100 trials, although the simulated outcomes were drawn from a 50-50 theoretical probability distribution. If we apply the LLN to both simulations by increasing the number of trials to 1,000, we will get a 49.1-50.9% outcome for 1 and 0. If we continue to increase the number of trials until we get to 5 million, we will eventually get a 50%-50% outcome for 1 and 0, which is the same as the theoretical probability of the outcomes.

Monte Carlo simulations rely upon this remarkable property of the LLN to draw deductions about the behavior of real-world occurrences by simulating multiple samples of the phenomena and analyzing their probability distribution. Another way to think of the Monte Carlo simulation approach is that it uses a large sample of independently drawn random variables from the same probability distribution as the underlying real-world phenomenon to estimate the most likely value of the real-world phenomena. Such real-world phenomena in finance include stock prices, portfolio outcomes, capital project outcomes, and risk outcomes.

Monte Carlo Simulation of Stock Prices

Given what we now know about the benefits of the Monte Carlo simulation, let us revisit our simulation of the sample path for the S&P 500 index. In our previous program, we simulated a single sample path. Our Monte Carlo extension to the SAS code creates an outer loop that will allow us to replicate the sample path n number of times. The optimal number of sample paths to simulate is determined by the Central Limit Theorem, which states that as the sample size becomes increasingly larger, the distribution of the sample means will be approximately normal

$\bar{X} \sim N\left(\mu, \dfrac{\sigma^2}{n}\right)$. The distributions of the sum of the samples will also be approximately normal

$\sum X \sim N\left(n\mu, n\sigma^2\right)$. The optimal number of repetitions n is the value that generates the best possible convergence between the sample statistics and the unknown real-world characteristics that we are simulating, given the computational resources at our disposal. Going by LLN, we also know that the properties of this distribution will be the same as the real-world occurrence that we are simulating. Hence, our best estimate of each month's return and stock price will be the mean of all the returns and prices simulated for that month.

Program 4.10 shows the SAS code that implements the Monte Carlo simulation of the sample path for the S&P 500 index. To create our 1,000 sample paths, we created an outer DO loop around the code for the single price path simulation shown in Program 4.8. Each path is delineated by the SAMPLEID variable, which stores the index of each iteration of the outer loop. In essence, we are simulating 1,000 values of each month of the S&P 500 index levels from its returns. We also include the code for the SGPLOT procedure that was used to plot 1,000 simulated sample paths. Notice in the SERIES statement that SAMPLEID was specified as the GROUP variable for invoking the plots of each series.

Program 4.10: Simulating the Sample Paths for the S&P 500 Index Using the Monte Carlo Approach

```
%let /*Montecarlo Simulation of S&P 500 Levels*/
%let smean=0.0067658;
%let ssd = 0.04465726;
%let inprice=3756.07;
%let nreps=1000;/*number of repetitions*/

data simul10;
      format Date monyy.;
      keep Date sampleID Fmret Sumret Price;
      InitDate = '2Jan2021'd;
      Sumret=&smean-&ssd *0.5;

      do sampleID=1 to &nreps;
            do iter=1 to 24; /*number of replication*/
                  Date=intnx('month',InitDate,dt,'end');/*Simulating Dates*/
                  Fmret =rand("normal",&smean,&ssd);/*Simulating Monthly Returns*/
                  Sumret =sumret+fmret; /*Cumulating the returns*/
                  Price =&inprice*exp(sumret);/*Continuously compounded Prices*/
                  dt+1;
                  output;
            end;

            dt=0;
            sumret=0;
      end;

      label
            Fmret='Simulated Monthly Returns'
            Price = 'Simulated Monthly Index Level'
            Sumret = 'Cumulative Monthly Returns'
            sampleID = 'Sample ID';
run;
```

```
/*Graphing Simulated SP500 Levels*/
proc sgplot data=simul10;
       inset "January 2021 to December 2022"
       /title="Monte Carlo Simulation of S&P 500 Index Levels" position=top
       textattrs=(family="Times New Roman" color=darkblue size=12 ) valuealign=center;
       series x=Date y=Price / group=SampleID;
       xaxis grid;
       yaxis grid values=(2000 to 9000 by 1000);
       ;
run;
```

Output 4.10: Simulated Sample Paths for the S&P 500 Index Using the Monte Carlo Approach

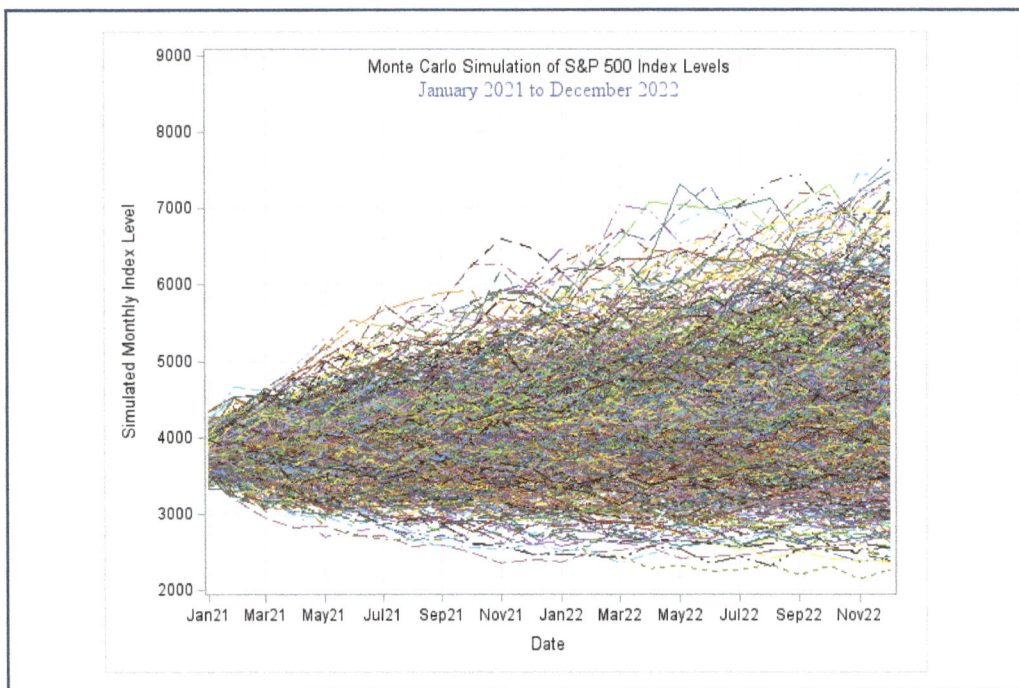

Output 4.10 shows the plots of the simulated 1,000 sample paths for the index. A quick scan of the plotted sample paths suggests that the index is unlikely to end above 6,000 or below 3,000 on December 31st, 2022. The bulk of the paths appear to converge around the 4,000 regions. From an investment decision-making point of view, we can see that the likelihood of obtaining a portfolio performance from a long position in the index over the two-year forecast period that is above 60% (above 6,000) or below -20% (below 3,000) is very low.

We can obtain the average path of the index over the 24 months and distribution statistics of the final value of the index on December 31st, 2022, by implementing the SAS code shown in Program 4.11. In the SAS code, we first sort the data by the date variable using the SORT procedure. We then compute the average simulated price for each month. The values of the average prices are then plotted on the series plot using the SGPLOT procedure. We used the MEANS procedure to compute the statistics of the simulated value of the index on the final month by including the (WHERE=(DATE='31DEC22'D)) option in the PROC MEANS statement.

Program 4.11: Calculating the Average Path of the S&P 500 Index

```
/*Calculating Average Path of the S&P 500 Index*/
proc sort data=simul10 out=ssimul10;
      by Date;
run;

proc means data=ssimul10 mean noprint;
      by date;
      var price;
      output out=out_simul10 mean=Price;
run;

proc sgplot data=out_simul10;
      inset "Average Path from January 2021 to December 2022"
      /title="Monte Carlo Simulation of S&P 500 Index Levels" position=top
      textattrs=(family="Times New Roman" color=darkblue size=12 ) valuealign=center;
      series x=Date y=Price;
      xaxis  grid valuesformat= monyy. values=('31Jan21'D to '31Dec22'D by month);
      yaxis grid values=(2000 to 6000 by 1000);
run;

proc means data=simul10(where=(Date='31Dec22'D))  mean std min max median  p5
      p10 q1 q3 p95 p99 qmethod=os;
      var Price;
run;
```

Output 4.11: Average Path of the S&P 500 Index from Monte Carlo Simulations

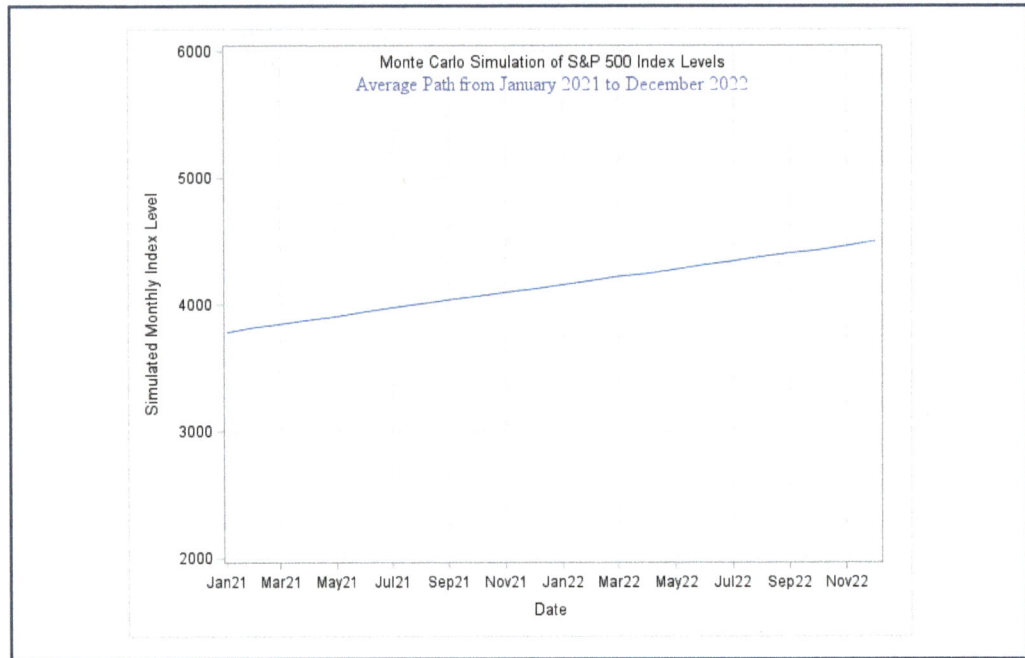

The average forecast we obtained from the simulations suggests that the value of the index will be around 4,500.52 on December 31st, 2022. However, this clearly did not occur. The actual value of the index on December 31st was 3,839.50. Herein lies one of the weaknesses of Monte Carlo and indeed all simulations. In general, simulations are best suited for normal market conditions. They tend to perform poorly in abnormal market conditions such as bear markets, recessions, and during financial crises. In 2022, the US stock market experienced a sustained period of negative returns culminating in an annual return of -19.6 %. Such market conditions are not well-suited for Monte Carlo simulations. There are special types of simulations that rely on Extreme Value Theory and Copulas that examine how financial assets will perform when markets are at an extreme. We will discuss these methods in Chapter Five.

Table 4.8: Descriptive Statistics from the Monte Carlo Simulations S&P 500 Index

Analysis Variable: Price Simulated Monthly Index Level										
Mean	Std Dev	Minimum	Maximum	Median	5th Pctl	10th Pctl	Lower Quartile	Upper Quartile	95th Pctl	99th Pctl
4500.52	977.74	2269.18	7627.03	4422.75	3029.11	3285.32	3797.4	5072.19	6281.63	7151.9

Monte Carlo Simulations for Capital Budgeting

Another common application of Monte Carlo simulation is for capital budgeting analysis. Capital investments are financial outlays by firms in long-term assets. These assets are the primary source of value-adding cash flows to the firm. Indeed, the market value of every capital project undertaken by the firm is theoretically the present value of all future net cash flows that will accrue to the firm as a result of the project.

Not all projects are value-adding; therefore, managers have to be very discerning when assessing which projects to pursue. Most managers select capital projects based on one of the following selection criteria: the net present value of the cash flow (NPV), the internal rate of return (IRR), the payback and discounted payback period (PP), and the profitability index (PI), to name a few.

Since the project decisions that managers are making will have future ramifications for the firm, it is often expedient for them to build additional layers of robustness in the selection criteria that they use for the decision. These additional layers of robustness include sensitivity analysis, scenario analysis, and real options analysis. Sensitivity analysis assesses the impact of one key variable at a time on the project outcome, while scenario analysis assesses the project's outcomes under multiple business environment conditions (typically three: worst-case, base-case, and best-case). In each case, one or more key variables are changed simultaneously. Real options analysis assesses the value and impact of managerial flexibility on the overall project outcome. Such flexibilities might include the option to change the scale, scope, or duration of the project in response to future prevailing conditions.

Sensitivity and scenario analyses usually entail assessing the impact of a limited number of changes to the key variables on the overall project outcome. Monte Carlo simulations are used in capital budgeting to extend our understanding of how far future deviations can be from the forecast of our key variables and how those deviations can impact our estimate of the project's decision criteria. We will start by specifying NPV as our primary investment criterion. The common rule for selecting projects using the NPV is to select all projects that have positive NPV, if there is no funding constraint. NPV is the sum of the present value of all future cash flows created by the project less its acquisition cost. Its general formula is written as:

$$NPV = -C_0 + \sum_{t=1}^{n} \frac{CF_t}{(1+r)^t} \tag{4.28}$$

where C_0 is the project's acquisition cost, CF_t the future cash flows accruing to the project, and r the financial cost of the capital that is used to fund the project.

Capital Budgeting Analysis in SAS

Before we implement the Monte Carlo simulation for capital budgeting, let's explore how we can use SAS for capital budgeting analysis. It turns out that SAS has a large number of built-in finance

Table 4.9: Project Information for NPV Analysis

Year	Cash Flow
0	-$53,000
1	15,800
2	13,100
3	16,700
4	19,700
5	14,300
Required Return	13%

functions.[10] We can build simple and complex financial worksheets using these functions, the DATA step, and SAS procedures such as COMPUTAB.

Let's start with the basic application of the capital budgeting functions in SAS. Suppose we have a five-year project with the cash flows shown in Table 4.9. Let us assess the suitability of the project for investment by computing the NPV and IRR of the project.

Program 4.12 implements a simple capital budgeting analysis in SAS using the DATA step and the built-in finance function for NPV and IRR. The project cash flows are stored in the CAPBUD1 data sets. The computation of the NPV and IRR are also done in the DATA step and stored within the same CAPBUD1 data set. By customizing our PROC PRINT statement, we highlight the computed values separately from the input value.

Program 4.12: Using SAS for Basic Capital Budgeting Calculations

```
/*Calculating NPV and IRR Using SAS*/
data capbud1;
      format CF0 nlmny12.2  CF1 nlmny12.2 CF2 nlmny12.2
             CF3 nlmny12.2 CF4 nlmny12.2 CF5 nlmny12.2 Rate percent8.2;
      Rate=0.13;
      CF0=-53000;
      CF1=15800;
      CF2=13100;
      CF3=16700;
      CF4=19700;
      CF5=14300;
      NPV=finance('npv',rate,cf1,cf2,cf3,cf4,cf5)+cf0;
      IRR=finance('irr',cf0,cf1,cf2,cf3,cf4,cf5);
      format NPV nlmny12.2 IRR percent8.2;
run;
```

---

[10] To see all of the built-in finance functions in SAS visit the FINANCE function page on in SAS® 9.4 and SAS® Viya® 3.5 Programming Documentation.

```
title 'Capital Expenditure Worksheet';

proc print data=capbud1 noobs;
     var CF0 CF1 CF2 CF3 CF4 CF5 Rate;
     var NPV IRR/style(data)={just=l fontweight=bold };
run;

title;
```

The output of the SAS code, which is shown in Output 4.12, indicates that our sample project will be value-adding, due to its positive NPV ($2,659.31) and IRR (15.0%) that is greater than its cost of capital (Rate).

Output 4.12: Capital Expenditure Worksheet

Capital Expenditure Worksheet

CF0	CF1	CF2	CF3	CF4	CF5	Rate	NPV	IRR
($53,000.00)	$15,800.00	$13,100.00	$16,700.00	$19,700.00	$14,300.00	13.00%	**$2,659.31**	**15.00%**

Program 4.12 used a simple cash flow problem to showcase some finance functions in SAS. Now let us build a more sophisticated capital budgeting problem in SAS using the DATA step and the COMPUTAB procedure. We will then write a SAS macro to combine the two SAS statements into n number of loops to create our Monte Carlo simulation. By doing this, we are better able to examine the scope of the deviations from the forecasted cash flows.

Capital Project Problem

Suppose the managers of ABA Manufacturing Inc. are analyzing a potential capital project. The project will have a 4-year tax life, with an initial cost of $5,245,000. The project will be depreciated using straight-line depreciation to zero over the 4-year life. The asset will have no residual value at the end of the project. The project will require an initial investment of $132,000 in working capital, subsequent years' working capital requirement will be 2% of annual sales. The company's corporate income tax rate is 21%, and the required rate of return on the project is 12.3%. The company expects to sell 120,000 units of the products in the first year at $35 per unit and raise the price each year by about 5%. The variable cost per unit of product is $12. The company expects this cost to grow by 3% each year. The general administrative expenses for the four years are expected to be approximately $550,000 per year. A summary of the project estimates is shown in Table 4.10.

Before we invoke PROC COMPUTAB, our first task is to place the project information in a SAS data set, which can then be called up in PROC COMPUTAB to create the capital budget worksheet. The SAS code for this step is shown in Program 4.13A.

Table 4.10: Project Information for NPV Analysis (ABA Manufacturing Inc.)

Project Information	Amount
Initial Cost	$5,245,000
Tax Life	4
Selling Price/Unit	$35
Variable Cost / Unit	$12
Fixed Cost	$550,000
Initial Working Capital	$132,400
Annual Working Capital/Sales Ratio	2%
Required Rate of Return	12.3%
Tax Rate	21%
# of Items Sold	120,000.00

Program 4.13A: Storing Key Project Data Using the DATA Step

```
/*Capital Budgeting Worksheet in SAS*/
/*Storing Key Project Info in Dataset*/
data pinfo;
     IC=   5245000;
     TL= 4;
     SPU= 35;
     CPU= 12;
     FC=   550000;
     NWC= 132400;
     RR=   0.123;
     TR=   0.21;
     QTY  = 120000;
run;
```

Creating a complex capital budgeting worksheet using PROC COMPUTAB involves two steps. In the first step, we will define the columns (years) and rows (income statement and cash flow statement items, and decision criteria). This is then followed by populating the cells with the appropriate calculations (for example, *revenue = quantity sold x sales price per unit*). The cash flow statement that we construct in this example is different from the statement of cash flows that are typically found in financial statements (sources and uses of cash). The cash flows that are estimated for capital project analysis are the cash that is theoretically available for distribution to the firm's investors (free cash flow). It is calculated as:

$$CF_t = OCF_t - CAPEX_t - WCR_t$$

(4.29)

where OCF_t which is calculated as $OCF_t = EBIT_t - Taxes_t + Depreciation_t$ is the operating cash flow. $CAPEX_t$ which can be calculated as the change in the values of the gross fixed asset $\left(CAPEX_t = \Delta Gross\_Fixed\_Asset_t \right)$ is the annual capital expenditure required for the project, and WCR_t which is calculated as the change in network capital $\left(\Delta NWC \right)$ is the short-term capital requirement to close the gap between when cash is expended and received by the firm during the operating year. Given these inputs, it is straightforward to think of free cash flow $\left(CF_t \right)$ as the cash that a firm can distribute to its investors after it has met all its operational and investing obligations. In capital budgeting settings, cash flow worksheets are normally built using inputs obtained from the pro forma income statement and balance sheet. They could also be forecasted directly, but the former approach (which we will show shortly) provides higher precision and more granularity on the project's key variables.

Program 4.13B: Using PROC COMPUTAB for Capital Budgeting Analysis

```
/*Creating Capital Budget Worksheet Using PROC COMPUTAB*/
title 'ABA Manufacturing Inc.';
title2 'Capital Expenditure Worksheet ';

proc computab data=pinfo out=capbud2;
      col YR0 YR1 YR2 YR3 YR4 /'Year' f=10.2;
      col  YR0/ 'Zero' zero=' ';
      col  YR1/ 'One';
      col  YR2/ 'Two';
      col  YR3/ 'Three';
      col  YR4/ 'Four';

      /*Defining Pro-forma Income Statement Items*/
      row Rev /'Income Statement' 'Sales' format= nlmny16.2;
      row COGS /'Cost of Sales'  format= nlmny16.2;
      row GP  /'Gross Profit' dol ul format= nlmny16.2;
      row DP /'Depreciation' format= nlmny16.2;
      row SGA  /'General Expense' ul format= nlmny16.2;
      row EBT /'Taxable Income' ul format= nlmny16.2;
      row Tax  / 'Taxes'  format= nlmny16.2;
      row NI  /'Net Income' dol dul format= nlmny16.2 skip;

      /*Defining Cash Flow Worksheet Items*/
      row OCF /' '
             'Cash Flow Estimation:'
             'Project Cash Flows' 'Operating Cash Flow' format= nlmny16.2;
      row CAPEX /'Capital Expenditure'  format= nlmny16.2 zero=' ';
      row WCR /'Working Capital Requirement'  format= nlmny16.2  zero=' ';
      row CF/ 'Net Project Cash Flow' dol dul format= nlmny16.2 skip;
```

```
      /*Defining Decision Criteria*/
      row NPV /' '
            'NPV Calculation:'
            'Net Present Value' format= nlmny16.2 zero=' ';
      row IRR/'Internal Rate of Return'  LJC format=percent8.2 zero=' ';

      /*Populating Income Statement Items with Values*/
colcalc:

      /*Revenue of 5% per year and cost increase of 3%*/
      if REV then do;
            YR1=QTY*SPU;
            YR2=YR1*1.05;
            YR3=YR2*1.05;
            YR4=YR3*1.05;
      end;

      if COGS then do;
            YR1=QTY*CPU;
            YR2=YR1*1.03;
            YR3=YR2*1.03;
            YR4=YR3*1.03;
      end;
rowcalc:

      if  _COL_>1  then do
            GP=REV-COGS; /*Gross Profit*/
            DP = IC/TL;  /*Annual Depreciation*/
            SGA = FC;    /*Selling and General Administrative*/
            EBT = GP-DP-SGA; /*Taxable Income*/
            TAX =TR*EBT;             /*Income Taxes*/
            NI = EBT-TAX;   /* Net Income*/

            /*Cash Flow Begins Here*/
CashFlows:
            OCF = EBT+DP-TAX; /*Can also be NI+DP*/
            WCR = 0.02*Rev;
      end;

      /*Controls to enter only values for initial date*/
      if _col_=1 then do;

            /*Initial CAPEX and WCR*/
            CAPEX = ic;
            WCR =NWC;
      end;

      CF = OCF-CAPEX-WCR;

      /*Decision Critieria*/
Decisions:
      npv=cf;
      irr=cf;
```

```
colcalc2:
    if npv then do;
            tempnpv =finance('npv',rr,yr1, yr2, yr3, yr4)+yr0;
            yr0=tempnpv;
            yr1=0;  yr2=0; yr3=0; yr4=0;

    end;

    if IRR then do;
            tempirr =finance('irr',yr0, yr1, yr2, yr3, yr4);
            yr0=tempirr;
            yr1=0;  yr2=0; yr3=0; yr4=0;
    end;
run;

title;
title2;
```

Program 4.13B shows the SAS code for the COMPUTAB procedure. The code begins by invoking the procedure and specifying the input data set (PINFO) and output data set (CAPBUD2). Next, the five columns that represent the project years are defined using the COL statements. Then, each row and its labels and formats in the pro-forma income statement are defined using the ROW statements. Next, the rows for the cash flow table are also defined. The rows for computing the NPV and IRR are then defined.

The column block calculation statements are used to specify the formula for calculating the row values of the elements of each column that depend on other columns. For example, Year 1 revenue is calculated as the quantity of unit sold (QTY) times the sales price per unit (SPU), while Year 2 to Year 4 revenues are compounded from previous years (column) revenue using a 5% growth rate. The row calculation block statement is used to specify the row calculations that depend on other rows. For example, the gross profit row (GP) is computed from the sales (REV) and cost of goods sold (COGS) rows.

The IF statements are used to control when and where in each column and row calculations should be performed. For example, the IF REV statement instructs SAS to perform the revenue calculation described above only on the revenue line item on the Pro forma income statement, while the IF _COL_=1 statement instructs SAS to record the capital expenditure (CAPEX) and working capital requirement (WCR) of $5,245,000 and $132,400 respectively into the Year 0 column only. Notice the subsequent years' WCRs are calculated as 2% of the annual revenue for that year. The annual free cash flows for each period are computed using the specification in Equation (4.29). The NPV and IRR of the projects are computed using the built-in FINANCE function in SAS. The computation for both criteria is first done using the temporary variables TEMPNPV and TEMPIRR. The values of the computation are then recorded in the desired rows and columns using the IF programming statement.

The results obtained from invoking the COMPUTAB procedure are shown in Output 4.13. The proforma financial statements show a project that is generally profitable and cash flow rich due to its high annual depreciation charge (a noncash expense that is added back to operating cash flow). The $1.01 million NPV and 20.79% IRR both suggest that the project should be accepted. It is important to note here that the proforma income statement and cash flow statement are forecasts of future financial outcomes that are due to the project under scrutiny. However, before committing the firm to a significant cash outlay, it is probably worthwhile to examine the impact of deviations in one or more variables on our NPV and IRR. Concerning these variables, an important question to ask is what values of these variables are the firm most likely to see once the project is implemented.

Output 4.13: Capital Expenditure Worksheet from PROC COMPUTAB

ABA Manufacturing Inc.
Capital Expenditure Worksheet

	Year Zero	Year One	Year Two	Year Three	Year Four
Income Statement					
Sales		$4,200,000.00	$4,410,000.00	$4,630,500.00	$4,862,025.00
Cost of Sales		$1,440,000.00	$1,483,200.00	$1,527,696.00	$1,573,526.88
Gross Profit		$2,760,000.00	$2,926,800.00	$3,102,804.00	$3,288,498.12
Depreciation		$1,311,250.00	$1,311,250.00	$1,311,250.00	$1,311,250.00
General Expense		$550,000.00	$550,000.00	$550,000.00	$550,000.00
Taxable Income		$898,750.00	$1,065,550.00	$1,241,554.00	$1,427,248.12
Taxes		$188,737.50	$223,765.50	$260,726.34	$299,722.11
Net Income		$710,012.50	$841,784.50	$980,827.66	$1,127,526.01
Cash Flow Estimation:					
Project Cash Flows					
Operating Cash Flow		$2,021,262.50	$2,153,034.50	$2,292,077.66	$2,438,776.01
Capital Expenditure	$5,245,000.00				
Working Capital Requirement	$132,400.00	$84,000.00	$88,200.00	$92,610.00	$97,240.50
Net Project Cash Flow	($5,377,400.00)	$1,937,262.50	$2,064,834.50	$2,199,467.66	$2,341,535.51
NPV Calculation:					
Net Present Value	$1,010,243.46				
Internal Rate of Return	20.69%				

To answer this question, we will bring to bear the power of the Monte Carlo simulation. Before we create the simulation, we will need to select which variable to anchor our simulation on. Firms that operate in commoditized markets are price takers but can adjust their output levels to market conditions. For these firms, prices are more random than production levels. Firms with pricing power are more likely to see randomness in the number of products or services purchased by customers. We will assume that ABA Manufacturing falls in the latter category. Hence, we will anchor our simulation on randomness in the quantity of the product the firm will sell in the first year.

To extend Program 4.13B for Monte Carlo simulations, we will rely on a simple SAS programming trick, which is to build a macro wrapper around the program. The macro wrapper will create a program loop, which will rerun the SAS code in the DATA step and PROC COMPUTAB statement for the number of trials in the Monte Carlo simulation. For each iteration, the macro stores the simulated values of the quantity sold, NPV, and IRR in the SIMUL11 SAS data set by invoking the PROC APPEND statement. The SIMUL11 data set can then be analyzed using any of the descriptive statistics procedures in SAS. Due to the large number of computations and the results that will be created, it is probably a good idea to suppress the printing of the results from each iteration by specifying the NOPRINT option in the PROC COMPUTAB statement.

Program 4.14: Using SAS to Implement Monte Carlo Simulation for Capital Investment Analysis

```
/*SAS Macro to Implement Monte Carlo Simulation of Capital Budgeting*/
%macro capsimul(nrep); /*specify number of reps*/
       proc datasets nodetails nolist;
              delete simul11;
       run;

       %local  i nrep; /*local macro variable*/

       %do i=1 %to &nrep;

/*******Reused Same Code from Program 4.14****/

data pinfo;

QTY = 12000 *(1+rand("normal",0,0.1)) ;/*simulating quantity sold*/

run;

proc computab data=pinfo out=capbud2 noprint;

/****Reused Code Ends Here***/

       /*Merge project info data with cap budgeting results*/
       data _simul_;
              merge pinfo(keep=QTY) capbud2(obs=1 keep=NPV IRR);
              sampleID=&i;
       label QTY= 'Quantity Sold' NPV='Net Present Value' IRR='Internal Rate of Return';
              format NPV nlmny16.2 QTY best10.2 IRR percent8.2;
       run;

       /*updated table with results from new iteration*/
       proc append base=simul11 data=_simul_ force;
       run;

%end;
%mend;

/*Macro invoked to do 1000 repetitions*/
%capsimul(1000);
proc tabulate data=simul11;
       var qty npv irr;
       table qty*F=bestn10.2 npv*F=dollar15.2 irr*F=percent8.2,(min median mean max  p5
        p10 );
run;
```

Table 4.11: Decision Criteria Results for Project Analysis

Variable	Minimum	Median	Mean	Maximum	5th Pctl	10th Pctl
QTY	86,243.76	120,677.27	120,114.57	159,357.19	100,366.38	104,245.52
NPV	-$921,728	$1,049,006	$1,016,801	$3,262,774	-$113,448	$108,567
IRR	4.11%	21.00%	20.64%	37.94%	11.32%	13.23%

Program 4.14 shows the abbreviated SAS code that was used for the implementation of the Monte Carlo simulation. Most of the code is a repetition of the code in Program 4.13B; therefore, only references to the original code are included to save space.[11] Observe that we have now incorporated randomness in the simulation via the DATA step that was used to create the PINFO data. The quantity sold was simulated from a normal distribution with a mean that is equivalent to the initial value of 120,000 units and a standard deviation that is equal to 10% of the mean quantity sold. The only input required for the CAMPSIMUL macro is the number of trials (NREP) required for the simulation [%macro CAPSIMUL(NREP)]. Notice that a PROC DATASET statement is also included at the beginning of the macro. This will delete the current version of the SIMUL11 data set and replace it with a new version every time the macro is invoked.

To view the descriptive statistics of the simulated data, we invoked the TABULATE procedure. The results obtained for implementing the procedure are shown in Table 4.11.

From the table, we can observe that although the project's average NPV is slightly over one million dollars, it could fall as low as -$922 thousand and be as high as $3.26 million. To give the managers more confidence in the NPV estimate, let's graph the distribution of the simulated NPV using the histogram option in the SGPLOT procedure as shown in Program 4.15.

Program 4.15: Plotting the Distribution of Project's NPV Using PROC SGPLOT

```
/*SAS Code to Graph Project's NPV Distribution*/
proc sgplot data=simul11;
     inset "NPV Distribution (Monte Carlo Simulation)"/title="ABA Manufacturing Inc."
      position=top
     textattrs=(family="Times New Roman" color=darkblue size=12 ) valuealign=center
     titleattrs=(family="Times New Roman" color=darkblue size=12 weight=bold)
     labelalign=center;
     histogram npv / nbins=20 dataskin=matte fill transparency=0.8
     fillattrs=(color=bipb );
     density npv/ legendlabel= "(Normal Density Plot for Project's NPV)";
     yaxis values=(0 to 20 by 2.5);
run;
```

---

[11] The full code is included in accompanying program file to Chapter Four, which can be found in the book's GitHub repository.

The results shown in Table 4.11 and the histogram shown in Output 4.15 imply that in over 90% of the simulation, the project will result in a positive NPV. The company needs to sell approximately 103 thousand units of the product in the first year to realize a positive NPV from the project. Our simulation shows that there is more than a 90% probability that the company will exceed this threshold. Altogether, these statistics should give managers some reassurance to proceed with the project. It is important to reiterate that to go by these numbers, we are assuming historically normal operating conditions during the course of the project. If operating conditions deviate significantly away from historic norms due to unforeseen events such as major economic downturns, natural disasters, health crises, or industry disruption, then there would be a low chance that the simulated project outcomes will manifest during the course of the project.

Output 4.15: Simulated NPV Distributions Using Monte Carlo Approach

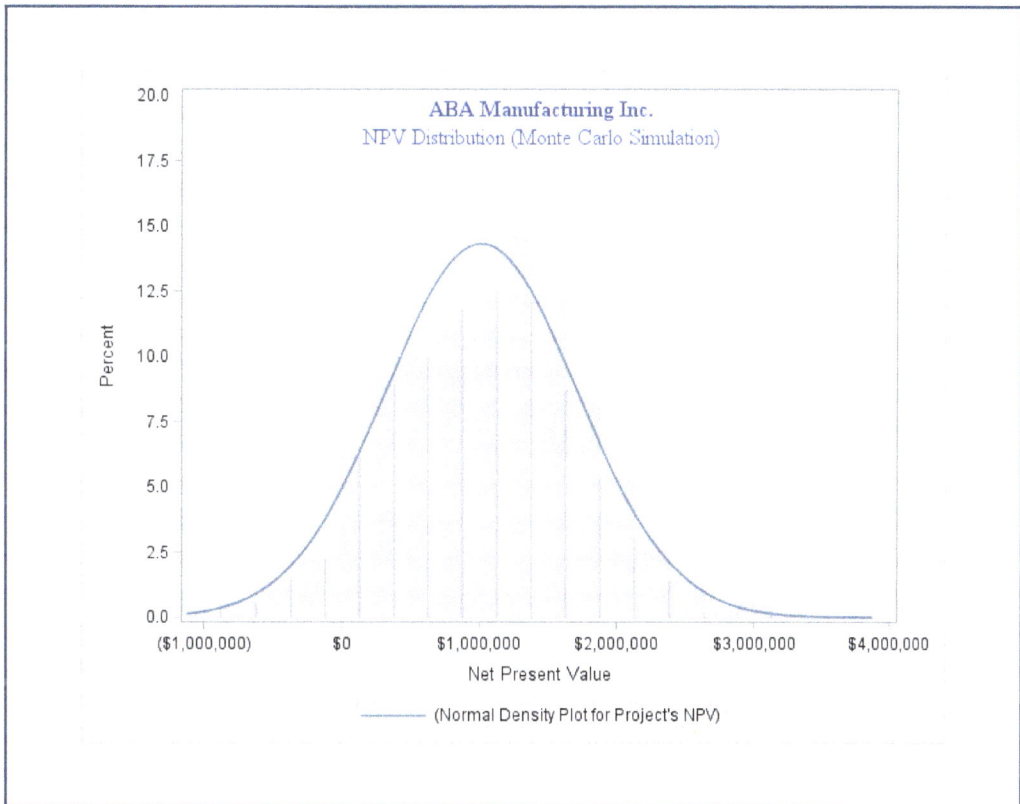

You can build a more robust capital budget worksheet and dashboard using PROC COMPUTAB. The value proposition in such an endeavor will be in the repeated use case. All you would need to generate a worksheet for a new project will be the data set that contains the new project information.

Exercises

1. John would like to play a lottery that involves a simultaneous roll of two six-sided dice. He would win $1,000 if he rolls 3 and 4. Write a SAS program to simulate the dice roll and graph the histogram of the probability of winning the lottery.
   a. In general, what is his chance of rolling the winning combination of numbers in one trial?
   b. In general, what is his chance of rolling the winning combination of numbers in 10 trials?
   c. Do his odds of winning improve if he plays the game 100 times?

   > **Hint:** There is a menu option to implement this in SAS Studio (Combinatoric and Probability).

2. The SAS data set SPX_Daily contains the daily levels and returns on the S&P 500 index.
   a. Write a SAS program to fit the normal distribution to the daily returns (DRET) on the index.
   b. Write a SAS program to simulate 1000 daily returns using the parameters that you estimated from Part A. Use a random seed value of 54321.
   c. Compare the distribution of the actual daily returns to the distribution of the simulated data using the UNIVARIATE procedure.
      i. Is the mean and standard deviation of the simulated data the same as the actual data?
      ii. Is the shape of the simulated data the same as the actual data?
      iii. What does the result imply about the normality of daily stock returns?
   d. Write a SAS program to draw the histogram of the monthly index returns (SPX_RET). Compare the histogram for daily returns to the monthly returns.
      i. Does sampling frequency have any impact on the distribution of S&P 500 returns?
      ii. Do investors face more risk from investing in the index on a daily basis versus a monthly basis? What could explain the differences between outcomes?

3. Write a SAS program to extract the daily returns on the S&P 500 from 01/02/2012 to 12/31/2021 from the SPX_Daily data.
   a. Write a SAS program to calculate the mean and standard of daily returns for the 10-year period.
   b. Write a SAS program to simulate 1,000 sample paths for one year of daily index prices. Use a random seed value of 54321. (This program will use a lot of computer resources.)

   > **Hint:** Modify Program 4.10 to convert the frequency of the simulation to daily. Set the date frequency to day or week using the following code:
   > ```
   > Date=intnx('weekday',InitDate,dt,'end')
   > ```

   c. Use the SGPLOT procedure to graph the 1,000-sample path. Set the Date on the X axis and Index Level on the Y axis. (This program will use a lot of computer resources).

    i. What is the highest simulated value of the index at the end of the year? How likely are you to obtain this result in the real world (what probability is the simulation estimating for this value)?

    ii. What is the lowest simulated value of the index at the end of the year, and how likely are you to obtain this result in the real world (what probability is the model estimating for this value)?

    iii. What is the most likely value of the stock at the end of the year? Support your answer with the appropriate statistics.

    iv. Compare your results to the actual value of the index on December 31st, 2022. How close is your simulated value to the actual value? What could explain the difference between the actual and the simulated values?

4. Sims Energy is evaluating a potential gas field development project. The company estimates that the gas field will have a four-year operational and tax life. The company expects to spend $33.2 million to acquire and develop the field. The gas field along with the associated equipment that will be used to extract the gas will be depreciated using straight-line depreciation to zero over the four-year life when the company expects the gas reserves in the field would be completely depleted. Due to the associated cost of cleanup and restoration, the company does not expect any additional cash flow from the disposal of the field at the end of the project (in other words, the asset will have no residual value at the end of the project). The project will require an initial investment of $322,000 in working capital, and the subsequent years' additional working capital requirement will be 2% of the total annual production cost. The company's corporate income tax rate is 21%, and the required rate of return on the project is 11.3%. The company expects to produce 10 billion cubic feet (10 million MCF) of natural gas in the first year. It expects the yield to decline by 20% each year until the end of the project. Natural gas is a commodity, so the company is a price taker. The current price of natural gas is $2.40 per 1000 cubic feet (1 MCF) of gas, and the unit cost of producing the same cubic feet is about $0.40. The fixed operating cost of the field is expected to be approximately $933,000 per year. A summary of the project estimates is shown in the table below.

Table 4.12: Project Information for NPV Analysis (Sims Energy Corp.)

Project Information	Amount
Initial Cost	$33,322,000
Tax Life	4
Price/1000 CCF	$2.40
Cost /1000 CCF	$0.40
Fixed Operating Cost	$933,000
Initial Working Capital	$322,000
Annual Working Capital/Production Ratio	2%
Required Rate of Return	11.3%
Tax Rate	21%
Initial Production Capacity	10,000,000.00 MCF

a. Write a SAS program to save all the project information in a data set called SIMINF.
b. Write a SAS program to create the capital budgeting worksheet for Sims Energy using PROC COMPUTAB. On the worksheet, show the pro-forma income statement and cash flow statement for the project. Save the output in a data set called SIMPROJ.
   i. What financial trends do you observe in terms of the revenue, cost, profitability, and cash flow for the project?
   ii. What are the major sources of cash for the project?
   iii. What are the NPV and IRR of the project?

> **Hint:** Modify Program 4.14 Pay attention to references to the data set. The names of data sets are not same. You might need to create a row in the income statement for output levels. They will not be same in every year.

c. Prices of natural gas are determined in the financial market. Over the past five years, the average price of natural gas was $2.856 per 1,000 CCF with a standard deviation of $0.6413. Use this information to write a SAS macro to implement a Monte Carlo simulation that would examine the impact of volatility in natural gas prices on the project's financial viability. Use 1000 replications. Set each year's natural gas prices to fluctuate independently of other years (that is, simulate prices for each operating year separately).
   i. How high and low could gas prices fluctuate during the life of the project?
   ii. What are the average net income and cash flow from the simulation?
   iii. What are the maximum and minimum NPVs and IRRs that you obtained from the simulation?
   iv. What is the most likely NPV and IRR from the NPV?

> **Hint:** Modify Program 4.15. Pay attention to the references to the data set. The names of data sets are not same. You will create a new row from price levels. They will not be the same in all years now that you have to simulate each one separately.

d. Given all that you now know about the project, should the company still proceed with it? What macroeconomic, demographic, social, and technological trends should the company also consider besides the worksheet and simulation results?

Chapter 5: Using Simulations for Risk Management

Using Simulations for Risk Management

Financial risk management is the practice of identifying, analyzing, assessing, and responding strategically to randomly occurring events that have the potential to cause economic harm to the organization. Financial risk can arise out of a myriad of other risk events such as operational risk, market risk, interest rate risk, liquidity risk, credit risk, reputational risk, and more recently identified risk sources such as climate and environmental risks. Data science tools such as simulations are a natural fit for implementing all four aspects of financial risk management.

In Chapter Four, we showed how simulations can be used to study the impact of the quantity of the product sold on the NPV of the proposed capital project, and can also be used to study the sample path of the S&P 500 index over a period. In both cases, a special type of simulation that is known as Monte Carlo simulation was used to analyze and assess the behavior of randomly occurring events (quantity sold and stock returns, respectively) that might have significant economic ramifications for the organization. We also pointed out that Monte Carlo simulations perform poorly in non-normal operating and market conditions.

In this chapter, we will examine some applications of simulations for assessing risk exposures at the tails of the distributions. For most risk managers, the behavior of the portfolio or project at the lower tail of the distribution is often the greater concern. Fortunately, there are other methods for examining the behavior of financial variables at the tails of their distributions. In reality, many of these methods also use simulations in their framework. The methods include extreme value theory (EVT), Copulas, and Severity distribution (SD) to name a few.

The extreme value theory is concerned with the stochastic behavior of the events that occur in the tails of the distribution. For example, a portfolio manager might be interested in the distribution of the maximum returns that were obtained from a collection of portfolios of randomly selected stocks.

Copulas are used to model the stochastic properties of multivariate distributions and the dependency among their marginal distributions. For example, a credit risk analyst might be interested in studying the dependency between the distributions of the loan losses in the bank's portfolio of auto loans and mortgage loans, particularly when one of the loan portfolios is experiencing a significantly high number of defaults.

The Severity approach fits distributional parameters to the variable values at the specified quantiles of the distribution. These quantiles are typically those at the tails of the distributions. For example, an insurance company might be interested in measuring the degree (severity) of losses in the risk portfolio when those risks manifest. We will use the severity approach in a subsequent example. For now, let us examine the EVT and Copula approaches.

Extreme Value Theory (EVT)

In the EVT approach, the random variable is assumed to have different distributional properties at its tails such that the behavior of the random variable is significantly different when it is farther from the center of its distribution. In general, high-impact, but low-frequency events are mostly found at the tails of the distribution. However, Gaussian distributions such as the normal distribution are not well suited for modeling these types of events because the probabilities they assign to them are so low that one might be led to erroneously believe that they have extremely low chances of occurring when in reality they do have some chance of occurring as the window of opportunity increases in a real-world setting.

For example, the probability of observing a one-month return on the S&P 500 index that is four standard deviations lower than the mean return of 0.67% return is 0.003% or one in 31,754 months (if we assume that the log returns on the index follow the normal distribution). In reality, a one-month return above this threshold was observed in one out of the 374 months in our SPX_RET data set (0.27% probability).

Extreme value theory is a statistical method of analyzing extreme values in a known distribution by using some type of limiting (asymptotic) distribution to model the patterns of occurrence of these extreme values. Limiting distribution is the probability distribution in which a collection of random variables from a known probability distribution converges as the sample size increases. If we assume that the extreme values of interest are independent and identically distributed (i.i.d), then we can apply some type of limiting distribution to analyze their patterns of occurrence. Two categories of extreme values that are commonly modeled using limiting distributions are minimum and maximum values.

Generalized Extreme Value Distribution

Suppose X_t is a collection of the random variables that are i.i.d. The limiting distribution of the collection of maximum or minimum values X_t can be described by the Generalized Extreme Value (GEV) distribution as shown in Equation (5.1).

$$F\left(x;\theta,\sigma,\xi\right) = \exp\left\{-\left[1+\xi\left(\frac{x-\theta}{\sigma}\right)\right]^{-1/\xi}\right\} \tag{5.1}$$

where θ is the location parameter, σ is the scale parameter, and ξ is the shape parameter.

The GEV distribution encompasses the three commonly used limiting distributions (Gumbel, Fréchet, and Weibull distributions). Depending on the value of the shape parameter, the GEV distribution resolves into one of these three distributions:

- When $\xi = 0$, the GEV is equivalent to the Gumbel distribution (Type I extreme value distribution).
- When $\xi > 0$, the GEV is equivalent to the Frechet distribution (Type II extreme value distribution.
- When $\xi < 0$, the GEV is equivalent to the Weibull distribution (Type III extreme value distribution).

The Gumbel distribution is commonly used to model the limiting distribution for the maxima or minima of a normal distribution, while the Frechet distribution is used to model the limiting distribution for the maxima and minima of the Student's *t*-distribution. The Weibull distribution is used more often as the limiting distribution of the maxima and minima of the beta distribution.

Since the normal distribution is more commonly used in finance, let us explore how to simulate the extreme values that are more likely to be found in the tails of the distribution. We are particularly interested in distributions that model both the maxima and minimum of the sequence of the random variable. Therefore, we will select the Gumbel distribution, by specifying $\xi = 0$ when we simulate values from the GEV distribution. We will also need to specify the location (θ) and scale (σ) parameters.

Program 5.1: Simulating Block Maxima and Minima Returns of S&P 500 Returns

```
/*Simulating Maximum and Minimum values of Index returns*/
%let mu=0.0067658;
%let ssd =0.04465726;

data simul13;
        call streaminit(4321);
        array xnum{1000} x1-x1000;

        do j = 1 to 1000;
                do I = 1 to 1000;
                  xnum[i]=rand''norma'',&mu, &ssd);
                end;

                xmax = max(of x1-x1000);
                xmin =min(of x1-x1000);
                output;
        end;

run;

proc univariate data=simul13;
        var xmin xmax;
        histogram xmin/gumbel kernel;
        histogram xmax/gumbel kernel;
run;
```

```
proc sgplot data=simul13;
      inset""Simulated Maximum and Minimum Stock Return""/title"" Distribution of 1-Month
      S&P 500 Index Stock Retur"" position=top
      textattrs=(family""Times New Roma"" color=darkblue size=12 ) valuealign=center
      titleattrs=(family""Times New Roma"" color=darkblue size=12 weight=bold)
      labelalign=center;
      histogram xmin/ legendlabel''Minimum Value'' dataskin=matte transparency=0.3;
      histogram xmax / legendlabel''Maximum Value'' dataskin=matte transparency=0.3;
      xaxis label=''Simulated Value'';
      yaxis values=(0 to 25 by 5);
run;
```

To derive some idea of what the values for these two parameters should be, let us start by
simulating 1,000 samples of S&P 500 index returns and then proceed to derive the minimum and
maximum values from each sample using Program 5.1. In the SAS program, we use the ARRAY
statement to create a 1,000-column array, using the array X1 to X1000. Notice that there are two
DO statements in the loop. The outer DO statement is used to repeat the simulation over the one
thousand sample size, while the inner DO statement invokes the RAND function to simulate the
1,000 values for each column of the array.

Output 5.1A: Simulated Distributions of Maximum and Minimum Returns of the S&P 500 Index

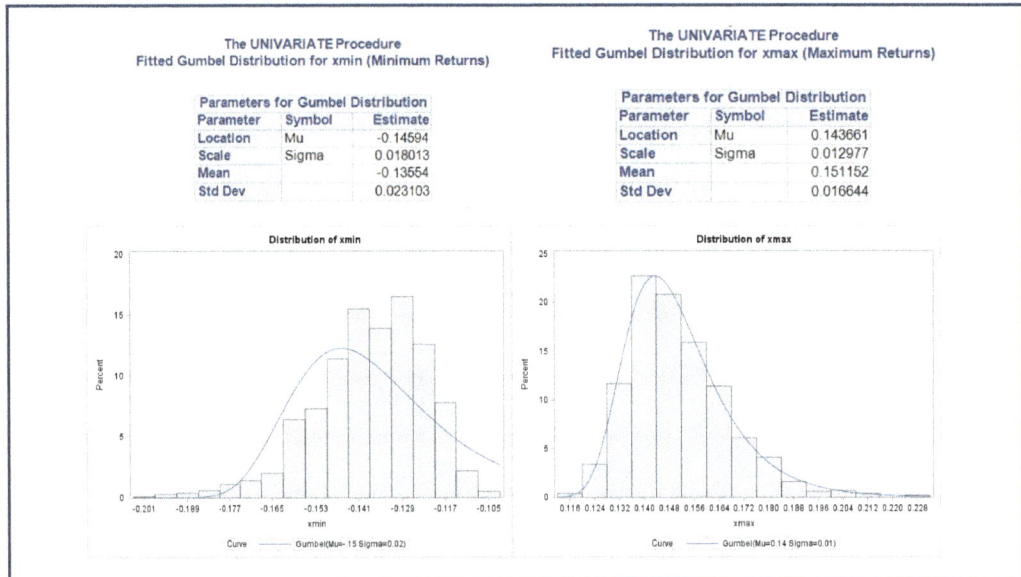

The UNIVARIATE Procedure
Fitted Gumbel Distribution for xmin (Minimum Returns)

Parameters for Gumbel Distribution

Parameter	Symbol	Estimate
Location	Mu	-0.14594
Scale	Sigma	0.018013
Mean		-0.13554
Std Dev		0.023103

The UNIVARIATE Procedure
Fitted Gumbel Distribution for xmax (Maximum Returns)

Parameters for Gumbel Distribution

Parameter	Symbol	Estimate
Location	Mu	0.143661
Scale	Sigma	0.012977
Mean		0.151152
Std Dev		0.016644

For each column, the maximum and minimum values are stored in the XMAX and XMIN
variables, respectively, using the MAX and MIN functions. The location and shape parameters
of the minimum and maximum values are calculated by fitting the parameters of the Gumbel

distribution to the simulated maximum and minimum values using the UNIVARIATE procedure as shown in Program 5.1. For each variable (maximum and minimum), the HISTOGRAM statement was invoked, and the GUMBEL option was specified to instruct SAS to fit each series to the Gumbel distribution.

Output 5.1A shows the parameter estimates that were obtained from fitting the Gumbel distribution to both the XMIN and XMAX variables. The location parameter for the minimum returns is -0.14594, while the shape parameter is 0.018013. For the maximum returns obtained from each sample, the location parameter is 0.143661, while the shape parameter is 0.012977. Notice in the results that the absolute values of the shape and location parameters are not the same for both distributions. This suggests that the shape and location of the limiting distribution of the maximum and minimum values are not the same. You can also observe the difference in the features of their distributions in the histogram plots for both variables.

We will also use the SGPLOT procedure to graph the distributions of values of both series (minimum and maximum) in one chart. Notice how the peaks of the distribution of the maxima are greater than the peaks of the minima.

Output 5.1B: Simulated Distributions of Maximum and Minimum Returns of the S&P 500 Index

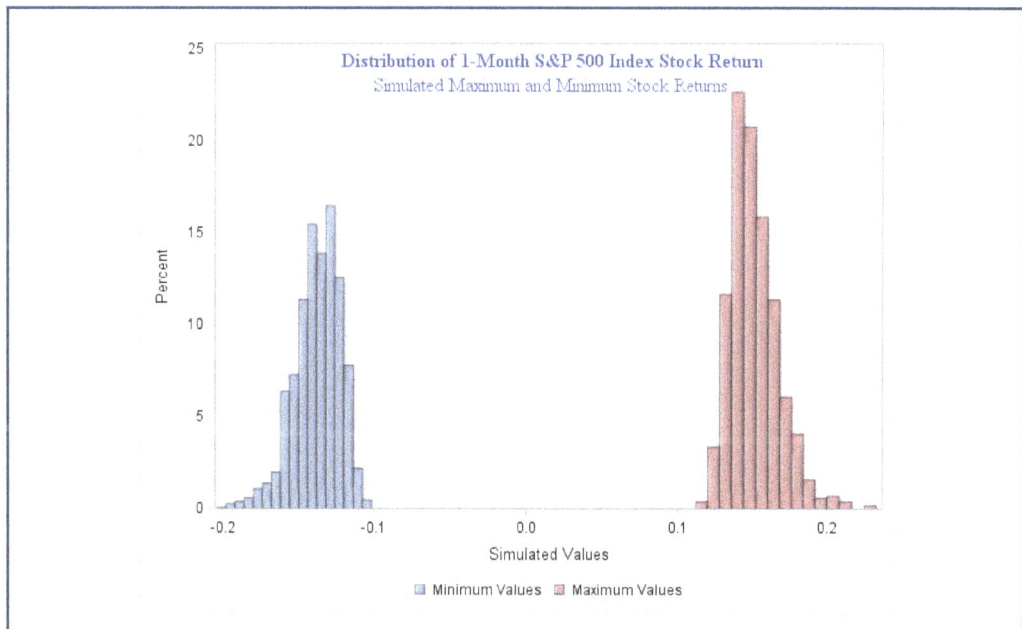

Now that we have the Gumbel distribution parameters that we need, let us go ahead and simulate the distribution of extreme negative returns using the location and shape parameters. Program 5.2 shows the SAS code that was used to implement the simulation. We also simulated

1,000 normally distributed returns to give some context to how these extreme returns can manifest in the real world. Since the Gumbel distribution is a special case of the GEV distribution, we also simulated its values from the GEV distribution by setting the shape parameter of the GEV distribution to zero.[1]

Program 5.2: Simulating Extreme Negative Returns from Gumbel and GEV Distributions

```
/*Simulating Extreme Negative Returns from Gumbel Distribution*/
%let n=1000;
%let mun     = -0.14594;  /* location parameter */
%let sigman = 0.018013; /*Shape Parameter*/
%let mean=0.0067658; /*Mean of Normal distribution*/
%let ssd =0.04465726;/*STDEV of Normal distribution*/

data simul14;
       call streaminit(4321);

       do k=1 to 1000;
               xgumb = rand('gumbel',&mun,&sigman);
               xgev= rand('extrvalue',&mun,&sigman,0);
               xnorm=rand('normal',&mean, &ssd);
               output;
       end;

       label
               xgumb ='Simulated Minimum Gumbel Returns'
               xgev ='Simulated Minimum GEV Returns'
               xnorm ='Simulated Normal Returns';
run;

proc sgplot data=simul14;
       inset "Minimum Stock Returns from Gumbel Distribution"/title=" Simulating Extreme
         1-Month S&P 500 Index Stock Returns" position=top
       textattrs=(family="Times New Roman" color=darkblue size=12) valuealign=center
       titleattrs=(family="Times New Roman" color=darkblue size=12 weight=bold)
       labelalign=center;
       histogram xgumb/dataskin=matte fill transparency=0.3 legendlabel='Extreme Negative
       Monthly Returns';
       histogram xnorm/dataskin=matte fill transparency=0.3 legendlabel='Normal Monthly
       Returns';
       xaxis label= 'Simulated Returns Values' values=(-0.2 to 0.2 by 0.05);
       yaxis values=(0 to 35 by 5);
run;
```

---

[1] You can simulate values directly from the Gumbel distribution by replacing 'EXTRVALUE' with 'GUMBEL' in the RAND statement.

Table 5.1: Extreme Value Statistics

Variable	Mean	Minimum	Median	Maximum
Simulated Minimum Gumbel Returns	-13.59%	-18.07%	-13.98%	3.10%
Simulated Minimum GEV Returns	-13.54%	-17.94%	-13.95%	-3.06%
Simulated Normal Returns	0.74%	-12.20%	0.72%	14.93%

The average returns obtained directly from the Gumbel and the special case Gumbel distributions are quite similar, but different from the simulated returns from the normal distribution, as shown in Table 5.1. For each simulated series, we also computed the averages for the minimum, median, and maximum returns.

Notice that the minimum return (approximately three standard deviations lower than the mean) that was obtained from the normal distribution is much higher than the values from the Gumbel distributions (approximately four standard deviations lower than the mean). The probability of obtaining a negative return that is four standard deviations lower than the mean using the normal distribution is approximately zero, while the probability of achieving the same outcome using the Gumbel distribution is 1.6%, which is much closer to what we observed in the sample data.

In Output 5.2, we graph the histogram of the simulated returns from both the Gumbel and normal distributions on the same plot to show the differences in the distributional properties of both returns. You will observe that the probability density plot of minimum returns that was derived from the Gumbel distribution is distinctively different from the probability density of the returns that were obtained from the normal distribution.

Output 5.2: Simulated Minimum S&P 500 Index Return Using Gumbel Distribution

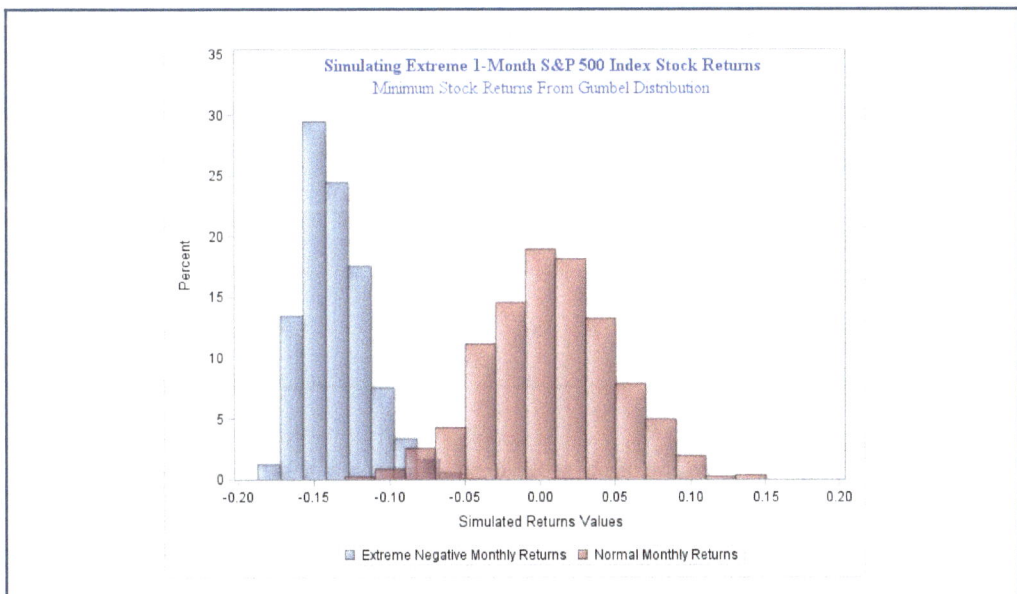

Value at Risk (VaR) Using GEV Distribution

Calculating the Value at Risk (VaR)[2] of a financial position using the GEV distribution can be achieved by implementing the following expression:

$$VaR = \begin{cases} \theta_n - \dfrac{\sigma_n}{\xi_n}\left\{1-\left[-n\log(1-p)\right]^{-\xi_n}\right\} & \xi_n \neq 0 \\ \theta_n - \sigma_n \log\left[-n\log(1-p)\right] & \xi_n = 0 \end{cases}$$

(5.2)

where θ_n and σ_n are the location and scale parameters of the simulated maximum distribution and n is the size of each sample drawn.

Program 5.3 shows the DATA step that was used to calculate the 90%, 95%, and 99% one-month VaR for the S&P 500 Index. Since $\xi_n = 0$ in the Gumbel distribution, the second expression in Equation (5.2) was used. The estimated VaRs are saved in the GEVVAR data set. The PRINT procedure is then used to invoke the printing of the values in the GEVVAR data set.

Program 5.3: Value at Risk Using the GEV Distribution

```
/*Calculating Value at Risk Using the GEV Distribution*/
%let n=1000;

/*From the output of Program 5.1*/
%let mun    = 0.143661;  /* Upper location parameter */
%let sigman = 0.0129773; /*Upper Shape Parameter*/

data gevvar;
        VaR90=&mun-&sigman*log(-&n*log(1-0.1));
        VaR95=&mun-&sigman*log(-&n*log(1-0.05));
        VaR99=&mun-&sigman*log(-&n*log(1-0.01));
        label
                var90 ='90% VaR'
                var95 ='95% VaR'
                var99 ='99% VaR';
        format var90 percent8.2  var95 percent8.2  var99 percent8.2;
run;

title ' One-Month Value-at-Risk for the S&P 500 Index';

proc print data=gevvar noobs label;
run;

title;
```

[2] The Value at Risk of a portfolio can also be defined as the maximum amount of market-related losses the portfolio (under normal market conditions) can incur within a window of time with a degree of confidence. The 99% VaR estimates the maximum loss the portfolio can incur with 99% confidence during a window of time. VaRs are quantiles of the distribution at the (1-VaR threshold).

The VaR estimates, which are shown in Output 5.3 indicate that there is a 10-percent probability of losing at least 8.32% or a one-percent chance of losing at least 11.37% on the index position in a given month.

Output 5.3: Computing Value-at-Risk Using Simulation and GEV Distribution

One-Month Value-at-Risk for S&P 500 Index		
90% VaR	95% VaR	99% VaR
8.32%	9.26%	11.37%

To get a complete picture of how much capital is at risk when losses exceed the threshold, it is a good idea to also calculate the average value of the returns that exceed the VaR threshold. This is known as the Expected Shortfall (ES). For the GEV distribution, the ES specification is written as:

$$ ES_p = \begin{cases} \theta + \dfrac{\sigma}{p\xi}\left\{\left[\Gamma\left(1-\xi-\log(p)\right)-p\right]\right. & \xi \neq 0 \\ \theta + \dfrac{\sigma}{p}\left[\mathrm{li}\left(p\right)-p\log\left(-\log(p)\right)\right] & \xi = 0 \end{cases} \tag{5.3} $$

where Γ is the incomplete gamma function (CDF of the gamma distribution) and li is the logarithmic integral function. The literature on the ES specification above is still emerging and the logarithmic integral function is not yet available in SAS. The technical complexity of writing the functions to implement them is beyond the scope of the book. The formula is provided for references only.[3]

Generalized Pareto Distribution

Another EVT class of distribution is the Generalized Pareto Distribution (GPD). The GPD is a continuous probability distribution that is used to model the tails of other probability distributions. In the same construct as the GEV distribution, the GPD is also defined by three parameters: θ the location parameter, σ the scale parameter, and ξ the shape parameter. The GPD is used to model the behavior of a random variable X when its values exceed a defined threshold u. The distribution function for the values above the threshold, which is also known as the conditional excess distribution is expressed as:

$$ F_\theta\left(y\right)=P\left(X-\theta\leq y\mid X>\theta\right),0\leq y<x_{max}-\theta \tag{5.4} $$

---

[3] Interested readers should review "Conditional Value-at-Risk for Uncommon Distributions" by Valentyn Khokhlov (2018).

where θ is the threshold, $y = x - \theta$ are the exceedances, and x_{max} is the maximum value of X in the F distribution. The GPD can be viewed as the distributions of the values of the random variable X that are in excess of some threshold θ as long as the threshold is sufficiently high enough. In this method (which is also known as Peak Over Threshold (POT)), only values that are in excess of the threshold are included in the GPD, which makes it well-suited for modeling extreme returns in financial assets. The cumulative distribution function for the GPD can be written as:

$$F_u(y) = \begin{cases} 1 - \left[1 + \xi \left(\dfrac{x - \theta}{\sigma} \right) \right]^{-\frac{1}{\xi}}, & \xi \neq 0 \\[3mm] 1 - \exp\left[-\left(\dfrac{x - \theta}{\sigma} \right) \right], & \xi = 0 \end{cases} \tag{5.5}$$

The GPD is a generalization of the uniform distribution, exponential distribution, and Pareto distribution. When $\xi = -1$, the GPD is equivalent to a uniform distribution; when $\xi = 0$ and $\theta = 0$, it is equivalent to the exponential distribution, and when $\xi > 0$ and $\theta = \sigma / \xi$, it is equivalent to the Pareto distribution, with an equivalent scale parameter of σ / ξ and a shape parameter of $1 / \xi$.

Simulating Data from the Generalized Pareto Distribution

Simulating data from the GPD can be implemented in multiple ways. Since the uniform, exponential, and Pareto distributions are special cases of the GPD, we can simulate the data for which of the special cases we are interested in by specifying it in the RAND function. Let us simulate data from the uniform and exponential distributions and fit both series to the GPD distribution using the UNIVARIATE procedures as shown in the SAS code in Program 5.4. You should note that although we specified the CDF of the GPD in Equation (5.5), the values that we will simulate will be derived from the inverse of the distribution, which is shown in Equation (5.6).

$$F_\theta^{-1}(y) = \begin{cases} \theta + \dfrac{\sigma}{\xi}\left[U^{-\xi} - 1 \right], & \xi \neq 0 \\[3mm] \theta - \sigma \log(U), & \xi = 0 \end{cases} \tag{5.6}$$

where $U \in [0,1]$ are derived from the simulated values of a uniformly distributed random variable. The values of the scale parameter (%SIGMA) and shape parameter (%XI), which we specified as macrovariables in the simulation, were obtained from the estimation of the distribution of returns in the lowest tenth percentile of the monthly returns of the S&P 500 index returns. We will shed more light on the computation of the parameters in the GPD-VaR section, which will be discussed shortly.

Since $\xi \neq 0$, we will use the first expression in Equation (5.6) to compute the values of our GPD distributed values. We will set $\xi = -1$ to compute the values of the uniformly distributed GPD values. We will use the second expression to compute the values for the exponentially distributed GPD. Remember that in all special cases, the threshold parameter θ is set to zero because we are simulating the excess distribution of this value.[4]

Program 5.4: Simulating Data from the Generalized Pareto Distribution (GPD)

```
/*Simulating Data from Special Cases Of GPD*/
%let n = 1000;
%let sigma =0.03153;
%let xi = 0.0000000105367;
%let xuni=-1;

data GPD;
call streaminit(4321);
      do i = 1 to &n;
            /* Generalized Pareto Parameters(scale=sigma, shape=xi) */
            u = rand('uniform');
            xguni=&sigma/&xuni*(u**(-&xuni)-1);
            xgexp=-&sigma*log(u);
            xgpd = &sigma/&xi *(u**(-&xi)-1);
            output;
      end;

      drop i;
      label
            xguni= 'Uniform Generalized Pareto Distributed Returns'
            xgexp ='Exponential Generalized Pareto Distributed Returns'
            xgpd = 'Generalized Pareto Distributed Returns';
run;

ods graphics on;
proc univariate data=gpd;
      var  xguni xgexp xgpd ;
      histogram xguni/ pareto (sigma=&sigma alpha=&xuni);
      histogram xgexp/pareto(sigma=&sigma alpha=&xi);
      histogram xgpd/pareto(sigma=&sigma alpha=&xi);
      ods select Histogram ParameterEstimates;
run;
```

We also fitted the probability density curve for each special case of the GPD we simulated by specifying the values of σ and ξ in the PARETO option of the HISTOGRAM statement. The PARETO option is used to request the fitted generalized Pareto density curves on the plotted histograms. The UNIVARIATE procedure will compute and plot the maximum likelihood estimates of the shape and scale parameters if you do not specify these parameters.

---

[4] The SAS code in Program 5.4 that is on the book's GitHub page also simulates values directly from the uniform, exponential, and Pareto distributions. Compare the results from those simulations with the values reported in Output 5.4.

Output 5.4: Simulated Data from the Generalized Pareto Distribution

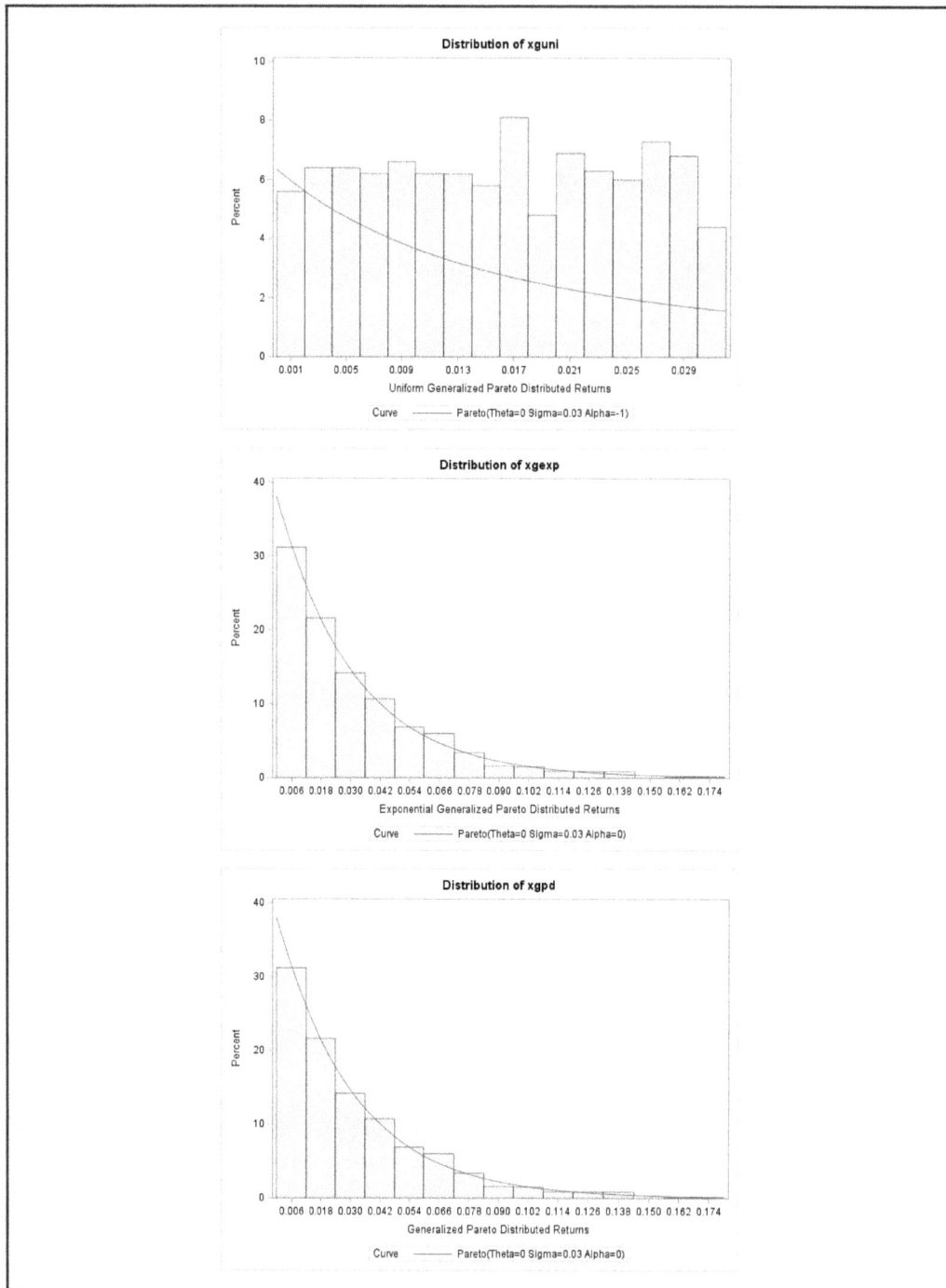

The plots of the probability densities of the exponential and GPD distribution look similar, while the uniform distribution plot is obviously different as shown in Output 5.4. The estimated scale parameters (sigma) for both distributions are also close in value, while their shape parameters (alpha) are slightly different.[5] Remember that we simulated values from all three distributions using the same scale parameters, but different shape parameters. The exponential distribution assumes that $\xi = 0$, which is very close to the $\xi = 1.05E - 08$ we specified for the GPD. The uniform distribution that assumes $\xi = -1$ displays the well-known rectangular shape of the probability density curve of the distribution for the simulated values.

Value at Risk Using the Generalized Pareto Distribution (GPD)

Now that we have laid out some theoretical and empirical demonstrations for the GPD applications, let us move on to applying it to the risk management problems that we tackled in Programs 5.1 and 5.2. GPD is also used to model the distribution of a financial position when estimating its value at risk (VaR). Under the GPD, the VaR for a specified period of time is derived from the quantile function of the GPD and can be written as:

$$VaR_q = F^{-1}\left(1-p\right) = \begin{cases} \theta + \dfrac{\sigma}{\xi}\left(\left(\dfrac{n}{N_0}p\right)^{-\xi} - 1\right) & \xi \neq 0 \\[2em] \theta + \sigma \log\left(\dfrac{n}{N_0}(1-p)\right) & \xi = 0 \end{cases} \tag{5.7}$$

where n represents the number of returns and N_θ denotes the number of returns that exceed threshold θ. Let us also get a complete picture of how much capital is at risk when losses exceed the VaR threshold, by calculating the average value of the returns that exceed the VaR, which we previously introduced as the Expected Shortfall (ES). For the GPD, the expression for ES is written as:

$$ES_q = \frac{VaR_q}{1-\xi} + \frac{\sigma - \xi\theta}{1-\xi} \tag{5.8}$$

To get started with our VaR modeling, let us define the threshold θ that will be used to derive our excess distribution. From a risk management point of view, the negative tails of the distribution are of primary concern. However, the GPD does not allow for negative values; hence, we would need to transform our negative excess distribution to positive values to estimate the

---

[5] To derive the maximum likelihood estimates of the shape and scale parameters, delete the specified distribution parameters from the PARETO option, then rerun the procedure.

parameters of the GPD distribution. Let us select θ such that only values in the lowest tenth percentile of the distribution are included in our excess distribution. One way to determine the optimal threshold is to construct a mean excess plot. The mean excess plot graphs the mean of excess values over the range of threshold. For our example, the value of the lowest tenth percentile of return is -5.26%. In Program 5.5, we used PROC MEANS and specified P10 in the options to obtain the threshold value for the tenth percentile. We then used the DATA step to create macro variables (from the output of the MEANS procedure) for the threshold (%MU) and its absolute value (%THRESH), which we will reference in future calculations. Absolute values of the monthly returns below the threshold are included in the excess distribution (EXMRET) while monthly returns that exceed this value are discarded in the subsequent DATA step.

Program 5.5: Estimating Excess Return Distribution

```
/*Estimating the threshold of the GPD Distribution*/
%datapull(spx_ret,spx_ret.sas7bdat);

proc means data=spx_ret p10;
      var mret;
      output out=threshold P10= / autoname;
run;

/*Creating macro variable with data step*/
data _null_;
      set threshold;
      call symput('mu',mret_p10);
      call symput('thresh',-mret_p10);
run;

/*Create excess distributions of returns*/
data exspx;
      set spx_ret;
      where mret<&mu;
      exmret=abs(mret-&mu);/*absolute values*/
run;
```

Output 5.5: 10th Percentile Return

The MEANS Procedure

Analysis Variable : Mret Monthly Returns
10th Pctl
-0.0520676

In Program 5.6, the SEVERITY procedure is used to assess the excess distribution and to fit the parameters of the GPD to the data. From the output of the program, the value of the shape parameter (ξ) is 1.0536E-8, which is approximately zero, while the value of the scale parameter (σ) is 0.03153. We also estimated the values of both parameters using the NLMIXED procedure and arrived at the same estimates. In the NLMIXED procedure, the parameters of the distributions are estimated based on the specified log-likelihood function.[6] Therefore, we are confident that the estimates are robust to the estimation approach.[7]

Program 5.6: Estimating the Parameters of GPD Using PROC SEVERITY

```
/*Estimating parameters of distribution using PROC SEVERITY*/
proc severity data=exspx crit=aicc outest=sevest(where=(_type_='EST'))
      print=all plots (histogram)= all;
      loss exmret;
      dist gpd;
      nloptions tech=quanew maxiter=200;
run;

/*Creating macro variable with data step*/
data _null_;
      set sevest;
      call symput('ssigma',theta);
      call symput('sxi',xi);
run;
```

Output 5.6: Parameter Estimate of GPD Using PROC SEVERITY

Fit Statistics

-2 Log Likelihood	-181.81558
AIC	-177.81558
AICC	-177.46264
BIC	-174.59375
Kolmogorov-Smirnov	0.65826
Anderson-Darling	0.44059
Cramer-von Mises	0.07973

Parameter Estimates

Parameter	DF	Estimate	Standard Error	t Value	Approx Pr > |t|
Theta	1	0.03153	0.00525	6.00	< 0001
Xi	1	1.05367E-8			

---

[6] The third approach that we used is the UNIVARIATE procedure. The HISTOGRAM/PARETO statement is used to invoke the MLE estimates of the parameters of the GPD. The scale and threshold parameters are the same, while the shape parameter is much greater than the values derived from the SEVERITY and NLMIXED procedures. The estimated value of the threshold parameter (Theta) is zero as expected because we are fitting the GPD to an excess distribution.

[7] SAS code for the PROC NLMIXED estimation is in the SAS program file for the chapter on the book's GitHub repository.

Output 5.6: Parameter Estimate of GPD Using PROC SEVERITY (Continued)

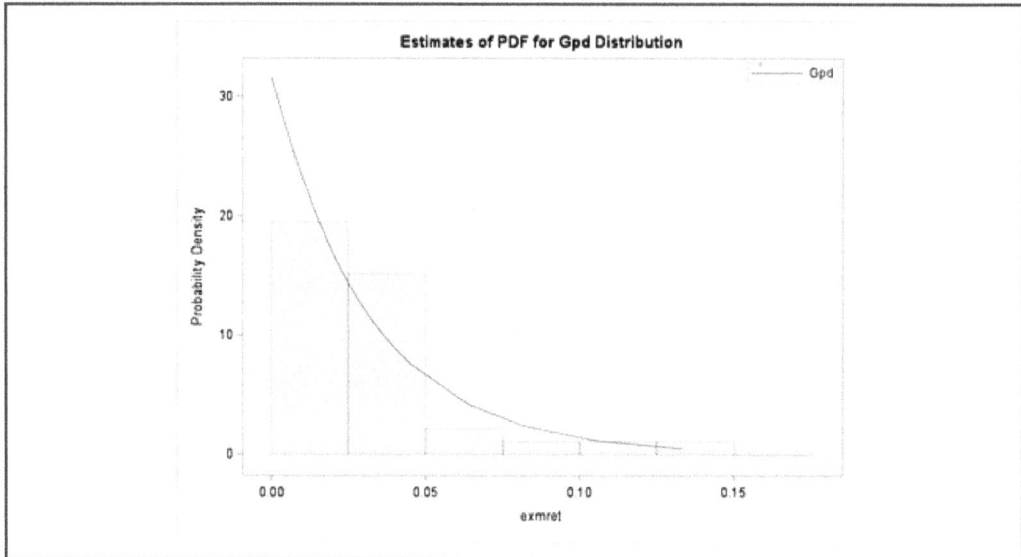

Using the same method that we used in the GEV VaR, Program 5.7 shows the DATA step that was used to calculate the 90%, 95%, and 99% one-month VaR and expected shortfall for the S&P 500 Index. Since $\xi_n = 0$ in the GPD distribution, the second expression in Equation (5.8) was also used.

Program 5.7: Value at Risk (VaR) and Expected Shortfall (ES) Using the GPD

```
/*Calculating GPD VaR*/
data gpdvar;
       VaR90= &mu-&ssigma*log((37*0.1/187));
       VaR95= &mu-&ssigma*log((37*0.05/187));
       VaR99= &mu-&ssigma*log((37*0.01/187));
       ES90 = Var90/(1-&sxi)+(&ssigma-&sxi*&thresh)/(1-&sxi);
       ES95 = Var95/(1-&sxi)+(&ssigma-&sxi*&thresh)/(1-&sxi);
       ES99 = Var99/(1-&sxi)+(&ssigma-&sxi*&thresh)/(1-&sxi);
       label
               var90 ='90% VaR' var95 ='95% VaR' var99 ='99% VaR'
               es90 ='90% Expected Shortfall' es95 ='95% Expected Shortfall' es99 ='99%
           Expected Shortfall';
       format var90 percent8.2 var95 percent8.2 var99 percent8.2
               es90 percent8.2 es95 percent8.2  es99 percent8.2;
run;

title ' One-Month Value-at-Risk for the S&P 500 Index';

proc print data=gpdvar noobs label;
run;

title;
```

The VaR estimates reported in Output 5.7 indicate that there is a ten-percent probability of losing at least 7.16%, a five-percent probability of losing at least 9.34%, and a one-percent chance of losing at least 14.4% on a long position in the index in a given month. The values are somewhat greater than those from the GEV-VaR. The average losses above the VaR thresholds for the 90%, 95%, and 99% thresholds are 10.31%, 12.50%, and 17.57%, respectively.

Output 5.7: Computing Value-at-Risk Using Simulation and GPD Distribution

One-Month Value-at-Risk for the S&P 500 Index					
90% VaR	95% VaR	99% VaR	90% Expected Shortfall	95% Expected Shortfall	99% Expected Shortfall
7.16%	9.35%	14.42%	10.31%	12.50%	17.57%

Copulas

Copulas are used to examine the relationships between two or more random variables. Copula functions link marginal distributions of two or more variables by linking the quantile functions of their uniform marginal distribution to a joint distribution function. This joint distribution function can then be used to estimate the parameters that measure their joint dependences. A common approach to measuring the strength of the association between two or more variables is correlation. However, linear correlation assumes the strength of the relationship between the variables is the same at every quantile of the distribution. In reality, correlations between financial variables are not static; they tend to change over time. They also tend to increase significantly in highly volatile periods and when asset returns are extreme. These evident patterns in financial data make the common correlation measures such as the Pearson linear correlation unreliable for statistical inference because it is susceptible to outliers. Ranked correlations that measure the strength of the association between two ranked variables are less susceptible to outlier values. They can also be estimated directly from copulas of the joint multivariate distribution. The theoretical framework for copulas is as follows.

Suppose X is a vector that contains a collection of random variables. Then according to Sklar's (1973) Theorem, the joint distribution function for $X = (X_1, \ldots, X_d)$ with continuous marginal cumulative distribution functions $F_1, \ldots, F_d$ can be expressed as:

$$G(X) = C\left(F_1(x_1), \ldots, F_d(x_d)\right) \tag{5.9}$$

where $C : [0,1]^d \to [0,1]$ represents the *d*-dimensional copula that is the multivariate distribution of the vector of random variables with the uniformly distributed marginal distribution. Such that:

$$C\left(u_1, \ldots, u_n\right) = G\left(F_1^{-1}(u_1), \ldots, F_n^{-1}(u_1)\right) \tag{5.10}$$

where $u_1 = F_1(x_1)$ and F_1^{-1} are the quantile functions of the marginals.

Conceptually, copulas couple the marginal CDF distribution u_1 to the joint distribution G. Copulas rely on two interesting properties of marginal distributions. The first is that the marginal distribution $(F_1(x_1),...,F_d(x_d))$ as shown in Equation (5.9) of a random variable is uniformly distributed. This means that the CDF of a random variable will follow a uniform distribution regardless of the underlying distribution of the variable. Therefore, we can analyze the relationship between two or more random variables at the CDF level even if they do not share the same underlying distribution. Copulas are the joint CDF of the functions of the uniformly distributed values of the CDF of the random variable. The second property states that we can extract the values of the random variables in line with their underlying distributions by applying the relevant inverse CDF or quantile function to the values of the uniform random variable as shown in Equation (5.10). Altogether, these two properties form the theoretical framework of the copula technique.

You can transform the uniformly distributed values of the CDF of one random variable into any other distribution by applying the inverse CDF of that distribution to the uniformly distributed values of the CDF. Copula functions link the marginal distributions of two or more random variables using the correlation structure to create a joint multivariate distribution of the uniform marginals. Their respective marginal distribution can be reengineered by applying the relevant inverse CDF of the uniform marginals. Using the same process, we can simulate values from a joint multivariate distribution by first simulating values from the copula-linked joint multivariate distribution of the uniform marginals and then transforming the values to the relevant distribution by applying the inverse CDF.

There are two broad categories of copula functions: the elliptical copulas such as Gaussian and Student's-t (also known as Student copula), and the Archimedean copulas functions such as the Clayton, Gumbel, and Frank copulas. Elliptical copulas are radially symmetric because they are copulas of elliptical marginal distributions such as the normal and the Student's-t distributions, although the Student copula has fatter tails than the Gaussian copula. Archimedean copulas are flexible form copula functions that are capable of modeling a wide range of dependence. Some Archimedean copulas such as the Frank copula are symmetric, while others such as Clayton and Gumbel are asymmetric. In the Clayton copula, there is more dependence at the negative tails than at the positive tails of the distribution, while in the Gumbel copula, there is more dependence at the positive tails than at the negative tails of the distribution.

The COPULA procedure in SAS can be used to fit all the elliptical and Archimedean copulas listed above. The procedure can also be used to simulate data from their joint multivariate distributions, as well as to analyze the dependence between the variables. PROC MODEL can also be used to fit copulas to multivariate data. However, the features in it are not as robust as the ones in PROC COPULA. Consequently, we will use the COPULA procedure for the estimation that we will perform shortly.

Copula literature is very broad, and the concept is technically challenging for a novice in the data science domain. For brevity, we will focus only on the Student copula in this book. The Student copula can be written as:[8]

$$C_\theta\left(u_1,...,u_n\right) = t_{v,\Sigma}\left(t_{v,1}^{-1}(u_1),...,t_{v,n}^{-1}(u_n)\right) \qquad (5.11)$$

where $t_{v,\Sigma}$ is the multivariate Student's t distribution with a correlation matrix Σ with v degrees of freedom. The coefficients of the tail dependence λ_L and λ_u can be written as:

$$\lambda_L = \lambda_u = 2t_{v+1}\left(-\sqrt{\frac{(v+1)(1-\rho)}{(1+\rho)}}\right) \qquad (5.12)$$

where ρ is the correlation coefficient between two random variables. The rank correlation of uniform marginals of the two random variables, which is also known as Kendall $\rho_\tau\left(u_i,u_j\right)$, can then be written as:

$$\rho_\tau(u_i,u_j) = \frac{\arcsin(\rho_{ij})}{\pi/2} \qquad (5.13)$$

Copula Application in Finance

Copulas have a wide range of applications in finance. These include portfolio risk management, pricing of baskets of linked securities, credit risk, and operational risk analyses.

Let us explore the application of copula-based simulation for portfolio risk management. Specifically, we will construct a copula for the returns of an equally weighted portfolio of five financial stocks (American Express, Bank of America, Citigroup, Goldman Sachs, and JP Morgan Chase). We will then use the copula to analyze the dependence amongst their returns as well as generate simulated returns from their joint multivariate distribution. We will conclude the exercise by using the simulated return to estimate the market risk (Value-at-Risk) exposure of the portfolio.

To get started, let us download the FINPORT.SAS7BDAT data set from the book's GitHub site by invoking our DATAPULL macro **%DATAPULL(finport,finport.sas7bdat).** Verify that the data set has been downloaded into your WORK library before running Program 5.8. The program fits the Student copula to the monthly returns of the five financial stocks by invoking the FIT statement.

---

[8] The derivation of the multivariate cumulative distribution function and probability density function is beyond the scope of this book. Readers should review Sutradhar (1986) to learn more about the multivariate Student's-t distribution. You should also visit SAS® 9.4 and SAS® Viya® 3.4 Programming Documentation for the COPULA procedure to learn more about how SAS estimates the Student copula at https://documentation.sas.com/doc/en/pgmsascdc/9.4_3.4/etsug/etsug_copula_details06.htm.

SAS does not estimate copula parameters for elliptical copulas such as the Student copula. In lieu, the numerical outputs from the implementation of the code are the degree of freedom parameters and the correlation matrices for the Pearson and Kendall correlations. The PLOTS option is used to request the bivariate correlations and tail dependence plots of the marginal distributions for the returns using both original data and the data in the uniform distribution form.

Program 5.8: Using Copulas to Simulate Returns from Multivariate Student's-T Distribution

```
/*Estimating and Simulating Returns from Student-T Copula*/
%datapull(finport,finport.sas7bdat);

proc copula data = finport;
      var raxp rbac rc rgs rjpm;

      /* fit T-copula to Monthly stock returns*/
      fit T /
            marginals = empirical
            method    = MLE
            /*Generate Plots (Chi - tail dependence plot)*/
      plots (chi) = (datatype = both);

      /* simulate 10000 observations*/
      simulate /
            ndraws = 10000
            seed   = 4321
            out    = simulR
            plots(chi) = (datatype = original);
run;
```

We invoke the SIMULATE statement to simulate 10,000 observations of the monthly returns of the five stocks and to save the simulated values in the SIMULR data set. The PLOTS option is used again to request the bivariate correlations and tail dependence plots of the marginal distributions for the returns using the distribution of the original data.

Output 5.8: Parameter Estimates from Student's-T Copulas

Parameter Estimates				
Parameter	Estimate	Standard Error	t Value	Approx Pr > |t|
DF·	3.978093	1.019344	3.90	<.0001

Correlations Matrix					
	RAXP	RBAC	RC	RGS	RJPM
RAXP	1.0000	0.5164	0.5700	0.5437	0.5459
RBAC	0.5164	1.0000	0.8409	0.8168	0.8717
RC	0.5700	0.8409	1.0000	0.8334	0.8417
RGS	0.5437	0.8168	0.8334	1.0000	0.8396
RJPM	0.5459	0.8717	0.8417	0.8396	1.0000

Kendall Correlations Matrix					
	RAXP	RBAC	RC	RGS	RJPM
RAXP	1.0000	0.3454	0.3861	0.3659	0.3677
RBAC	0.3454	1.0000	0.6360	0.6085	0.6740
RC	0.3861	0.6360	1.0000	0.6273	0.6369
RGS	0.3659	0.6085	0.6273	1.0000	0.6344
RJPM	0.3677	0.6740	0.6369	0.6344	1.0000

From the output, we can see that Pearson and Kendall's correlations are greater between the stock returns of Bank of America, Citigroup, Goldman Sachs, and JP Morgan than the stock returns of American Express. All of the banks in the former group have significant trading and investment banking exposure, while American Express is mostly focused on consumer and commercial banking. Figure 4.5 displays the scatter plot of the raw and transformed stock returns of the five banks. The transformed returns are the uniformly distributed marginals of each stock return. The transformed returns of RAXP have a more scattered distribution relative to the returns of the four other financial companies. The plot of the transformed returns of RBAC, RC, RGS, and RJPM shows a stronger relationship between their marginals.

Figure 5.1: Correlations and Tail Dependence Plots

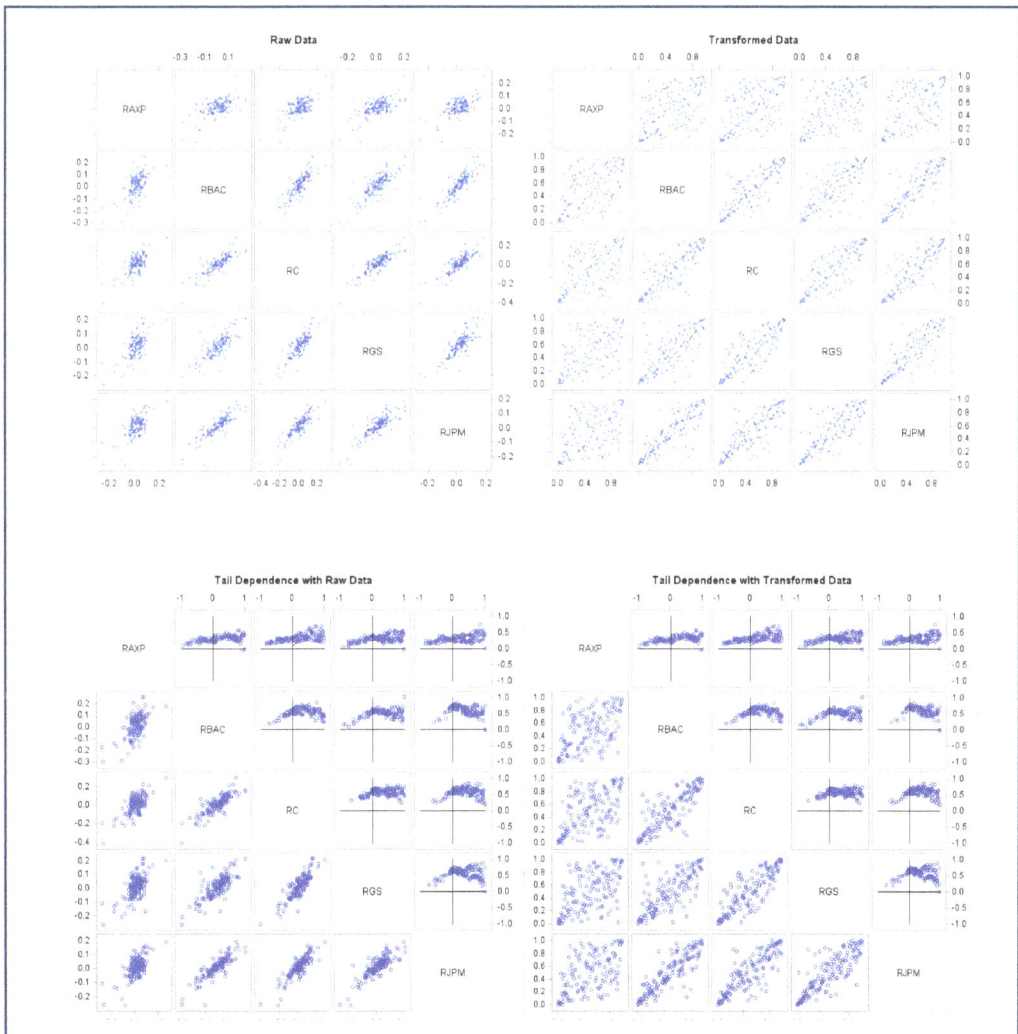

The tail dependence plots show higher dependence at the center and right tails of the distribution of both the raw and transformed data than at the left tails. This means that their stock returns are more likely to move together during normal and good times than during bad times.

Portfolio Construction and Value at Risk

Let us construct the returns of the equally weighted portfolio of the five stocks in the SIMULR data set using Program 5.9. Since the raw returns for each stock are in log form, we should also transform them into simple returns to allow for comparison with the portfolio returns. To derive the 99%, 95%, and 90% value-at-risk (VaR) for the portfolio and the stock return of each bank, we used the TABULATE procedure. The 99%, 95%, and 90% VaRs are the 1st, 5th, and 10th percentile of the simulated values for each variable. The 99% VaRs for the five banks and the equally weighted portfolio of their stocks are close in magnitude. Citigroup and Bank of America have higher 95% and 90% VaRs. In line with its business model, the 95% and 90% VaRs for American Express are the lowest among the five stocks. It is also lower than the VaR of the Portfolio.[9]

Program 5.9: Portfolio Construction and Value at Risk Using Copulas

```
/*SAS Code to Construct Portfolio and Estimate VaR*/
data Port_ret(drop=i);
      set simulR;
      array sret{5} raxp rbac rc rgs rjpm;

      /*Calculating Equally Weighted Portfolio Returns*/
      PortR=0;

      do i=1 to 5;
            PortR=PortR+0.2*(exp(sret[i])-1);
      end;

      /*Transforming Log Returns in Simple Returns*/
      rnaxp=exp(raxp)-1;
      rnbac=exp(rbac)-1;
      rnc=exp(rc)-1;
      rngs=exp(rgs)-1;
      rnjpm=exp(rjpm)-1;
      label rnaxp ='American Express' rnbac ='Bank of America'
            rnc = 'Citi Group' rngs ='Goldman Sachs' rnjpm='JPMorgan Chase' PortR=
'Equally-Weighted Portfolio';
run;

title 'Value at Risk for Portfolio of Financial Stocks';

proc tabulate data=Port_Ret;
      var rnaxp rnbac rnc rngs rnjpm PortR;
      table (rnaxp rnbac rnc rngs rnjpm PortR), (p1 p5 p10)*{format=percent8.2};
            keylabel p1='99% VaR' p5='95% VaR' p10='90% VaR';
run;

title;
```

---

[9] Unlike the previous VaR estimates, we report these VaRs using negative values because they represent the lowest 1st, 5th, and 10th percentile of the distributions of the returns of these stocks.

Output 5.9: Value at Risk (VaR) for Portfolio of Financial Stocks

Value at Risk for Portfolio of Financial Stocks			
	99% VaR	95% VaR	90% VaR
American Express	(22.61%)	(9.12%)	(4.32%)
Bank of America	(25.40%)	(15.28%)	(11.43%)
Citi Group	(28.84%)	(16.60%)	(10.34%)
Goldman Sachs	(21.76%)	(13.10%)	(7.90%)
JPMorgan Chase	(22.78%)	(11.27%)	(6.51%)
Equally-Weighted Portfolio	(20.55%)	(11.39%)	(7.62%)

Resampling Techniques

In this section, we will examine another way to generate data for both descriptive and inferential statistics. Unlike the simulation approach where we rely on the theoretical distribution to generate artificial data, in resampling, we rely on the empirical distribution of the data to generate our artificial data set for further analyses. The resampling technique is the process of drawing repeated sub-samples from an existing sample. The motivation behind this approach is the same law of large numbers (LLN) and the central limit theorem. Recall that the LLN states that the distribution of large samples that are independent and identically distributed tends to converge to the distribution of the underlying population. Since the LLN did not constrain the source of the sample, we can theoretically reuse a sufficiently large sample that is drawn from the same population as our source for creating the sampling distribution. The sampling distribution that is created from the collections of the samples of random variables that are drawn from the main sample should be approximately the same as those of the underlying population.

Resampling is also beneficial for predictive modeling when the data set is not sufficiently large enough to be split into training and validation data sets without significant degradation in the model performance. In such instances, computer-intensive resampling methods can be used so that all the data can be used for both fitting and honest assessment.

Bootstrapping

Bootstrapping is one of the most commonly used resampling techniques. It uses the sampling distribution of the sub-samples to draw statistical inferences about the population. In your statistics course, you might have encountered the two main categories of probability-based sampling techniques (with replacement and without replacement).[10] In general, the bootstrapping technique uses the sampling with replacement approach. This means sub-samples are drawn from another sample repeatedly to create the sampling distribution as

---

[10] Probability-based sampling technique can also be classified into simple random, stratified, cluster, and systematic.

Figure 5.2: Bootstrap Distribution of Sample Statistics

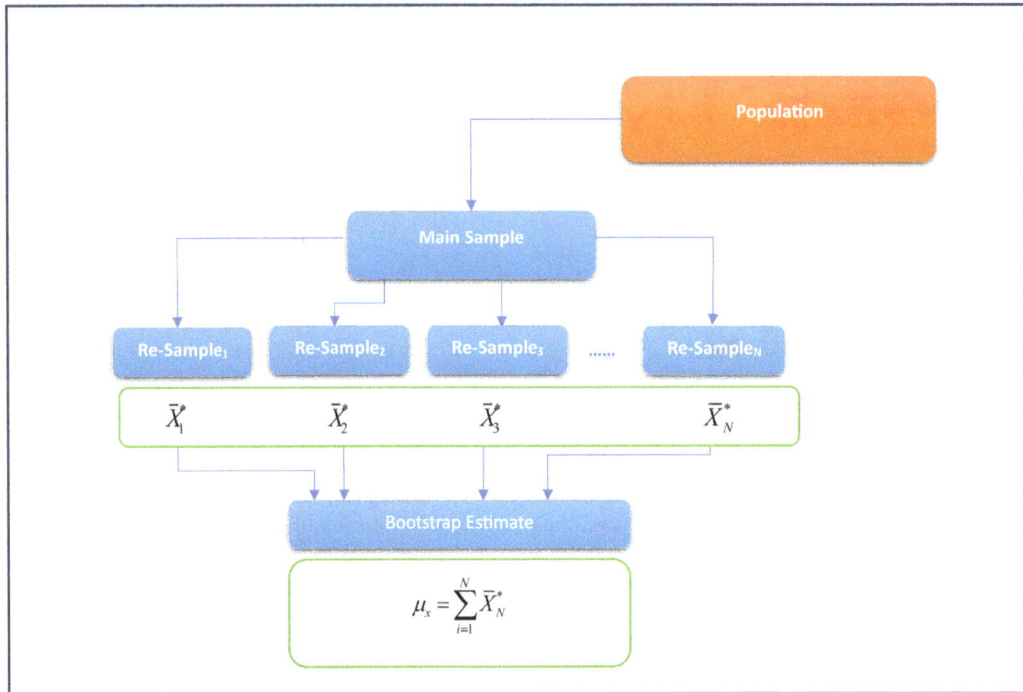

shown in Figure 5.2. The mean of the sampling distribution would be approximately equal to the unknown population mean.

There are three broad categories of Bootstrapping techniques:

- **Nonparametric Bootstrapping**: This is the simplest form of resampling technique. In this approach, the sub-sample is simply drawn with replacement from the larger sample repeatedly. Descriptive and inferential statistics are then calculated from the sampling distribution for the statistics of interest. Nonparametric bootstrapping does not require specific assumptions about the distribution of the sample, beyond the asymptotic normality of the parameter estimates from the resampled data.
- **Parametric Bootstrapping**: This approach to bootstrapping assumes that the sample comes from a known distribution. Therefore, it relies on the parameter estimates drawn from the sample to estimate the unknown population parameters. This is achieved by simulating new sets of data repeatedly using the main sample parameter estimate to create the sampling distribution of the parameter estimate of the sub-sample. Descriptive and inferential statistics are then calculated from the sampling distribution for the statistics of interest.
- **Semi-Parametric Bootstrapping**: This approach places less weight on the accuracy of the parameters of the main sample to reflect the true population characteristic. Hence,

it resamples the residuals from the fitted model and randomly applies those residuals to the fitted values of the dependent variable to create a set of synthetic values of the dependent variable. The model is then refitted repeatedly to obtain the sampling distribution of the parameter estimates.

Bootstrapping in SAS

There are several ways to implement bootstrapping in SAS. The preferred approach depends on the degree of sophistication and the need for flexibility to modify the procedure. Let us describe each of the approaches before proceeding to demonstrate their applications for finance in SAS.

- **Basic Bootstrapping**: Basic bootstrapping such as nonparametric bootstrapping can be done using the DATA step, PROC SURVEY SELECT, and PROC IML.
- **Advanced Bootstrapping**: A quick way to implement parametric and nonparametric bootstrapping is to use one of the many SAS procedures that support bootstrapping. The names of most of these procedures have SURVEY prefixes attached to them, such as SURVEYREG, SURVEYLOGISTICS, SURVEYMEANS, and SURVEYIMPUTE, to name a few.[11]

Bootstrapping Applications in Finance

Financial data scientists would find bootstrapping techniques useful for tackling a variety of analytics and statistical tasks in which they are uncertain about the distribution of the population. These include bootstrapping asset returns, portfolio optimizations, risk management, and option pricing. One important issue to note before applying bootstrapping techniques to financial market data is that asset returns tend to exhibit autocorrelations as shown in the previous chapters. However, to draw inferences from the bootstrap distribution, we need to assume that the sample distribution is constructed from i.i.d returns. Therefore, some adjustment to the basic bootstrapping technique is required before we can apply it to financial data. A common type of adjustment to bootstrapping technique is resampling using blocks of data rather than on an observation-level basis.

Block bootstrapping, as it is commonly known, divides the main sample into n-number blocks of data. This n-number of blocks could be non-overlapping, moving blocks, or stationary blocks. Each block represents a finite amount of data from the main sample. For non-overlapping and moving blocks, the number of observations within each block is fixed, while for stationary blocks, the number of observations is not.

---

[11] You can learn more about SAS procedures that use bootstrapping techniques by visiting the SAS/STAT® 14.3 User's Guide for the SURVEY procedures at https://documentation.sas.com/doc/en/statcdc/14.3/statug/statug_introsamp_sect002.htm.

Bootstrapping Stock Returns

Let us perform a simple bootstrapping example using PROC SURVEYSELECT. We will start by pulling a sample data set (SPX_RET) from the book's GitHub repository using the %DATAPULL macro.[12] The SPX_RET data set contains the monthly returns on the S&P 500 index from 1992 to 2022. Before you proceed to the next step, verify that the data set has been downloaded by checking your WORK library.

Program 5.10 shows the SAS code that was used to invoke the PROC SURVEYSELECT statement for the simple bootstrapping example. The sampling method used is the simple random sample as indicated in the SRS statement. There are 1,000 samples drawn, with each sample containing 12 observations. The PROC MEANS statement is used to calculate the mean of each sample. The distribution of the calculated means obtained from the one thousand samples is the sampling distribution of the means. The ODS EXCLUDE ALL statement suppresses the printing of all the outputs, while the ODS EXCLUDE NONE reactivates the printing option. The second PROC MEANS statement is used to calculate the mean of the sample means, which is our best estimate of the unknown population mean. The distribution of the sample means is also graphed using the SGPLOT procedure.

Program 5.10: Simple Bootstrapping Using PROC SURVEY SELECT

```
/*Simple Bootstrapping using SURVEY SELECT*/
%datapull(spx_ret,spx_ret.sas7bdat);

proc surveyselect data=spx_ret out=bootsamp1
        method=urs sampsize=12 reps=1000 seed=12345;
run;
ods exclude all;/*Suppress printing of listing outputs*/

proc means data=bootsamp1 mean std;
        by replicate;
        var mret;
        ods output summary=bootstats1;
run;

ods exclude none; /*Reactivates print of listing outputs*/

proc means data=bootstats1 mean stderr;
        var mret_Mean;
run;

proc sgplot data=bootstats1;
        inset "Basic Bootstrapping (URS)"/title="Distribution of the Sample Means of
        Bootstrapped S&P 500 Index Monthly Returns " position=top
```

---

[12] The code for the %DATAPULL macro can be found in Program 2.2. Run the macro first (if you have not done so already) before invoking it using the macro statement.

```
          textattrs=(family="Times New Roman" color=darkblue size=12 ) valuealign=center
          titleattrs=(family="Times New Roman" color=darkblue size=12 weight=bold)
           labelalign=center;
          histogram mret_mean/ nbins=20 dataskin=matte fill transparency=0.8
          fillattrs=(color=blue );
          density mret_mean/ legendlabel= "(Normal Density Plot for Sample Means)";
          yaxis values=(0 to 25 by 5);
 run;
```

Output 5.10: Bootstrapped Distribution of Sample Means of the Monthly Returns of the S&P 500 Index

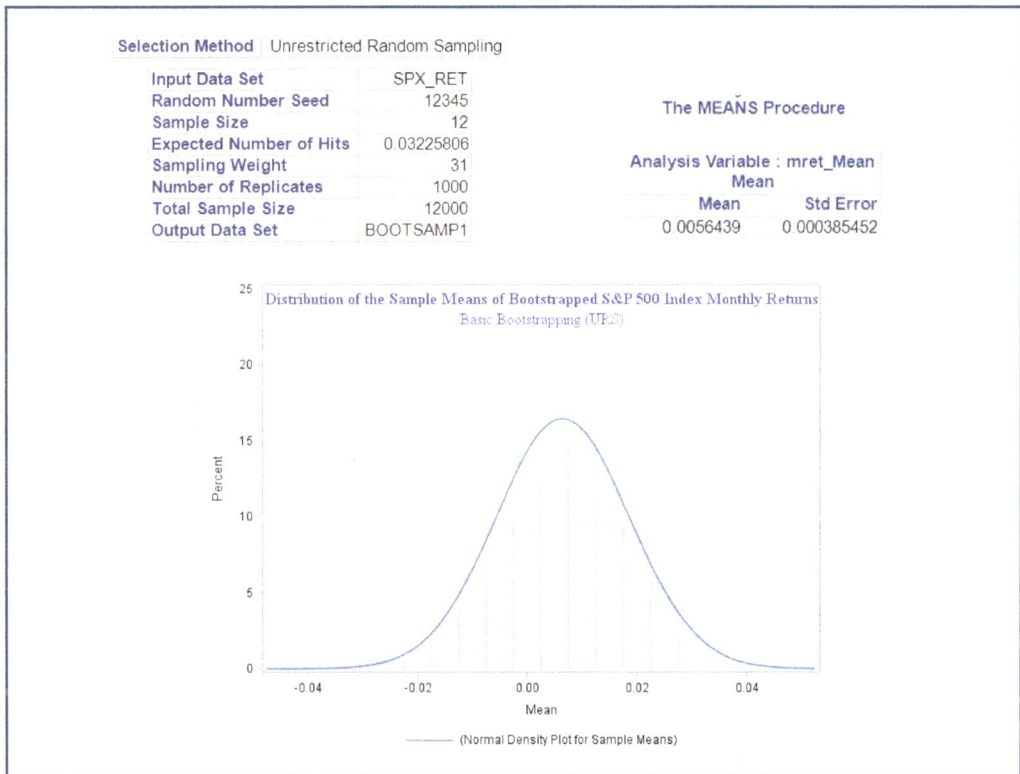

Selection Method | Unrestricted Random Sampling

Input Data Set	SPX_RET
Random Number Seed	12345
Sample Size	12
Expected Number of Hits	0.03225806
Sampling Weight	31
Number of Replicates	1000
Total Sample Size	12000
Output Data Set	BOOTSAMP1

The MEANS Procedure

Analysis Variable : mret_Mean
Mean

Mean	Std Error
0.0056439	0.000385452

Distribution of the Sample Means of Bootstrapped S&P 500 Index Monthly Returns
Basic Bootstrapping (URS)

—— (Normal Density Plot for Sample Means)

Output 5.10 shows the results obtained from implementing the code for our simple bootstrap procedure. Notice in the bootstrap report that 12 samples, each containing 1,000 randomly sampled observations, were derived from our main sample of stock return data. You should note that the main sample only contains 372 observations of monthly returns, which were then resampled repeatedly by the procedure to obtain the 1,000 observations in each sample. The average monthly logarithmic return for the index based on simple bootstrapping is 0.56%. With continuous compounding, that amount would yield approximately 7.0%, which is the annual price return (without dividend reinvestment) on the index from 1960 to 2022.[13]

Now that we have shown an example of basic bootstrapping, let us move on to explore block bootstrapping techniques using the same SPX_RET data set. The block bootstrapping approach we will explore is the non-overlapping block bootstrapping technique. We will examine two methods for implementing non-overlapping block bootstrapping: the PROC SURVEYSELECT approach and the PROC IML approach.

The PROC SURVEYSELECT approach is intuitively simpler and faster to implement, so we will start with it first. To get started, we will divide our main sample into *n*-number of sequential blocks of equal sizes. Let us specify a block size of 12 (in other words, 12 observations per block). Our main sample consists of 372 observations, which means there are 31 blocks in the main sample. Program 5.11A shows the SAS code that is used to implement blocking bootstrapping using PROC SURVEYSELECT. We first assign a block ID to the observations in the main sample. We created a new variable BLOCK in the SPX_RET data set. The variable assigns a block ID to each observation by invoking the CEIL function. This function returns the smallest integer that is greater than or equal to the input argument. In this case, we divide the observation number (_n_) by 12 to obtain a float that is then rounded to the next whole integer. For example, when _n_ =3, _n_/12=0.25, which when rounded up to the nearest integer will be equal to 1. Indeed, all values of _n_ from 1 to 12 will have block ID of 1, _n_ from 12 to 24, block ID of 2, and so on.

With the block ID set, we can then reinvoke the SURVEYSELECT procedure to resample the SPX_RET data set on a block-by-block basis (in other words, a single draw will consist of a block of 12 sequential observations). We request the block sampling option using the CLUSTER statement and specify the BLOCK variable as the ID for cluster sampling. We also specify a random seed value of 12345 and a sample of 1 to allow us to compare the block sampling approach in PROC SURVEYSELECT against the block sampling approach in PROC IML. Let us review the first randomly selected block in the BOOTSAMP2 data set by using the PROC PRINT statement. Notice that the first block selected was 19, which consists of 12 months of returns from January to December of 2010. We can also analyze the distributional properties of the bootstrapped data by reinvoking the PROC MEANS and SGPLOT statements. Notice that the average monthly mean returns, and the standard error of the means are slightly greater than those obtained from the basic bootstrapping approach.

---

[13] You should review the BOOTSAMP1 data set to see the number of times each observation in the main sample data set was sampled into each of the 12 bootstrapped samples.

Program 5.11A: Block Bootstrapping Using PROC SURVEYSELECT

```
/*Block Bootstrapping Using SAS*/
data aspx_ret;
     set spx_ret;
     block =ceil(_n_/12);
run;

proc surveyselect data=aspx_ret out=bootsamp2
     method=urs sampsize=1 reps=1000 seed=12345;
     cluster block;
run;

proc print data=bootsamp2 (obs=13);
run;

ods exclude all;

proc means data=bootsamp2 mean std;
     by replicate;
     var mret;
     ods output summary=bootstats2;
run;

ods exclude none;

proc means data=bootstats2 mean stderr;
     var mret_Mean;
run;
```

Output 5.11A: Block Bootstrapped Value of Returns from the Time Series of S&P 500 Index Returns

The SURVEYSELECT Procedure	
Selection Method	Unrestricted Random Sampling
Sampling Unit Variable	block

Input Data Set	ASPX_RET
Random Number Seed	12345
Sample Size	1
Expected Number of Hits	0 03225806
Sampling Weight	31
Number of Replicates	1000
Total Sample Size	1000
Output Data Set	BOOTSAMP2

Obs	Replicate	block	Date	Price	Mret	NumberHits
1	1	19	31JAN10	1073.87	(3.77%)	1
2	1	19	28FEB10	1104.49	2.81%	1
3	1	19	31MAR10	1169.43	5.71%	1
4	1	19	30APR10	1186.69	1.47%	1
5	1	19	31MAY10	1089.41	(8.55%)	1
6	1	19	30JUN10	1030.71	(5.54%)	1
7	1	19	31JUL10	1101.6	6.65%	1
8	1	19	31AUG10	1049.33	(4.86%)	1
9	1	19	30SEP10	1141.2	8.39%	1
10	1	19	31OCT10	1183.26	3.62%	1
11	1	19	30NOV10	1180.55	(0.23%)	1
12	1	19	31DEC10	1257.64	6.33%	1
13	2	31	31JAN22	4515.55	(5.40%)	1

The MEANS Procedure

Analysis Variable : Mret_Mean
Mean

Mean	Std Error
0.0056788	0.000451474

In Program 5.11B, we show the SAS code to implement block bootstrapping of the monthly index returns using the IML procedure. The macro variables &SS and &NRP specify the sample size and the number of replications, respectively. The data, which had 372 observations, was first reshaped into a 12 by 32 (row x column) matrix. Each row of the matrix can now be sampled as a block using the SAMPLE statement. Because we selected the same random seed, we can see in the program output that the first block selected is also Block 19. The mean and standard error from the IML approach is also the same as those obtained from the SURVEYSELECT approach. Indeed, the sampling distributions of the means that were obtained from both approaches are the same, as shown in the output of the IML procedure.

Program 5.11B: Block Bootstrapping Using IML

```
/*Block Bootstrapping Using IML*/
%let ss = 12; /*sample size*/
%let nrp =1000; /*Number of replications*/

proc iml;
    call randseed(12345);
    use aspx_ret;/*Same data set as SURVEY SELECT*/
    read all var {'Date' 'Price' 'mret' 'Block'};
    close;
    n=nrow(mret);
    ss=&ss;
    m=n/ss;
    ys=shape(mret,m,ss);
    sid = sample(1:nrow(ys), &nrp);
```

```
        yb=sid'||ys[sid,];/*include sid to show sampleID*/
        ybc=ys[sid,];
        smean=(mean(ybc'))';/*Calculate mean of each sample*/
        ssd =((std(smean)))/sqrt(&nrp);/*Calculate stdev of each sample*/
        bsmean=mean(smean); /*Mean of means calculation*/
        create bootsamp3 from yb;
        append from yb;
        close bootsamp;
        create bootstats3 from smean;
        append from smean;
        close bootstats3;
        print ("Block Bootstrapping Using PROC IML");
        colnames = "obs1":"obs12";
        print (yb[1:2,1])[label='Block ID']  (yb[1:2, 2:13])[format=percent8.2
colname=colnames]; /*Print first 13 obs*/
        print ("Descriptive Statistics");
        print (bsmean)[label='Mean'] (ssd) [label='Std Error']; /*Standard error of sample
means*/
quit;

proc sgplot data=bootstats3;
        inset "Block Bootstrapping (RS)"/title Distribution of the Sample Means of
          Bootstrapped S&P 500 Index Monthly Returns " position=top
        textattrs=(family="Times New Roman" color=darkblue size=12 ) valuealign=center
        titleattrs=(family="Times New Roman" color=darkblue size=12 weight=bold)
        labelalign=center;
        histogram col1/nbins=20 dataskin=matte fill transparency=0.8
        fillattrs=(color=blue);

/*Block Bootstrapping Using IML*/
        density col1/ legendlabel= "(Normal Density Plot for Sample Means)";
        yaxis values=(0 to 25 by 5);
        xaxis  label= 'Mean';
run;
```

Output 5.11B: Distribution of Sample Means of S&P 500 Monthly Returns Using Block Bootstrapping

Block Bootstrapping Using PROC IML

Block ID	obs1	obs2	obs3	obs4	obs5	obs6	obs7	obs8	obs9	obs10	obs11	obs12
19	(3.77%)	2.81%	5.71%	1.47%	(8.55%)	(5.54%)	6.65%	(4.86%)	8.39%	3.62%	(0.23%)	6.33%
31	(5.40%)	(3.19%)	3.51%	(9.21%)	0.01%	(8.77%)	8.72%	(4.34%)	(9.80%)	7.68%	5.24%	(6.08%)

Descriptive Statistics

Mean	Std Error
0.0056788	0.0004515

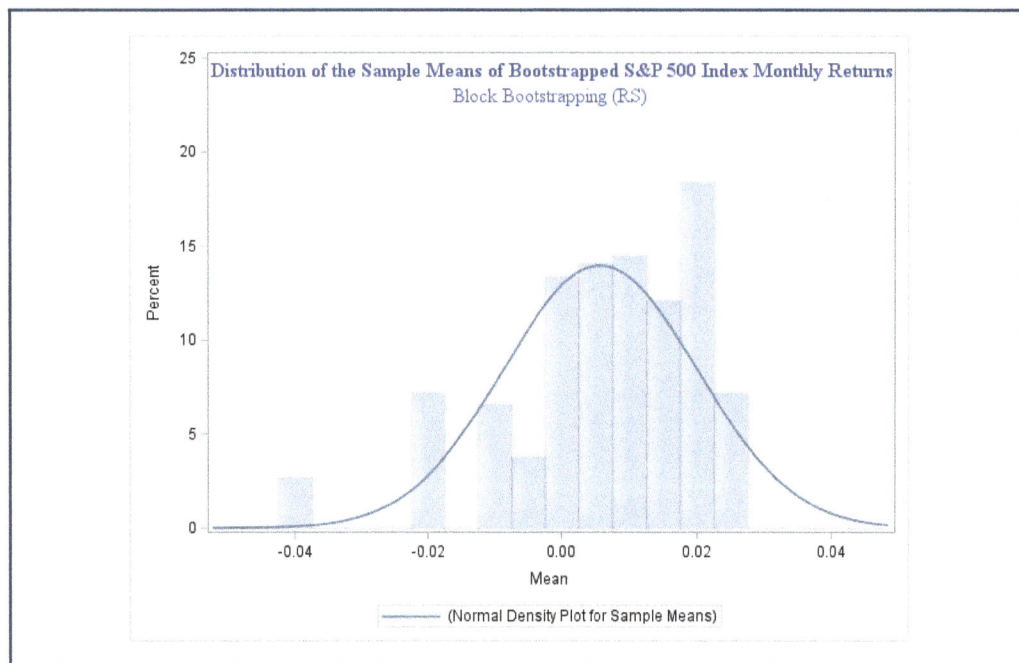

Also, notice that the sampling distribution of the block bootstrapped values is significantly different from the basic bootstrapping. That's because block bootstrapping allows for within-the-block correlation and independence across the blocks. The higher variability in the sample means obtained across the block is because we set a sample size of one block for the replication to allow us to compare the outputs from the SURVEYSELECT and IML procedures. If we increase the sample size for the block's sample to more than one, we will obtain the expected bell-shaped distribution as shown in Figure 5.3.

Now that we are familiar with the workings of bootstrapping, let us explore some practical applications of the methodology in finance settings. We will start by using bootstrapping to examine the finite sample properties of option prices.

Bootstrapping Option Prices

Financial options are derivative securities that give the holder the right to buy (call option) or sell (put option) an underlying asset, at a specified price (strike or exercise price), within a specified period of time (expiration date). The two common types of options are American options (which give the holder the right to exercise the option at any time until the expiration date) and European options (which can only be exercised on the expiration date). Option sellers (writers) must complete the transaction if the buyer (holder) chooses to exercise the option during the

Figure 5.3: Distribution of Sample Means Using Block Bootstrapping

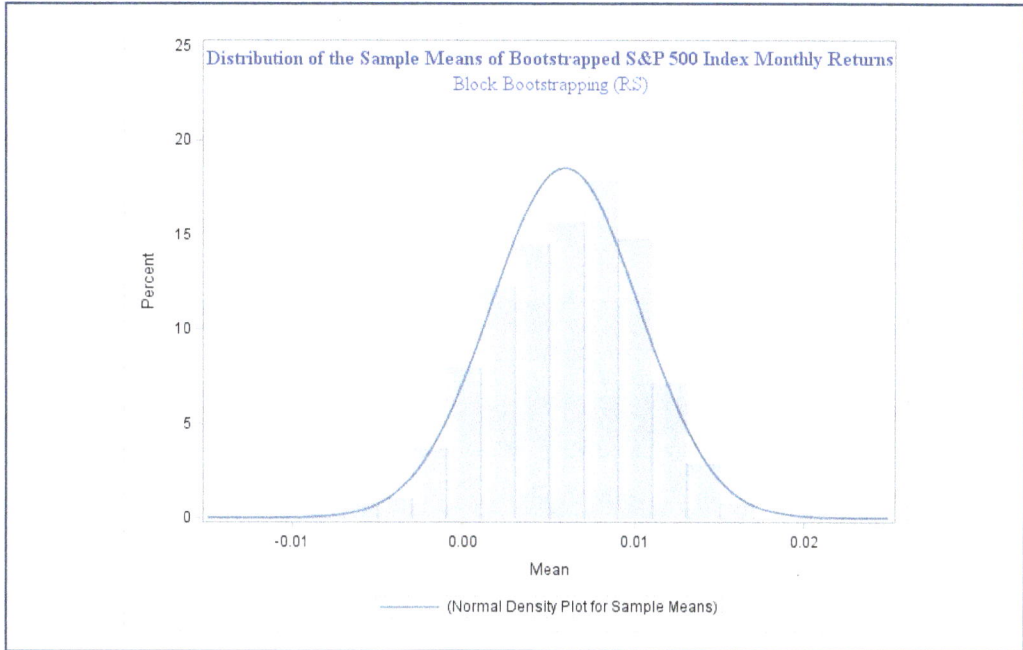

term of the option.[14] There are options on various classes of underlying securities, such as stock, equity index, foreign exchange, futures, interest rate, and commodities, to name a few.[15]

For our analysis, we will examine bootstrapping applications for equity index option contracts. US Equity index options are European-style options, so their values can be estimated using the Black-Scholes option pricing formula shown in Equation (5.14).

$$C\left(S_t, t\right) = N(d_1)S_t - N(d_2)Xe^{-r(T-t)}$$
$$P\left(S_t, t\right) = N(-d_2)Xe^{-r(T-t)} - N(-d_1)S_t$$

(5.14)

---

[14] Options contracts are either physically settled (exchange of cash for the underlying security) or cash-settled (in which the counterparty with a net positive (negative) position will receive (pay) the difference between the current market value of the security and the exercise price) from (to) the exchange.
[15] You can learn more about options by visiting the website of the largest option exchange in the US. The Chicago Board Options Exchange (CBOE) at https://www.cboe.com/.

$$\text{where } d_1 = \frac{LN\left(\frac{S_t}{X}\right) + \left(r + \frac{\sigma^2}{2}\right)(T-t)}{\sigma\sqrt{T-t}}, \quad d_2 = \frac{LN\left(\frac{S_t}{X}\right) + \left(r - \frac{\sigma^2}{2}\right)(T-t)}{\sigma\sqrt{T-t}}$$

- $C(S_t,t)$ and $P(S_t,t)$ are the values of the call and put options, respectively;

- S_t is the current price of the stock;

- X is the exercise price;

- $(T-t)$ is the time to maturity of the option (Theta);

- σ is the volatility of the underlying stock (Vega);

- r is the risk-free rate of interest (Rho);

- $N(d_1)$ and $N(d_2)$ are the cumulative distribution functions for a standard normal distribution for d_1 and d_2, respectively.

From the above, we can deduce that the price of an option depends on the following factors:

- The current price S_t of the underlying asset relative to the exercise price X. Because the option will only be valuable if it is advantageous for the holder to exercise.

- The sensitivity of the option price to the change in the price of the underlying (Delta, $\Delta = \frac{\partial C}{\partial S}$).

- The rate of change of the sensitivity (Gamma, $\Gamma = \frac{\partial^2 C}{\partial S^2}$).

- The time remaining to expiration (Theta, $\frac{\partial C}{\partial t}$).

- Prevailing interest rate (Rho, $\frac{\partial C}{\partial r}$).

- The volatility of the underlying security's price (Vega, $\frac{\partial C}{\partial \sigma}$).

Notice that some of the variables in the expression in Equation (5.14) also appeared in the Itô process and GBM expression, which can be found in the stochastic process sections of Chapter Three. This is because the Black-Scholes model was derived from the GBM using Itô's Lemma.

Table 5.2: S&P 500 Index Option Valuation Inputs

S&P 500 Index Option Valuation Inputs		
Exercise Price	XP	3844.16
Risk-free rate	rf	4.34%
Current Price	price	3844.16
Volatility	vol	19.03%
Time to Expiration (N/362.25)	time	0.08761

Option Valuation in SAS

It is gratifying to know that SAS users do not need to implement the option valuation formula above manually because SAS has built-in functions that implement the Black-Scholes formula. The BLKSHCLPRC function calculates the theoretical price of European-style call options, while the BLKSHPTPRC function calculates the price of the European-style put options on stocks.[16] For each function, we will need to provide five inputs, in line with the Black-Scholes model shown in Equation (5.14). These are the exercise price, the time to expiration (in years), the current stock price, the annualized risk-free rate, and the annualized volatility of the asset.

Let us start with an example in which we calculate the theoretical values of at-the-money (ATM) call and put options on the S&P 500 index on December 30th, of the current year using the Black-Scholes option valuation function in SAS. The option price is considered at-the-money if the intrinsic value of the option is zero (in other words, the market price and the exercise price of the underlying security are the same). We will assume that both options will expire on January 31st of the following year (32 days to expiration). Other inputs to the valuation such as exercise price, stock price, risk-free rate, and volatility of the index are shown in Table 5.2.

Program 5:12: Pricing Index Options Using SAS Option Valuation Functions

```
/*SAS Program to Calculate Black-Scholes Options Prices*/
data optionv;
      XP     = 3844.16;
      rf     = 0.04339;
      price  = 3844.16;
      vol    = 0.19031;
      time   = 0.087611225;
      c=BLKSHCLPRC(xp,time,price,rf,vol);
      p=BLKSHPTPRC(xp,time,price,rf,vol);
```

---

[16] SAS also has the BLACKCLPRC and BLACKPTPRC functions that calculate the theoretical prices of the European-style call and put options on futures, respectively.

```
        label
                XP      =       'Exercise Price'
                rf      =       'Risk free rate'
                price   =       'Current Price'
                vol     =       'Volatility'
                time    =       'Time'
                C ='Call Price'
                P ='Put Price';
        format rf percent8.2 vol percent8.2 time best8.2 c dollar8.2 p dollar8.2;
run;

/*SAS Program to Calculate Black-Scholes Options Prices*/
proc print data=optionv noobs label;
        title 'Valuing S&P 500 Index Options';
        var XP rf      price vol time;
        var c p /style(data)=[fontweight=bold  backgroundcolor=liggr];
run;
title;
```

Program 5.12 shows the SAS code that was used to calculate the theoretical value of the index option on December 30th. The code uses the DATA step to first store all of the relevant variables, which are shown in Table 5.2. The built-in option valuation functions in SAS were then used to compute the prices for both the call and put options in the index. Next, the PRINT procedure is used to display the inputs and computed options prices in the output window.

Output 5.12: Index Options Pricing Using SAS Option Valuation Functions

Valuing Equity Options on the S&P 500 Index

Exercise Price	Risk free rate	Current Price	Volatility	Time	Call Price	Put Price
3844.16	4.34%	3844.16	19.03%	0.087611	$93.70	$79.12

Output 5.12 shows the results obtained from running the code. The last two columns report the calculated theoretical values of the call and put options on the index. You will notice that the calculated price of the call option is greater than the price of the put option, despite both having the same strike price and expiration date. This is due to the parity (no arbitrage) condition. It turns out that you can create a synthetic put (call) option by combining a call (put) with a short (long) position in the stock and investing (borrowing) the present value of the exercise price at the risk-free rate over the time to expiration of the contract as shown in the expressions in Equation (5.15).

$$P = C - S_t + Xe^{-r(T-t)}$$
$$C = P + S_t - Xe^{-r(T-t)}$$

(5.15)

You should consider modifying Program 5.12 to verify that the parity formula shown in Equation (5.15) actually holds for the call and put option contracts on the index.

Now that we have developed some understanding of how options are priced, let us apply our bootstrapping technique to tackling one of the issues with the BSM model. It's important to note that the volatility input to the model is unobservable at the time of the pricing and must be estimated from the data. It is common to use historical data to do the estimation as in the previous example; however, this approach is susceptible to estimation error. To guard against this problem, we can construct a bootstrap distribution of stock prices over the sample period and use the volatility estimate from that bootstrap distribution as our proxy for the true population volatility.

Program 5.13 shows the SAS code for estimating the bootstrap distribution of the volatility of the S&P 500 Index returns. Because we are now sampling from a shorter window of opportunity to capture the prevailing conditions more accurately in the capital market, the block size has been reduced from 12 months to 6 months and the sample size to 3. We use the SURVEYSELECT procedure to resample the historical stock returns data 1,000 times using block bootstrapping. We then calculated the volatility of each sample using the PROC MEANS statement.

Program 5.13: Bootstrapping the Volatility of Stock Prices for Option Valuation

```
/*Bootstrapping Option Prices*/
data cspx_ret;
        set spx_ret(where=(date>'31dec17'd));
        block =ceil(_n_/6);
run;

proc surveyselect data=cspx_ret out=bootsamp4
        method=urs sampsize=3 reps=1000 seed=54321;
        cluster block;
run;

ods exclude all;
proc means data=bootsamp4 mean std;
        by Replicate;
        var  Price Mret;
        ods output summary=bootstats4
                (keep= replicate price_mean price_stddev Mret_mean Mret_StdDev);
run;

ods exclude none;
%let time=32; /*Time to expiration in days*/
%let rf=0.04340;/*Annualized Risk-free rate*/
%let price = 3844.16; /*Current Stock and Exercise Price*/

data optionvalue;
        set bootstats4;
        by replicate;
        exp=&time/365.25;/*calculating expiration in years)*/
        Sigma = mret_stddev*sqrt(12); /*Annualized monthly volatility*/
        CallP =BLKSHCLPRC(&price,exp,&price,&rf,sigma);
```

```
        PutP  =BLKSHPTPRC(&price,exp,&price,&rf,sigma);
        label CallP = 'Call Price' PutP='Put Price' Sigma ='Volatility';

run;

title 'Valuing Equity Options on the S&P 500 Index';
proc tabulate data=optionvalue;
        var Sigma CallP PutP;
        table  (mean stderr ),(Sigma*F=percent8.2  CallP*F=dollar8.2 PutP*F=dollar8.2);
label CallP = 'Call Price' PutP='Put Price' Sigma ='Volatility';
            Keylabel StdErr='SE';
run;

proc sgplot data=optionvalue;
        inset "Block Bootstrapped Stock Return Volatility"/title=" Distribution of One
        Month S&P 500 Index Option Prices" position=top
        textattrs=(family="Times New Roman" color=darkblue size=12 ) valuealign=center
        titleattrs=(family="Times New Roman" color=darkblue size=12 weight=bold)
        labelalign=center;
        histogram CallP/ nbins=20 dataskin=matte fill transparency=0.8
        fillattrs=(color=blue );
        histogram PutP/ nbins=20 dataskin=matte fill transparency=0.8
        fillattrs=(color=depk);
        density CallP/ legendlabel= "(Normal Density Plot for Call Prices)";
        density PutP/ legendlabel= "(Normal Density Plot for Put Prices)";
        yaxis values=(0 to 35 by 5) ;
        xaxis  label= 'Option Prices' valuesformat=dollar8.2;
run;
title;
```

The sampling distributions of the ATM call and put options were calculated using the option valuation functions in the subsequent DATA step. Unlike the code in Program 5.12, where we stored the inputs to the option valuation function in the same data set, here we used macro variables because we will be generating 1,000 values of prices for each option. With the options price computed, the TABULATE procedure was then used to compute the averages of the options prices derived from the sampling distributions. Finally, the sampling distributions of both option prices were depicted on histograms using the SGPLOT procedure.

Output 5.13 shows the averages of the option prices that were derived using the block bootstrapping technique. The average prices for the call and put options that were obtained from our sampling distributions were $90.94 and $76.35, respectively, which are slightly lower than the average prices computed using the fixed valuation inputs. You will also notice that the average value of the volatility input for our bootstrap valuation model is also lower than the value of the fixed input model. The lower volatility value is one of the reasons the option prices we obtained from the bootstrap model are lower than those from the fixed input model.

Output 5.13: Option Pricing Using Bootstrapped Volatility

Valuing Equity Options on the S&P 500 Index

	Volatility	Call Price	Put Price
Mean	18.42%	$90.94	$76.35
SE	0.13%	$0.57	$0.57

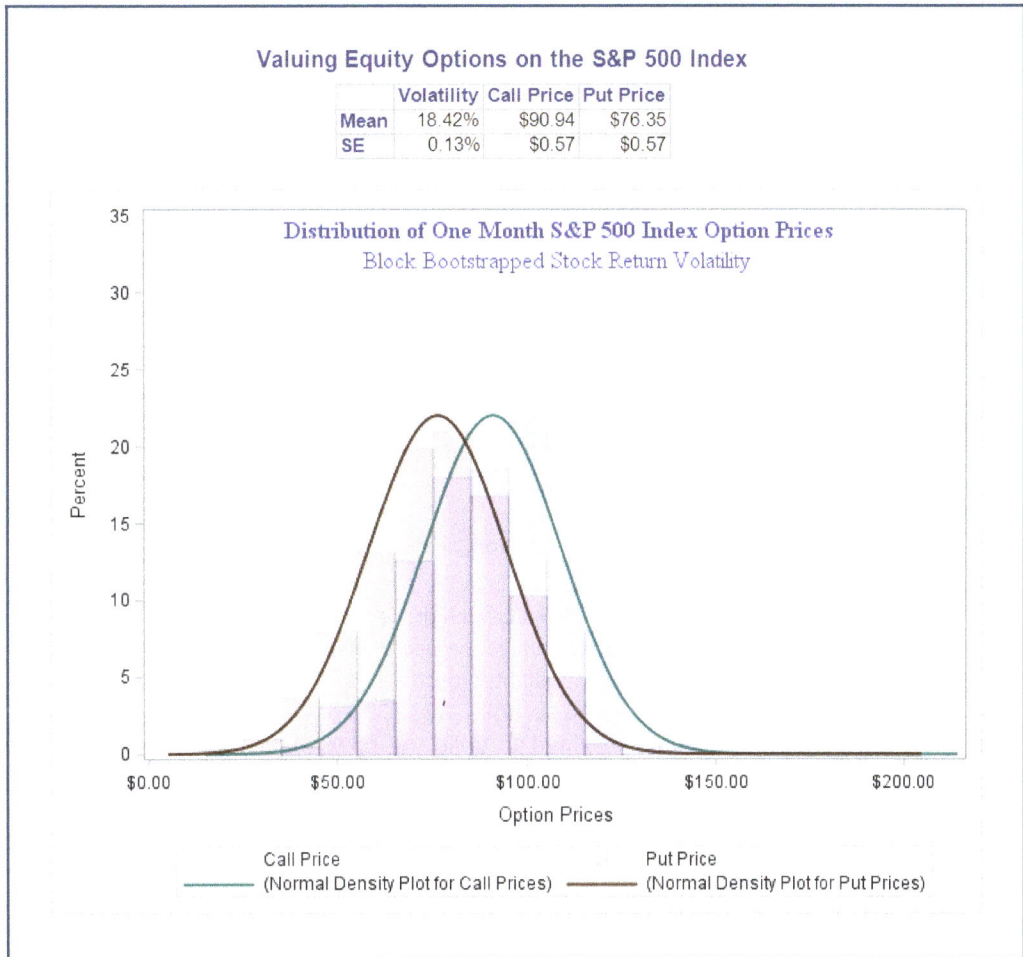

Distribution of One Month S&P 500 Index Option Prices
Block Bootstrapped Stock Return Volatility

Call Price
(Normal Density Plot for Call Prices)

Put Price
(Normal Density Plot for Put Prices)

Exercises

1. The data set DIVERSIFIED contains five years (January 2017 to December 2021) of monthly returns for five asset classes: stocks, bonds, crude oil, gold, and bitcoin.
   a. Use the SGPLOT procedure to construct a series plot that overlays the monthly returns for each asset class on the same graph.
      i. Which asset class appears to be most volatile during the period?
      ii. Which asset class appears to be the least volatile during the period?
   b. Use the UNIVARIATE procedure to estimate the descriptive statistics for each asset class. Request the histogram for each asset class and fit the normal CDF to the returns of each asset class.

      i. What are the average monthly returns and standard deviations of each asset class during the sample period?

      ii. From the histogram, which asset class has the highest and lowest dispersion?

  c. Write a SAS program to fit the Student copula to the returns of the five asset classes. Request the tail dependence plot as well as the scatter plots of the relationships between the asset classes (SET DATATYPE=BOTH). Also, simulate 1,000 returns from the joint distribution of their returns. Save the simulated data in the SIMULRET data file.

      i. Which combination of asset classes has the highest linear and ranked correlations?

      ii. Which combination of asset classes has the lowest linear and ranked correlations?

      iii. Observe the tail dependence plot using both the raw and simulated data. Which combination of asset classes has higher dependence at the left tail and the right tails?

      iv. Is the direction of tail dependence the same at the left and right tails of the distribution?

        • What are the implications of these results on investment opportunities in highly volatile periods?

> **Hint:** Modify Program 5.8. Pay attention to the variable names.

2. Using the SIMULRET data set from the COPULA procedure, write a SAS program that uses the DATA step to create a new data set named PORTRET. Include in your SAS code, the formula to calculate an equally weighted portfolio (EQPORTR) of the five asset classes, and a not-equally weighted portfolio (NEQPORTR). The weights assigned to each asset class in the not-equally weighted portfolio are shown in the table below.

Asset	Stocks	Bonds	Oil	Bitcoin	Gold
Weight	60%	20%	5%	5%	10%

  a. Write a SAS program that uses the TABULATE procedure to calculate the 90%, 95%, and 99% Value-at-Risk (VaR) for the five asset classes and the equally and not-equally weighted portfolios.

      i. Which asset class has the highest and lowest market risk?

      ii. Does the equally weighted portfolio have higher market risk than the not-equally weighted portfolio? What can explain the difference in their market risk exposure?

> **Hint:** Modify Program 5.9. Pay attention to the variable names. Create an array of weights for the not-equally weighted portfolio. Then use the array to calculate your returns by the modifying the portfolio calculations for the equally weighted.

  b. Write a SAS program that uses PROC SGPLOT to graph the histogram of the returns of the equally and non-equally weighted portfolios.

      i. Do the histograms imply that there are benefits to strategic diversification (not equally weighting the portfolios) over naïve diversification (equally weighting the portfolios)?

Chapter 6: Predictive Analytics in Finance

Predictive Modeling

In Chapter One, we described predictive analytics as the process of using data and an assortment of advanced statistical methods to predict future events, behaviors, and trends. Although the literature on predictive analytics is quite large, there are not that many that have presented their finance applications. In this chapter, we will explore some of these predictive methods but mostly focus on their applications in the finance domain.[1] As highlighted in the previous chapter, many of the topics that will be presented in this chapter are based on well-established econometric and statistical theories. You will probably encounter more mathematical constructs and notations. As in previous chapters, readers who are less proficient in mathematical statistics should focus on the general concepts, which are mostly provided at the end of every topic, and the accompanying SAS program as they go through the chapter.

Financial data scientists use predictive models to test out theories, forecast future realizations of some variables of interest, and predict the outcome of response variables to changes in the realizations of their covariates or explanatory variables. In general, predictive models fall into two broad categories. The first category of predictive models is those that are based on inferential statistics and/or econometric modeling. Statistical and econometric models set out to prove or disprove theoretical abstraction about real-world phenomena. As described in Chapter One, the starting point in this approach is the theory that would be tested. This is then followed by applying statistical or econometric models on data collected from the subset of the population to draw inferences about the validity of the theory proposed for the population. Once the theory is established, it is inherent that the model used can also be used to predict the variable of interest in the population. For example, asset pricing models are used by both academics and practitioners. Academics use them to test asset pricing theories, while practitioners use them to make predictions concerning asset returns once those theories become well-established. The most common of these theories is the well-known capital asset pricing model (CAPM). The CAPM, which assumes a linear relationship between risk and expected return, is typically tested

---

[1] Readers who are interested in acquiring an in-depth knowledge of the econometric models discussed in this chapter should consult Econometrics by Fumio Hayashi and Introductory Econometrics by Jeffrey Wooldridge. Those with an interest in analytics and machine learning models should review End-to-End Data Science with SAS® by James Gearheart, and Machine Learning in Finance: From Theory to Practice by Matthew Dixon, Igor Halperin, and Paul Bilokon.

using linear regression models. In subsequent sections of this chapter, we will explore a set of econometric models and their use for predictive modeling.

The second category of predictive models is those that are based on the machine learning approach. Here, the goal is not to test out theories, but to find relationships, trends, and patterns that are buried in the data obtained from real-world phenomena. Machine learning harnesses the power of advanced computing, statistical programming, and big data to achieve these outcomes. As highlighted in Chapter One, predictive analytics has grown to encompass the use of a wide range of statistical algorithms, data modeling techniques, and artificial intelligence applications such as machine learning and deep learning. Going back to asset pricing models, it is important to note that many of the statistical models that are used for asset pricing are based on modeling the covariances between some risk factors and the expected returns. The challenge with this approach is that the degree of mispricing increases as the number of risk factors increases or when the relationship between the risk factors and the dynamics of the expected returns is non-linear.[2] Because machine learning is unencumbered by the theory, it is best equipped to capture hidden relationships that can exist between the returns on financial assets and their risk factors.

Beyond asset returns, machine learning is also used in the financial services industry to optimize operational activities. These include transaction automation (such as trading, underwriting, and portfolio construction), risk management (portfolio, credit, liquidity, and operational), client management (acquisition, retention, and upselling), regulatory compliance, and enforcement, to name a few. We will explore two categories of analytics models that use the machine learning approach in Chapter Seven.

Statistical Versus Machine Learning Models

Although machine learning has its roots in statistical, mathematical, and computer programming, in practice, machine learning modeling is a distinct field from statistical modeling. Table 6.1 provides a summary of the similarities and differences between statistical and machine learning approaches to predictive modeling.

Methods of Estimation

Regardless of the predictive modeling approach that we use, it is also important to familiarize yourself with how statistical models and computational algorithms actually uncover relationships in the data or generate predictions. In this context, the models can be parametric or nonparametric. Parametric models use a set of assumptions (probability distributions and underlying stochastic process) to define the relationships between the predictors and the response (target) variable. Using these assumptions, the parameters that best satisfy

---

[2] Read more about this in Odusami (2023).

Table 6.1: Comparing Statistical Learning with Machine Learning

Characteristics	Modeling Methods	
	Statistical	**Machine Learning**
Modeling Objective	Confirmatory	Discovery
Data Requirement	Small to moderate	Large
Features Modeling	Additive	Additive, Nonadditive
Parameter Size	Small to moderate	Large
Data Segmentation	In-sample and Out-of-sample	Training, Validation, and Test
Model Construction	In-sample	Training data
Model Assessment Data	In-sample	Validation data
Accuracy	Confidence interval	Fit statistics
Inference Deduction	P-values	Prediction accuracy

some criteria are derived heuristically using some method of estimation. For statistical and econometric modeling, the three commonly used methods of estimation are the Least Square (LS), Maximum Likelihood (MLE), and the Method of Moments (MM).

Nonparametric models, however, do not require specific assumptions about the probability distribution of the underlying phenomena. Instead, they rely on fitting specific density functions to the data or computing the posterior probability directly from the data. The fitted model or the calculated posterior probability is then used to derive estimates of the parameters of interest.

You should note that parameter estimates can be derived using both parametric and nonparametric models. The main difference between the two is the need to assume a specific probability distribution and to define a specific mapping function that links the predictors to the response variable, both of which are required when using the parametric method of estimation. Nonparametric models do not have these constraints; hence their parametric specifications are typically not fixed. It is quite possible for the size of the model (number of parameters) in the nonparametric models to grow with the size of the data. Furthermore, statistical and machine learning approaches use both parametric and nonparametric estimation methods.

Parametric Method of Estimation

Parametric models typically have a finite set of parameters; hence, the model results tend to have a higher degree of interpretability than nonparametric models. They are also easier to implement and require less computational resources than nonparametric models. However, they are relatively less flexible than nonparametric models. Because the parametric method of estimation requires us to assume a probability distribution before estimating the model, there is also the risk we might misspecify the distribution for the data. The conceptual frameworks of

Figure 6.1: Methods of Estimation

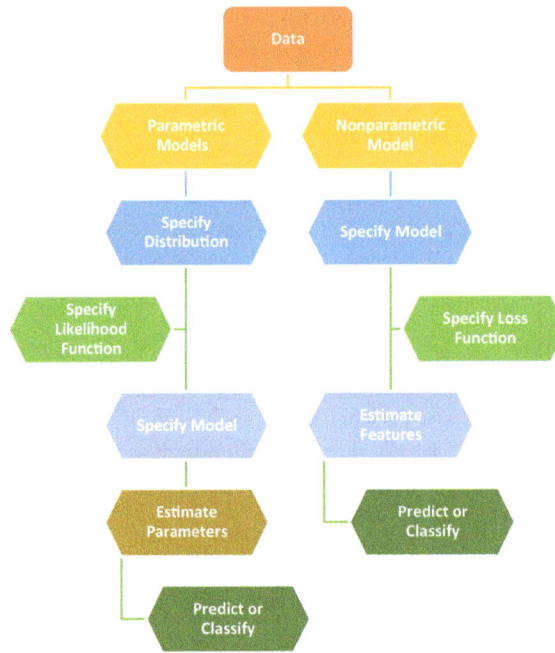

the three common types of parametric methods of estimation (least square models, maximum likelihood estimation, and method of moments) are described in the sections that follow.

Least Square

Least square models (LS) use an estimation process that finds the parameter space that minimizes the sum of squared residuals (that is, the sum of the squared difference between the predicted and observed values of the response variable). Let Y represent the vector of the response variable, X the matrix of the covariates, and β the vector of parameters such that the i-th element of Y can be expressed as $y_i = x_i\beta + \varepsilon_i$. We can write the residual of the regression as follows:

$$\varepsilon_i = y_i - x_i\hat{\beta} \tag{6.1}$$

ε_i is the residual for observation i and x_i is the ith row element of X. The sum of the squared error (SSE) is calculated from the regression using the following equation:

$$SSE(\hat{\beta}) = \sum_{i=1}^{N}(y_i - x_i\hat{\beta})^2 \tag{6.2}$$

Then the least square estimator of the parameter β is the $\hat{\beta}$ that minimizes the function:

$$\hat{\beta}_{LS} = \underset{\hat{\beta}}{\operatorname{argmin}}\left[SSE\left(\hat{\beta}\right)\right] \tag{6.3}$$

Notice that $SSE\left(\hat{\beta}\right)$ is a quadratic function of the $\hat{\beta}$. Therefore, a graph with $SSE\left(\hat{\beta}\right)$ as the Y-variable and $\hat{\beta}$ as the X-variable will be a U-curve. The partial derivative (w.r.t $\hat{\beta}$) of the $SSE\left(\hat{\beta}\right)$ function at its minimum will have a slope of zero. Solving the partial derivative function at its minimum for $\hat{\beta}$ yields the values of the parameter space that generates the least square of errors.

> The least-square estimator of the regression function is the parameter space that yields the lowest sum of squared residuals. The values of this parameter space are obtained by deriving the partial derivative of the function at the lowest value. The partial derivative of the SSE at the lowest point is zero. Solving the equation for the parameter space yields the corresponding (least square) values of the parameters at that threshold.

If we fit a regression line through a scatter plot of Y and X variables, then the least square estimator is the one that minimizes the dispersion of the plots around the regression line. The lower the dispersion of the plots around the line, the lower the SSE, and consequently the better the fit of the parameter to the model under consideration.

Figure 6.2 displays a scatter plot of the monthly excess return on the financial services sector against the market risk premium. Also shown on the scatter plot is the fitted regression line, along with its 95% confidence and prediction limits. Notice that the location of the line appears to be optimal in terms of the lowest dispersion of the observations from the line.

There are various types of least-square models. The most widely used among these types of models is the ordinary least square (OLS), which is also commonly known as simple or multiple regression. The main assumptions of the OLS models include a linear relationship between the response variable and the regressors, independence between the residual and the regressors (orthogonality), constant variance (homoscedasticity), and no multicollinearity.[3] Statistical and machine learning models such as linear regressions, non-linear regressions, and least absolute shrinkage and selection operator (LASSO) use the least square approach. Least square models are intuitively simple to implement and would suffice for simple predictive modeling problems.

---

[3] Orthogonality implies that the independent variables are uncorrelated with the residuals from the regression. Homoscedasticity implies that the variance of the residual is constant across all observations. Multicollinearity exists when the independent variables are correlated. Chapter Three shows how violating these assumptions could impair some of the statistical properties of the model under consideration.

Figure 6.2: Fitting Regression Line for Stock Return

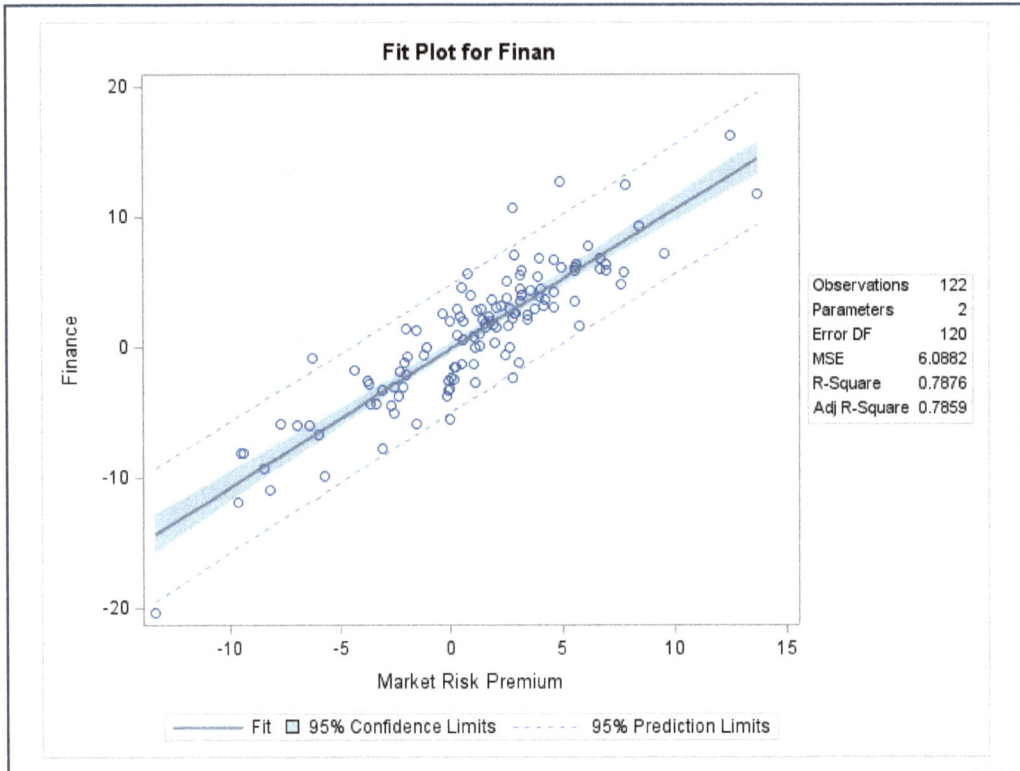

They are not well suited for modeling complex problems, classification problems, or modeling censored data.

Maximum Likelihood Estimation

The maximum likelihood estimation (MLE) approach to estimating the model parameters searches for the parameter space that maximizes the likelihood that the observed data is drawn from the assumed probability distribution. Another way to describe the MLE is that the approach searches for point estimates of the parameter space such that the observed data is most likely to fit the probability distribution specified for it.

From a mathematical construct point of view, the MLE is presented as follows. Let Y represent the vector of the independent and identically distributed sequence of the response variable. Also let $f(Y,X)=f(Y,X;\phi)$ represent the probability density of the realization of (Y,X) at the true parameter vector ϕ, where X is the matrix of the covariates. $f(Y,X;\phi)$ is also called the likelihood of (Y,X) and ϕ the likelihood function of (Y,X). The ML estimate of ϕ is the parameter space that maximizes the likelihood function of the realizations of (Y, X). If we assume that the parameter vectors θ and ω are subsets of ϕ such that $\phi = (\theta, \omega)$, we can write the joint density $f(Y, X; \phi)$ of the sequence of the random variables (Y, X) as a product of the conditional density $f(Y \mid X; \phi)$ and the marginal density $f(X; \omega)$.[4]

$$f(Y, X; \hat{\phi}) = f(Y \mid X; \hat{\theta}) \cdot f(X; \hat{\omega}) \tag{6.4}$$

where $\hat{\phi}$, $\hat{\theta}$, and $\hat{\omega}$ are estimates of the parameter vector ϕ and it subsets θ and ω. If we assume that θ and ω are not related functions, the density function (likelihood) in Equation (6.4) can be written in terms of the elements of Y as:

$$\prod_{i=1}^{n} f\left(y_i, x_i; \hat{\phi}\right) = \prod_{i=1}^{n} f\left(y_i \mid x_i; \hat{\theta}\right) \cdot \prod_{i=1}^{n} f\left(x_i; \hat{\omega}\right) \tag{6.5}$$

If we ignore the second term,[5] the optimization process of the MLE will then involve the search only in the domain of θ, since Y is assumed to be fixed. Therefore, we can rewrite the density function as a likelihood function of θ as follows.

$$L_n\left(\theta\right) = \prod_{i=1}^{n} L\left(\theta \mid y_i\right) = \prod_{i=1}^{n} f\left(y_i \mid x_i; \theta\right) \tag{6.6}$$

The aim of the MLE can then be described in terms of β as the search for the parameter space $\hat{\beta}$ that maximizes the likelihood function such that:

$$\hat{\theta}_{MLE} = \underset{\hat{\theta}}{\operatorname{argmax}} L\left(\theta \mid Y\right) \tag{6.7}$$

The likelihood function is often transformed into a log form for computational ease because of the small values of the probability density functions (PDF) for each observation while preserving the monotonicity of the function. By using the log transformation, the likelihood becomes an additive sum of the PDF. The log form of Equation (6.7) can be written as:

$$\ln(\theta) = \log L_n\left(\theta\right) = \sum_{i=1}^{n} \log L\left(\theta \mid y_i\right) = \sum_{i=1}^{n} \log f\left(y_i; \theta\right) \tag{6.8}$$

To find the maximum likelihood value, the derivative of the likelihood function is obtained w.r.t θ in the same manner as the least square. While the specification of the functional form of

---

[4] Using Bayes' rule.
[5] Given that Y is independent across observations of X, it is unlikely that the second term will have significant impact on the value of ϕ. This approach is one of the many other approaches that can be used to derive the maximum likelihood formula. You might come other approaches in different text. However, the general construct of the MLE remains the same.

the maximum likelihood entails finding the maximum, the implementation is normally performed by searching for the parameter space that minimizes the negative log-likelihood.

$$\hat{\theta}_{MLE} = \underset{\hat{\theta}}{\operatorname{argmin}}\left[-L(\theta \mid Y)\right] \qquad (6.9)$$

The partial derivative of the negative log-likelihood function at its minimum (also known as the score function) will have a slope of zero. Solving the score function $L'_n(\theta \mid Y)$ for $\hat{\theta}$ yields the values of the parameter space that consequently yields the maximum likelihood value.

If we assume that (Y, X) follows a normal distribution, we can denote Y as:

$$Y = N\left(X\beta, \sigma^2 I_n\right) \qquad (6.10)$$

where β and σ^2 are subsets of the parameter vector θ. We can now substitute for $f(y_i; \theta)$ with the logarithm of the conditional density (using the normal PDF) of Y given X as shown in Equation (6.11).

$$\log L_n\left(\hat{\theta}\right) = \log L_n\left(\hat{\beta}, \hat{\sigma}^2\right) = -\frac{n}{2}\log(2\pi) - \frac{n}{2}\log\left(\hat{\sigma}^2\right) - \frac{1}{2\hat{\sigma}^2}\sum_{i=1}^{n}\left(y_i - x_i\hat{\beta}\right)^2 \qquad (6.11)$$

> Although the mathematical construct of the MLE can appear complex, the intuition behind the approach is relatively straightforward. Given a functional for $y_i = x_i\beta + \varepsilon_i$ for the random variable Y, the MLE specifies a density function $f(y_i \mid x_i; \theta)$ for the variable and then searches for the values of the parameter space $\hat{\theta}$ that best fit the data to the distribution. The best fit is determined when the probability of fit is maximized.

Many statistical and machine learning models use the maximum likelihood approach to estimation. Statistical models that use maximum likelihood include probit, logit, and censored regression, while machine learning models that use the same include neural network models, linear discriminant analysis, and logistic regressions.

Method of Moments

Unlike the MLE, which uses assumptions of the distribution of the random variable to estimate the model parameters, the Method of Moment (MM) uses assumptions about a set of moment specifications for the data-generating process. The MM then estimates the parameters of the model or data-generating process that best fit the sample moments of the model to the specified (theoretical) moments of the data.

The most common moment assumption used under the MM is based on the orthogonality condition, which states that a set of population moments is all equal to zero. To further explain how MM works, consider the least square residual specified in Equation (6.1). The orthogonality condition for the population residual as specified under the ordinary least square (OLS) assumption is that the mean of the residual is zero and that each realization of the residual is uncorrelated with the regressor x_i as shown below.

$$E(\varepsilon) = 0, \ \ E(x_i, \varepsilon) = 0, \ \ i = 1, ..., n \tag{6.12}$$

We can generalize the moment expression in Equation (6.12) in terms of a set of population moments conditions $E[G(x_i, \beta)] = 0$, where β is the parameter space. The corresponding sample moments can be written as follows:

$$g_n(\hat{\beta}) = \frac{1}{n} \sum_{i=1}^{n} g(x_i, \hat{\beta}) \tag{6.13}$$

Thus, the method of moment estimator β for the population moment is simply the parameter space $\hat{\beta}$ that solves the system of sample moments equations $g_n(\hat{\beta}) = 0$. From an algebraic standpoint, for a solution to be feasible, the number of moment conditions q must be the same as the number of parameters p in the parameter space $\hat{\beta}$. This is known as the order condition for identification.

Let's replace the second OLS orthogonality condition in Equation (6.12), with the expression in Equation (6.1). The resulting expression is now:

$$E(x_i, \varepsilon) = E(x_i, y_i - x_i \beta) = E\left[x_i\left(y_i - x_i \hat{\beta}\right)\right] = 0 \tag{6.14}$$

And the sample moment condition can then be written as:

$$\frac{1}{n} \sum_{i=1}^{n} x_i \varepsilon_i = \frac{1}{n} \sum_{i=1}^{n} x_i\left(y_i - x_i \hat{\beta}\right) = 0 \tag{6.15}$$

The MM estimator β is the $\hat{\beta}$ that solves the system of equations, and it is equivalent to the OLS estimator shown in Equation (6.3). In reality, the OLS estimator is a special case of the method of moment estimators.

As shown in Chapter Three, the orthogonality condition for the residual term is often violated in financial data such that $E(x_i, \varepsilon) \neq 0$. In this case, we can side-step the problem by replacing x_i with an instrumental variable z_i that is correlated with x_i but orthogonal to the residual term. The population moment condition can then be written in the form.

$$E(z_i, \varepsilon_i) = E\left[z_i\left(y_i - x_i \hat{\beta}\right)\right] = 0 \tag{6.16}$$

The sample moment condition is analogous to the expression in Equation (6.16) and is shown as follows:

$$\frac{1}{n}\sum_{i=1}^{n}z_i\varepsilon_i = \frac{1}{n}\sum_{i=1}^{n}z_i\left(y_i - x_i\hat{\beta}\right) = 0 \tag{6.17}$$

Remember that our initial population moment conditions are defined as $E\left[G(x_i,\beta)\right]$.

Consequently, their analogous sample moment conditions can be defined as $g(x_i,\hat{\beta}) = g\left(\hat{\beta}\right)$.

$$g\left(\hat{\beta}\right) = \frac{1}{n}\sum_{i=1}^{n}z_i\left(y_i - x_i\hat{\beta}\right) = 0 \tag{6.18}$$

The estimation approach shown above is known as instrumental variable regression and is also a special case of the method of moment estimation. There are many other special cases of the method of moment estimation. Indeed, we can show that the maximum likelihood estimation (MLE) is also a special case of the MM estimator by setting the score function $L_n'\left(\beta\,|\,Y\right)$ of the MLE to equal zero.

$$\frac{1}{n}\sum_{i=1}^{n}L_n'\left(\beta\,|\,Y\right)_i = 0 \tag{6.19}$$

Generalized Method of Moment (GMM)

Algebraically it is infeasible to derive a solution to the moment conditions when the number of orthogonality conditions p is less than the number of parameters q (under identification). However, when q is greater than p, we face an overidentification problem because we now have more equations than parameters, which increases the chance that we might obtain more than one solution. One way to estimate the unknown parameter vector in the presence of overidentification is to specify a weighting matrix W_n that is symmetric and positive definite such that we can find a parameter space θ that will bring the solutions $Q_n(\theta)$ as close as possible to zero. The GMM estimator is then defined as the value of θ that minimizes.

$$Q_n(\theta) = g_n(\theta)' W_n g_n(\theta) \tag{6.20}$$

The optimization problem for the GMM estimator can then be written as:

$$\hat{\theta} = \operatorname*{argmin}_{\hat{\theta}} Q_n(\theta) \tag{6.21}$$

Comparing Parametric Methods of Estimation in SAS Using PROC MODEL

Let us perform a quick comparison of the different parametric methods of estimation in SAS using PROC MODEL. PROC MODEL is a workhorse estimation procedure in SAS/ETS. It is capable of estimating and analyzing various types of model specifications, including linear and non-linear models. It can also be used to simulate data and generate forecasts from a variety of model specifications. For our example, we will use PROC MODEL to estimate the industry beta for the financial services sector using the single index model. The index model regresses the excess returns ER_{it} for the security or portfolio on the excess market return MRP_t as shown in Equation (6.22).

$$ER_{it} = \alpha_i + MRP_t + \varepsilon_{it} \qquad (6.22)$$

In Program 6.1, we show the SAS program that was used to estimate the raw beta of the financial services sector using the single-index model. By default, PROC MODEL tries to fit linear equations using the OLS approach. We can request the MLE and GMM approaches by specifying additional FIT statements as shown in the code.

Program 6.1: Fitting Parametric Index Models of Stock Returns Using PROC MODEL

```
/*SAS code to show different parametric methods of estimation*/
%datapull(industr,industr.sas7bdat);

proc model data=industr;
      finance = constant +beta*mrp;
      fit finance / ols; /*OLS*/
      fit finance / fiml; /*MLE*/
      fit finance / gmm;/*GMM*/
run;
```

The output of the programs shows that the values of the parameter estimate from all three approaches are the same. However, their standard errors and consequently their test statistics are slightly different due to the differences in the methods used to calculate the standard errors.

Output 6.1: Index Models of Stock Returns

Nonlinear OLS Parameter Estimates				
Parameter	Estimate	Approx Std Err	t Value	Approx Pr > |t|
constant	-0.09484	0.2293	-0.41	0.6799
beta	1.066036	0.0505	21.10	<.0001

Nonlinear FIML Parameter Estimates				
Parameter	Estimate	Approx Std Err	t Value	Approx Pr > |t|
constant	-0.09484	0.2232	-0.42	0.6717
beta	1.066036	0.0422	25.24	<.0001

Nonlinear GMM Parameter Estimates				
Parameter	Estimate	Approx Std Err	t Value	Approx Pr > |t|
constant	-0.09484	0.2437	-0.39	0.6978
beta	1.066036	0.0597	17.84	<.0001

In reality, both the OLS and MLE are special cases of GMM where a probability distribution is specified for the data-generating process. For both estimations, we assumed that the errors are normally distributed to be able to draw statistical inferences from the estimation results.[6] However, only the MLE directly applies the properties of the distribution (via the likelihood function) in estimating the parameters of the model. You should also note that both the GMM and MLE are iterative procedures, meaning that they start with an initial guess of the value of parameters, and then use one of the many optimization algorithms to conduct a numerical search for the parameter space that results in the highest likelihood values for the MLE and the lowest degree of violation of the orthogonality conditions for the GMM. In contrast, the OLS model is not iterative. It is simply the algebraic solution to a functional specification of the parameters of the model that is expressed as the search for the minimum of the sum of squared residuals.

Nonparametric Method of Estimation

Under the nonparametric method of estimation, we do not assume any specific distribution for the data. Rather the distributional properties of the data and the parameter estimates (or model features) are derived directly from the data itself using some type of estimator. In general, it is common to provide some guidance for the estimation process to know how well the nonparametric model fits the given data set by specifying a loss function. One way to think about the loss function is that it is the penalty for a bad fit to the data. Thus, analogous to the optimization process in the parametric models, the optimization process for nonparametric models would typically also seek to minimize these loss functions. It is also possible to impose additional penalties for model complexity to prevent overfitting. Hence, the optimization problem for the loss function can be generalized as:

$$\underset{f}{\operatorname{argmin}} \frac{1}{N} \sum_{i=1}^{n} L\left(f\left(x_i\right), y_i\right) + R\left(f\right) \qquad (6.23)$$

where L is the mapping of the function of the feature variables $f\left(x_i\right)$ to the target outcome y_i and $R\left(f\right)$ is the penalty function for model complexity. For models that require the estimation of parameter space, we can rewrite the expression above in terms of the parameter vector β as follows:

$$\underset{\beta}{\operatorname{argmin}} \frac{1}{N} \sum_{i=1}^{n} L\left(f_\beta\left(x_i\right), y_i\right) + R\left(\beta\right) \qquad (6.24)$$

Although there are many types of loss functions, in general, they fall into these three categories: regression loss functions, classification loss functions, and distribution-based loss functions.

---

[6] In reality, you do not need normally distributed variables to estimate the parameters of the model in least square regressions. The assumption of normality of the error term is needed to derive statistical inferences from the estimates.

Regression-based loss functions include mean absolute error (MAE), mean squared error (MSE),[7] and Huber loss (HL) to name a few. Classification loss functions include binary loss (zero-one), perceptron loss, cross-entropy, hinge loss, and logarithmic loss, to name a few. Distribution- or density-based (entropy) loss functions include binary cross-entropy, weighted cross-entropy, and balanced cross-entropy, to name a few.

The simplest type of nonparametric estimator is the histogram, which constructs the probability density of a variable by obtaining the relative frequencies of binned data sets. From a predictive modeling point of view, it is more common to use density estimators that allow for a more flexible way of binning the data (bandwidth or smoothing parameter), which is what kernel density estimators provide. Besides density estimators, another nonparametric method of estimation is to use the posterior probability of obtaining the values of the parameter space from the data to estimate the model parameters.[8] This is because the posterior probability distribution of the parameter space that is obtained from the data will converge to its true value according to Doob's theorem, as long as the prior probability of obtaining the parameter space is nonzero. This is a fairly rigorous concept, but the general idea is as follows.

> If we have a predetermined probability of how the parameter space explains the data, as we encounter more data, we can examine how well it matches that prior belief and update our beliefs accordingly. The more data we get, the more we refine our belief and parameter space. After reviewing enough data, we will arrive at a well-calibrated parameter space along with our belief in how well it matches the data.

Although nonparametric models can help us avoid the risk of specifying the wrong probability distribution for the data, they also come with their challenges. Nonparametric models require more observations than parametric models. Because there are typically no restrictions on the number of parameters, they have a higher risk of overfitting the model to the data than parametric models. The greater number of parameters could also make model interpretability more challenging than in the case of parametric models.

Kernel Density Estimation

Kernel density estimators (KDE) are the most commonly used nonparametric method of estimation in predictive modeling. Unlike histograms that have non-overlapping bins with a fixed width, the KDE generates the probability distribution of the data by applying moving windows of adjustable bin sizes (smoothing bandwidth) over the distribution of the data. The probability distribution is obtained by fitting the density function (kernels) at every observation of the

---

[7] The mean squared error (MSE) loss function is calculated as the average of the Sum of Squared Residual (SSE) shown in Equation (6.2). This implies the least square estimation approach is also a special case of a loss function.

[8] Think of this as the probability of obtaining the parameter space β, given the data. This approach is based on Bayes' Theorem.

data. Therefore, the probability distributions that are generated by kernel densities are smooth functions, which is unlike the bar-shaped distribution that is obtained from the histogram. One way to think of kernel density estimation is as moving histograms of a small sample of the data that are plotted at each observation. Successive peaks of the histogram are then joined together to create a distribution plot. The general framework for kernel density estimation is as follows. Given a set N dimensional random variable $\{x_1, x_2, ..., x_n\}$, the probability density $\hat{p}(x)$ for the sequence of the values $x \in R$ can be obtained from a fixed-width kernel density estimator K and fixed bandwidth parameter h as follows.

$$\hat{p}(x) = \frac{1}{Nh} \sum_{i=1}^{N} K\left(\frac{X_i - x}{h}\right) \tag{6.25}$$

The kernel function measures the closeness of x to X_i, in terms of whether it is in the specified bandwidth $\{x - h; x + h\}$ and if so, how close is it to x. From the above, it is evident that the bandwidth is integral to the shape of the kernel density. The greater the bandwidth, the smoother the kernel density. However, extremely large bandwidth might oversmooth the data, such that the salient characteristics of the data might be lost. Extremely low bandwidth may lead to under-smoothed data, which will increase the risk of overfitting the data. One way to select the best optimal bandwidth is to compute the Mean Integrated Squared Error (MISE) and select the bandwidth that minimizes its value.

There are various types of kernel functions. They include Gaussian (normal) kernels, rectangular (uniform) kernels, and Epanechnikov kernels to name a few. The default kernel function used in PROC UNIVARIATE, when the KERNEL statement is invoked is the Gaussian Kernel function and is written in the form. [9]

$$K(x) = \frac{1}{\sqrt{2\pi}} \exp\left(\frac{x^2}{2}\right) \tag{6.26}$$

Estimating Kernel Densities in SAS

There are two ways to estimate kernel densities in SAS. With PROC UNIVARIATE, you can request the estimation of the univariate kernel density by invoking the HISTOGRAM statement and specifying the KERNEL option. With PROC KDE, you can estimate both univariate and bivariate kernel densities. Program 6.2 shows the SAS code to estimate the kernel densities of the monthly returns of the financial services sector using the PROC UNIVARIATE and HISTOGRAM statements.

---

[9] Interested readers should visit the SAS reference page for Kernel Density Estimate at https://documentation.sas.com/doc/en/pgmsascdc/9.4_3.5/procstat/procstat_univariate_details60.htm.

Program 6.2: Using PROC UNIVARIATE to Estimate Kernel Densities of Stock Returns

```
/*Estimating Kernel Densities Using PROC UNIVARIATE*/
title 'Distribution of Financial Services Industry Returns';

proc univariate data=industr noprint;
      histogram  finance/
            kernel(c = 0.5 1 2
            noprint
            k=normal)
            odstitle = title;
run;
```

The KERNEL statement is invoked to request the plots of the kernel densities for three bandwidths (0.5, 1, and 2) shown in Output 6.2. The 'C' statement is used to specify the bandwidth. Notice how the bandwidth selected affects the shape of the kernel densities. The lower the value of the bandwidth selected, the more closely the kernel density fits the histogram. Amongst the three bandwidth choices displayed on the graph, 1.0 appears to have the best fit to the data.

Output 6.2: Kernel Densities of Stock Returns

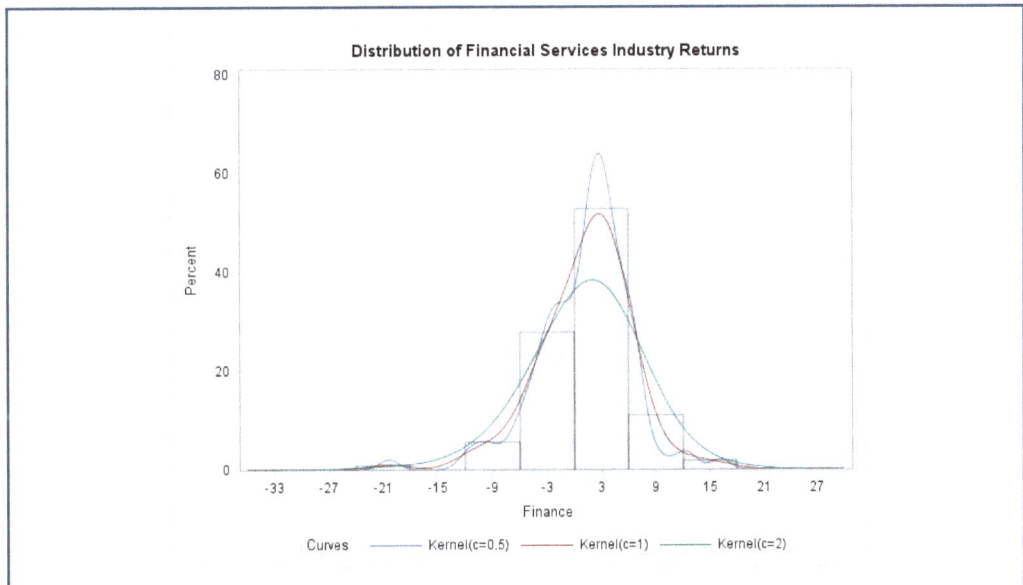

In Program 6.3, the SAS code that was used to graph the multivariate kernel densities for the monthly returns of the financial sector and the stock market is shown. In this example, we used the KDE procedure. The UNIVAR statement is used to request the univariate kernel densities for both variables, while the BIVAR statement is used to request the bivariate kernel density for both variables. BWM is the bandwidth multiplier that specifies the bandwidth of the kernel density.

The PLOTS=DENSITYOVERLAY statement is used to request the overlay plots of their respective univariate kernel densities, while the second PLOTS=ALL statement is used to request the graphs of the various types of bivariate kernel densities that are available in SAS. They include contour, histogram, and surface plots of the bivariate kernel densities.

Program 6.3: Using PROC KDE to Estimate Univariate and Bivariate Kernel Densities of Stock Returns

```
/*Estimating Univariate Bivariate Kernel Densities Using PROC KDE*/
title 'Distribution of Financial Services Industry and Market Returns';
ods graphics on;

proc kde data=industr;
      univar finance(bwm=1) mrp(bwm=1) /plots=densityoverlay;
      bivar finance mrp/ plots=all;
run;
```

Output 6.3: Univariate and Bivariate Kernel Densities of Stock Returns

Output 6.3 shows the results obtained from invoking the procedure. The first plot is the overlaid univariate density plots for the excess returns of the financial services sector and the market risk premium. The second graph is the contour plot of the bivariate kernel density of both variables, while the third and fourth graphs are the bivariate surface plot and histogram of the two variables. Overall, the plots show a joint distribution that is correlated and skewed to the left tails of the finance variable.

Kernel Regression

Now that we have established the conceptual framework of KDE, let us generalize the approach to a predictive modeling problem by proposing the conditional expectation of the response variable Y relative to its predictors X as follows:

$$m(X) = E(Y \mid X) \tag{6.27}$$

where $m(\bullet)$ is the unknown nonlinear function of the predictor variables. We can write the above in a nonparametric regression form as follows.

$$y_i = m(x_i) + \varepsilon_i \tag{6.28}$$

With $E(\varepsilon_i) = 0$ and $Var(\varepsilon_i) = \sigma^2$. m is the smoothing function of the predictor variables. Given what we know about x_i, one way to predict each y_i is to estimate the kernel at each realization of x_i using only the observations that are close to it. The best estimate of y_i as expressed in the form of $\hat{m}(x)$ is then the weighted mean of y_i near the point x_i, with the weights depending on the value of x_i and the bandwidth h. In reality, the weights are calculated as the ratio of the joint density of x_i and y_i at each point in x, adjusted by the marginal density of x_i. This ratio is known as the Nadaraya-Watson Kernel Regression estimator and is expressed as:

$$\hat{m}(x) = \sum_{i=1}^{n} \underbrace{\frac{K\left(\dfrac{X_i - x}{h}\right)}{\displaystyle\sum_{i=1}^{N} K_h\left(\dfrac{X_i - x}{h}\right)}}_{\equiv w_i} y_i = \sum_{i=1}^{n} w_i \cdot y_i \tag{6.29}$$

where w_i are the weights assigned to each value of y_i for all observations of x_i that fall into the interval $\{x - h; x + h\}$.[10]

From a conceptual point of view, the approach used by kernel regression can be explained as the process of predicting the response variable by estimating the weighted sum of all the values of the response variable that are observed within a given bandwidth of the predictor x_i. The

---

[10] You can learn more about kernel density estimation by visiting Rick Wicklin's blog, The DO Loop at https://blogs.sas.com/content/iml/2018/08/29/kernel-regression-in-sas.html.

greater the bandwidth, the smoother the regression line (that is, theoretically more values of the response variable are included in calculating the averages). Furthermore, observations that are closer to each other are given relatively higher weights in making predictions than those that are far apart.

K-Nearest Neighbor Methods

While the kernel weight shown in Equation (6.29) uses fixed bandwidth, we can relax this restriction to allow for averaging over the kth nearest points. For example, we can opt to average over the $\left(1^{st},\ 2^{nd},\ 3^{rd},...,k^{th}\right)$ nearest observations of each observation x_i. This approach is called the K_n Nearest Neighbor (KNN) method. The averaging method of the KNN regression assigns equal importance to the contribution of each neighbor to the estimate of Y regardless of their distance to the point of estimate.

Locally Estimated Scatter Plot Smoothing (LOESS)

One way to adjust for the role of distance in the estimate of y_i is to weigh the average contribution of each KNN neighbor to the estimate of y_i by its distance to the point of estimation x_i. The LOESS approach combines the smoothing parameters of the kernel regression with the nearest neighbor group (bucket) of the KNN. Furthermore, concerning the functional form of $y_i = m(x_i) + \varepsilon_i$, in the LOESS approach, we can specify a linear or polynomial form for $m(\cdot)$. In a k-dimensional (k-d) feature space, the bucket that contains all of the feature variables is divided into rectangular hierarchical child cells iteratively until the child cell has less than the specified number of vertices. The LOESS method then performs a weighted least square at all of the vertices of each terminal child cell. The weights are a decreasing function of the distance from the vertices, while the smoothing parameter represents the fraction of the data that is included in the local regression. In the direct implementation, all of the observations are included in the regression; however, this is computationally intensive. Another approach is to perform the fit using samples drawn from the data, and then blend the fitted values with the predicted values at the vertices of the k-d tree cell.

Implementing Kernel-Based Regression in SAS

SAS currently does not have a built-in procedure to directly estimate kernel regressions. However, you can implement kernel regression using SAS/IML modules for weighted polynomial regression (visualize a weighted regression in which you use the PDF function to compute the kernel weights). The kernel regression module computes the kernel regression at a vector of points.[11] Alternatively, the LOESS procedure can be used to estimate local regression-type models and fit linear and polynomial function forms of $m(x_i)$. PROC LOESS can generate predicted values for the response variables, as well as confidence intervals for the predictions. It can also be used to score new data sets.

---

[11] Examples of the code to implement kernel regression using SAS/IML can be found on The DO Loop at https://blogs.sas.com/content/iml/2018/08/29/kernel-regression-in-sas.html.

Program 6.4: Fitting Index Model of Stock Returns Using PROC LOESS

```
/*Using PROC LOESS to Fit the Index Model*/
ods graphics on;
%datapull(industr,industr.sas7bdat);
%datapull(finscore,finscore.sas7bdat);

proc loess data=industr plots=all;
      model finance=mrp/ all details  degree=1
            smooth=0.1;
      score data=finscore /clm print(var=finance);
run;
```

Program 6.4 shows the SAS code that was used to estimate the LOESS regression for the index model. Although it is not used here, the DIRECT statement can be invoked to request local regression at all points. The default degree of the polynomial is one. You can request a quadratic polynomial by setting DEGREE=2. SMOOTH=0.1 specifies the values of the smoothing parameter. The default value is 0.5. We selected 0.1 to highlight an example of an overfitted function. The smooth value of 1 will result in a fit plot that is similar to the regression line of the OLS. The SCORE statement is specified to request the scoring of the FINSCORE data set.

Output 6.4: Index Model of Stock Returns Using PROC LOESS

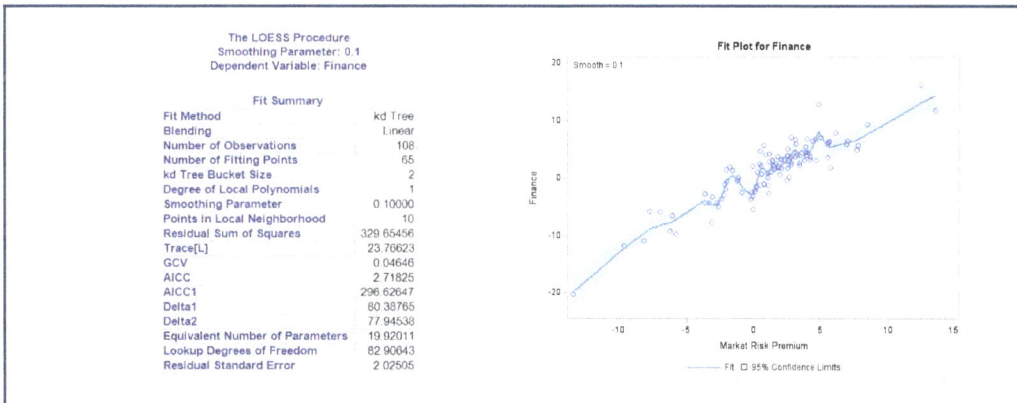

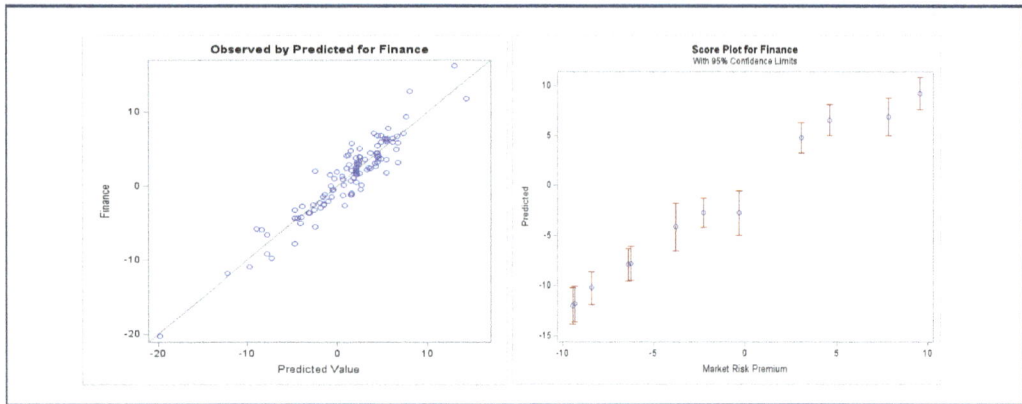

Output 6.4 shows the results and plots that were obtained from implementing Program 6.4. The Fit Summary table shows the value of the smoothing parameter and some associated statistics. It shows the fit method as the KD tree with a linear blending method. There are 65 fitting points in the KD tree with 10 points in the local neighbor group. The equivalent number of parameters in the model is approximately 20. You will notice on the Observed by Predicted Plot that the dispersion of prediction around actual values is much closer than those from the linear regression model. The Score Plot shows the predictions and the confidence intervals for the industry returns for the holdout data in the FINSCORE data set.

Generalized Maximum Entropy

The generalized maximum entropy (GME) method of estimation is based on the principle that to determine the true distributions of a random variable subject to some constraints imposed by the available information about the distribution of the data, we should apply the distribution with the highest entropy. Understanding the concept of entropy is crucial for financial data scientists because it is a commonly used optimization criterion in the data science domain.

Entropy is the degree of randomness in a variable, and it is generally defined by its probability distribution. From a predictive modeling point of view, entropy can be viewed as the degree of uncertainty in the probability distribution of a random variable. Thus, we can map it to the quality of information that can be obtained from observing or modeling the variable. Higher entropy implies higher uncertainty, and consequently, lower information quality, while lower entropy implies vice versa. The aim of predictive models that use entropy specification as their loss function is to maximize the entropy of the model features. The mathematics of entropy is conceptually easy to comprehend. If we assume a finite discrete set of outcomes for a random variable, then its Shannon entropy (or simply entropy) $H(X)$ can be calculated as:

$$H(X) = -\sum_{x \in X} p(x_i) \log(p(x_i))$$

(6.30)

where $p(x_i)$ is the probability of obtaining the ith outcome from a n number of possible outcomes. The information quality of each outcome is measured by the negative logarithms of the probabilities $-\log(p(x_i))$. Thus, it is decreasing in $p(x_i)$ and converges to zero when $p(x_i) = 1$. Entropy is maximized if all outcomes of the random variable have equal probabilities (as in the case of a uniform distribution). Entropy also increases as the number of outcomes increases if all outcomes have equal probability.

> Think of entropy as how surprising the realization of an outcome is. Events that have a high probability of occurring will not convey significantly high information value to the observer (lower surprise), in contrast to events that have low probabilities of occurring (high surprise).

Following this reasoning, cross-entropy can also be defined as the difference between the probability distributions for a given random variable over the same set of outcomes.

$$H(p,q) = -\sum_{i=1}^{n} p(x)\log q(x)$$

(6.31)

From a predictive modeling point of view, cross-entropy can be extended to measure prediction accuracy or divergence. This is known as relative entropy or Kullback-Leibler (KL) Divergence. Relative entropy[12] (actual versus predicted) measures the degree to which one distribution diverges from another distribution, given that one of the distributions is the true distribution. If we assume that the true distribution is p, then relative entropy $D(p,q)$ is the entropy loss by assuming that the distribution is q instead.

$$D(p,q) = H_p(x) - H_q(x) = \sum_{i=1}^{n} p(x)\log \frac{p(x)}{q(x)}$$

(6.32)

Since predictive modeling usually entails more than one variable, it is useful to also consider the entropy relationship amongst variables. If we consider the case of two random variables X and Y, then their joint entropy $H(X,Y)$ can be written as:

$$H(X,Y) = -\sum_{x \in X}\sum_{y \in Y} p(x,y)\log[p(x,y)]$$

(6.33)

In this case, entropy is the information value from the joint realizations of both variables. We can also formulate the conditional relationship between Y and X using entropy. Here, the quest is to

---

[12] Also known as Kullback-Leibler (KL) Divergence.

find the information quality that is required to describe Y given that X is known. The formula to calculate conditional entropy is as follows.[13]

$$H(Y \mid X) = -\sum_{x \in X}\sum_{y \in Y} p(x,y)\log[p(y \mid x)] = H(X,Y) - H(X) \qquad (6.34)$$

It can be shown that X will increase the entropy of Y only if it contains information that is irrelevant to describing Y. Think of this construct in these terms – the more information about Y that is contained in X, the less surprise we can derive from the realization of Y, given what we already know about X. If Y is completely determined by X, then the entropy of Y given X will be zero. Therefore, a good approximation of the information value of any predictor variable as a feature of Y is to assess its contribution to the conditional entropy of Y.

The application of the above concepts to the generalized maximum entropy estimation is as follows. Suppose the response variable Y can be specified by the general linear model $Y = X\beta + \varepsilon$. Y represents the vector of the response variable, X the matrix of the covariates, β the vector of unknown parameters, and ε the residual term. We can reparametrize our vector of unknown parameters and the residual terms as $\beta = Zp$ and $V\omega$, respectively such that our linear model can then be written as follows.

$$Y = XZp + V\omega \qquad (6.35)$$

where Z is specified as the matrix of boundaries (support) for the possible values of the parameter space β and V the boundaries (support) of the values of the residual term ε .

p is the probability associated with the support Z values and ω the weights assigned to the support V . The values of Z are usually distributed to be symmetrical around the possible values

of β such that for the kth feature variable, its parameter β_k can be written as $\beta_k = \sum_{j=1}^{J} z_{jk} p_{jk}$

(that is, the sum of the products of the probabilities and possible values of β).

The values for the boundaries for each residual term in V are also chosen such that the error distribution is symmetric with zero mean, and the same across all observations.

Since the Z and V are predetermined, our optimization problem statement can be formulated as finding the values p and ω that maximize the cross entropy $H(p,w)$. Following our definition of the GME approach:

$$Max\ H(p,w) = -p\log(p) - w\log(w) \qquad (6.36)$$

---

[13] Applying Bayes' rule to the joint entropy $H(X,Y)$ allows us to derive the conditional entropy $H(Y \mid X)$ and marginal entropy $H(X)$.

Subject to the following:

$$Y = X\beta + \varepsilon = XZp + Vw \tag{6.37}$$

Hence, our GME estimators $\beta_{GME} = Z\hat{p}$ and $\varepsilon_{GME} = Z\hat{w}$ can be derived by solving the first-order conditions of the constrained optimization problem.

> The GME estimation approach searches for the values of the unknown parameters or feature space that yields the largest entropy. The parameter space is respecified as a product of the preselected values and their associated probabilities. The error is also respecified as a product of the preselected values and their associated probabilities. The optimization then searches for parameter and error probabilities that yield the maximum entropy. Once the probabilities are estimated, the unknown parameters and model errors can be derived from the sum of the product of the probabilities and the preselected values. For example, for a two-boundary case,
>
> $$\beta_k = \sum_{j=1}^{J=2} z_{jk} p_{jk} = z_{1k} p_{1k} + z_{2k} p_{2k}.$$

Notice that GME does not require us to make any assumption about the distribution or impose moment conditions, although you can choose to do the latter. The generalized maximum entropy estimation approach is particularly valuable for predictive modeling task that involves a large number of features, given the challenge that we face in terms of determining the true multivariate probability distribution of the model. It can be used for both parametric and nonparametric models, as well as for supervised and unsupervised learning models.

The ENTROPY procedure in SAS is currently offered in experimental form. Nevertheless, let's explore how we can apply it in a predictive model. We will revisit the industry beta regression that was shown in Equation (6.22) and Program 6.1. To provide some guidance for our GME optimization, we will set supports and priors (in parentheses) for both the market risk premium [0.5(0.5) to 1.5(0.5)] and the error term [-1.0 (0.5) to 1.0 (0.5)]. It is unlikely that the beta of the financial services industry will be outside the range of 0.5 to 1.5, given its correlation with the economy, so we are confident that the estimated beta should fall within this range. The -1.0 and +1.0 for the error term are chosen arbitrarily.[14]

---

[14] By default, PROC ENTROPY sets 5 support points for the parameters (PRIOR statement) and the error term (ESUPPORTS). The values of the support points are calculated from the OLS regression. Visit https://documentation.sas.com/doc/en/etscdc/14.2/etsug/etsug_entropy_syntax10.htm and https://documentation.sas.com/doc/en/etscdc/14.2/etsug/etsug_entropy_syntax11.htm to review the methods.

Program 6.5: Fitting Index Model of Stock Return Using PROC ENTROPY

```
/*Estimating an Index Model Using PROC ENTROPY*/
proc entropy data= industr maxiter=50 outp=entprob plots=all;
      priors mrp  0.5(0.5) 1.5(0.5);
      model finance = mrp /esupports= (-1.0(0.5) 1.0(0.5));
run;

proc print data=entprob;
run;
```

Program 6.5 shows the SAS code that was used to estimate the index model. The PRIOR statement was used to specify the support for the parameter estimates, while the ESUPPORTS statement was used to do the same for the error. We used the default five support options for the intercept term. The estimated probabilities for the GME parameters are saved in the ENTPROB data set and printed using the PRINT statement.

Output 6.5: Estimating an Index Model of Stock Returns Using the ENTROPY Procedure

GME Summary of Residual Errors							
Equation	DF Model	DF Error	SSE	MSE	Root MSE	R-Square	Adj RSq
Finance	2	120	730.6	5.9884	2.4471	0.7876	0.7859

GME Variable Estimates					
Variable	Estimate	Approx Std Err	t Value	Approx Pr > |t|
mrp	1.066035	0.0501	21.27	<.0001
Intercept	-0.09483	0.2274	-0.42	0.6774

Output 6.5 shows the generalized maximum entropy estimate for our index model. Notice that the parameter estimates of the model are the same as the ones we derived from the parametric methods of estimation. The standard errors are different because of the different methods of computing the covariance matrix of the parameter estimates. The default option in the procedure is the generalized maximum entropy.

In Table 6.2, we show how the coefficients of the GME estimator are derived from the estimated probabilities and the prior support specified for the model. The beta estimates for the financial services sector are the probability-weighted sum of the estimated betas and the specified supports. Notice that probabilities for both coefficients sum to one (for example, 0.43397+0.56603=1.0).

The values of the parameter estimates obtained from the GME estimator are equivalent to the estimates derived from the OLS, FIML, and GMM estimators. In Chapter Seven, we will explore some machine learning models that use the entropy specification for their optimization loss functions.

Table 6.2: Calculating the Estimates of the Generalized Maximum Entropy Parameters

	GME Parameter Estimations					
Variable	**NSupport**	**Support**	**Prior**	**Probability**	**Intercept** (Support x Prob)	**MRP** (Support x Prob)
MRP	2	0.500	0.5	0.43397		0.216985
MRP	2	1.500	0.5	0.56603		0.849045
INTERCEPT	5	-1.099	0.2	0.23602	-0.25948	
INTERCEPT	5	-0.550	0.2	0.21645	-0.11898	
INTERCEPT	5	0.000	0.2	0.19851	0.00000	
INTERCEPT	5	0.550	0.2	0.18206	0.10008	
INTERCEPT	5	1.099	0.2	0.16696	0.18356	

$$\beta_k = \sum_{j=1}^{J} z_{jk} p_{jk} = \quad -0.09483 \qquad 1.06603$$

Types of Predictive Models

Financial data scientists use predictive models to achieve a variety of organizational tasks and objectives. The common types of models and their applications are described in the following segment.

Classification Models

Classification models are used to categorize outcomes or events into groups using the characteristics that these events or outcomes share in common with other variables. For example, classification models are used to classify loan applications into successful and unsuccessful applicant pools based on the characteristics of the potential borrower such as credit score, income, and loan duration, to name a few. Classification models can be used for both ordinal and nominal groupings and can be in the form of supervised, unsupervised, and reinforcement learning models.[15] They can also be in the form of parametric, nonparametric,

---

[15] The first chapter of the book presents various types of machine learning models. We will highlight their practical applications in more detail in Chapter Seven.

and semi-parametric models. Predictions from classification models are either in a discrete form in which an observation is assigned to a particular group or in the form of probabilities that observations fall into a particular group. Common types of classification models include decision trees, random forests, logistic regressions, support vector machines (SVM), neural networks, and Bayesian classifier networks.

Regression Models

Regression models are used to estimate the magnitude of outcomes or events. Using our previous loan applicants pool as an example, a regression model can be used to estimate the interest rate to charge on the loans that are offered to successful applicants using a similar set of characteristics. Regression models are used to predict interval response variables. These predictions can be in the form of point estimates or prediction intervals. The input to regression models can be in the form of continuous or discrete variables. As shown in the previous section of the chapter, they can be estimated using both parametric and nonparametric models. Most regression models are in the form of supervised learning models. Common types of regression models include linear regression, data mining regression, least angle regression, neural network, and support vector regression (SVR).

Dimension Reduction Models

While classification models predict events or outcomes of the same variable, dimension reduction models are used in the data preprocessing phase of the analytics life cycle to reduce the number of variables in the high-dimensional data set before feeding them into the final predictive model. The three types of dimension-reduction procedures are principal component analysis, factor analysis, and cluster analysis.

Principal component analysis, which is the most common approach, uses matrix algebra to reduce the dimension of the data by finding the dominant pattern in the matrix of explanatory variables. The dominant pattern is defined by the variance of the transformed values relative to the untransformed data. Factor analysis aims to find underlying common variables that can explain observed patterns in a group of variables.

Clustering models are used to group observations in a data set based on the characteristics that they share in common. Clustering models are commonly used for data exploration, dimension reduction, outlier detection, segmenting outcomes, and as a complement to factor analysis, to name a few. Most clustering models are based on unsupervised learning techniques, but there are a few supervised clustering techniques. In reality, there is a proliferation of clustering techniques and consequently many approaches to their implementation. There are parametric and nonparametric clustering models, as well as models that are based on hierarchy, centroid, and density-based clusters, to name a few. The main difference between the two approaches is that principal component analyses are used to group variables, while cluster analyses are used to group observations.

Forecasting Models

Forecasting models are used to predict the future values of variables of interest using their current and past realizations as predictors. These models attempt to answer a basic question in terms of what the future value of the variable of interest will look like, given what we know about its current and past values. For example, forecasting regression could be used to forecast the future default rate on a loan portfolio using the historical default rates. Unlike the previous two models, which are not necessarily based on time series data, forecasting models rely purely on time series data to generate future forecasts. In Chapter Three, we highlighted a few statistical models that are commonly used for forecasting. These include Autoregression (AR), Autoregressive Integrated Moving Average (ARIMA), and Seasonal Autoregressive Moving Average (SARIMA) models. In this chapter, we add to that list the Vector Autoregressive (VAR) and Vector error correction (VECM) models.

Time Index Forecasting Models

Unlike forecasting models that use current value and past values of the variable to forecast future values, the time index models use time indices as their primary predictor variable, and as such they are particularly useful for forecasting events or outcomes that are mostly time dependent. These include events or outcomes whose values increase or decrease monotonically over time, as well as those with non-monotonic changes over time (such as those with cyclicality, seasonality, and stationarity). For example, a bank could use a time index forecasting model to forecast the future size of its loan portfolio if the loan portfolio has been growing monotonically over time. Common types of time index forecasting models include the Autoregressive Integrated Moving Average (ARIMA), exponential smoothing, and Prophet models.

Outlier Models

Outlier models are used to detect events or outcomes that deviate from the norm. They deviate from the general classification model in the sense that the models employed here operate from a baseline, and only aim to decipher events or outcomes that deviate from it. Hence, they are often regarded as single-class classification models. Outlier models are mostly employed to detect anomalous events such as fraudulent activities, intrusion detection, and employee churning, to name a few. In the past, outlier analyses were performed using univariate statistical methods. Recent advances in data science have led to the introduction of more robust approaches. These include Support Vector Data Description, which constructs an n-dimensional feature (predictors) space (hypersphere) around the normal outcome or events. Outlier events or outcomes are defined as those that fall outside the boundaries of the hypersphere.

Predictive Modeling in SAS

There are various means to implement predictive modeling in SAS. For those accessing SAS using desktop clients such as Enterprise Guide and SAS 9.4 or web applications such as SAS Studio, statistical predictive modeling can be implemented if you have an active license to SAS/STAT and SAS/ETS. Machine learning modeling can also be implemented in Enterprise Guide, SAS Studio, and Enterprise Miner if you have an active license to SAS Enterprise Miner. You should be aware that SAS Viya is now the flagship analytics engine for SAS. Although the SAS Viya engine operates on a different architecture than SAS 9.4, you can still access it using Enterprise Guide, SAS Studio, and Enterprise Miner. Base SAS procedures also run seamlessly in the SAS Viya environment. However, due to the wider availability of SAS Studio, Enterprise Guide, and Enterprise Miner, we will stick to these applications for our demonstrations. You can check the list of SAS products that are licensed to your site by submitting the following SAS program and checking the log.

Program 6.6: SAS Code to Verify Current SAS License on Machine

```
proc product_status;
run;
```

If you are accessing SAS through SAS OnDemand for Academics, then you should note that access to SAS/STAT, SAS/ETS, and SAS Enterprise Miner are available in that windowing environment. Many of the exercises that we will perform in subsequent sections of this chapter would require an active license to SAS/STAT and SAS/ETS. If you do not have an active site license, you should consider signing up for free access to SAS Studio through SAS OnDemand.[16] Table 6.3 provides a summary of some of the predictive models that are available in SAS and the SAS product licenses that are required to implement them.

Statistical Predictive Models in SAS

Now that we have established a rigorous framework of the fundamentals of predictive modeling using some basic examples such as linear regression models, let us proceed with examples of how other statistical predictive models that are listed in Table 6.3 can be implemented in SAS.

Classification Models

As discussed earlier, classification models are generally used to predict categorical or discrete events. You should note that categorical events can be mutually or non-mutually exclusive in nature. Mutually exclusive outcomes imply that only one outcome can occur at a reference point

---

[16] To access SAS Studio for free on the web, visit: https://welcome.oda.sas.com/. Create a free SAS profile, which will provide you access to SAS Studio and 5GB of free data storage for your personal files.

Table 6.3: Predictive Models Options in SAS 9.4

SAS Product	Modeling Problem	Model Types	Procedures	Estimation Method	Distribution
	Regression	Regression	REG, GLM, NLIN, QUANTREG	LS, MLE, GMM	Parametric
		Regression	LOGISTIC, PROBIT, TOBIT	MLE	Parametric
		Discriminant Analysis	DISCRIM, CANDISC	MLE	Parametric
	Classification	Tree	DTREE, HPSPLIT	Entropy	Nonparametric
		Principal Component	PRINCOMP, FACTOR	PCA	Nonparametric
	Dimension Reduction	Cluster Analysis	CLUSTER, FASTCLUS, VARCLUS	PCA	Nonparametric
SAS/STAT	Time-to-Event	Survival Analysis	ICLIFETEST, ICPHREG, LIFEREG, LIFETEST, PHREG, SURVEYPHREG	MLE	Parametric and Nonparametric
	Regression	System Models, Multivariate Regression	SYSLIN, VARMAX	LS, MLE	Parametric
	Classification	Qualitative and Limited Dependent Variable	QLIM	MLE	Parametric
	Forecasting	Autoregression	AUTOREG, ARIMA	LS, MLE	Parametric
SAS/ETS	Time Index Forecasting	ARIMA, Exponential Smoothing	ARIMA, ESM, UCM	LS, MLE	Parametric
	Regression	Regression	Linear, Autoneural	MLE	Parametric
			LARS, DMINE	LS	Parametric
	Classification	Trees	Decision Tree, Forest, Gradient Boosting	Entropy	Nonparametric
		Kernel	Support Vector Machine	Entropy	Nonparametric
SAS Enterprise Miner (Procedures are presented as nodes)		Regression	Logistics, Data Mining, Autoneural	MLE	Parametric
	Clustering	Cluster Analysis	Variable Clustering, Cluster	PCA	Nonparametric

from a range of probable outcomes. The distribution of these probable and mutually exclusive outcomes is called the multinomial distribution. A special case of the multinomial distribution is the binomial distribution in which there are only two possible outcomes in each trial. We will focus on the models for these types of events in the book. There are statistical models for predicting events with multinomial outcomes. In reality, many of them are extensions to the models of binary outcomes. Therefore, establishing a strong foundational knowledge of the statistical framework of binary choice models is essential before delving into multinomial models.[17]

Binary Choice Models

The most common types of classification models are binary choice models. They are used to model response variables Y with dichotomous outcomes as a function of a set of predictor variables $X = [X_1, X_2, ..., X_k]$. Categorically, the response variable can be any outcome where there are only two possibilities (for example, employed or unemployed, pass or fail). Examples of dichotomous response variables in financial settings include loan approval, directional movement in stock prices, the payoff of derivative securities, and event risk, to name a few. Numerically, binary choice outcomes are typically labeled as 0 or 1, where each value represents either of the dichotomous states that the response variable can take. Binary choice models attempt to describe the conditional distribution of the response variable Y, given a set of explanatory variables X. However, the functional form of the expected value $E[Y|X] = f(X\beta)$ of binary choice models is unlike those in the linear regression models, given the discreteness in the values of the response variable. You will notice in Figure 6.3 that Y can only take on the values of 0 or 1, given the values of the explanatory variables X.

In reality, binary choice models are inherently non-linear models. The linear form is an outcome of the transformation used in the specified form of $f(X\beta)$ in the binary choice model. The two commonly applied functional forms are the Probit models, which use the standard normal cumulative distribution function, and the Logit models (also known as logistic regression), which use the logistic cumulative distribution function. Therefore, the upshot of the functional transformation used in binary choice models is not the prediction of the values of the actual outcomes themselves but the probability that the outcome is realized or otherwise (that is, the probability that an observation is either 1 or 0).

Classifications are then derived based on an ascribed probability threshold. Let us consider the probability that an outcome of the response variable $p(y_i = 1)$ can be modeled by the following expression:

$$p(y_i = 1 | x_i) = f(u_i)$$
(6.38)

---

[17] The discussion of the statistical models of non-mutually exclusive events is beyond the scope of the book.

Figure 6.3: Binary Choice Models Specification

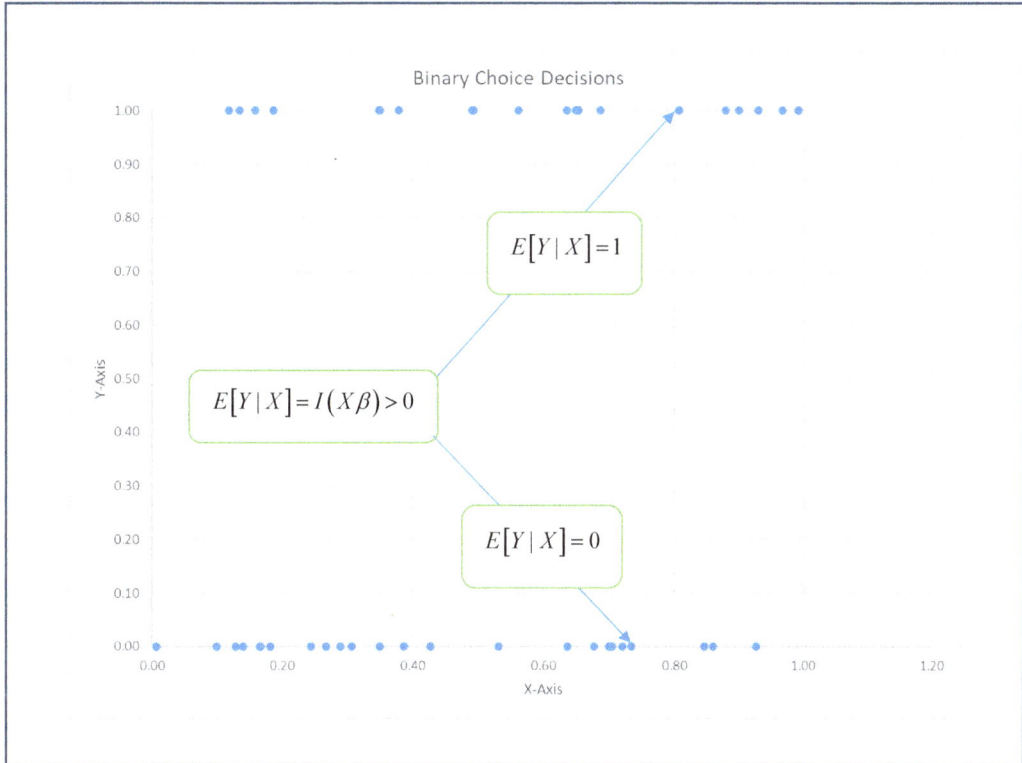

where u_i represents some parametric form of the predictor variables as shown in the expression below:

$$u_i = \beta_0 + \beta_1 x_{i1} + \beta_2 x_{i2} + ... + \beta_k x_{ik} + \varepsilon_i \qquad (6.39)$$

Probit Model

The functional form $f(u_i)$ of the Probit model specification for $P(Y = 1 \mid X)$ can be written as:

$$p(y_i = 1 \mid x_i) = f(u_i) = \Phi\left(\beta_0 + \beta_1 x_{i1} + \beta_2 x_{i2} + ... + \beta_k x_{ik}\right) \qquad (6.40)$$

where Φ represents the standard normal cumulative distribution function.

Figure 6.4: Link Functions for Binary Choice Models

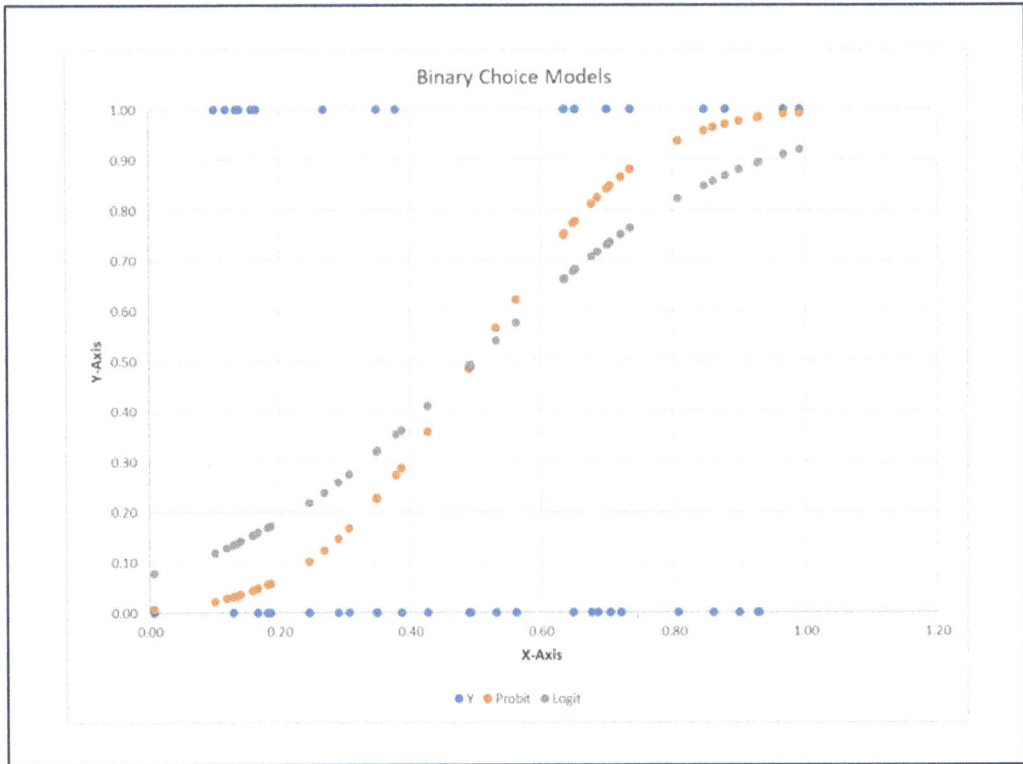

Logit Model

Likewise, the functional form $f(u_i)$ for the Logit model's specification for the same outcome applies the logistic cumulative distribution function and can also be written as:

$$p(y_i = 1 \mid x_i) = f(u_i) = \frac{1}{1 + \exp\left(-\left(\beta_0 + \beta_1 x_{i1} + \beta_2 x_{i2} + \ldots + \beta_k x_{ik}\right)\right)} \tag{6.41}$$

Probit and logit models are both estimated using the maximum likelihood method. Although both models can be extended to model response variables with more than two outcomes (multinomial probit and logit), for now, we will stick to a two-outcome setting. While the directional impact of the marginal effect of each predictor on the overall probability of the response variable can be inferred, the actual values of the effect itself cannot be directly inferred because the relationship between Y and X is non-linear. To calculate the impact, it is common to estimate the effect at the average value of the X or in the case of the logit to present it in the form of the log ratio of success to failure (also known as log odds).

$$\log\left(\frac{p(y_i = 1)}{1 - p(y_i = 1)}\right) = \beta_0 + \beta_1 x_{i1} + \beta_2 x_{i2} + \ldots \ldots + \beta_k x_{ik} \tag{6.42}$$

Figure 6.4 shows the plots of the link functions $f(u_i)$ for both the logit and probit models for randomly simulated values of the X and Y variables. You will notice that both link functions share similar S- or sigmoid curve shapes. Both functions are symmetrically distributed between zero and one, although the logit link function also has fatter tails than the probit link function.

Estimating Classification Models in SAS

Several procedures in SAS can be used to estimate binary choice models but PROC PROBIT and PROC LOGISTIC are the two more commonly used procedures. PROC PROBIT and PROC LOGISTIC can both estimate Probit and Logit models. PROC QLIM and PROC GLM can also estimate both types of models.

Predicting Long-Term Profitability Using PROBIT and LOGIT Models

The SAS data set SPX_Profit contains the financial and operational characteristics of the firms in the S&P 500 index. Let us explore if there are distinguishing characteristics that can predict whether a firm will be a profitable investment over a number of years. Because firms with poor long-term performance represent a small proportion of the firms in the index, the dichotomous variable PRET5 was created by re-coding the five-year stock return (RET5Y) for each firm in the index as 1 for positive long-term return and 0 for negative long-term stock return. The predictor variables for our binary choice model consist of a set of financial, operational, and governance characteristics of the firm. They include the logarithm of market capitalization, the log of the number of employees, the tenure of the CEO, cost of capital, and percent of the stock held by institutional shareholders, to name a few.

PROC PROBIT

Program 6.7 shows the SAS code that was used to implement the PROBIT procedure for the predictors of the long-term profitability of large publicly listed firms. The PROBIT and LOGISTIC procedures model the events with the lowered ordered value. Specifying EVENT= '0' informs the procedures to model the negative long-term returns outcomes as the lower ordered value. Although PROC LOGISTIC is more commonly used than PROC PROBIT to model binary choice response variables, the procedure has some of the same appealing features that are available in PROC LOGISTIC. First, you can specify the distribution function using the DIST= option in the model statement. Specifying the logistic distribution (LOGISTICS) in the model statement will invoke the estimation of the LOGIT model. The STORE statement can also be used to store the estimated model, which can then be used to score a new data set when it is called up in the PLM procedure. The EFFECT PLOT statement is used to request plots that overlay the fitted values on interaction plots of the covariates. The CONTOUR option overlays the fitted values at multiple thresholds of the Log of Employees (on the Y axis) and the percent of shares held by institutional investors (on the X axis).

Program 6.7: Fitting Probit Model of Long-term Firm Profitability Using PROC PROBIT

```
/* Using PROC PROBIT to Estimate the Determinants of Long-term Stock
Return*/
%datapull(profit,spx_profit.sas7bdat);
ods graphics on;

proc probit data=spx_profit plot=all;
      class ceoduality sector;
      model pret5(event='0') =  ceo_tenure logmcap logemp
              Instshrout pe esg wacc age ceoduality sector;
      effectplot contour( x=Instshrout y=logemp);
run;
```

Output 6.7: Determinants of Long-term Firm Profitability Using PROC PROBIT

Type III Analysis of Effects

Effect	DF	Wald Chi-Square	Pr > ChiSq
CEO_Tenure	1	5.1239	0.0236
Logmcap	1	29.8207	<.0001
Logemp	1	9.4005	0.0022
Instshrout	1	7.5336	0.0061
PE	1	0.1725	0.6779
ESG	1	8.4953	0.0036
WACC	1	1.4616	0.2267
Age	1	0.1000	0.7518
CEODUALITY	1	0.0007	0.9787
Sector	10	24.3968	0.0066

Fit for PRET5

Fit computed at CEO_Tenure=7.124 Logmcap=24.32 PE=34.31 ESG=21.44 WACC=8.025
Age=37.91 CEODUALITY=Y Sector=Utilities

Analysis of Maximum Likelihood Parameter Estimates

Parameter		DF	Estimate	Standard Error	95% Confidence Limits		Chi-Square	Pr > ChiSq
Intercept		1	12.0229	2.6737	6.7826	17.2632	20.22	<.0001
CEO_Tenure		1	-0.0348	0.0154	-0.0650	-0.0047	5.12	0.0236
Logmcap		1	-0.6380	0.1168	-0.8670	-0.4090	29.82	<.0001
Logemp		1	0.2622	0.0855	0.0946	0.4298	9.40	0.0022
Instshrout		1	-0.0157	0.0057	-0.0269	-0.0045	7.53	0.0061
PE		1	-0.0009	0.0022	-0.0053	0.0035	0.17	0.6779
ESG		1	0.0398	0.0136	0.0130	0.0665	8.50	0.0036
WACC		1	-0.0912	0.0754	-0.2391	0.0567	1.46	0.2267
Age		1	0.0008	0.0027	-0.0044	0.0061	0.10	0.7518
CEODUALITY	N	1	-0.0047	0.1780	-0.3537	0.3442	0.00	0.9787
CEODUALITY	Y	0	0.0000					
Sector	Communication Services	1	2.2200	0.5703	1.1023	3.3377	15.15	<.0001
Sector	Consumer Discretionary	1	1.2802	0.5455	0.2110	2.3493	5.51	0.0189
Sector	Consumer Staples	1	0.8622	0.5526	-0.2210	1.9454	2.43	0.1187
Sector	Energy	1	0.8932	0.5999	-0.2825	2.0689	2.22	0.1365
Sector	Financials	1	1.2111	0.5169	0.1980	2.2242	5.49	0.0191
Sector	Health Care	1	1.3281	0.5282	0.2928	2.3633	6.32	0.0119
Sector	Industrials	1	0.6410	0.5358	-0.4091	1.6911	1.43	0.2315
Sector	Information Technology	1	1.3334	0.5651	0.2259	2.4409	5.57	0.0183
Sector	Materials	1	0.8639	0.5708	-0.2547	1.9826	2.29	0.1301
Sector	Real Estate	1	1.8775	0.6420	0.6191	3.1359	8.55	0.0035
Sector	Utilities	0	0.0000					

Output 6.7 shows the Type III Analysis of Effects and the Maximum Likelihood Parameter Estimate tables. Also shown in the output is the Effect Plot, which shows the effect of the interaction between the number of employees and institutional share ownership on profitability. The Wald statistics shown on the Type III Analysis of Effect table indicate that CEO tenure, market capitalization, employee size, institutional share ownership, ESG score, and the sector in which the company operates are predictors of profitability. The signs of the coefficients of these variables that are shown in the Parameter Estimate table suggest that companies with longer CEO tenure, higher market capitalization, and a higher proportion of institutional ownership are less likely to have negative long-term returns, while companies with higher ESG scores, a higher number of employees, are in the communication services, consumer discretionary, financial, health care, information technology, and real estate are more likely to have negative long-term return.

PROC LOGISTIC

PROC LOGISTIC invokes the LOGISTIC procedure for estimating and classifying binary, ordinal, and nominal response variables. Although it shares many features with the PROBIT procedure, it has more features and options that make it well-suited for modeling categorical outcomes.

The PROC LOGISTIC statement (which is accompanied by a suite of options) is used to invoke the procedure. The CLASS statement is used to specify the categorical predictor variables. The CODE statement is used to write the scoring code from the estimation into a SAS program file. The MODEL statement is used to specify the names of the response variable and its predictors. The statement is accompanied by options that define the model specification (LINK), effect selection criterion (SELECTION), significance level for effect selection (SLENTRY, SLSTAY), model-fitting specification (TECHNIQUE, FCONV), confidence interval (ALPHA, CLODDS), display classification (CTABLE), ROC curve computation, diagnostic, display, and computational methods. The ODDSRATIO statement can be used to request several types of odds ratios. Several types of hypotheses testing, and test of parameter estimates can also be performed using the CONTRAST, ESTIMATE, EXACT, and TEST statements. You can compare the performance of multiple models using the ROC curve by using the ROC and ROCCONTRAST statements. The SCORE statement creates a SAS data set that contains all the data used in the estimation, along with the posterior probabilities of the response variable. In reality, there are more features in PROC LOGISTIC than we can discuss in this section alone.[18]

Program 6.8 shows the SAS code that was used to implement the LOGISTIC procedure for the predictors of the long-term profitability of large firms.

---

[18] It is highly recommended that you visit The LOGISTIC Procedure User's Guide page for a more detailed description of the numerous features of the procedure at https://documentation.sas.com/doc/en/ pgmsascdc/9.4_3.3/statug/statug_logistic_overview.htm.

Program 6.8: Fitting Logit Model of Long-term Firm Profitability Using PROC LOGISTIC

```
/* Using PROC LOGISTIC to Estimate the Determinants of Long-term Stock Return*/
ods graphics on;

proc logistic  data=spx_profit plot=all;
      class ceoduality sector;
      model pret5(event='0') = CEO_Tenure logmcap logemp
              Instshrout pe esg wacc age ceoduality sector;
      effectplot contour(x=Instshrout y=logemp);
run;
```

The results for the LOGISTIC procedure, which are shown in Output 6.8A through Output 6.8E, are quite similar to those for the PROBIT procedure (Output 6.7). Indeed, the same determinants of profitability were selected in both models. Output 6.8A shows the Type III Analysis of Effects. The significant variables shown on the Type III Analysis of Effect table for the logit model are the same as those shown on the same Type III Analysis of Effect table for the Probit model (CEO tenure, market capitalization, employee size, institutional share ownership, ESG score, and sector), although their test statistics were slightly different. Output 6.8B presents the Analysis of Maximum Likelihood Parameter Estimates table. As expected, the results shown in the table are also similar to those from the Probit model.

Output 6.8C shows the table of Odds Ratio Estimate. Although they use different link functions, the shapes of the functions are quite similar, as shown in Figure 6.4. The Logit is preferred over the Probit because the marginal effect of each predictor on the response variable is easier to describe using the log-odds ratio than in the Probit model. In Probit models, it is often estimated at thresholds such as the mean of the continuous predictor variable or relative to some reference value of the categorical predictor variable. Since the relationship in binary choice models is non-linear, the marginal effect of the Probit will not be the same at different values of the predictor variables. Log odds are linear models of the predictor variables; hence, the marginal effects of the log odds are static at every value of the response variable. The odds ratio can be extracted from the log-odds by exponentiating the parameter estimates of the log-odd model.

Output 6.8A: Determinants of Long-term Firm Profitability

Type 3 Analysis of Effects			
Effect	DF	Wald Chi-Square	Pr > ChiSq
CEO_Tenure	1	4.9351	0.0263
Logmcap	1	26.9124	<.0001
Logemp	1	8.3066	0.0040
Instshrout	1	7.0940	0.0077
PE	1	0.1097	0.7405
ESG	1	7.4812	0.0062
WACC	1	1.5646	0.2110
Age	1	0.1758	0.6750
CEODUALITY	1	0.0222	0.8814
Sector	10	20.3644	0.0260

Output 6.8B: Parameter Estimates from Logistics Regression

Parameter		DF	Estimate	Standard Error	Wald Chi-Square	Pr > ChiSq
				Analysis of Maximum Likelihood Estimates		
Intercept		1	23.3532	4.8262	23.4142	<.0001
CEO_Tenure		1	-0.0657	0.0296	4.9351	0.0263
Logmcap		1	-1.1304	0.2179	26.9124	<.0001
Logemp		1	0.4797	0.1665	8.3066	0.0040
Instshrout		1	-0.0272	0.0102	7.0940	0.0077
PE		1	-0.00136	0.00409	0.1097	0.7405
ESG		1	0.0687	0.0251	7.4812	0.0062
WACC		1	-0.1863	0.1489	1.5646	0.2110
Age		1	0.00202	0.00483	0.1758	0.6750
CEODUALITY	N	1	-0.0241	0.1616	0.0222	0.8814
Sector	Communication Services	1	1.8871	0.5158	13.3824	0.0003
Sector	Consumer Discretionary	1	0.2932	0.4289	0.4673	0.4942
Sector	Consumer Staples	1	-0.4953	0.5402	0.8405	0.3593
Sector	Energy	1	-0.4165	0.7824	0.2835	0.5944
Sector	Financials	1	0.2277	0.3829	0.3537	0.5520
Sector	Health Care	1	0.2701	0.4304	0.3938	0.5303
Sector	Industrials	1	-0.7789	0.4523	2.9654	0.0851
Sector	Information Technology	1	0.3661	0.4856	0.5684	0.4509
Sector	Materials	1	-0.3739	0.5457	0.4695	0.4932
Sector	Real Estate	1	1.1852	0.8080	2.1513	0.1424

Output 6.8C: Log-Odds Ratio from PROC LOGISTIC

Effect		Point Estimate	95% Wald Confidence Limits	
		Odds Ratio Estimates		
CEO_Tenure		0.936	0.884	0.992
Logmcap		0.323	0.211	0.495
Logemp		1.616	1.166	2.239
Instshrout		0.973	0.954	0.993
PE		0.999	0.991	1.007
ESG		1.071	1.020	1.125
WACC		0.830	0.620	1.111
Age		1.002	0.993	1.012
CEODUALITY N vs Y		0.953	0.506	1.795
Sector	Communication Services vs Utilities	57.501	5.468	604.737
Sector	Consumer Discretionary vs Utilities	11.681	1.170	116.595
Sector	Consumer Staples vs Utilities	5.309	0.528	53.439
Sector	Energy vs Utilities	5.744	0.458	72.012
Sector	Financials vs Utilities	10.940	1.233	97.043
Sector	Health Care vs Utilities	11.414	1.202	108.421
Sector	Industrials vs Utilities	3.998	0.413	38.722
Sector	Information Technology vs Utilities	12.564	1.174	134.497
Sector	Materials vs Utilities	5.994	0.567	63.393
Sector	Real Estate vs Utilities	28.501	1.979	410.462

Output 6.8D displays the Effect Plot for the logit model. The Effect Plot shows the interaction of the two predictors (institutional share ownership and log number of employees) on the probability of long-term profitability. The red dots show unprofitable firms, while the blue dots show profitable firms. Notice the increasing number of red dots as the log number of employees increases and the decreasing number of red dots as the percentage of institutional ownership increases.

Output 6.8D: Contour Effect Plot

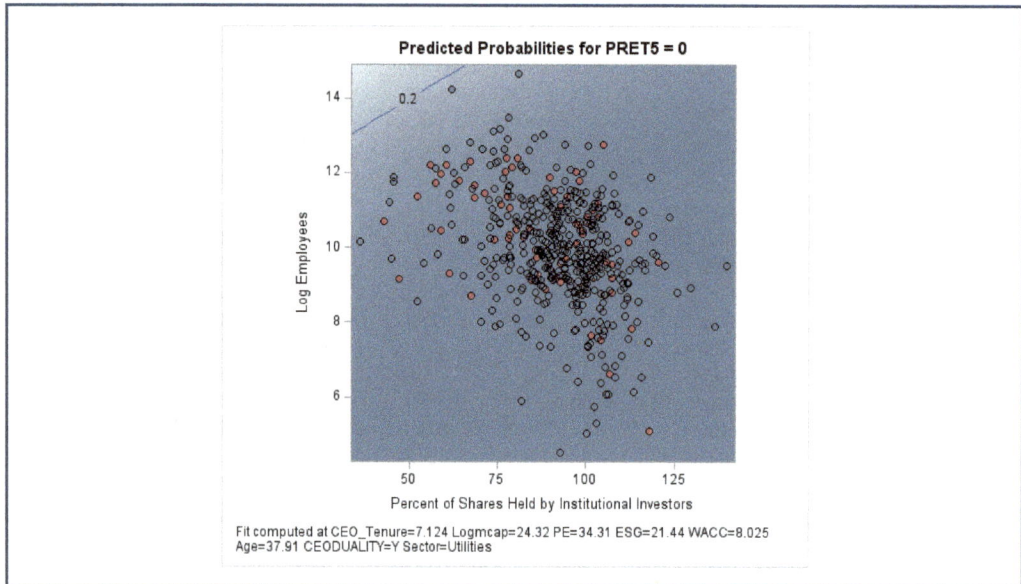

Receiver Operating Characteristics (ROC)

Output 6.8E shows the Receiver Operating Characteristics (ROC) curve of the logistic regression. The ROC curve plots the true positive rate (sensitivity) of the model against the false positive rate (1-Specificity) at different cutoff points. It is a commonly used statistic to measure the discriminating ability of binary classification models at different classification thresholds. For example, at a low classification threshold (let's select the probability of a negative return of 10%), the model will invariably incur a high rate of false positive classification relative to true positive, because of the low discriminating power. As the classification threshold increases, the model is better able to distinguish between true positive and false positive up to a point, before the model starts to experience diminishing discriminatory ability from the increased number of false negatives classification. The blue line plots the proportion of true positives to false positives relative to a random classifier, which is indicated by the 45-degree line drawn through the coordinates (0,0) and (1,1).

Another way to use the ROC curve to evaluate the accuracy of the model is to compute the Area Under the ROC (AUROC) curve or the Area Under the Curve (AUC as it is more commonly called). The AUC is the aggregate measure of the model performance. It is the integral of the area under the ROC curve over the range of 0 to 1. The AUC of the diagonal line is 0.5; therefore, a good model should have an AUC of above 0.5. The higher the AUC above this threshold, the more accurate the model is in its classification. Since the AUC of our logit model is 0.825, we are fairly confident of its predictive accuracy.

Output 6.8E: Receiver Operating Characteristic (ROC) Curve

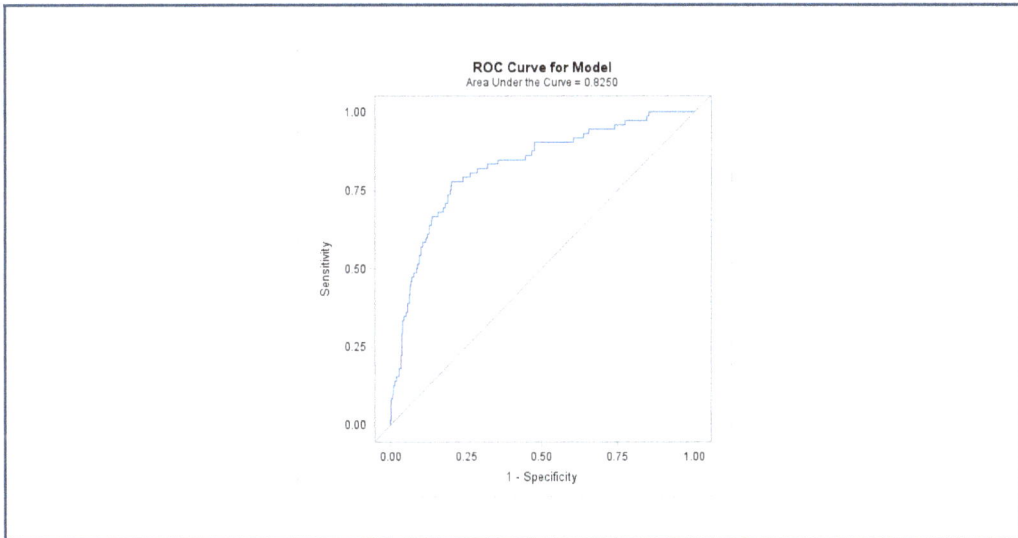

Discriminant Analysis

The classification approach used by linear discriminant analysis (LDA) is slightly different from the MLE optimization of the probit and logit models. In the LDA framework, the objective is to model the distribution of the explanatory variables given the classification observed in the response variable. This is achieved by deriving a linear parameterization of the feature variables that maximizes the distance between the value functions of each class. Besides data classification, LDAs are also used for dimension reduction; however, we will focus on the classification applications of LDAs alone.

It turns out that there is more than one approach to implementing the LDA. The Fisher discriminant analysis (also called first-stage linear discriminant analysis) searches for the parameter space that maximizes the variance between classes relative to the variance of the data from the same class.

$$\arg\max_{w} \ D(w) = \frac{w'S_B w}{w'S_W w} \tag{6.43}$$

where S_B is the between the class variance, S_B is the within the class variance, and w is the transformation matrix whose eigenvalue maximizes the value function $D(\cdot)$. The Gaussian or normal discriminant analysis, which is the generalization of the Fisher's LDA, uses conditional expectation and the Bayes rule to assign observations to classes. Since PROC DISCRIM, which is the SAS procedure that implements discriminant applies the latter approach, we will focus on the normal discriminant analysis from now on.

In the normal discriminant analysis approach, the feature variables are assumed to be multivariate and normally distributed in each class; hence, they can only be in the form of continuous variables.[19] Let y_j denote each classification from the J-number of class labels. Denote $X = (x_1, x_2, ..., x_N)$ as the feature matrix, where x_i represents the ith row element (sample) of X with M-dimensional features. To keep things simple, we will assume $J = 2$, such that y_1 and y_2 represent the two possible classes with M-dimensional features. Consider a value function $p(x_i, y_j = j)$, which measures the likelihood of x_i belonging to the class j. Drawing from the Bayes optimal classifier, the discriminant score for assigning x_i to class $j = 1$ is given by:

$$D_j = p(x_i, y_j = 1) - p(x_i, y_j = 0) > T \tag{6.44}$$

> The Bayes optimal classifier rule is a common approach that is used to reduce the risk of assigning x_i to the wrong classification. According to the classifier rule, the risk is lower if the probability of x_i being in that classification is greater than the probability of x_i being in a different classification. The greater the distance D_j between the two probabilities, the lower the chances of making a wrong classification.

Since we assumed that x_i is multivariate normally distributed in both y_1 and y_2, then the optimal specification for the value functions $p(x_i, y_j = 1)$ and $p(x_i, y_j = 0)$ is the multivariate normal density function. Hence, we can rewrite our value function for our discriminant score in terms of the multivariate normal density function as follows.[20]

$$D_j = \left[\left(x_i - u_{y=1} \right)' \Sigma_{y=1}^{-1} \left(x_i - u_{y=1} \right) + \log \left| \Sigma_{y=1}^{-1} \right| \right] - \left[\left(x_i - u_{y=0} \right)' \Sigma_{y=0}^{-1} \left(x_i - u_{y=0} \right) + \log \left| \Sigma_{y=0}^{-1} \right| \right]$$

$$+ \log \frac{p(y_j = 1)}{p(y_j = 0)}$$

$$\tag{6.45}$$

---

[19] There are some types of discriminant analysis that allow for discrete variables. They are called discriminant correspondence analysis. Their description is beyond the scope of this book.
[20] The notations are the matrix form of the log-density of the normal distribution.

where $\Sigma_{y=j}$ is the within the class variance, $u_{y=j}$ is the mean of the observations in class j , and $p(y_j = j)$ is the prior probability of y_j. The expression above is known as the quadratic discriminant analysis (QDA). However, if we assume that both classifications have equal variance $\Sigma_{y=0} = \Sigma_{y=1} = \Sigma$, then D_j can be written in the form:

$$D_j = w'x + c > T \tag{6.46}$$

where $w = \Sigma^{-1}\left(u_{y=1} - u_{y=0}\right)$ and $c = w'\left(u_{y=1} + u_{y=0}\right) + \log\dfrac{p(y_j = 1)}{p(y_j = 0)}$.

It is common to use $T = 0$ as the threshold for assigning the observation to the default class. The discriminant score D_j is calculated from the linear combination of the values of the feature variables, as shown below.

$$D_j = w'x_i + c > 0 \tag{6.47}$$

Thus, for our two class problems, the sample x_i is assigned to class $y_j = 1$ if $w'x_i > c$ and class $y_j = 0$. The vector w can now be regarded as the discriminant vector that projects x_i to class j (that is, fits the value of x_i to class j). Since higher D_j reduces our risk of misclassification, the optimization problem in the normal discriminant analysis framework is to find the $w = f\left(u_1, u_{0,} \Sigma\right)$ that maximizes the value of D_j.

$$\arg\max_{w} D_j = w'x_i + c \tag{6.48}$$

The LDA can also be estimated using a nonparametric approach. The nonparametric approach is particularly useful when the discriminant information cannot be found in the means of the classes (such as in the cases of where the means of classes are equal, thereby making it impossible to calculate $w = \Sigma^{-1}\left(u_{y=1} - u_{y=0}\right)$). In this approach, the value function is derived using kernel functions ϕ of x_i. This approach, which is also known as the Kernel Fisher discriminant analysis, uses kernel functions to map the linear feature space of x_i into a non-linear space using some transformation function ϕ.[21] The value function is similar to the Fisher LDA and is written as:

$$\arg\max_{w} D(w) = \frac{w'S_B^{\phi}w}{w'S_w^{\phi}w} \tag{6.49}$$

---

[21] Kernel estimation methods and the common types of kernel functions are described in the previous section of this chapter.

S_B^ϕ and S_w^ϕ are the kernel-based between class variance and the within-class variances, respectively.

> The mathematical construct of the kernel approach is fairly rigorous. However, the general concept is the same as in every LDA approach. We aim to find the discriminating vector w of parameters that best separates the classes, given our prior knowledge of the class.

Firm Profitability Revisited

Now that we have developed the theoretical foundation for linear discriminant analysis, let's apply the approach to the classification problems that we previously explored using the probit and logit models. Here we use discriminant analysis to identify the numerical features space that best classifies a firm into the profitable and unprofitable group. Discriminant analysis can be performed in SAS using the CANDISC, DISCRIM, and STEPDISC procedures. The DISCRIM procedure can implement a wide range of discriminant analysis approaches (including parametric and nonparametric estimation). PROC CANDISC performs canonical discriminant analysis,[22] while PROC STEPDISC performs the stepwise discriminant analysis. You should note that both the CANDISC and the DISCRIM procedures do not perform variable selections. Hence, all potential discriminating variables that are included in the model specification will also remain in the final model, regardless of their discriminating ability. Therefore, it is more efficient to use the STEPDISC procedure as a prelude to the CANDISC and DISCRIM procedures. Let's revisit the classification problem that we explored in Programs 6.8A and 6.8B. Discriminant analysis can only analyze numerical feature variables, so our explanatory variables for identifying long-term stock returns will exclude the categorical variables we used in PROC LOGISTIC and PROC PROBIT.

PROC STEPDISC

Program 6.9A shows the SAS code for the STEPDISC procedure, which uses the iterative parametric stepwise LDA (with forward-step selection) model to select the final set of feature variables. Program 6.9B shows the SAS code that uses the DISCRIM procedure to estimate the parametric LDA, while Program 6.9C shows the SAS code for the nonparametric approach to estimating LDA using the same DISCRIM procedure.

---

[22] Canonical discriminant analysis derives canonical variables that summarizes the between-class variations in the same manner as principal component analysis summarizes total variation. Canonical coefficients are the correlation coefficients derived from the linear combination of the variables that has the highest possible multiple correlation with the groups.

Program 6.9A: Stepwise Discriminant Analysis Model of Long-Term Profitability

```
/*Using PROC STEPDISC to Preselect the Determinant of Long-Term Stock
Returns*/
%datapull(profit,spx_profit.sas7bdat);

proc stepdisc data=spx_profit include=0 short;
     class pret5;
     var ceo_tenure logmcap logemp
          Instshrout pe esg wacc age;
run;
```

Output 6.9A: Selection Summary from Stepwise Discriminant Analysis Model of Long-Term Profitability

										Average Squared	
	Number				Partial			Wilks'	Pr <	Canonical	Pr >
Step	In	Entered	Removed	Label	R-Square	F Value	Pr > F	Lambda	Lambda	Correlation	ASCC
1	1	WACC		Weighted Average Cost of Capital	0.0282	14.44	0.0002	0.97182377	0.0002	0.02817623	0.0002
2	2	Logmcap		Log Market Cap	0.0215	10.93	0.0010	0.95091396	< .0001	0.04908604	< .0001
3	3	Logemp		Log Employees	0.0447	23.22	< .0001	0.90839011	< .0001	0.09160989	< .0001
4	4	Instshrout		Percent of Shares Held by Institutional Investors	0.0267	13.56	0.0003	0.88416824	< .0001	0.11583176	< .0001

The STEPDISC statement invokes the stepwise discriminant analysis of the specified data. The procedure uses either the F test from the analysis of covariance or changes in the squared partial correlation for predicting the variable when new variables are added to the existing set of variables. Variables can enter or leave the model through forward, backward, or stepwise selection. The default selection criterion is the stepwise method. You can specify the significance level for adding (SLE=) and keeping (SLSTAY=) a variable in the model. You can also specify the number of feature variables in the options by invoking INCLUDE=n, where n is the number of feature variables you desire in the final model and the minimum number of feature variables in the final model (STOP=n). In Program 6.9A, the SHORT option is invoked to suppress the printout of all iterations besides the final iteration of the STEPDISC procedure. Overall, four variables (as shown in the results) were selected for the final LDA.

PROC DISCRIM

In Program 6.9B, the DISCRIM procedure is invoked to create a classification model of feature variables that can distinguish firms with positive long-term returns from firms with negative long-term returns. The DISCRIM statement has more options and features than the STEPDISC statement. These include the options to include a new data set to be scored (TESTDATA), test for the homogeneity of the within-class variance (POOL=), estimate parametric and nonparametric (METHOD), and implement canonical discriminant analysis (CANONICAL), to name a few. The PRIOR statement is used to specify the prior probability of the classifications. The two available options are EQUAL and PROPORTIONAL (which is based on the relative frequency of the response variable in the data set).

Program 6.9B: Parametric Linear Discriminant Analysis Model of Long-Term Profitability

```
/*Using PROC DISCRIM (Parametric Method) to Estimate the Determinants of Long-Term Stock
Returns*/
proc discrim data=spx_profit method=normal crossvalidate
outstat=distat outd=discore  outcross=cvalid posterr distance anova manova pool=yes
canonical ncan=2;
       class pret5;
       var logmcap logemp Instshrout wacc;
       priors proportional;
run;
```

You can judge the classification accuracy of the DISCRIM procedure by specifying any combination of the three validation options. CROSSLIST displays the cross validation for each observation. CROSSLISTERR displays the cross-validation error for misclassified observation only, while the CROSSVALIDATE option generates a confusion matrix, which shows the true positive, false positive, true negative, and false negative predictions of the model. This is achieved using a contingency table that matches the predicted classification against the actual classification. Two types of Classification Summary tables are produced by invoking the CROSSVALIDATE statement. The Resubstitution Summary using the Linear Discriminant Function table is based on classification results obtained from an in-sample classifier, while the Cross-validation Summary using Linear Discriminant Function table shows the results from an out-of-sample classifier.

The in-sample classifier applies a discriminant function that is calculated from all observations in the data set, while the out-of-sample classifier applies a discriminant function that is calculated from all observations except for the one that is being classified. In general, the error rate from the Resubstitution classifier is usually lower than the error rate from the cross-validation classifier.

Output 6.9B: Parametric Linear Discriminant Model of Long-Term Profitability

Linear Discriminant Function for PRET5			
Variable	Label	0	1
Constant		-451.59103	-476.14272
Logmcap	Log Market Cap	34.49078	35.56105
Logemp	Log Employees	-3.18214	-3.64479
Instshrout	Percent of Shares Held by Institutional Investors	1.28404	1.32571
WACC	Weighted Average Cost of Capital	-0.44957	-0.26615

Resubstitution Summary using Linear Discriminant Function Cross-validation Summary using Linear Discriminant Function

Number of Observations and Percent Classified into PRET5			
From PRET5	0	1	Total
0	48	25	73
	65.75	34.25	100.00
1	122	307	429
	28.44	71.56	100.00
Total	170	332	502
	33.86	66.14	100.00
Priors	0.5	0.5	

Number of Observations and Percent Classified into PRET5			
From PRET5	0	1	Total
0	48	25	73
	65.75	34.25	100.00
1	123	306	429
	28.67	71.33	100.00
Total	171	331	502
	34.06	65.94	100.00
Priors	0.5	0.5	

Error Count Estimates for PRET5			
	0	1	Total
Rate	0.3425	0.2844	0.3134
Priors	0.5000	0.5000	

Error Count Estimates for PRET5			
	0	1	Total
Rate	0.3425	0.2867	0.3146
Priors	0.5000	0.5000	

Output 6.9B shows excerpts of the results obtained from implementing the code of the DISCRIM procedure. You will notice on the Linear Discriminant Function for PRET5 table that market capitalization, institutional share ownership, and cost of capital are more strongly associated with profitability, while the number of employees is more related to unprofitability. The confusion matrices reported in the output show a fair classification accuracy for the parametric model. You will also notice on the Resubstitution Summary table that 34.25% of the unprofitable firms were wrongly classified as profitable and 28.44% of the profitable firms were classified as unprofitable. A comparable set of results can be observed in the Cross-validation Summary table (34.25% and 28.67% for false negative and false positive rates, respectively). The average accuracy for the Resubstitution Summary and Cross-validation Summary are also approximately the same (31.34% and 31.36%, respectively). The average posterior probability of a true negative prediction is 73.96% (unprofitable firms that are correctly classified as unprofitable), while the average posterior probability of a false positive is 65.47% (unprofitable firms that are incorrectly classified as profitable). The average posterior probability of false negative (profitable firms that are incorrectly classified as unprofitable) is 62.47%, while the average posterior probability of true positive (profitable that are correctly classified as profitable) is 70.99%. This could be caused by any of the following reasons: wrong variable selection for the model, wrong discriminant function, or wrong distribution assumed for the data.

Program 6.9C: Nonparametric Linear Discriminant Analysis Model of Long-Term Profitability

```
/*Using PROC DISCRIM (Nonparametric Method) to Estimate the Determinants of Long-Term Stock
Returns*/
proc discrim data=spx_profit method=npar kernel=normal r=.1 crossvalidate
        outstat=distat outd=discore outcross=cvalid posterr distance anova manova pool=yes;
        class pret5;
        var logmcap logemp Instshrout wacc;
        priors equal;
run;
```

In Program 6.9C, we show the SAS code that implements the discriminant analysis using the nonparametric approach. To request the nonparametric approach in the options that accompany the PROC DISCRIM statement, you will need to specify METHOD=NPAR and the type of distribution (KERNEL=). We chose the normal kernel with a radius value of 1. We also set the PRIORS to be PROPORTIONAL.

Notice in the results shown in Output 6.9C that the prediction accuracy has now significantly improved over the parametric discriminant analysis. The Resubstitution Summary table shows a 100% accuracy for unprofitable classification, while the Cross-validation Summary table has about 20.52% error rate.

Output 6.9C: Nonparametric Linear Discriminants of Long-Term Profitability

Resubstitution Summary using Normal Kernel Density

Number of Observations and Percent Classified into PRET5

From PRET5	0	1	Total
0	73	0	73
	100.00	0.00	100.00
1	0	429	429
	0.00	100.00	100.00
Total	73	429	502
	14.54	85.46	100.00
Priors	0.14542	0.85458	

Error Count Estimates for PRET5

	0	1	Total
Rate	0.0000	0.0000	0.0000
Priors	0.1454	0.8546	

Cross-validation Summary using Normal Kernel Density

Number of Observations and Percent Classified into PRET5

From PRET5	0	1	Total
0	13	60	73
	17.81	82.19	100.00
1	43	386	429
	10.02	89.98	100.00
Total	56	446	502
	11.16	88.84	100.00
Priors	0.14542	0.85458	

Error Count Estimates for PRET5

	0	1	Total
Rate	0.8219	0.1002	0.2052
Priors	0.1454	0.8546	

Dimension Reduction Models

Although factor analysis and principal component analysis are also used in machine learning for data preprocessing, the origins of both methodologies are in statistical theory. Therefore, we will explore their conceptual framework and estimation under statistical predictive models.

Factor Analysis

In factor analysis, dimension reduction is achieved by exploring whether a set of latent variables may be responsible for the variability observed in a group of variables that are related. From a financial data science point of view, factor analysis is particularly useful for exploring the drivers of the performance of a portfolio of assets. Indeed, the factor investing approach, which involves constructing portfolios to capture the reward to a specific set of risk factors, has its roots in factor analysis. These risk factors are typically grouped into three categories: macroeconomic, fundamental, and statistical factors.

In effect, the three most widely used pricing models can be viewed as factor models. The capital asset pricing model (CAPM) is a single-factor model of macroeconomic risk premised on the idea that an asset's return is linearly related to its exposure to systematic risk (measured by beta). The arbitrage pricing theory (APT) is a multifactor model premised on the notion that asset returns have a linear relationship to a collection of macroeconomic risk factors, while the Fama-French factor model combines macroeconomic and fundamental risk factors to derive a three-factor model of systematic risk, firm size, and the relative value of the firm's asset. Although macroeconomic and fundamental factor models rely on mostly observable factors or factor betas, statistical factors are inherently latent and can only be deduced from the returns of the assets using statistical procedures such as principal component analysis and factor analysis.

Factor analysis examines the covariances of the structure of a collection of variables. It decomposes the covariance into common variance (common factors) and unique variance (unique factors). The observed values of the variables are then modeled as the function of the common and unique factors. Factor analysis can be implemented using maximum likelihood estimation, principal factor analysis, and principal component analysis. The maximum likelihood approach is more commonly used, so we will explore that approach in this section.[23]

Let R_t be a $N \times 1$ vector representing a collection of observed excess asset returns $\left[R_{1,t}, R_{2,t}, ..., R_{N,t} \right]^T$ at time t with a covariance matrix $Cov(R_t) = \Sigma_R$. Also, let f_t be the $K \times 1$ matrix of common factors with $E(f_t) = 0$ and $Cov(f_t) = \Omega_f$, and ε_t be the current value of a $N \times 1$ matrix of unobservable stochastic error terms with $E(\varepsilon_t) = 0$ and covariance $Cov(\varepsilon_t) = \psi_\varepsilon$. Then the factor model of R_t in terms of f_t and ε_t can be written as:

$$R_t = \alpha + \beta f_t + \varepsilon_t \qquad (6.50)$$

where α and β are $N \times 1$ vector and $N \times K$ matrix of constants, respectively.

The equation above is specified as a cross-sectional regression model at the time t. Notice that the expression above is similar to the common regression models. It turns out that factor analysis also uses the maximum likelihood estimation methods for the factor loadings that we will derive shortly. Since we are using the maximum likelihood approach, we will need to make additional assumptions about the properties of the variables. For now, let's assume that the common and unique factors are independent (in other words, the common factors are independent of each other and independent of the unique factors) and that all random variables are normally distributed. Furthermore, let's write the function of R_t in terms of its demeaned values $R_t^d = R_t - \alpha$ as shown below.

$$R_t^d = \beta f_t + \varepsilon_t \qquad (6.51)$$

---

[23] We will discuss principal component analysis in the next section of this chapter.

If we assume that R_t and R_t^d have the same covariance Σ_R, then we can write the covariance of the observable variables as:

$$Cov\left(R_t^d\right) = \Sigma_R = Cov\left(\beta f_t\right) + Cov\left(\varepsilon_t\right)$$
$$= \beta' \Omega_f \beta + \psi_\varepsilon \qquad (6.52)$$

Replacing the terms with the covariances of the latent factors and further assuming that $\Omega_f = I_k$ results in:

$$Cov\left(R_t\right) = \Sigma_R = \beta\beta' + \psi_\varepsilon \qquad (6.53)$$

The equation above implies that the covariance of the collection of variables can be written as the sum of the product of the factor loading matrix β and the covariance of the residuals ψ_e. We can write the likelihood function of R_t as:

$$L\left(\alpha, \Sigma_R\right) = p\left(R_1, R_2, ..., R_T \mid \alpha, \Sigma_x\right) = \prod_{t=1}^{T} p\left(R_t \mid \alpha, \Sigma_R\right) \qquad (6.54)$$

And the log-likelihood function as:

$$L_n\left(\alpha, \Sigma_R\right) = -\frac{TK}{2}\log\left(2\pi\right) - \frac{T}{2}\log\left(\Sigma_R\right) - \frac{1}{2}\sum_{t=1}^{T}\left(R_t - \alpha\right)' \Sigma_R^{-1}\left(R_t - \alpha\right) \qquad (6.55)$$

From the above, we now know that factor analysis is the end result of deriving the maximum likelihood estimates of the $\alpha, \beta, \psi_\varepsilon$ subject to the constraint that the covariance matrix $\Sigma_R = \beta'\beta + \psi_e$ is the sum of the common and unique factors.

$$\left(\hat{\alpha}, \hat{\Sigma}_R\right) = \underset{\alpha, \Sigma_R}{\arg\max} \, L_n\left(\alpha, \Sigma_R\right)$$
$$\text{subject to} : \Sigma_R = \beta\beta' + \psi_\varepsilon \qquad (6.56)$$

If we standardized the original variables such that $z_{j,t} = \dfrac{R_{j,t} - \alpha_j}{\sigma_{jj}}$, then Σ_R will no longer be a covariance matrix, but now a correlation matrix with the diagonals showing the correlation of the jth variable with itself written as the $s_{jj} = \sum_{k=1}^{K} \beta_{jk}^2 + \psi_{jj} = 1$. We can infer from this expression that the terms of the diagonal of Σ_R are equal to the sum of the squared factor loading (partial correlations) between the variables and unique factors (residual correlations). Thus, factor analysis can be viewed as the estimate of the correlations between variables that are due to the common variance and those that are due to the uniqueness of the variables.

Factor Extraction and Interpretation

To achieve dimension reduction, it is necessary to determine the optimal number of meaningful factors to extract from the estimation. This is done through either the principal component analysis, common factor analysis, or maximum likelihood factor analysis. The principal component analysis approach (which we will discuss shortly) extracts the factors in their order of diminishing contributions to the overall variance. The principal component analysis approach is applicable if we assume that no unique variance exists and that the total variance is equal to the common variance. Hence, principal component analysis selects the factors based on the eigenvalues of the covariance matrix. The common factor analysis (also known as principal factor analysis) selects the factors that best capture the common variance of the data. The maximum likelihood factor analysis (which follows the approach discussed in the preceding subsection) forms the factors from the linear combinations of the variables and the estimated parameters. The parameter estimates are selected such that they are most likely to have resulted in the observed correlations matrix.

Factor Rotation

Factor rotation is used to interpret the factor loadings. Remember that factors are combinations of the original variables, and it is common to see the same variables appear in multiple factors. This makes the interpretation of the latent process more challenging. Factor rotation simply tilts the axes of the factors such that variables with marginal relationship to the factor are minimized and those with larger correlations are maximized. This helps to simplify the structure of the factor matrix and thereby ensures a more lucid interpretation of the features of the factors. There are two main types of factor rotation methods: orthogonal factor rotation, which assumes independence amongst factors, and oblique factor rotation, which assumes factors are correlated. Each method can be implemented using a variety of approaches. However, the discussion of the approaches is beyond the scope of this book.

> Factor analysis is a variable reduction technique that examines whether a set of unobservable variables may be responsible for the variability in a set of observable variables that are related. The unobservable variables (factors) are derived from linear combinations of the observable variables using a variance decomposition technique. The variance decomposition technique splits the covariances of the observable variables into common variances (common factor or communality) and unique factors.

Three approaches to extracting the factors and their betas from the decomposed variance are the principal factor analysis, principal component analysis, and maximum likelihood factor analysis. The extracted common factors, which are the main variables of interest are then manipulated using rotation techniques to enhance their interpretability and to reduce the likelihood that the factors would overlap in terms of the unobservable features that are being examined. Orthogonal rotation yields distinct factors that are unrelated, while oblique factor rotation allows for a small degree of correlation between the factors if it would lead to better interpretability.

Factor Analysis in Portfolio Management

Two common applications of factor analysis in the investment domain are portfolio factor analysis, which is a statistical attribution model of the factor exposures of investment portfolios, and the construction of factor mimicking portfolios, which are portfolios that replicate the attributes of individual assets, funds, or non-tradable factors such as macroeconomic trends. The factors can be observable variables such as macroeconomic and fundamental factors, or unobservable factors that are derived through statistical estimation.

Portfolio Factor Analysis

Portfolio factor analysis seeks to understand the underlying source of the portfolio performance using statistical models. Therefore, its aim generally lends itself to the factor analysis approach. The link between factor analysis and portfolio factor models goes as follows. Suppose $R_t = \left[R_{1,t}, R_{2,t}, ..., R_{N,t} \right]^T$ can be specified as the collections of the excess returns on a set of N investable assets in our portfolio, which we denote as $R_{p,t} = w'R_t$. Furthermore, let us denote $w = \left[w_1, w_2, ..., w_N \right]$ as the vector of portfolio allocations in $R_{p,t}$, that has exposures to K number of factors. For simplicity, we will assume that $K = 1$. If R_t follow the same specification as Equations (6.50) and (6.51), then our portfolio return can be written as:

$$R_{p,t} = w'\alpha + w'\beta_f f_t + w'\varepsilon_t$$
$$R_{p,t} = \alpha_p + \mathrm{B}'_f f_t + \varepsilon_{p,t} \qquad (6.57)$$
$$\text{where: } \alpha_p = w'\alpha, \ \mathrm{B}'_f = w'\beta_f, \text{ and } \varepsilon_{p,t} = w'\varepsilon_t$$

Notice that the above is the portfolio equivalent of the excess returns of our asset universe (shown in Equation (6.51)), which can also be written in its demeaned excess return form as $R^d_{p,t} = \left(R_{p,t} - \alpha_p \right)$. If the previous assumption that our factors are orthogonal to the error term still holds and that R_t and R^d_t have the same covariance Σ_R, then the covariance of our portfolios can also be written as:

$$Cov\left(R_{p,t}\right) = Cov\left(B'_f f_t\right) + Cov\left(\varepsilon_{p,t}\right)$$
$$w'\Sigma_R w = w'\beta_f \Omega_f w \beta'_f + w'\psi_\varepsilon w \qquad (6.58)$$
$$w'\Sigma_R w = w'\beta_f \beta'_f w + w'\psi_\varepsilon w$$

You can see that the above equations are also similar to Equations (6.52) and (6.53), except that we are accounting for the covariance of our portfolio, and not the individual assets. Recall that we have previously assumed that $\Omega_f = I_k$ in Equation (6.53). This means that our factor portfolio variance can be expressed as: $w'\Sigma_R w = w'\beta\beta'w + w'\psi_\varepsilon w$. Solving for $B'_f = w'\beta_f$ in Equations (6.57 and 6.58) links the overall returns and risk of the portfolio to its exposures to the risk factor f_t. The factor analysis approach can be used to derive the unique common factor loading (beta) and factor realizations f_t. The factors can also be rotated using an orthogonal matrix H (where $HH' = I$) such that it yields the most interpretable and unique factors and factor loadings as shown below.

$$R_t = \alpha + \beta_f HH'f_t + \varepsilon_t$$
$$= \alpha + \beta_f^* f_t^* + \varepsilon_t \qquad (6.59)$$

where $\beta_f^* = \beta_f H$ and $f_t^* = H'f_t$.

Factor Mimicking Portfolios

A factor mimicking portfolio is a financially engineered portfolio of tradeable assets that is constructed to earn the risk premium of a non-tradable factor. The financially engineered portfolio is designed to be strongly correlated with the non-tradeable factor, such that changes in the non-tradable factor are then tracked by the returns of the mimicking portfolio. Factor mimicking portfolios are also used in academic research to test various asset pricing theories. The renowned Fama-French three-factor model is based on the application of the factor-mimicking portfolio theory. The High-Minus-Low (HML) portfolio is constructed to harvest the so-called value premium by buying the stocks of top book-to-market quintile stocks (value stock) and shorting the stocks of the bottom quintile book-to-market stocks (growth stocks). Conversely, the Small-Minus-Big (SMB) portfolio is constructed to harvest the so-called size premium by buying the stocks of the bottom quintile market capitalization stocks (small-cap stocks) and shorting the portfolio of stocks of the top quintile market capitalization stocks (large-cap stocks). Other factors have been introduced besides the HML and SMB factors; they include momentum, volatility, cash flow, quality, and more recently climate risk factors.

The factor analysis approach is one of the various methods that can be used for constructing factor-mimicking portfolios. To get started, let us review Equation (6.57) once again. From the equation, we can observe that to track our factor as closely as possible, it is generally a good idea to minimize the distance between the expected excess return $E(R_{p,t})$ on our mimicking portfolio and the factor premia $E(f_t)$ we want to earn. This implies that the allocation that yields the optimal mimicking portfolio should be such that it minimizes the mispricing error $\alpha_p = w'\alpha = E(R_{p,t}) - B_f E(f_t)$. Furthermore, we also want the mimicking portfolio to have maximum exposure to the factor such that its volatility and the factor's volatility are the same $w'\beta_f = B_f$. Together, these requirements can be formulated as an optimization problem for the factor mimicking portfolio as shown below:

$$(\hat{w}) = \arg \min_{w} w' \Sigma_R w$$
$$\text{subject to} : w'\beta_f = B_f$$

(6.60)

Σ_R is a weighting matrix that is included in the problem to control the relative importance of each mispricing component of returns. Equation (6.60) is now a constrained variance-minimization problem that can be solved using non-linear optimization, which will be discussed in Chapter Eight. To attain our desired maximum factor exposure, the portfolio is specified to have unit-beta $(B_f = 1)$ exposure to the factor it aims to mimic and zero exposure to other factors. It is also common to rescale $\hat{w}$ such that $\hat{w}_k' 1_N = \sum_{i=1}^{N} w_i = 1$ to conform with the standard nomenclature for specifying portfolio allocations.[24] The associated return to the factor $\hat{f}_t$ (which is sometimes called the factor premium or factor realization) can now be written as:

$$\hat{f}_t = \left(\hat{B}_f' \Sigma_R^{-1} B_f \right)^{-1} \hat{B}_f' \Sigma_R^{-1} R_t = \hat{w} R_t$$

(6.61)

Another standard approach for constructing mimicking portfolios that is called the maximum correlation approach is based on the mean-variance efficiency theory, which states that for the mimicking portfolio to be mean-variance efficient, it must be the minimum variance portfolio with the highest possible (or prespecified) correlation with the pertinent risk factor and no linkages with other risk factors. This implies that the allocation that maximizes the mimicking portfolio's correlation (or yields the desired factor exposure) with the desired factor will also be the same allocation that minimizes the portfolio variance. The mathematical specification for this approach is similar to the one shown in Equation (6.60).

---

[24] The approach described in this section is known as the least mispricing approach. Be aware that there are other methods for constructing factor mimicking portfolios, such as the maximum correlation, machine learning, and principal component factor analysis approach. In reality, both the least mispricing and the maximum correlation approaches yield the same vectors of portfolio weights.

In the mispricing approach, the factor realization $\hat{f}_t$ is typically derived from a two-step estimation process. For macroeconomic factors that are directly observable, the factor loadings are first derived using a time series regression model of the portfolio returns on the pertinent factor. A second pass cross-sectional regression is then used to derive the factor realizations.[25] For fundamental factor portfolios, the factor betas are assumed to be directly observable characteristics of the assets, while the factor realizations are not. Therefore, we can respecify the linear regression model as the regression model of the portfolio returns on the factor betas, to derive the pertinent factor realizations. Fundamental factor models can be estimated using a variety of methods. These methods include the BARRA and Fama-French approaches. The BARRA approach treats the observable asset-specific attributes as the factor betas. At each time t, the factor realizations are then estimated using weighted least square regression of the asset returns on the factor-beta.[26] [27] In the Fama-French approach, the factor realizations are derived from sorting the assets into quintiles based on specific fundamental factors. The factor realization is then the net return from a portfolio that holds a long position in the assets in the top quintile and a short position in the assets in the bottom quintile. The factor betas are estimated from regressing the asset returns on the derived factor realization. The factor realizations in statistical factor models are unobservable and therefore must be derived from the returns of the assets (which are observable) using factor analysis or principal components analysis.

Implementing Factor Analysis in SAS

The three types of factor analyses highlighted in the previous section can be implemented in SAS using PROC FACTOR. Input data for PROC FACTOR can be in raw data form. It can also be in correlation or covariance matrix form. Two types of output data sets are generated by the procedure. The OUT statement creates an output data set that includes the original data and the factor scores, while the OUTSTAT statement creates a data set that contains a set of estimation statistics. This includes communalities, eigenvalues, correlations, and scoring coefficients, to name a few. The procedure also generates a suite of plots, which includes the initial and rotated factor patterns, as well as the scree plot and the path diagram.

---

[25] In the first pass, the factor betas are estimated using time-series regressions of the asset returns on the factors. In the second step, the risk premium for each factor is then derived by estimating a cross-sectional regression of the average returns of each asset on the estimated factor beta.

[26] The weighting matrix $\sum_R$ is set to equal to an identity matrix in the ordinary least approach, the diagonal of the covariance matrix in the weighted least square approach, and the full covariance matrix in the generalized least square approach.

[27] In the Fama-French approach, the factor realizations are derived from sorting the assets into quintiles based on the specific fundamental factors. The factor realization is the net return from a portfolio that holds a long position in the assets in the top quintile and a short position in the assets in the bottom quintile.

Maximum Likelihood Factor Analysis of the Stock Returns of the Banking Industry

The BANK data set contains the monthly stock returns for the 15 US banks that are currently included in the S&P 500 Index. The data set includes the monthly stock returns of major Wall Street banks such as JP Morgan Chase and Citi Group, as well as regional banks such as Zions and Fifth-Third Bank. Let us attempt to model the set of latent statistical factors that can explain the co-variability of these stocks over time using PROC FACTOR. Program 6.10 shows the SAS code that was used to implement the statistical factor analysis on the 15 stock returns. It is crucial to reiterate at this point that the data set we will use contains only the monthly stock returns of 15 stocks and no other information. Hence, our aim in this exercise is to explore if the model can discern commonalities in the underlying firms by simply observing the statistical patterns of price changes in the stocks over the five-year period.

PROC FACTOR

The METHOD=ML option is used to request the maximum likelihood factor analysis. ML can be changed to PRINCIPAL or P to request the principal component analysis or PRIN to request the iterated principal factor analysis. The SCORE option is used to request the scoring coefficient or factor betas for the model. The NFACTORS=4 option is used to specify the criteria for selecting the number of factors. Although the Varimax (Orthogonal) rotation method is more commonly used, we will select an Oblimin (Oblique) rotation method to simplify the interpretation of the factor realizations. The Oblimin method that we will use is the Quartimin rotation method. PLOTS=ALL invokes the plot of the accompanying ODS graphs (Scree plot, Proportion of Variance Explained, Factor Patterns, and Path Diagram). The OUT=FACTFACTORS and OUTSTAT=FACTSTATS are used to request the factor scores and the estimation statistics. The PATHDIAGRAM statement is used to specify the numerical format and graphical layout of the path diagram. The FUZZ=0.3 option specifies the minimum factor loading estimate that is required for displaying the corresponding link between a variable and factor (the default value is 3). The ARRANGE=GRIP option specifies the algorithm for laying out the variables in the path diagram. SCALE=0.85 specifies the magnification (above 1) or reduction (below 1) in the size of the nodes relative to the design dimension.

Program 6.10: Maximum Likelihood Factor Analysis of Bank Stock Returns

```
/*Estimating a Statistical Factor Model of Bank Stocks Returns Using PROC FACTOR*/
%datapull(banks,banks.sas7bdat);
ods graphics on;

proc factor data= banks method=ml
        score nfact=4 priors=smc heywood
        rotate=quartimin plots=all
        outstat = factstats out=factfactors;
        var rbac rwfc rpnc rjpm rusb rc rtfc rhban rmtb rrf rzion rfitb rcfg rkey rcma;
        pathdiagram  fuzz=0.3 arrange=grip scale=0.85 title='Quartimin-Rotated Path
Diagram' ;
run;
```

Output 6.10A: Scree Plot, Variance Explained Plot, and Statistical Test of Factors of Bank Stock Returns

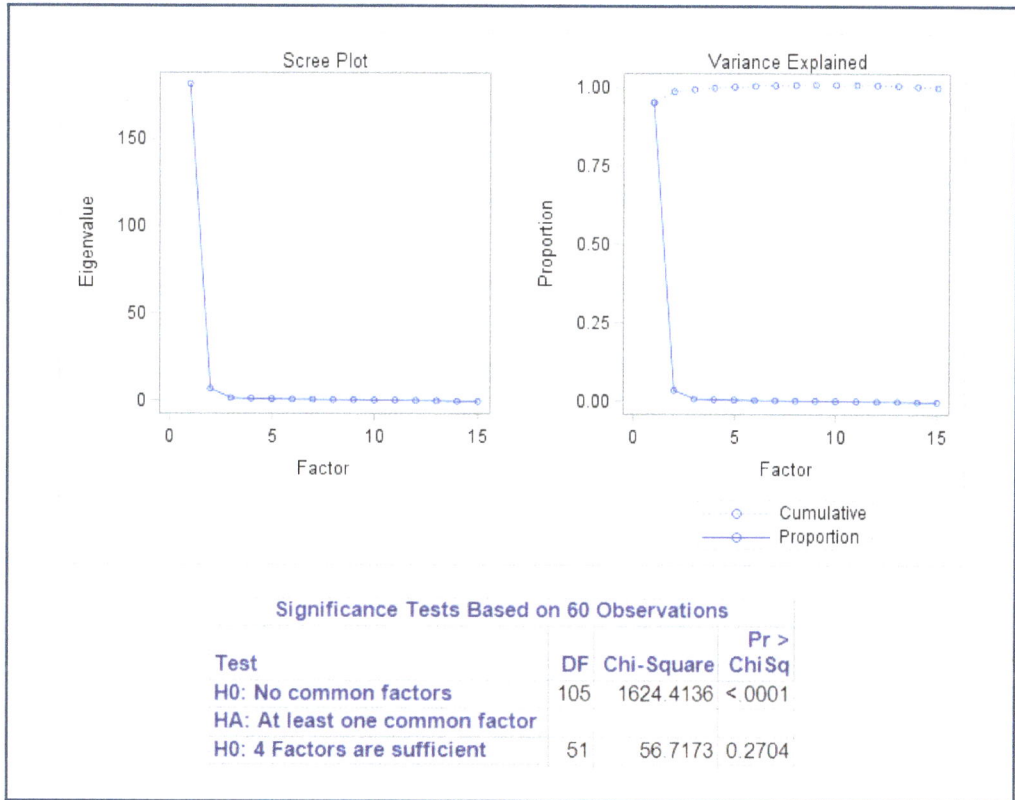

Significance Tests Based on 60 Observations			
Test	DF	Chi-Square	Pr > ChiSq
H0: No common factors	105	1624.4136	<.0001
HA: At least one common factor			
H0: 4 Factors are sufficient	51	56.7173	0.2704

PROC FACTOR generates a lot of outputs, due to the variety of factor extraction and rotation methods that it supports. We will focus only on those relevant to our goal of deriving a set of latent factors that can explain the monthly changes in the prices of these 15 stocks. First, we can observe on the Scree plot of the eigenvalues of each factor and the Proportion of Variance Explained plot (in Output 6.10A) that almost all of the variability in the returns of the 15 stocks can be explained by the four factors. Indeed, 95% of the variability in the returns can be explained by the first factor alone. Furthermore, the Chi-square test of the null hypothesis that no common factor exists for the fifteen stocks is rejected in favor of the notion that at least one common factor. The test of the second hypothesis that states that the four-factor specification is adequate fails to reject the null. So, we can be confident that our four-factor specification is adequate for modeling the latent common factor for the returns of the 15 banking stocks.

Output 6.10B: Factor Patterns and Rotated Factor Patterns

	Factor Pattern	Factor1	Factor2	Factor3	Factor4
RBAC	Bank of America Corp	0.00000	0.94121	0.12604	-0.18008
RWFC	Wells Fargo & Co	0.02204	0.80412	0.30446	-0.25341
RPNC	PNC Financial Services Group Inc	0.01235	0.93494	0.13592	-0.13673
RJPM	JPMorgan Chase & Co	-0.19822	0.98016	-0.00000	0.00000
RUSB	US Bancorp	0.10588	0.90180	0.17991	-0.11574
RC	Citi Group	-0.03664	0.87775	0.28059	-0.16325
RTFC	Truist Financial Corp	0.29278	0.87316	0.25783	-0.00149
RHBAN	Huntington Bancshares Inc.	0.16764	0.90572	0.23546	0.14117
RMTB	M&T Bank Corp	0.30746	0.76898	0.32066	-0.00015
RRF	Regions Financial Corp	0.24470	0.89856	0.25618	0.10749
RZION	Zions Bancorp NA	0.27961	0.86412	0.29271	0.01234
RFITB	Fifth Third Bancorp	0.38059	0.92474	-0.00000	0.00000
RCFG	Citizens Financial Group Inc	0.24526	0.91756	0.21156	0.03015
RKEY	KeyCorp	0.19371	0.92664	0.26500	0.00644
RCMA	Comerica Inc	0.37909	0.83676	0.26436	0.09863

	Rotated Factor Pattern (Standardized Regression Coefficients)	Factor1	Factor2	Factor3	Factor4
RBAC	Bank of America Corp	0.00119	0.92065	0.10848	0.00587
RWFC	Wells Fargo & Co	0.00022	0.92735	-0.06945	-0.12256
RPNC	PNC Financial Services Group Inc	0.10941	0.81278	0.09045	0.03264
RJPM	JPMorgan Chase & Co	0.02520	0.83266	0.11250	0.30919
RUSB	US Bancorp	0.29224	0.63319	0.07216	-0.02035
RC	Citi Group	0.10921	0.86232	-0.07965	0.00858
RTFC	Truist Financial Corp	0.80327	0.15262	0.03328	-0.05579
RHBAN	Huntington Bancshares Inc.	0.92838	0.03291	-0.02827	0.15367
RMTB	M&T Bank Corp	0.85053	0.05751	-0.04506	-0.09268
RRF	Regions Financial Corp	0.96900	0.00348	-0.00969	0.07247
RZION	Zions Bancorp NA	0.84327	0.12805	-0.01290	-0.04254
RFITB	Fifth Third Bancorp	0.69939	0.12562	0.33925	-0.06192
RCFG	Citizens Financial Group Inc	0.78133	0.17933	0.06055	0.01603
RKEY	KeyCorp	0.72169	0.28330	-0.00623	0.02180
RCMA	Comerica Inc	1.10194	-0.17425	0.02745	-0.03174

Output 6.10B shows the Factor Pattern table, which reports the raw factor betas, and the Rotated Factor Pattern table, which shows the standardized rotated factor betas for the 15 stocks. Notice that the monthly returns of the largest US banks (JP Morgan Chase, Bank of America, Wells Fargo, Citi Bank, US Bank, and PNC) appear to be driven by Factor 2, while the rest of the banks on the list, which mostly are regional banks, appear to be driven by Factor 1. Factor 3 appears to have a weak negative relationship with all stocks, except for Fifth-Third Bank. The same pattern is evident in Factor 4, except for JP Morgan Chase. JP Morgan Chase is the largest bank in the US with significant operations in other areas of the financial services sector besides banking, while Fifth-Third is possibly the largest pure-play regional bank in the index. In terms of interpretability, Factor 1 is mostly a measure of the exposure to the relatively smaller and diverse pool of regional banks, while Factor 2 is mostly a measure of exposure to the large nationwide and Wall Street banks. Factors 3 and 4 appear to represent bank-specific statistical exposures.

The Factor Pattern is a scatter plot of the factor loadings coordinates (Factor 1 loadings on the X axis, and Factor 2 loadings on the Y axis) for each variable. Notice the clustering of the plots around the highest quartile of Factor 2. It is difficult to distinguish the factor groupings of the banks because the returns of all banks in the sample have high Factor 2 loadings. You can observe the difference in the factor loadings (for Factor 1 and Factor 2) of the bank returns between the Initial Factor Pattern and Rotated Factor Pattern plots shown in Output 6.10C. By tilting the axes of the factors and allowing for up to 0.9 correlations, the Quartimin rotation is now able to distinguish the stock return patterns of the large banks from those of the regional banks in the respective factor loadings.

Output 6.10C: Factor Patterns and Rotated Factor Patterns Plot

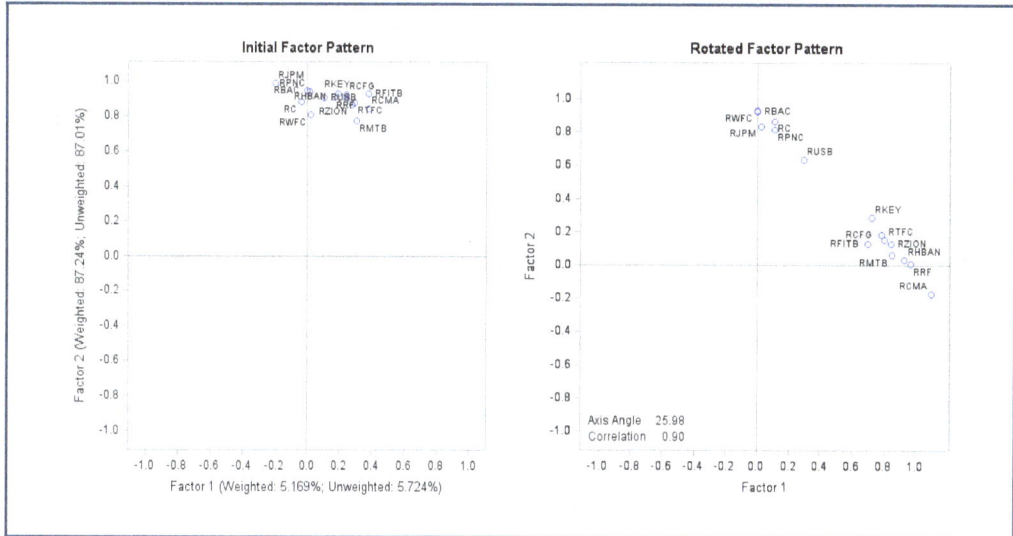

Output 6.10D: Communality and Weights

Final Communality Estimates and Variable Weights		
Total Communality: Weighted = 155.21474 Unweighted = 13.716977		
Variable	Communality	Weight
RBAC	0.93419181	15.1949039
RWFC	0.80400462	5.1000128
RPNC	0.91142758	11.2878755
RJPM	1.00000000	Infty
RTFC	0.91460833	11.7113585
RHBAN	0.92381077	13.1280569
RUSB	0.87022198	7.7056738
RMTB	0.78869030	4.7327840
RC	0.87716905	8.1446207
RRF	0.94446957	18.0103130
RZION	0.91071288	11.2012387
RFITB	1.00000000	Infty
RCFG	0.94772988	19.1294816
RKEY	0.96644771	29.7988998
RCMA	0.92349252	13.0695234

The communality table displayed in Output 6.10D shows the percentage of variation in each stock return that is explained by the factors. The values range from 78.86% for M&T Bank Corp to 100% for JP Morgan Chase and Fifth Third Bancorp.

Output 6.10E shows the path diagram for the Quartimin-Rotated factors. The double-arrow connectors show the correlations among the factors. Although all four factors are correlated, the degrees of their correlations are not the same as shown by numerical values on each link. For example, the correlation between Factor 1 and Factor 2 is 0.9, while the correlation between Factor 1 and Factor 4 is 0.02. On the other hand, the correlation between Factor 2 and Factor 4 is 0.83. The double-arrow link on each variable shows the factor variance and error variance of each variable. The numerical values on the single-arrow link to each variable show the factor loadings of each variable.

Output 6.10E: Path Diagram for Quartimin-Rotated FactorsPrincipal Component Analysis

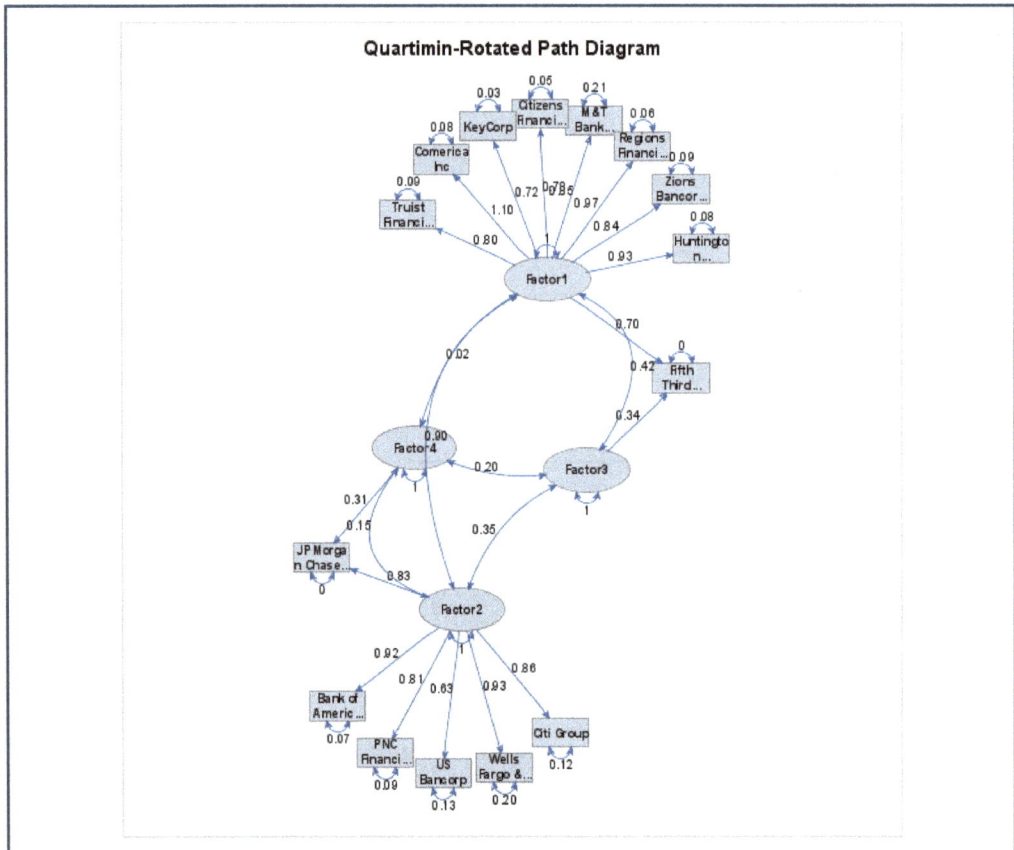

Quartimin-Rotated Path Diagram

Principal Component Analysis

Principal component analysis (PCA) reduces the size of a high-dimensional data set by projecting the data set into a lower-dimensional space. The process creates a synthetic data set with a lesser number of explanatory variables called principal components while preserving as much as possible the variation in the original data set. Hence, the PCA approach attempts to find the set of synthetic variables that most explain the variances in the raw data. The first variable derived from the projection has the highest variance, followed by the variable with the second highest variance, and so on in that order.

In reality, there is more than one method for deriving PCA variables. Nevertheless, the actual construct of the PCA is typically implemented using matrix algebra. We will denote $X = \left(x_1, x_2, ..., x_p \right)$ as the feature matrix with n rows and p columns where x_j is the vector of n-observation of the jth feature variable. The principal component analysis summarizes X into the matrix $Z = \alpha X^d = \sum_{j=1}^{p} \alpha x_j^d$, where $\alpha = \left[\alpha_1, \alpha_2, ..., \alpha_p \right]$ is a collection of vectors of constants, $X^d = \left[x_1^d, x_2^d, ..., x_n^d \right]$ is the demeaned (centered) vector of the jth feature variable, and αX^d are the projections (transformation) of X into the $m \le p$ dimensional space variable Z. Let us denote the covariance of Z as equivalent to $Z'Z = \alpha' \Sigma \alpha$, where Σ is the covariance matrix of X^d. Then j^{th} principal components of X are α_j that maximize $\alpha_j' \Sigma \alpha_j$ and is written as:

$$\hat{\alpha}_j = \arg \max_{\alpha} \alpha_j' \Sigma \alpha_j$$

$$\text{s.t } \alpha_j' \alpha_j = 1$$

(6.62)

It can be shown using LaGrange multiplier optimization that the principal components of X are the eigenvectors of the Σ, and the maximizing vectors are those with the largest eigenvalue λ.[28] Therefore, it is feasible to reduce the dimensionality of the data when the number of eigenvalues required to explain the total variance in the raw data is less than the number of variables in the raw data $m \le p$.

> The principal component analysis is a variable reduction technique that creates a smaller set of synthetic variables from the raw data. The synthetic variables (principal component) are derived from linear combinations of the original variables. The coefficients of the linear transformation are the eigenvectors of the correlation or covariance matrix of the raw data. The principal components are selected in descending order, from those with the largest eigenvalue to those with the lowest eigenvalue. The eigenvalues are equivalent to the variances of the principal components. The procedure aims to obtain the number of principal components that fully explain all of the variations in the raw data, without using all of the variables that currently exist in it.

---

[28] Eigenvector of a matrix is the transformation of the matrix that results in the multiple of the vector. The multiple is the eigenvalue. If V is the eigenvector of matrix A, then $AV = \lambda V$, where λ is the eigenvalue of A.

Variable Selection

There are many ways to select the informative principal components to retain. One approach is to select the components with eigenvalues that are greater than one because these components account for the greater variance that is contributed by more than one variable (also known as the Kaiser rule). Another approach is to select the number of components that result in at least 70–80% of the cumulative proportion of variance explained (PVE rule). A third approach is to select the components using the Scree plot. Components are selected until no further significant decline in the eigenvalue is observed on the Scree plot (elbow rule).

Implementing Principal Component Analysis in SAS

PROC PRINCOMP and PROC FACTOR can be invoked to implement principal component analysis in SAS. The PRINCOMP procedure is simpler and slightly faster to use and can analyze larger problems than the FACTOR procedure. Input data for PRINCOMP can be in raw form. It can also be in correlation or covariance matrix form. Output data includes the original data and the principal component scores. The procedure also generates estimation statistics, which include the eigenvectors and eigenvalues as well as a suite of plots, which includes the proportion of the variance explained by each principal component.

PROC PRINCOMP

Let's apply the PRINCOMP procedure to the SPX_PROFIT data set. Program 6.11 shows the SAS program that was used to implement the principal component analysis on the set of explanatory variables that will be used to identify the determinant of long-term stock return. We aim to create a set of synthetic variables that can explain the variation in the 11 explanatory variables selected. The explanatory variables include the log of revenue, the log of market capitalization, the log number of employees, the log number of shares outstanding, company age, beta, gender diversity score, and the tenure of the CEO, to name a few.

Program 6.11: Principal Component Analysis of the Determinants of Long-Term Stock Return Using PROC PRINCOMP

```
/* Principal Component Analysis of the Determinants of Long-Term Profitability Using PROC
PRINCOMP */
%datapull(profit,spx_profit.sas7bdat);
ods graphics on;

proc princomp data  = spx_profit standard
out=pcscores(label="original data and principal components scores for work.spx_profit")
outstat=pcstats(label="principal components statistics for work.spx_profit")
        prefix='comp#'n              vardef=df
        plots(only)=scree
        plots(only)=matrix
        plots(only)=patternprofile
        plots(only)=pattern ;
        var logrev logmcap logemp logshrout age beta esg pct_wboard pe ceo_tenure logvol;
run;
```

OUT=PCSCORES stores the original variables and the principal components in the PCSCORE SAS data set. OUTSTAT=PCSTATS stores all the statistics created by the procedure in the PCSTATS SAS data set. PREFIX='COMP#'n specifies the prefix for the names that SAS gives to the estimated principal components. VARDEF=DF specifies that the degrees of freedom should be used as the divisor for calculating the variances and standard deviations. The PLOTS statement specifies the types of ODS graphs that should be produced by the statement. They include the Scree plots of the eigenvalues, the Proportion of Variance Explained by each principal component, and the Matrix plots of the principal component scores.

Output 6.11A: Principal Component Analysis of the Determinants of Long-Term Stock Return

Eigenvalues of the Correlation Matrix

	Eigenvalue	Difference	Proportion	Cumulative
1	3.24558994	1.80255803	0.2951	0.2951
2	1.44303192	0.37748077	0.1312	0.4262
3	1.06555115	0.04029113	0.0969	0.5231
4	1.02526002	0.01550189	0.0932	0.6163
5	1.00975813	0.15882823	0.0918	0.7081
6	0.85092990	0.03191243	0.0774	0.7855
7	0.81901748	0.11399082	0.0745	0.8599
8	0.70502665	0.28175018	0.0641	0.9240
9	0.42327647	0.19306008	0.0385	0.9625
10	0.23021640	0.04787446	0.0209	0.9834
11	0.18234194		0.0166	1.0000

Eigenvectors

		comp1	comp2	comp3	comp4	comp5	comp6	comp7	comp8	comp9	comp10	comp11
Logrev	Log Revenue	0.486472	-.026617	0.031397	0.039874	-.227293	-.029661	-.084105	0.243614	0.178331	-.254552	0.737902
Logmcap	Log Market Cap	0.433454	0.210970	0.008380	0.208268	-.094731	-.132379	-.053702	0.070284	-.708485	-.319745	-.292667
Logemp	Log Employees	0.405107	0.013172	0.163964	-.033040	-.453857	0.236078	-.088105	0.289120	0.344029	0.329948	-.476913
Logshrout	Log Shares Outstanding	0.448292	0.106312	-.105837	-.104231	0.302866	-.165418	-.004847	-.291240	-.159894	0.708785	0.183818
Age	Age	0.145892	-.408161	0.205965	0.457988	-.080899	0.473328	0.163690	-.545223	-.044050	-.033102	0.047578
Beta	Systematic Risk	-.099513	0.510795	0.010500	-.330005	-.167420	0.572388	0.419873	-.002607	-.222344	0.046504	0.191348
ESG	ESG Score	0.111817	-.383594	-.545536	0.128172	0.267328	0.214916	0.402312	0.484140	-.076642	0.058899	-.055426
PCT_Wboard	Percent of Women on Board	0.095841	-.109475	0.735215	-.090840	0.347008	-.176263	0.466845	0.242902	0.007123	-.024568	-.030884
PE	Price to Earnings Ratio	-.049142	0.381314	0.144575	0.460241	0.491292	0.369046	-.397151	0.263395	0.098632	0.055600	0.044415
CEO_Tenure	Tenure of CEO	-.097859	0.394997	-.119428	0.591563	-.225400	-.363451	0.468663	-.035446	0.228015	0.118515	0.018738
Logvol	Log Trading Volume	0.381469	0.235047	-.212160	-.194870	0.350749	0.035820	0.148311	-.325576	0.450893	-.444135	-.251762

The PRINCOMP procedure also generates a lot of output. For now, we will focus on the tables of the eigenvalues and eigenvectors of the principal components, which are shown in Output 6.11A, and the Scree, Proportions and Cumulative Proportion of Variance, and the Component Pattern plots, which are shown in Output 6.11B. The range of eigenvalues of the principal component is from 0.182 to 3.245. The values of the eigenvectors show that log revenue, log market cap, log number of employees, and log number of shares outstanding are highly correlated with the first principal component. Indeed, the log of revenue was omitted from the PROBIT and LOGIT models to reduce the likelihood of multicollinearity-induced bias. Concerning the selection of the meaningful components for further analyses, components 1 to 5 will be selected if we apply the Kaiser rule (components 1–6 using the 80% PVE rule and components 1–7 by the elbow rule).

Output 6.11B shows the Scree plot of the eigenvalues that were previously reported in the Eigenvalue table. Notice how quickly the values reduce from the first to the second principal component, and from the fifth to the subsequent principal components. The Variance Explained plot shows that 80% of the variance is explained by the first six principal components and over

90% by the first ten principal components. The Component Pattern Profiles show the correlation of each variable with the principal components. For example, the plot of the second principal component (in red) shows that the component is positively correlated with beta, but negatively correlated with Age.

Output 6.11B: Scree Plot, Variance Explained Plot, and Component Profile Patterns

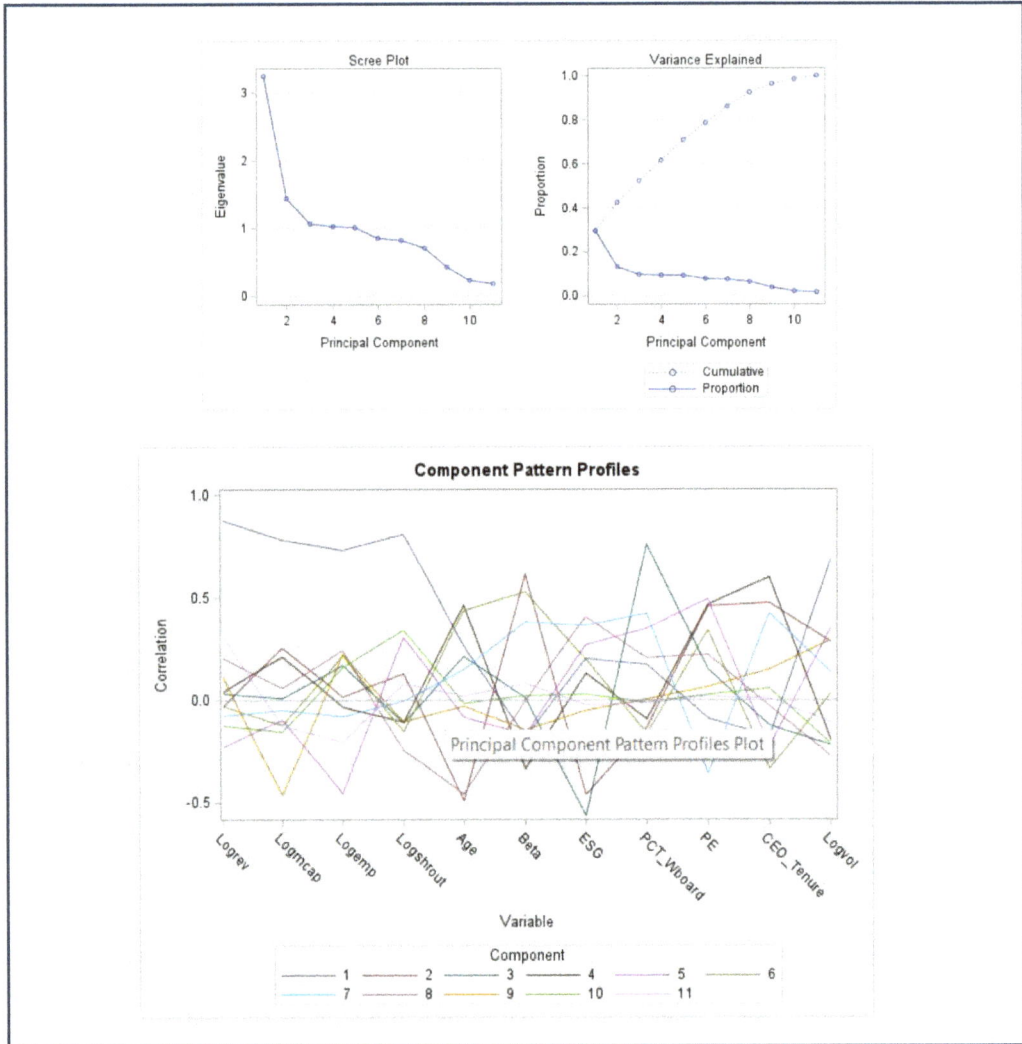

Now that the principal component analysis has been performed on the raw data, readers should consider re-estimating the previous probit and logit models, replacing the raw variables with the selected principal components.

Time to Event Models

In business settings, the magnitude of the event of interest (such as the financial impact of a default) is not the only concern of decision-makers. In many cases, the organization might also be interested in when the event of interest is most likely to occur and the factors that can influence the duration to the event. These types of insights can assist the organization in strategically deploying resources to mitigate the impact of events with potentially adverse outcomes such as loan default or to seek investment opportunities if the event of interest will lead to potentially positive outcomes such as post-bankruptcy reorganization. The time-to-event analysis is generally referred to as survival analysis.

Survival Analysis

Survival Analysis is the statistical study of the time to an event of interest. The predictive component of these types of studies models the factors that can influence the duration to the event or the probability that the event will happen at a specific window of time. Survival analysis is commonly used in the healthcare domain; however, there are many uses of the approach in financial settings as well. In particular, survival analysis is used in the insurance industry to model life expectancy, and in the investment industry to model time to default or delinquency on credit obligations or the occurrence of other risk events such as corporate actions and trade execution. The response variable in survival analysis is time, and since the time variable in many survival analysis studies is not normally distributed, regression-based models that rely on the assumption of normality are unsuitable for modeling these types of events.

A common feature of survival analysis data is censoring. Censoring occurs when we are unable to observe the outcome of interest in the study subjects due to a variety of reasons. This could be due to the sample period ending before the event of interest occurs in some subjects, or the subject's removal from the sample due to the occurrence of unrelated events that make further data collection impossible (right censoring). It is also possible for the event of interest to have occurred in the subject before the data is collected, which then makes it impossible to determine the true time of the event (this is called left censoring). Interval censoring happens when the event of interest occurs between two points in time in the observation period; however, we are unable to determine the exact point in time. Left censoring and interval censoring are not common in financial settings, so we will focus primarily on right censoring.

Three important items of interest in survival analysis are the survival function, hazard function, and probability density function. The survival function is the probability that the event of interest will not occur to the subject until after a reference time has passed (that is, the subject survives the event beyond the referenced time). Analogous to it is the hazard function, which is the probability that an event of interest will occur at the instantaneous point in time, given that it has not occurred in the past (that is, the subject will experience the event at that instantaneous point in time). The last item of interest is the probability density function, which is the frequency of occurrence of the event of interest per unit of time.

Let's apply survival analysis to model the event risk on credit obligations. We will define T as the time to the credit event of interest. The survival function that a credit obligor will not default or be delinquent on a credit obligation at time t can be expressed as:

$$S(t) = P(T > t), 0 < t < \infty \qquad (6.63)$$

Survival function does not rule delinquency or default in perpetuity, it is simply the probability that delinquency or default on the credit obligation will happen at a future date beyond time t. This implies that that $S(t)$ is a decreasing function of time. The greater the window of time, the higher the chances that delinquency will indeed occur in that window rather than at some future point in time. A complement to the survival function is the cumulative distribution function, which describes the probability that the credit event will occur within the window of time.

$$F(t) = 1 - S(t) = P(T < t) \qquad (6.64)$$

Given what we know from the above, we can write the probability density function that delinquency occurs at exactly time t as:

$$f(t) = -\frac{dS(t)}{dt} = \lim_{\Delta t \to 0} \frac{P(t \leq T \leq t + \Delta t)}{\Delta t} \qquad (6.65)$$

In Equation (6.65), the default time T is assumed to occur within the instantaneous interval t to $t + \Delta t$ as $\Delta t \to 0$. The hazard function that defines the probability of default or delinquency at time t, given no history of prior default or delinquency, can now be written as:

$$h(t) = \lim_{\Delta t \to 0} \frac{P(t \leq T < t + \Delta t \mid T \geq t)}{\Delta t} = \frac{f(t)}{S(t)} \qquad (6.66)$$

In contrast to the survival function, the hazard function can increase or decrease over time depending on the characteristics of the subjects and underlying factors that explain the dynamics of those characteristics over time. The cumulative hazard function $H(t)$, which is the accumulated risk of delinquency up to the reference time, is written as:

$$H(t) = \int_0^\infty h(t)\, d(t) = -\log(S(t)) \qquad (6.67)$$

The relationship between the survival function and the cumulative hazard function can also be written in terms of the survival function as follows:

$$S(t) = \exp(-H(t)) \qquad (6.68)$$

Censored observations in the credit portfolio under study will include obligors who fully repaid their loans during the study period or did not default on their loan before the end of the study period. Therefore, we can denote the censoring indicator δ_i at the censoring time C_i for all borrowers that fall into these two categories as equal to zero and those that defaulted on their credit obligations as equal to one as shown in the following expression.

$$\delta_i = \begin{cases} 1 : T_i \le C_i \\ 0 : T_i > C_i \end{cases} \tag{6.69}$$

T_i is the survival time, which is unobservable when the subject is censored. We can generalize the observable time for the subject i as $U_i = \min(T_i, c_i)$. In reality, we are able to observe both U_i and δ_i (in other words, the time at the point of measurement and whether the subject is censored or not). Thus, our likelihood function is proportional to the time of the event and the probability that the subject is censored.

> Since the items of interest in survival analysis are mostly probabilities of the event of interest, they can be specified using likelihood functions that reflect the probability that the event of interest might occur in the future in the subject i that has been censored or the probability that the event will occur instantaneously if the subject has not been censored.

If we assume that t_i is *i.i.d* and has a probability distribution $f(t_i)$, then its density function can be written as:

$$L_i(F) = f(t_i) = \begin{cases} f(t_i) & \text{if } \delta_i = 1 \\ S(t_i) & \text{if } \delta_i = 0 \end{cases}$$

$$= \left[f(t_i) \right]^{\delta_i} \left[S(t_i) \right]^{1-\delta_i} = \left[f(t_i) \right]^{\delta_i} \left[1 - F(t_i) \right]^{1-\delta_i} \tag{6.70}$$

We can also denote the density function in terms of the parameter space θ as $f(u_i; \theta)$, where f is a known distribution and θ an unknown parameter space. The likelihood function for all cases can then be written as:

$$L(F) = \prod_{i=1}^{n} L_i(F) = \prod_{i=1}^{n} \left\{ f(u_i; \theta)^{\delta_i} \left[1 - F(u_i; \theta) \right]^{1-\delta_i} \right\} \tag{6.71}$$

This specification allows us to model the likelihood of the time to event as a function of a set of conditional distribution parameters. The specification can also be extended to model the conditional distribution as a function of a set of explanatory variables and associated parameters as we will see shortly. The log-likelihood of the above can be written as:

$$L_n(\theta) = \sum_{i=1}^{n} \left(\delta_i \log\left[f(u_i; \theta) \right] - (1 - \delta_i) \log\left[1 - F(u_i; \theta) \right] \right)$$

$$= \sum_{i=1}^{n} \left(\delta_i \log\left[h(u_i; \theta) \right] \right) - \sum_{i=1}^{n} \left(H(u_i; \theta) \right) \tag{6.72}$$

The maximum likelihood estimator of the survival function is the parameter space $\hat{\theta}$ that maximizes $L_n(\theta)$ and it is written as:

$$\hat{\theta}_n = \arg\max\ L_n(\theta) \tag{6.73}$$

Survival analysis models can be estimated using both parametric and nonparametric approaches. For the parametric approach, the two commonly specified probability density functions are exponential and Weibull distributions. The Weibull distribution allows the hazard function to monotonically increase or decrease over time, while the exponential distribution which is a special case of the Weibull distribution assumes that the hazard function is constant over time.

Nonparametric estimators of the hazard functions include the Kaplan-Meier's estimator, which calculates the survival function as a fraction of the borrowers who have not defaulted at a time t. It is written as:

$$\hat{S}(t) = \prod_{i:t_i \leq t}\left(1 - \frac{d_i}{n_i}\right) \tag{6.74}$$

where t_i is the time at which at least one credit default or delinquency occurs. d_i is the number of defaults or delinquencies that occurred at the time t_i, and n_i represents the number of borrowers that are yet to default at the same time. The Kaplan-Meier's survival curve is used to graph the probability of survival (no credit default) on the Y axis against time on the X axis.

The cumulative hazard function and its corresponding standard errors can also be estimated using the Nelson-Aalen estimator. This is written as:

$$\hat{H}(t) = \sum_{t_i < t} \frac{d_i}{n_i} \tag{6.75}$$

Proportional Hazard Model

Another useful application of survival analysis in the credit risk domain is using the model to investigate the link between the time to event (in this case default or delinquency) and a set of predictor variables. This is usually done using Cox proportional hazard models. The Cox proportional hazard model specifies the time-to-event as a function of one or more risk factors or exposures (prognostic variable). In the model, the hazard rate, which is the response variable, represents the number of events per unit of time. The assumptions of the Cox proportional hazard model include that the effects of the prognostic variable on the hazard rate are constant over time and multiplicative with respect to the relationship between the predictors and the hazard. The model also assumes independence of survival time between subjects in the sample and that the hazard ratio, which is the ratio of the hazard function to the baseline hazard, is constant over time. The model can be written as:

$$h(t) = h_0(t)\exp\left(\beta_1 x_1 + ... + \beta_p x_p\right) \tag{6.76}$$

where $h(t)$ is the hazard function that is determined by the set of prognostic variables, $(x_i,...,x_p)$ is the matrix of covariates, and $(\beta_i,...,\beta_p)$ is the vector of hazard parameters to be estimated. $h_0(t)$ is the baseline hazard rate that corresponds to the value of the hazard when all x_i are equal to zero. One way to think about the relationship between the parameter estimate and the hazard function is to evaluate them in the context of the log hazard ratio

$$\left[\log\left(\frac{h(t)}{h_0(t)}\right)=\beta_1 x_1 +,...+\beta_p x_p\right]$$. Analogous to the odds ratio in logistic regression, the

marginal effect of a unit change in the covariate on the log hazard ratio, given that all other covariates are held constant can then be derived from the parameter estimate β_i .

Estimating Survival Analysis Models in SAS

SAS/STAT software contains a suite of procedures that can be used for various types of survival analysis. In general, the procedures fall into two categories; the first category, which typically will have a 'TEST' suffix in the procedure name (such as ICLIFETEST and LIFETEST), is used to perform nonparametric survival analysis. The second category, which has the 'REG' suffix in the procedure name, is used to estimate parametric and regression analysis of survival data. It includes the ICPHREG, LIFEREG, PHREG, and SURVEYREG procedures. In this chapter, we will explore the LIFETEST procedure, which performs a nonparametric estimate of the survivor function using the Kaplan-Meier method or the life-table method, and the PHREG procedure, which implements regression analysis of survival data using the Cox proportional hazard model.

Besides computing the nonparametric estimates of the survivor function, we can use the LIFETEST statement and the PLOT option in PROC LIFETEST to generate the survivor curves, hazard functions, and cumulative incidence rate, to name a few. The LIFETEST statement can also be used to estimate the cumulative hazard function using the Nelson-Aalen estimator (NELSON option) as well as to store the output data from the procedure into a SAS data set. The TIME statement is used to specify the failure time variable and the censoring variable, while the STRATA statement is used to specify the variables that define the strata levels, as well as to compare the survivor curves from multiple groups. The TEST statement is used to test the relationship between the failure times and a set of numeric exposure variables.

PROC PHREG has more robust capabilities for survival analysis than the LIFETEST procedure. Besides fitting the multiplicative Cox model, it can also perform a wide range of analyses and estimations, including fitting frailty models, testing linear hypotheses about the regression parameters, estimating customized hazard ratios, fitting logistic regression analysis for matched case-control, and performing variable selection for the choice model. The procedure also generates a set of Receiver Operating Characteristics (ROC) related plots that can be used to evaluate the fit of the model, as well as a set of baseline function plots such as the cumulative hazard and survival function plots.

Modeling Time to Delinquency for Peer-to-Peer Lending Borrowers

Now that we have established some baseline knowledge about the implementation of survival analysis in SAS, let us demonstrate the real-world application of PROC LIFETEST and PHREG by applying both procedures to a relatively small sample (10,000 observations) of loan portfolio data that was obtained from the Lending Club data. The Lending Club loan data is a well-recognized, open-source data set that contains millions of records of anonymized loan performance data from borrowers who obtained crowdfunded loans through the platform. The sample data set obtained from the larger repository of the Lending Club data set is saved in the LCLOANS. sas7bdat data set on the book's GitHub repository.

Unfortunately, not all borrowers (obligors) fulfill their commitments to repay the monthly amount when due. In our data set, a borrower is classified as delinquent (STATUS=1) if the borrower has not paid the monthly amount due for more than 30 days. This is a subjective threshold that is selected only for practical convenience in this exercise. In reality, the threshold might vary across organizations in line with their business objective, but it is common to use 30 days as the threshold. Our aim in this exercise is to study the time to delinquency (TIMETD variable) using survival analysis.

A borrower is right censored if the borrower is current on the loan, has fully repaid, or is less than 30 days late on the payment. Time to delinquency (TIMETD) is the months that have passed between when the loan was issued and when the borrower defaults. Although the data set has over 150 variables, we selected 14 prognostic variables for our covariates. We will define the survival function of a lending club borrower as the probability that the borrower will not become delinquent in the referenced month. Along this same line, the hazard function for the borrower can also be defined as the probability that the borrower will be delinquent during the referenced month.

PROC LIFETEST

Program 6.12A shows a simple SAS code that was used to implement the LIFETEST procedure on the LCLOAN data set. The ODS GRAPHICS ON statement invokes the ODS graphs that accompany the LIFESTEST procedures. They include the survival function (S or SURVIVAL), the cumulative hazard function (LS or LOGSURV), the log of negative logs (LLS or LOGLOGS), and the hazard function (H or Hazard). The ATRISK option requests the number of borrowers who are still at risk of being delinquent at time t (n_i). The KERNEL=EPANECHNIKOV option specifies that the nonparametric estimate of the hazard function should be based on the Epanechnikov kernel density function.[29] The METHOD= PL (or KM) option specifies that the survivor function must be computed using the Kaplan-Meier (also known as Product-Limit) method. The other methods that can be specified include the Life-Table method (also known as actuarial) (LT, ACT, LIFE), the Breslow (BRESLOW), and the Fleming-Harrington method (FH). INTERVALS=0 to 50 by 1 specifies

---

[29] The Epanechnikov kernel density is the default option in LIFETEST, so specifying it is optional. The other Kernel density options are UNIFORM and BIWEIGHT.

the interval for computing the survivor function. If not specified, it will be calculated at each time index, which might result in a survival function table with missing entries if no event occurs at that time. OUTSURV=SDATA is used to save the estimated survival function in a SAS data set. The TIME=TIMETD*STATUS (0) is used to specify the TIMETD as the time variable and STATUS as the censoring variable, with zero indicating that the observation has been right censored.

Program 6.12A: Estimating Survival Function of Credit Obligors Using PROC LIFETEST

```
/*Estimating the Survival Functions of Credit Obligors Using PROC LIFETEST*/
%datapull(loans,lcloans.sas7bdat);
ods graphics on;

proc lifetest data=lcloans plots=(s(atrisk),ls,lls,h(kernel=epanechnikov) cif)
      method=pl nelson  intervals=0 to 50 by 1  outsurv=sdata;
      time timetd*status(0)/;
run;
```

Output 6.12A, which was obtained from the procedure, shows the Kaplan-Meier estimates of the survival function and the Nelson-Aalen cumulative distribution function (Failure) along with the standard error of the survival function. It also shows the cumulative hazard function and its standard errors, as well as the cumulative number of borrowers who become delinquent and the number of borrowers at risk of delinquency over time. As expected, an increasing number of borrowers become delinquent over time resulting in a monotonically decreasing survivor function and increasing cumulative hazard function. The hazard function, however, is not monotonically increasing. It initially increases for the first 10 months, then declines steadily up to the 36 months, which is then followed by a dramatic spike in subsequent months. This is due in part to the differences in terms of the loans that are taken by the borrowers. The term of the Lending Club loans can either be for 36 months or 60 months. The spike in the hazard function is likely due to a significant increase in the delinquency rate from the 36-month borrowers as their loans reach maturity. We will explore this issue in Program 6.12B.

Output 6.12A: Survival Function of Credit Obligors Using PROC LIFETEST

	Survival Function and Cumulative Hazard Rate							
	Product-Limit				Nelson-Aalen			
timetd	Survival	Failure	Survival	Standard Error	Cumulative Hazard	Cum Haz Standard Error	Number Failed	Number Left
0.0000	1.0000	0		0	0		0	10000
1.0000	0.9988	0.00120		0.000347	0.00120	0.000347	12	9961
2.0000	0.9960	0.00403		0.000636	0.00404	0.000638	40	9856
3.0000	0.9921	0.00791		0.000892	0.00793	0.000898	78	9721
4.0000	0.9885	0.0115		0.00108	0.0116	0.00109	113	9595
5.0000	0.9827	0.0173		0.00132	0.0175	0.00134	169	9457
6.0000	0.9770	0.0230		0.00152	0.0232	0.00156	223	9292
7.0000	0.9712	0.0288		0.00170	0.0291	0.00175	277	9121
8.0000	0.9636	0.0364		0.00192	0.0370	0.00198	348	8925
9.0000	0.9564	0.0436		0.00210	0.0444	0.00219	413	8728

Output 6.12B: Survival and Hazard Functions of Credit Obligors Using PROC LIFETEST

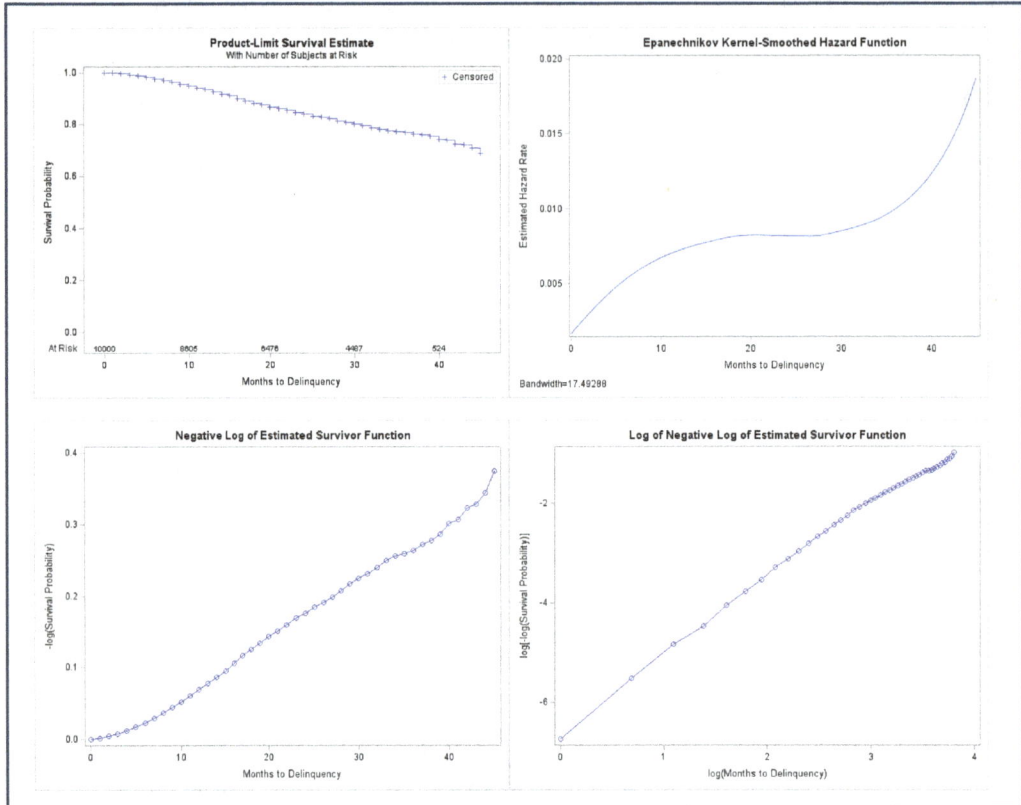

Further evidence in support of the values shown in the table can be found on the ODS plots produced by the LIFETEST procedure (shown in Output 6.12B). The Product-Limit Survival Estimate (Kaplan-Meier's curve) shows the declining survivor function. The Epanechnikov Kernel-Smooth Hazard Function is the hazard function of the borrower pool. The Negative Log of Estimated Survivor Function is the cumulative hazard function. The Log of Negative Log of Estimated Survivor Function graphs the log of the cumulative hazard function against the log of time to delinquency.

In Program 6.12B, we modify the SAS code in Program 6.12A to compare the survivor, hazard function, and cumulative hazard functions of borrowers with 36- and 60-month loans using the STRATA statement. We also test the null hypothesis that the survivor functions are the same for both loan terms by invoking the TEST=(LR LOGRANK) option in the STRATA statement. The likelihood ratio and the LOGRANK test are requested. Furthermore, we use the TEST INT_RATE DTI to examine the effects of interest rate and debt-to-income ratio on survivor time. OUTTEST is used to save the estimated test statistics in the SEST SAS data set.

Program 6.12B: Comparing Survival Function of Credit Obligors Using PROC LIFETEST

```
/*Comparing the Survival Functions of Credit Obligors Using PROC LIFETEST*/
ods graphics on;

proc lifetest data=lcloans method=pl plots=(s h ls lls) notable outtest=sest intervals=0
to 50 by 1 outsurv=sdata;;
      time timetd*status(0);
      strata term/order=internal test=(lr logrank);
      test dti int_rate;
run;
```

Output 6.12C: Comparing Survival Function of Credit Obligors Using PROC LIFETEST

Summary of the Number of Censored and Uncensored Values

Stratum	term	Total	Failed	Censored	Percent Censored
1	36	6671	987	5684	85.20
2	60	3329	785	2544	76.42
Total		10000	1772	8228	82.28

Testing Homogeneity of Survival Curves for timetd over Strata

Rank Statistics

term	Log-Rank
36	-147.89
60	147.89

Covariance Matrix for the Log-Rank Statistics

term	36	60
36	390.818	-390.818
60	-390.818	390.818

Test of Equality over Strata

Test	Chi-Square	DF	Pr > Chi-Square
Log-Rank	55.9636	1	<.0001
-2Log(LR)	57.4056	1	<.0001

In the summary table shown in Output 6.12C, we learn that about two-thirds of the loans in the sample mature in 36 months compared to one-third that mature in 60 months. The log-rank and likelihood ratio tests reject the null hypothesis that the survival curves of both loan terms are the same. Further evidence in support of the rejection of the null can be seen in the ODS graphs produced by the procedure and shown in Output 6.12D.

Output 6.12D: Comparing Survival and Hazard Functions Between Groups of Credit Obligors Using PROC LIFETEST

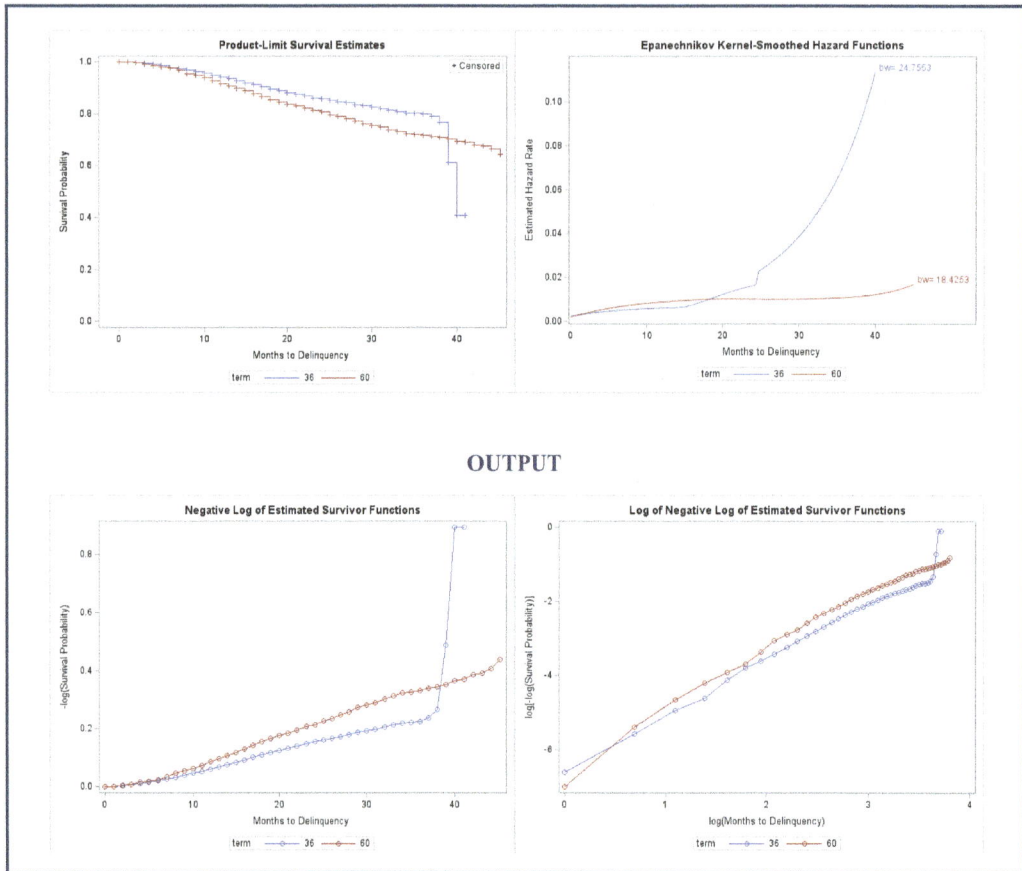

The plots show marked differences in the survivor functions, cumulative hazard functions, and hazard functions for both loan terms. As expected, the survivor functions for the 36-month loans converge and fall dramatically once the loans reach maturity (that is, the probability of surviving today and defaulting at a later date in the future is zero, because there is no future once the loans mature). In contrast, the survivor function of the 60-month loans continues to steadily decline beyond the 40-month window until the observation is right censored. You can also notice the stunning increase in the hazard functions of the 36-month loans as they near maturity.

Output 6.12E shows the result of the Wilcoxon and log-rank tests of the association of the covariates with the time-to-delinquency. For both tests, two sets of rank statistics are reported. A univariate rank statistic is first computed, and then the sequence of test statistics for joint effect is then displayed. The first variable in the sequence of the joint statistics is the variable with the largest univariate statistics. The results of the univariate test indicate that both debt-to-income ratio and interest rate have statistically significant associations with time to delinquency.

However, the joint test based on the sequential addition of variables indicates that the debt-to-income ratio does not significantly improve on interest rate in terms of the joint significance of both variables in predicting time-to-delinquency. It is possible that both variables might be representing the same underlying factors (loan affordability) that lead borrowers to default on their loans.

Output 6.12E: Statistical Test of Survival and Hazard Functions Between Groups of Credit Obligors Using PROC LIFETEST

Rank Tests for the Association of timetd with Covariates Pooled over Strata

Univariate Chi-Squares for the Wilcoxon Test

Variable	Test Statistic	Standard Error	Chi-Square	Pr > Chi-Square
dti	-1907.6	325.4	34.3741	<.0001
int_rate	-37.2281	1.4649	645.9	<.0001

Covariance Matrix for the Wilcoxon Statistics

Variable	dti	int_rate
dti	105862	98
int_rate	98	2

Forward Stepwise Sequence of Chi-Squares for the Wilcoxon Test

Variable	DF	Chi-Square	Pr > Chi-Square	Chi-Square Increment	Pr > Increment
int_rate	1	645.9	<.0001	645.9	<.0001
dti	2	646.3	<.0001	0.4509	0.5019

Univariate Chi-Squares for the Log-Rank Test

Variable	Test Statistic	Standard Error	Chi-Square	Pr > Chi-Square
dti	-2098.5	363.0	33.4185	<.0001
int_rate	-40.9361	1.6204	638.2	<.0001

Covariance Matrix for the Log-Rank Statistics

Variable	dti	int_rate
dti	131776	118
int_rate	118	3

Forward Stepwise Sequence of Chi-Squares for the Log-Rank Test

Variable	DF	Chi-Square	Pr > Chi-Square	Chi-Square Increment	Pr > Increment
int_rate	1	638.2	<.0001	638.2	<.0001
dti	2	638.7	<.0001	0.5023	0.4785

PROC PHREG

Program 6.13 shows the SAS code that was used to fit the Cox proportional hazard model of time-to-delinquency for the lending club data using PROC PHREG. The procedure has quite a vast number of features, but many are unrelated to the typical needs of a financial data scientist. Hence, we will focus on those features that are required to estimate the survival analysis model that we are considering. The PLOT= (SURVIVAL CUMHAZ ROC) option is used to request the ODS plot for the survival and cumulative hazard functions, and the ROC curve, respectively. The ROCOPTIONS (AT=0 to 40 BY 10) is used to request the ROC curves at 0, 10, 20, 30, and

40 months of loan durations. The CLASS statement is used to specify categorical variables in the model. They include the application type (APPLICATION_TYPE), the credit grade (GRADE), the duration of the loan (TERM), the homeownership status (HOME_OWNERSHIP), the type of income verification (VERIFICATION_STATUS), and the duration of employment (EMP_LENGTH).

Program 6.13: Estimating Proportional Hazard Model of Credit Obligors Using PROC PHREG

```
/*Estimating Proportional Hazard Models of Credit Obligors Using PROC PHREG*/
ods graphics on;

proc phreg data=lcloans plots=(survival cumhaz roc auc)
        rocoptions(at=0 to 40 by 10) simple;
        class application_type grade term purpose home_ownership verification_status
        emp_length;
        model timetd*status(0)= loan_amnt int_rate annual_inc dti pub_rec application_type
        total_acc revol_util grade term purpose home_ownership      verification_status
        emp_length / selection=stepwise slentry=0.25 slstay=0.15 details;
run;
```

The numerical variable in the model includes the amount borrowed (LOAN_AMNT), the total number of credit accounts (TOTAL_ACC), the interest rate charged to the borrower (INT_RATE), the annual income of the borrower (ANNUAL_INC), the borrower's debt-to-income ratio, and the number of public records which the borrower has. The MODEL statement is used to specify the time to delinquency variable (TIMETD) and the censoring variable (STATUS) and their interaction with the prognostic variables. The SELECTION=STEPWISE statement requests an iterative step selection process to narrow the prognostic variables in the model to only the ones with a statistically significant relationship with time.

Output 6.13A: Proportional Hazard Model of Credit Obligors Using PROC PHREG

Model Fit Statistics		
	Without	With
Criterion	Covariates	Covariates
-2 LOG L	31112.240	30365.573
AIC	31112.240	30393.573
SBC	31112.240	30470.291

Testing Global Null Hypothesis: BETA=0			
Test	Chi-Square	DF	Pr > ChiSq
Likelihood Ratio	746.6669	14	<.0001
Score	804.3080	14	<.0001
Wald	697.6709	14	<.0001

Type 3 Tests			
Effect	DF	Wald Chi-Square	Pr > ChiSq
int_rate	1	30.0692	<.0001
total_acc	1	11.9986	0.0005
revol_util	1	5.4618	0.0194
grade	6	36.2132	<.0001
term	1	11.8989	0.0006
home_ownership	2	31.6470	<.0001
verification_status	2	16.8559	0.0002

Output 6.13A: Proportional Hazard Model of Credit Obligors Using PROC PHREG (Continued)

Parameter		DF	Parameter Estimate	Standard Error	Chi-Square	Pr > ChiSq	Hazard Ratio	Label
int_rate		1	13.51599	2.46483	30.0692	<.0001	741173.5	
total_acc		1	0.00687	0.00198	11.9986	0.0005	1.007	
revol_util		1	-0.24220	0.10364	5.4618	0.0194	0.785	
grade	A	1	0.60083	0.54896	1.1979	0.2737	1.824	grade A
grade	B	1	0.94600	0.47410	3.9815	0.0460	2.575	grade B
grade	C	1	1.04626	0.40995	6.5137	0.0107	2.847	grade C
grade	D	1	0.96903	0.34955	7.6852	0.0056	2.635	grade D
grade	E	1	1.02598	0.31067	10.9063	0.0010	2.790	grade E
grade	F	1	0.76159	0.27473	7.6846	0.0056	2.142	grade F
term	36	1	0.19010	0.05511	11.8989	0.0006	1.209	term 36
home_ownership	MORTGAGE	1	-0.29331	0.05237	31.3717	<.0001	0.746	home_ownership MORTGAGE
home_ownership	OWN	1	-0.09570	0.07881	1.4745	0.2246	0.909	home_ownership OWN
verification_status	Not Verified	1	-0.29375	0.07156	16.8497	<.0001	0.745	verification_status Not Verified
verification_status	Source Verified	1	-0.09365	0.05370	3.0410	0.0812	0.911	verification_status Source Verified

Analysis of Maximum Likelihood Estimates

Output 6.13A shows the fit statistics, Type 3 Test table, and the Analysis of Maximum Likelihood Estimates table obtained from estimating the Cox proportional hazard model. The test statistics shown on the Type 3 test table suggest that interest rate, the total number of credit accounts, credit utilization ratio, the credit quality of the borrower, the purpose of the loan, and the homeownership status of the borrower are significant determinants of time to delinquency. The Analysis of Maximum Likelihood Estimate table shows that the hazard rate of delinquency is associated with higher interest rates, debt to income, the total number of accounts, shorter loan duration, less-than-perfect credit (lower than an 'A' grade), and loans for non-vacation-related purposes. Borrowers with higher revolving balances, who own a home (paid-off or mortgage), and borrowers with verified income or no verification[30] have lower default frequency than the baseline borrower. The hazard ratio shows the change in the hazard function of delinquency between two groups (A and B) in which the difference between the groups is a unit of the prognostic variable. For example, a one-unit increase in the number of revolving accounts will increase the hazard of delinquency by 1.007.

Output 6.13B shows the plots of the survivor function and cumulative hazard function for a reference borrower (with the prognostic characteristics shown in the Reference Set of Covariates for Plotting table). The output also shows the time-dependent receiver operating characteristics (ROC) curves that plot the sensitivity (true positive) against the 1-specificity (false positive) at various points in the term of the loans. The survivor and cumulative hazard functions graphs show a monotonic decline in the survival probability and a steady increase in the cumulative

[30] Lending Club independently verifies borrowers' income using three methods. 'Verified' borrowers include those whose income source and amount are both verified. 'Source Verified' borrowers are those borrowers whose income source only is verified, and unverified borrowers are those with no verification. Lender Club appears to apply more stringent verification methods to weaker borrowers than stronger borrowers, which explains why the hazard rate is higher for fully verified borrowers, relative to 'source verified' and 'unverified' borrowers.

hazard of delinquency over the duration of the loan term. The time-dependent receiver operating characteristics (ROC) curves examine the ability of the model to accurately discriminate between borrowers in good standing and borrowers in delinquency over the duration of the loan. The areas under the plots show a consistent performance in the model's ability to distinguish between the two groups across time.

Output 6.13B: Survivor Function, Hazard Function, and ROC Curves

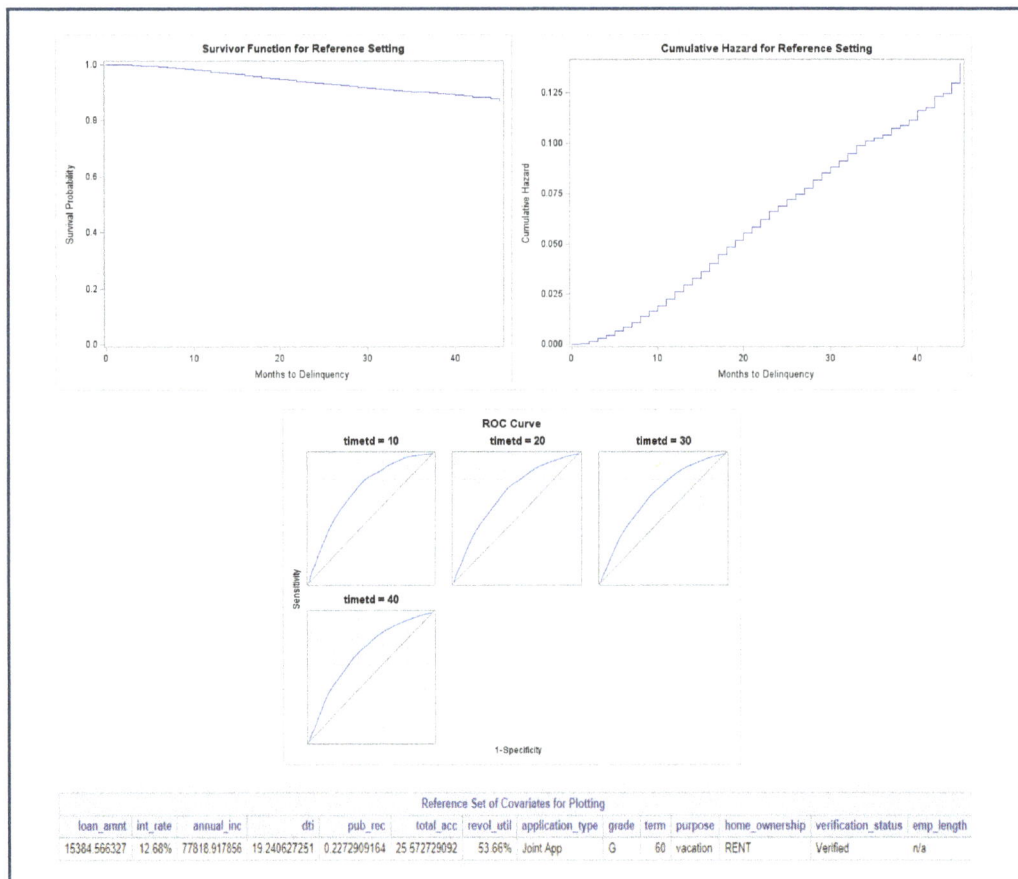

	loan_amnt	int_rate	annual_inc	dti	pub_rec	total_acc	revol_util	application_type	grade	term	purpose	home_ownership	verification_status	emp_length
	15384.566327	12.68%	77818.917856	19.240627251	0.2272909164	25.572729092	53.66%	Joint App	G	60	vacation	RENT	Verified	n/a

Reference Set of Covariates for Plotting

Forecasting Models

There are various types of forecasting models. One way to categorize them is based on whether they use single dependent variables (univariate models) or multiple dependent variables (system models). The aim of univariate forecasting models is typically to forecast the future value of a single dependent variable while the system models aim to forecast multiple dependent variables simultaneously. Many of the common univariate forecasting models such as ARIMA, time series regression, and Autoregression have been presented in Chapters Three and Four. Therefore, we will focus on system models and other types of univariate forecasting models in subsequent sections of this chapter.

System Models

Many statistical models assume unidirectional relationships between the predictor variables and the response variables. However, many economic and financial variables dynamically influence each other over time. These effects can occur in the form of a simultaneous feedback loop that arises from changes in investment opportunities across financial markets or through lead-lag relationships that could be between macroeconomic factors and the policy reactions to those factors (such as inflation and interest rates). The problem with modeling these variables with univariate models is that the residuals of the univariate model might now be correlated with the response variable itself since it is also a predictor of the predictor variable. The parameter estimates that are derived from univariate models where simultaneity bias exists will themselves be biased and inconsistent (over or underestimate the value of the true parameter) due to the endogeneity problem (that is, the covariance of the predictor variable with the residual is no longer zero) that now exists in the error term. For predictive purposes, it is important to account for these features using special techniques. One of those techniques is to model the relationship in a multi-equation approach. Commonly used multi-equation models for financial data science include simultaneous equation models (SEM) and vector autoregression models (VAR).

Simultaneous Equation Models

Simultaneous equation models (SEM) are employed in a multivariate framework when two or more variables have bi-directional contemporaneous relationships, and you need to model one variable as a predictor of the other variable. The models might also include other exogenous variables. Although SEMs are not commonly used in predictive modeling, it is worth exploring their applications for statistical modeling for research purposes. Consider a bivariate system of equations consisting of $y_{1,t}$ and $y_{2,t}$, where both variables are jointly determined in their respective equations. Furthermore, let us allow the regression equation for the response variable to also include a set of exogenous regressors. We can formulate the bivariate system of equations as follows:

$$y_{1,t} = \beta_{10} + \alpha_1 y_{2,t} + X_{1t}\beta_1 + \varepsilon_{1,t}$$
$$y_{2,t} = \beta_{20} + \alpha_2 y_{1,t} + X_{2t}\beta_2 + \varepsilon_{2,t}$$

(6.77)

where $X_{1t}\beta_1 = \left[x_{11,t}\beta_{11} + x_{12,t}\beta_{12} +,.....+ x_{1k,t}\beta_{1k} \right]$ and

$X_{2t}\beta_1 = \left[x_{21,t}\beta_{21} + x_{22,t}\beta_{22} +,.....+ x_{2k,t}\beta_{2k} \right]$ are the tth row vectors of exogenous regressors.

In the regression equation system, you will notice that both response variables are contemporaneously affected by the other response variable. We can model a system such as this using a variety of approaches. These include two-stage (2SLS) and three-stage (3SLS) least squares, as well as limited information and full information maximum likelihood. The 2SLS and 3SLS require the use of instrumental variables. Concerning the $y_{1,t}$ equation, the appropriate instrumental variable will be a variable that is correlated with $y_{2,t}$ but uncorrelated with the residual terms $\varepsilon_{1,t}$. Furthermore, the variable must not already be included in $y_{1,t}$ the equation. This is known as the identification condition. In general, you will need the number of excluded exogenous variables to be greater than the number of endogenous variables from the $y_{1,t}$ equation. In the implementation of the 2SLS for $y_{1,t}$, we first regress the endogenous response variable $y_{2,t}$ against the instrumental variable to obtain its predicted value $\hat{y}_{2,t}$. The predicted value $\hat{y}_{2t}$ is then used in the $y_{1,t}$ equation, in place of the y_{2t}, $\left[y_{1,t} = \beta_{10} + \alpha_1 \hat{y}_{2,t} + X_{1,t} \beta_1 + \varepsilon_{1,t} \right]$. Because $\hat{y}_{2,t}$ is the expected value of $y_{2,t}$ given its instruments, which are uncorrelated with $\varepsilon_{1,t}$, then $\hat{y}_{2,t}$ satisfies the condition for estimating $y_{1,t}$ using OLS. Hence, the term the two-stage (2SLS) least square.

Modeling the Relationship Between Stock Returns and Trading Volume

Now, let's consider a joint predictive model of daily stock returns and daily trading volume. In this setup, it is evident that there would be a feedback loop between the two variables. Anecdotally, you would expect higher volume to cause large swings in prices and large price movements to drive higher trading volume. Hence, modeling these two variables must be done in a simultaneous equation system setup. In the model specification, daily index returns (DRET) is regressed on the daily change in aggregate bond market yield (RBOND), daily change in oil prices (ROIL), daily change in the US dollar exchange rate (REXR), and daily change (DVRET) and lagged daily change (LVRET) in trading volume. Daily change in trading volume (DVRET) is regressed on the daily (DRET) and lagged (LRET) daily index return, daily change in US equity VIX (RVIX), gold VIX (RGVIX), and oil VIX (ROVIX).

$$DRET_t = \beta_{10} + \alpha_1 VRET_t + \beta_{11} LVRET_t + \beta_{11} RBOND_t + \beta_{11} ROIL_t + + \beta_{11} REXR_t + \varepsilon_{1t}$$
$$VRET_t = \beta_{10} + \alpha_1 DRET_t + \beta_{11} LDRET_t + \beta_{11} RVIX_t + \beta_{11} RGVIX_t + + \beta_{11} ROVIX_t + \varepsilon_{1t} \qquad (6.78)$$

The instrument variables used include all the regressors although it is possible to specify similar regressors in both equations as long as there are more exogenous regressors than the number of endogenous regressors. However, the exogenous regressors in both equations are not the same in this case.

Estimating Simultaneous Equations in SAS

Three commonly used SAS procedures for modeling SEMs are PROC MODEL, PROC SYSLIN, and PROC CALIS. PROC MODEL is a workhorse SAS procedure that can model a wide variety of relationships among the variables in a system of one or more linear and nonlinear equations.

These include linear and nonlinear SEM models. PROC SYSLIN is a tailored solution for modeling SEMs, while PROC CALIS is a more general procedure for modeling latent variables in an equation system. For more complex modeling problems, PROC MODEL requires fairly more code writing than PROC SYSLIN. However, PROC SYSLIN allows at most one latent variable, the error term, in each equation, while PROC CALIS allows several latent variables to appear in an equation. From a predictive analytics perspective, PROC SYSLIN is relevant as it writes predicted and residual values to an output SAS data set. On the other hand, PROC CALIS is used for path analysis and causal modeling. Furthermore, PROC SYSLIN and PROC MODEL provide more methods of estimation (including OLS, SUR, 2SLS, 3SLS, LIML, and FIML, to name a few) than PROC CALIS.[31]

PROC SYSLIN

Program 6.14 shows the SAS code that was used to jointly model the daily returns and trading volume of the S&P 500 index. The SAS procedure invoked for the estimation is PROC SYSLIN. However, the SYSLIN procedure can be used to estimate simultaneous equation systems using a wide range of approaches, including the 2SLS, 3SLS, FIML, and LIML approaches, which were highlighted earlier. In the example, we request the 2SLS option after the DATA statement. The OUT option is used to specify the SAS data set to save the predicted values of both series. The ENDOGENOUS statement is used to specify the two endogenous variables, while the INSTRUMENT statement is used to specify the instrument variables for the 2SLS. The MODEL statement specifies the equation for each model. Notice the differences between the list of the regressors in the return and the volume equations. The OUTPUT statement is used to request the creation of the estimation results (in this case the predicted values of returns and volume), while the PREDICTED option is used to assign a variable name to the saved values of predicted response variables.

Program 6.14: Using PROC SYSLIN to Model the Determinant of Stock Return and Volume

```
/*Using PROC SYSLIN to Model the Determinant of Stock returns and Trading Volumes*/
%datapull (market,market_data.sas7bdat);
ods graphics on;

proc syslin data=market_data 2sls out=predicted;
        endogenous dret vret;
        instruments rbond roil rexr rvix rgvix rovix ldret lvret;
return:
        model dret= vret lvret rbond roil rexr;
        output predicted=pdret ;
volume:
        model vret= dret ldret rvix rgvix rovix;
        output predicted=pvret;
run;
```

---

[31] You can learn more about the differences between the SYSLIN and CALIS procedures at https://go.documentation.sas.com/doc/en/pgmsascdc/9.4_3.4/statug/statug_introcalis_sect047.htm.

The results shown in Output 6.14 show a strong statistical connection between the two response variables. Lower stock market returns are more likely to occur on days with higher trading volumes, while lower stock market returns, and volume today are more likely to precipitate higher trading volume on the following day. This result matches relatively well with anecdotal patterns. On average, trading volume on the index is slightly higher on the day with negative index returns and on days that follow trading days with negative returns on the index. The return regression also shows that today's return is negatively correlated with the previous trading day's return and volume. It is also negatively correlated with the exchange rate, but positively correlated with oil price changes.

Trading volume is positively correlated with the levels of volatility in the stock and gold markets, but not with the crude oil market.

Output 6.14: Determinants of Stock Return and Volume

The SYSLIN Procedure
Two-Stage Least Squares Estimation

Model	RETURN
Dependent Variable	DRET
Label	Daily Index Return

Analysis of Variance

Source	DF	Sum of Squares	Mean Square	F Value	Pr > F
Model	5	0.220407	0.044081	34.93	< .0001
Error	3486	4.399480	0.001262		
Corrected Total	3491	0.481418			

Root MSE	0.03553	R-Square	0.04771
Dependent Mean	0.00041	Adj R-Sq	0.04634
Coeff Var	8720.14102		

Parameter Estimates

Variable	DF	Parameter Estimate	Standard Error	t Value	Pr > |t|	Variable Label
Intercept	1	0.000621	0.000603	1.03	0.3028	Intercept
VRET	1	-0.20637	0.019757	-10.45	< .0001	%Chg in Daily Volume
LVRET	1	-0.07307	0.007622	-9.59	< .0001	Lagged Daily Change in Volume
RBOND	1	-0.24043	0.186011	-1.29	0.1962	%Chg AGG Bond Yield
ROIL	1	0.042851	0.021875	1.96	0.0502	%Chg Oil Price
REXR	1	-0.93663	0.184396	-5.08	< .0001	%Chg in USD Exchange Rate

The SYSLIN Procedure
Two-Stage Least Squares Estimation

Model	VOLUME
Dependent Variable	VRET
Label	%Chg in Daily Volume

Analysis of Variance

Source	DF	Sum of Squares	Mean Square	F Value	Pr > F
Model	5	4.328018	0.865604	25.86	< .0001
Error	3486	116.7052	0.033478		
Corrected Total	3491	112.9084			

Root MSE	0.18297	R-Square	0.03576
Dependent Mean	0.00036	Adj R-Sq	0.03438
Coeff Var	50939.1427		

Parameter Estimates

Variable	DF	Parameter Estimate	Standard Error	t Value	Pr > |t|	Variable Label
Intercept	1	-0.00218	0.003144	-0.69	0.4885	Intercept
DRET	1	7.209778	1.368437	5.27	< .0001	Daily Index Return
LDRET	1	0.023214	0.278399	0.08	0.9335	Lagged Daily Index Return
RVIX	1	1.099012	0.149922	7.33	< .0001	%Chg VIX
RGVIX	1	0.258208	0.063403	4.07	< .0001	%Chg Gold VIX
ROVIX	1	0.021493	0.066419	0.32	0.7463	%Chg Oil VIX

Vector Autoregression

Unlike simultaneous equations that explore contemporaneous feedback loops between response variables, vector autoregression (VAR) assumes that feedback arises out of the lagged values of the response variables such that each response variable is a function of its own lagged values as well as the lagged values of other response variables. VARs are the multivariate extension of the univariate autoregressive models. Besides modeling the relationship between two or more response variables, VAR can be used for forecasting as well as analyzing various statistical relationships between variables – these include causality, cointegration, impulse response, forecast error decomposition, and dynamic simultaneous equations. VAR models can also include exogenous variables, as well as their lags in the multivariate regression framework. There are several other extensions to VAR models such as the addition of conditional volatility specification to the mean equation to form the multivariate GARCH-VAR (MGARCH-VAR) and panel data VAR.

Although its origin is in econometrics, machine-learning implementations of VAR have also emerged in recent years due to the versatility of the VAR framework. Furthermore, because many financial and economic time series tend to comove, it is cardinal that all financial data scientists develop competencies in implementing VAR models. Let $Y_t = \begin{bmatrix} y_{1,t}, y_{2,t}, \dots y_{k,t} \end{bmatrix}$ be a k-dimensional time series vector. The mathematical framework of the pth order VAR model of Y can be described by the following multivariate regression equation system.

$$Y_t = C + \Pi_1 Y_{t-1} + \Pi_2 Y_{t-2} + \dots + \Pi_p Y_{t-p} + \varepsilon_t \tag{6.79}$$

Although it is common to define VAR models using matrix algebra shown above, we will proceed with a simple bivariate VAR model with one autoregressive lag. The bivariate VAR system of equation consisting of $y_{1,t}$ and $y_{2,t}$, where each variable is described by its own lag and the lagged realization of the other variable, is described as follows.

$$y_{1,t} = c_1 + \pi_{11}^1 y_{1,t-1} + \pi_{12}^1 y_{2,t-1} + \varepsilon_{1,t}$$
$$y_{2,t} = c_2 + \pi_{11}^2 y_{1,t-1} + \pi_{12}^2 y_{2,t-1} + \varepsilon_{2,t} \tag{6.80}$$

π_{ij}^i is the coefficient of the autoregressive lags of the first variable, while π_{ji}^j is the coefficient of the autoregressive lags of the second variable. For example, π_{11}^1 as shown in Equation (6.80) is the coefficient of the first autoregressive lag of the first variable in the first equation, and π_{12}^1 is the coefficient of the first autoregressive lag of the second variable in the first equation. Equation (6.80) can also be extended to include a set of exogenous variables but for now, we will continue with the model specification that contains endogenous variables $y_{1,t}$ and $y_{2,t}$ alone.

The estimation of VAR models can be performed using the least square or the maximum likelihood methods. Most simple VAR models can be estimated using the least square approach. VAR models that have been augmented with additional parameter specifications such as the multivariate GARCH-VAR, often involve estimating a lot of parameters and due to this, they are typically estimated using maximum likelihood.

As presented earlier, the VAR specification in Equation (6.80) can be used to explore various statistical relationships between the two endogenous variables. For example, we can use the model to explore the causal relationship between $y_{1,t}$ and $y_{2,t}$. Causal relationships exist between two variables if past values of one variable can explain the current or future values of another variable after controlling for its lags.

This implies that there is information about current values of $y_{1,t}$ that cannot be found in its lagged values but can be found in past values of $y_{2,t}$ (that is, past values of $y_{2,t}$ predict current values of $y_{1,t}$).

We can also use VARs to study the effects of shocks to one response variable on the other response variables in the system. This type of study is particularly useful from a policy analysis point of view. For example, a multi-asset class portfolio manager might be interested in studying the impact of shocks to one asset class on the other asset classes in the portfolio. In the VAR framework, the analysis of shock transmission from one variable to another is called the impulse response function (IRF). The impulse response function analyzes the impact of the one standard deviation (two standard deviations in VARMAX) change in the value of one variable on the other variables in the system. This analysis is performed both in terms of the magnitude of the shock and in the persistence of the shock. An extension to this approach is to measure how much a shock to one variable contributes to the variance (forecast error) of the other variables in the systems. This is known as variance decomposition or forecast error decomposition.

The last application of VAR we will explore is forecasting and prediction confidence. Since VARs can be used to establish causality, it is quite logical that we can also apply them for predictive and forecasting purposes. In general, the forecasting approach of VAR models follows the same approach as the univariate models, although in a system format. The estimated parameters of the models are simply used to predict future values of all of the response variables up to the specified lead time in an iterative manner.

Now that we have established the theoretical framework of the VAR, let's use the model to examine the relationship between unemployment and personal consumption in the US. Private consumption accounts for about 68% of the US GDP. Ceteris paribus, an increase in aggregate consumption should lead to an increase in aggregate production (GDP), which should increase aggregate employment (lower unemployment). Increased aggregate employment should lead to increased aggregate income, which will also fuel an increase in consumption. The transmission of the effects of changes in employment to consumption or vice versa is not necessarily contemporaneously determined; hence, the relationship can be modeled in the following VAR framework:

$$pce_t = c_1 + \pi_{11}^1 pce_{t-1} + \pi_{12}^1 unrate_{t-1} + \varepsilon_{1,t}$$

$$unrate_t = c_2 + \pi_{11}^2 pce_{t-1} + \pi_{12}^2 unrate_{t-1} + \varepsilon_{2,t}$$

(6.81)

where pce_t and $unrate_t$ represent monthly personal consumption expenditure and unemployment, respectively. Although the order p of the lagged variables specified in Equation (6.81) can be greater than 1, we will keep the specification to a single lag framework to simplify the analysis.

Estimating Vector Autoregression Models in SAS

PROC VARMAX is the workhorse procedure for estimating VAR models in SAS. The capabilities of the procedure are quite extensive. They include modeling various types of VAR specifications and statistical relationships, as well as the ability to use various types of estimation methods and statistical tests.[32] You can also estimate VAR models using the MODEL procedure. However, the VAR modeling features that are included in the MODEL procedure are not as robust as those included in the VARMAX procedure.

PROC VARMAX

Program 6.15 shows the SAS code that was used to implement the VAR model of the monthly change in US personal consumption expenditure and the unemployment rate. Both variables are stored in the CONSWORK SAS data set. The PLOTS option was used in the PROC VARMAX statement to request a plot of the monthly forecast and the impulse response function for both variables. The MODEL statement includes the options P=1 (METHOD=ML) and PRINT=(IMPULSE (12) DECOMPOSE(12)), which specify the relationship to be modeled, the order of the autoregressive terms, the maximum likelihood method of estimation, and the printing of the impulse and variance decompositions, respectively. The CAUSAL statement requests the causality test of the null that Group 2 variables do not Granger-cause the Group 1 variables. The OUTPUT statement specifies the number of forecast months (LEAD=12) and the data set to store the forecast in (OUT=FORE). The COINTEG statement is used to fit a vector error correction model to the data. Vector error correction models assess whether two or more variables are COINTEGRATED (in other words, they share long-term relationships even if they appear to be nonstationary in the short term).

The model examines whether there is some linear combination of the variables that is stationary of some order. If such a linear combination exists, then the variables might have a long-term stable relationship, even if they temporarily deviate from it in the short term. From an investing point of view, this might create opportunities to exploit temporary deviations in the values of asset classes that share stable long-term relationships when they momentarily deviate from their equilibrium relationships. Other options in the VARMAX procedure include the GARCH statement, which is used to fit multivariate generalized autoregressive conditional heteroscedasticity models, and the RESTRICT and TEST statements that are used to invoke several types of hypotheses tests.

---

[32] It is highly recommended that readers visit https://documentation.sas.com/doc/en/pgmsascdc/9.4_3.4/ etsug/etsug_varmax_toc.htm to review the full range of the capabilities of the VARMAX procedure.

Program 6.15: Modeling the Relationship Between Unemployment and Consumption Using PROC VARMAX

```
/*Modeling the Relationship between Unemployment and Consumption*/
%datapull (conswork,conswork.sas7bdat);
ods graphics on;

proc varmax data=conswork plots=all;
      id date interval=month;
      model  pce unrate = / p=1 method=ml print=(impulse(12) decompose(12));
      causal group1=(pce) group2=(unrate);
      causal group1=(unrate)  group2=(pce);
      output lead= 12 out=forecast;
run;
```

The result shown in Output 6.15A shows strong bidirectional relationships between personal consumption and the unemployment rate as well as with their respective lagged values using the *p*-values of the parameter estimates as the point of reference. This finding is further buttressed by the *p*-values of the Granger causality tests. The parameter estimates and the impulse response function plots imply that an increase in personal consumption leads to a lower unemployment rate. Interestingly, an increase in the unemployment rate (AR1_1_2 coefficient) is also associated with an increase in consumption. This is most likely due to the delayed effect or consumption stickiness.

Output 6.15A: Relationship Between Unemployment and Consumption

The VARMAX Procedure

Type of Model	VAR(1)
Estimation Method	Maximum Likelihood Estimation

Model Parameter Estimates

Equation	Parameter	Estimate	Standard Error	t Value	Pr > |t|	Variable
PCE	CONST1	0.00223	0.00069	3.25	0.0013	1
	AR1_1_1	0.45403	0.07943	5.72	0.0001	PCE(t-1)
	AR1_1_2	0.07396	0.01186	6.23	0.0001	UNRATE(t-1)
UNRATE	CONST2	0.01456	0.00436	3.34	0.0009	1
	AR1_2_1	-4.29420	0.50470	-8.51	0.0001	PCE(t-1)
	AR1_2_2	-0.35313	0.07540	-4.68	0.0001	UNRATE(t-1)

Granger-Causality Wald Test

Test	DF	Chi-Square	Pr > ChiSq
1	1	39.00	<.0001
2	1	72.67	<.0001

Test 1: Group 1 Variables: PCE
Group 2 Variables: UNRATE

Test 2: Group 1 Variables: UNRATE
Group 2 Variables: PCE

The stickiness of consumption is also shown in the impulse response functions (shown in Output 6.15B) for the unemployment rate. The plots show that it takes approximately four months for two standard deviation shocks to unemployment to completely negate consumption growth. In contrast, two standard deviation shocks to consumption will push unemployment significantly down in the following month, followed by an uptick two months later, then further downward in the third and fourth months. Shocks to consumption growth do not appear to be long-lasting on consumption itself. The immediate effect occurs in the following month, which is then followed by a reversion to the mean. This might be due to the seasonality effect.

Output 6.15B: Impulse Response Functions from PROC VARMAX

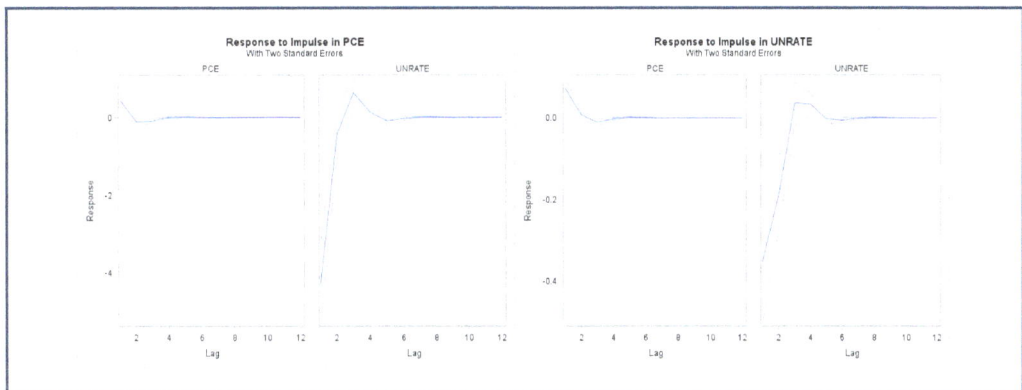

Output 6.15C: Forecasting Using PROC VARMAX

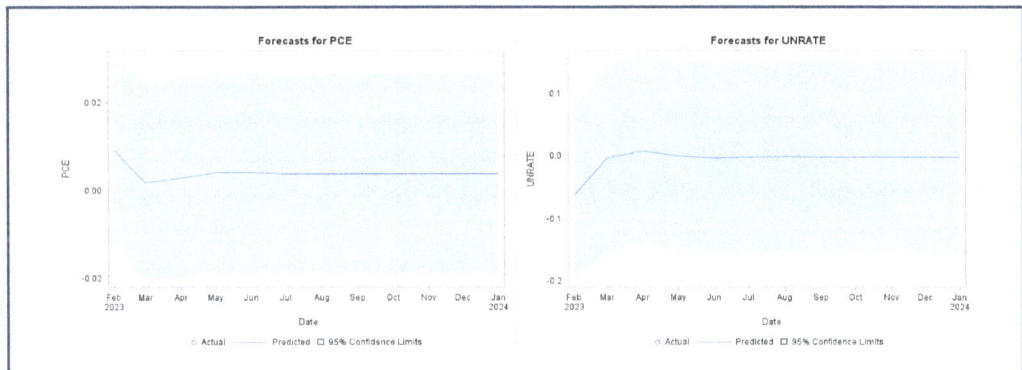

Output 6.15C shows the monthly forecasts of consumption growth and unemployment from the model. The charts show a small decline in consumption in the first quarter of 2023, followed by a relatively steady but low growth in consumption for the rest of the year. For unemployment, the forecast shown on the graph implies little to no change in the unemployment level (zero growth forecast) throughout the entire year.

Time-Index Forecasting Models

In Chapters Two and Three, we explored the applications of some univariate time series models such as the ARIMA, AUTOREG, and X13 models from a modeling point of view. It turns out that these models can also be used for forecasting purposes as well. Let us also explore two additional time series models that are popularly used for forecasting purposes. These are the exponential smoothing model and the unobserved component model.

Exponential Smoothing Models

Exponential smoothing (ESM) models generate forecasts of the future values of a variable from the weighted averages of past observations of the same variable. In this approach, recent lags of the variable are given more weight in the forecast than long-past lagged observations. The decreasing weights applied to the past observation use smoothing parameters that exponentially decrease over time. In its most basic form, which is known as the simple exponential smoothing model (SESM), we assume that the variables follow a purely stochastic process that is devoid of trends and seasonality. Suppose y_t is the raw data to be smoothed, which has an initial value y_0, then the specification of the SESM is as follows:

$$S_{t+1} = \alpha y_t + (1 - \alpha) S_{t-1} \tag{6.82}$$

where $\alpha\,(0 \le \alpha \le 1)$ is the exponential smoothing parameter and S_t is the forecasted value of the variable at time t. In reality, the SESM is actually a special case of an ARIMA (0,1,1) model. The SESM can also be modified to account for trends in the data through the use of double exponential smoothing functions. In this approach, both the trend and stochastic components of the time series are smoothed separately and then combined to create the forecast of the time series. The mathematical expression of the double exponential model (DESM) is as follows. Let L_t be the estimate of the levels and T_t be the estimate of the trend at time t. The double exponential smoothing (also known as Holt's method) functions of y_t are:

Level smoothing:
$$L_t = \alpha y_t + (1 - \alpha)\left[L_{t-1} + T_{t-1}\right] \tag{6.83}$$

Trend smoothing:
$$T_t = \beta\left(L_t - L_{t-1}\right) + (1 - \beta)T_{t-1} \tag{6.84}$$

Forecast equation:
$$S_{t+m} = L_t + mT_t \tag{6.85}$$

where $\alpha\,(0 \le \alpha \le 1)$ is the exponential smoothing parameter for the level, $\beta\,(0 \le \beta \le 1)$ is the exponential smoothing parameter for the trend, and m is the forecast window. When $m = 1$, we obtain a one-period ahead forecast window that is characterized by $S_{t+1} = L_t + T_t$. The DESM is equivalent to an ARIMA (0,2,2) model.[33]

---

[33] ARIMA(0,1,1) model has one lag and one autoregressive moving average.

Lastly, ESM can be generalized to also account for seasonality and trends in the forecast through the use of triple exponential smoothing. In this approach, a third smoothing function that accounts for seasonality is added to the forecasting system using either additive or multiplicative seasonality.[34] The mathematical expression of the triple exponential model (TESM) that uses the additive seasonality is as follows. Let L_t be the estimate of the levels, T_t be the estimate of the trend, and I_t be the estimate of the seasonality components (with duration p) at time t. Then the triple exponential smoothing (also known as the Holt-Winters method) functions of y_t are:

Level smoothing:
$$L_t = \alpha\left(y_t - I_{t-m}\right) + \left(1 - \alpha\right)\left[L_{t-1} + T_{t-1}\right]$$
(6.86)

Trend smoothing:
$$T_t = \beta\left(L_t - L_{t-1}\right) + \left(1 - \beta\right)T_{t-1}$$
(6.87)

Seasonality smoothing:
$$I_t = \gamma\left(y_t - L_t\right) + \left(1 - \gamma\right)I_{t-p}$$
(6.88)

Forecast equation:
$$S_{t+m} = L_t + mT_t + I_{t-p+1+(m-1)\bmod p}$$
(6.89)

where $\alpha\left(0 \leq \alpha \leq 1\right)$ is the exponential smoothing parameter for the level, $\beta\left(0 \leq \beta \leq 1\right)$ is the exponential smoothing parameter for the trend, $\gamma\left(0 \leq \gamma \leq 1\right)$ is the seasonality smoothing parameter for the seasonality component, and m is the forecast window. Just as in the case of double exponential smoothing, we obtain the period ahead forecast, when $m = 1$. The expressions for the level, seasonality, and forecast equations for multiplicative seasonality are:

Level smoothing:
$$L_t = \alpha\left(\frac{y_t}{I_{t-m}}\right) + \left(1 - \alpha\right)\left[L_{t-1} + T_{t-1}\right]$$
(6.90)

Seasonality smoothing:
$$I_t = \gamma\left(\frac{y_t}{L_t}\right) + \left(1 - \gamma\right)I_{t-p}$$
(6.91)

Forecast equation:
$$S_{t+m} = \left(L_t + mT_t\right) \cdot I_{t-p+1+(m-1)\bmod p}$$
(6.92)

The parameters of the exponential smoothing models are generally estimated using a variant of the least square approach, although it is possible to apply other estimation methods such as maximum likelihood. For the least square approach, the estimation objective is to search for the smoothing parameters that best minimize the sum of squared prediction errors.

---

[34] Additive seasonality is used if seasonal changes are calculated using absolute values, while multiplicative seasonality is used if seasonal changes are calculated using multiples.

Figure 6.5: SAS Time Series Forecasting System

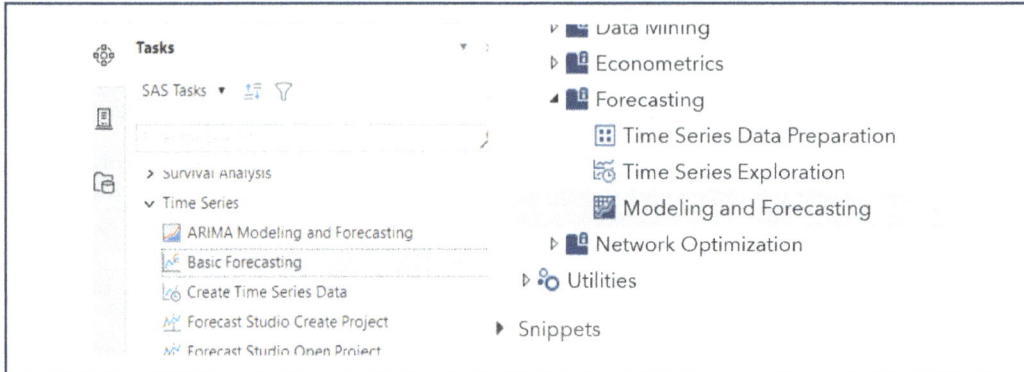

> ESM is a conceptually simple approach to forecasting, regardless of the ESM method used. The basic approach is to generate forecasts of the future values of a time series from the sum of its time series components. In the forecast, more weights are assigned to recent past values of the applicable time series components (trend, seasonality, and levels) than the distant past values.

Estimating Exponential Smoothing Models in SAS

Exponential smoothing models can be estimated in SAS using PROC ESM or the Time Series Forecasting System. The Time Series Forecasting System is a point-and-click interface for invoking ARIMA and exponential smoothing models and would suffice for many ESM implementations. It can be invoked in Enterprise Guide (shown on the left in Figure 6.5) by clicking on SAS Tasks and then selecting Time Series, followed by selecting Basic Forecasting. In SAS Studio (shown on the right in Figure 6.5), click Task and Utilities and then select Forecasting, followed by selecting Modeling and Forecasting.

Forecasting Monthly Trading Volume of the S&P 500 Index

Monthly trading volume is a technical indicator that signals the intensity of the directional move in the prices of a security. For example, rising prices in high-volume stocks are typically indicative of high buying pressure from investors, while declining prices are indicative of selling pressures. Forecasting volume trends might therefore be insightful in terms of future price movement. So, let's explore the use of the ESM procedure for forecasting the monthly trading volume of the S&P 500. For this exercise, we will reuse the SAS data set (RSPX_MONTHLY. SAS7BDATA) that contains the monthly price and volume data on the index.

PROC ESM

Let us also write the SAS code for the ESM procedure to estimate the exponential smoothing model. You will recall that in Chapter Three, we decomposed the monthly volume of the S&P 500 into its trends and seasonal components using the X13 procedure. In Program 6.16, we will generate 24-month forecasts of the monthly trading volume on the S&P 500 index using the simple, double, and additive triple exponential smoothing model. In the SAS code, the LEAD=24 option in the PROC ESM statement is used to specify 24 months forecast lead time, while the BACK=12 specifies that the forecast should start 12 periods before the final observation in the data set. The ESM procedure generates a large number of ODS graphs. We can request a plot of only the forecasted series by using the PLOT=FORECASTSONLY option. The OUTEST option is used to save the smoothing parameters in a SAS data set.

The ESM procedure can analyze time series data in various frequencies. For forecasting purposes, it is helpful to specify the time index variable and frequency of the data using the ID and INTERVAL statements, respectively. The actual estimation and forecasting are invoked by using the FORECAST statement. The MODEL option is used to specify the type of ESM that will be estimated and used in producing the forecast. The ESM procedure can estimate simple, double, linear (Holt's), and Winter's (additive and multiplicative) methods, to name a few. It can also transform the data using log, square, and logistic transformations.

We will estimate the simple, Holt's, and multiplicative Winter's models in Program 6.16. The OUTSTAT= is used to request the fit statistics of each model for comparison purposes. The procedure does not print the parameter estimates by default; you can request it along with other statistics by invoking the PRINT= ALL in the PROC ESM statement. The PRINT procedure is used to display the collated parameter estimates and fit statistics from the three ESM procedures.

Program 6.16: Forecasting Monthly Trading Volume for the S&P 500 Index Using PROC ESM

```
/*Forecasting the Monthly Trading Volumes of the S&P 500 using Exponential
Smoothing Models*/
%datapull(spx,rspx_monthly.sas7bdat);
ods graphics on;

proc esm data=rspx_monthly back=12 lead=24 plot=forecastsonly
outest=sesmparms outstat=sesmstats print=all;
    id date interval=monthly;
    forecast volume /model=simple;
run;

proc esm data=rspx_monthly back=12 lead=24 plot=forecastsonly
outest=desmparms outstat=desmstats print=all;
    id date interval=monthly;
    forecast volume /model=linear;
run;
```

```
proc esm data=rspx_monthly back=12 lead=24 plot=forecastsonly
outest=tesmparms outstat=tesmstats print=all;
      id date interval=monthly;
      forecast volume /model=multwinters;
run;
```

The values of the level smoothing parameter are significant for all three models. For the simple ESM and Holt's double ESM, the coefficients are approximately 0.4. The values of the same coefficient for the Holt-Winters ESM are slightly higher (0.46). The trend smoothing parameter is significant, while the seasonality smoothing parameter is significant in the multiplicative Holt-Winters ESM. The abbreviated fit statistics show that Holt-Winters ESM appears to have the best fit to the data.

Output 6.16A: Forecasts of Monthly Trading Volume for the S&P 500 Index

Forecasting S&P 500 Volume Using Simple ESM

Obs	_NAME_	_TRANSFORM_	_MODEL_	_PARM_	_EST_	_STDERR_	_TVALUE_	_PVALUE_
1	Volume	NONE	SIMPLE	LEVEL	0.39956	0.029784	13.4154	1.4168E-33

Forecasting S&P 500 Volume Using Holt Double ESM

Obs	_NAME_	_TRANSFORM_	_MODEL_	_PARM_	_EST_	_STDERR_	_TVALUE_	_PVALUE_
1	Volume	NONE	LINEAR	LEVEL	0.39923	0.029786	13.4032	0.00000
2	Volume	NONE	LINEAR	TREND	0.00100	0.002347	0.4261	0.67029

Forecasting S&P 500 Volume Using Additive Holt-Winters Triple ESM

Obs	_NAME_	_TRANSFORM_	_MODEL_	_PARM_	_EST_	_STDERR_	_TVALUE_	_PVALUE_
1	Volume	NONE	WINTERS	LEVEL	0.49401	0.031142	15.8630	0.00000
2	Volume	NONE	WINTERS	TREND	0.00865	0.005571	1.5529	0.12133
3	Volume	NONE	WINTERS	SEASON	0.06023	0.017187	3.5041	0.00052

Fit Statistic from Forecasting S&P 500 Volume Using ESM

Obs	_NAME_	_REGION_	DFE	N	NOBS	NMISSA	NMISSP	NPARMS	TSS	SST	SSE	MSE
1	Volume	FIT	361	362	362	0	0	1	1.3339E23	3.2276E22	3.0324E21	8.3768E18
2	Volume	FORECAST	12	12	12	0	0	0	2.5603E21	2.4234E19	5.5779E19	4.6483E18

Obs	_NAME_	_REGION_	DFE	N	NOBS	NMISSA	NMISSP	NPARMS	TSS	SST	SSE	MSE
1	Volume	FIT	360	362	362	0	0	2	1.3339E23	3.2276E22	3.0335E21	8.3798E18
2	Volume	FORECAST	12	12	12	0	0	0	2.5603E21	2.4234E19	5.0417E19	4.2014E18

Obs	_NAME_	_REGION_	DFE	N	NOBS	NMISSA	NMISSP	NPARMS	TSS	SST	SSE	MSE
1	Volume	FIT	359	362	362	0	0	3	1.3339E23	3.2276E22	2.3116E21	6.3856E18
2	Volume	FORECAST	12	12	12	0	0	0	2.5603E21	2.4234E19	2.3889E19	1.9908E18

Output 6.16B: Plots of Forecasts of Monthly Trading Volume for the S&P 500

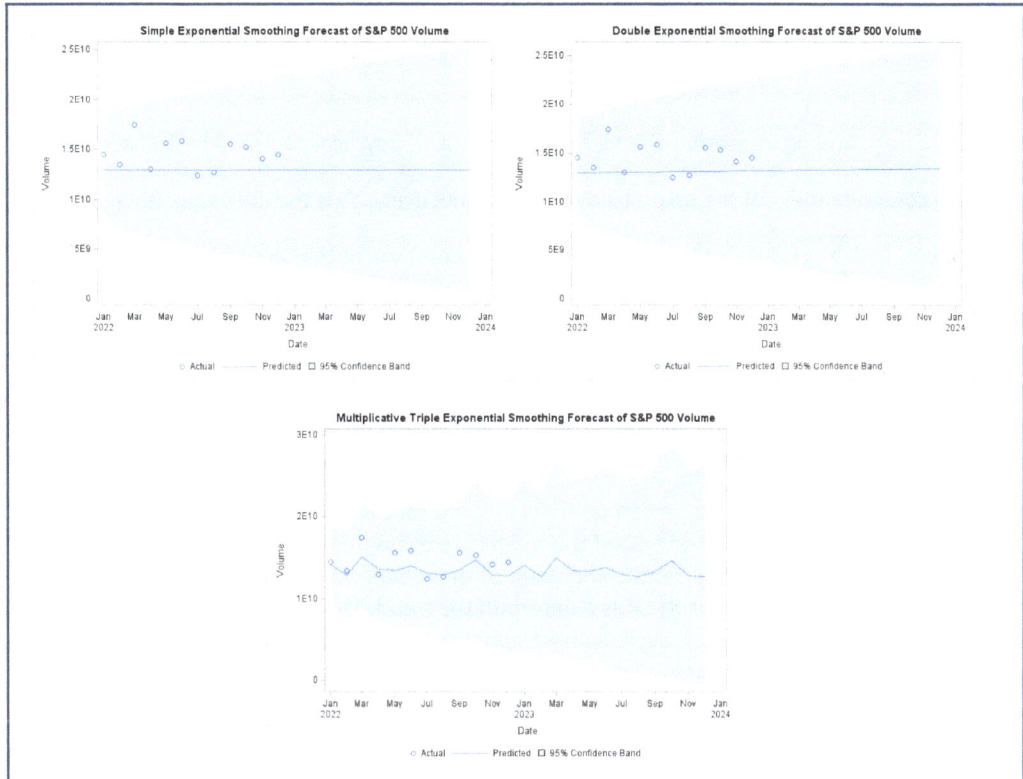

Further evidence in support of this statistic can be found in the forecast plots for the three models. The Simple and Holt's double ESM generate straight-line forecasts, while the Holt-Winters ESM includes seasonality in its forecast to account for the periodicity of the seasonal components. The titles of the graphs shown in Output 6.16B have been edited using the ODS Graphics Editor.

Unobserved Component Model

Unobserved component models (UCM) are also based on the time series decomposition principle that we discussed in Chapter Two. The UCM incorporates time series decomposition (trend, seasonality, cyclicality, and irregularity) into a multiple regression framework, thereby creating a forecasting model that can capture the time series properties of the response variables as well as any predictive information that is embedded in its exogenous regressors. From a regression modeling perspective, the trend, seasonal, and cyclical components can be viewed as time-varying regression coefficients, while the irregular component can be viewed as the residuals of the regression model. We assume that these components are unobservable and hence must be estimated from the data. The mathematical expression of the UCM model is as follows:

$$y_t = \mu_t + \varphi_t + \gamma_t + r_t + \sum_{j=1}^{m} \beta_j x_{j,t} + \varepsilon_t$$

$$\varepsilon_t \sim iid \ N\left(0, \sigma^2\right)$$

(6.93)

Where μ_t, φ_t, and γ_t represent the trend component T_t, cyclical component C_t, and seasonal component S_t of the response variable, respectively. r_t is the autoregressive component, and $\sum_{j=1}^{m} \beta_j x_{j,t}$ is the multiple regression component that accounts for the contribution of the exogenous variables to the forecast of y_t. We assume that the residual term ε_t is the irregular component I_t and that it follows the Gaussian white noise process with zero mean and variance σ^2. In the UCM, the trend, seasonal, regression, and nonstationary cycle components account for the structural dynamics of the response variable, while the stationary cycle and autoregressive components account for the transitory dynamics of the same variable.[35] The time series components of the model are estimated using some type of stochastic specifications. For example, the trend component of the model can be specified as a random walk process (with or without drift) or as a deterministic trend. The cycle components can be specified as either a deterministic cycle with a frequency parameter, an autoregressive moving average process, or a time-varying trigonometric cycle. The seasonal component is specified either as a fixed seasonal dummy, time-varying seasonal dummy, fixed trigonometric season disturbance, or time-varying seasonal disturbance.

UCMs are also treated as state space models because the dynamics of the response variable are in part controlled by unobservable (latent) processes. In the state space framework, Equation (6.93) is the observation equation that links the response variable y_t to the state matrix that consists of the vector of unobserved time series components $\left[\mu_t, \varphi_t, \gamma_t, r_t\right]$ and exogenous regressors $\sum_{j=1}^{m} \beta_j x_{j,t}$.

The state space analysis aims to learn more about the hidden processes from the observed process and the specification of the system; therefore, the parameter estimates of the hidden process are invariably linked to the estimates of the state process. In the state space estimation, filtering is performed to remove measurement errors between the true value of the hidden variables and the observed variable. Forecasting can also be done to estimate the future values of the hidden and observed variables and smoothing to estimate past values of the hidden variable, given what we currently know about the future and current values of the variable.

---

[35] The functional forms of the various specifications for each component are not provided here. Visit the SAS/ETS User's Guide for PROC UCM at https://documentation.sas.com/doc/en/pgmsascdc/9.4_3.5/etsug/etsug_ucm_details01.htm to review them.

From a forecasting point of view, one of the advantages of the state space approach is that the filtering method (known as the Kalman filter) is used to produce the one-step ahead forecast of the state vector, which is then also used to generate a one-step-ahead forecast of the response variable. The Kalman filtering recursively generates the forecast of the future values of the response variable by updating the weights it assigns to each prediction based on the accuracy of the prediction once the observed value is realized. More weights are assigned to predictions with greater accuracy in making future predictions.

Due to the large number of parameters and the complex specifications to be estimated, UCMs are typically estimated using a special case of the maximum likelihood approach. The all-encompassing functional forms and flexibility to include or exclude any of the time series components discussed earlier in the estimated models make UCMs a compelling approach for forecasting time series data.

Estimating Unobserved Component Models in SAS

The UCM procedure in SAS/ETS can estimate and generate forecasts from unobserved component models. The procedure has many functional features, including many that are typically found in other regression-based procedures. These include the MODEL statement that is used to specify the response variable and its predictors. The time series components of the UCM and its specifications can be requested by invoking the respective UCM statements. For example, the random walk trend, cycle, and seasonal components can be incorporated into the model by including the LEVEL, CYCLE, and SEASON statements, respectively in the code for the procedure. The AUTOREG statement is used to request the autoregressive component of the model. You can request lead and backstep forecasts using the LEAD= and BACK= statements. The UCM can also implement nonlinear models of the relationship between the response variables and its exogenous regressors (SPLINEREG), as well as nonlinear seasonal patterns (SPLINESEASON). In the same manner as the ESM procedure, the UCM procedure generates a large number of ODS graphs. However, many of the plots are linked with a specific UCM statement. For example, the FORECAST statement can be accompanied by the PLOT=FORECASTS to plot the multi-step-ahead forecast.

Forecasting Monthly Stock Index Returns using the UCM Model

Let us apply the UCM to forecast the monthly returns (WIL5000) of the Wilshire 5000 index, which tracks the performance of all publicly listed firms in the US. The index is a broad-based, market value-weighted benchmark and provides the most comprehensive view of the conditions in the US equity market. The SAS data set CONSWORK contains the monthly returns of the index and a set of explanatory variables that include the monthly US unemployment rate (UNRATE) and personal consumption expenditure (PCE), as well as the yields on the 10-year US treasury (T10YR) and junk bonds (JBY) as our exogenous regressors.[36]

PROC UCM

Program 6.17 shows the SAS code that was used to estimate the UCM for the monthly returns on the Wilshire 5000 index. The irregular, level, cycle, and seasonal components of the time series of return are requested using their respective statements. The BACK=24 and LEAD=24 options in the FORECAST statement were used to create a holdout sample of 24 months to assess the accuracy of the forecasting model. Creating a holdout sample is particularly useful for validating the efficacy of predictive models. When applied in investment settings, data in the holdout period can also be used for backtesting the model. The OUTEST=UCMPARMS option in the ESTIMATE statement specifies that the parameters and time series components of the model should be saved in the UCMPARMS SAS data set.

Program 6.17: Forecasting Monthly Returns of the Wilshire 5000 Index Using PROC UCM

```
/*Generating Monthly Forecasts of the Wilshire 5000 Index Returns Using UCM*/
%datapull (conswork,conswork.sas7bdat);
ods graphics on;

proc ucm data=conswork;
        id date interval=monthly;
        model will5000 = t10yr unrate pce jby;
        irregular;
        level;
        cycle;
        season type=dummy length=12;
        estimate outest=ucmparms;
        forecast back=24 lead=36 plot=(decomp decompvar forecasts );
        nloptions tech=dbldog maxiter=200;
run;

proc print data=ucmparms;
run;
```

The results of the estimation, which are shown in Output 6.17A suggest that the model appears to fit the data relatively well. The final estimates of the free parameter table show that the 10-year treasury bill and junk bond yields have statistically meaningful roles in predicting the determinant of contemporaneous equity market return. The Significance Analysis of The Time Series Components shows that the irregular and to some extent cycle components are the main time series drivers of the dynamics of the Wilshire 5000 index return. Small-capitalization stocks

---

[36] PROC UCM requires values of the predictors to produce out-of-sample forecasts, so we will stick with in-sample estimates. You can generate an out-of-sample forecast by specifying the response variable alone in the MODEL statement.

have the largest representation in the index, and junk bonds are highly speculative fixed-income products. They are generally known to have higher correlations with stocks than with investment-grade bonds.

Output 6.17A: Fit Statistics from UCM Model of Stock Index Returns

Component	Parameter	Estimate	Approx Std Error	t Value	Approx Pr > |t|
Irregular	Error Variance	0.00096160	0.0001148	8.38	<.0001
Level	Error Variance	0.00000436	3.58094E-6	1.22	0.2232
Season	Error Variance	0.00000949	8.8207E-6	1.08	0.2817
Cycle	Damping Factor	0.94351	0.07006	13.47	<.0001
Cycle	Period	2.34893	0.07263	32.34	<.0001
Cycle	Error Variance	0.00001107	9.6265E-6	1.15	0.2504
T10YR	Coefficient	0.04447	0.02547	1.75	0.0808
UNRATE	Coefficient	0.05700	0.03712	1.54	0.1246
PCE	Coefficient	-0.18385	0.26016	-0.71	0.4798
JBY	Coefficient	-0.42466	0.02554	-16.62	<.0001

Final Estimates of the Free Parameters

Significance Analysis of Components (Based on the Final State)

Component	DF	Chi-Square	Pr > ChiSq
Irregular	1	4.26	0.0389
Level	1	1.60	0.2058
Cycle	2	0.47	0.7919
Season	11	18.51	0.0706

Output 6.17B shows various plots from the UCM procedure. The Out-of-Sample plot compares the forecast (line) with the actual values (dots) in the holdout period (January 2021 to January 2023). Although the actual values and the predicted values are not equal, the directions however are mostly accurate. In reality, it is relatively easier to predict the direction of the market than the actual values of the performance of the market in each period. We will explore directional prediction (classification) in Chapter Seven. The Smoothed Trend plot shows elements of cyclicality in the performance of the market in the first decade, but little evidence of cyclicality in the immediate past decade. The Sum of Smoothed Trend and Regression Effect plot appears to have a better fit to the data than just the time series component alone. Overall, by allowing for explanatory variables in the forecasting framework, the UCM provides a richer platform than the PROC ESM approach, which relies only on the current and past realizations of the response variable to forecast its future values.

Output 6.17B: Forecast Plots of Monthly Returns of the Wilshire 5000 Index

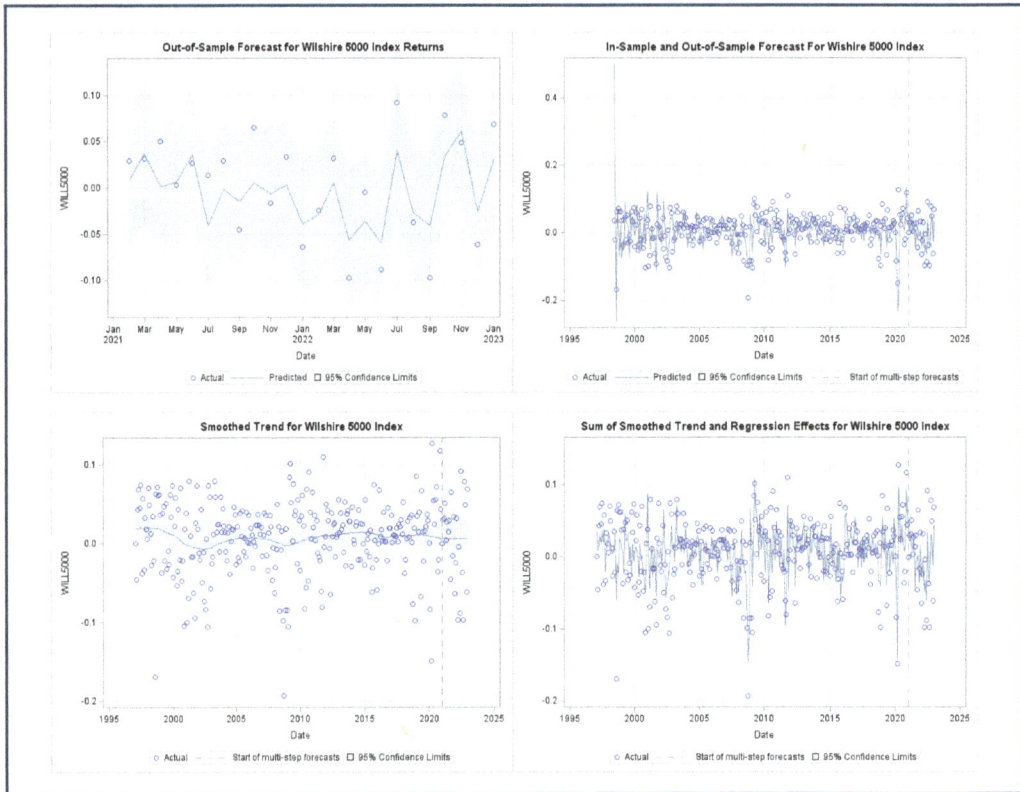

Other Statistical and Econometric Procedures

Although we have reviewed a considerable number of procedures in this chapter, you should be aware that there are more statistical and econometric procedures available in SAS than the ones we have discussed. All econometric procedures that are available in SAS are included in the SAS/ ETS software. Statistical procedures, including the ones we discussed, are included in the SAS/ STAT software.[37] Both SAS/ETS and SAS/STAT are components of the SAS 9.4 system. They are also available in the SAS Viya environment. Furthermore, SAS now offers high-performance versions of some of the econometric and statistical procedures described in this chapter. We will discuss some of these high-performance SAS procedures in Chapter Seven.

---

[37] You can review all of the econometric procedures that are available in the SAS/ETS software by visiting SAS/ETS 15.3 User's Guide at https://documentation.sas.com/doc/en/pgmsascdc/v_047/etsug/etsug_intro_ sect001.htm and the statistical procedures available in SAS/STAT software by visiting the SAS/STAT User's Guide at https://documentation.sas.com/doc/en/pgmsascdc/9.4_3.5/statug/titlepage.htm.

Exercises

1. The SAS data set INDUSTR.SAS7BDAT contains the monthly returns for 17 industries, five risk factors (market risk premium and the Fama-French, which are HML and SMB, RMW, and CMA factors), and the risk-free rate. The HML variable represents the risk premium earned for growth potential, while SMB represents the risk premium for size, with smaller firms receiving a higher premium than large firms. RMW (Robust Minus Weak) represents the risk premium for operating profitability, with lower profitability firms receiving a higher premium, while CMA represents the risk premium for the investment strategy of the firm, with firms that have a conservative investment strategy earning a higher premium than firms with aggressive investment strategy.

   a. Write a SAS program to estimate the following single-factor index model using OLS, Maximum Likelihood, and the GMM approach for the food and steel industry returns.

   Equation One: $ER_{it} = \alpha + \beta_m MRP_t + \varepsilon_t$

   i. Compare the estimate of the market betas obtained from the steel industry to the beta from the food industry from all three methods of estimation. Are they the same or different?

   ii. Compare the estimate of the beta from the steel industry to the beta of the food industry. Which industry has the highest systematic risk?

   iii. What would be the market beta of the portfolio that consists of 50% of the food services sector fund and 50% of the steel industry sector fund?

   b. Now extend the model from a single factor to a multifactor model by writing the SAS code to estimate the following regression specification (use all three parametric methods).

   Equation Two: $ER_{it} = \alpha + \beta_m MRP_t + \beta_s SMB_t + \beta_H HML_t + \beta_R RMW_t + \varepsilon_t$

   i. Which industry is mostly comprised of small, mid, or large-cap stocks? Which of the two industries is most likely to consist of growth stocks?

   c. Write a SAS program to estimate and superimpose the univariate kernel densities of the excess returns of the food industry and the steel industry on the market risk premium.

   i. What does the kernel density indicate about the riskiness of each industry relative to the market?

   d. Add the SAS code to request the bivariate kernel density of the returns of the food and steel industries.

   i. What do the scatter plot and kernel density plot show about the clustering of extreme returns for the two industries? Compare your results to the bivariate density of the financial services and the stock market that is shown in Output 6.3.

2. The SAS data set LCLOANSAMP.SAS7BDAT contains a sample of 3,400 observations of the loan portfolio data of Lending Club Inc. In the previous section of the chapter, we used the data to demonstrate how to estimate survival analysis models in SAS. Let's examine if the predictors of time-to-delinquency will be the same predictors for the delinquency event itself.

a. Write a SAS code to estimate a LOGIT model of the determinants of delinquency. The dependent variable that categorizes the status of the borrower as delinquent or otherwise is STATUS (where 1 implies delinquent and 0 implies that the borrower is not). The potential predictor variables for the LOGIT model are:

```
LOAN_AMNT ANNUAL_INC DTI PUB_REC APPLICATION_TYPE TOTAL_ACC
REVOL_UTIL REVOL_UTIL TOTAL_ACC OPEN_ACC GRADE TERM PURPOSE
HOME_OWNERSHIP VERIFICATION_STATUS EMP_LENGTH
```

In the options for the MODEL statement, set the event category to be modeled to 1, the classification probability (PPROB) to 0.5, the LINK=LOGIT, SELECTION to BACKWARD, and SLSTAY to 0.05.

   i. Which variables were selected from the backward selection process as the significant predictors of default?

   ii. What type of association does each of the selected variables have with the probability of delinquency? For example, are borrowers with a higher debt-to-income (DTI) ratio more likely to become delinquent than borrowers with a lower DTI?

   iii. By how many units does having a mortgage reduce the odds of default compared to renting a home?

b. Change the link function to PROBIT and the selection criteria to STEPWISE. Run the model again and review your results.

   i. Are your new results consistent with the results in Part A of the question?

   ii. Review the ROC curve produced by both estimations. Do the graphs show classification models with high predictive abilities?

3. Let's apply the linear discriminant analysis approach to model the classification problem that we examined in Question 2. Remember that LDA only accepts numerical predictor variables. So, you can only select numerical predictors from the list shown in Question 2.

a. Write a SAS code to estimate a linear discriminant analysis (LDA) model to classify the status of the borrowers in the Lending Club loan sample (LCLOANSAMP.SAS7BDAT). Set the method of estimation to NORMAL to request the parametric estimation of the LDA model. Include the option to generate the confusion matrix, the posterior error of classification, and the pool test of within the group covariance. Also, set the priors to proportional.

   i. Is the accuracy of the LDA classifier higher than those of the logistic or probit classifiers?

   ii. Not all variables selected by the LDA appear in the final models of the logistic and probit classifiers. Why did this occur?

b. Write a SAS program for the LDA procedure that you can use to narrow down the number of predictors before including them in the model for the DISCRIM procedure.

   i. Did preselecting the variable improve the accuracy of the PROC DISCRIM model?

c. Modify the PROC DISCRIM statement by changing the method of estimation from parametric to nonparametric. Specify a normal kernel density function and radius value of 1.

   i. Did applying a nonparametric method of estimating the LDA improve the accuracy of the classification?

4. A multi-asset portfolio manager would like to know if there is a common factor that is driving the daily returns of the stock, bond, crude oil, and forex markets. The SAS data set MARKET_DATA.SAS7BDAT contains the daily return from the five markets as well as other variables that might be of interest.

   a. Write a SAS program to estimate the factor analysis model of the daily returns of the four markets. In your code, select the principal component method of factor extraction. Set the minimum eigenvalue for a factor to be retained to 1. Rotate the factors using the QUARTIMAX method and request the plot of all graphs.

      i. How many factors were retained based on the eigenvalue of the factors?

      ii. Use the Variance Explained plot to determine the proportion of the total variance that is explained by each factor, and the cumulative value of the variance explained. Are the two factors selected using the eigenvalues sufficient from a dimension reduction point of view?

      iii. What variables are positively related to both factors, and what variables are negatively related?

      iv. Compare the initial Factor Pattern plot to the Rotated Factor Pattern plot. Which variables are mostly related to rotated factor 1 and factor 2?

      v. Does the Path diagram confirm these relationships? What common macroeconomic factors could be associated with factor 1 and factor 2?

   b. Quartimax is an orthogonal factor rotation method. Replace it with Quartimin, which is an oblique factor rotation method.

      i. Did the change in the rotation method improve the uniqueness of each factor?

      ii. Examine the communality estimates.

   c. What insight did you obtain from the factor analysis as a manager of a multi-asset portfolio?

5. Does stock market performance affect consumer confidence or does consumer confidence affect stock market performance? The SAS data set TRADEM.SAS7BDAT contains a set of macroeconomic, consumer sentiment, and stock market variables. Let's use the data set to examine this question by estimating a vector autoregression (VAR) model of the US stock market return (WILL5000IND) and the University of Michigan Consumer Sentiment Survey (UMCSENT).

   a. Write a SAS program to estimate a VAR model of WILL5000IND and the UMCSENT. Specify that all plots should be produced. Set the ID to DATE and the INTERVAL to MONTHS. Set the autoregressive coefficient P to 1. Also, request the maximum likelihood method of estimation and the impulse response and variance decomposition for up to 6 lags.

      i. What do the results tell us about the relationship between the stock market and consumer confidence?

      ii. What does the result indicate about the relationship between current changes in consumer confidence and future changes in consumer confidence?

      iii. What does the result indicate about the relationship between the current performance of the stock market and the future performance of the market?

      iv. Review the impulse response table and plots for both variables. What do they suggest about the impact of two standard deviations (positive and negative) shock to consumer sentiment on future changes in consumer sentiments and future returns on the stock market? Repeat the same analysis for two standard deviations (positive and negative) shock to the Wilshire 5000 index.

    v. How long do shocks to either variable persist in the system?

b. Modify the SAS code to request a bivariate Granger causality test for the WILL5000 and UMCSENT (that is, the null that WILL5000 does not Granger cause UMCSENT, then do the same for UMCSENT to WILL5000).

    i. Which of these variables is most likely impacting the other?

    ii. From an investing perspective, what is the significance of the direction of causality? Should investment decisions be made in part by the changes in levels of consumer sentiment?

6. A global macro hedge fund manager would like to conduct a two-year forecast of the US gross domestic product (GDP). The SAS data set GDP.SAS7BDAT contains quarterly real and nominal GDP from 1947 to October 2022.

a. Write a SAS program to generate 12 quarterly forecasts of nominal US GDP using the simple exponential smoothing model (SESM). Set the ID to DATE and the INTERVAL to QUARTERLY. Also, set the forecast of the lead to 16 and back forecast to start two years (8) before the final observation in the data set. If you prefer, you can request the forecast plot by specifying PLOT=FORECASTONLY. Use the PRINT=ALL option to request the printing of the parameter estimates and the fit statistics of the model.

    i. What are the level and trend weights that were estimated by the model?

    ii. Going by the back period forecast, how close is the forecast of the SESM to the actual levels of the GDP? What could explain the poor forecasting accuracy of the model?

    iii. Change the backstep forecast to 2 and the lead period to 10. Did that improve the accuracy of the forecast?

b. It is unlikely that GDP will grow at a constant rate in every quarter. So, let's include trend and seasonality smoothing in the forecast by estimating the triple exponential smoothing (TESM) with multiplicative smoothing. Write a SAS program to estimate a TESM forecasting model of GDP for 10 quarters, starting with a back forecast of 2 quarters.

    i. What are the level, trend, and seasonality weights estimated by the model?

    ii. Did the forecast of the GDP improve with the TESM model, relative to the SESM model?

Chapter 7: Machine Learning Models in Finance

Machine Learning in Finance

In Chapter Six, we examined a suite of statistical models that are commonly used in finance settings. In this chapter, we will turn our attention to machine learning models. As underscored in Chapter One, machine learning models can be categorized into supervised and unsupervised models. Supervised models learn about the predictable features of the target variable from a collection of input variables. Unsupervised models such as clustering models learn about common features that the input variables share and then use those features to group cases in the data. The insights or groups produced by unsupervised models are sometimes used as preliminary steps in predictive modeling. For example, customers can be clustered into homogeneous groups based on sales of different items. Then a model can be built to predict the cluster membership based on more easily obtained input variables. Supervised learning models include point estimation algorithms such as regression models, and classification algorithms such as logistic regressions, decision tree, random forest, artificial neural network, and support vector machines.

While unsupervised learning models include clustering algorithms and dimension reduction models, in reality, many of the statistical models we have discussed also have machine learning applications. In Table 6.1, we highlighted the features that distinguish machine learning from statistical modeling. The primary aim of machine learning is discovery; hence, there is less emphasis on drawing inferences, but more on the accuracy of the predictions and the relevance of the clustering and dimension reduction obtained for other predictive or business purposes.

In Chapter One, we also pointed out that machine learning is one of the subfields of artificial intelligence. Other subfields of artificial intelligence include deep learning (a subfield of machine learning), computer vision, expert systems, natural language processing, generative algorithms, and quantum computing. Indeed, innovations in all fields of artificial intelligence are moving at such a fast rate that they are poised to redefine many aspects of life and business in general. Many of the subfields of artificial intelligence rely on machine learning methods in their implementation, so all financial data scientists must understand their conceptual framework. Remember that one of the pervasive uses of machine learning algorithms in finance is for developing and implementing trading strategies. Therefore, in this chapter, it will be advantageous to discuss the machine learning models in SAS from the perspective of developing an algorithm-based trading strategy.

Developing an Algorithm-Based Trading Strategy

The applications of predictive algorithms and computer intelligence models in trading are motivated by the idea that markets are not fully efficient in either the weak form or the semi-strong form. Therefore, the aim of machine learning implementations in investment settings is to train the algorithms to quickly discern trading signals from a set of information and to deploy them swiftly in the markets. These signals include latent market trends such as momentum, mean reversion, and sentiments; or anomalies in the market that create opportunities for transitory mispricing of securities, which can then be exploited using statistical arbitrage or market making. There are four broad categories of data that are commonly used for training machine learning algorithms in investment settings. They include technical indicators, fundamental indicators, macroeconomic and financial indicators, and sentiment indicators.

Technical Indicators

Technical indicators are usually some statistical measures that describe past patterns of price movements and trading volumes, which the algorithm then attempts to use to predict future patterns of price movements. It includes prices, adjusted prices, returns, volumes, and successive patterns of price movements. Common types of technical indicators include the money flow index (MFI), relative strength index (RSI), simple moving average price (SMA), volume weighted average price (VWAP), and open interests. The use of technical indicators is driven by the belief that the market price of a security reflects every relevant piece of information about the financial and non-financial conditions of the issuer of the security and that the patterns of how these prices change are somewhat predictable. In reality, most technical indicators are simply statistical measures of the interaction (balance or imbalance) between the supply and demand for the security.

Fundamental Indicators

Fundamental indicators are information about the financial conditions of the firm. Think of this as any firm-specific information that an investor would like to know before investing in or divesting from the firm. This category would include the firm's or portfolio's financial metrics, the relative value of the firm, and the financial and operational risk of the firm, to name a few. If valuations are connected to the firm's financial conditions, then changes in the financial condition of the firm will precipitate changes in the value of the firm's stock. Therefore, the aim of machine learning, in this case, is to train the algorithm such that it can quickly discern trade signals from the public disclosure of such information. Clearly, these types of implementations require highly sophisticated algorithms[1] and automation to deploy them successfully in investment settings.

---

[1] Such as algorithms for natural language processing that can read and parse financial disclosures in both written and audio forms into meaningful investment signals.

Macroeconomic and Financial Indicators

Financial markets react to changes in macroeconomic factors. Furthermore, because financial markets are linked, they also react to changes in the prevailing conditions in other markets. Machine learning algorithms can be trained to exploit these dynamic relationships in a few ways. One approach is to train the algorithm to exploit the delay in the reaction in one market to events in another market or to changes in the macroeconomic indicators. Another approach is to train the algorithm to discern and exploit transitory deviations in the long-term relationship between the markets. In view of these possibilities, macroeconomic and financial market data such as inflation, bond yields, interest rates, exchange rates, commodity prices, volatility measures, and indicators from other markets are also included in the universe of data that are fed to the algorithm.

Sentiment Indicators

Sentiment indicators measure investor psychology in terms of their general perception of the level of risk and/or profit opportunities in the market. They defer from technical indicators in the sense that while technical indicators measure past and current trends, sentiment indicators are measures of the current posture or views (bullish or bearish) that investors hold about future market conditions. Therefore, they might contain nuggets of information that the algorithms can exploit to make predictions about future market outcomes. Examples of sentiment indicators include the renowned CBOE volatility index, social media posts, the Bullish Percent Index (BPI), and the Put/Call ratio, to name a few.

A Caution on Algorithm-Based Investment Strategies

Before we proceed any further, it is worthwhile to mention that the success rate for market-predicting algorithms is very low. If it were high, I probably would not have had the time and/or the motivation to write this book.

The journey of algorithm-based investment strategy is long and laden with many obstacles. Before an algorithm is deployed in live investment settings, it must first succeed in identifying exploitable relationships and trends in the model-building phase. Whether the identified trends or relationships will be transient or long-lasting usually depends on whether there is an underlying theory that can explain the discovery. Relationships and trends that have no underlying theoretical motivations will most likely be transitory or are random occurrences that might not be exploitable in real-world settings.[2] If the findings from the algorithm pass this test, then it must succeed in a backtesting scenario. In this phase, the model is deployed on historical data to see how it would have performed in the past. Since the past is not a perfect realization of

---

[2] For example, numbers generated by lottery vending machine periodically would win the lottery. But that does not necessarily imply that the random number generator in the vending machines have better insights than you manually picking your own numbers.

the future, if the model is successful in the backtest, it must also outperform in simulated real-time (paper trading) settings before it is finally deployed in live trading settings with real money.

Given all of these hurdles, it is easy to comprehend why only a few machine-learning models will ultimately be successfully deployed in live settings. In reality, the few successful models often degrade very quickly in their predictive ability. Therefore, financial data scientists who ply their trade in this space must be conditioned to accept that the analytic life cycle of algorithm-based investing is fraught with many challenges and compressed at the deployment phase of the cycle. With that said, it is still very valuable for all financial data scientists to develop competencies in how machine learning can be deployed in investment settings. And we will do that moving forward.

Conceptualizing our Trading Strategy

Suppose we are interested in developing an algorithm that can exploit one or some of the latent trends that have been documented in academic and professional studies. These trends could be momentum, mean reversion, and sentiments. We aim to develop an algorithm that can sift through a large amount of financial, macroeconomic, sentiment, and technical data to help us predict the direction of the S&P 500 index before the market opens the next day. Specifically, we aim to classify whether the index will rise or fall at the close of the next day, given the information that we have at the close of today's trading day. If we can develop such an algorithm, then we can exploit it by holding positions in the S&P 500 index futures today depending on the prediction made by the algorithm for tomorrow.

For example, if the algorithm predicts that the index will rise (fall) at the close of business tomorrow, then we can enter into a long (short) position in the index futures when the futures market opens later that day. Between 4:00 PM when the stock market closes and 5:00 PM when the futures market opens, we will update our model with the new information from today's market activities. We will then close out the position at the market open (5:00 PM) and enter into a new futures position based on the prediction the algorithm will make for the subsequent day. This is a straightforward, easy-to-implement, and easy-to-evaluate trading strategy, assuming we can successfully develop this algorithmic trading model.

Data

To implement our classification model for the S&P 500 index, our predictor variables will include a set of fundamental indicators (such as the P/E ratio) and technical indicators (including Money flows, Relative Strength Indicators, Moving Average Prices, and the daily returns of the index). Since we are working with mostly daily data, we are limited in the number of macroeconomic variables that we can use. Nevertheless, our macroeconomic variables include initial jobless claims and the Conference Board leading economic index, to name a few. Financial market indicators include the daily returns of indices from the major capital markets around the world, using the MSCI indices from Asia, and Europe, as well as daily changes in the prices of

Table 7.1: Predictor Variables

Predictor Variables	
Technical Indicators	
Open-to-Open Price Return	5-Day Moving Average Price
Close-to-Close Price Return	10-Day Moving Average Price
Trading Volume	30-Day Moving Average Price
Money Flow Net-Block	3-Day RSI
Money Flow Net Non-Block	9-Day RSI
Total Call Open Interest	14-Day RSI
Total Put Open Interest	30-Day Historical Volatility
Fundamental Indicator	
Price Earnings Ratio (P/E)	
Macroeconomic and Financial Market Indicators	
Term Spread	Federal Funds Target Rate
Default Spread	Initial Jobless Claims Index
US Dollar Forex Rate	Leading Economic Indicator Index
Sentiment Indicators	
Historical Call Implied Volatility	Historical Put Implied Volatility
CBOE VIX Volatility Index	

commodities, and exchange rates. Our sentiment indicators are the CBOE VIX index and the number of open interests in the call and put options on the S&P 500 index. The algorithm we aim to develop will be trained using the predictor variables described above and a binary target variable, which denotes the next-day directions of the S&P 500 index. Days with positive index performance are labeled as "1", while days with negative performance are labeled as "0". All the variables that will be used for building the model are in the SPXRAW.sas7bdat data set. The data set that will be used to backtest the champion model is the SPXSCORE.sas7bdat. Both data sets are located in the book's GitHub repository.

SAS Environment Options

From this point forward, we will show both the SAS Studio and SAS Enterprise Miner demonstration of the procedures we will highlight in each subsection. Chapter One of the book discusses some of the features that make Enterprise Miner more appealing for machine learning applications in comparison to SAS Studio. However, we will show both the Enterprise Miner steps and the SAS program that can be used to obtain similar outputs in SAS Studio. As you will see shortly, most of the demonstrations we will perform in SAS Enterprise Miner will be done in the process flow diagram using pre-built code packages that are called nodes. We will also store the code that we write and the tasks that we will invoke for each demonstration using the process flow feature of SAS Studio. You should note that SAS constantly adds new features to all of its analytics products, so this is probably a good point to specify that the versions of both products that we will use for our demonstrations are SAS Studio 3.8 and Enterprise Miner 15.2.[3]

Classical Versus High-Performance Computing Procedures

Many of the machine learning procedures in Enterprise Miner and SAS Studio operate in either the conventional computing environment or the distributed computing environment called high-performance (HP) mode. In the HP mode, the procedure runs using parallel processing in either multithreaded single-machine mode or distributed multiple-machine mode. This approach is particularly beneficial when working with a large data set and developing models with a significantly large number of features. The workload is distributed and managed across multiple machines to deliver faster results. The high-performance procedure versions also include SAS statements for data mining and machine learning implementations. These include SAS statements that can be invoked to:

- Partition the data into training, validation, and test data sets.
- Create a score code that can be used for scoring the data.
- Extract ODS tables that contain machine learning-related fit statistics.

These appealing features make the HP procedures in the SAS Studio and HPDM nodes in the Enterprise Miner the default options that will be selected for our modeling tasks in both SAS environments. All HP procedures in SAS Studio have the HP prefix (for example, HPLOGISTICS, HPLMIXED). HP procedures in Enterprise Miner can be found under the HPDM (high-performance data mining) tab shown in Figure 7.1.

Importing Our Data Into SAS

To access your data set in SAS Enterprise Miner, it needs to be placed in a built-in library named EMSAS. To keep things simple, we will also use the same library to do most of our demonstrations in SAS Studio. Since the **%DATAPULL** macro imports data from the repository

---

[3] All of the subsequent demonstrations can also be implemented in SAS Viya. The workflow in SAS Viya is slightly different from Enterprise Miner and SAS Studio. But as noted earlier, both Enterprise Miner and SAS Studio have interfaces to connect directly with SAS Viya. The SAS Studio in the SAS Viya environment uses a different version nomenclature (current version is 5.2) and does not have some of the features in SAS Studio for SAS 9.4. The demonstration of the SAS Viya implementation of these steps is beyond the scope of this book.

Figure 7.1: HPDM Tab in Enterprise Miner

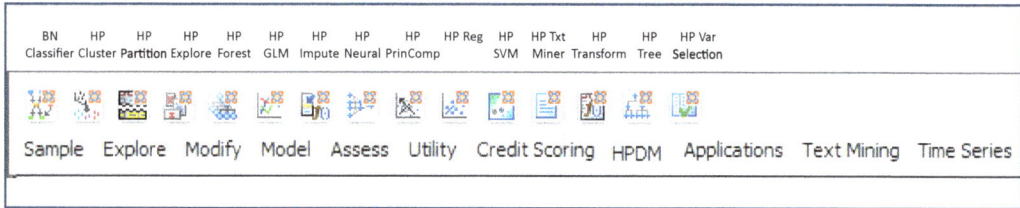

only into the WORK library, we will need to copy the data into the EMSAS library before it can be analyzed. Program 7.1 shows the SAS code that can be used to download the raw and scoring data sets from the GitHub repository and place them into the EMSAS library. Use the PROC CONTENTS statement to verify that the data have both been retrieved and stored in the EMSAS library after running the program. The EMSAS is a permanent library, so you will be able to access the data in subsequent SAS sessions without re-downloading them.

Program 7.1: Importing Data from GitHub Using the %DATAPULL Macro

```
/*Importing Required Data Sets into Your SAS Environment*/
%datapull(spxraw,spxraw.sas7bdat);
%datapull(spxscore,spxscore.sas7bdat);
data emsas.spxraw ;set work.spxraw ;run;
data emsas.spxscore ;set work.spxscore;run;
```

Creating Process Flow Diagrams

A process flow is a collection of one or more linked SAS objects. Examples of SAS objects include data sets, SAS programs, queries, tasks, and results. Each object is represented in the process flow by an icon called a node. Process flows are available in SAS Studio, Enterprise Guide, and Enterprise Miner. The equivalent feature of process flow in SAS Viya is called pipelines.

There are many benefits of using process flows to manage your data science project. First, process flows enable you to visually observe the sequence of the relationships between the objects in your projects. Second, you can create and run multiple independent process flows in the same SAS project. You can also create sub-process flows from another process flow. Lastly, you can generate the SAS programs from the nodes in the process flow. The code in the SAS program is created in the order in which it runs in the process flow. Process flows is one of the many project management tools in SAS that makes it the preferred platform for all data science projects.

Enterprise Miner

Create a new project using the File menu. Follow the prompts to complete the process. To connect to the data in the EMSAS library, right-click the Data Sources icon in the Project Panel area. Select Create Data Source. Click Next, until you get to Select a SAS Table. Click Browse

Figure 7.2: Importing Data into Enterprise Miner

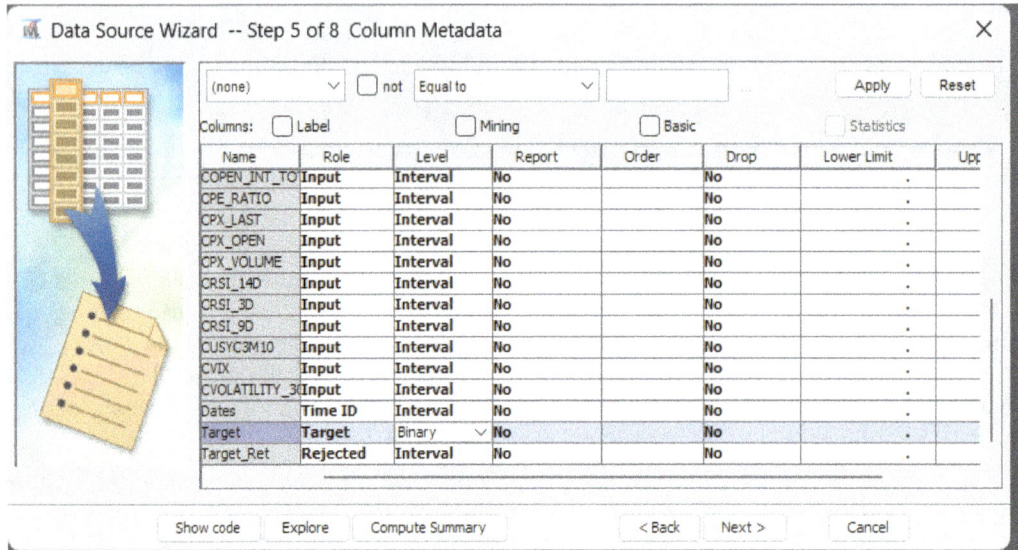

to launch the Select a SAS Table window. Click the SASUSER library and then double-click the SPXRAW data set. Click Next. Review the Table Properties, then click Next. Pause at the Data Source Wizard (Figure 7.2) to review and adjust the roles of the variables in the data set. Scroll to the bottom. Then change the level of the Target variable to Binary. The Target_Ret variable is the actual value of the index return on the next trading day. Since we are only predicting the direction and not the magnitude, we should change the role of the Target_Ret variable to Rejected.

You can review descriptive statistics from each variable by clicking the Compute Summary button. Scroll to the right to review the summary statistics generated by SAS Enterprise Miner. Once you are done, click Next until Step 9 of 9. Then click Finish. Repeat the same steps for the SPXSCORE data set until Step 9 and change the value of the Role drop-down box to Score. Then click Finish. To create a diagram, right-click the Diagrams button in the Project Panel, then click Create New Diagram. Name the diagram SP500. Drag and drop the SPXRAW data set on the diagram to bring your data set into the project area.

In the SAS Studio environment (Figure 7.3), make sure you have selected Visual Programmer as the default perspective. Then click the ellipsis next to the Visual Programmer option and select New Process Flow. Navigate to the EMSAS Library. Then drag and drop the SPRAW data set in the Process Flow area. Save your Process Flow by clicking on the Save icon.

Figure 7.3: Importing Data into SAS Studio

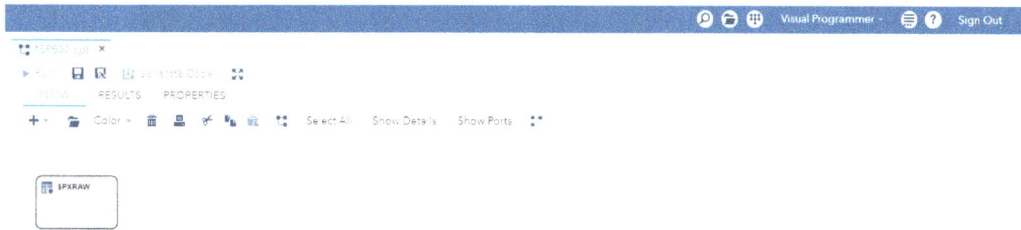

Data Partitioning

One of the best practices in developing machine learning models is to iteratively build and assess the model using different sets of data. Data partitioning is the process of randomly dividing the master data set into training and validation sub-data sets. As mentioned earlier, in an investment setting, a third data set is also retained for backtesting purposes. The third subsample of data is often called "test data" in the data science domain. Data partitioning helps to reduce the risk of overfitting the model to the training data set. By iteratively using a separate set of data to evaluate the accuracy of the model that the algorithm is creating, we increase the likelihood that the model can be generalized to new sets of data or deployed to achieve the intended modeling objectives in live settings.

Because we are working with time-indexed data, a special technique might be required when creating our training and validation data sets to avoid look-ahead bias. One approach is to split the data into training and validation data sets using a date threshold. In this approach, the data in the later subperiod is used to validate the model built using data from the prior period. While this approach may be sufficient for pure time series models, it might not work well for classification models that require the response variables to be on the same row as the feature variables.[4] Indeed, many of the classification algorithms that we will examine are not designed to model lead/lag relationships. Therefore, such transformations must be done on the data before feeding it into the model.

In our SPXRAW data set, the values of the target variable for the next day have been placed on the same row as the predictor variables using PROC EXPAND. Furthermore, the classification problem is relatively straightforward and requires a single-period set of information. So, the risk of look-ahead bias is very low if we randomly sample observations for our training and validation

---

[4] You can also apply the k-fold validation method, in which the data is split into k-partitions. The model is then built iteratively trained using a rolling window of k-1 partitions with the last partition serving as the validation data set in each attempt. However, this approach will work only if we assume that our data is independent across time, which might not necessarily hold for time series data.

Figure 7.4: Data Partitioning in Enterprise Miner

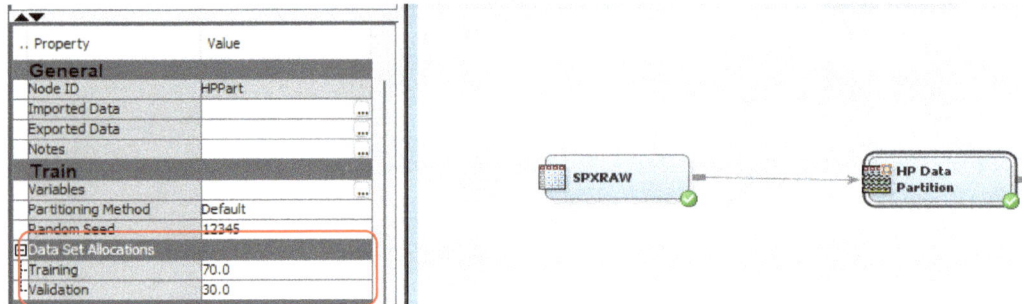

data set. However, the data in the holdout period, which we will use for backtesting is not randomly sampled. The data for the modeling subperiod is from January 3rd, 2011, to December 31st, 2020, and consists of 2,501 observations divided into 70% (1,751 observations) training data set and 30% (750 observations) validation data set. The back-testing (holdout) sub-period, which is from January 1st, 2021, to July 29th, 2022, contains 396 daily observations.

SAS Enterprise Miner

Click the HPDM tab, then drag and drop the high-performance data partitioning node on the diagram. Connect it to the SPXRAW data set. In the Properties Panel shown in Figure 7.4, change Training to 70 and Validation to 30 under the Data Set Allocations. Specify the Random Seed value of 54321. The default random sampling for binary target variables is stratified random sampling. So, we will leave the setting as it is. Right-click the node and select Run.

SAS Studio

Click Tasks and Utilities. Then click Tasks, and then Data to reveal the DATA step menu in SAS Studio. Drag and drop the Partition Data menu onto the Process Flow. (See Figure 7.5.) Double-click the code node and make sure that EMSAS.SPXRAW is selected in the Select a Table drop-down box. Click Roles to show the drop-down area. In the Stratify By cell, click on the + sign to add a column. Then select Target as the variable to stratify by. Increase the Number of Partitions to 2. Then set the Proportion of Cases for partitions 1 and 2 to 0.7 and 0.3, respectively. Specify the random seed value of 54321. Change the data set name to SPXRAWP and name the Variable name for partition value to PARTITION and the ID value for partition 1 and partition 2 data to 1 and 2. Then run the program.

Figure 7.5: Data Partitioning in SAS Studio

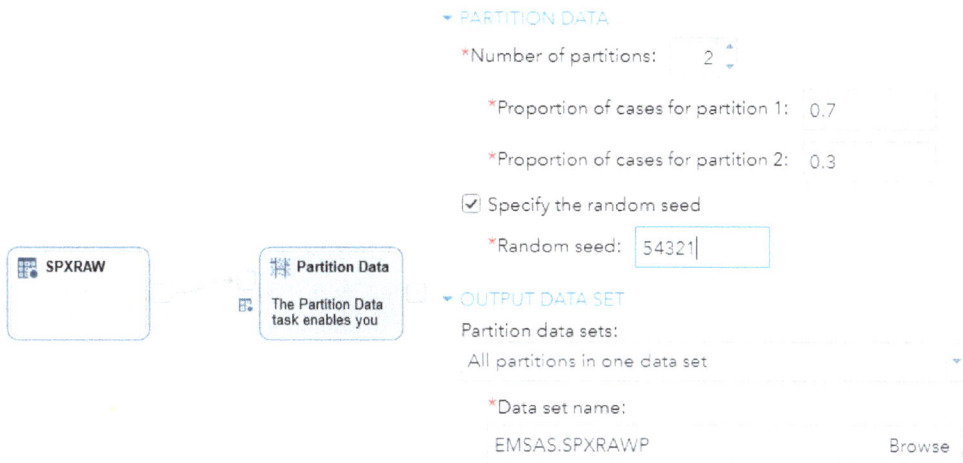

▾ PARTITION DATA

*Number of partitions: 2

    *Proportion of cases for partition 1: 0.7

    *Proportion of cases for partition 2: 0.3

☑ Specify the random seed

    *Random seed: 54321

SPXRAW   Partition Data

    The Partition Data task enables you

▾ OUTPUT DATA SET

Partition data sets:

All partitions in one data set

    *Data set name:

    EMSAS.SPXRAWP   Browse

Supervised Learning Models for Predicting Stock Price Movements

The two broad categories of supervised learning algorithms are parametric algorithms and nonparametric algorithms. Remember that parametric algorithms often use a set of assumptions to define the relationship between the predictors and the target variable. These assumptions inherently define the mapping functions that the algorithm learns to build the prediction model for the target variable. Nonparametric algorithms do not make specific assumptions about the relationship between the predictor variables and the target variable. Hence, they do not require a specific mapping function and can estimate the unknown function that could be of any form.

Hyperparameter Tuning

All of the algorithms in SAS Studio and Enterprise Miner have default settings for options that control the learning process used by the algorithms. These options are called hyperparameters. Unlike model parameters that are estimated by algorithms, hyperparameters are model options that are specified in advance by the data scientist and are used to train the model. They could potentially impact the values of the parameters that are estimated by the algorithms. They are particularly useful because they serve as scaffolds that the algorithm uses in the learning process. Hyperparameters are used in both supervised and unsupervised learning algorithms. In Enterprise Miner, the available hyperparameters for each node can be found in its Properties Panel. In SAS Studio, they are typically the options that accompany the listed SAS statement for the procedure. For example, one of the hyperparameters for the decision tree is the maximum depth of the tree. This controls the level of complexity of the tree.

Parametric Algorithms

Parametric algorithms that are employed in supervised learning models include point estimate models such as linear regression (OLS), regularized regression (RR), neural network models (NN), logistic regression (when probability estimates are the desired output), and generalized linear models (GLM), while classification models include logistic regression (LR) (which we have already discussed in Chapter Six), neural network models (NN), and data mining regression (DM). In the following subsection, we will discuss and demonstrate the most commonly used parametric models for classifications, which are logistic regression, generalized linear models, and neural network models. The data mining regression and variable clustering regressions are extensions of the logistic regression. They differ only in the types of inputs that are fed into the model. Classical logistic regression uses raw data as inputs, while the data mining and variable clustering regressions are fed transformed variables as inputs. In SAS Enterprise Miner, the transformation is automatically performed in the Data Mining node, while the variable clustering approach transforms the variable using the Variable Clustering node before feeding the data into the Regression node. There are no high-performance nodes for either approach. However, we will experiment with them in the practice exercise for this chapter.

Logistic Regression

For logistic regression, the functional form for the classification problem relies on estimating a vector of parameters to calculate the probability that our response variable y_{t+1} takes on the value of 1 or zero. The probability distribution that is used in this case is the logistic cumulative distribution function and can be written as:

$$p(y_{t+1} = 1 \mid x_t) = \frac{1}{1 + \exp\left(-\left(\beta_0 + \beta_1 x_{1t} + \beta_2 x_{2t} + \ldots + \beta_k x_{kt}\right)\right)} \tag{7.1}$$

Classification is then performed based on the probability of exceeding a certain threshold. The most common probability threshold for classification problems is fifty percent $p(y_{t+1} = 1 \mid x_t) \geq 0.5$. We can infer the directional impact of the marginal effect of each predictor on the overall probability of the response variable; however, the values of the marginal effect cannot be directly inferred because the relationship between y_t and x_t is non-linear. Therefore, they are mostly presented in the form of the log ratios of success to failure (also known as log odds).

$$\log\left(\frac{p(y_{t+1} = 1)}{1 - p(y_{t+1} = 1)}\right) = \beta_0 + \beta_1 x_{1t} + \beta_2 x_{2t} + \ldots + \beta_k x_{kt} \tag{7.2}$$

The HPLOGISTICS Procedure

PROC HPLOGISTICS is a high-performance version of the LOGISTICS procedure that we examined in Chapter Six. Some notable features of the HPLOGISTICS procedure include the PARTITION statement that is used to specify how the data should be divided into the training, validation, and test data sets. The CODE statement is used to request the scoring code from the fitted model. The scoring code can be used to score existing or new data. In a subsequent section, we will also combine the score code from the HPLOGISTICS procedure with the scoring code from other procedures to create the Ensemble model.

Two mutually exclusive options can be used to save the scoring code to a physical location on your machine. The CATALOG option is used to specify the location of the generated code using up to four level name options (CATALOG=libref.catalog.entry.type). The FILE option (which is the preferred option) is used to specify the location to store the scoring code. In the example below, the temporary folder (`file="%sysfunc(pathname(work))/"`) for the WORK library is specified. This implies that your scoring code will not be available in your next SAS session unless you rerun the model. You can specify a different location if you would like to keep a permanent copy of the scoring code. In the SAS OnDemand environment, the location will be (`"/home/userid/userfolder/"`), while in the Windows environment, it will be (`"C:\Users\userid\userfolder\"`).

The FORMAT option specifies the numeric format for the regression coefficient, while the GROUP option specifies the identity for the array names and statement labels. You should specify different GROUP options if you plan to combine the scoring codes for multiple procedures in one DATA step as the default array names and statement labels are the same for some procedures (for example, HPLOGISTICS and HPGENSELECT). The IMPUTE option is used to request predictions for missing or invalid covariates, while the RESIDUAL option is used to request the calculation of the residuals for the current model. It will not produce residuals for the scoring data set, which does not contain a target variable. The HPLOGISTICS procedure generates the receiver operating characteristics (ROC) curve by default. We discussed the ROC curve in Chapter Six; we will revisit the topic in the subsequent section of this chapter.

SAS Enterprise Miner

Drag and drop the HP Regression node onto your diagram. Connect it to the output port of your data partition node. In the Properties panel, the default regression type for binary target variables is logistic regression. In the Model selection area, select Backward as the Selection Method and Significance Level as the Selection Criterion. Right-click the node, then update the path and run the node after the path has been updated. Review the results from the estimation by right-clicking the node and clicking Results. You will find a suite of tables, graphs, and outputs in the Results. Pay attention to the Variable Selection, Fit Statistics, and Parameter Estimates windows. Together, they show the overall performance of the model and the variables and their effects on the prediction. We will analyze some of these metrics in the model comparison section.

SAS Studio

Click the + · icon in your process flow. Then select SAS Program to create a programming node in your process flow. Connect the input port of the node to the output port of your Partition

data node. Double-click the node. Copy and paste the SAS program below into the code area, then run it. Click the Node tab and type in "HP Reg" in the Name area. Save your Process Flow
► Run 🖫 🖳 .

Program 7.2A: Classifying Stock Price Movement Using PROC HPLOGISTICS

```
/*Classifying Stock Market Directions Using High-Performance Logistic Procedure*/
/*Use Macro Variable to create a list of predictor variables*/
%let var_list=CCSIBBB CFDTR CFXRATE CHIST_CALL_IMP_VOL CHIST_PUT_IMP_VOL CINJCJC CLEI
        CMF_NET_BLCK CMF_NET_NON_BLCK CMOV_AVG_10D CMOV_AVG_30D CMOV_AVG_5D
        COPEN_INT_TOTAL_CALL COPEN_INT_TOTAL_PUT CPE_RATIO CPX_LAST CPX_OPEN;

ods graphics on;
proc hplogistic data=EMSAS.SPXRAWP;
        id Dates Partition;
        class Target;
        model Target=&var_list. /cutpoint=0.5 link=logit;
        partition rolevar=partition(train='1' validate='2');
        selection method=backward(slstay=0.1)  details=all;
        code file ="%sysfunc(pathname(work))/logscore.sas" group=HPLOG;
        output out=plogout /allstats;
        ods output PartFitStats=logstats;
run;
```

CUTPOINT=0.5 specifies the threshold for classifying the predicted Target as "1". The backward selection method with a 10% level of significance for keeping a potential predictor in the model is specified using SLSTAY=0.1. SAS ODS output can also be invoked to create SAS data sets from ODS tables generated by the procedure. In this example, we used the ODS statement to create an output data set LOGSTATS from the PARTFITSTATS ODS table. We will combine these with the fit statistics from other models and review them together in the model comparison section, which we will perform shortly.

The DATA step below the procedure contains the SAS code that was used to combine the prediction output (PLOGOUT) from the procedure with the partitioned input data set (SPXRAWP) for subsequent analyses. We will also try to replicate some of the visualizations in SAS Enterprise Miner by computing a set of variables that can be used to produce the classification matrix and perform model diagnostics and comparison.

Program 7.2B: Classifying Stock Price Movement Using PROC HPLOGISTICS

```
/*Comparing Predicted to Actual Outcomes*/
proc sort data=plogout; by dates; run;
proc sort data=emsas.spxrawp; by dates;run;
data logout;
        merge plogout emsas.spxrawp;
        by dates;
```

```
/*****************************************************
The code below is repeated in other Models.
*****************************************************/

        if (Pred < 0.5) then
                P_Target = 0;
        else P_Target = 1;
   format Classification $10. Role $9. Model $15.;
    if (Target = P_Target) then Classification = 'Correct';
        else Classification = 'Incorrect';
        if Partition = '1' then
                Role ='Train';
        else Role ='Validate';
   if P_Target = 1 and Target=1 then TP=1; else TP='';
   if P_Target = 1 and Target=0 then FP=1; else FP='';
   if P_Target = 0 and Target=1 then FN=1; else FN='';
   if P_Target = 0 and Target=0 then TN=1; else TN='';
   label TP='True Positive' FP='False Positive' FN='False Negative' TN='True Negative';

/*****************************************************
End of repeated code
*****************************************************/

  Model='HP Logistics';
run;
```

Results

Click the Result tab to view the results of the HPLOGLISTIC procedure. The estimation generates a lot of output. To save space and time, we will perform a summary of the results. However, I encourage you to spend some time reviewing all of them on your own.

Scrolling to the bottom of the result will reveal the fit statistics of the final model and the variables selected for the model. The variables selected include Historical implied volatility on call options, Leading Economic Indicator Index, Money Flow, Open interests on Call and Put options, PE ratio, and the CBOE Implied Volatility Index (VIX). Notice the signs of the relationships between the variables and the direction of the market. In particular, positive changes in implied volatility of call options, leading economic index, and open interest on call options increase the probability that the market will end higher the next trading day. Positive changes in open interest on put options, money flow, PE ratio, and the VIX index imply negative stock market movement on the next trading day. The signs of the variables are consistent with expectations and the theory of market behavior. Positive news and higher investor optimism are generally correlated with higher price movements in the market.

Output 7.2: Estimated Coefficients of Selected Variables from PROC HPLOGISTICS

Parameter Estimates					
Parameter	Estimate	Standard Error	DF	t Value	Pr > |t|
Intercept	0.2037	0.04925	Infty	4.14	<.0001
CHIST_CALL_IMP_VOL	2.7810	1.4618	Infty	1.90	0.0571
CLEI	71.6809	40.9855	Infty	1.75	0.0803
CMF_NET_BLCK	-0.02232	0.01195	Infty	-1.87	0.0618
COPEN_INT_TOTAL_CALL	5.9001	2.5545	Infty	2.31	0.0209
COPEN_INT_TOTAL_PUT	-5.8796	2.5521	Infty	-2.30	0.0212
CPE_RATIO	-19.5541	6.7053	Infty	-2.92	0.0035
CVIX	-5.1794	1.5181	Infty	-3.41	0.0006

Generalized Linear Model (GLM)

GLM is a broad category of models that can be used to model linear and non-linear relationships between the response variable and its covariates. This innovative approach to predictive modeling divides the problem into three components.

- **Random component**: This specifies the conditional distribution for the response variable, which could be normal, Poisson, or binomial as in the case of our classification problem.
- **Structural component**: This specifies a linear predictor relationship between the response variable and its predictors. The relationship could be a pure linear function such as $\eta_{t+1} = \beta_0 + \beta_1 x_{1t} + \beta_2 x_{2t} + ... + \beta_k x_{kt}$ or a curvilinear function such as $\eta_{t+1} = \beta_0 + \beta_1 x_{1t} + \beta_2 x_{2t}^2 + ... + \beta_k x_{kt}^2$. The key point here is that the parameterization must be in a linear form.
- **Link function**: This describes how the random and the structural components are connected. This is done by linking the expected value of the random component to some functional form of the structural component using a smooth and invertible linearizing function that is typically denoted by $g(\cdot)$. For example, a linear link function between a normally distributed response variable, which has a linear relationship with its predictor will take the form of $\mu_{t+1} = E(y_{t+1} | x_t)$, which is the linear regression model.

$$g\left(u_{t+1}\right) = E\left(y_{t+1} \mid x_t\right) = \eta_{t+1} = \beta_0 + \beta_1 x_{1t} + \beta_2 x_{2t} + ... + \beta_k x_{kt} \qquad (7.3)$$

Common types of link functions include the identity, log, log-log, inverse, logit, probit, and inverse Gaussian, to name a few. Furthermore, because the function is invertible, its inverse (which is known as its mean function) can be derived as:

$$\mu_{t+1} = g^{-1}\left(\eta_{t+1}\right) = g^{-1}\left(\beta_0 + \beta_1 x_{1t} + \beta_2 x_{2t} + ... + \beta_k x_{kt}\right) \qquad (7.4)$$

> The GLM procedure uses a link function to connect some type of linear specification of the predictor variables to some function of the response variable that has a known distribution. By using this approach, we avoid the need for the response variable and its predictors to share the same multivariate distribution. While the response variable itself might not vary linearly with the predictors, however, by construct, the function of the response variable will vary linearly with the predictors in the GLM framework.

The HPGENSELECT Procedure

PROC HPGENSELECT is a high-performance procedure for building and fitting generalized linear models (GLM) in SAS. Although the HPGENSELECT procedure shares many statements with HPLOGISTICS (such as CLASS, CODE, PARTITION, MODEL, SELECTION, and PERFORMANCE), its capabilities extend to modeling response variables from the exponential family of distributions such as the Poisson, Normal, and Tweedie. The MODEL statement is used to specify the relationship between the response variable and its predictors. It includes options such as DISTRIBUTION, which is used to specify the distribution of the response variable, and LINK, which is used to specify the link function. The RESTRICT statement is used to impose restrictions on the model for hypothesis testing. The SELECTION statement is used to specify the method and criteria for selecting the final model.

SAS Enterprise Miner

Drag and drop the HP GLM node onto your diagram. Connect it to the output port of your data partition node. In the Properties panel, the default probability distribution for the binary target variable is the binomial distribution. Change the Link function for the binary target variable from Logit to Probit. In the Model selection area, select Backward as the Selection Method and Significance Level as the Selection Criterion. Right-click the node, then update the path and run the node after the path has been updated. Review the results from the estimation by right-clicking on the node and clicking Results. You will find a suite of tables, graphs, and outputs in the Results. Pay attention to the Variable Selection, Fit Statistics, and Parameter Estimates windows.

SAS Studio

Click the ＋ icon in your process flow. Then select SAS Program to create a programming node in your process flow. Connect the input port of the node to the output port of your Partition data node.

Double-click the node. Copy and paste the SAS program below into the Code area, then run it. Click the Node tab and type "HP GLM" in the Name area. Save your Process Flow ▶ Run 🖫 🖳 .

You will notice that the HPGENSELECT procedure shares similar features with the HPLOGISTIC procedure. This is because logistic regression is a special case of the GLM. Rather than re-estimate a logit model, let's use LINK=PROBIT to specify a probit model for the link function in the model statement. Just as in the case of the HPLOGISTIC procedure, the PARTITION statement is used to specify how the data should be divided into the training, validation, and test data sets. The CODE FILE= statement specifies the location where the scoring code should be stored. SAS ODS output can also be invoked to create SAS data from the ODS tables generated by the procedure. In this example, we used the ODS statement to create an output data set (GLMSTATS) from the FITSTATISTICS ODS table.

Program 7.3: Classifying Stock Price Movement Using PROC HPGENSELECT

```
/*Classifying Stock Market Directions Using High-Performance GLM Procedure*/
proc hpgenselect data=EMSAS.SPXRAWP;
        class Target;
        id dates partition;
        partition role=Partition (validate='2');
        model Target (event='1')= &var_list./dist=binary link=probit;
/* Macrovariable list*/
                selection method=backward(slstay=0.1) details=all;
                output out=pglmout role=partrole / allstats;
           code file="%sysfunc(pathname(work))/glmscore.sas" group=HPGLM ;
           ods output fitstatistics=glmstats(where=(Step is missing));
run;

/*Comparing Prediction to Actual Outcomes*/
proc sort data=pglmout; by dates; run;
proc sort data=emsas.spxrawp; by dates;run;
data glmout;
merge pglmout emsas.spxraw;

/*********************************
Same code as Program 7.2B
*********************************/

        if (Pred < 0.5) then
                P_Target = 0;
        else P_Target = 1;
   format Classification $10. Role $9. Model $15.;
   if (Target = P_Target) then Classification = 'Correct';
        else Classification = 'Incorrect';
        if Partition = '1' then
                Role ='Train';
        else Role ='Validate';
```

```
if P_Target = 1 and Target=1 then TP=1; else TP='';
if P_Target = 1 and Target=0 then FP=1; else FP='';
if P_Target = 0 and Target=1 then FN=1; else FN='';
if P_Target = 0 and Target=0 then TN=1; else TN='';
label TP='True Positive' FP='False Positive' FN='False Negative' TN='True Negative';
model='HP GLM';
run;
```

Results

Click the Result tab to view the results of the HPGENSELECT procedure. The estimation also generates a lot of output. To save space and time, we will perform a summary of the results. Again, I encourage you to spend some time reviewing all of them on your own. Scrolling to the bottom of the result will reveal the fit statistics of the final model and the variables selected for the model (shown in Output 7.3). Notice in the results that the same set of variables that were selected in the HPLOGISTIC procedure is also selected by the HPGENSELECT procedure. The HPGENSELECT procedure does not automatically classify target variables. So, the misclassification rate is not provided with its fit statistics. We will manually calculate it using the DATA step below the procedure. The DATA step combines the prediction output (PGLMOUT) from the procedure with the partitioned input data set (SPXRAWP) for subsequent analyses.

Output 7.3: Estimated Coefficients of Selected Variables from PROC HPGENSELECT

Parameter Estimates					
Parameter	DF	Estimate	Standard Error	Chi-Square	Pr > ChiSq
Intercept	1	0.127218	0.030716	17.1542	<.0001
CHIST_CALL_IMP_VOL	1	1.737973	0.899699	3.7316	0.0534
CLEI	1	44.497572	25.500261	3.0450	0.0810
CMF_NET_BLCK	1	-0.013527	0.007261	3.4705	0.0625
COPEN_INT_TOTAL_CALL	1	3.657141	1.562036	5.4815	0.0192
COPEN_INT_TOTAL_PUT	1	-3.644063	1.561064	5.4492	0.0196
CPE_RATIO	1	-12.155272	4.046818	9.0220	0.0027
CVIX	1	-3.224110	0.938655	11.7980	0.0006

The steps to create a program node for each procedure are the same and many of the high-performance procedures share similar SAS statements, moving forward we will only highlight those that are unique to the procedure.

Artificial Neural Network

Artificial neural network models estimate the outcomes of the response variable y_{t+1} using a set of combination and activation functions. Although we will be applying it to a classification problem in this book, you should note that artificial neural network models have a variety of applications beyond classification problems. They are also used for predictions, controls, and optimization. Indeed, they can model complex latent relationships due to the flexible form of the framework that they use. However, their ability to achieve these outcomes comes at a cost, which is the lack of model transparency. In reality, artificial neural networks are one of the most common black-box algorithms currently in use.

There are various specifications of artificial neural network algorithms, such as the feed-forward, backpropagation, radial basis function neural network, and convolution neural network. However, the most common architecture is the feed-forward approach with multi-layer perceptron. In the feedforward approach shown in Figure 7.6, unidirectional flows of information occur through a fully connected network of neurons. It starts with an input layer where the data is standardized using weights, then followed by a hidden layer in which the data is further transformed using hidden-layer activation functions,[5] before finally passing through the output layer where the actual prediction or classification is made using the output or target layer activation functions.

Figure 7.6: Feed-Forward Neural Network with One Hidden Layer

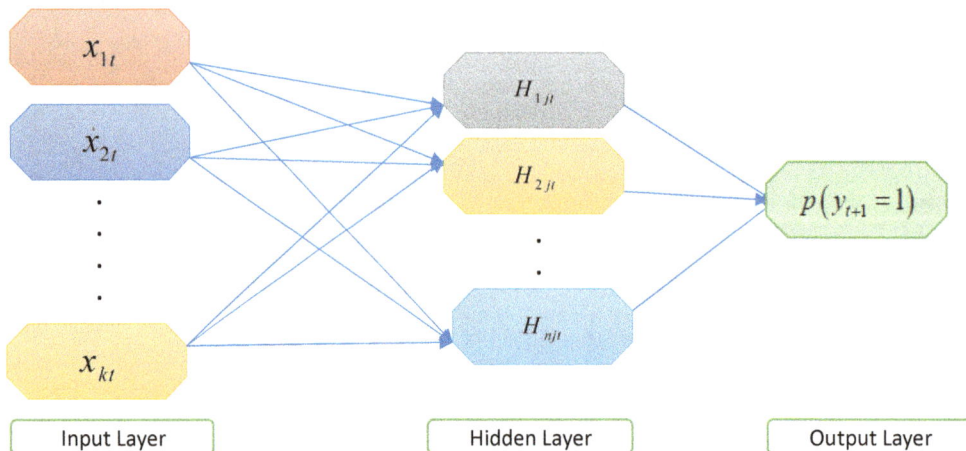

---

[5] Three common categories of activation functions include: the ridge activation functions such as the linear, sigmoid, and hyperbolic functions; the radial activations functions such as Gaussian and quadratic functions; and the folding activation functions such as the SoftMax functions.

Suppose the values obtained from each hidden layer are stored in a vector H_j, where j is the referenced layer. Let n represent the number of nodes in each layer. Furthermore, let σ_j represent the activation function for the jth layer and β_j represent scalar values called bias. W_j is the weighting matrix of the jth layer with the number of rows equals the number of nodes in the $j^{th} - 1$ layer. Then the functional form for the classification problem in the feed-forward neural network approach using the same probabilistic framework for the outcomes of y_{t+1} can be written as:

$$p(y_{t+1} = 1 \mid x_t) = g^{-1}(y_{t+1}) = \sigma_k \left(\beta_k + \ldots + W_3 \sigma_2 \left(\beta_2 + W_2 \sigma_1 \left(\beta_1 + W_1 x_t \right) \right) \right) \quad (7.5)$$

There are also multiple types of activation functions. They include the logistic or sigmoid function, the hyperbolic tangent function, the sine and cosine functions, and the SoftMax function, to name a few. The sigmoid activation function is written as $\sigma(z) = \dfrac{1}{1 + \exp(-z)}$, while

the hyperbolic tangent function is $\sigma(z) = \tanh(z) = \dfrac{2}{1 + \exp(-2z)} - 1$. The SoftMax function is

$$\sigma(z)_i = \frac{\exp(z_i)}{\displaystyle\sum_{j=1}^{n} \exp(z_j)} \ .$$

The SoftMax activation function converts a vector of raw outputs from the neurons in the output layer into a vector of probabilities scores by scaling them to fall between 0 and 1. The sigmoid and SoftMax functions are mostly used in the output or target layer, while the hyperbolic tangent, identity, sine, and cosine functions are more commonly used in the hidden-layer activation functions.

Neural network models do not use selection methods to filter out variables with low information values; therefore, you should note that all input variables are used in the artificial neural network model. You should preselect the variables before feeding them into the algorithm using other methods if you desire this feature.

> It is helpful to think of neural network models as functions of functions in which recipient nodes in each consecutive layer consist of the sum of the weighted values of the predictors from the nodes in the previous layer. The process continues recursively until the data is passed to the output layer for the actual prediction to be made using the activation function in the layer.

The HPNEURAL Procedure

The estimation of the various architectures of neural network models can be invoked in SAS using the high-performance HPNEURAL procedure. The ARCHITECTURE statement specifies which types of architecture should be used for training the model. The options include logistics, multilayer perceptron (MLP) with one or more hidden layers, and multilayer perceptron with direct connections between the input and output layers. The CODE statement is used to output the scoring code for the procedure in the same manner as the previous procedures. The HIDDEN statement is used to specify the number of hidden layers in the model, the number of neutrons in each layer, and the activation (ACT) function for each layer. Each hidden layer must be specified by a separate HIDDEN statement. The activation function available in each hidden layer includes cosine (COS), identity (IDENTITY), and tangent (TANH). The INPUT statement specifies the list of predictor variables and their measurement levels (LEVEL=NOM|INT). The NOM and INT options specify the nominal and interval measurement levels, respectively. The TARGET statement specifies the target variable and its measurement level (LEVEL =NOM|INT). Other options in the TARGET statement include the activation functions (ACT=COS|EXP|IDENTITY|TANH) that are used for interval targets. The default activation function for nominal targets is the SoftMax function. The STD option specifies whether interval targets should be standardized and the types of standardization to use (RANGE, ZSCORE, NONE). The ERROR option specifies the error function (GAMMA, NORMAL, POISSON) to apply to interval target variables. The TRAIN statement specifies how the procedure handles the training data in estimating the network weights that will be used to predict the target variable. The SCORE statement specifies that the procedure should write the actual target and predicted target values into a SAS data set that is specified in the OUT= option. You can also request that the model parameters be saved in a SAS data set specified in the MODEL= option. WEIGHT specifies whether the inverse of the fraction of time that the target class occurs in the data should be used to weight the training observation.

SAS Enterprise Miner

Drag and drop the HP Neural node onto your diagram. Connect it to the output port of your data partition node. In the Properties panel, set Use Inverse Priors to Yes and set the Architecture to User-Defined. Then change the number of Hidden Layers to 1. Click the Ellipsis in front of the Hidden Layer Option and set the Activation Function for the layer to TANH and the Number of Neurons to 3. The default activation function for binary classification variables is SoftMax, so we will leave it as is. We will also leave the remaining hyperparameters at their default settings. Right-click the node, update the path, then run the node after the path has been updated.

SAS Studio

Click the $+$ icon in your process flow. Then select SAS Program to create a programming node in your process flow. Connect the input port of the node to the output port of your Partition data node. Double-click the node. Copy and paste the SAS program below into the Code area, then run it. Click the Node tab and type "HP Neural" in the Name area. Save your Process Flow

► Run

Program 7.4: Classifying Stock Price Movement Using PROC HPNEURAL

```
/*Classifying Stock Market Directions Using HP Neural Network Procedure*/
/*Creating numeric partition variable*/
data emsas.spxrawn;
set emsas.spxrawp;
npartition = input(partition,2.);
run;

ods graphics on;
proc hpneural data=emsas.spxrawn;
        architecture mlp;
        input &var_list.;/* Macrovariable  list*/
        id dates partition;
        target target/level=nom;
        hidden 3/act=tanh;
        train numtries=3 outmodel=model_spxwrap  maxiter=1000;
        weight  _inverse_priors_;
        partition rolevar=npartition(validate=2);
        code file ="%sysfunc(pathname(work))/neuralscore.sas";
        score out=pneuralout;
        ods output fitstatistics=neuralstats;
run;

/*Comparing Prediction to Actual Outcomes*/
proc sort data=pneuralout;by dates;
proc sort data=emsas.spxrawn;by dates;
run;
data neuralout;
merge pneuralout emsas.spxrawn;
by dates;

/********************************
Same code as Program 7.2B
********************************/
        if (Pred < 0.5) then
                P_Target = 0;
        else P_Target = 1;
   format Classification $10. Role $9. Model $15.;
    if (Target = P_Target) then Classification = 'Correct';
        else Classification = 'Incorrect';
        if Partition = '1' then
                Role ='Train';
        else Role ='Validate';
  if P_Target = 1 and Target=1 then TP=1; else TP='';
  if P_Target = 1 and Target=0 then FP=1; else FP='';
  if P_Target = 0 and Target=1 then FN=1; else FN='';
  if P_Target = 0 and Target=0 then TN=1; else TN='';
  label TP='True Positive' FP='False Positive' FN='False Negative' TN='True Negative';

Model='HP Neural';
run;
```

The DATA step before the PROC HPNEURAL statement was used to transform the partition variable into numeric values because the HPNEURAL procedure only accepts numeric values for the partition variable. Notice in the SAS code that the HIDDEN statement is followed by 3, which specifies that one hidden layer that contains three neurons should be used. ACT=TANH specifies the activation function for the hidden layer. The TRAIN statement specifies that the training data specified in the PARTITION statement should be used to determine the network weights that best predict the target in the training data without overfitting it. The SCORE and OUT statements specify that the predictions from the model should be stored in the PNEURALOUT data set. WEIGHT _inverse_priors specify the inverse of the fraction of times that the target class occurs should be used to weight the training observation.

Results

Neural network models are black box models; therefore, they have very few interpretable results. The HPNEURAL procedure generates the list of hyperparameters and the fit statistics of the model. The HP Neural Node in SAS Enterprise Miner creates more output. So, let's review some of the outputs of the node.

Output 7.4A shows the link graph from the procedure. Notice that all 24 predictor variables are used in the model. Each of the variables is linked to the three neurons in the hidden layer, which are then fed into the single neuron in the target (output) layer for the actual prediction.

Output 7.4B shows a heat map of the total weights of each predictor variable and each neuron in the hidden layer. The redder the color, the more positive the weight that is assigned to the variable. The bluer the color, the more negative the weight that is assigned to the variable. Notice that the variables with deep red weights (positive changes in implied volatility of call options, leading economic index, and open interest on call options) are the same as those with a higher probability of a positive stock market outcome in the PROC LOGISTIC and GLM models, while the variables with deep blue colors (open interest on put options, money flow, PE ratio, and the VIX index) are the same as those with a higher probability of the negative stock market outcome in the same models. In terms of the contributions of the three neurons in the hidden layer to the target layer, you can observe that H1 and H2 have higher weights in predicting the target outcome than H3.

Output 7.4A: Link Graph Obtained from HP Neural Node

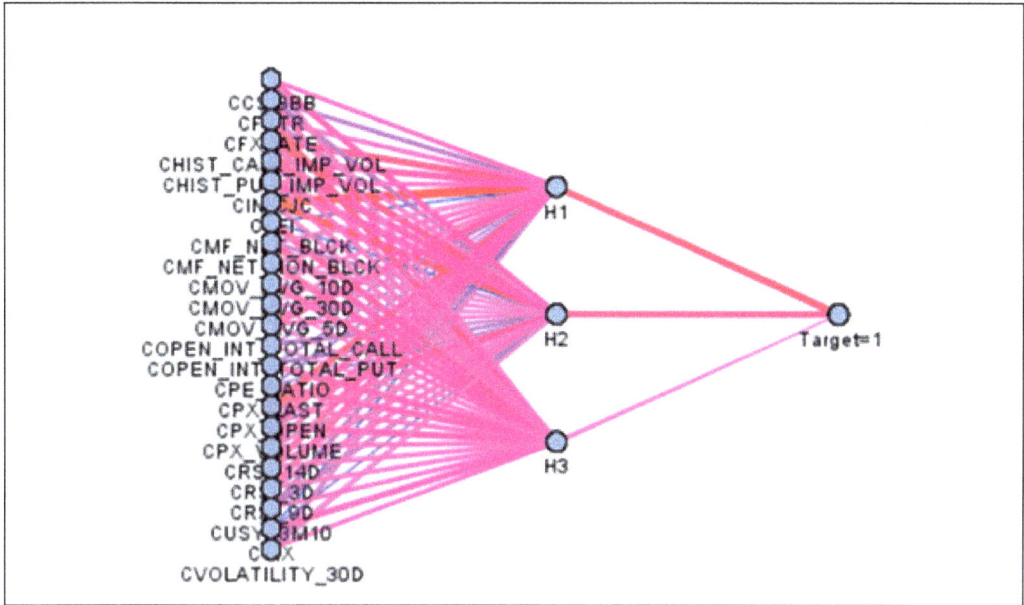

Output 7.4B: Variable Weights Obtained from HP Neural Node

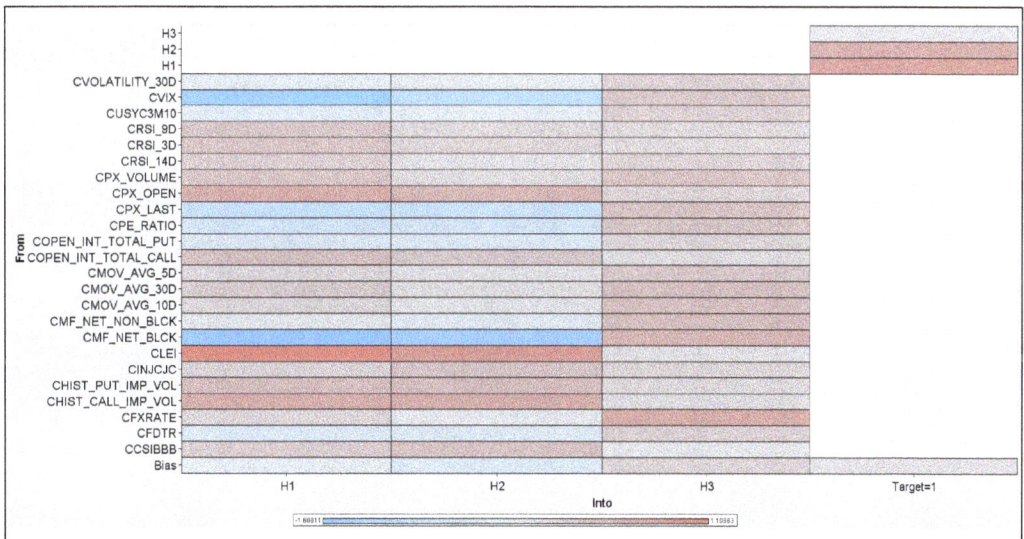

Nonparametric Algorithms

Nonparametric algorithms usually make few to no assumptions about the relationship between the predictor variables and the target variable. Hence, they do not require a specific mapping function. This implies that nonparametric algorithms can be trained to model complex and salient relationships between the predictors and the response variable. Because they learn the mapping function directly from the data itself, nonparametric algorithms typically require more observations than parametric algorithms. Common types of nonparametric algorithms include decision trees (DT), random forests (RF), and Support Vector Machines (SVM).

Decision Tree

The decision tree algorithm is a type of supervised learning algorithm that makes predictions or classifications through hierarchical segmentation of the predictor variables. Each segmentation (node) is determined by a splitting rule such that the classification yields the best assessment measure when the splitting rule is applied to the validation data set. These measures (also known as impurity functions) include entropy, the Gini coefficient, misclassification error, and information gains.

In the decision tree framework, the objective is to classify our unknown outcome with a k-dimensional vector of features x (which might include both real $(x_j \in \mathbb{R})$ and/or categorical data $(x_j \in \mathbb{C})$ into one of the classes of the set $y = \{1, 2, ... n\}$. This is done by training the algorithms on the collection of data $S = \{(y_{t+1}, x_{1,t}, x_{2,t}, \ .\ .\ ., x_{k,t}); t = 1, .\ .\ ., T\}$. At each node, the algorithm decides on the variable to split on and the location of the split that minimizes the selected impurity measure. This task is then performed recursively until some stopping rule is satisfied.

Overall, the classifier divides the predictors x into v disjoint nodes, $\{G_1, ..., G_v\}$. Let

$p(q\,|\,r) = \dfrac{1}{n_r}\sum_{x_i \in G_r} 1\{y_{t+1} = q\}$ be the proportion of the qth class at the rth leaf node of the tree

and n_r the number of observations at the leaf node r. Then our classifier can be written as:

$$h(x) = \arg\max_q p(q\,|\,r), \text{ where } x \in G_r \qquad (7.6)$$

Furthermore, let $l_s(h) = \dfrac{\left|\{i \in [n] : h(x_t) \neq y_{t+1}\}\right|}{n}$ denote the proportion of y_{t+1} that is

misclassified in the training data set S and $R(l_s)$ represent a strictly convex type of impurity function of the empirical error. Then for $n = 2$ classes, $(\text{i.e. } y_{t+1} = 1 \text{ or } y_{t+1} = 0)$, the optimal classification rule for the decision tree with M number of leaf nodes is achieved by finding the $h^*(x)$ that minimizes the regularized impurity function shown below:

$$\underset{h(x)}{\text{argmin}} \sum_{r=1}^{|M|} R_r(l_s) + \lambda |M| \tag{7.7}$$

where λ is the tuning parameter for model complexity. If we select the misclassification rate as our impurity function, then $R_r(l_s) = 1 - \max_r(p(q|r))$ at the rth leaf node. Hence, the goal of the objective function of the decision tree is to find the splitting rule that minimizes the empirical classification errors.

The decision tree generates the classification of the response variable using a sequential set of splitting rules (starting from the root node) that are designed to achieve some optimization goal (for example, homogeneity of the observations in each group after the split). Each split is done using the feature variable (decision node) and each branch represents a decision rule. The culmination of all splitting rules is the terminal node (leaf node), which represents the outcome of the sequence of decision rules. Another way to think of the decision tree is as a flow chart, with a sequence of decision points that culminates in a classification or prediction decision of the values of the response variable.

The HPSPLIT Procedure

The HPSPLIT procedure is a high-performance procedure for building decision tree-based models for classification and regressions in SAS. Classification trees are used for modeling categorical response variables, while regression trees are used to model continuous variables. The splitting rules available in the procedure include impurity functions (such as entropy, the Gini coefficient, and residual sum of squares) and statistical tests (such as Chi-square, F test, and CHAID).

The PROC HPSPLIT statement is accompanied by a large number of options that fall into two categories. The basic options (such as DATA, which specifies the predictor data set; INTERVALBINS, which specifies the number of bins for continuous variables; the CVCC, which requests a table for the results of the cost-complexity pruning; NODES, which requests a table that describes the nodes of the final tree; and NSURROGATE, which specifies the number of surrogate rules to apply) consist of general hyperparameters for the estimation and options to control the outputs from the estimation. The splitting options (such as ASSIGNMISSING, which specifies how missing values in the predictor variables are handled; the MAXBRANCH, which specifies the maximum number of leaves per node; and the MAXDEPTH, which specifies the maximum depth of the tree) consist of hyperparameters that control the tree splitting process.

The CLASS statement is used to specify which of the predictor variables should be treated as a categorical variable. The CODE statement serves the same purpose as in other HP procedures. The GROW statement specifies the criterion for growing the tree. This is the loss function that the algorithm attempts to minimize as it grows the tree. The MODEL Statement specifies the target variable and its predictors, while the OUTPUT statement specifies the data set where the predictions of the algorithm and the matching ID variables in the input data are stored. The PRUNE statement specifies the method for pruning the maximal tree into the final subtree. The pruning option includes C45, Cost Complexity, and reduced errors such as Misclassification or Average Squared Errors. The RULES statement specifies the file where the rules for the final tree should be saved.

SAS Enterprise Miner

Drag and drop the HP Tree node onto your diagram. Connect it to the output port of your data partition node. In the Properties panel, set the Nominal Target Criterion to Entropy, Use Input Once to Yes, the Minimum Leaf Size to 1, and the Surrogate Rule to zero. Also, set the Subtree Method to Assessment and the Selection Method to Automatic. Finally, set the Nominal Target Assessment to Misclassification and the Minimum Subtree to Yes. Update the path and then run the node after the path has been updated.

SAS Studio

Click the ＋▾ icon in your process flow. Then select SAS Program to create a programming node in your process flow. Connect the input port of the node to the output port of your Partition data node. Double-click the node. Copy and paste the SAS program below into the Code area, then run it. Click the Node tab and type in HP Tree in the Name area. Save your Process Flow
▸ Run   🖫 🖳 .

Program 7.5: Classifying Stock Price Movement Using PROC HPSPLIT

```
/*Classifying Stock Market Directions Using HP Decision Tree Procedure*/
ods graphics on;
proc hpsplit data=emsas.spxrawp  maxbranch=2 splitonce
      intervalbins=100 maxdepth=10 mincatsize=1 mindist=0.01 alpha=0.2 leafsize=1
nsurrogates=0
      assignmissing=popular;
      id dates partition;
      class target;
      model target = &var_list.;
      grow entropy;
```

```
/*Prune based on misclassification and select subtree with lowest misclassification*/
        prune  misc / min;
        partition rolevar=partition(train='1' validate='2');
        code file ="%sysfunc(pathname(work))/splitscore.sas";
        rules file="%sysfunc(pathname(work))/rules.txt";
        output out=ptreeout;
        ods output treePerformance=treestats;
run;

/*Comparing Predictions with Actual Outcome*/
proc sort data=ptreeout; by dates; run;

data treeout;
merge ptreeout emsas.spxraw;
by dates;

/********************************
Same code as Program 7.2B
********************************/

        if (Pred < 0.5) then
                P_Target = 0;
        else P_Target = 1;
    format Classification $10. Role $9. Model $15.;
    if (Target = P_Target) then Classification = 'Correct';
        else Classification = 'Incorrect';
        if Partition = '1' then
                Role ='Train';
        else Role ='Validate';
    if P_Target = 1 and Target=1 then TP=1; else TP='';
    if P_Target = 1 and Target=0 then FP=1; else FP='';
    if P_Target = 0 and Target=1 then FN=1; else FN='';
    if P_Target = 0 and Target=0 then TN=1; else TN='';
    label TP='True Positive' FP='False Positive' FN='False Negative' TN='True Negative';

  Model='HP Tree';
run;
```

Notice in the SAS code that the NSURROGATE option is set to zero, MAXBRANCH is set to 2, SPLITONCE is requested, and missing values are to be assigned to the largest leaf (ASSIGNMISSING=POPULAR). GROW ENTROPY requests that the tree should be grown using entropy. The PRUNE MISC/MIN request that the tree should be pruned to minimize the misclassification rate. The files for the scoring code and splitting rules are both saved in the physical location of the WORK library.

Results

Notice in Output 7.5A that the algorithm continues to build the tree until the maximum depth (10) is reached. Although it is not showing in the output, the tree at this depth has over 100 nodes and 54 leaves. In reality, if the maximum depth had not been set to 10, it would have continued splitting the tree until it could not find a split to reduce the impurity any further.[6] As shown on the Misclassification Rate Pruning Plot, the maximum depth (10) would lead to a tree that overfits the training data but cannot be generalized to the other data set such as the validation data set. While the tree continues to fit better to the training data after 33 leaves, the misclassification rate for the validation data starts to increase beyond this point. Hence, the full tree was pruned back to the tree shown in Output 7.5B.

Output 7.5A: Misclassification Rate Pruning

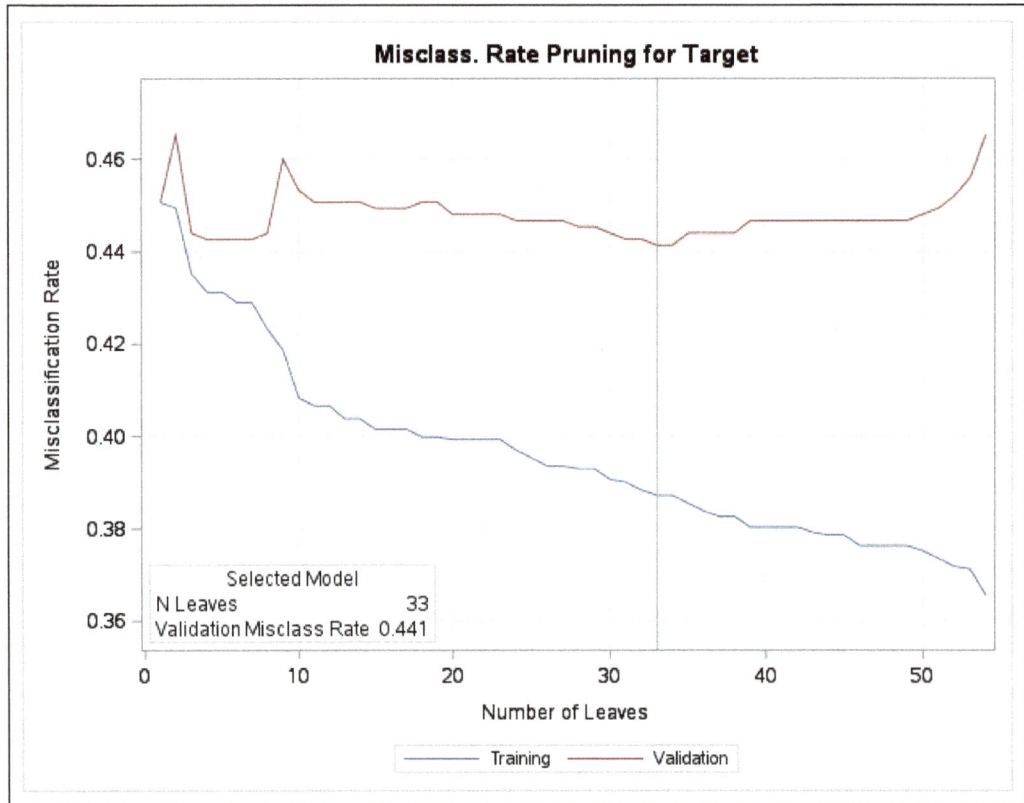

---

[6] Without the depth restriction, the maximum depth of the tree would have been 24 with over 317 leaves. This explains why the decision tree algorithm is sometime referred to as a "greedy algorithm." It continues to choose the locally optimal outcome at each step until it runs out optimal choices to select. The problem with this approach is that the sequence of local optimal choices may not necessarily lead to a global set of optimal choices if the algorithm is not properly calibrated. This is why the fully constructed decision tree is often pruned using the desired optimal global criterion.

Output 7.5B: Pruned Decision Tree from PROC HPSPLIT

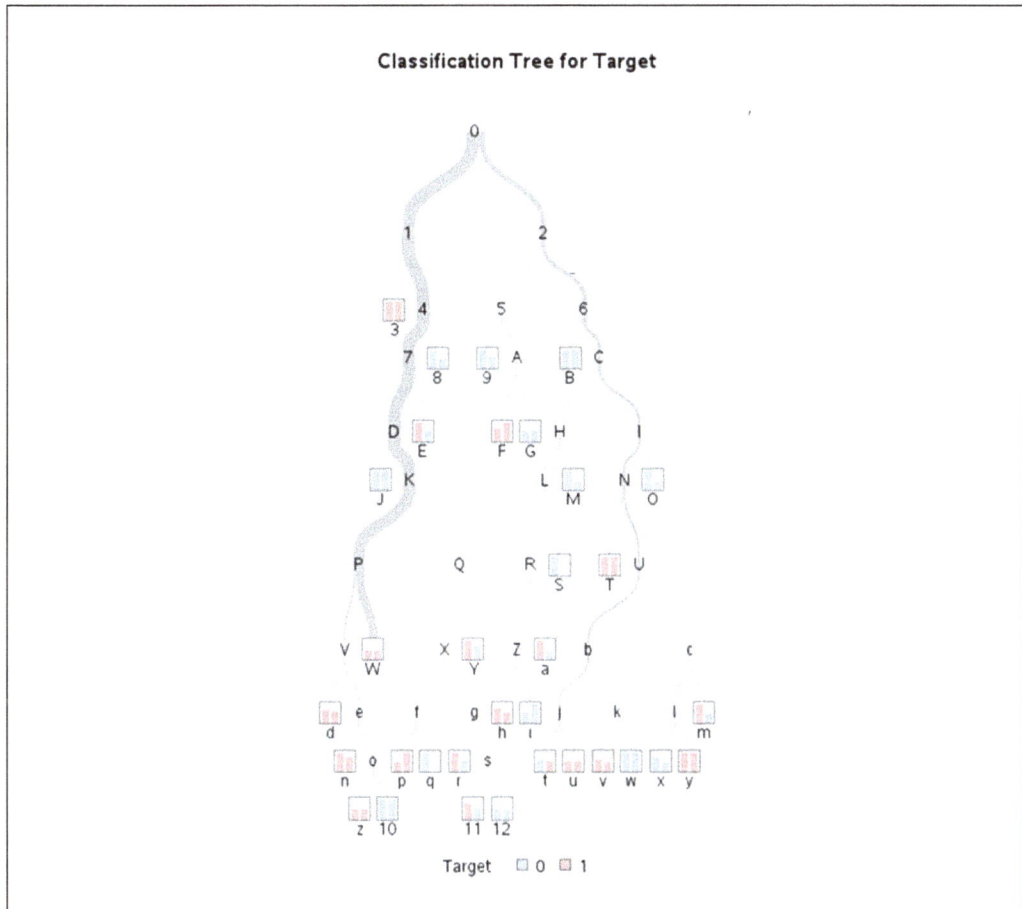

Classification Tree for Target

The classification tree shown in Output 7.5B has 65 nodes and 33 leaves.[7] The bar charts in each leaf (represented by the boxes with colored graphs) show the proportion of actual observations for each target classification in the training and validation data set. For example, the bar charts in the terminal leaf at the third node suggest that 100% of the observations in both the training and validation data have the target value=1. The splitting rule followed by the algorithm to arrive at these classifications can be found in the RULES.TXT file. You can also request the Node Information table (shown in Output 7.5C) by accompanying the PROC HSPLIT statement with a NODES=DETAIL option.

---

[7] Shown in the Information Table, which is not included. You can verify this by counting the number of boxes on the tree with colored graphs.

To arrive at node=3,[8] the algorithm first splits the data based on whether the percent change in net money flow from non-block trades is less than or greater than 7.17%. Days with less than 7.17% are split into the third node. It then conducts a final split at node=3 based on whether the percent change in initial jobless claims is less than or greater than 9.9%. The next trading day after a day with more than a 10% drop in initial jobless claims is then classified as a positive stock market day.[9]

The width of the branches shows the proportion of observations that go into each node after a split has occurred. Notice that the nodes on the left (starting with node=1) have thicker widths down to node=W. The W node has 870 and 382 observations from the training and validation data sets, respectively. This is about half of all observations in both data sets.

Output 7.5C: Abbreviated Node Information from PROC HPSPLIT

		Node Information					
			Training Data			Validation Data	
ID	Path	Count	0	1	Count	0	1
0	Root Node	1751	0.4506	0.5494 *	750	0.4507	0.5493
1	Root Node	1751	0.4506	0.5494	750	0.4507	0.5493
	CMF_NET_NON_BLCK < 0.0716704 or Missing	1223	0.4285	0.5715 *	543	0.4420	0.5580
2	Root Node	1751	0.4506	0.5494	750	0.4507	0.5493
	CMF_NET_NON_BLCK >= 0.0716704	528	0.5019 *	0.4981	207	0.4734	0.5266
3	Root Node	1751	0.4506	0.5494	750	0.4507	0.5493
	CMF_NET_NON_BLCK < 0.0716704 or Missing	1223	0.4285	0.5715	543	0.4420	0.5580
	CINJCJC < -0.098817	8	0.0000	1.0000 *	1	0.0000	1.0000

The ranking of the predictor variables (based on the validation data set) in terms of their usefulness for classifying the next-day direction of the stock market is shown in the Variable Importance Table (shown in Output 7.5D). It turns out that they are mostly the same set of variables that were selected in the previous parametric models. Although it now includes two additional variables (the percent change in the 5-day Moving Average Price and the percent change in the US spot exchange rate).

---

[8] SAS uses base 62 convention to the name the nodes. The first 10 nodes (0-9), followed by the next 26 nodes (A-Z). The next 26 nodes are (a-z), then followed by (10-19), and then (1A-1Z), and so on. The last (65th) node on the tree is 12.

$$10(0-9)+26(A-Z)+26(a-z)+3(10-12) \ or \ 12 = 1(62 \ nodes)+2(3 \ nodes).$$

[9] You should note that initial jobless claims are released on a weekly basis, so most days will record 0 as the value for this variable. Furthermore, a 10% drop in initial claims is a rare event, hence the low number of observations recorded at this node (8 in the training data set and 1 in the validation data set).

Output 7.5D: Variable Importance from PROC HPSPLIT

		Training		Validation		Relative	
Variable	Variable Label	Relative	Importance	Relative	Importance	Ratio	Count
CPX_OPEN	Open Price	0 7210	2 1328	1 0000	1 3309	1 3870	2
CINJCJC	Initial Jobless Claims Index	0 7458	2 2061	0 9981	1 3284	1 3384	2
CHIST_CALL_IMP_VOL	Hist Call Implied Volatility	0 9570	2 8309	0 8512	1 1329	0 8895	3
CMOV_AVG_5D	Moving Average 5 Day	0 9646	2 8533	0 6736	0 8966	0 6984	3
CFXRATE	US Spot Forex Index	1 0000	2 9581	0 6231	0 8293	0 6231	2
CLEI	Leading Economic Indicator Index	0 5446	1 6109	0 5862	0 7802	1 0765	1
CPE_RATIO	Price Earnings Ratio (P/E)	0 7325	2 1669	0 4305	0 5730	0 5877	2
CMF_NET_BLCK	Money Flow Net-Block	0 9441	2 7927	0 0000	0	0 0000	2

Output 7.5E: Abbreviated Node Information from PROC HPSPLIT

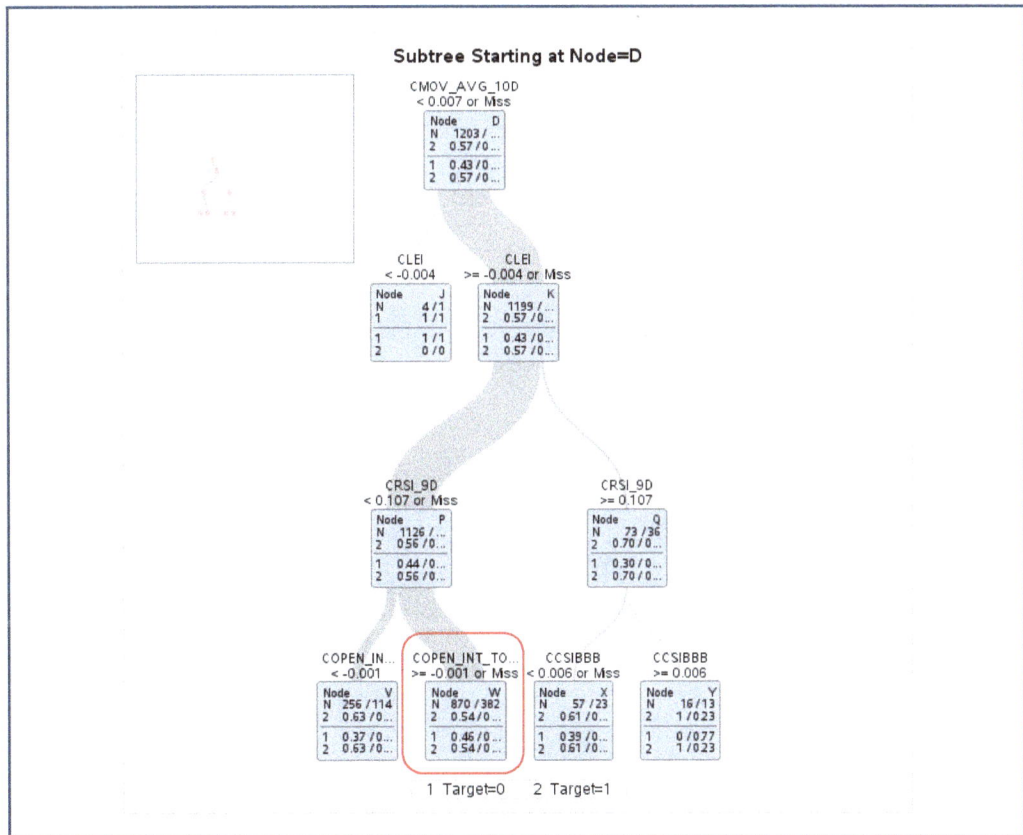

You can conduct a further drill-down assessment of the tree by selecting subtrees from the main tree. By default, a subtree starting at the root node is displayed by the procedure (as shown in Output 7.5E). However, you can request the subtree plot to start at any node of your choice and for up to the number of available branches. For example, a customized subtree plot that starts at the fifth and up to three sub-branches can be requested using the PLOT=(ZOOMEDTREE(NODE=('D') DEPTH=3). On the customized plot, you can view the number of observations in each node for both the training and validation data set, as well as the distribution of the target variable based on the splitting rule that created the node. For example, in Node W, there are 870 and 382 days in the training and validation data sets, respectively. Approximately 54% of the 870 days in the training data set are positive stock market days, while 46% are not.

Support Vector Machine

The support vector machine (SVM) is a machine learning algorithm that uses hyperplanes in *n*-dimensional space to predict or classify events of interest. The SVM algorithm attempts to fit the best separation lines through the *n*-1 dimensional space and within a threshold value (margin) that yields the best classifications using linear or nonlinear transformation of the input variables. These transformations are achieved using kernel functions.

Figure 7.7: SVM Hyperplanes in Two-Dimensional Plane

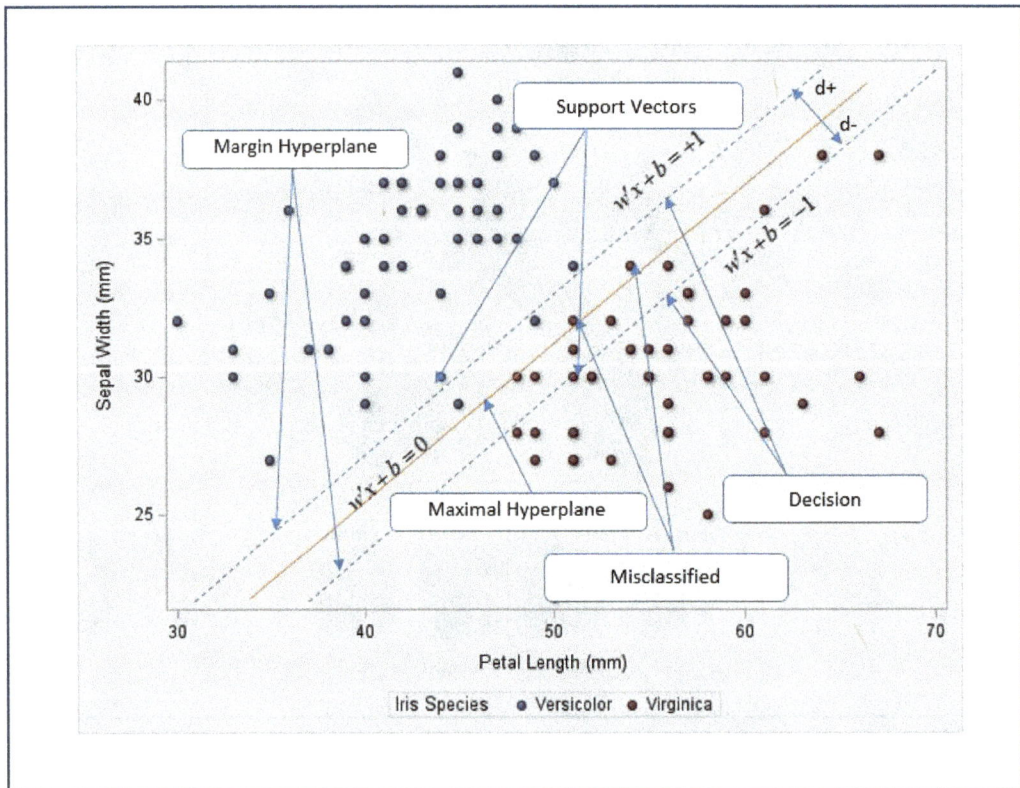

Let us denote $y_i = \pm 1$ as the prediction of the direction of the price movement of the S&P 500 tomorrow, where $y_i = +1$ if the index rises on the next trading day and $y_i = -1$ if the index falls on the next trading day. Then our classifier can be specified as any separating hyperplane function of x_i such as:

$$h(x_i) = sign(w'x_i + b)$$ (7.8)

where w is a classification vector that is normal to the hyperplane and b is the bias term. $y_i = +1$ when $w'x_i + b \geq +1$ and $y_i = -1$ when $w'x_i + b \leq -1$. The optimization problem in SVM is to find the normalizing vector w and bias term b that maximizes the distance (margin) between the closest points (support vectors) on the separating hyperplanes. In reality, the hard margin linear classifier $h(x_i)$ shown above is only optimal if the training data are linearly separable.[10]

Furthermore, in its current form, the objective function is difficult to optimize because observations may not be linearly separable, or some observations may not lie on the correct side of the separating hyperplane as shown in Figure 7.7. Hence the classification problem in SVM is typically formulated as a constrained optimization problem that maximizes the margin $\left[\max \gamma(w,b)\right]$ subject to the constraint that all observations must lie on the correct side of the hyperplane $\left[y_i\left(\hat{w}'x_i + \hat{b}\right) \geq 1\right]$.

$$\max_{w,b} \gamma(w,b) \ s.t. \ y_i\left(\hat{w}'x_i + \hat{b}\right) \geq 1$$ (7.9)

We note here that the distance between the hyperplane is maximized when the norm $\|w\|$ is minimized since the geometric distance between a point x and the decision boundary is $\frac{b}{\|w\|}$. Hence, the objective function $\gamma(w,b)$ is often rescaled and rewritten as a minimization function of the norm $\min_{w,b}\|w'w\|$. Furthermore, we can relax the constraint that all observations lie on the correct side of the hyperplane by respecifying the constrained optimization as an unconstrained minimization problem with a soft margin. This entails replacing the constraint with a hinge loss function that is specified as $\max(0, 1 - y_i(w'x_i + b))$. $\lambda\|w'w\|$ now becomes a penalty function as shown in the equation below. Given a hinge loss function defined above, the optimal SVM classifier for the prediction of the next day direction of the S&P500 index can then be written as:

---

[10] All observations of the response variables with same classification lie below or above the appropriate separating hyperplane.

$$\underset{w,b}{\arg\min}\left[C\sum_{t=1}^{n}\max\left(0,1-y_{i}\left(w'x_{i}+b\right)\right)+\lambda\left\|w'w\right\|\right] \qquad (7.10)$$

λ is a tuning parameter, which determines the trade-off between model complexity and the correct fit to the data, and C is a weight parameter. The SVM is inherently a linear learning algorithm; therefore, linearly inseparable data must be transformed to make them linear. This typically requires some nonlinear combination of the data and a mapping function to project the data onto a higher dimensional space where they can be linearly separable. This approach is computationally expensive. The kernel trick avoids the need to explicitly map the data to the high-dimensional plane using the two-step computation. Instead, it employs kernel functions that directly lead to the same results without the need for extensive computation. Suppose the classification vector W can be defined as the dot product of the feature variables x_t such that

$$w^{*}=\sum_{i}^{n}\alpha_{i}y_{i}x_{i}\ .[11]$$

For linearly inseparable data, we can project the expression in Equation (7.10) onto a higher dimensional space by replacing the terms in the equation with the kernel transformation of the normalizing vector as shown below:

$$h(x_{i})=sign\left(\sum_{i=1}^{n}\alpha_{t}^{*}y_{i}k\left(x_{i},x_{j}\right)+b\right) \qquad (7.11)$$

where α_{i} are weights assigned to each observation in the training data set during the optimization by the algorithm. Unused observations are assigned weights $\alpha_{i}=0$, while used observations are assigned weights $\alpha_{i}>0$. Although the SVM does not directly compute the probability $p(y_{t+1}=1\,|\,x_{t})$, it can be inferred from the classification score obtained from Equation (7.1) using the logistic link function.

---

[11] Plugging in for w in Equation (7.10) results in the $sign\left(\sum_{i}\alpha_{i}y_{i}x_{i}'x_{j}+b\right)$. We can respecify the dot product $x_{i}'x_{j}$ in high-dimensional space using the kernel trick that denotes $k\left(x_{i},x_{j}\right)=\varphi\left(x_{i}\right)\varphi\left(x_{j}\right)$. Common kernel functions include the linear: $K\left(u,v\right)=u'v$, polynomial: $K\left(u,v\right)=\left(u'v+1\right)^{p}$, radial basis: $K\left(u,v\right)=exp\left[-p\left(u-v\right)2\right]$, and sigmoid: $K\left(u,v\right)=tanh\left[p*\left(u^{T}v\right)+q\right]$, where p is the kernel scale parameter and q is the kernel location parameter, and u and v are successive data points in the sample.

Figure 7.8: Optimal SVM Hyperplane After Projecting Data onto Three-Dimensional Plane

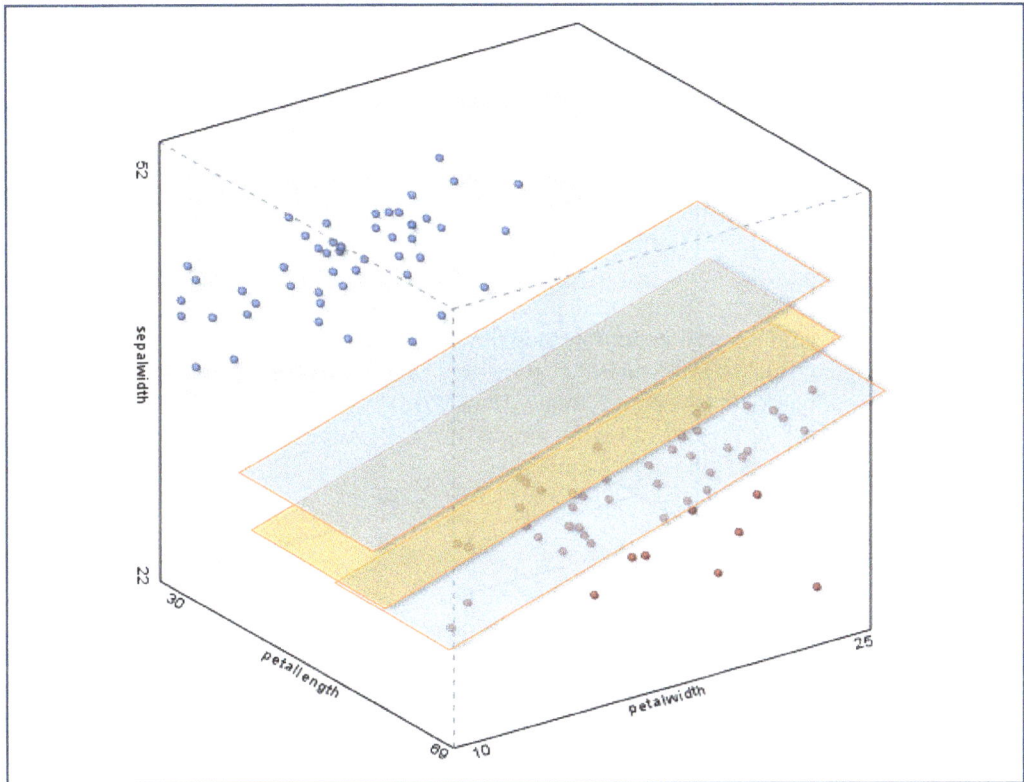

In review, the objective of the SVM is to find the kernel space $h^*(x_i)$ that maximizes the distance in the separation hyperplane. This is done by projecting the data onto a high dimensional space (as shown in Figure 7.8) using kernel transformation of the data, such that the data can then be linearly separable using the hyperplane. The optimization then attempts to find the hyperplane boundaries between the data that best minimizes a predefined loss function.

SVM is another type of black box algorithm. In reality, projecting a vector of n-dimensional features onto higher-dimensional spaces will lead to a significant loss in interpretability. Although the conceptual framework of SVM is relatively straightforward in the sense that it applies some discriminating functions to separate the classes, trying to extract the marginal contribution of each predictor to the discriminating vector is much harder due to the kernel transformation that is required to project the vectors onto the higher dimension. Users will have to rely on the fit statistics to gauge how well the algorithm performs the classification or apply newer methods such as partial dependence and individual conditional expectation plots, or the Local

Interpretable Method-Agnostic Explanation (LIME) and Kernel SHAP values. These features are currently not available in SAS Studio and Enterprise Miner but are available in the SAS Viya platform.[12]

The HPSVM Procedure

The HPSVM procedure is a high-performance procedure for modeling categorical response variables using the SVM approach. The procedures support both continuous and categorical input variables. The HPSVM statement includes options for specifying the two types of optimization technique it supports (namely: Interior Points [IPOINT] and Active Sets [ACTIVESET]),[13] as well as the penalty value (C=), which must be greater than 0. The KERNEL statement specifies the types of kernel functions that the algorithm should use. The default kernel function is the linear kernel function (LINEAR). Other kernel functions include the polynomial (POLYNOM), the radial basis (RBF), and the sigmoid (SIGMOID). The INPUT statement specifies the list and types of variables using the LEVEL option (NOMINAL or INTERVAL). The TARGET statement names the target variable whose values PROC HPSVM tries to predict. The target variable must be binary and different from the variables in the INPUT statement.

SAS Enterprise Miner

Drag and drop the HP SVM node onto your diagram. Connect it to the output port of your data partition node. In the Properties panel, set the penalty to 20, then click on the ellipsis next to the Interior Point Options. Change the value of the Kernel Property to Polynomial and the Polynomial Degree to 3. Update the path and then run the node after the path has been updated.

SAS Studio

Click the + icon in your process flow. Then select SAS Program to create a programming node in your process flow. Connect the input port of the node to the output port of your Partition data node. Double-click the node. Copy and paste the SAS program below into the Code area, then run it. Click the Node tab and type in "HP SVM" in the Name area. Save your Process Flow

► Run

---

[12] The discussion of these concepts is beyond the scope of this book. However, you can learn more about model interpretability using these methods by visiting SAS interpretability blog at https://blogs.sas.com/content/tag/interpretability/ or reviewing a 2018 SAS Global Forum Proceeding's paper by Ray Wright at https://support.sas.com/resources/papers/proceedings18/1950-2018.pdf.

[13] We will discuss the interior point and active set method in Chapters Eight and Nine where optimization methods are presented.

Program 7.6: Classifying Stock Price Movement Using PROC HPSVM

```
/*Classifying Stock Market Direction Using HP Support Vector Machines Procedure*/
ods graphics on;
proc hpsvm data=emsas.spxrawp method=ipoint;
        id dates partition;
        input &var_list. /level=interval;
        kernel polynom/ degree=3;
        target target/;
        penalty C=20.0;
        partition  rolevar=partition(validate='2');
        code file ="%sysfunc(pathname(work))/svmscore.sas";
        output out=psvmout;
        ods output fitstatistics=svmstats;
run;

/*Comparing Prediction to Actual Outcomes*/
proc sort data=psvmout;
        by dates;
run;

data svmout;
        merge psvmout emsas.spxraw;
        by dates;
        /*****************************
        Same code as 7.2B
        *****************************/
        if (Pred < 0.5) then
                P_Target = 0;
        else P_Target = 1;
        format Classification $10. Role $9. Model $15.;

        if (Target = P_Target) then
                Classification = 'Correct';
        else Classification = 'Incorrect';

        if Partition = '1' then
                Role ='Train';
        else Role ='Validate';

        if P_Target = 1 and Target=1 then
                TP=1;
        else TP='';

        if P_Target = 1 and Target=0 then
                FP=1;
        else FP='';

        if P_Target = 0 and Target=1 then
                FN=1;
        else FN='';

        if P_Target = 0 and Target=0 then
                TN=1;
        else TN='';
        label TP='True Positive' FP='False Positive' FN='False Negative' TN='True Negative'
        Model='HP SVM';
run;
```

The KERNEL=POLYNOM/DEGREE=3 statement specifies that a third-degree polynomial kernel should be used to transform the data into a higher dimension. The PENALTY statement and the option C=20 are used to specify the maximum penalty value of 20. A lower penalty value increases the number of constraint violations, which reduces the accuracy of the model.

Results

Output 7.6 shows the fit statistics from the HP SVM Node in SAS Enterprise Miner. There are 1,537 support vectors, with 1,374 vectors lying on the margin. The norm of the longest vector is 33.22 and the value of the bias terms is 15.69. The large decline in the accuracy, error, sensitivity, and specificity of the model algorithm shows a higher propensity to overfit the training data, relative to the validation data. Since the SVM is a black box algorithm, we will revisit the fit statistics shortly, in the model comparison section.

Output 7.6: Fit Statistics from HP SVM Node

Description	Train		Validation
Number of Observations Read		2501	
Number of Observations Used		1741	742
Number of Input Interval Variables		24	
Number of Input Class Variables		0	
Number of Input Class Variable Levels		0	
Number of Effects		24	
Columns in Data Matrix		24	
Columns in Kernel Matrix		2925	
Inner Product of Weights		1926.942	
Bias		-15.6846	
Total Slack (Constraint Violations)		1353.884	
Norm of Longest Vector		33.21969	
Number of Support Vectors		1537	
Number of Support Vectors on Margin		1374	
Maximum F		7.055144	
Minimum F		-15.5808	
Accuracy		0.633544	0.559299
Error		0.366456	0.440701
Sensitivity		0.902413	0.844828
Specificity		0.308376	0.214286

Random Forest

The random forest algorithm is a nonparametric supervised learning algorithm that builds an ensemble of independent and identically distributed decision trees. The algebraic derivation of the mathematical expression of the random forest is beyond the scope of this book. However, the general logic of the procedure is relatively straightforward to describe. The random forest approach collects predictions or classifications for the target variable from a collection of randomly created decision trees. The trees are constructed using various subsets of the data and feature variables. To ensure that the trees are uncorrelated, the random forest uses bagging and feature randomness. The final prediction or classification for the target variable is made by voting and the cumulation of the predictions of the individual trees.

Random Forest is particularly prone to overfitting the training data as you will see in the results section. Therefore, it is important to carefully tune the hyperparameters of the algorithm during the training process. This might require you to iteratively estimate and perform some model diagnostics before arriving at the final random forest model. Random Forest is also a black box model in the sense that there is not a lot of transparency in terms of the marginal effects of the predictor variables on the classification outcome. While we can derive the summative importance of each variable in arriving at a classification, we cannot visualize the splitting rules from the algorithm in the same way as we would using the decision tree algorithm.

The HPFOREST Procedure

The HPFOREST procedure is a high-performance procedure that gathers predictions or classifications from a collection of distinctly created decision trees. Independence between the trees is derived by randomly selecting a collection of input variables into each tree and randomly sampling the observations that are used to construct the trees.

The options that accompany PROC HPFOREST, which is the SAS statement that invokes the procedure, include ALPHA, which specifies the p-value for the test of association of a potential predictor with the target variable; BALANCE=YES|NO, which specifies whether the splitting criterion should ensure that the observations in each target class are equal; CATBINS, which specifies the maximum number of categories to allocate to nominal predictor variables in implementing the association test; and VARS_TO_TRY, which specifies the number of variables to try when splitting nodes in each tree. Other options include IMPORTANCE, which is used to request the variable importance, and INBAGN, which specifies how many observations should be used to train each tree. Alternatively, you could specify that a fraction of the observation should be used to train each tree by using INBAGFRACTION or TRAINFRACTION.[14] PRUNEFRACTION, which specifies the fraction of training observations that can be used to prune trees, and SCOREPROLE, which specifies the collections of observations that should be used to make predictions for new observations. This could be all the values that have the same roles (DEFAULT), all observations in the INBAG sample (INBAG), out-of-bag sample (OOB), or in the validation data set (VALID). The TARGET statement specifies the target variable, while the INPUT statement specifies the list of predictor variables. The SCORE statement saves the predicted values and ID variables into a SAS data set, while the SAVE statement is used to specify the file name and the location to save the scoring code created by the procedure.

SAS Enterprise Miner

Drag and drop the HP Forest node onto your diagram. Connect it to the output port of your data partition node. In the Properties panel, set the Number of Variables to Consider to 10, the Proportion of OBS to 0.3, and the Maximum Depth to 10. We will apply the default settings in the Properties panel for the rest of our hyperparameters and model options. Go ahead and update the path and then run the node after the path has been updated.

---

[14] Although INBAGN and (INBAGFRACTION or TRAINFRACTION) achieve the same objective, they are mutually exclusive and cannot be specified together. Doing so will result in an error message.

SAS Studio

Click the ➕▾ icon in your process flow. Then select SAS Program to create a programming node in your process flow. Connect the input port of the node to the output port of your Partition data node. Double-click the node. Copy and paste the SAS program below into the Code area, then run it. Click the Node tab and type "HP Forest" in the Name area. Save your Process Flow

▶ Run 🖫 🖳 .

Program 7.7: Classifying Stock Price Movement Using PROC HPFOREST

```
/*Classifying Stock Market Directions Using HP Random Forest Procedure*/
ods graphics on;

proc hpforest data=emsas.spxrawp
        maxtrees=100 vars_to_try=10 seed=12345 inbagfraction=0.3
        maxdepth=10 leafsize=1 alpha=0.05 scoreprole=oob;
        id dates partition;
        target target/level=binary;
        input &var_list. /level=interval; /* Macrovariable list*/
        partition rolevar=partition(train='1' validate='2');
        save file ="%sysfunc(pathname(work))/forestscore.sas";
        score out=pforestout;
        ods output fitstatistics=pforeststats modelinfo=forestinfo;
run;

/*SAS Code to the obtain the fit statistics for the selected number of trees*/
data _null;
        set forestinfo(where=(parameter='Actual Trees'));
        call symput("treenum",setting);
run;

data foreststats;
        set pforeststats(where=(Ntrees=&treenum));
run;

/*Comparing Prediction to Actual Outcomes*/
proc sort data=pforestout;        by dates;run;
proc sort data=emsas.spxrawp; by dates;run;

data forestout;
        merge pforestout emsas.spxrawp;
        by dates;
/*****************************
Same code as Program 7.2B
*********************************/

        if (Pred < 0.5) then
                P_Target = 0;
        else P_Target = 1;
    format Classification $10. Role $9. Model $15.;
```

```
    if (Target = P_Target) then Classification = 'Correct';
       else Classification = 'Incorrect';
       if Partition = '1' then
              Role ='Train';
       else Role ='Validate';
    if P_Target = 1 and Target=1 then TP=1; else TP='';
    if P_Target = 1 and Target=0 then FP=1; else FP='';
    if P_Target = 0 and Target=1 then FN=1; else FN='';
    if P_Target = 0 and Target=0 then TN=1; else TN='';
    label TP='True Positive' FP='False Positive' FN='False Negative' TN='True Negative'
       model='HP Forest';
run;
```

Many of the options that we show in the code are the default values of the hyperparameters of the model. It is shown here to highlight how they can be tuned to improve the fit of the model to the data. However, we will set the INBAGFRACTION to 0.3, the MAXDEPTH to 10, and SCOREPROLE=OOB. The ODS table for the FITSTATISTICS statement generates fit statistics for the collections of all forest samples created. In the following DATA step, we first extract the ID for the forest that was eventually used for the predictions and classification, from the ODS table called MODELINFO. A macrovariable (&TREENUM) is then assigned to the row name ACTUAL TREES. The values of the fit statistic for the actual tree in the FITSTATISTICS table are then called up in the subsequent DATA step that was used to create the FORESTSTATS table.

Results

Output 7.7A shows the plot of the misclassification rates for the series of trees. Notice how the misclassification for the training data dropped significantly after about 10 trees. In contrast, the misclassification rates for the validation and OOB data stayed relatively the same as the number of trees in the forest grew. Remember that the random forest performs classification using bootstrapped samples of the trees in the forest. Since the law of large numbers states that the sampling distribution of independently drawn samples from the same distribution will converge to its true population distribution, the averages of the predictions from the random forest are expected to converge to a limit as the number of trees in the forest increases. However, in terms of evaluating the accuracy of a model that should be generalized to new data, it is best to use either the validation or OOB data set to make such decisions (as specified in SCOREPROLE=OOB in the PROC HPFOREST statement).

Output 7.7A: Misclassification Rates and Number of Trees Using HP Forest Node

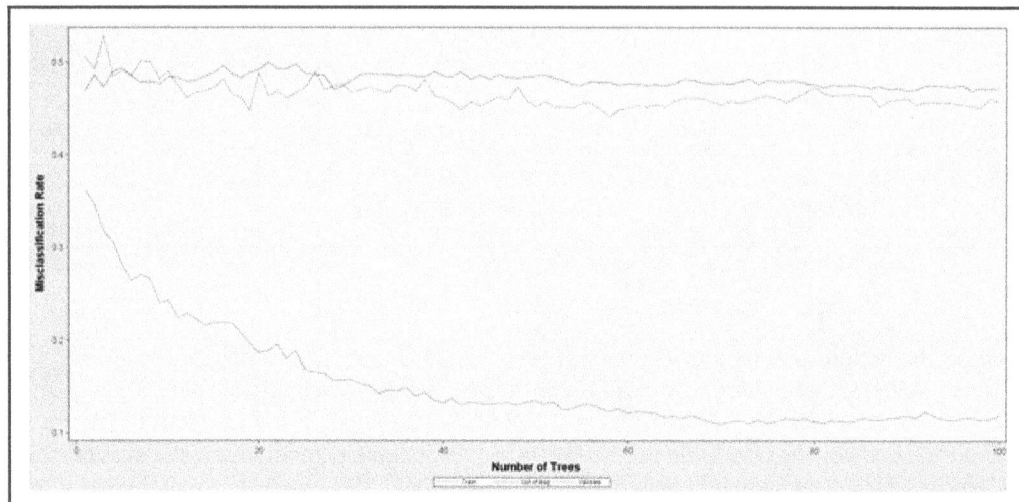

Output 7.7B shows the variable importance of the predictors using the Gini Impurity Index and Margin. The Gini Impurity Index compares the sum of the errors in the splitting rule without the variable in the model with the sum of the errors of the model with the variable included in the splitting rule. The greater the reduction in the errors, the more information value the variable has for predicting the target. Margin calculates the difference in the probability of true classification using the variable to the maximum probability of alternate classification. The logic behind this measure is that the greater the relevance of the variable in predicting the right classification, the greater its margin relative to the wrong classification. The variables are sorted in ascending order, from the lowest absolute values of the Gini and Margins to the highest absolute values. In this context, the lowest variables on the Loss Reduction Variable Importance table have the highest importance. A few of the variables at the bottom of the table were selected in the other models that we previously examined. These include the VIX volatility index, the open-to-open daily return, the open interest on put options on the index, and money flows, to name a few.

Output 7.7B: Variable Importance from PROC HPFOREST

		Loss Reduction Variable Importance					
Variable	Number of Rules	Gini	OOB Gini	Valid Gini	Margin	OOB Margin	Valid Margin
CFDTR	2	0.000024	-0.00002	-0.00003	0.000047	-0.00000	-0.00001
CLEI	98	0.001840	-0.00223	-0.00189	0.003680	-0.00068	-0.00040
CHIST_CALL_IMP_VOL	351	0.007128	-0.00747	-0.00662	0.014265	-0.00023	0.00059
CINJCJC	411	0.007263	-0.00805	-0.00598	0.014526	-0.00093	0.00091
CRSI_14D	711	0.012334	-0.01178	-0.01248	0.024667	0.00066	-0.00064
CPE_RATIO	740	0.013439	-0.01362	-0.01333	0.026877	-0.00010	-0.00049
CPX_LAST	950	0.016793	-0.01787	-0.01617	0.033587	-0.00091	0.00071
CHIST_PUT_IMP_VOL	948	0.018363	-0.02047	-0.01643	0.036726	-0.00178	0.00166
CRSI_3D	1197	0.021169	-0.02151	-0.02138	0.042338	-0.00054	-0.00045
CRSI_9D	1250	0.020576	-0.02179	-0.02054	0.041152	-0.00117	0.00042
CCSIBBB	1021	0.020043	-0.02227	-0.02039	0.040086	-0.00166	-0.00053
COPEN_INT_TOTAL_CALL	1262	0.023028	-0.02244	-0.02241	0.046065	0.00025	0.00013
CMOV_AVG_10D	1245	0.024686	-0.02301	-0.03055	0.049372	0.00168	-0.00502
CMOV_AVG_5D	1208	0.022225	-0.02374	-0.02200	0.044450	-0.00172	0.00039
CMF_NET_NON_BLCK	1227	0.024568	-0.02396	-0.02183	0.049136	0.00047	0.00247
CMF_NET_BLCK	1252	0.024340	-0.02405	-0.02168	0.048680	-0.00018	0.00307
CFXRATE	1234	0.024882	-0.02512	-0.02511	0.049765	-0.00006	-0.00027
CMOV_AVG_30D	1251	0.024028	-0.02633	-0.02421	0.048055	-0.00277	-0.00008
COPEN_INT_TOTAL_PUT	1424	0.025665	-0.02637	-0.02492	0.051330	-0.00067	0.00102
CPX_VOLUME	1555	0.027846	-0.02753	-0.02691	0.055692	0.00059	0.00128
CPX_OPEN	1588	0.028093	-0.02795	-0.02861	0.056187	-0.00054	-0.00090
CUSYC3M10	1825	0.030274	-0.03091	-0.03056	0.060547	-0.00052	-0.00032
CVIX	2174	0.034182	-0.03560	-0.03574	0.068364	-0.00045	-0.00101
CVOLATILITY_30D	2966	0.042310	-0.04074	-0.04139	0.084619	0.00150	0.00141

The Ensemble Model

The machine learning approach to modeling the relationships between variables is unconstrained by theory; thus, they provide more flexibility than the inferential statistical approach. For example, machine learning methods can infer the relationship between variables by combining the predictions obtained from multiple models and algorithms to yield potentially more accurate predictions. Predictions obtained from the combined (ensemble) model may be drawn from the cumulative votes or average predictions of all the algorithms fed into the ensemble model. Therefore, the final prediction from the ensemble model will arise out of the concordance or dissonance of the predictions of the algorithms that are fed into it. The ENSEMBLE node is only available in SAS Enterprise Miner; however, the SAS code to implement ensemble models can be written in SAS Studio.

SAS Enterprise Miner

Click the Model Tab. Then drag and drop the Ensemble node onto your diagram. Connect its input port to the output ports of the nodes of all of the previous models. We will apply the default settings in the properties panel for our estimation (Use the average of predicted probabilities). So go ahead and update the path and then run the node after the path has been updated.

> You must first run all five procedures (HPLOGISTICS, HPGENSELECT, HPNEURAL, HPSPLIT, and HPSVM) before invoking the Ensemble node or code because the ENSEMBLE.SAS program file will also call up the scoring code for these models. Each code is used to rescore the SPXRAWP data file to calculate the posterior probabilities of the events (1 and 0) for each model. It then calculates the posterior probabilities of the ensemble model by taking the averages of the posterior probabilities of the five models. Just like in the previous demonstrations, the scoring codes for the five models are saved in the physical location of your WORK library using the `"%sysfunc(pathname(work))/*******.sas"` macro. You will need to edit these lines in the ENSEMBLE.SAS file if you have changed the physical locations of your scoring code.

SAS Studio

Click the `+ˇ` icon in your process flow. Then select SAS Program to create a programming node in your process flow. Connect the input port of the node to the output ports of the nodes of all of the previous models. Double-click the node. Copy and paste the SAS program below into the code area, then run it. Click the Node tab and type "Ensemble" in the Name area. Save your Process Flow `► Run 🖫 🖳` .

Program 7.8: Classifying Stock Price Movements Using the ENSEMBLE Model

```
/*Classifying Stock Market Directions Using Ensemble Model*/
%datapull(Ensemble,Ensemble.sas);/*Pull Ensemble code file from GitHub*/

/*Ensemble Code includes scoring from previous models: HPLOGISTICS, HPGENSELECT, HPNEURAL,
HPTREE, HPSVM*/

data PEnsemble;
set emsas.spxrawp;
%include "%sysfunc(pathname(work))/Ensemble.sas";
/***Average of the posterior probabilities from the models is first calculated**
 **Classification is then performed using the 50% threshold***/
run;

/*Comparing Prediction to Actual Outcomes*/
data Ensembleout;
set PEnsemble;
```

```
/**********************************
Same code as Program 7.2B
**********************************/

   Model='Ensmbl';

        if (Pred < 0.5) then
                P_Target = 0;
        else P_Target = 1;
   format Classification $10. Role $9. Model $15.;
    if (Target = P_Target) then Classification = 'Correct';
        else Classification = 'Incorrect';
        if Partition = '1' then Role ='Train';
        else Role ='Validate';
   if P_Target = 1 and Target=1 then TP=1; else TP='';
   if P_Target = 1 and Target=0 then FP=1; else FP='';
   if P_Target = 0 and Target=1 then FN=1; else FN='';
   if P_Target = 0 and Target=0 then TN=1; else TN='';
   label TP='True Positive' FP='False Positive' FN='False Negative' TN='True Negative';
run;
```

The SAS code shown in Program 7.8 performs a series of tasks. First, it downloads the ENSEMBLE. SAS file from the book's GitHub repository and stores it in the physical location of your WORK library using the **%datapull** macro. The first DATA step then scores in the partitioned datafile SPXRAWP using the downloaded code by invoking the %INCLUDE statement. Because %INCLUDE is a global statement and global statements are not executable, the %INCLUDE statement cannot be used with conditional logic. Therefore, another DATA step is used to implement the conditional logic statements for classifying the direction of the stock market on the following day. In the same manner, as with other models, the code for classifying the outcome based on the estimated average probabilities are the same as those shown in Program 7.2B.

Results

Output 7.8 shows the percentages of the predicted events (positive stock market movement) and the percentage of nonevent (negative stock market movement) in both the training and validation data sets. The graphs show compact distributions of probabilities of obtaining either outcome. There were very few observations with a higher (lower) than 65% (35%) chance of a positive stock market outcome in both the training and validation data set. The same pattern is also evident for the negative stock market outcomes. The vast majority of the classifications done by the model are based on probabilities of positive and negative stock market outcomes that hover around the 50% range. This suggests a relatively low signal-to-noise ratio for classifying the direction of the stock market and further alludes to how difficult it is to predict the future direction of the stock market.

Output 7.8: Percentage of Events (Target=1) and Nonevents (Target=0) from Ensemble Node (Training)

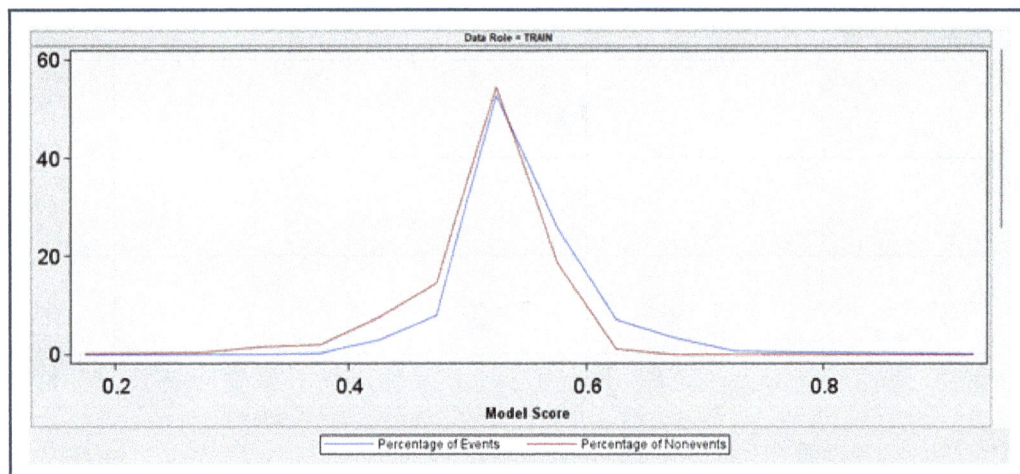

Output 7.8: Percentage of Events (Target=1) and Nonevents (Target=0) from Ensemble Node (Validation)

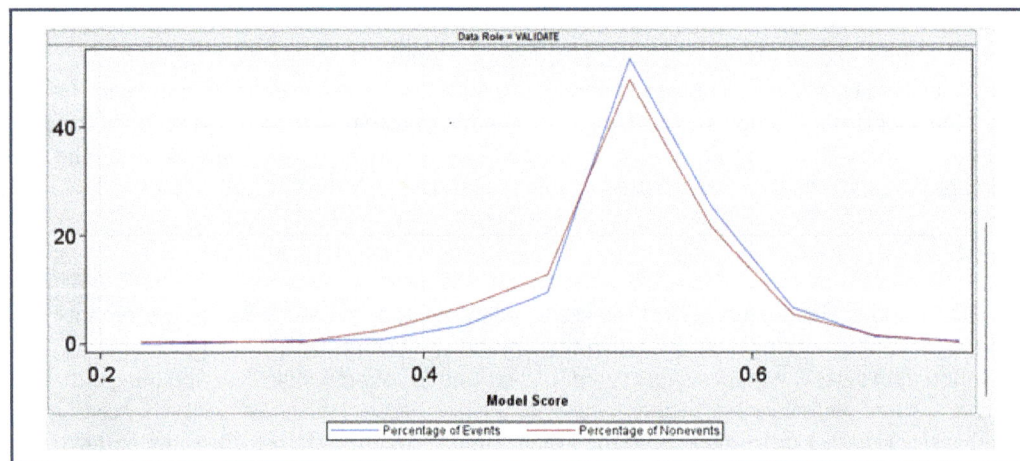

Unsupervised Learning Algorithms

Unsupervised learning algorithms are fed unlabeled data and tasked with discerning whether commonalities exist between them. What distinguishes this approach from other learning techniques is the minimal level of human intervention that is needed in the iterative process. The algorithm is essentially tasked with sifting through the data to find common patterns or hidden groupings that exist in it without prior knowledge of such structures or patterns.

Table 7.2: Unsupervised Learning Algorithms

Algorithm	Classical		High Performance	
	PROC Statement	EM Node	PROC Statement	EM Node
Variable Clustering	VARCLUS	Variable Clustering		
K-mean Clustering	CLUS	Cluster	HPCLUS	HP Cluster
Principal Component Analysis	PRINCOMP	Principal Component	HPPRINCOMP	HP Principal components
Binning	BINNING	Transform Variable	HPBIN	HP Transform

The optimization processes used by unsupervised learning algorithms are also similar to those used by supervised learning algorithms. The algorithms recursively regroup the data, such that each iteration increasingly leads to a further reduction in a specified loss function or an increase in a specified likelihood function until no further improvement in the desired objective can be attained. Although they are not often used for predictive or classification modeling, they can be used for portfolio construction or portfolio attribution.

In the previous section of this chapter, we discussed the optimization problems in factor analysis, and principal component analysis and showed how they can be used to create factors mimicking portfolios. In machine learning, unsupervised algorithms are typically used for cluster analysis (PROC HPCLUS) and dimensionality reduction (PROC HPPRINCOMP). The output from other dimension reduction algorithms (such as PROC HPBINNING and PROC HPVARCLUS) can also be fed as input to the predictive models. Although we will not go into much of the details of these procedures, you should experiment with them to see whether augmenting the supervised learning algorithm with inputs from the unsupervised learning algorithms can yield better performance than the seven supervised learning algorithms we have discussed so far. Table 7.2 shows the SAS procedures and equivalent nodes in SAS Enterprise Miner for a set of unsupervised algorithms.

Model Selection Criteria

There are three categories of model selection criteria, namely: classification, data mining, and statistical measures. Although we will mostly use classification measures to select our final model, it is worth examining the two other categories of selection criteria.

Classification Measures

In general, fit statistics for classification problems can be categorized into the measures of accuracy, precision, recall, and specificity of the algorithms.

a. **Accuracy:** This evaluates the model's overall ability to yield the correct classification relative to all the classifications made by the model (that is, the ratio of the sum of true positives [TP] and true negatives [TN] to the sum of true positives [TP], true negatives [TN], false positives [FP], and false negatives [NP]).

$$\text{Accuracy} = \frac{\text{TP} + \text{TN}}{\text{TP} + \text{TN} + \text{FP} + \text{FN}} \tag{7.12}$$

You are most likely to see this statistic reported in SAS and other common statistical software as the total **misclassification rate**, which is 1–Accuracy of the model.

b. **Precision:** This assesses the model's ability to correctly predict the actual target outcome from all the predictions of the target outcome made by the model (that is, the ratio of TP to the sum of TP and FP).

$$\text{Precision} = \frac{\text{TP}}{\text{TP} + \text{FP}} \tag{7.13}$$

c. **Recall (sensitivity):** This measures the ability of the model to correctly predict the positive target outcomes from the actual number of positive outcomes that occur in the data set. (that is, the ratio of TP to the sum of TP and FN).

$$\text{Recall} = \frac{\text{TP}}{\text{TP} + \text{FN}} \tag{7.14}$$

Since we are interested in both the up and down movements in the returns of the S&P 500, we will also include the specificity measure.

d. **Specificity:** This measures the ability of the model to accurately predict the true negative outcomes (days with negative returns) for the target variable from the actual realizations of all negative outcomes that occur in the data set.

$$\text{Specificity} = \frac{\text{TN}}{\text{TN} + \text{FP}} \tag{7.15}$$

e. **Confusion matrix:** This is a crosstabulation of the actual classification of the response variable against the predicted classification from the model. In binary classification problems, a confusion matrix is used to obtain a quick overview of the accuracy or biases in the predictions of the model. The top left quadrant of the matrix displays the true positives, the top right displays the false positives, the bottom left displays the false negatives, while the bottom right displays the true negatives.

Decision Criterion

All classification measures assess the ability of the model to correctly classify a given outcome, relative to the larger pool of outcomes, hence the model with the highest classification measure of choice is typically selected. To successfully implement the algorithmic trading strategy on all trading days, regardless of the direction of the market, the optimal algorithm must be able to accurately predict both TP and TN events. Hence, the main model selection criterion for

Table 7.3: Confusion Matrix

		Predicted Class	
		1	0
Actual Class	1	True Positive (TP)	False Positive (FP)
	0	False Negative (FN)	True Negative (TN)

this study is the accuracy statistic (misclassification rate or 1–Accuracy), which measures the proportion of true positive and true negative (false negatives and false positives) predictions made by the algorithm for the validation data set.

Data Mining Measures

Data mining measures generally assess the algorithms based on some predefined modeling objectives. They defer from classification measures in the sense that they do not necessarily measure the exactness of the prediction but the proximity or improvement over some specified thresholds.

a. **Gain:** This calculates the percentage of events in the decile relative to the random percentage of events in the decile.
b. **Lift:** This is the ratio of the percentage of correct responses within each decile to the baseline percentage of responses.
c. **Cumulative Lift:** This is the cumulative ratio of correct classifications within each decile to the baseline percentage of responses.
d. **Profit:** This measure calculates the total profit per decile if the profit option is available in the selection criteria in the properties panel.
e. **Cumulative Profit:** This measure calculates the cumulative total profit per decile.
f. **Receiver Operating Characteristics (ROC)**: This measure calculates the ratio of the true positive rate (sensitivity) to the false positive rate (1–Specificity) for each decile.
g. **Area Under the ROC Curve (AUROC)**: This measure calculates the ability of the algorithm to correctly order each observation into the right grouping (that is, the probability that random negative return days are positioned to the left of the actual positive return day). This is done by estimating the sum of consecutive trapezoidal sections of the regions below the ROC curve.
h. **Gini Impurity Index**: This is equal to 2AUROC–1. The measure calculates the probability of incorrectly classifying a randomly selected observation.

Decision Criterion

Depending on the selection criterion, the model with the lowest Gini impurity index or highest Gain, Lift, Cumulative Lift, Profit, Cumulative Profit, ROC, and AUROC is usually selected.

Statistical Measures

Statistical measures are similar to data mining measures in terms of objectives. However, they use statistical measures as the basis to assess model performance.

    a. **Average Squared Error (ASE):** This is the ratio of the sum of squared error SSE to the sample size N, SSE / N

    b. **Akaike Information (AIC) and Bayesian Information Criteria (BIC):** Both measures estimate the prediction error of a model by calculating a penalized objective function where the penalty is a function of the number of parameters. Both measures impose a trade-off between additional model parameters and sampling variability. The mathematical formulas for the statistics are:

$$AIC = -2 \cdot Ln(L) + 2K \qquad (7.16)$$

$$BIC = -2 \cdot Ln(L) + K \bullet Ln(N) \qquad (7.17)$$

where $Ln(L)$ is the log-likelihood of the model, N is the sample size, and K is the number of parameters in the model.

Decision Criterion

For each statistical measure, the model with the lowest score is usually selected. For the case of average squared error, lower values imply a lower deviation between the predicted value and the actual value. The likelihood functions of both the AIC and BIC also include the deviation scores for each predicted value; hence, lower values are more desirable than higher values.

Model Comparison

Let us now proceed to demonstrate how we can implement model comparison in both SAS Enterprise Miner and SAS Studio. It is relatively easier to implement model comparison in SAS Enterprise Miner because it involves using drag-and-drop menus. We will have to do a fair amount of programming to replicate these features in SAS Studio.

SAS Enterprise Miner

The Model Comparison node in SAS Enterprise Miner can compare and select the champion model using any of the criteria described earlier. Click the Assess Tab. Then drag and drop the Model comparison node onto your diagram. Connect its input port to the output ports of the nodes of all of the previous models. In the Properties panel, change the Selection and HP Selection Statistics to the Misclassification Rate. Then change the Selection table to Valid. Right-click and run the node.

The Model Comparison node in SAS Enterprise Miner computes all three categories of model selection criteria, as well as a suite of graphs that are commonly used for model diagnostics (such as classification charts, ROC curves, and lift and gains charts). It also automatically selects the champion model based on the assessment criteria specified in the Properties panel and pushes the scoring code of the model to the Scoring node, which will be used to score the data from our backtesting period. We will discuss the results from the Model Comparison node along with results from the SAS Studio approach.

SAS Studio

Replicating all of the features in the Model Comparison in SAS Studio will require a significant amount of SAS programming steps. First, we will use PROC PRINT and PROC SGRENDER to print the ODS fit statistics table that was previously obtained from the models. The Ensemble model does not have an ODS fit statistics table but will compare its performance against the other algorithms using multiple DATA steps, and the TABULATE, SGRENDER, and LOGISTICS procedures. Although we will discuss each programming step separately, you can run all of the code in one node.

So, go ahead and click the ➕˙ icon in your process flow. Then select SAS Program to create a programming node in your process flow. Connect the input port of the node to the output ports of the nodes of all of the previous models. Double-click the node. Copy and paste all the code in Programs 7.9 to 7.13 into the code area, then run it. Click the Node tab and then name the node as "Model Comparison" in the Name area. Save your Process Flow ▶ Run 🖫 🖳 .

Program 7.9A: Using PROC PRINT to Display Summary of Fit Statistics from Competing Models

```
/*Print the Summary of the Fit Statistics from the Estimations*/
proc print data=logstats;
      title 'Logistic Regression Statistics';

proc print data=glmstats;
      title 'GLM Regression Statistics';

proc sgrender data=neuralstats template=HPDM.HPNEURAL.FitStatistics;
      title 'Neural Network Statistics';

proc print data=treestats;
      title 'Decision Tree Statistics';

proc sgrender data=svmstats template=HPDM.HPSvm.FitStatistics;
      title 'Support Vector Machine Statistics';

proc print data=foreststats;
      title 'Random Forest Statistics';
run;

title;
```

Program 7.9A shows the SAS code that can be used to print the previously saved ODS tables of fit statistics from the three parametric and three nonparametric models. The PROC SGRENDER statement was used to print the fit statistics tables for the neural network and SVM because their ODS tables were saved using their variable names and not their label. The SGRENDER procedure produces graphical output using the ODS template that is created with the Graph Template Language (GTL). Run the program. The outputs are not shown in the text but do review the results from each algorithm in your SAS Studio environment. In subsequent SAS code, we will combine many of these results and present them side-by-side for all algorithms.

Program 7.9B: Generating Summary of Model Accuracy Using DATA Step and PROC TABULATE

```
/*Merging Predictions and Classifications for Further Analysis*/
data Modelcomp1;
 set logout(keep=dates model target role p_target classification TP FP FN TN)
       glmout(keep=dates model target role p_target classification TP FP FN TN)
       neuralout(keep=dates model target role p_target classification TP FP FN TN)
       treeout(keep=dates model target role p_target classification TP FP FN TN)
       svmout(keep=dates model target role p_target classification TP FP FN TN)
       forestout(keep=dates model target role p_target classification TP FP FN TN)
       Ensembleout(keep=dates model target role p_target classification TP FP FN TN);
run;

/*Using Proc Tabulate to Compute the Classification Accuracy*/
proc tabulate data=Modelcomp1;
       class model classification role;
       table  classification*(pctn<classification>=''),Model='Comparing Model
Classification Accuracy'*role ;
run;
```

Program 7.9B shows the SAS code that was used to combine the predictions and classification from all seven algorithms. Notice that the DATA step used a SET statement instead of a MERGE statement. Using the SET statement allows us to stack the results from each algorithm using the same column and call up the results from the algorithm that we need by referencing the model column of the MODELCOMP1 data set. The TABULATE procedure is then used to compare the overall accuracy of each algorithm, which is shown in Output 7.9. Accuracy is the measure of the percentage of correct classification (TP+TN) or incorrect classifications (FP+FN) relative to all classifications made by the algorithms. The results are presented for both the training and validation data sets.

Output 7.9: Comparing Accuracy of Model Classifications

	Ensemble		HP Forest		HP GLM		HP Neural		HP Regression		HP SVM		HP Tree	
	Role		Role		Role		Role		Role		Role		Role	
	Train	Validate	Train	Validate	Train	Validate	Train	Validate	Train	Validate	Train	Validate	Train	Validate
Classification														
Correct	58.31	57.33	94.80	56.80	56.77	53.47	54.60	54.27	56.94	53.47	61.96	56.93	57.00	55.73
Incorrect	41.69	42.67	5.20	43.20	43.23	46.53	45.40	45.73	43.06	46.53	38.04	43.07	43.00	44.27

Comparing Model Classification Accuracy

Output 7.9 shows the results from the TABULATE procedure. For the training data, the accuracy rate of the algorithms ranges from 54.6% for the HP Neural model to 94.8% for the HP Forest algorithm. For the validation data, the accuracy rate ranges from 53.47% for the HP Regression to 57.33% for the Ensemble Model. Although the values are not precisely the same, the same pattern of results can be found in the Fit Statistics table that is shown in the result area of the Model Comparison Node in Enterprise Miner. In Program 7.10, we use the SGPANEL procedure to create a grouped classification chart for all the algorithms we examined. This chart is similar to the classification chart that can be found under the view menu of the results of the Model Comparison node in Enterprise Miner.

Program 7.10: Using PROC SGPANEL to Generate a Classification Chart for All Algorithms

```
/*Plotting the Classification Table for All Models*/
proc sort data=Modelcomp1 out=Plotdata;
     by Model Role;
run;

/*Using PROC SGPANEL to Produce Cluster Performance Graphs*/
ods graphics / reset width=6.4in height=4.8in imagemap;
title 'Classification Chart for Machine Learning Algorithms';

proc sgpanel data=Plotdata pctlevel=cell ;
     panelby role model/ onepanel rows=2 noheaderborder novarname
             colheaderpos=bottom spacing=2;
     vbar Target / group=Classification groupdisplay=stack stat=percent
     transparency=0.10 ;
     colaxis label='Target';
     rowaxis label='Prediction Percent';
run;
title;
```

Output 7.10: Panel of Column Charts Displaying Classification Accuracy for All Models

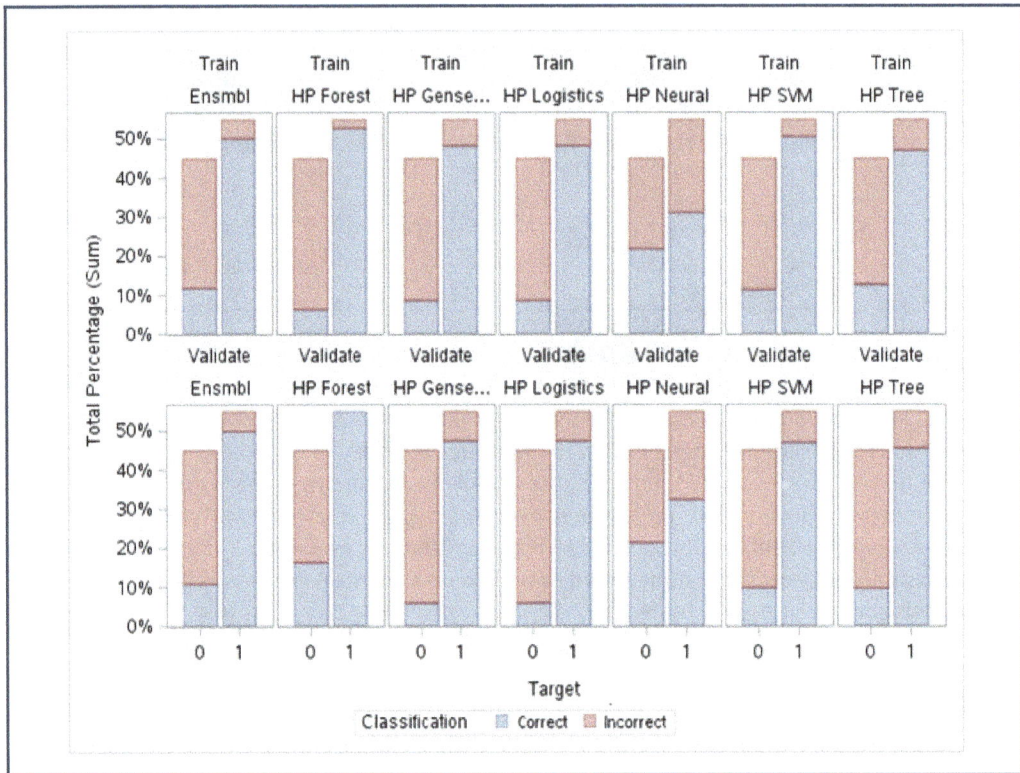

The visualization produced by the SAS code is shown in Output 7.10. Overall, the chart shows that all the algorithms do relatively well in predicting positive stock market days, but relatively poorly in predicting days with negative stock market returns. The pattern of prediction accuracy is relatively stable in both the training and validation data sets. This arises in part from the fact that the signal-to-noise ratio tends to be higher on days with positive stock market returns than on days with negative stock market returns. From an analytics life cycle point of view, it means that future revisions to the model should place more emphasis on improving the true negative rates of all of the algorithms. Since accuracy is the main model selection criterion for this project, our champion model will be the Ensemble model, which has the lowest misclassification rate in the validation data set. The Ensemble model was also automatically selected by the Model Comparison node in Enterprise Miner.

Although the Ensemble has been selected as the champion model, it is important to further analyze the results from all models to uncover evidence of systematic prediction errors, overfitting, and bias, as well as the rationale for the prediction accuracy of the champion and unsuccessful models. From a profit and risk management perspective, a model that misclassifies a small number of high financial impact days in the stock market might not necessarily be better than one that does extremely well on those days but misclassifies a relatively large number of small financial impact days. We will perform further diagnostics of all models before scoring our backtesting data with the scoring code of the Ensemble model.

Program 7.11: Comparing Confusion Matrices Using PROC TABULATE

```
/*Using Proc Tabulate to Compute the Classification Matrix*/
proc tabulate data=Modelcomp1;
     class model target p_target role;
     table  role*Target='Target',
     Model='Comparing Model Classification
     Matrix'*(pctn<P_Target>='Predicted')*P_Target=''  ;
run;
```

In Program 7.11, the TABULATE procedure is used to produce the Confusion (Classification) matrix for all algorithms. In the TABLE statement, the actual outcome of the stock market is crosstabbed against the classification made by each model and then stacked based on the data role of the observation. The PCTN<P_TARGET> *P_TARGET statement is used to request the cell-by-cell percentage of the count of the row variable (that is, the percentage of 1 [0] that is classified as 1 [0] by each algorithm).

Output 7.11: Comparing Confusion Matrices for All Models

		Ensemble		HP Forest		HP GLM		HP Neural		HP Regression		HP SVM		HP Tree	
		Predicted		Predicted		Predicted		Predicted		Predicted		Predicted		Predicted	
		0	1	0	1	0	1	0	1	0	1	0	1	0	1
Role	Target														
Train	0	18.12	81.88	88.59	11.41	18.76	81.24	39.80	60.20	19.26	80.74	25.35	74.65	8.87	91.13
	1	8.73	91.27	0.10	99.90	12.06	87.94	33.26	66.74	12.16	87.84	8.00	92.00	3.53	96.47
Validate	0	16.86	83.14	16.27	83.73	13.31	86.69	37.57	62.43	13.31	86.69	21.89	78.11	6.80	93.20
	1	9.47	90.53	9.95	90.05	13.59	86.41	32.04	67.96	13.59	86.41	14.32	85.68	4.13	95.87

Output 7.11 displays the Confusion matrix for all algorithms. The table provides more evidence about the innate weakness of the algorithms examined, which is the very low values of the true negative rate. Recall from the Percentage of Event Plots that the distributions of the predicted probabilities for both outcomes are relatively compact and around 50%. This means that classifications are extremely sensitive to small changes in the threshold. Raising the threshold for probability to classify a stock market day as positive by 3% for the Ensemble model will raise the percent of the true negative by 20% but cause the percentage of true positive to fall by approximately the same. The net effect on the model accuracy dropped by 1% in the training data and 2% in the validation data.

Program 7.12 uses PROC SQL statements to generate a summary of the measures and statistics from the algorithms. The PROC PRINT statement is then used to report the summary of the statistics for all algorithms.

Program 7.12: Generating Summary of Classification Measures Using PROC SQL

```
/*Using Proc SQL to Calculate Classification Measures*/
proc sql;
      create table modelcomp2 as select Role as Role, Model as  Model,
              (sum(TP)+sum(TN))/(sum(TP)+sum(TN)+sum(FP)+sum(TN)) as Accuracy ,
              1-(sum(TP)+sum(TN))/(sum(TP)+sum(TN)+sum(FP)+sum(TN))
              label="Misclassfication Rate" as Misclass , sum(TP)/(sum(TP)+sum(FP)) as
              Precision, sum(TP)/(sum(TP)+sum(FN)) as Sensitivity,
              sum(TN)/(sum(TN)+sum(FP)) as Specificity, 1-sum(TN)/(sum(TN)+sum(FP))
              label="1-Specificity" as MSpecificity from plotdata group by Role, Model;
              quit;

title 'Summary of Fit Statistics from Estimated Models';

proc print data=modelcomp2 label style(header)=[width=0.8 in textalign=center]noobs;
      var Role model;
      var Accuracy Misclass Precision Sensitivity Specificity
      Mspecificity/style(data)=[textalign=center];
      format Accuracy best4.2 Misclass best4.2 Precision best4.2 Sensitivity best4.2
      Specificity best4.2 Mspecificity best4.2;
run;
title;
```

Output 7.12A: Summary of Classification Measures for All Models

		Summary of Fit Statistics from **Estimated Models**					
Role	Model	Accuracy	Misclassification Rate	Precision	Sensitivity	Specificity	1-Specificity
Train	Ensemble	0.56	0.44	0.58	0.91	0.18	0.82
Train	HP Forest	0.68	0.32	0.91	1	0.89	0.11
Train	HP GLM	0.56	0.44	0.57	0.88	0.19	0.81
Train	HP Neural	0.55	0.45	0.57	0.67	0.4	0.6
Train	HP Regression	0.56	0.44	0.57	0.88	0.19	0.81
Train	HP SVM	0.58	0.42	0.6	0.92	0.25	0.75
Train	HP Tree	0.56	0.44	0.56	0.96	0.09	0.91
Validate	Ensemble	0.56	0.44	0.57	0.91	0.17	0.83
Validate	HP Forest	0.56	0.44	0.57	0.9	0.16	0.84
Validate	HP GLM	0.54	0.46	0.55	0.86	0.13	0.87
Validate	HP Neural	0.55	0.45	0.57	0.68	0.38	0.62
Validate	HP Regression	0.54	0.46	0.55	0.86	0.13	0.87
Validate	HP SVM	0.56	0.44	0.57	0.86	0.22	0.78
Validate	HP Tree	0.55	0.45	0.56	0.96	0.07	0.93

Output 7.12A shows the results of the invocation of the PRINT procedure. The table contains a summary of the classification measures. We can obtain a more complete picture from the Statistic Comparison table (shown in Output 7.12B), which can be obtained from the results of the Model Comparison node in SAS Enterprise Miner. The table contains the classification, data mining, and statistical measures from all the algorithms we examined. Overall, the Ensemble model outperforms other algorithms based on most of the assessment measures. It has a lower ASE, higher ROC, and lower misclassification rate.

Output 7.12B: Statistics Comparison Table for Validation Data

Data Role	Target Variable	Target Label	Fit Statistics ▼	Statistics Label	Ensmbl	HPTree	KPSVM	HPGLM	HPReg	HPDMForest	KPNNA
Valid	Target	Daily Directio...	VKS	Valid: Kolmog...	0.106	0.067	0.086	0.068	0.068	0.048	0.083
Train	Target	Daily Directio...	KS	Train: Kolmog...	0.225	0.174	0.277	0.125	0.151	1	0.094
Train	Target	Daily Directio...	BINNED_KS	Train: Bin-Ba...	0.53	0.596	0.515	0.555	0.543	0.57	0.53
Train	Target	Daily Directio...	WRONG	Train: Numbe...	688	694	639	775	761	0	800
Valid	Target	Daily Directio...	VWRONG	Valid: Number...	319	324	329	336	336	343	352
Valid	Target	Daily Directio...	VSSE	Valid: Sum of...	367.3691	386.3805	371.0414	374.1077	374.3052	383.7372	373.9638
Valid	Target	Daily Directio...	VRESPC	Valid: Cumula...	59.21053	59.17065	61.84211	50	55.26316	57.45614	55.26316
Valid	Target	Daily Directio...	VRESP	Valid: Percent...	55.26316	55.70973	68.42105	44.73684	63.15789	61.32376	44.73684
Valid	Target	Daily Directio...	VRASE	Valid: Root Av...	0.494557	0.507192	0.497023	0.499072	0.499204	0.505454	0.498976
Valid	Target	Daily Directio...	VNOBS	Valid: Sum of...	751	751	751	751	751	751	751
Valid	Target	Daily Directio...	VMISC	Valid: Misclas...	0.424767	0.431425	0.438083	0.447403	0.447403	0.456724	0.468708
Valid	Target	Daily Directio...	VMAX	Valid: Maximu...	0.701111	1	0.821293	0.757429	0.795107	0.83	0.768947
Valid	Target	Daily Directio...	VLIFTC	Valid: Cumula...	1.076685	1.07596	1.124538	0.909201	1.004906	1.044784	1.004906
Valid	Target	Daily Directio...	VLIFT	Valid: Lift	1.004906	1.013027	1.24417	0.813496	1.148464	1.115113	0.813496
Valid	Target	Daily Directio...	VKS_PROB	Valid: Kolmog...	0.508	0.351	0.516	0.515	0.514	0.491	0.517
Valid	Target	Daily Directio...	VKS_BIN	Valid: Bin-Bas...	0.109	0.067	0.082	0.053	0.069	0.048	0.076
Valid	Target	Daily Directio...	VGINI	Valid: Gini Co...	0.121	0.098	0.094	0.018	0.037	0.022	0.079
Valid	Target	Daily Directio...	VGAIN	Valid: Gain	7.668536	7.596032	12.4538	9.079903	0.490633	4.478357	0.490633
Valid	Target	Daily Directio...	VDIV	Valid: Divisor...	1502	1502	1502	1502	1502	1502	1502
Valid	Target	Daily Directio...	VDISF	Valid: Freque...	751	751	751	751	751	751	751
Valid	Target	Daily Directio...	VCAPC	Valid: Cumula...	10.89588	10.88855	11.38015	9.200969	10.16949	10.57304	10.16949
Valid	Target	Daily Directio...	VCAP	Valid: Percent...	5.084746	5.125835	6.2954	4.116223	5.811138	5.64238	4.116223
Valid	Target	Daily Directio...	VBINNED_K...	Valid: Bin-Bas...	0.531	0.567	0.516	0.521	0.52	0.495	0.511
Valid	Target	Daily Directio...	VAUR	Valid: Roc Ind...	0.56	0.549	0.547	0.509	0.519	0.511	0.54
Valid	Target	Daily Directio...	VASE	Valid: Averag...	0.244587	0.257244	0.247032	0.249073	0.249204	0.255484	0.248977

Program 7.13A: Using the DATA Step to Collate Model Predictions

```
/*Merging Data for ROC Curves*/
data Modelcomp3;
      merge
      logout(rename=(Pred=Log_Pred P_Target=Log_Target Classification=Log_class))
      glmout(rename=(Pred=Glm_Pred P_Target=Glm_Target Classification=Glm_class))
       treeout(rename=(P_Target1=Tree_Pred P_Target=Tree_Target
       Classification=Tree_class))
      svmout(rename=(P_Target1=SVM_Pred P_Target=SVM_Target Classification=SVM_class))
      forestout(rename=(P_Target1=Forest_Pred P_Target=Forest_Target
      Classification=Forest_class))
      neuralout(rename=(P_Target1=Neural_Pred P_Target=Neural_Target
      Classification=Neural_class))
      Ensembleout(rename=(P_Target1=Ens_Pred P_Target=Ens_Target
      Classification=Ens_class));
      by dates;
run;
```

You can replicate the ROC curves from the Model Comparison in SAS Studio by using the DATA step and LOGISTICS procedure. In Program 7.13A, the DATA step is first used to merge the posterior probabilities and the classifications produced by each algorithm with the target outcome. The LOGISTIC procedure is then invoked in Program 7.13B to compute the ROC and AUROC and to overlay the computed ROC curves for all algorithms on a single graph. The procedure is estimated for each data partition but only the code for the validation data set is shown. To obtain the same graph for the training data, change the value of the ROLE='VALIDATE' to ROLE='TRAIN'. In terms of the AUROC, the HP Forest had the highest AUROCC for the training data set, while the HP NEURAL did slightly better than the Ensemble model with the validation data set.

Program 7.13B: Comparing ROC Curves from Fitted Models Using DATA Steps and PROC LOGISTIC

```
/*Using PROC LOGISTICS to Compare ROC Curves*/
%let _ROCOVERLAY_ENTRYTITLE = Comparing ROC Curves (Data Role=Validate);

proc logistic data=modelcomp3 (where=(role='Validate'));
      model target(event='1')=Log_Pred GLM_Pred Neural_Pred
            Tree_Pred SVM_Pred    Forest_Pred Ens_Pred / nofit;
      roc 'HPReg' pred=Log_Pred;
      roc 'HPGLM' pred=GLM_Pred;
      roc 'HPNNA' pred=Neural_Pred;
      roc 'HPTree' pred=Tree_Pred;
      roc 'HPSVM' pred=SVM_Pred;
      roc 'HPForest' pred=Forest_Pred;
      roc 'Ensmbl' pred=Ens_Pred;
      ods select ROCOverlay;
run;
%symdel _ROC_ENTRYTITLE;
```

One of the many assessment plots created by the Model Comparison node is the ROC curves for all algorithms. Output 7.13A shows a general decline in the predictive power of the model from the training to the validation data set. For the training data set, the graphs show a more pronounced higher ratio of sensitivity to 1–Specificity as the classification threshold increases and a flatter curve for the validation data set. Although the sensitivity of the algorithms stayed relatively the same in both the training and validation data sets, the specificity of the algorithms declined in the validation data, leading to the lower ratios of the sensitivity to 1–Specificity that is evident on the graph.

Output 7.13A: ROC Curves from Fitted Models Using Model Comparison Node

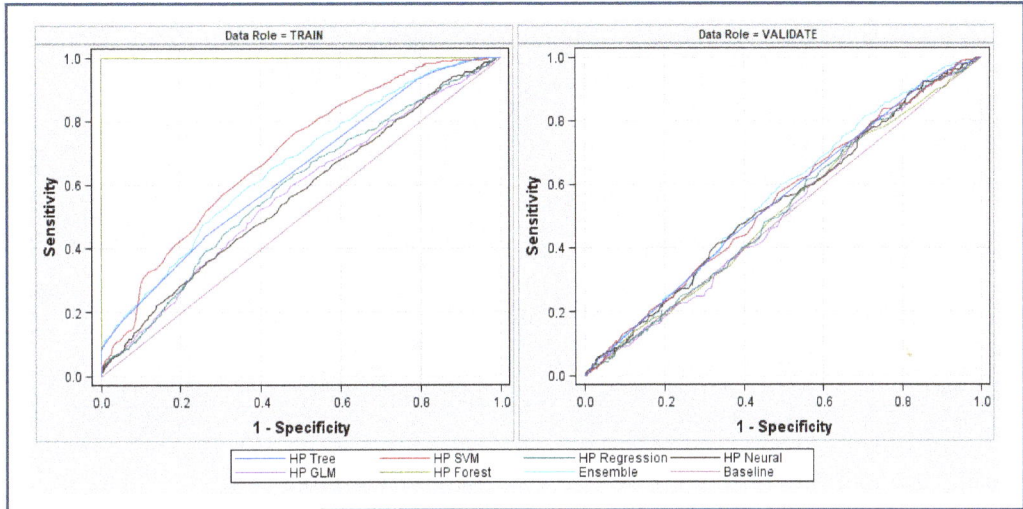

Output 7.13B: ROC Curves from Fitted Models Using PROC LOGISTIC

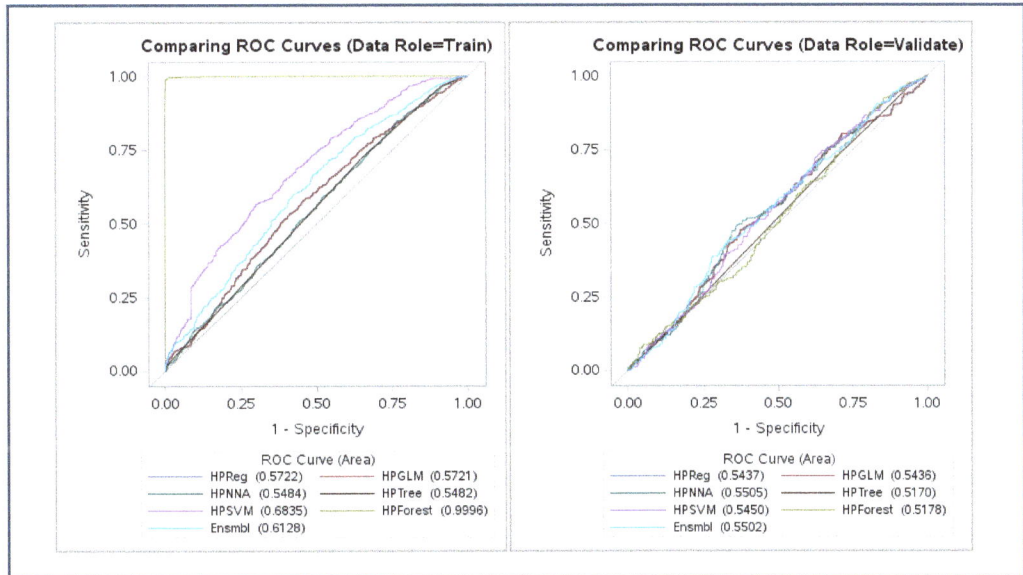

Overall, the 56% accuracy rate for the Ensemble model is a relatively adequate accuracy rate, given how difficult it is to predict stock market outcomes. It is quite unrealistic to expect market prediction algorithms to have a very high accuracy rate, given the relatively high level of efficiency and the random manner in which news arrives in the US market. The goal of active portfolio management is to outperform a benchmark on a risk-adjusted basis. Thus, if our

Figure 7.9A: SAS Studio Process Flow Diagram

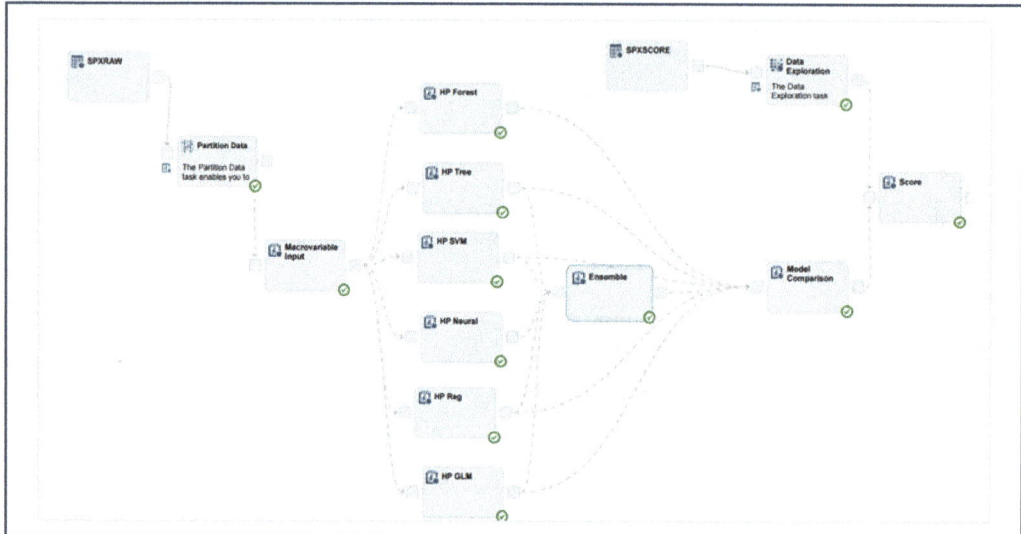

Ensemble model can outperform a passive position in the S&P 500 index, it would have achieved its objective. We will assess if this is indeed the case in the next section.

Process Flow Diagram

Figure 7.9A shows the process flow diagram created in SAS Studio for the project. While Figure 7.9B shows the process flow diagram in SAS Enterprise Miner. Remember that each node contains code packages that you can run together or as a sequence of connected steps. From an operational perspective, using process flow will facilitate the automation of your machine learning project. All you need to do is log in to your SAS environment and run the flow to achieve end-to-end functionality.

Backtesting our Algorithmic Strategy Against a Passive Investment Strategy in the S&P 500 Index

To assess the efficacy of the best-fit algorithm in an investment setting, we will backtest the model using data from the holdout subperiod, which is from January 2nd, 2021, to July 31st, 2022.[15] First, we create two hypothetical investment portfolios, each with an initial portfolio value of $1 million. For the first portfolio, we will construct an investment strategy where trade signals for the next day will be drawn from the predictions of the Ensemble model at market close for

---

[15] Recall that machine learning algorithms suffer from model degradation as the model ages. Therefore, they may not be well-suited for an extensively long backtesting period. (See Young and Steel, 2022.)

Figure 7.9B: SAS Enterprise Miner Process Flow Diagram

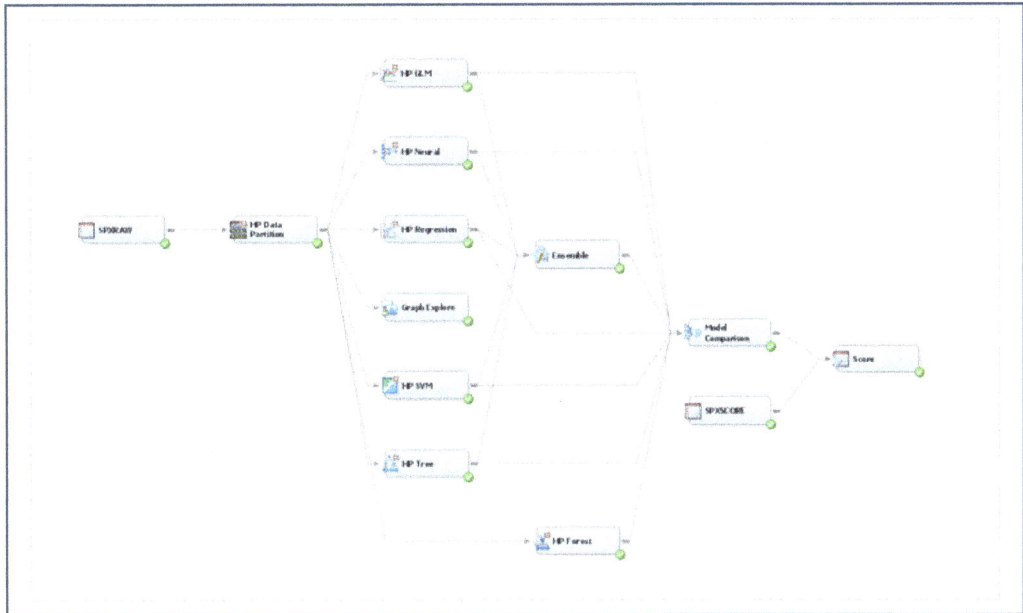

the current day. If the algorithm predicts that the S&P 500 index will close higher the next trading day, we will enter into a long position (enter into a short position if the model predicts otherwise) in a three-month S&P 500 E-mini futures contract (priced at 50 multiplied by the closing value of the S&P 500 index) when the futures markets open (at 5:00 PM Mondays to Thursdays and 6:00 PM on Sundays) each day and close out the position at the next open of the futures market. Each day, between the duration of the closing of the stock market and the opening of the futures market, we recursively update the Ensemble model with the new information from the market activities and then implement the trading signal obtained from the model.

To benchmark this strategy, for the second portfolio, we will construct a passive portfolio of a hypothetical $1 million investment in an S&P 500 index mutual fund on January 2nd, 2021, and keep the portfolio over the same holdout period. At the end of the holdout period, we will examine if the algorithmic portfolio can outperform the passive index position on an absolute and risk-adjusted basis.

It turns out that you don't need a significant cash outlay to hold positions in the S&P 500 E-Mini futures. You are only required to post the initial margin requirement (which is about 5.5% of the notional value of the position at inception) and keep the maintenance margin of approximately 5%. This means you can potentially invest the remaining amount (about $940,000) in a risk-free asset and still earn additional returns while keeping your exposure to the stock market relatively the same as someone with all of their money tied in the index portfolio. However, to ensure that the comparison with the passive strategy is unbiased, we will assume that the futures position is fully funded and earns zero interest on cash. The total contract size for each day will depend on the value of the futures position at 5:00 PM. More contracts are purchased if the previous trade resulted in a gain in portfolio value, while fewer contracts are purchased if the ending position resulted in a loss in the portfolio value. You should note that all futures contracts have expiration dates. We will simply roll the position into the next available maturity at the end of the quarter. Transaction costs for the fully funded futures position are insignificant in absolute terms (on average around 20 basis points per year) and still cheaper than a long-only position in the index as shown by a study conducted by the Chicago Mercantile Exchange (CME) group.[16] Consequently, we will ignore transaction cost, as it would have little to no impact on the ending value of the portfolio.

The SPXSCORE data set contains the scoring data for the backtesting period. The data set contains all of the variables in our raw data and the daily open-to-open and close-to-close prices of the three-month S&P 500 E-Mini futures contract.

Program 7.14A: Scoring Holdout Data Using Scoring Code from Champion Model

```
/*Backtesting the Champion Model Using its Scoring Code*/
/*Pull Scoring Code for Ensemble Model from GitHub*/
%datapull(Ensemble,Ensemble.sas);

/*Scoring Holdout Data Using DATA Step*/
data pscorespx;
      set emsas.spxscore;
      %include "%sysfunc(pathname(work))/Ensemble.sas";
run;

data scorespx;
      set pscorespx;
      format Classification $10. CMatrix $8.;
      if (I_Target=Index_out) then do;
            Classification='Correct';
            Algo_ret=abs(OTO_FRet);/*Open-to-Open Futures Return*/
      end;
      else do;
            Classification='Incorrect';
            Algo_Ret=-1*abs(OTO_FRet);
      end;
      EXAlgo_Ret=Algo_Ret-RF; /*Excess Algorithmic Return*/
      EXIndex_Ret=Index_Ret-RF;/*Excess Index Return*/
      if I_Target=1 and  Index_out=1 then CMatrix='TP';
      if I_Target=1 and  Index_out=0 then CMatrix='FP';
      if I_Target=0 and  Index_out=1 then CMatrix='FN';
      if I_Target=0 and  Index_out=0 then CMatrix='TN';
```

```
label CMatrix='Prediction Condition'
Algo_Ret='Algorithmic Returns';

        /*Cumulative Returns*/
        Sumiret+Index_Ret; /*Passive Index Buy and Hold*/
        Sumaret+algo_Ret;  /*Algorithmic Based*/
        IndexVal =1000000*exp(sumiret); /* Index Portfolio Value*/
        AlgoVal = 1000000*exp(sumaret);/* Algorithmic Portfolio Value*/
        format IndexVal dollar16.2 AlgoVal dollar16.2;
        label IndexVal= 'Index Portfolio Values' AlgoVal ='Algorithmic Portfolio Values';
run;
```

Program 7.14A pulls the scoring code for the Ensemble model from the GitHub repository. It then uses the DATA step and the INCLUDE statement to score the SPXSCORE data set using the downloaded ENSEMBLE.sas file. A second DATA step is then used to compute the daily returns from the algorithmic trade that was made using the model predictions. Be aware that, unlike the passive portfolio that moves in tandem with the index, the return from the algorithmic portfolio is determined by the accuracy of the predictions. The portfolio will earn a positive return regardless of the direction of the stock market, as long as the prediction of the algorithm is in line with the market outcome. Consequently, the portfolio will earn a negative return if it misclassifies the market outcome regardless of the actual outcome on the next trading day. This means that it is possible for the algorithmic portfolio to make money when the market is down (true negative classification), and to lose money when the market is up (false positive classification). In short, the algorithmic portfolio earns positive returns only when it makes true positive and true negative classifications, regardless of the market outcome. The code for the DATA step concludes by calculating the daily values of both the algorithmic and passive portfolios using continuously compounded returns over the holding period.

Program 7.14B: Plotting Classification Accuracy in Backtesting Period Using PROC SGPLOT

```
/*Graphing Classification Accuracy Using PROC SGPLOT*/
ods graphics / reset width=6.4in height=4.8in imagemap;

proc sgplot data=Scorespx;
    title height=12pt "Prediction Accuracy (Backtesting Period)";
vbar Index_Out / group=Classification groupdisplay=stack stat=percent dataskin=crisp;
    yaxis grid label="Prediction Percent";
run;

ods graphics / reset;
title;
```

Program 7.14B shows the SAS code for the SGPLOT procedure that was used to create a bar chart of the prediction outcomes for the data in the holdout subperiod using the Ensemble model. The bar chart that was created from invoking the procedure is shown in Output 7.14. Evident on the graph is the same pattern of prediction accuracy that we observed in the training and validation data sets. The Ensemble model does relatively well when classifying trading days with positive returns but continues to perform poorly with classifying trading days with negative returns.

Output 7.14: Classification Accuracy from Ensemble Model During Backtesting Period

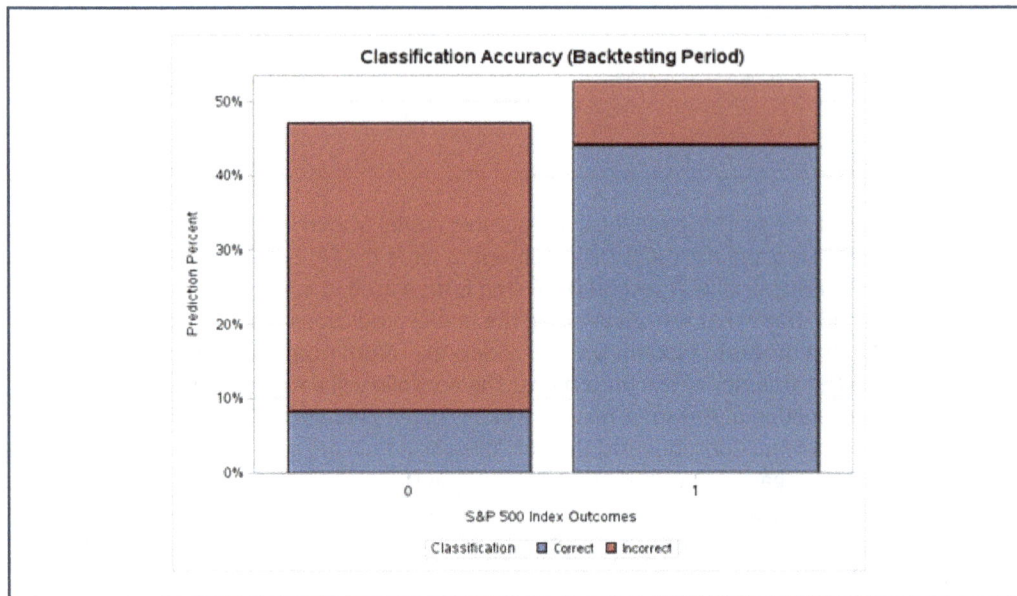

Let's examine the financial impact of this lopsided accuracy rate on the overall performance of the algorithmic portfolio. Program 7.15 shows the code for the REPORT procedure that was used to generate the performance report for the algorithmic and passive portfolios. PROC REPORT extends the capabilities of PROC TABULATE, FREQ, MEANS, SUMMARY, and PRINT by allowing for custom calculations, conditionals, and formatting in creating a report. Although it is fairly complicated to work with, the functionality it provides makes it suitable for building our performance report table. In the code for the procedure, a side-by-side performance report for both the algorithmic and passive portfolio is presented, along with conditional and custom calculations. The conditional and custom calculations were used to create the row for the total, annualized means and standard deviations of returns, and the Sharpe ratios of both strategies.

Program 7.15: Portfolio Performance Reporting Using PROC REPORT

```
/*Comparing Portfolio Performance Using PROC REPORT*/
proc report data=scorespx nowd ;
columns ('Backtesting the Performance of Algorithmic Portfolio Relative to Passive
Index Strategy'(CMatrix
(('Algorithmic Portfolio'(Algo_Ret=Asum Algo_Ret=Amean Algo_Ret=Astd AAmean AAstd
ExAlgo_Ret=EXAmean ExAlgo_Ret=EXAstd  ASharpe))
('Index Portfolio' (Index_Ret=Isum Index_Ret=Imean Index_Ret=Istd AImean AIstd
ExIndex_Ret=EXImean ExIndex_Ret=EXIstd ISharpe))) ));
```

```
        define Cmatrix/group style(header)=[textalign=left]   left;
/*****************Algorithmic Portfolio Calculations****************/
        define Asum/analysis sum format=percent8.2 'Total Return' center;
        define Amean/analysis mean format=percent8.2 'Mean Daily Return' center
noprint;
        define Astd/analysis std format=percent8.2 'Standard Deviation' center noprint;
        define AAmean/computed format=percent8.2 'Annualized Mean' center;
        compute AAmean;
        AAmean =amean*252;
        endcomp;
        define AAstd/computed format=percent8.2 'Annualized Standard Deviation' center;
        compute AAstd;
        AAStd =Astd*sqrt(252);
        endcomp;

        /*Calculating Mean Excess Return and Standard of Excess Return*/
        define ExAmean/analysis mean format=percent8.2  noprint ;
        define EXAstd/analysis std format=percent8.2 noprint ;

        define ASharpe/computed format=best6.2 'Sharpe Ratio' center;
        compute ASharpe;
         if Amean>0 then ASharpe=EXAmean/ExAstd;
        endcomp;

/*****************Passive Portfolio Calculations*****************/
        define Isum/analysis sum format=percent8.2 'Total Return' center;
        define Imean/analysis mean format=percent8.2 'Mean Daily Return' center noprint;
        define Istd/analysis std format=percent8.2 'Standard Deviation' center noprint;
        define AImean/computed format=percent8.2 'Annualized Mean' center;
        compute AImean;
        AImean =Imean*252;
        endcomp;
        define AIstd/computed format=percent8.2 'Annualized Standard Deviation' center;
        compute AIstd;
        AIstd =Istd*sqrt(252);
        endcomp;

         /*Calculating Mean Excess Return and Standard of Excess Return*/
        define EXImean/analysis mean  format=percent8.2  noprint;
        define ExIstd/analysis std  format=percent8.2 noprint;

        define ISharpe/computed format=best6.2  'Sharpe Ratio' center;
        compute ISharpe;
        if CMatrix='Total' then ISharpe=EXImean/EXIstd;
        endcomp;
        rbreak after / summarize style=[font_weight=bold  ] ;
         compute Cmatrix;
         if CMatrix='' then
              CMatrix='Total';
        endcomp;
run;
```

Output 7.15 shows the performance report generated from Program 7.15. Overall, we can see that the algorithmic portfolio outperformed the passive index portfolio on an absolute and risk-adjusted basis (using the Sharpe ratio as the measure of risk-adjusted return). The total return earned by the algorithmic portfolio exceeded the passive portfolio by approximately 8% during the backtesting period. The total return during the backtesting period for the algorithmic portfolio was 18.78%, compared to 10.70% for the passive index portfolio. The average daily return on the algorithmic portfolio is about 0.05% (not shown in the table), which accumulates to about 11.95% annualized return. In comparison, the average daily return of the passive index portfolio was about 0.03%, which accumulates to approximately 6.81% on an annualized basis. Interestingly, the risks of both portfolios are quite similar, with the algorithmic portfolio having slightly lower daily and annualized standard deviations. The outsized return performance and relatively lower risk of the algorithmic portfolio explain why the Sharpe ratio of the algorithmic portfolio is almost twice the value of the passive portfolio.

Output 7.15: Performance Report from Backtesting Algorithmic Portfolio

Backtesting the Performance of Algorithmic Portfolio Relative to Passive Index Strategy								
	Algorithmic Portfolio				Passive Portfolio			
Prediction Condition	Total Return	Annualized Mean	Annualized Standard Deviation	Sharpe Ratio	Total Return	Annualized Mean	Annualized Standard Deviation	Sharpe Ratio
FN	(34.82%)	(258.1%)	12.59%	.	26.29%	194.9%	9.78%	.
FP	(121.1%)	(198.1%)	12.26%	.	(135.0%)	(220.9%)	13.41%	.
TN	32.54%	248.5%	12.91%	1.2072	(26.92%)	(205.6%)	14.84%	.
TP	142.1%	204.7%	11.71%	1.0949	146.4%	210.8%	10.99%	.
Total	**18.78%**	**11.95%**	**17.96%**	**0.0375**	**10.70%**	**6.81%**	**18.14%**	**0.0193**

Performance Attribution

So why did the Ensemble model perform better than the passive strategy? First, let's examine the prediction accuracy of the algorithm for the classification threshold. The ensemble model successfully classified most of the trading days with positive returns (TP), and a few of the trading days with negative returns (TN). Notice that the total return of the TP days is relatively the same for both approaches, while the total return for the TN days is not. The algorithm captured about 15% of the possible returns that could have been earned if it was 100% accurate on the trading days with negative index returns. The average daily return (not shown in the table) for the algorithmic portfolio on the TP days is 0.81%, while the average daily return on the TN days is 0.99%. The algorithm made a lot of false positive (FP) classifications but incurred a relatively lower cost per misclassification than the lower number of false negative (FN) classifications that it made. The average return on FP days (0.79%) is much lower than the average return on FN days (1.02%). The accuracy rate of the algorithm actually fell to about 52.5% in the backtesting period. In all, it correctly classified 208 days and incorrectly classified 188 days out of the 396 days in the backtesting period. Nevertheless, it gained 174.64% from its accurate classifications and lost 155.9% from incorrectly classifying the outcomes of the next trading days, thereby netting an 18.78% total return.

Program 7.16: Graphing the Correlation Between Posterior Probabilities and Actual Index Return Using PROC SGPLOT

```
/* Using SGPLOT Procedure to Graph the Relationship Between Posterior Probabilities and
Actual Index Return*/
proc sgplot data=scorespx;
        title height=12pt "Predicted Probabilities of Positive Market Movement";
        scatter x = index_ret y=P_Target1/group=I_Target markeroutlineattrs=( thickness=1)
markerattrs=(symbol=circlefilled size=10);
        reg x = index_ret y=P_Target1/  clm;
        yaxis label='Predicted Probabilities';
        xaxis valuesformat=percent8.2 values=(-0.04 to 0.03 by 0.01);
run;
```

Next, we will examine whether the estimated posterior probabilities from the models are correlated with the actual magnitude of returns on the next trading day. It will be valuable to know if the algorithm is only useful for predicting a certain range of market movements and not all possible movements. That way we can adjust our classification threshold to account for such properties. Program 7.16 shows the SAS code that was used to generate a scatter plot of the posterior probability and the actual next-day return on the index.

In Output 7.16A, the posterior probabilities are graphed on the Y axis, while the actual index return on the next trading day is plotted on the X axis. Ideally, you would like to see all red dots on the bottom left quadrants and all blue dots on the top right quadrants of the plot. Such an outcome would imply that the right posterior probabilities were estimated for each outcome. However, the substantial number of blue dots in the upper left quadrant shows that the algorithm consistently assigned high probabilities of positive movement to days with actual negative price movement, even on some days with pronouncedly negative price movements. The model also assigned low probabilities of positive price movements to days with pronouncedly positive price movements as seen from the red dots in the bottom right quadrant of the plots. However, a large number of the blue are in the TP quadrant, and the estimated posterior probabilities assigned for each dot in that quadrant appear to be positively correlated to the magnitude of the returns on the index on the next trading day.

Output 7.16A: Correlation Between Posterior Probabilities and Actual Index Return

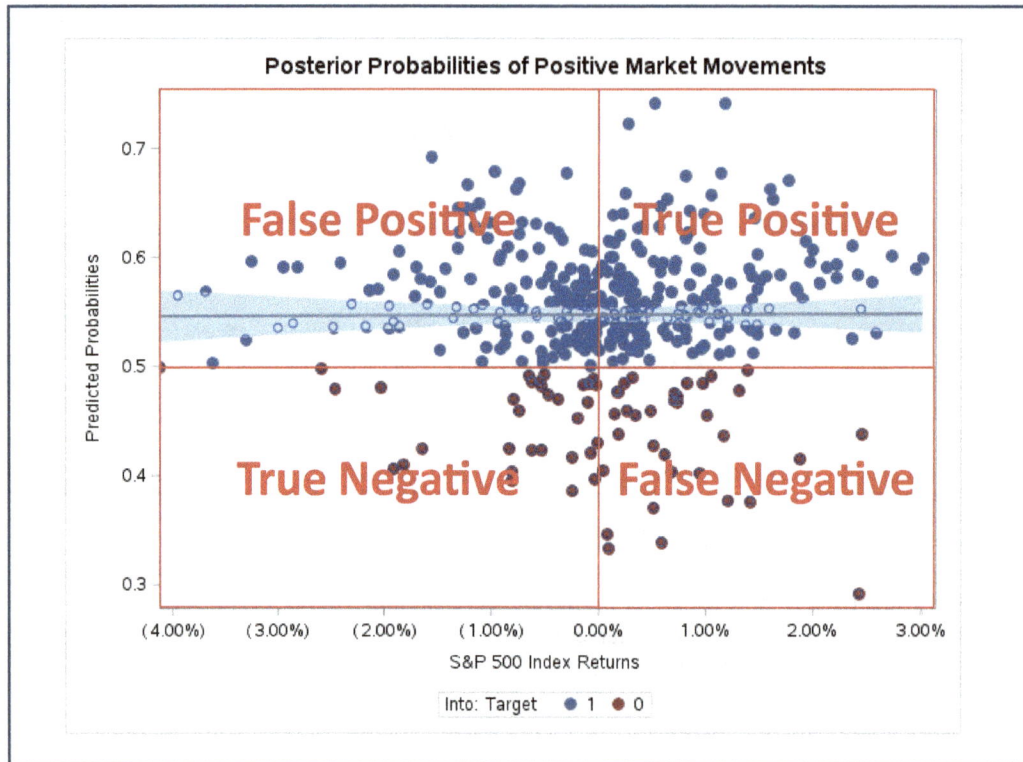

In Output 7.16B, we examined whether changing the classification threshold will lead to an improvement in the alignment of the predicted probabilities with the actual magnitude of the next-day returns of the index that we observed. We reproduced the plot of the posterior probabilities on the Y axis and the actual index return on the next trading day on the X axis using a 40% probability of positive return on the index as the classification threshold. You will notice on the new plot that the lower classification threshold resulted in significantly higher numbers of both TP and FP days.

Output 7.16B: Correlation Between Posterior Probabilities and Actual Index Return (40% Threshold)

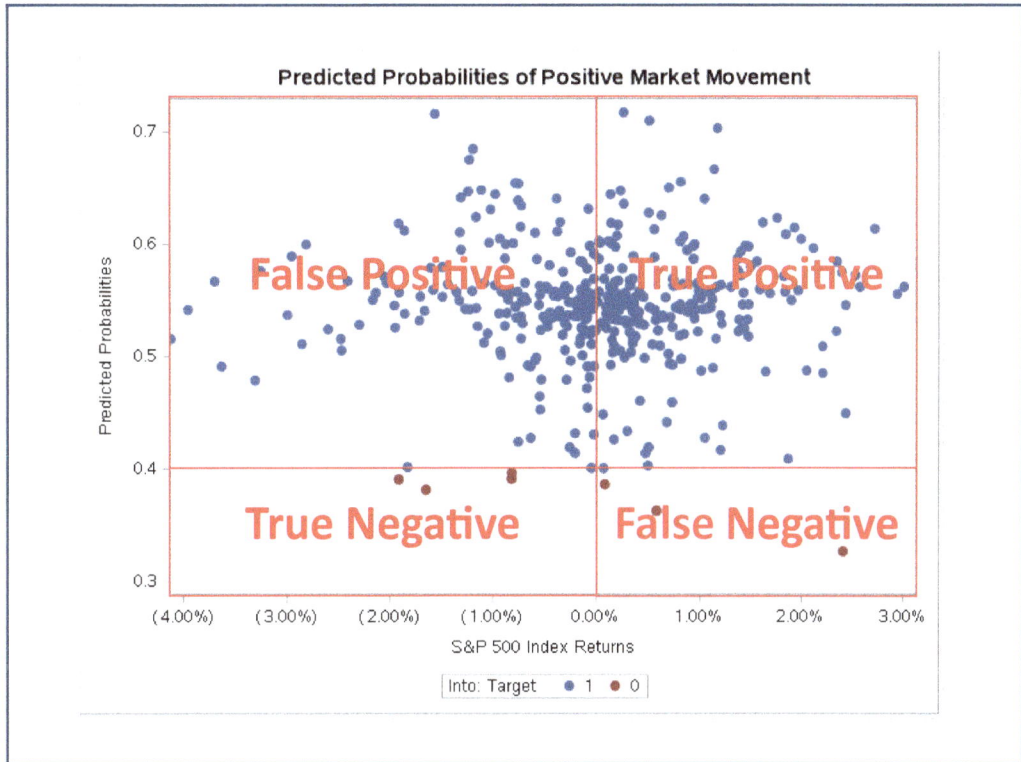

Almost all the positive stock market days were correctly classified at the threshold (202 out of 209 days). However, that outcome came at a significant cost. There are about 52.78% positive trading days in the holdout period. At the 50% classification threshold, 83.7% of those days were already correctly classified. Reducing the threshold to 40% increased the number of TP days by 27, but also the number of FP days by 30. The lower classification threshold would result in a 51.24% gain in total returns from the higher TP and lower FN days, but a 61.26% loss in returns from the higher FP and lower TN days. The combined net effect from changing the classification threshold is a total performance of 8.53% as shown in Output 7.16C. This value is not only lower than the total return from the 50% classification threshold but also lower than the return obtained from the passive strategy.

Although we still stick with our initial classification threshold of 50%, we recommend that readers experiment with different classification thresholds by modifying Program 7.14A. Add the code line: IF P_TARGET1>= "Replace with your desired threshold (in decimals)" THEN I_TARGET=1; ELSE I_TARGET=0; below the FORMAT statement in the code for the DATA step.

Output 7.16C: Portfolio Performance at 40% Positive Return Classification Threshold

	Performance of Algorithmic Portfolio at 40% Classification Threshold								
	Algorithmic Portfolio								
Prediction Condition	Total Return	Mean Daily Return	Standard Deviation	Annualized Mean	Annualized Standard Deviation	Sharpe Ratio	Days	Days (%)
FN	(9.28%)	(1.33%)	1.10%	(334.20%)	17.46%	.	7	1.77%
FP	(151.70%)	(0.82%)	0.78%	(207.80%)	12.46%	.	184	46.46%
TN	1.88%	0.63%	0.53%	157.80%	8.49%	1.1632	3	0.76%
TP	167.70%	0.83%	0.73%	209.20%	11.63%	1.1274	202	51.01%
Total	8.53%	0.02%	1.13%	5.43%	17.97%	0.0147	396	100.00%

Periodicity in Performance

Next, we will examine how the model performs in different market environments. Does the algorithm perform better in all market conditions or only when the market is volatile, calm, rallying, crashing, or correcting? This is a particularly valuable insight that can impact the overall usefulness of the algorithm. For example, the algorithm might only be useful in market conditions that are unlikely to repeat in the near term such as during the COVID-19 pandemic.

Program 7.17: Comparing Portfolio Values (Algorithm-Based Versus Index Strategy) Using PROC SGPLOT

```
/*Comparing Portfolio Values Using PROC SGPLOT*/
proc sgplot data=scorespx;
      title height=14pt "Daily Portfolio Values";
      series x=Dates y=IndexVal/;
      series x=  Dates y=AlgoVal;
      yaxis label='Daily Portfolio Values';
run;
title;
```

Program 7.17 shows the code for the SGPLOT procedure that was used to graph the daily values of the algorithmic and passive portfolios. Notice the extent of the outperformance of the algorithm relative to the passive strategy from January to September 2021 as shown on the graph in Output 7.17. The algorithm's performance subsequently collapsed during the short correction that occurred in November 2021. It outperformed again during the end-of-year rally. And then underperformed during the correction that started in January 2022. The model did not capture the short rally that occurred between March and April of 2022. The outperformance of the algorithm then grew significantly between May and July 2022. Overall, these patterns suggest that most of the model's performance is constrained to periods of upward-trending markets. The model incurs large losses during down-trending markets because of the high number of false positive classifications. Investors who trade on these false positive signals will hold a long position in E-Mini futures contracts when the correct strategy should have been to hold a short position. Such a model could lead to catastrophic loss in portfolio values during market crashes.

Lastly, using the futures position was also instrumental in achieving the outperformance. Because index futures trade almost 24 hours a day, we can immediately exploit the insight we gain from the algorithm after the equity market closes. If we had waited until the next morning to trade on the signals we obtained from the algorithm by buying or short selling an S&P 500 Exchange Traded Fund (ETF) at market open, we would have earned approximately 11% return, which is about the same as holding a passive index position.

Output 7.17: Comparing Portfolio Values from Algorithmic Versus Passive Index Strategies

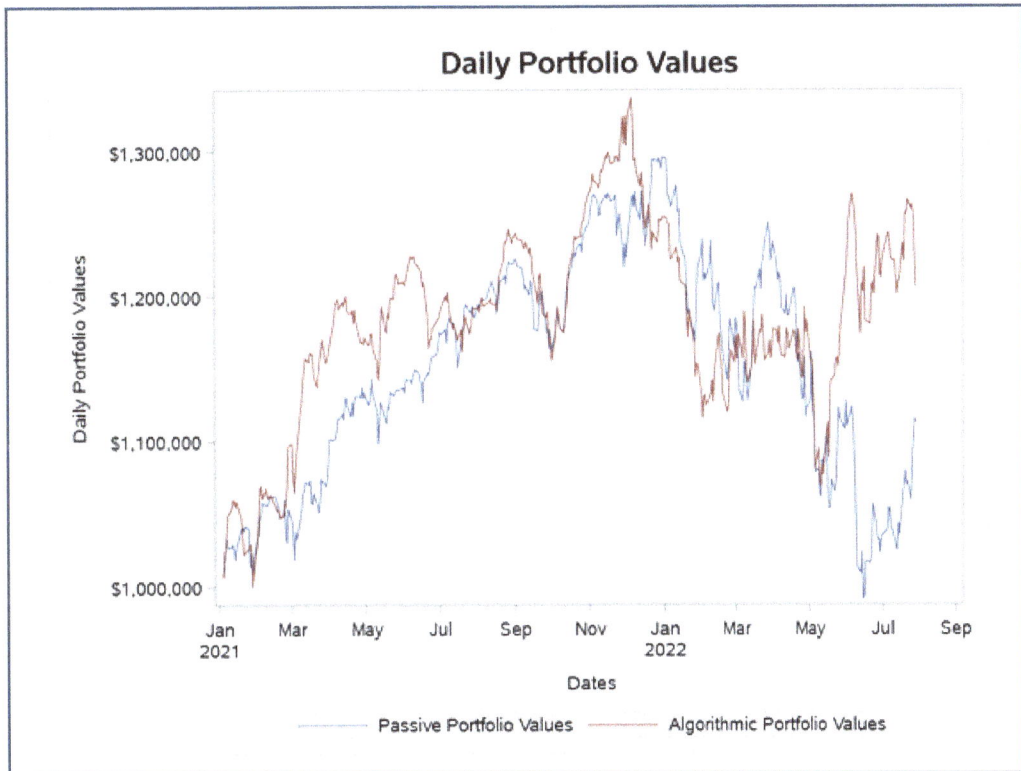

Closing Thoughts

Remember that backtesting of trading strategies is done in a controlled environment where all factors of the model have been predetermined. These conditions might not hold in the real world when you deploy the model. Hence, there is a need to further test the model in a live paper trading setting before placing actual money at risk. Although this is purely an academic exercise, there is some truth about the ability of algorithms to predict the next-day direction of the market. This explains why more than 70% of the trading that occurs on US exchanges is driven by computer intelligence systems. Predicting the direction of a broad-based market index is one of the many implementations of algorithms that are used in investment settings.

As more sophisticated algorithms are developed and more computational resources are brought to bear, one can only expect algorithms to have even more prominent roles in investment and financial services in general. While high predictive accuracy might be necessary to deploy algorithms in other settings, in reality, such restriction is unnecessary for investing purposes. You just need a model that can make better predictions than humans and other actors (including algorithms) in the financial marketplace, particularly during periods of consequential market movements.

It is important to note that timing and the actual investment products used might have also played a role in the results that we obtained. Predicting stock market outcomes remains a challenging endeavor. However, the net gain of 8% from correctly classifying 20 extra days and the possibility of further fine-tuning the model to improve on the false positive classifications is a strong motivation for those who ply this trade to continue developing better and more sophisticated trading algorithms.

Exercises

This exercise requires SAS/STAT and SAS Enterprise Miner licenses. However, you will work mostly in the SAS Studio environment.

1. Let us examine another method to implement our machine learning model for classifying the direction of the stock market. This approach entails a fair degree of automation. However, we will need to set up the data before calling up the SAS Rapid Predictive Modeler (RPM).
   a. Create a new process flow in SAS. Insert a programming node.
   (SKIP this step if you have already downloaded the data into your EMSAS Library.)
   b. Use the %DATAPULL macro to download the two SAS data sets (SPXRAW and SPXSCORE) from the book's GitHub repository. (See Program 7.1). Remember to run the DATAPULL macro first before invoking it with the %DATAPULL macro statement.

   ```
   /*Importing data set into your SAS Environment*/
   %datapull(spxraw,spxraw.sas7bdat);
   %datapull(spxscore,spxscore.sas7bdat);
   data emsas.spxraw ; set work.spxraw ;run;
   data emsas.spxscore; set work.spxscore;run;
   ```

   c. Navigate to the EMSAS Library. Then drag and drop the SPRAW data set in the Process Flow area. Save your Process Flow by clicking the Save icon.
   d. Click Tasks and Utilities. Scroll down and click the Data Mining icon. Then drag and drop the Rapid Predictive Modeler onto your process flow. Connect the control port of your SPXRAW data set to the control port of the Rapid Predictive Modeler.

e. Double-click the model. Verify that the EMSAS.SPXRAW is selected under DATA. If not, then click the Select a Table icon, and navigate to your EMSAS Library to select the SPXRAW data set.

f. Click the + sign next to the Dependent variable to launch the Select a Column. Select Target and then click OK.

g. Under ADDITIONAL ROLES, click the + sign next to "Variables to exclude from the model." Then select Target_Ret.

h. Click the +sign next to the ID variables, then select Dates.

i. Next, click the OPTIONS Tab. Under Model, select Advance in the drop-down menu for Modeling Method. Select Standard and Additional Reports in the drop-down menu for REPORT. Check all the boxes under Additional Reports.

j. In the OUTPUT tab, you can choose to save your Enterprise Miner Project or skip that option. Click Export the scoring code. Then navigate to a folder on your server where you would like to save the scoring code. Click also on the Score input data set. Keep the default location, which is your WORK Library.

k. Run the Rapid Predictive Modeler. Be aware that the procedure takes a fair amount of time to run.

l. Review the results from the estimation.

   i. Which variables were selected as important? Are they similar to the ones that we discussed earlier in the text?

   ii. Compare the ROC chart from the RPM to the ROC Chart we discussed earlier. Did the RPM produce better classification results (sensitivity and specificity)?

   iii. Review the Scorecard points generated by the RPM. Which variables have high scorecard points for high values? Which variables have low scorecard points for high values? What does this mean in terms of the ability of the variable to predict the next day's direction of the market?

   iv. Review the Classification Matrix. Are the classification patterns the same as we previously discussed?

   v. Review the Fit Statistics. What are the misclassification rates of the model for both the training and validation data sets? Are they better than those from the earlier section of this chapter?

   vi. Which algorithm did the RPM select as the champion model? Is it the same as the Ensemble model? Why did the RPM select the model? What type of improvement does the RPM approach provide over the step-by-step method we examined in the chapter text?

   vii. What are the potential pitfalls of the RPM approach over the step-by-step approach?

m. Navigate to the folder you selected to save your scoring code. Usually, it is the "/home/user/folder/". A subfolder (with a randomly generated name) would have been created by the RPM, with the scoring code in it. Double-click the subfolder and right-click the SCORE.SAS file, then select view properties. Copy the address of the file in the Location area of the pop-up box. Connect a program node to your RPM. Write a SAS program to score the SPXSCORE data set with the scoring code from the champion model to replicate the performance reports shown in Output 7.14 to Output 7.17. Remember to use the %INCLUDE statement in your DATA step. Note that the classification performed by the scoring code can be found in the EM_DECISION column of the output file.

> To modify Program 7.14, replace the fileref in %include with the correct path to the file containing the scoring code "***path/score.sas". Change every instance of I_TARGET to EM_DECISIONS. You can reuse Programs 7.14B to 7.17 in their current form.

i. Did the RPM model perform better or worse than the Ensemble model in terms of misclassification, profit, and estimating the right posterior probabilities?
ii. Review the algorithmic portfolio values of the RPM. How risky is the algorithmic portfolio, relative to the one discussed earlier?
iii. How high is the model risk of RPM's algorithmic strategy relative to the passive strategy?
iv. How high is the model risk of RPM's algorithmic strategy relative to the step-by-step algorithmic strategy?

Chapter 8: Introduction to Financial Optimization

Introduction to Optimization

In Chapter Six, we highlighted various types of estimation methods that rely on optimization. In those instances, the optimization problem involved obtaining some parameters of the population that best satisfied some predefined criteria. In this chapter, we will examine optimization from a different perspective. Here, the aim of optimization is to derive the values of a set of decision variables that best satisfy some criteria.

From a business point of view, organizations use optimization as a mathematical tool to achieve their business objectives in the most efficient manner possible. Therefore, optimization is used for making decisions on how to allocate organizational resources to maximize desired organizational objectives such as profit, or minimize undesirable outcomes such as risks or costs. Since most business decisions often have financial implications, the use of optimization techniques to arrive at such decisions is very common in the finance domain. Moreover, many optimization problems require financial data as inputs; therefore, financial data scientists must also be familiar with this domain.

Optimization is sometimes called prescriptive analytics in the data science domain. Unlike predictive analytics, which provides insight into what the outcome would be given a set of inputs, prescriptive analytics approaches the problem from an alternate perspective. Here, the insights from the analytic models are the optimal set of inputs that will result in the desired outcome.

There are many applications of optimizations in financial settings. In corporate finance settings, optimization is used for project selection, financial planning, competitive bidding, and strategic acquisitions. In banking settings, optimization is used for risk management, client management, business process improvement, and transaction automation.

One of the most common applications of optimization in financial settings is in the investment area. The well-known modern portfolio theory (MPT) proposes that investors select portfolios based on their assessment of the trade-off between the expected returns on the portfolios (mean) and the risks of holding the portfolios (variance). According to the theory, rational risk-averse investors who seek to maximize their wealth in a given period will prefer to hold portfolios that provide the highest level of return for a given level of risk, or the lowest level of risk for a given level of return. The mathematical framework of the MPT (also known as the mean-variance optimization) relies on optimization to construct these dominant (efficient) portfolios of assets. The practical success of this theory in investment settings can be seen in its wide-spread usage in many of the portfolio optimizers that are used in the investment management industry.

Besides portfolio allocations, optimization is also used for portfolio replication. In this instance, the portfolio manager uses optimization to construct a replica portfolio (using fewer assets) that can mimic the attribute of a portfolio and benchmark that consists of a larger number of assets. Optimization is also used for risk management and governance in an investment setting. In this instance, the desired portfolio outcome (expected return) is optimized against some type of operational constraints that might be set internally by the organization's risk governance framework or by virtue of regulatory oversight (such as the Basel Accords). Another application of optimization in investment settings is for the construction of portfolios to match the parameters (such as cash flow, duration, maturity, or value) of liabilities that the organization expects to fulfill at some point in the future (such as pension benefits or life insurance benefits payout).

In all of these instances, optimization helps financial decision-makers determine the best course of action to pursue to achieve the desired objectives. In subsequent sections of this chapter, we will explore different types of optimization methods and their applications to various finance problems. If you have read the previous chapters of this book, you should be familiar with many of the mathematical concepts that will be presented in this chapter. Readers who have not done so or are less proficient in mathematical statistics should focus on the general concepts, which are mostly provided at the end of every topic, and the accompanying SAS program as they go through the chapter.

Structure of Optimization Problems

In general, optimization problems can be constrained or unconstrained. In unconstrained optimization, the aim is to find the best solutions (maximum or minimum of a function) over its entire domain without any restrictions on the range of the decision variables. In constrained optimization, the aim is to find the best outcome within the bounds of some constraints that have been imposed on the decision variables. It is more common to frame optimization problems that are used in business settings as constrained optimization. Indeed, many of the business applications of optimization methods used today have their roots in operation research, which is a branch of management that emphasizes the use of analytical methods in decision-making. Therefore, their applications in the finance domain are often aligned with the framework used in the operation research field.

In general, the mathematical framework of optimization problems is described as follows. Consider a business problem defined by a real value function $f(x)$ and a set of real value constraints $S \subset \mathbb{R}^n$. The optimization problem can then be defined as the search for the $x^* \in \mathbb{R}^n$ that solves:

$$min \mid max \ f(x)$$
$$\text{s.t.} \quad x \in S;$$

(8.1)

where x is an array of decision variables, the function $f(x)$ is defined as the objective function and is analogous to many of the objective functions we discussed in Chapters Six and Seven, and S is the feasible region whose boundary and limit are defined as a collection of functions $C(x)$.

Feasibility

The optimization problem is deemed infeasible if we are unable to derive the array of decision variables that satisfies S. Infeasibility can arise because the regions defined by the boundaries of the intersection constraints constitute an empty array of decision variables or because the characteristics of the decision variables in the feasible region are incompatible with the requirements of the problem (for example, the optimal values of the decision variables are continuous; however, the problem requires integer solutions). From a business perspective, infeasibility might arise because of resource constraints or the selection of unrealistic targets.

Boundedness

An optimization problem is deemed as unbounded if there is no limit to the value $f(x)$ can take, usually because there are no constraints or bounds on the decision variables. Hence, the problem can be improved upon indefinitely. Most unbounded problems are such that the problem can only be improved in perpetuity in only one direction, such that there are no minimum (maximum) values of $f(x)$, but maximum (minimum) values. When multiple minimums or maximum values of $f(x)$ exist, then values of $f(x)$ that are minimum or maximum relative to other points in proximity are called local minimums or local maximums. The value of $f(x)$ that is minimum or maximum relative to all points in $f(x)$ are called the global minimum or global maximum. Therefore, an unbounded maximization (minimization) problem could have no maximum (minimum) and still possess a minimum (maximum). It is also possible to have an unbounded problem without maximums or minimums; however, this is more likely to be caused by problems that are incorrectly formulated.

Feasible regions with bounds have both upper and lower limits, while unbounded feasible regions have either upper or lower limits, but never both. From a business perspective, the boundaries of the feasible region are usually determined by organizational, contractual, operational, or regulatory constraints. For example, the Investment Company Act of 1940 allows mutual funds to borrow only up to a third (33.33%) of the fund asset. Hence, the boundaries of the feasible region for debt as a decision variable for a mutual fund will be between 0 and 33.33% of the fund's assets.

Smoothness

Optimization problems that consist of smooth functions are those in which both the objective function and constraints are differentiable, and their derivatives are continuous. From a business perspective, a differentiable objective function characterizes a business outcome (objective values) whose marginal values can be obtained by incremental changes to the decision variables. A continuous function is one in which a small change in the decision variables induces a small change in the objective values of the function. Problems with nonsmoothed functions are those with either discontinuous objective functions or discontinuous constraints. Although smoothness is extremely desirable in optimization, problems with nonsmoothed functions can still be tackled using special types of optimization algorithms.

Convexity

A strictly convex optimization problem possesses a single minimum, which inherently implies that such a point is also the global minimum. A convex function is an upward-bowed function such that a line segment between two points on the graph of the function will always lie above the graph. A strictly convex function will have a unique minimum because the curve will have a single minimum value. The second derivatives of convex functions are positive because they have first derivatives that are increasing in the values of the decision variables. Convexity is a desired property in optimization because it guarantees that an array of optimal values can be found simply by using a gradient descent approach in our search for the values of the decision variables that yield the best solutions. All other optimization problems that do not satisfy this condition are nonconvex, which implies that any minima obtained from the optimization might not necessarily be the global minimum. It is important to note that the concept of strict convexity can also be applied to a maximization problem since the negative of a strictly concave (downward bowed) function $g(x) = -f(x)$ is a strictly convex function.

Optimization Procedures in SAS

SAS Optimization software is a package of SAS procedures that can be used for solving a wide range of optimization problems. These include:

- PROC CLP – used for solving constraint satisfaction problems (CSPs) with linear, logical, and global constraints.
- PROC OPTLP and PROC MILP – used for solving linear programming and mixed-integer linear programming problems, respectively, using data tables that conform to the Mathematical Programming System (MPS) format.
- PROC OPTQP – used for solving optimization problems with quadratic objective functions and a set of linear constraints.
- PROC OPTNETWORK – includes a set of graph theory and network optimization algorithms that are used in complement to the generic optimization algorithms.
- PROC OPTMODEL – a full-fledged procedure that includes the solvers for all the previously listed problems. It also includes capabilities for managing and maintaining optimization models.

All financial optimization problems explored in this chapter can be easily solved using the OPTMODEL procedure. Hence, we will mostly focus solely on its usage for solving various financial problems moving forward.

PROC OPTMODEL

Although PROC OPTMODEL is native to the SAS environment, it is invoked using a modeling language that is distinct from the other SAS procedures you have encountered in the past. The modeling language is divided into three categories: the PROC statement used to invoke the procedure; the declaration statements used to define the parameters, variables, constraints, and objective functions of the problem to be solved; and the programming statements, which consist of a suite of commands that are used to read the data (in SAS format) for the problem into the model or to write the outputs of the optimization into a SAS data set. Programming statements are also used to set parameter values, generate text output, and invoke the appropriate solver for the optimization problem that is under scrutiny. Consider the optimization problem shown in Equation (8.2).

$$\min f(x,y) = 7x + 5y$$
$$\text{s.t.} \quad 4x + 3y \geq 19$$
$$x + y <= 5 \quad (8.2)$$
$$x \geq 0, \; y \geq 0$$

The mathematical presentation of the optimization shown above can be written in the OPTMODEL modeling language and solved using the procedure as shown in Program 8.1.

Program 8.1: Simple PROC OPTMODEL Problem

```
/*Using PROC OPTMODEL to Solve a Simple Optimization Problem*/
proc optmodel;
     var x >= 0 , y >= 0;
     min f = 7*x +5*y;
     con 4*x + 3*y >= 19;
     con  x + y <= 5;
     solve;
     print x y;
quit;
```

In the SAS code above, the PROC OPTMODEL statement is used to invoke the OPTMODEL procedure. The VAR, MIN, and CON statements are the declaration statements that are used to define the decision variables (x and y), the objective function $(\min f)$, and the two constraints, respectively. The SOLVE, PRINT, and QUIT statements are used to invoke the SOLVER, PRINT the output from the OPTMODEL procedure, and terminate the procedure, respectively.

Output 8.1: Results from Simple PROC OPTMODEL

The OPTMODEL Procedure

Problem Summary	
Objective Sense	Minimization
Objective Function	f
Objective Type	Linear
Number of Variables	2
Bounded Above	0
Bounded Below	2
Bounded Below and Above	0
Free	0
Fixed	0
Number of Constraints	2
Linear LE (<=)	1
Linear EQ (=)	0
Linear GE (>=)	1
Linear Range	0
Constraint Coefficients	4

The OPTMODEL Procedure

Solution Summary	
Solver	LP
Algorithm	Dual Simplex
Objective Function	f
Solution Status	Optimal
Objective Value	33
Primal Infeasibility	0
Dual Infeasibility	0
Bound Infeasibility	0
Iterations	0
Presolve Time	0.00
Solution Time	0.00

x	y
4	1

Output 8.1 shows the results from invoking the OPTMODEL procedure. The Problem Summary table is shown on the left-hand side, while the Solution Summary table is shown on the right-hand side. Notice the description of the problem as shown in the Problem Summary table includes the type of optimization, the number of variables, the number, and types of bounds, as well as the number and types of constraints. Also included are the free and fixed parameters and the constraint coefficients. The Solution Summary table displays the type of solver (LP), the algorithm used (dual simplex), the name of the objective function (f), the solution status (Optimal), and the optimal value of the objective function (33). Also reported are the infeasibility statuses (Primal, Dual, and Bound) of the optimization. However, because this problem has an optimal solution, the Primal, Dual, and Bound infeasibilities are all zeros. We will discuss the primal and dual problems in a subsequent subsection of this chapter. Lastly, the Solution Summary also reports the optimal values of the x and y decision variables, which are 4 and 1.

Types of Optimization Problems

Optimization problems vary in the types of decision variables (discrete or continuous), and the types of functions (linear or nonlinear, continuous, or discontinuous). For example, an optimization problem can consist of linear functions of discrete or continuous variables, or nonlinear functions of continuous variables. The combinations of these features define the characteristics of the optimization problem and the algorithms that can be used to solve them. All optimization problems can be classified into two broad categories: linear optimization problems and non-linear optimization problems. Linear optimizations are performed on linear objective functions subject to linear constraints. In cases where a collection of continuous objective functions and constraints include non-linear functions, then the optimization problems are defined as non-linear optimization problems.

Linear Optimization or Programming

In linear programming (LP), the mathematical optimization problem consists of a collection of linear objective functions and linear constraints, which could be equality or inequality types of constraints. In its standard form, the LP problem is to minimize an objective function, subject to a finite set of constraints and is expressed as:

$$\min \quad c'x$$
$$\text{s.t.} \quad Ax \geq b, x \geq 0$$

(8.3)

where c, A, and b are matrices of constants, and b represents the variables to be determined. In business settings, it is common for x to represent some decisions, choices, or input levels that are controllable by the firm. Whereas the constants c, A, and b represent the set of uncontrollable features of the problems. These could be operational methodology as in the case of c, resource or regulatory constraints as in the case of b, or operational constraints as in the case of A. Mathematically, these constraints can be imposed on the problems as bound constraints or as linear equality or inequality constraints.

The assumptions of linear programming include:

- **Linearity or Proportionality:** Each variable contributes proportionally in terms of its value to both the objective function and the constraint.
- **Additivity:** The contribution of each variable to the objective function is independent of the contribution of other variables. There are no synergistic or antagonistic interactions among the variables.
- **Certainty:** All parameters of the LP model are known and do not change in the model.
- **Finiteness:** The number of decision variables and constraints is finite.
- **Divisibility:** The decision variables can take on fractional values.

Linear programming problems where the decision variable can only be integers (for example, the number of assets in a portfolio or clients to serve) are called integer linear programs (ILP), while those in which some decision variables can only be integers are called mixed integer linear programs (MILP). Regardless of the LP problem we are tackling, you should note that the decision variables must be real values, and the objective function and constraints must be linear equations.

Simple Bond Portfolio Allocation Problem

Let us start with a simple linear programming approach to a bond portfolio management scenario. The portfolio manager must decide how to efficiently allocate $1 million of capital between two bonds to maximize the yield on the portfolio while keeping the duration of the portfolio to no more than six years. Suppose both bonds have the same credit risk, but different durations. The YTM on Bond x_1, which has a duration of 4.5 years is 4.0%, while the YTM on Bond x_2, which has a duration of 8.0 years is 6.0%. x_1 and x_2 represents the portfolio weights in each bond. The optimal solution to this problem is the allocations to each bond that maximize the portfolio yield within the set duration constraints. Before we introduce the SAS code for the problem, let us also impose a short selling constraint such that $x_1 \geq 0$ and $x_2 \geq 0$. The mathematical representation of the portfolio optimization problem is as follows:

$$\max \ Z = 4x_1 + 6x_2$$
$$\text{s.t.} \qquad 4.5x_1 + 8.0x_2 \leq 6.0$$
$$x_1 + x_2 = 1.0 \tag{8.4}$$
$$x_1 \geq 0 \text{ and } x_2 \geq 0$$

Because linear programming problems are usually constructed with inequality constraints, we can write $x_1 + x_2 = 1$ as a system of two inequality constraints (for example, $x_1 + x_2 \geq 1$ and $x_1 + x_2 \leq 1$). Furthermore, we can multiply $x_1 + x_2 \geq 1$ by -1, to convert it into a less-than-constraint $\left(x_1 + x_2 \leq 1 \right)$. We can now rewrite our optimization problem in its primal form as follows.

$$\max \ Z = 4x_1 + 6x_2$$
$$\text{s.t.} \qquad 4.5x_1 + 8.0x_2 \leq 6.0$$
$$x_1 + x_2 \leq 1.0$$
$$- x_1 - x_2 \leq -1.0$$
$$x_1 \geq 0 \text{ and } x_2 \geq 0 \tag{8.5}$$

Figure 8.1 displays the feasible (shaded) region for the optimal solutions to the bond portfolio allocation problem. The boundaries of the region are defined by the intersections of the plots of the constraints with each other and with both axes (since $x_1 \geq 0$ and $x_2 \geq 0$). Notice that values of x_2 that are greater than 0.8 (80%) or less than 0.0 are infeasible because they lie outside the region. The same infeasibility condition applies to the values of x_1 that are greater than 1.0 (100%) or less than 0.0. Thus, the search for the optimal values of x_1 and x_2 for our portfolio allocation problem must lie within the boundaries of (0.0,0.0), (0.0,0.75), (0.6,0.4), and (1.0,0.0).

Figure 8.1: Feasible Region

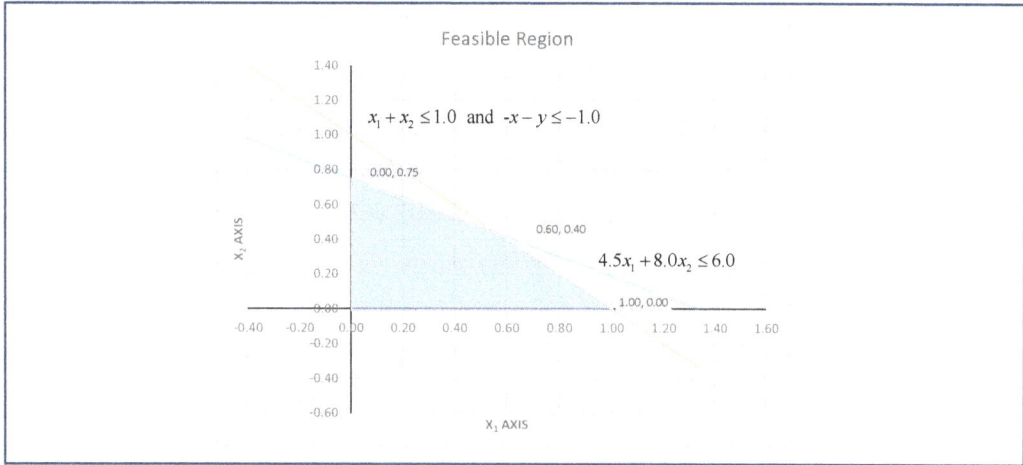

The two algorithms that are commonly used for solving linear programming problems are the simplex method and the interior point method. The simplex algorithm solves linear optimization problems by iterating across the boundaries of the feasible regions until an optimal solution is found. The interior point approach solves the optimization problems by iterating from inside the feasible region toward the boundaries until the optimal condition is satisfied. In general, the interior point solution is more efficient than the simplex method in solving complex and non-linear optimization problems. In Chapter Seven, the interior point method was introduced as one of the optimization methods of the support vector machine (SVM) algorithm. In reality, the SVM is a classification model that is based on the quadratic optimization problem. We will discuss quadratic optimization and the interior point method in subsequent sections of this chapter.

Simplex Method

The simplex framework starts by transforming the equation system into a standard form such that the objective function (if applicable) is changed from a minimization problem into a maximization problem. All linear inequality must also be in the form of less-than or equal-to and all variables must be nonnegative. Nonnegative slack variables (s_1, s_2, s_3) are then added to the constraint equations to transform them from inequality constraints to equality constraints as shown in Equation (8.6) below.

$$
\begin{aligned}
\max \ &Z \\
\text{s.t.} \quad &Z - 4x_1 - 6x_2 = 0.0 \\
&4.5x_1 + 8.0x_2 + s_1 = 6.0 \\
&x_1 + x_2 + s_2 = 1.0 \\
&x_1 + x_2 + s_3 = -1.0 \\
&x_1, x_2, s_1, s_2, s_3 \geq 0.
\end{aligned}
$$

(8.6)

Table 8.1: Simplex Tableau One

LHS	x_1	x_2	s_1	s_2	s_3	Z	RHS	Ratio Test
	-4.0	-6.0	0.0	0.0	0.0	1.0	0.0	
x_2	4.5	8.0	1.0	0.0	0.0	0.0	6.0	0.75
	1.0	1.0	0.0	1.0	0.0	0.0	1.0	1
	1.0	1.0	0.0	0.0	1.0	0.0	1.0	1

The next step in the simplex algorithm is the creation of a tableau of the equation system as shown in Table 8.1. The tableau consists of the coefficients of the variables in the objective function and constraints equation written in tabular form. The column headings are variable names, while the row entries are the coefficients of each variable in the objective function and the respective constraint equation as shown below. Furthermore, let us refer to the first column, which we will use to keep track of the pivot row as the left-hand-side (LHS) column, while the column before the last column on the right, which contains the values of the equation constants as the right-hand-side (RHS) column.

With our first simplex tableau now set, an optimality check is performed to examine if the coefficients of the variables in the first row are positive. If the coefficients are not, then the values of the variable are not the optimal values. The optimal solution can be found from a set of standardized coefficients of the variables that yields the highest objective function using a recursive process. The process starts with the selection of a pivot column (the variable corresponding to the column with the lowest coefficient in the objective function row, which in our case, is the variable x_2 that has a coefficient of -6.0). For the pivot column, a pivot row is then selected (the row of the variable with the lowest ratio of the coefficient of the pivot column

and the constraint column, $\min\left\{\dfrac{6.0}{8.0}, \dfrac{1.0}{1.0}, \dfrac{1.0}{1.0}\right\}$).[1] The pivot element is the value of the pivot variable that is at the intersection of the pivot row and pivot column (8.0). The coefficient of the pivot element is then standardized to the value of 1 by dividing the entire row by the value of the selected pivot element as shown in Table 8.2.

To optimize the x_2 variable in the first constraint equation, each element on the non-pivot row is then standardized by adding the product of the negative value of the element of the pivot column and the corresponding pivot row to the values of each element in the Simplex Tableau One. (For example, for the first element of the first column, the calculation will be $[-(-6.0*0.563)-4.0]=-0.625$). Notice that all the values of the pivot variable in the non-pivot row are now set to zero. This makes x_2 a basic variable.[2] Also, notice that the Z column has one

---

[1] Notice that the variable with the lowest ratio is also x_2 (0.75). The minimum of the ratios shows the extent to which the pivot variable can be increased without causing the other variables to become negative.
[2] A basic variable is a variable with a value of 1 in one of the rows of the pivot column and a corresponding value of zero for the variables in other rows of the same column.

Table 8.2: Standardizing Pivot Rows

x_2	4.5/8.0	8.0/8.0	1.0/8.0	0.0/8.0	0.0/8.0	0.0/8.0	6.0/8.0	0.75
	0.563	1.00	0.125	0.00	0.00	0.00	0.75	

Table 8.3: Simplex Tableau Two

LHS	x_1	x_2	s_1	s_2	s_3	Z	RHS	Ratio Test
Z	-0.625	0.000	0.750	0.000	0.000	1.000	4.500	-0.625
x_2	0.563	1.000	0.125	0.000	0.000	0.000	0.750	0.563
	0.438	0.000	-0.125	1.000	0.000	0.000	0.250	0.438
	0.438	0.000	-0.125	0.000	1.000	0.000	0.250	0.438

Table 8.4: Simplex Tableau Three

LHS	x_1	x_2	s_1	s_2	s_3	Z	RHS	Ratio Test
Z	-0.625	0.000	0.750	0.000	0.000	1.000	4.500	
x_2	0.563	1.000	0.125	0.000	0.000	0.000	0.750	1.333
x_1	0.438	0.000	-0.125	1.000	0.000	0.000	0.250	0.571
	0.438	0.000	-0.125	0.000	1.000	0.000	0.250	0.571

row with a coefficient with a value of 1. The element of the RHS column for the Z row shows the value of the objective function as the system is being optimized. The corresponding rows for each basic variable show the value of the variable at that point in the optimization.

You can also observe that after the first iteration, $Z = 4.50$ and $x_2 = 0.75$. We can check whether the problem is optimized by revisiting the coefficients of the variables in the objective function row. You will notice on that row that the coefficient of the x_1 variable is still negative, which implies that the problem is not yet optimized. Since the element of the x_1 variable in the same column is the lowest, this column will now become our new pivot column for the second round of optimization. Dividing the RHS column by the new pivot column (x_1) and selecting the row with the minimum ratio gives us our new pivot row, which is the row for the second constraint equation.

We can now standardize the second pivot row by dividing the elements of the entire row with the value of the new pivot element (0.438).

The x_1 variable in the second constraint equation is then optimized by adding to each element of the non-pivot rows, the product of the negative value of the element of the new pivot column times the corresponding new pivot row as shown in Simplex Tableau Three.

Table 8.5: Standardizing Pivot Rows

x_1	0.438/0.438	0.000/0.438	-0.125/0.438	1.000/0.438	0.000/0.438	0.000/0.438	0.250/0.438	**0.57**
	1.000	0.000	-0.286	2.286	0.000	0.000	0.571	

Table 8.6: Simplex Tableau Four

LHS	x_1	x_2	s_1	s_2	s_3	Z	RHS	Ratio Test
Z	0.000	0.000	0.571	1.429	0.000	1.000	4.857	
x_2	0.000	1.000	0.286	-1.286	0.000	0.000	0.429	1.33
x_1	1.000	0.000	-0.286	2.286	0.000	0.000	0.571	0.57
	0.000	0.000	0.000	-1.000	1.000	0.000	0.000	0.57

Now, notice on the fourth simplex tableau, that the coefficients of the objective function row are now positive, which implies that we have reached the optimal values of the decision variables. The elements of the RHS column and its corresponding rows for the coefficients of x_1, x_2, and Z are now at the optimum values of the objective function and the two decision variables. In terms of the bond portfolio allocation problem, the values of x_1 and x_2 indicate that approximately 57% ($570,000) of the portfolio should be allocated to Bond x_1 and approximately 43% ($430,000) to Bond x_2. The expected return of the optimized portfolio is 4.86%. If you attempt to locate the allocation on the graph shown in Figure 8.1, you will see the coordinates of the optimal values of x_1 and x_2 are within the vicinity of the point of the plots of the two constraints.

Now that we have discussed the conceptual framework of linear programming, we will proceed to solve the same problem using the OPTMODEL procedure. Program 8.2 shows the SAS code for solving the linear optimization problem. In the SAS code, the declaration statements (VAR, MAX, CON) were used to set up the model. Specifically, the VAR statement is used to specify the decision variables along with their nonnegative bounds. The MAX statement specifies the objective function, and the two CON statements specify the maximum duration constraint and the full investment portfolio constraint. The programming statements (SOLVE, PRINT, and EXPAND) were used to invoke the solver and to request the print of various outputs from the procedure. Namely, the SOLVE statement was used to request the primal simplex solver. You should note that the default solver for the LP problem is the dual simplex solver. The first PRINT statement was used to request the printing of the optimal values of the decision variables (x_1 and x_2). The EXPAND statement was used to request the printing of the variables, objectives, implicit variables, and constraints used in the primal form of the LP Program. If you do not specify a name for each of your constraints, the procedure will utilize a predefined anonymous array of constraints (_ACON_) and a predefined numeric parameter (_NACON_), which contains the number of the anonymous constraint. The BODY suffix refers to the expression of the constraints in the standardized form.

Program 8.2: Using PROC OPTMODEL to Solve Simple Optimization Problem

```
/*The Primal Simplex Method in PROC OPTMODEL*/
proc optmodel;
     var x1 >= 0.0 , x2 >= 0.0;
     max Z = 4*x1 +6*x2;
     con 4.5*x1 + 8*x2 <= 6.0;
     con x1 + x2= 1.0;
     solve with lp / algorithm=ps;
     print x1 x2;
     print _ACON_.dual _ACON_.body;
     expand;
quit;
```

Output 8.2: Using PROC OPTMODEL to Solve Bond Allocation Problem

EXPAND Statement Output

```
Var x1 >= 0
Var x2 >= 0
Maximize Z=4*x1 + 6*x2
Constraint _ACON_[1]: 4.5*x1 + 8*x2 <= 6
Constraint _ACON_[2]: x1 + x2 = 1
```

The OPTMODEL Procedure

Problem Summary

Objective Sense	Maximization
Objective Function	Z
Objective Type	Linear
Number of Variables	2
Bounded Above	0
Bounded Below	2
Bounded Below and Above	0
Free	0
Fixed	0
Number of Constraints	2
Linear LE (<=)	1
Linear EQ (=)	1
Linear GE (>=)	0
Linear Range	0
Constraint Coefficients	4

The OPTMODEL Procedure

Solution Summary

Solver	LP
Algorithm	Primal Simplex
Objective Function	Z
Solution Status	Optimal
Objective Value	4 8571428571
Primal Infeasibility	0
Dual Infeasibility	0
Bound Infeasibility	0
Iterations	0
Presolve Time	0 00
Solution Time	0 00

x1	x2
0 57143	0 42857

[1]	_ACON_.DUAL	_ACON_.BODY
1	0 57143	6
2	1 42857	1

Duality

It turns out that for every linear programming problem that is written in its primal form, there is a corresponding version of the problem that can be written in its dual form if certain conditions are met. This is a particularly useful concept in linear programming because any feasible solution to the dual problem gives the bound of the value of the objective function in its primal problem form. Consider an LP problem written in the primal form using matrix algebra as follows:

$$\max \quad c'x$$
$$\text{s.t.} \quad Ax \le b, x \ge 0 \tag{8.7}$$

Then the dual of the problem can be written as follows:

$$\min \quad b'y$$
$$\text{s.t.} \quad A'y \le c, y \ge 0 \tag{8.8}$$

where y is a vector of positive multiplicative scaling factors such that $c'x \le y'Ax \le b'y$. Since $x \ge 0$, then some algebraic combination of the elements of y defines the upper bound of the objective function $c'x$. Notice that the approach to find the values of the elements of y that will define the upper bound of the primal objective function is also an LP program since we will be minimizing the values of the elements. Hence, the maximum value of the objective function of the primal LP problem is equivalent to the minimum value of the objective function of the corresponding dual LP program.

$$\max \quad c'x = \min \quad b'y \tag{8.9}$$

The same requirement applies to the minimization problem in its primal form, in the sense that the algebraic combination of the elements of y will also define the lower bound of the primal objective function. Therefore, the minimum value of the objective function of the primal LP problem will be equal to the maximum value of its corresponding dual problem. You can create dual LP problems from the primal form, by creating a variable for each constraint in the primal problem, and a constraint for each variable in the primal problem. The dual form of our bond allocation LP problem can be written in the following form.

$$\min \quad 6y_1 + y_2$$
$$\text{s.t.} \quad 4.5y_1 + y_2 \ge 4.0 \tag{8.10}$$
$$8.0y_1 + y_2 = 6.0$$

Although we will not go much deeper into the mathematics of duality,[3] it is important to familiarize yourself with the duality theorems of linear programming that encompass the concept

---

[3] If you are interested gaining a deeper knowledge of duality and its implementation in SAS, please review the SAS Optimization documentation at http://documentation.sas.com/doc/en/pgmsascdc/9.4_3.2/ casmopt/casmopt_optmodel_details50.htm

we have just discussed. The weak duality theorem states that if x is a feasible solution to the LP problem in its primal form, and y is a feasible solution to the LP problem in its dual form, then if the dual problem is infeasible, the primal problem is unbounded. If the primal problem is unbounded, then the dual problem is infeasible.

Program 8.3: Solving the Dual of an Optimization Problem Using PROC OPTMODEL

```
/*Solving the Dual of an Optimization Problem using PROC OPTMODEL*/
proc optmodel;
      var y1 >= 0.0 , y2 >= 0.0;
      min Z = 6*y1 +y2;
      con 4.5*y1 + y2 >=4.0;
      con  8.0*y1 + y2= 6.0;
      solve with lp / algorithm=ps;
      print y1 y2;
      print _ACON_.dual _ACON_.body;
      expand;
quit;
```

If both the dual and primal problems are feasible and bounded, and $c'x = b'y$, the x must be the optimal for the primal LP and y the optimal for the dual LP. Drawing from the above, the strong duality theorem states that if a linear programming problem in its primal form has an optimal solution, then the same problem expressed in the dual form will also have an optimal solution with the value of its objective function equal to that of the primal problem.

In the SAS code shown in Program 8.3, we rewrote the SAS code in Program 8.2 to solve the dual LP program using the primal simplex algorithm. Remember that the default algorithm for solving the LP problem in the OPTMODEL procedure is the dual simplex algorithm, so rewriting the primal problem in its dual form would not be necessary in practice as the procedure automatically does the conversion before solving the LP problem. The code shown in Program 8.3 is for demonstration purposes. In reality, the dual of the dual LP problem is the primal form of the same problem. Therefore, if you do not specify ALGORITHM=PS with the dual form of the LP program, the OPTMODEL procedure will by default convert the dual form back to its primal (dual of the dual) before solving it.[4]

Notice that the value of the objective function for the dual LP problem is the same as the value for the primal LP problem that is shown in Output 8.2. However, the optimal values of the decision variables (y_1 and y_2) are values of the duals of the constraint of the primal problem. While the optimal values of the primal problem are the values of the duals of the constraints of the dual problem. This reinforces our previous assertion that the dual of the dual LP problem is the primal LP problem.

---

[4] You can verify this statement by replacing the ALGORITHM=PS statement with ALGORITHM=DS statement or just specify the SOLVE statement alone, since the default algorithm is the dual simplex method.

Output 8.3: Results from Solving the Dual of an Optimization Problem

The OPTMODEL Procedure

Problem Summary	
Objective Sense	Minimization
Objective Function	Z
Objective Type	Linear
Number of Variables	2
Bounded Above	0
Bounded Below	2
Bounded Below and Above	0
Free	0
Fixed	0
Number of Constraints	2
Linear LE (<=)	0
Linear EQ (=)	1
Linear GE (>=)	1
Linear Range	0
Constraint Coefficients	4

The OPTMODEL Procedure

Solution Summary	
Solver	LP
Algorithm	Primal Simplex
Objective Function	Z
Solution Status	Optimal
Objective Value	4.8571428571
Primal Infeasibility	0
Dual Infeasibility	0
Bound Infeasibility	0
Iterations	0
Presolve Time	0.00
Solution Time	0.00

y1	y2
0.57143	1.4286

[1]	_ACON_.DUAL	_ACON_.BODY
1	0.57143	4
2	0.42857	6

EXPAND Statement Output

```
Var y1 >= 0
Var y2 >= 0
Minimize Z=6*y1 + y2
Constraint _ACON_[1]: 4.5*y1 + y2 >= 4
Constraint _ACON_[2]: 8*y1 + y2 = 6
```

Integer Linear Programming (ILP)

You might have noticed in the previous problem that the optimal values of the decision variables can take fractional or decimal values. However, in the real world, there are many instances where the optimal values of the decision variables must be integers. For example, the number of customers to serve or the unit of products to make or purchase. In these cases, we will need to use a special type of linear programming that is called integer linear programming (ILP). In reality, integer linear programming is simply an additional constraint that is imposed on an LP problem that the optimal values of all the decision variables must be integers. In instances where only some values of the decision variables must be integers, the problem is called a mixed integer linear program (MILP).

Although they are conceptually simple to understand, solving ILP and MILP problems is more challenging than LP problems because the search for the optimal solutions to these types of

Figure 8.2: Feasible Regions of Integer Linear Programming Problem

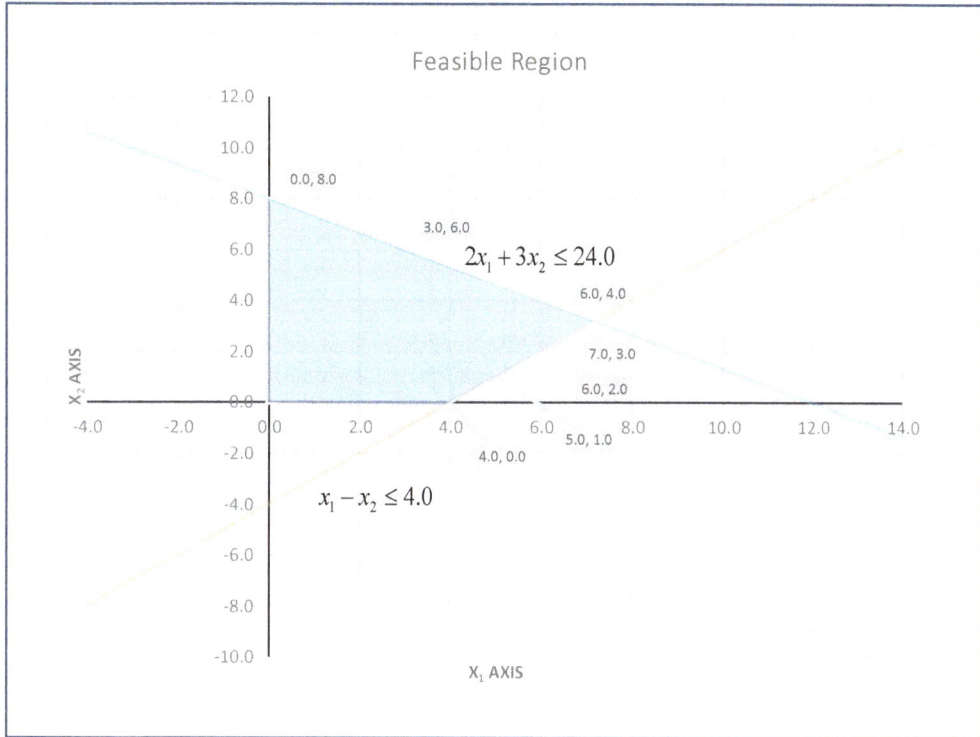

problems is no longer continuous but a jump from one feasible coordinate of integer values to another feasible combination of integer values. Fractional values between these integer points, which in theory could be optimal for an ordinary LP problem, are no longer so, because of the integer constraint. Hence, solving these problems is more challenging due to the further restrictions on what could constitute a feasible region. Consider the ILP problem in Equation (8.11).

$$\begin{aligned}
\text{max} \quad & 4x_1 + 3x_2 \\
\text{s.t.} \quad & 2x_1 + 3x_2 \leq 24 \\
& x_1 - x_2 \leq 4 \\
& x_1 \geq 0, x_2 \geq 0, \ x_1 \ \text{integer}, \ x_2 \ \text{integer}
\end{aligned}$$

(8.11)

The feasible solutions to the ILP problem are the seven integer coordinates shown in Figure 8.2. They are [0,8], [3,6], [6,4], [7,3], [6,2], [5,1], and [4,0]. If we try to solve the problem using the simplex algorithm by relaxing the integer constraint, the optimal value of the decision variables would be [7.2,3.2]. However, the ILP problem cannot have fractional optimal values. Nevertheless, the optimal values from the simplex algorithm will be a reliable starting point for the search for the optimal values that satisfy the ILP requirement. The optimal integer values for the decision variables may lie between the nearest integers to 7.2 and 3.2, which will be [7,3] and [8,4]. These sets of values form the branch and boundaries of the new search for the optimal solution to the LP problem. However, [8,4] are outside the boundaries of the feasible region. Therefore, the best path for the search will be in the direction of the [7,3], which are the nearest integer feasible points for the optimization. It turns out that from the 7 feasible points shown earlier, [7,3] yields the highest value for the objective function $4(7)+3(3)=37$ and thus will be optimal integer values for the decision variables. The approach we just described is called the branch and bound algorithm.

Branch and Bound Method

The branch and bound first solves the ILP problem as a regular LP problem without the integer restriction. It then recursively computes the lower and upper bound of the optimal values over these regions, and reoptimizes the problem, shrinking the boundaries in each iteration, until a feasible set of integers is reached. If no other feasible set of integers can result in a better value of the objective function, then the candidate feasible integer solution will be selected as the optimal solution. The branch and bound algorithm is also used to solve both ILP and MILP problems. For MILP problems, the integer restriction is also initially relaxed. Branching and bounding are then performed using only the decision variables with integer restrictions.

Profit Maximization Problem

Now that we have established a foundation in ILP, let us proceed to other sophisticated applications of ILP in business settings. An auto manufacturer that makes three types of vehicles (Sedans, SUVs, and Trucks) is trying to determine the optimal combination of vehicles to produce each month that will result in maximum profitability for the company. To make each vehicle, the company requires labor hours, equipment hours, and raw materials. The information concerning the units of each resource that is consumed in making each type of vehicle and the sales prices for each type of vehicle are shown in Table 8.7.

Table 8.7: Problem Data for Profit Optimization

	Labor	Equipment	Materials	Sales Price
Sedan	40	35	40	$26,000.00
SUVs	50	45	60	$37,500.00
Trucks	60	60	75	$45,000.00
Resource Cost and Availability				
	Labor	Equipment	Materials	
Cost/Unit	$50.00	$35.00	$400.00	
Available Units	1,000,000	2,000,000	2,000,000	

Problem Statement

Before we implement the SAS code to solve the optimization problem, it might be helpful to review the conceptual framework of the problem. Remember the main aim of the company is not necessarily to produce vehicles, but to maximize its profitability. The types and units of vehicles produced each month are merely the avenues by which the company can achieve this objective. Therefore, they will be decision variables that will be optimized to maximize our profit function. The total revenue for the units of each type of vehicle produced less the total cost of the units of the resources consumed in producing each type of vehicle will form the objective function that would be maximized. The finite number of each resource available to produce any combination of the units of vehicle types including 1,000,000 hours of labor, 2,000,000 equipment hours, and 2,000,000 units of raw materials will be used to form the constraints for the problem. We can summarize our objective function and constraints as follows:

$$\begin{aligned}
\text{Maximize} \quad & \text{Profit} = \text{Revenue} - \text{Production Cost} \\
\text{s.t.} \quad & \text{Labor Units } (Sedans, \; SUVs, \; Trucks) \le 1,000,000 \\
& \text{Equipment Units } (Sedans, \; SUVs, \; Trucks) \le 2,000,000 \qquad (8.12) \\
& \text{Material Units } (Sedans, \; SUVs, \; Trucks) \le 2,000,000 \\
& N(Sedans) \ge 0, \; N(SUVs) \ge 0, \; N(Trucks) \ge 0
\end{aligned}$$

Program 8.4: Solving ILP Problem (Profit Maximization) Using PROC OPTMODEL

```
/* Using PROC OPTMODEL for Integer Linear Programming (ILP) Problem */
proc optmodel;
     /* declare variables */
     var Sedans >= 0 integer, SUVs >= 0 integer, Trucks>=0 integer;

     /* declare constraints */
     con Labor: 40*Sedans + 50*SUVs+ 60*Trucks <= 1000000;
     con Equipment: 35*Sedans + 45*SUVs + 60*Trucks<=2000000;
     con Materials: 40*Sedans + 60*SUVs + 75*Trucks <= 2000000;

     /* declare objective */
     max NetProfit = 26000*Sedans + 37500*SUVs + 45000*Trucks
            - 50 * (40*Sedans + 50*SUVs+ 60*Trucks)
            - 35 * (35*Sedans + 45*SUVs + 60*Trucks)
            - 400 * (40*Sedans + 60*SUVs + 75*Trucks);
     expand;
     solve;
     print Sedans SUVs Trucks;
quit;
```

Program 8.4 shows the SAS code that could be used to find the type and the optimal number of vehicles to produce. In the code, the decision variables are the optimal number of each vehicle type to produce. It is highly unlikely that the company will be able to sell a fractional unit of a vehicle; hence, we also impose the constraint that the optimal number of each vehicle produced must be integers.

In line with Equation (8.12), the CON statement was used to declare three constraint equations and the MAX statement to declare the objective function. The EXPAND statement is used to request the printing of the specified constraint, variable, implicit variable, or objective function in the current problem after expanding aggregation operators, substituting the current value for parameters and indices, and resolving constant subexpressions. The SOLVE statement is used to request the algorithm to solve the integer LP problem specified. The default algorithm for solving integer LP problems in SAS is the Branch and Cut algorithm. The Branch and Cut algorithm is an extension of the Branch and Bound algorithm. The algorithm adds cutting planes to the Branch and Bound algorithm to define the integer boundaries in the search for the optimal solution to the ILP problem. Branch and Cut are also used to solve mixed integer linear problems.

Output 8.4: Results from ILP Problem Using PROC OPTMODEL

The OPTMODEL Procedure

Problem Summary

Objective Sense	Maximization
Objective Function	NetProfit
Objective Type	Linear
Number of Variables	3
Bounded Above	0
Bounded Below	3
Bounded Below and Above	0
Free	0
Fixed	0
Binary	0
Integer	3
Number of Constraints	3
Linear LE (<=)	3
Linear EQ (=)	0
Linear GE (>=)	0
Linear Range	0
Constraint Coefficients	9

The OPTMODEL Procedure

Solution Summary

Solver	MILP
Algorithm	Branch and Cut
Objective Function	NetProfit
Solution Status	Optimal
Objective Value	188500000
Relative Gap	0
Absolute Gap	0
Primal Infeasibility	0
Bound Infeasibility	0
Integer Infeasibility	0
Best Bound	188500000
Nodes	1
Solutions Found	6
Iterations	3
Presolve Time	0.00
Solution Time	0.00

Sedans	SUVs	Trucks
0	20000	0

EXPAND Statement Output

```
Var Sedans INTEGER >= 0
Var SUVs INTEGER >= 0
Var Trucks INTEGER >= 0
Maximize NetProfit=6775*Sedans + 9425*SUVs + 9900*Trucks
Constraint Labor: 40*Sedans + 50*SUVs + 60*Trucks <= 1000000
Constraint Equipment: 35*Sedans + 45*SUVs + 60*Trucks <= 2000000
Constraint Materials: 40*Sedans + 60*SUVs + 75*Trucks <= 2000000
```

Output 8.4 shows the results that were obtained from invoking the OPTMODEL procedure and the accompanying declaration and programming statements. Notice that the optimal type of vehicle to make was SUVs and the optimal quantity of SUVs to make was 20,000 units. The objective value, which is the maximum profit that will be obtained from making 20,000 units of SUVs, is $188,500,000. You may wonder why the optimal solution does not include any units of Sedans and Trucks. That is because SUVs have the highest profit per unit of vehicle produced. Remember that LP assumes linearity and additivity; therefore, in the absence of a constraint or bounds that specify a greater than zero unit of the other vehicle types, the algorithm with simply optimize along the path that provides the highest increase in the objective value per unit increase in the values of the decision variable, which in this case is the SUV.

Using Arrays, Index Sets, and Data Sets in the OPTMODEL Procedure

So far, we have hardcoded data (prices, cost, quantity) into our model. For large problems, this approach may not be practical. A more efficient approach to setting up large and complex problems in SAS is to use arrays and index sets. The problem data can then be read into the model either in the form of arrays or as a SAS data set. Once this is performed, we can then use the matrix mathematical programming formulation of the OPTMODEL procedure to set up the problem. Before we proceed, let us define some key features of this approach.

- **Index Set:** In the same manner as mathematical set theory, index sets are employed in the OPTMODEL procedure to link the element of another set to the element of the index set. For example, an index set can be used to create a collection of production resources (labor, equipment, and materials) or vehicles (Sedans, SUVs, and Trucks). In the SAS program shown below, we specify an index set that is comprised of the three types of vehicles using the SET statement.[5] Remember that each element of the index set also has its own elements. For example, the sales price of each vehicle, which are elements of another set (sales_price) that can now be referenced from the Vehicle set as shown in the next line of code in the program.

Program 8.5A: Reading Data into PROC OPTMODEL

```
/*Reading Data into OPTMODEL Procedure*/
proc optmodel;
      set VEHICLES = /Sedan SUVs Trucks/;
      num sales_price {VEHICLES} = [26000 37500 45000];
      print sales_price;
```

---

[5] The SET statement in the OPTMODEL procedure is different from the SET statement used in the DATA step. In the DATA step, the SET statement is used to read rows from the referenced data set into the program data vector (PDV) for further manipulation.

- **Parameters:** These are the constants in the problem. They include the constants in both the constraints and the objective function. For example, the constraint equation for labor hours implies that you need 40 labor hours to produce one Sedan, while the objective function equation shows that the sales price of the Sedan line of vehicles is $26,000. Parameter names are usually specified using lowercase letters. Parameter names with spaces are linked using an underscore. When specifying parameters in the OPTMODEL procedure, it is essential that you indicate whether the data to be read into the parameter is a numeric (num) or string value (str).
- **Parameter Array:** Parameter arrays contain the element of the index set and the associated values of the elements of the parameters. For example, the parameter array for the sales prices will include each type of vehicle and its sales price.
- **Data:** These are the actual values of the parameters and parameter arrays. There are two ways to read data values into the problem in the OPTMODEL procedure. In the first approach, the data is simply read into each parameter space using matrix formulation as shown in Program 8.5A. In the second approach, the problem data already stored in SAS data set format is read into the model using the READ statement as shown in Program 8.5B.
- In the SAS code, the SAS data set named PRICE_DATA contains the types and sales prices of each vehicle type. In the OPTMODEL statements. The SET <STR> statement is used to specify the VEHICLES index set that consists of string elements. If you do not specify the string option, the default element of the index set will be numeric. The NUM sales_price specifies the parameter array into which the sales price data will be read from the PRICE_DATA data set. The READ DATA statement is then used to read the vehicle type (with Type as the index) into the index set and sales prices in the sales_price array.

Program 8.5B: Reading SAS Data into PROC OPTMODEL

```
/*Reading SAS Data Set into OPTMODEL Procedure*/
data price_data;
      input Type $ Price;
      datalines;
Sedan 26000
SUVs 37500
Trucks 45000
;
run;

proc optmodel;
      set <str> VEHICLES;
      num sales_price {VEHICLES};
      read data price_data into VEHICLES=[Type]
            sales_price=Price;
      print  sales_price dollar8.;
```

- **Implicit Variables:** You may have noticed in Program 8.4 that the same set of expressions was used to calculate the resource utilization constraint and the objective function. You can eliminate this repetitive task when dealing with complex problems by using implicit variable declarations. When an IMPVAR declaration is made, the procedure computes the value of the expression once and then substitutes the value into the model anytime the implicit variable is called up in the problem. Implicit variables declaration can be used to evaluate algebraic expressions that are written in equation or array formats. They are evaluated in the same way SAS evaluates algebraic expressions that are defined using the macrovariable statement %LET.

- **Local Dummy Parameter:** In some cases, it is also more efficient to eliminate the need to restate values of the index set when performing sequential calculations. In such instances, you can reference the index value using a local dummy parameter. Local dummy parameters are similar to the index variables used in iterative calculations. Each value of the local dummy parameter is linked to the value of the index set. Local dummy parameters are typically used in conjunction with aggregation operators.

- **Aggregation Operators:** These are used to combine the values of an expression that is evaluated over a collection of the members of a set. Aggregation operators that OPTMODEL modeling language supports include SUM, MAX, MIN, INTER, AND, OR, AND SETOF, and PROD. For example, the OPTMODEL statement "sum{p in VEHICLES} sales_price[p]" invokes the sum of the sales prices of the three types of vehicles ($26,000 + $37,500 + $45,000).

Program 8.5C: Demonstrating Programming Statements in PROC OPTMODEL

```
/*Reading Data into OPTMODEL Procedure*/
proc optmodel;
     set <str> VEHICLES;
     num sales_price {VEHICLES};
     read data price_data into VEHICLES=[Type]
          sales_price=Price;
     print  sales_price dollar8.;
     impvar Revenue= sum{p in VEHICLES} sales_price[p];
     print Revenue dollar8.;
quit;
```

Now that we have developed a general understanding of the framework for using arrays, index Sets, and SAS data sets in OPTMODEL modeling language, let us revisit our profit maximization ILP problem using this new approach. First, let us store our problem data in two SAS data sets. The RESOURCE_DATA SAS data set contains the input items, their unit cost, and the maximum unit available, while the PRODUCTION_DATA SAS data set contains the vehicle types, their sales prices per unit, the units of labor, equipment, and materials that are required to produce each unit.

Program 8.5D: Storing Problem Data in SAS Data Sets

```
/*Reading Data into OPTMODEL Procedure*/
data resource_data;
      format Items $10.;
      input Items $ Costs Available;
      datalines;
Labor   50 1000000
Equipment 35 2000000
Material   400 2000000
;
run;

data production_data;
      input Types $ Price Labor Equipment Material;
      datalines;
Sedan 26000 40 35 40
SUVs 37500 50 45 60
Trucks 45000 60 60 75
;
run;
```

Program 8.5E shows the SAS code of the OPTMODEL procedure for the profit maximization problem. SET <STR> RESOURCES, VEHICLE is used to declare the resources and vehicle index sets. The first two NUM statements are used to declare the parameter array for the sales prices of each vehicle, the unit cost of each production input, and the available units of each input item. The third NUM statement is used to create an array of the units of each input that is utilized in producing each vehicle type. The first READ statement is used to read the INPUT_DATA data set into the COSTS and AVAILABLE arrays using the input item as the index set. The second READ statement is then used to read the PRODUCTION_DATA data set into two arrays. In the first array, the local dummy parameter (r) was used to reach the product utilization data into the input array. The SALES_PRICE=PRICE statement was used to read sales prices into the SALES_PRICE array. Next, the PRINT statements are used to verify that the data sets were properly read into the correct arrays.

Program 8.5E: Solving an ILP Problem Using Index Sets in PROC OPTMODEL

```
/*Using Index Set, Arrays, and SAS data set in OPTMODEL Procedure*/
proc optmodel;
      set <str> RESOURCES,VEHICLES;
      num sales_price {VEHICLES};
      num costs{RESOURCES},available{RESOURCES};
      num inputs{VEHICLES,RESOURCES};

      /*read data price_data into index sets*/
      read data resource_data into RESOURCES=[Items]
            costs available;
      read data production_data into VEHICLES=[Types]
            {r in RESOURCES} <inputs[Types,r]=col(r)>  sales_price=price;
```

```
      /*Validate Data Read into Problem*/
      print costs available;
      print sales_price inputs;

      /*Declare Variables*/
      var Units{VEHICLES}>=0 integer;
      impvar Revenue=
            sum{p in VEHICLES} sales_price[p]*Units[p];
      impvar Usage {r in RESOURCES}=
            sum{p in VEHICLES} Units[p]*Inputs[p,r];
      impvar ProductCost=
            sum{r in RESOURCES} costs[r]*Usage[r];

      /*Declare Constraints*/
      con Utilization {r in RESOURCES}:
            Usage[r]<=available[r];

      /*Declare Objective*/
      max Profit = Revenue - ProductCost;
      expand;
      solve;
      print units usage;
quit;
```

Next, decision variables, which are the optimal units of the three types of vehicles to produce are declared using the VAR statement. This is then followed by declaring the three implicit variables (Revenue, Usage, and ProductCost) using the IMPVAR statements and local dummy variables. Notice that in the first IMPVAR statement, the aggregation is performed over the VEHICLE index set, while in the second IMPVAR statement, the aggregation is performed over both the VEHICLE and RESOURCES index sets (that is, total units of vehicle produced multiplied by the units of each input consumed in producing each vehicle). The last IMPVAR statement aggregates over the RESOURCES index set (that is, the total cost of all input items utilized to produce all units of vehicles). We can now declare the constraint using the CON statement and local dummy parameter and the objective function using the previously declared implicit variables. Lastly, the SOLVE and PRINT programming statements are then invoked to solve the ILP problem and to print the values of the optimal unit of vehicle type to produce and the unit of resources utilized at the optimal production level.

Output 8.5: Result from Solving ILP Problem Using Index Set in PROC OPTMODEL

The OPTMODEL Procedure

Problem Summary

Objective Sense	Maximization
Objective Function	Profit
Objective Type	Linear
Number of Variables	3
Bounded Above	0
Bounded Below	3
Bounded Below and Above	0
Free	0
Fixed	0
Binary	0
Integer	3
Number of Constraints	3
Linear LE (<=)	3
Linear EQ (=)	0
Linear GE (>=)	0
Linear Range	0
Constraint Coefficients	9

The OPTMODEL Procedure

Solution Summary

Solver	MILP
Algorithm	Branch and Cut
Objective Function	Profit
Solution Status	Optimal
Objective Value	188500000
Relative Gap	0
Absolute Gap	0
Primal Infeasibility	0
Bound Infeasibility	0
Integer Infeasibility	0
Best Bound	188500000
Nodes	1
Solutions Found	6
Iterations	3
Presolve Time	0.00
Solution Time	0.01

[1]	Units	Usage
Equipment		900000
Labor		1000000
Material		1200000
SUVs	20000	
Sedan	0	
Trucks	0	

EXPAND Statement Output

```
Var Units[Sedan] INTEGER >= 0
Var Units[SUVs] INTEGER >= 0
Var Units[Trucks] INTEGER >= 0
Impvar Revenue = 26000*Units[Sedan] + 37500*Units[SUVs] + 45000*Units[Trucks]
Impvar Usage[Labor] = 40*Units[Sedan] + 50*Units[SUVs] + 60*Units[Trucks]
Impvar Usage[Equipment] = 35*Units[Sedan] + 45*Units[SUVs] + 60*Units[Trucks]
Impvar Usage[Material] = 40*Units[Sedan] + 60*Units[SUVs] + 75*Units[Trucks]
Impvar ProductCost = 50*Usage[Labor] + 35*Usage[Equipment] + 400*Usage[Material]
Maximize Profit=Revenue - ProductCost
Constraint Utilization[Labor]: Usage[Labor] <= 1000000
Constraint Utilization[Equipment]: Usage[Equipment] <= 2000000
Constraint Utilization[Material]: Usage[Material] <= 2000000
```

Output 8.5 shows the results from invoking the OPTMODEL procedure. Notice that the results are quantitatively and qualitatively the same. There is more output generated from invoking the EXPAND statement in this approach than in the approach used in Program 8.5 due to the use of the implicit variables.

Mixed Integer Linear Programming (MILP) Problems

Let us consider a mixed integer linear programming problem where the decision variables include both integer and binary variables. We will slightly modify our vehicle production problem by including the option to add sales discounts to the prices of the previous year's model. Suppose the vehicle manufacturer has an inventory of unsold vehicles from the previous year. A common pricing strategy of most vehicle manufacturers is to sell older editions at a discount to the current year's model. Because some vehicle types are generally more sought after than others, we will assume that the company will not apply the same sales price discount (in percent) across all vehicles. Furthermore, due to accrual accounting rules, production cost is only realized when sales are recognized. Hence, we will recognize last year's production cost for the overstocked vehicles when their forecasted sales for this year for each model are recognized.

Let's add a few more complexities to the problem. Let's assume that offering a discount on last year's model will allow us to sell all of the inventory of overstocked vehicles; however, it will cannibalize some sales from this year's model by the percentage of sales that would be lost on the overstocked model of vehicles if we do not offer a discount on the overstocked inventory of last year's model. (In other words, offering a discount will lead to the sales of the entire stock of excess vehicle inventory, but we will lose sales on the current edition. Offering no discount will lead to a reduction in the proportion of the overstocked vehicle sold by the same magnitude.) To prevent the price discount from leading to suboptimal financial performance for this year, we will impose additional constraints on the problem. These include the constraint that discounting should have a net positive effect on the current year's profitability and that the minimum number of each vehicle to sell this year must be at least seven times more than the previous year's unsold inventory. Lastly, we imposed a constraint that the unit of vehicles to produce in the current period cannot be less than 4,000 units in order not to idle the plant. A summary of the additional information that is now included in the problem data is shown in Table 8.8.

Problem Statement

Our problem statement now involves two types of decision variables. The first set of decision variables is the units of the current year's model of the three types of vehicles that should be made. These will be the same set of integer variables we derived in the original problem. The

Table 8.8: Additional Problem Data for Profit Maximization Problem

	Labor	Equipment	Materials	Sales Price	Excess Units	Price Discount	Lost Sales
Sedan	40	35	40	$26,000.00	600	5%	35%
SUVs	50	45	60	$37,500.00	650	8%	25%
Trucks	60	60	75	$45,000.00	630	9%	35%

second set of decision variables consists of binary choice variables, which are the decision to offer a discount or otherwise on the previous year's edition of the vehicles. Our linear programming problem will follow the MILP approach because we are dealing with two types of decision variables (integer and binary). You can think of the binary decision variable as an ILP problem with an upper bound of 1 and a lower bound of 0.

You should note that just like ILP problems, MILP problems require both linear constraint and linear objective functions. With complex problems such as these, you run the risk of encountering a scenario where the analytical formula for the problem in its complex form is non-linear. You would need to linearize the equation in your programming statement before invoking the solver. Before we present the SAS program that we will use to solve the problem, let us reformulate the expression of the bounds of the decision variables for the optimization problem shown in Equation (8.12) to now include the added decision variable and its bounds.

$$
\begin{aligned}
&N(\text{Sedans}) \geq 4{,}000 \text{ integer, } N(\text{SUVs}) \geq 4{,}000 \text{ integer,} \\
&N(\text{Trucks}) \geq 4{,}000 \text{ integer} \\
&D(\text{Sedans}) \text{ binary, } D(\text{SUVs}) \text{ binary, } D(\text{Trucks}) \text{ binary}
\end{aligned}
\tag{8.13}
$$

where $D(\text{Sedans})$, $D(\text{SUVs})$, and $D(\text{Trucks})$ are binary decision variables that represent the choice of whether to discount or not. Program 8.6 shows the SAS code for solving the revised vehicle production problem. To save space, we will only highlight areas where modifications were made to Program 8.5. The full program is available on the book's GitHub site.

Program 8.6: Solving an MILP Problem with PROC OPTMODEL

```
/*Solving MILP Problems Using OPTMODEL Procedure*/
data production_data;
      input Items $ Price Labor Equipment Material Ounits rate lsp;
      datalines;
Sedan 26000 40 35 40 600 0.05 0.35
SUVs 37500 50 45 60 650 0.08 0.25
Trucks 45000 60 60 75 630 0.09 0.35
;
run;
%let minimum_unit=4000;

proc optmodel;
      set <str> RESOURCES,VEHICLES;
      num sales_price {VEHICLES};
      num costs{RESOURCES},available{RESOURCES};
      num inputs{VEHICLES,RESOURCES};
      num lsp{VEHICLES};
      num ounits{VEHICLES};
      num rate{VEHICLES};

      read data resource_data into RESOURCES=[Items]
            costs available;
```

```
      read data production_data into VEHICLES=[Items]
      {r in RESOURCES} <inputs[Items,r]=col(r)> ounits
       rate lsp sales_price=price;

      /*Declare explicit and implicit Variables*/
      var Units{VEHICLES}>=0 integer;
      var Discount{VEHICLES} binary;
             impvar Revenue=
             sum{p in VEHICLES}  (sales_price[p]*Units[p]);
      impvar AdjRevenue=
             sum{p in VEHICLES} ((Discount[p]*((1-rate[p])-0.1*lsp[p])+(1-
Discount[p])*(1-lsp[p]))*ounits[p]*sales_price[p]);

      impvar Usage {r in RESOURCES}=
             sum{p in VEHICLES} Units[p]*Inputs[p,r];
      impvar ProductCost=
             sum{r in RESOURCES} costs[r]*Usage[r];

      impvar AdjProductCost=
             sum{r in RESOURCES,p in VEHICLES} ((Discount[p]+(1-Discount[p])*(1-
lsp[p]))*(ounits[p]*Inputs[p,r]*costs[r]));

      /*Declare Constraints*/
      con Utilization {r in RESOURCES}:
             Usage[r]<=available[r];

      /*Declare Initial Objective Function*/
      max Profit = Revenue - ProductCost;

      /*Declare Additional Constraints*/
      con Erosion{p in VEHICLES}: (1/ounits[p])*units[p]>=7;
      con ProfitBound:AdjRevenue-AdjProductCost>=0;
      con Minimum_Units {p in VEHICLES}: Units[p]>=&minimum_unit;

      /*Declare Second Stage Objective Function*/
      max AdjProfit= Profit+AdjRevenue - AdjProductCost;
      expand;

      solve obj AdjProfit with milp/relobjgap=0;
      print units usage rate percent8. discount lsp percent8.;
     print Revenue dollar12. AdjRevenue dollar12. ProductCost dollar12. AdjProductCost
    dollar12.;
 quit;
```

SAS code for linear programming problems is sometimes difficult to comprehend because it is not standardized in the same way as most SAS statistical procedures. The programmer has some latitude in how the problem is set up in the OPTMODEL procedure, which may not be obvious to the readers of the program. It is possible for the code for the same problem to be written in a slightly different form. Nevertheless, let's walk through the version above to see how it is implemented in this example.

First, we modified the SAS program that was used to create the SAS data set named PRODUCTION_DATA and added three more columns (OUNITS, RATES, and LSP) to the PRODUCTION_DATA SAS data set, to include the additional problem data in the model. OUNITS represents the quantity of excess inventory of the older models of the vehicles. RATE is the price discount that will be applied to each vehicle type if discounting is chosen, and LSP is the proportion of excess inventory that will not be sold if a price discount is not offered. Next, additional numeric parameter arrays are introduced to the model (Ounits, Rate, LSP) using the NUM statements. We then specify our two decision variables (UNITS and DISCOUNT).

Next, we introduce two implicit variables (AdjRevenue and AdjProductCost) to capture the contribution of the decision to discount (or not) the prices of last year's vehicle model to the current year's revenue and production cost. The aim here is to distinguish the contribution of the unsold inventory to the overall profit from the current year's production levels. Notice how the mathematical program for the adjusted revenue (AdjRevenue) was written in linear form. In its complex form, the mathematical expression for the adjusted revenue would use an indicator function as shown below:

$$\text{AdjRevenue} = \sum_{i=1}^{N=3} \begin{cases} (D_i = 1)\big((\text{rate}_i - 0.1*\text{lsp}_i)*\text{ounits}_i*\text{sales\_price}_i\big) \\ (D_i = 0)\big((1-\text{lsp}_i)*\text{ounits}_i*\text{sales\_price}_i\big) \end{cases} \quad (8.14)$$

If a discount is not offered on the excess inventory $(D_i = 0)$, it will result in a loss in sales by the percentage $(1 - lsp_i)$ of the excess inventory, but no negative effect on the newer model sales. If the discount is offered $(D = 1)$ on a vehicle, then the additional revenue includes the units of the excess inventory sold and its negative effect on the sales of the newer models of the vehicle $(rate_i - 0.1*lsp_i)$. The indicator function creates non-linearity in the mathematical model for the problem in a way that is not supported by the OPTMODEL procedure. We avoid this problem by replacing $(D_i = 0)$ with $[1-(D_i = 1)]$ and calculating the sum of both expressions.[6] Notice that the original formula for the implicit variable for Revenue and ProductCost remains the same.

While it is not necessary, we created two objective functions. The first objective function is the same as the one in Program 8.5, which is to maximize profit. The second objective function, which maximizes the adjusted profit, builds on the first objective function by adding the additional revenue (AdjRevenue) and subtracting the additional cost (AdjProductCost) from the first objective function. We also added to the code a set of additional constraints (Erosion and Profit boundaries). The Erosion constraint imposes the condition that the unit of each vehicle sold in the current year must be at least seven times the units of excess inventory from the previous year, while the Profit boundary imposes the constraint that ensures that the additional units sold from the excess inventory should have no detrimental impact on the current year's profitability. Since we have two objective functions, we need to specify which objective function

---

[6] The realizations of the indicator variable are mutually exclusive and collectively exhaustive; therefore, the sum of both expressions should be the same as using an indicator variable. You can also achieve the same functional expression by imposing additional constraint on the problem.

we want to optimize when we invoke the solver. The SOLVE OBJ ADJPROFIT statement informs the solver to optimize the adjusted profit function.[7]

Let's turn our attention now to the results that are shown in Output 8.6. The Problem Summary table shows that we have six decision variables, which include the three integer variables that are bounded from below and the three binary variables that are bounded below and above. There are 10 constraints, including three less than and seven greater than. The Solution Summary table shows an optimal solution status, with an objective value (profit) of $190.46 million. The optimal units of current year vehicles to produce are now 11,348 SUVs, 4,200 Sedans, and 4,410 Trucks. Notice that for Sedans and Trucks, the optimal units of the current year model of both types of vehicles are equivalent to seven times the unit of excess inventory for the previous year. Regarding the decision to discount the prices of the previous year's model, the optimal choice is to discount only the prices of the Sedan and not the other two types of vehicles. The incremental benefit of this decision is an increase in profit of approximately $11.4 million.

Output 8.6: Result from Solving MILP Problem (Profit Maximization)

The OPTMODEL Procedure

Solution Summary

Solver	MILP
Algorithm	Branch and Cut
Objective Function	AdjProfit
Solution Status	Optimal
Objective Value	190456637 5

The OPTMODEL Procedure

Problem Summary

Objective Sense	Maximization
Objective Function	AdjProfit
Objective Type	Linear
Number of Variables	6
Bounded Above	0
Bounded Below	3
Bounded Below and Above	3
Free	0
Fixed	0
Binary	3
Integer	3
Number of Constraints	10
Linear LE (<=)	3
Linear EQ (=)	0
Linear GE (>=)	7
Linear Range	0
Constraint Coefficients	18

Relative Gap	0
Absolute Gap	0
Primal Infeasibility	0
Bound Infeasibility	0
Integer Infeasibility	0
Best Bound	190456637 5
Nodes	1
Solutions Found	5
Iterations	3
Presolve Time	0 00
Solution Time	0 01

[1]	Units	Usage rate	Discount	Isp
Equipment		922260		
Labor		1000000		
Material		1179630		
SUVs	11348	8%		0 25%
Sedan	4200	5%		1 35%
Trucks	4410	9%		0 35%

Revenue	AdjRevenue	ProductCost	AdjProductCost	Profit	AdjProfit
$733,200,000	$50,982,750	$554,131,100	$39,595,013	$179,068,900	$190,456,638

---

[7] You can simultaneously solve both objective functions by invoking the Local Search Optimization Solver (LSO), which is used for multi-objective optimizations. Replace the SOLVE statement in the code with the following code 'SOLVE WITH LSO OBJ (PROFIT ADJPROFIT);'.

Capital Budgeting Problem

Let's now apply MILP to a capital budgeting example. Suppose a manufacturing company is evaluating which combination of five potential capital projects (A, B, C, D, and E) will yield the highest net present value (NPV). For now, we will assume that all five projects have the same risk profile and consequently, the same discount rate. The cash flows for each project are shown in Table 8.9. Due to the limited funding opportunities, the company has implemented capital rationing such that the maximum amount that is available to fund all projects is $55,000, which is less than the $101,000 that is required to fund all five projects. Hence, the company must select the combination of projects that best maximizes NPV within the budgeting constraint that it faces.

Problem Statement

All of the information we need to calculate the NPV of each project has been provided in the problem data. Therefore, what needs to be optimized is the choice of projects we should assemble that will lead to the highest combined NPV. We can model our decision to include or not to include a project in the portfolio using binary choice variables. We should note that the projects are not mutually exclusive; therefore, in modeling our decision variables, we will assign a binary choice variable to all five projects. The outcome of the optimization will then be the collection of the binary outcomes assigned to all projects.

In Program 8.7 we show the SAS program that was used to solve the optimization problem using PROC OPTMODEL. We will start with the two DATA steps used to create the EQUIPMENT_DATA and the CASHFLOW_DATA data sets. We then use a macrovariable to set the upper boundary of the total project cost imposed by capital rationing. For the OPTMODEL procedure, we declare two index sets (PROJECT and CASHFLOW). For both index sets, the project ID (EQUIPMENT) is used as the index variable. The numeric DISCOUNT_RATE array of parameters is then declared and indexed to the PROJECT index set. The numeric parameter array named CASHFLOWS is also declared and indexed by the PROJECT and CASHFLOW index sets. The parameter array named YEAR is declared, indexed to the CASHFLOW index set, and populated with numeric values that represent the time of the cash flow occurrence. Next, the data from the EQUIPMENT_DATA

Table 8.9: Modeling Data for Capital Budget Problem

Project	Cash Flows					
	CF_0	CF_1	CF_2	CF_3	CF_4	CF_5
A	($10,000)	$3,000	$4,000	$3,500	$800	$0
B	($15,000)	$5,000	$7,000	$9,000	$8,000	$7,500
C	($20,000)	$5,000	$7,000	$10,000	$13,000	$15,000
D	($24,000)	$7,000	$8,500	$11,000	$13,000	$16,000
E	($32,000)	$8,000	$7,500	$14,000	$15,600	$23,000
Total	($101,000)	$28,000	$34,000	$47,500	$50,400	$61,500

and CASHFLOW_DATA data sets are read into the DISCOUNT RATE array and CASHFLOW array, respectively. The binary decision variable X is then declared.

In the mathematical programming for the problem, we create two implicit variables. The first implicit variable (CF) calculates the sums of the present values of each project cash flow, post-acquisition. The second implicit variable (COST) calculates the initial cost of acquiring each project. We impose the constraint that the sum of the initial costs must be less than the capital rationing limit. Notice that we manipulate the mathematical expression for the budget constraint to impose a lower bound on the total cost for the project by specifying a "less than" inequality for the negative value of the total capital budget. The objective function for the problem is declared as the sum of the product of the CF and the binary choice decision variable that maximizes the combined NPV.

Program 8.7: Solving Capital Rationing Problem Using PROC OPTMODEL

```
/*Solving Capital Expenditure with Capital Rationing problem using PROC
OPTMODEL*/
data equipment_data;
      input equipment $ discount_rate;
      datalines;
A 0.1
B 0.1
C 0.1
D 0.1
E 0.1
;
run;

data cashflow_data;
      input cf $ A B C D E;
      datalines;
cf0 -10000 -15000 -20000 -24000 -32000
cf1 3000 5000 5000 7000 8000
cf2 4000 7000 7000 8500 7500
cf3 3500 9000 10000 11000 14000
cf4 800 8000 13000 13000 15600
cf5 0 7500 15000 16000 23000
;
run;

%let max_budget=50000;

proc optmodel;
      set <str> PROJECT,CASHFLOW;
      num  discount_rate{PROJECT};
      num  cashflows{PROJECT,CASHFLOW};
      num  year{CASHFLOW} =[0 1 2 3 4 5];
```

```
    read data equipment_data into PROJECT=[equipment]
        discount_rate;
    read data cashflow_data into CASHFLOW=[cf]

        {r in PROJECT} <cashflows[r,cf]=col(r)>;

/*Declare Decision Variables*/
var X{r in PROJECT} binary;

/*Calculate PV of Cash flows*/
impvar cf{r in Project}=sum{p in CASHFLOW}
(cashflows[r,p]/(1+discount_rate[r])**year[p]);
/*Calculate Initial Capital Outlay*/
impvar cost{r in PROJECT} =sum{p in CASHFLOW} (if year[p]=0 then
X[r]*cashflows[r,p]);

/* declare constraints */
con Budget: sum{r in PROJECT} cost[r] >=-&max_budget;
/* declare objective */
max NPV  = sum{r in PROJECT} X[r]*cf[r];
expand;
solve;

/*Print Optimization Output*/
print X;
print Budget.lb dollar8.;
```

Output 8.7 shows the results of the optimization. The Problem Summary table shows the number and types of decision variables (5 binary variables), the number of constraints (1), and the constraint coefficients (5). The Solution Summary table shows the solver used (MILP), the algorithm (Branch and Cut), and the Solution Status (Optimal). Also shown are the value of the optimized objective function ($32,503), and the number of solutions found (1). The printout of the optimal values of the decision variables shows that Projects C (NPV=$16,037) and D (NPV=$16,647) were selected, while the rest of the projects (A, B, and E) were rejected.

You may wonder why Project E, which had the highest NPV was not selected. This is because Project E had the highest initial cost of acquisition ($32,000), compared to Projects C ($20,000) and D ($24,000). The combined cost of Projects C and D ($44,000) leaves us with about $11,000, which would have been enough to acquire Project A. However, because Project A is not a value-creating project, it was also not selected.

Output 8.7: Optimal Capital Rationing Decisions from PROC OPTMODEL

The OPTMODEL Procedure

Solution Summary

Solver	MILP
Algorithm	Branch and Cut
Objective Function	NPV
Solution Status	Optimal
Objective Value	32503 529938

The OPTMODEL Procedure

Problem Summary

Objective Sense	Maximization
Objective Function	NPV
Objective Type	Linear
Number of Variables	5
Bounded Above	0
Bounded Below	0
Bounded Below and Above	5
Free	0
Fixed	0
Binary	5
Integer	0
Number of Constraints	1
Linear LE (<=)	0
Linear EQ (=)	0
Linear GE (>=)	1
Linear Range	0
Constraint Coefficients	5

Relative Gap	0
Absolute Gap	0
Primal Infeasibility	0
Bound Infeasibility	0
Integer Infeasibility	0
Best Bound	32503 529938
Nodes	0
Solutions Found	1
Iterations	0
Presolve Time	0.00
Solution Time	0.00

[1] X		PNPV
A	0	$-791
B	0	$12,213
C	1	$16,037
D	1	$16,467
E	0	$16,926

Budget.LB

$-50,000

EXPAND Statement Output

```
Var X[A] BINARY
Var X[B] BINARY
Var X[C] BINARY
Var X[D] BINARY
Var X[E] BINARY
Impvar cost[A] = - 10000*X[A]
Impvar cost[B] = - 15000*X[B]
Impvar cost[C] = - 20000*X[C]
Impvar cost[D] = - 24000*X[D]
Impvar cost[E] = - 32000*X[E]
Maximize NPV=- 790.92958131*X[A] + 8861.3293294*X[B] + 18333.459824*X[C] + 14196.295396*X[D] + 12707.199095*X[E]
Constraint Budget: cost[A] + cost[B] + cost[C] + cost[D] + cost[E] >= -55000
```

Asset and Liability Management Problem

Suppose a pension fund that has the future funding obligations shown in Table 8.10A is trying to assemble a portfolio of bonds to meet the obligations. The price, coupon rate, and maturity of the bonds that can be purchased to finance future obligations are shown in Table 8.10B. Our aim here is to construct a laddered portfolio of bonds at the minimum cost that can meet the future cash flow obligations of the pension fund.

Table 8.10A: Pension Obligation Data for Asset-Liability Management Problem

Pension Obligations ('Thousand Dollars)								
Year	1	2	3	4	5	6	7	8	9
Obligation	34,000	28,000	29,000	26,000	32,000	35,000	40,000	42,000	45,000

Table 8.10B: Bond Universe Data for Asset-Liability Management Problem

Bond Information Table											
Bonds	A	B	C	D	E	F	G	H	I	J	K
Price	98	99	103	97	102	103	102	100	103	101	103
Coupon Rate	5	4.5	6	4.5	5	6.5	7	6	6	6	6
Maturity	1	2	2	3	4	5	5	6	7	8	9

It is unlikely that the units of bonds that will be purchased will generate exactly the dollar amount of cash that will be needed each year. Therefore, we will most likely generate more cash flow from our bond portfolio than we need in some years. Any surplus cash that we generate in each period can be reinvested until next year and will be used in part to offset the funding needed in that year. For now, let's assume that the reinvestment rate for the excess cash is zero.

Problem Statement

Our primary aim here is to derive the optimal units of each bond to include in the portfolio, such that the portfolio can meet the future cash flow obligations of the pension fund at the minimum cost possible. Our problem statement now involves two types of decision variables. The first set of decision variables is the units of bonds to purchase. Since bonds cannot be purchased in fractional amounts, these will be integer variables. The second type of decision variable is an auxiliary variable that we will use to compute the amount of excess cash to hold each year. This is a real variable; hence our optimization problem combines integer variables and real variables, which makes it a MILP problem. The objective function is to minimize the initial cost of funding the obligations. The constraints are multi-period in the sense that for each year, the bond portfolio must generate enough cash flow from the coupon and principal payments to meet the cash flow obligations.

We can write the mathematical formula for our optimization problem as follows. Let $X = [x_1,..,x_n]$ be a vector of the unit of n bonds to purchase, $P = [p_i,...,p_n]$ the vector of bond prices, $C = [c_i,...c_n]$, the coupon rate for each bond, and $PV = [pv_i,..., pv_n]$ the principal amount that is paid at maturity. Furthermore, let $CF = [cf_i,...cf_T]$ and $Z = [z_i,...,z_T]$ represent the pension obligations and excess cash received from bond payments. The optimization problem can now be written as:

$$Min \ \ CF_0 = \sum_{i=1}^{n} x_i p_i + z_0$$

$$s.t. \ \ \sum_{t=1}^{T} x_i c_{i,t} + x_i pv_{i,t} + z_t - z_{t-1} = cf_t, \ \forall \, t. \qquad (8.15)$$

$$Z \geq 0, X \geq 0 \ \text{integer.}$$

To keep things moving along, we have saved the problem data in two SAS data sets (BOND_DATA and OUTFLOWS). We will use the %DATAPULL macro to download them from the book's GitHub page into our WORK library as shown in Program 8.8. After invoking the OPTMODEL procedure, we declared two index sets. The CASHFLOW index set is used to account for future obligations, while the BOND index set references the characteristics of our bond universe. Notice that the CASHFLOW set is a numeric index set, while the BOND set is a string index set. Next, we declare the problem parameters. These are the YEAR and LIABILITIES, which are linked to the CASHFLOW index set, and the PRICE, COUPON, and MATURITY, which are linked to the BOND index set.

The problem data is then read into the procedure using the READ statement. Next, we declare the vectors of decision variables X and Z. Notice that X is indexed to BOND because its elements are the optimal units of each bond to purchase, while Z is indexed to a set of numbers starting from time $t = 0$ to T, where T is the last year of pension obligation payment. We then used implicit variables to calculate the annual coupon and principal payments to be received from the bond investment. Note that for each bond, coupon payments are received up until the maturity date, while principal payments are received only on the year of the bond's maturity. We also used implicit variables to compute the change in surplus cash in each period. The last implicit variable HOLDINGS is not required for the optimization but is calculated to show the total dollar value of each bond purchased. Next, we declared the constraint and objective function. Notice that we also included a slack variable in the objective function. We then invoked the MILP solver and PRINT statement to display the optimization results. Lastly, we used the CREATE statement to export the HOLDINGS data into a SAS data set and then created a pie chart using the SGPIE procedure.

Program 8.8: Solving Cash Flow Dedication ALM Problem Using PROC OPTMODEL

```
/*Using PROC OPTMODEL to solve Cash Flow Dedication Problem*/
%datapull(outflows,outflows.sas7bdat);
%datapull(bonds,bondsdata.sas7bdat);
proc optmodel;
```

```
      /* declare sets and parameters */
      set <num> CASHFLOWS;
      set <str> BONDS;
      num year{CASHFLOWS}, liabilities{CASHFLOWS};
      num price{BONDS},coupon{BONDS},maturity{BONDS};
      num mature{CASHFLOWS};

      /*Problem data from SAS  dataset*/
      read data outflows into CASHFLOWS=[_N_]
             year liabilities mature=_N_ ;

      *print outflow dollar8. mature;
      read data bondsdata into BONDS=[bond]
             price coupon maturity;

      /*Count the number of years of funding need*/
      impvar N=card(CASHFLOWS);

      /*Declare Decision Variables*/
      var X{i in BONDS} >=0 integer, Z{j in 0..N}>=0;

      /*Setup liability funding pattern (Coupon+Principal at maturity + surplus). Coupons
      received every year until maturity, Principal received at maturity    */

      impvar coupons {j in CASHFLOWS}=
             sum{i in BONDS} (if maturity[i]>=mature[j] then coupon[i]*10*X[i]);
      /*Coupons*/

      impvar Principal{j in CASHFLOWS}=
      sum{i in BONDS}(if maturity[i]=mature[j] then 1000*X[i]); /*Principal*/

      /*Surplus cash*/
      impvar Surplus{j in CASHFLOWS}=Z[j]-Z[j-1]; /*Surplus*/

      /*Dollar Value of Bond Purchased*/
      impvar Holdings {i in BONDS} = X[i]*price[i]*10;

      /*Declare Constraints Bond Cash Flows = liability funding+Surplus*/
      con Cfcon {j in CASHFLOWS}: coupons[j]+principal[j]-surplus[j]=liabilities[j]*1000;

      /*Declare Objective function*/
      min Totalcost =Z[0]+sum{I in BONDS} price[i]*10*X[i];
      solve with milp;
      expand;

      /*Print Optimization Output*/
      print Totalcost dollar12.;
      print X comma10. Holdings dollar12.;
      print Z dollar12. surplus dollar12.;

             /* write data to SAS  data sets */
      create data Holdings from [Bond]={j in BONDS: Holdings[j]}
             Holdings=Holdings;
quit;
```

Output 8.8A shows the results of the optimization procedure. The Problem Summary table shows that we have 21 decision variables, 11 of which are the units of bonds to purchase and 10 of which are the slack variables used to compute the excess cash in each payment period. Notice that there are 9 equality constraint equations in line with the nine years of pension payment obligations.

The Solution Summary table indicates that the MILP solver that was invoked was the Branch and Cut algorithm. The Solution Status indicates that the objective value ($233,339,350) is about 241.13 from the best bound ($233,339,103.87). The objective value is the total dollar amount of bonds that would be purchased to fund future obligations. Nine out of the 11 bonds were selected to be purchased in varying amounts, with bond K having the highest units and dollar allocations. You will observe that bonds C and F were not selected. That's because there are cheaper bonds (B and G) that had the same maturity as these two bonds, so they were selected instead. We also present the optimal bond allocations for our funding problem in the pie chart shown in Output 8.8B by invoking the SGPIE procedure and PIE statement as shown in Program 8.8.

Output 8.8A: Optimal Bond Portfolio for Cash Flow Dedication Problem Using PROC OPTMODEL

The OPTMODEL Procedure

Problem Summary

Objective Sense	Minimization
Objective Function	Totalcost
Objective Type	Linear
Number of Variables	21
Bounded Above	0
Bounded Below	21
Bounded Below and Above	0
Free	0
Fixed	0
Binary	0
Integer	11
Number of Constraints	9
Linear LE (<=)	0
Linear EQ (=)	9
Linear GE (>=)	0
Linear Range	0
Constraint Coefficients	70

The OPTMODEL Procedure

Solution Summary

Solver	MILP
Algorithm	Branch and Cut
Objective Function	Totalcost
Solution Status	Optimal within Relative Gap
Objective Value	233339350
Relative Gap	1 0548194E-6
Absolute Gap	246 13061434
Primal Infeasibility	3 547896E-16
Bound Infeasibility	0
Integer Infeasibility	0
Best Bound	233339103 87
Nodes	789
Solutions Found	2
Iterations	2815
Presolve Time	0.00
Solution Time	0.04

Totalcost
$233,339,350

[1]	X	Holdings
A	20,777	$2,036,146
B	15,816	$1,565,784
C	0	$0
D	17,529	$1,700,313
E	15,316	$1,562,232
F	0	$0
G	22,083	$2,252,466
H	26,637	$2,663,700
I	33,219	$3,421,557
J	37,220	$3,759,220
K	42,451	$4,372,453

[1]	Z	Surplus
0	$640	
1	$245	$-395
2	$0	$-245
3	$1,035	$1,035
4	$265	$-770
5	$695	$430
6	$9,315	$8,620
7	$1,715	$-7,600
8	$1,975	$260
9	$35	$-1,940

Output 8.8B: Bond Portfolio Allocations for Future Liability Funding

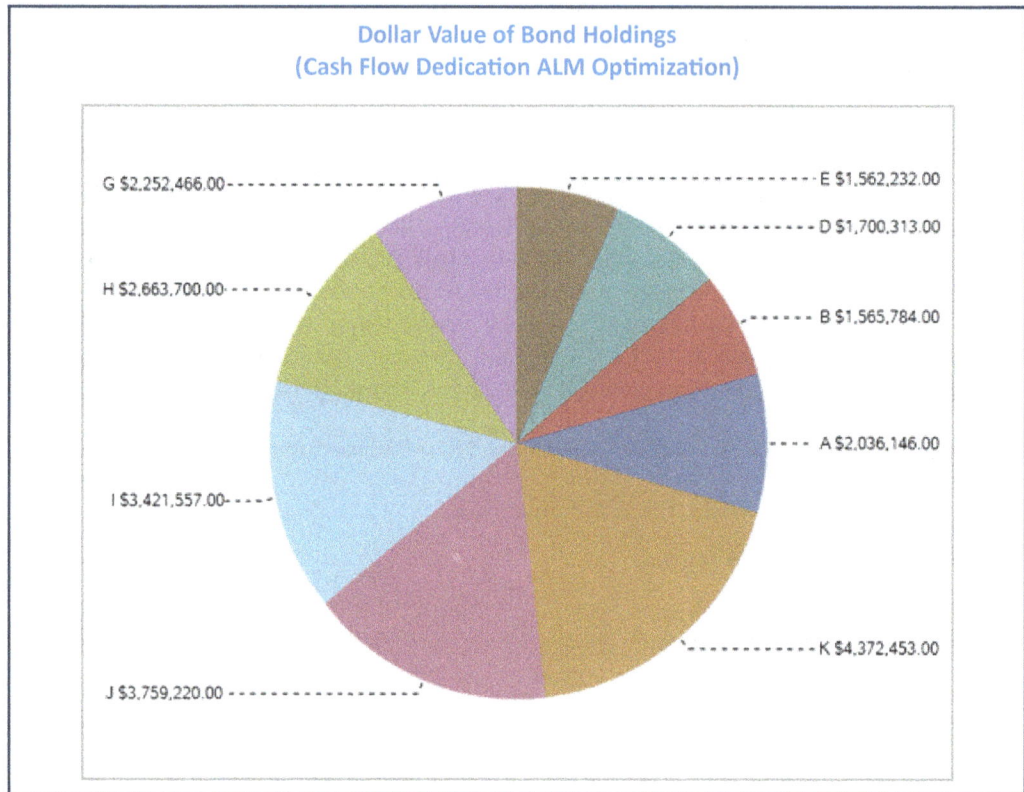

Dollar Value of Bond Holdings
(Cash Flow Dedication ALM Optimization)

G $2,252,466.00
E $1,562,232.00
D $1,700,313.00
H $2,663,700.00
B $1,565,784.00
A $2,036,146.00
I $3,421,557.00
K $4,372,453.00
J $3,759,220.00

Non-Linear Optimizations

As a financial data scientist, many of the complex problems you will encounter cannot be solved using linear programming methods. Any optimization problem that includes non-linear functions in either its objective function or constraints is usually regarded as a non-linear optimization problem. In general, nonlinear optimization problems are more challenging to solve than linear problems. Thankfully, there are many non-linear optimization methods that can be used to solve most of these problems. Non-linear optimization methods include quadratic optimization (or programming), which is commonly used in the portfolio management domain; stochastic optimization (or programming), which is used for solving portfolio risk management problems; robust optimization, which is used for solving optimization problems that have uncertainty in the input data; and conic optimization, which is used to solve optimization problems with constraints that come in the form of convex cones.

The general approach used by most solvers when tackling constrained nonlinear optimization problems is to reformulate them as an unconstrained optimization problem using the Lagrangian function[8]. Readers with a strong quantitative foundation will remember that the Lagrangian function imposes a penalty on the objective function via the constraint when the constraint is violated.

Let us momentarily consider an objective function $\min f(x)$ that is subject to a constraint $g(x) = b$. Then the Lagrangian of the objective function can be written as:

$$L(x, \lambda) = f(x) - \lambda(g(x) - b) \tag{8.16}$$

where λ is generally known as the Lagrangian multiplier. The Lagrangian function for problems with multiple constraints will include its corresponding multiplier for each constraint.[9] To find the minimum (maximum) of the constrained optimization, the Lagrangian approach examines stationary (saddle) points in the Lagrangian function by deriving the partial derivatives of the function with respect to the decision variable $\frac{\partial L}{\partial x} = 0$ and multiplier $\frac{\partial L}{\partial \lambda} = 0$. The system of equations that are obtained from these first-order conditions can then be solved to derive the candidate optimal values of the decision variables. The potentially optimal points are then subject to the optimality conditions specified in the Karush-Kuhn-Tucker (KKT) theorem. These conditions include:

- **Stationarity:** This implies that no further improvement in the objective function can be found beyond this point.
- **Complementary Slackness:** Only one of either primal or its corresponding dual inequality can be active at the point.
- **Primal Feasibility:** The candidate point is in the feasible region of the primal problem.
- **Dual Feasibility:** The Lagrangian multiplier for each constraint must be nonnegative. In the nonlinear programming problems that use Lagrangian functions, the multipliers are the corresponding dual variables of the primal problem. Positive Lagrangian multiplier values imply that constraint is active at the point under scrutiny, while negative values imply that it is not.

In view of the daunting mathematical context that is required to solve nonlinear optimization problems, it is gratifying to know that they can be readily solved using the OPTMODEL procedure. This is another feature that makes the procedure a compelling resource in the toolkit of every

[8] A general description of the Lagrangian approach to solving optimization problems is presented here. The mathematical presentation of the approach is beyond the scope of this book.
[9] Notice that the functional framework described here was employed in many of the nonparametric loss functions we explored in the previous chapter (such as kernel regression, decision tree, and support vector machines). It is also used in parametric methods of estimations that involve the use of shrinkage estimators such as the least absolute shrinkage and selection operator (LASSO) regression.

Figure 8.3: Feasible Region and Interior Point Iterations

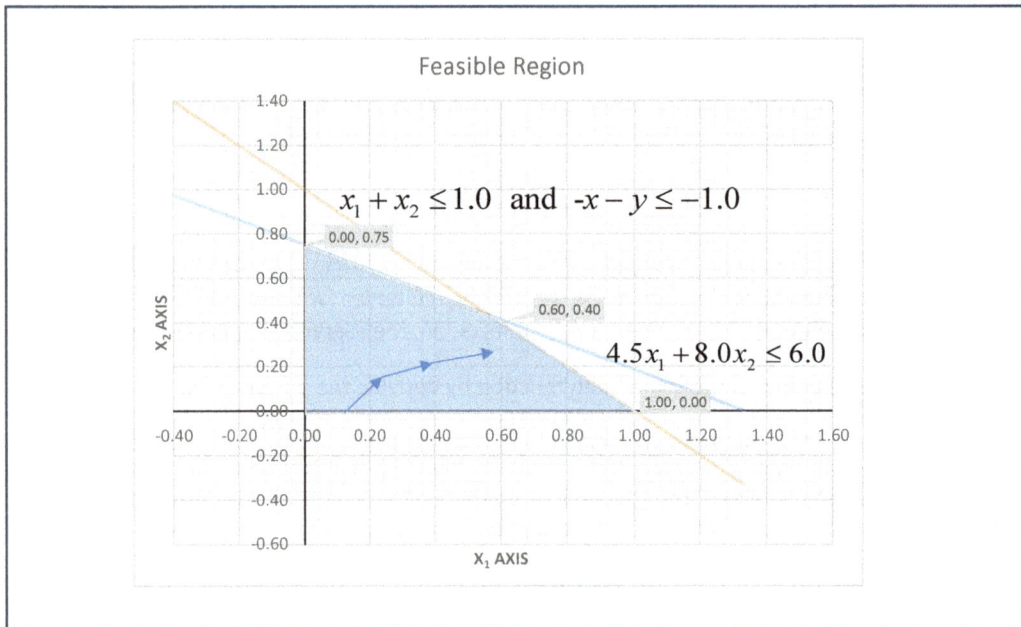

financial data scientist. Two types of solvers in the OPTMODEL procedure that are commonly used for nonlinear programming problems are the interior point method and active set.[10]

Interior Point Method

The interior point method (IPM) is a class of algorithms that are more commonly used to solve non-linear optimization problems than the simplex method because they are a relatively more efficient methodology for tackling large-scale problems. In reality, the IPM can solve both linear and non-linear optimization problems. Unlike the simplex that iterates across the bounds of the problem, the interior point algorithm solves the optimization problems by iterating from inside the feasible region toward the boundaries until the optimal condition is satisfied. Another difference between the IPM and the simplex algorithm is that the simplex method uses a slack variable in the constraint, whereas in the IPM, slack is imposed by including a logarithmic barrier function in the objective function. The constrained optimization is then respecified as an unconstrained optimization using the Lagrangian function. Although the objective function is unconstrained, the barrier function ensures that the optimal value of the objective function will

---

[10] The OPTMODEL procedure includes other solvers that are not presented here. You can learn more about them at https://documentation.sas.com/doc/en/pgmsascdc/9.4_3.5/ormpug/titlepage.htm.

remain in the feasible region. The search for the optimal solution is then performed via a central path, which depends on the parameter of the barrier function.

Consider a convex optimization problem defined as:

$$\min \quad c'x$$
$$\text{s.t.} \quad Ax \geq b, x \geq 0 \tag{8.17}$$

In the IPM, the constrained optimization problem above with inequality constraint is converted into a constrained objective function with equality constraints by specifying:

$$f_\mu(x) : c'x - \mu \sum_{i=1}^{N} \log(x_i)$$
$$\text{s.t.} \quad Ax = b \tag{8.18}$$

where μ is a real-valued parameter that is generally known as the barrier parameter. The optimal values of the decision variables are obtained by finding the μ and its corresponding x_u that minimizes the objective function using the Lagrangian function and the KKT conditions.

There are two common types of IPM: the primal barrier approach, which we just described, and the primal-dual IPM approach, which relies on the duality theorem. The primal-dual IPM simultaneously solves the primal and dual problems in a complementary approach. Remember that under the strong duality theorem, the optimal value of the primal objective function (minimum) is the same as the optimal value of the dual problem (maximum). This implies that the duality gap between the primal and dual problem is equal to 0. Furthermore, the upper bound of the primal problem will be equal to the lower bound of its corresponding dual problem, and vice versa. Hence, the goal of the primal-dual IPM is to find the optimal values of the primal and dual variables that satisfy the complementary set of constraints drawn from both the primal and dual problems.[11]

Active Set Method

The active set method of solving constrained optimization problems involves the iterative search across the feasible points by solving an equality-constrained optimization problem. The equality constraints are reformulated from all the inequality constraints that are active at the feasible point. It then iterates to another feasible point, while including another active constraint that was not present at the previous feasible point. The process continues until no other active constraint can be found. The Lagrangian function of the objective function and active constraints

---

[11] The general idea is presented in this section. The mathematics of the interior point method and primal-dual interior point is fairly rigorous and beyond the scope of this book as well. You can learn more about the algorithm at https://documentation.sas.com/doc/en/pgmsascdc/v_042/casmopt/casmopt_nlpsolver_details05.htm.

is then computed. Since constraints with negative Lagrangian multipliers are not active at the point of optimality, they are subsequently dropped from the problem before the candidate point is then subject to the KKT conditions to determine its optimality. The active set method is more efficient for small-scale nonlinear problems, while the interior point method is better suited to large-scale problems.

Quadratic Optimization

Quadratic optimization or programming is arguably the most common type of optimization you will encounter in financial data science activities. For example, quadratic programming is used in statistical models such as regression analysis and machine learning models such as support vector machines (SVM). Quadratic programming is used to solve optimization problems with quadratic objective functions and linear constraints. Consider the quadratic optimization problem shown below:

$$\min_{x} f(x) = x'Qx + c'x$$

$$\text{s.t.} \quad Ax = b, x \geq 0$$

(8.19)

Where $Q \in \mathbb{R}^n$, $A \in \mathbb{R}^n$, $B \in \mathbb{R}^n$, and $c \in \mathbb{R}^n$ are sets of given real values and $x \in \mathbb{R}^n$ is a set of decision variables. In the above problem, the objective function consists of a quadratic and linear component. In reality, linear programming is a special case of quadratic programming that results from $Q = 0$. However, quadratic programming problems are more challenging to solve because the objective function can take many shapes. For example, the objective function could be strictly convex (concave), in which case, it will possess a single minimum (maxima), which will be the global minimum (maximum). If the quadratic objective function is nonconvex (nonconcave), then it could possess multiple minima (maxima). The Karush-Kuhn-Tucker (KKT) conditions are commonly employed in many nonlinear solvers to determine whether a point in the feasible space that is a candidate for local minima or maxima satisfies the condition for global optimality.

In the finance domain, quadratic programming is commonly used to solve portfolio optimization problems. We will explore portfolio optimization in more detail in the next chapter. For now, let us show an example of how it can be applied to a simple convex optimization problem. Consider the minimization problem shown in Equation (8.20).

$$\min_{x,y} Z = x^2 + y^2 - 2x + 6y$$

$$\text{s.t.} \quad 3x + 8y \geq 25,$$

$$x+y \leq 5, x \geq 0, y \geq 0$$

(8.20)

We can show that Z is a strictly convex function of the x and y decision variables on the surface plot shown in Figure 8.4. The plot of Z shows a single unique minimum around the values of zero for x and y.

Figure 8.4: Surface Plot of Z-function

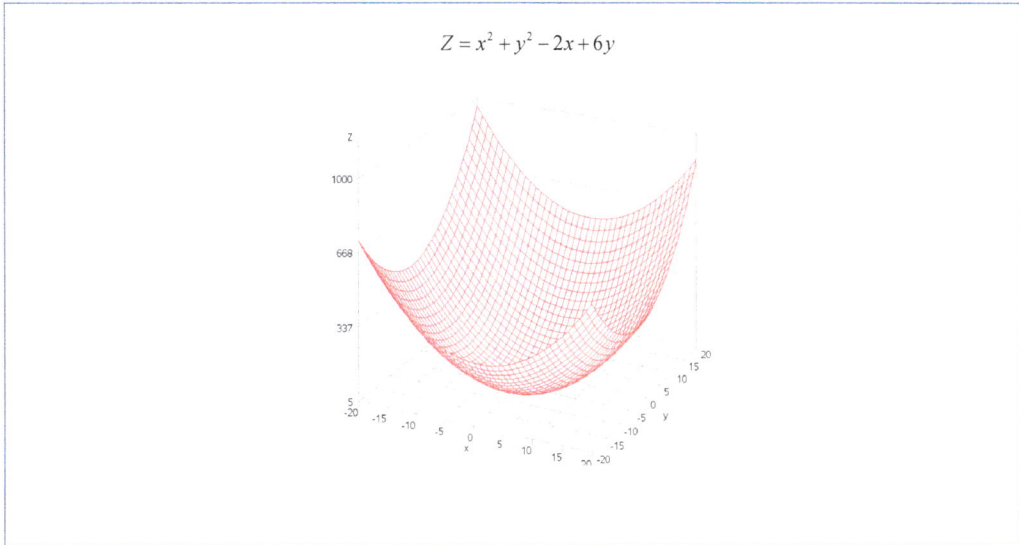

$$Z = x^2 + y^2 - 2x + 6y$$

In Program 8.9, we show the mathematical programming for the same quadratic optimization problem. We can also confirm the assertion that Z is strictly convex by reviewing the results of the unconstrained minimization of our objective function, which we invoked in the first SOLVE statement shown in the SAS code. The primal-dual interior point algorithm is the default solver for nonlinear optimization, so it is not necessary to specify it with the ALGORITHM=IP statement. Nevertheless, the statement is included to show you how to specify your solver of preference (for example, the active set).

Program 8.9: Solving Nonlinear Optimization Problem with PROC OPTMODEL

```
/*Solving Quadratic Optimization Problem using Interior Point Algorithm*/
proc optmodel;
      var x >= 0, y >= 0;
      min Z = (x**2)+(y**2)-2*x+6*y;
      solve with nlp obj z/algorithm=ip;
      print x x.dual y y.dual;
      con A:   3*x+8*y>=25;
      con B:   x+y <= 5;
      solve with nlp obj z/algorithm=ip;
      print x x.dual y y.dual;
      expand a;
      print A.dual A.body;
      print B.dual B.body;
quit;
```

Output 8.9: Optimal Solution to Nonlinear Optimization Problem from PROC OPTMODEL

The OPTMODEL Procedure

Solution Summary	
Solver	NLP
Algorithm	Interior Point
Objective Function	Z
Solution Status	Optimal
Objective Value	-0.999999971
Optimality Error	5E-9
Infeasibility	0
Iterations	4
Presolve Time	0.00
Solution Time	0.00

x	x.DUAL	y	y.DUAL
1	0 4.7564E-09	6	

The OPTMODEL Procedure

Solution Summary	
Solver	NLP
Algorithm	Interior Point
Objective Function	Z
Solution Status	Optimal
Objective Value	18.986302633
Optimality Error	5E-7
Infeasibility	0
Iterations	4
Presolve Time	0.00
Solution Time	0.00

x	x.DUAL	y	y.DUAL
2.8904	-3.278E-09	2.0411	-1.764E-08

A.DUAL	A.BODY
1.2603	25

B.DUAL	B.BODY
-0.00015568	4.9315

The optimal values of x and y (shown on the left-hand-side Solution Summary table) obtained from this optimization are 1 and 0, respectively. The objective value of the function at its global minimum is approximately -1.0. Next, we impose the two constraints (A and B) using the statement and then reinvoke the solver to apply the primal-dual interior point algorithm to the constrained optimization problem. The optimal values of x and y (shown on the right-hand-side Solution Summary table) from this optimization are now 2.89 and 2.014, respectively. And the objective value of the function at the new minimum is now 18.99. We can verify that the constraint is active by viewing the dual values of the constraint at this minimum. For minimization problems, positive dual values at the minimum imply that the greater than constraint is active, while negative dual values imply that less than constraint is active. The positive dual value of the A constraint and the negative value of the B constraint imply both constraints are active at the global minimum of this problem. You can verify this by checking the values of A.BODY and B.BODY. The BODY is the value of the simplified constraint expression. Notice that for A it is 25, which is equal to the lower bound of the $(\geq)$ A constraint, while the BODY value for B is 4.93, which is very close to the 5.0 upper bound of the $(\leq)$ B constraint.

Return-Based Style Analysis

In Chapter Two, we conducted numerical and visual performance attributions of a sample portfolio. Other types of performance attribution methods include those that use portfolio holdings analysis and those that use statistical analysis. Statistical performance attribution methods examine the risk factor exposures of the portfolio and their contributions to its overall performance. In Chapter Six, we introduced the portfolio factor model, which is a type of statistical model that is also used to conduct performance attribution. In the investment

Figure 8.5: Equity Style Box and Fixed Income Style Box

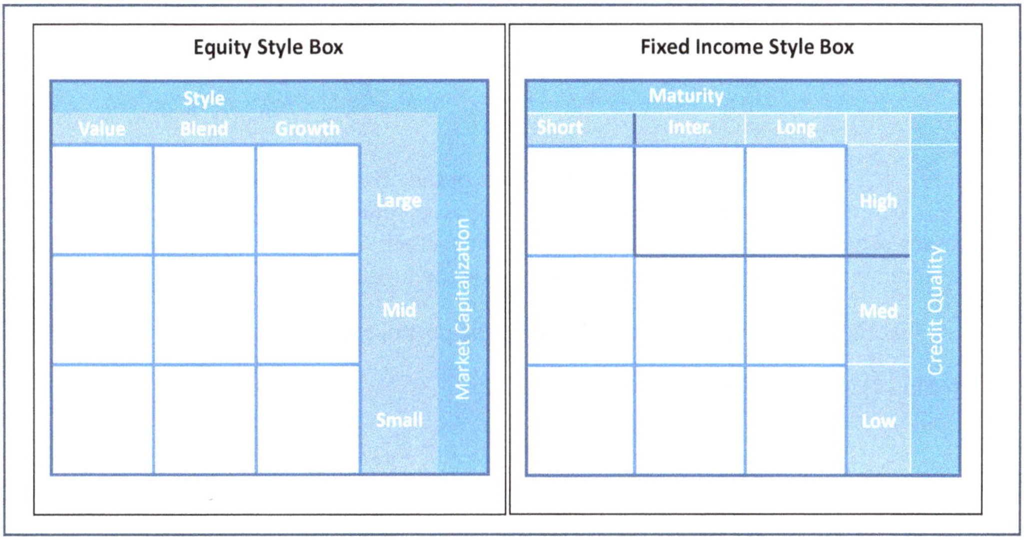

management industry, factor models are used to determine the set of observable fundamental factors that generated the performance of the portfolio.

Most portfolio managers include a portfolio style analysis in their performance report. Style analysis reports the investment choices of the portfolio manager in a style box, which is a nine-box grid that is spread across investment style (growth, blend, value) and market-capitalization (large-, mid-, and small-capitalization companies) for equity-based investment funds. For fixed-income funds, the same nine-box grid is spread across maturity (short, intermediate, and long) and credit quality (high-, medium-, and low-credit quality) as shown in Figure 8.5.

In reality, the spectrum of factors that can be measured using these types of analyses extends much farther than the nine-grid boxes shown in Figure 8.5 to include any observable style components of the investment manager's strategy, such as momentum, volatility, or quality. It could also include macroeconomic factors analysis such as interest rates, economic growth, inflation, and credit cycles. For now, we will focus solely on style-based analysis.

There are two types of style analysis: holdings-based and return-based. Holdings-based style analysis examines the characteristics of the entire component assets of the portfolio. These characteristics are aggregated to determine the overall style of the portfolio. The challenge with this approach is that it is time-consuming and financially expensive to implement, particularly for under-resourced investors. An alternate approach proposed by William Sharpe is a statistical-based approach called return-based style analysis. In this approach, the historical return of the portfolio is fitted against a select number of indices that represent various investment styles using quadratic optimization. The specification for the style factor model is as follows. Let $R_{i,t}$

denote the return of the component asset i of the portfolio at time t. The return-based factor model for the asset can be expressed as:

$$R_{i,t} = \left[\beta_{i,1}\tilde{F}_{1,t} + \beta_{i,2}\tilde{F}_{2,t} +,...+ \beta_{i,n}\tilde{F}_{n,t} \right] + \tilde{\varepsilon}_{i,t} \qquad (8.21)$$

where $\tilde{F}_{1,t}, \tilde{F}_{2,t},..., \tilde{F}_{n,t}$ are indicators of the values of the observable factors at each time index, $\tilde{\varepsilon}_{i,t}$ denotes the non-factor component of the asset return, and $\beta_{i,1}, \beta_{i,2},..., \beta_{i,n}$ denotes the sensitivity of the component asset to the factors. Although the specifications above are presented in the context of individual assets, they can be extended to portfolios of assets provided that the sum of the factor sensitivities of the portfolio equals one $\sum_{i}^{n} \beta_{p,j} = 1$, such that Equation (8.21) can now be rewritten as follows.

$$R_{p,t} = \left[\beta_{p,1}\tilde{F}_{1,t} + \beta_{p,2}\tilde{F}_{2,t} +,...+ \beta_{p,n}\tilde{F}_{n,t} \right] + \tilde{\varepsilon}_{p,t} \qquad (8.22)$$

In the above expression, the sum of the terms in the square bracket denotes the proportion of the portfolio's performance that can be explained by exposure to the style factors $\left(\tilde{F}_{1,t}, \tilde{F}_{2,t},..., \tilde{F}_{n,t} \right)$, while the residual component of the portfolio return $\tilde{\varepsilon}_{p,t}$ is the proportion of the portfolio's performance that can be attributed to the manager's security selection. When the returns of a benchmark portfolio are used as the style factor, $\tilde{\varepsilon}_{p,t}$ is often denoted as the tracking error of the portfolio.

Given a set of historical returns of the portfolio, and data on the style factor, we can assess to what extent the manager's portfolio performance is attributed to exposure to the set of style factors, versus the manager's prowess in security selection by implementing a constrained least square optimization that minimizes the collection of $\tilde{\varepsilon}_{p,t}$ over the set of historical returns.

$$\varepsilon_{p,t} = R_{p,t} - \left[\beta_{p,1}\tilde{F}_{1,t} + \beta_{p,2}\tilde{F}_{2,t} +,...+ \beta_{p,n}\tilde{F}_{n,t} \right] \qquad (8.23)$$

We can examine the extent to which the portfolio manager used an active or passive investment strategy by calculating the R-squared $\left(R^2 \right)$ of the constrained least square optimization, which we denote as:

$$R^2 = 1 - \frac{Var\left(\tilde{\varepsilon}_{p,t} \right)}{Var\left(R_{p,t} \right)} \qquad (8.24)$$

The higher the R-squared, the more of the portfolio performance that can be attributed to the allocation the portfolio manager made across the investing style factors.

Because many investment funds, such as mutual funds and pension funds often have short-selling restrictions, another restriction often placed on the model is that the factor sensitivities cannot be negative (that is, $\beta_{p,j} \geq 0$). Although the constraint can be relaxed for investment funds that are not restricted from using short-selling strategies, for those that are, the constraints prevent the use of the standard regression model for the estimation of the factor sensitivities. Instead, we will use quadratic optimization to derive the factor sensitivity of the sample portfolio.

Implementing Return-Based Style Analysis Using SAS

We use two steps to complete the implementation of the return-based style analysis in SAS. First, we will optimize our objective function using the OPTMODEL procedure. We will then calculate the R-squared of our model using the IML procedure. We will also visually display the derived factor weights using the SGPLOT procedure.

The SAS data set with the file name CONSTRAINED.SAS7BDAT contains the 60 months of monthly returns for the sample portfolio we examined in Chapter Two. Added to the data are the monthly values of the five Fama-French Factors, which are the MRP (Market Risk Premium), HML (High Minus Low factor), SMB (Small-Minus-Big factor), RMW (Robust Minus Weak factor), and CMA (Conservative Minus Aggressive factor). MRP is the excess return on the stock market, HML is the value factor, SMB factor is the size factor, RMW is a profitability factor, and CMA is the investment strategy factor (conservative versus aggressive). We will estimate the proportion of the sample portfolio return that is determined by the five factors using quadratic optimization. The objective function that we will optimize is the sum of the squared deviation of the tracking error, subject to a no short-selling constraint, and the constraint that the sum of the factor sensitivities must equal one as shown in Equation (8.25).

$$\min \sum_{t=1}^{T} \varepsilon_{p,t}^2$$

$$\text{s.t. } \sum_{i=1}^{n} \beta_{p,j} = 1, \ \beta_{p,j} \geq 0 \tag{8.25}$$

Program 8.10 contains the SAS program for implementing the return-based style analysis. First, we download our CONSTRAINED data set from the book's GitHub page using the %DATAPULL macro. We then invoke the OPTMODEL procedure. Next, we declare two index sets: the FUND index set, which uses the Date variable as its index variable (and therefore is a numeric index set), and the FACTOR index set, which uses the style factors as the index variable (and therefore is a string index set). We also declare two sets of parameters: PRETURNS and FACTORS. PRETURNS is the monthly portfolio returns. The parameter is indexed to the fund index set. The FACTORS parameter array is indexed to the FUND and FACTOR index sets. The FACTORS array contains the five style factors (MRP, SMB, HML, RMW, and CMA) that we will use in our style analysis. Next, we read the data from the CONSTRAINED data set into both the PRETURNS parameter and FACTORS parameter arrays using two READ statements. The decision variable (WEIGHTS), which represents the factor loadings of the portfolio, is then declared. We use the implicit variable TE to compute the tracking error for each month. We also impose the constraint that the sum of all factor loadings must equal one by using the CON statement. We then specify the objective function, which is to minimize the sum of the squared tracking error. We invoke the quadratic programming solver using the SOLVE statement. Although it is not necessary (because the procedure will automatically determine the formulation of the problem), you may prefer to use the SOLVE WITH QP statement instead.

Next, we use the CREATE statements to create two data sets. The FACTWEIGHT data set contains the optimal values of the factor loadings, while the RSQUARECAL data set contains the monthly values of the estimated tracking errors and portfolio returns. We then use the IML procedure to compute the R-Square and the SGPLOT procedure to construct a bar chart to display the optimal weight of each style factor.

Program 8.10: Solving Nonlinear Optimization Problem with PROC OPTMODEL

```
/*Implementing Return-Based Style Analysis using PROC OPTMODEL*/
%datapull(constr,constrained.sas7bdat);
proc optmodel;
        /* declare sets and parameters */
        set <num> FUND;
        set <str> FACTOR={'MRP', 'SMB', 'HML','RMW', 'CMA'};
        num Preturns {FUND};
        num Factors{FUND,FACTOR};

        /* read portfolio data from SAS data sets */
        read data Constrained into FUND=[Date] PReturns;

        *read data Constrained into FACTORS=[Month] PReturns;
        read data Constrained into [Date]
                {j in FACTOR} <Factors[Date,j]=col(j)>;

        /* declare variables */
        var Weights{FACTOR} >= 0;

        /*Calculate Portfolio Risk Measures*/
        impvar TE{i in FUND}=sum{j in FACTOR}(preturns[i]-Weights[j]*factors[i,j])**2;

        /* declare constraints */
        con Factor_Weights: sum {j in FACTOR} Weights[j] = 1;

        /* declare objective */
        min Fund_Factor = sum{i in FUND}TE[i];
        solve with QP;
        print Weights;

        /* write data to SAS data sets */
        create data factweight from [Factors]={j in FACTOR}
                Weights=Weights;
        create data RSquarecal from [date]={i in FUND} TE=TE PReturns= preturns;
quit;

/*Use PROC IML to compute R-Square*/
proc iml;
        use Rsquarecal;
        read  all into RR[colname=NumerNames];
```

```
        CR=RR[,2:3];
        VCV=cov(CR);
        print VCV;
        RSquare=1-VCV[1,1]/VCV[2,2];
        print RSquare[ format=percent8.2];
quit;
```

Output 8.10A: Return-Based Style Analysis Using PROC OPTMODEL and PROC IML

The OPTMODEL Procedure

The OPTMODEL Procedure

Problem Summary

Objective Sense	Minimization
Objective Function	Fund_Factor
Objective Type	Quadratic
Number of Variables	5
Bounded Above	0
Bounded Below	5
Bounded Below and Above	0
Free	0
Fixed	0
Number of Constraints	1
Linear LE (<=)	0
Linear EQ (=)	1
Linear GE (>=)	0
Linear Range	0
Constraint Coefficients	5
Hessian Diagonal Elements	5
Hessian Elements Below Diagonal	0

Solution Summary

Solver	QP
Algorithm	Interior Point
Objective Function	Fund_Factor
Solution Status	Optimal
Objective Value	0.680068484
Primal Infeasibility	1.2860512E-7
Dual Infeasibility	8.974097E-10
Bound Infeasibility	0
Duality Gap	2.2218604E-8
Complementarity	0
Iterations	6
Presolve Time	0.00
Solution Time	0.01

[1]	Weights
CMA	0.000000
HML	0.045874
MRP	0.803199
RMW	0.000000
SMB	0.150926

Covariance Matrix
0.0003392   -0.0002
-0.0002   0.002254

R-Square
84.95%

Output 8.10A shows the results we obtained from implementing Program 6.10. The Problem Summary table shows the characteristics of our optimization problem (Objective Sense=Minimization, Objective Function=FUND_FACTOR, and Objective Type=Quadratic). It also shows the number of variables and constraints. The Solution Summary table shows the type of Solver invoked (QP or quadratic solver), the Algorithm (Interior Point) the Solution Status (Optimal), and the Objective Value (0.68). Reported below the Solution Summary are the estimated weights of the style factors. About 80% of the observable factor exposure is from holding stocks in general by virtue of the MRP factor, 15.09% is due to holding a small capitalization tilt and 4.59% comes from the value tilt of the portfolio. Notice that the optimized weight of the CMA and RMW factors are both zero.[12]

---

[12] Consider reoptimizing the objective function without the constraint that the factor loadings must sum to 1.

The covariance matrix that we obtained from the IML procedure is shown below the output tables from the OPTMODEL procedures. The variance of PRETURNS and the tracking error are diagonal elements of the matrix, while their covariances are the off-diagonal elements. Notice the low covariance between the tracking error and the portfolio returns. This is consistent with the theory, which states that the $\tilde{\varepsilon}_{p,t}$ represents the unexplained variations in the model after accounting for the role of the observable factors. The R-square of the return-based style analysis is 84.95%, which suggests that about 15% of the portfolio performance is due to the manager's security selection abilities. It is important to note that this measure does not imply superior security selection skills for the manager. It is only an indicator of the (positive or negative) contribution from security selection to the overall portfolio performance.

In Output 8.10B, we graph the factor loadings of the portfolio on a vertical bar chart using the SGPLOT procedure. The VBAR statement specifies the FACTOR variables, and the RESPONSE option specifies the statistic of the variable we are plotting, which in our case are the derived weights for each factor. We use the COLORRESPONSE, COLORMODEL, NOSTATLABEL, DATASKIN, and LEGENDLABEL options to provide further customizations to the graph.

Output 8.10B: Return-Based Style Analysis Using PROC OPTMODEL and PROC IML

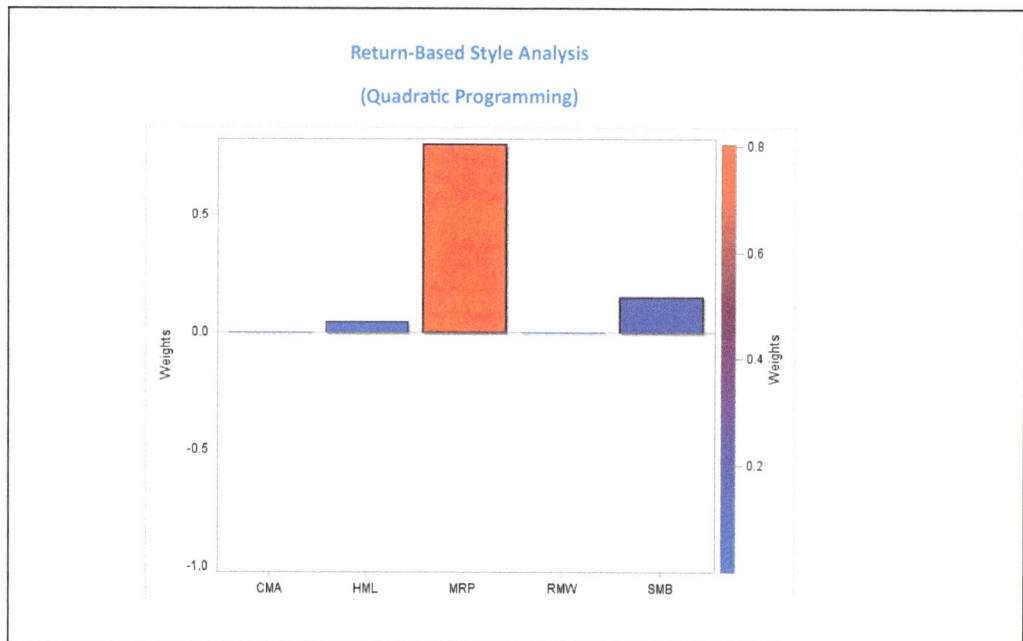

In conclusion, we have shown the vast potential of the OPTMODEL procedure for solving various optimization problems in the finance domain. In the next chapter, we will focus on its application for solving various types of portfolio optimization problems.

Exercises

1. Write the SAS code to solve the following set of mathematical optimization problems.

   a. $\max f = 4x + 3y + 6z$

        s.t. $3x + 5y + 2z \leq 15$

                    $5x + 6y - 4z \geq 10$

                    $x \geq 0, y \geq 0, z \geq 0$

   b. $\min f = 8x + 3y + 6z$

        s.t. $3x + 5y + 4z \leq 30$

                    $3x - 3y + 2z \geq 25$

                    $x \geq 0 \text{ integer}, y \geq 0 \text{ integer}, z \geq 0 \text{ integer}$

   c. $\min f = 3x^2 + 5y^2$

        s.t. $8x + 3y \leq 15$

                    $x \geq 0, y \geq 0$

2. Let's revisit our capital project selection problem. Modify the SAS program to change the objective function from maximizing total NPV to maximizing the total profitability index (PI) for the portfolio of projects. Include an implicit variable to calculate the total NPV of the selected projects.

   a. Compare the projects selected to the one selected for the maximizing NPV problem.
      i. Were the same projects selected, why and why not?
      ii. Are their NPVs the same?
   b. Now modify the initial program, changing the objective function from maximizing total NPV to minimizing the total costs of the project, subject to a minimum NPV of $49,000.
      i. Were the same projects selected, why and why not?
      ii. Are their NPVs the same?

3. Consider the cash flow dedication problem that we solved using Program 8.8. Modify the SAS code in the program to include a reinvestment rate of 2% for the surplus funds. Then reoptimize the objective function.

   a. Compare the objective value from this solution to the objective value shown in Output 8.8. Are the objective values different? What is the effect of the reinvestment opportunity on the new total cost for constructing the bond portfolio?
   b. Did including the reinvestment rate alter the optimal units of the bond purchased? What effect did it have on the bond ladder?

c. Suppose the reinvestment rate for the first five years, starting from the initial date is 2%, before rising to 3% for the remaining five years. Modify your SAS code to allow for a period-specific reinvestment rate. What impact did the increase in the reinvestment rate on the later years' surplus cash have on your initial cost and the bond ladder portfolio?

Chapter 9: Using SAS for Portfolio Optimizations

Modern Portfolio Theory (MPT) and Portfolio Optimization

Modern portfolio theory argues that given a universe of risky assets with a known probability distribution of expected returns over some holding period, rational utility-maximizing investors who are risk-averse will construct portfolios of risk assets using an optimized trade-off between the risk of the portfolio and the expected return to be earned by holding the portfolio. To put it more broadly, the theory states that rational risk-averse investors will seek the best risk-return trade-off for every level of risk or expected returns. Under this theory, the investor's portfolio decision is based solely on two factors, the expected return from the security (mean) and the risk of the security, which is measured by the variance of expected return (variance).[1] Hence, the MPT approach to portfolio construction is often called the mean-variance optimization (MVO).

From a practical point of view, deriving the best trade-off between risk and return is strictly an optimization problem in which the objective function and constraints can be calibrated to reflect the primary domain in which the investor prefers to optimize the portfolio. For example, suppose the investor desires to minimize the risk of the portfolio at a given level of return, then the objective function will be expressed in terms of the portfolio risk, while the desired level of return will be expressed in terms of the constraint as follows:

$$\min w' \sum w$$
$$\text{s.t.} \quad w'\text{E}(R) = \text{E}(P), w'1_N = 1$$

(9.1)

where $\text{E}(R)$ is a vector of expected returns for the universe of risky assets, Σ is the covariance matrix of the expected returns, and w is a vector of decision variables. In the MVO framework,

---

[1] Although it is not commonly used in the MPT framework, readers might also prefer to compare the portfolios using the coefficient of variation (CV). CV is a statistical measure of the dispersion of returns around its expected value and is calculated as the ratio of standard deviation to the expected return. However, you should note that there are some disadvantages to using CV for evaluating portfolio performance. CV should not be used to compare portfolio performance from different periods since the expected return (denominator) includes the risk-free rate of return, which might not be the same in both periods. CV will be undefined when the portfolio return is zero. Indeed, when the portfolio return is close to zero, CV will be extremely sensitive to the changes in portfolio mean.

w are the policy weights to be derived from optimizing the objective function. Furthermore, $\mathrm{E}(R)$ and Σ are arrays of predetermined parameters.

Notice the similarity between the formulation of Equations (8.20) and (9.1). That is because the product of the portfolio weights for the elements of the covariance matrix follows a quadratic form of w_i^2 (for the diagonal element of the covariance matrix) or $w_i w_j$ (for the off-diagonal elements of the covariance matrix) of the matrix.

If the investor seeks to maximize returns for a given level of risk, then the objective function for the optimization problem will be written in the domain of expected returns, while the desired risk level of the portfolio will be accounted for in the constraint as shown in Equation (9.2).

$$\max_{w} w'\mathrm{E}(R)$$

$$\text{s.t.} \quad w'\sum w \leq Q, w'1_N = 1 \tag{9.2}$$

Although the optimization problem in Equation (9.2) does not have a quadratic objective function, it is still a nonlinear programming problem because the constraint is nonlinear. Indeed, both optimization problems are nonlinear and can be solved by one of the many nonlinear solvers that are available in the OPTMODEL procedure. Notice that the portfolio optimization formulas shown in Equations (9.1) and (9.2) follow the same structure as all of the previous optimizations we have tackled, in the sense that they are both comprised of objective functions and a set of constraints. This means that our portfolio optimization problems can be solved using mathematical programming.

Mean-Variance Optimization

Let us revisit our sample portfolio from Chapter Two. You will recall that the portfolio consists of 63 stocks, spread over 11 GIC sectors, and all three categories of market capitalizations. The stock tickers and monthly historical returns, standard deviation of monthly returns, and current portfolio weights for the stocks in the portfolio are shown in Table 9.1. Let us reallocate the weights of the sample portfolio using the MVO framework.

Return Maximization

Our objective in this optimization problem is to determine the set of allocations that would maximize the expected monthly return of the portfolio, subject to a maximum portfolio risk (which is measured by the standard deviation of monthly return) of 4.5%. The mathematical formulation of our portfolio optimization problem is shown as follows:

$$\max_{w} \mathrm{E}(R_p) = \sum_{i=1}^{n} w_i \mathrm{E}(R_i)$$

$$\text{s.t.} \quad \sigma_p = \sqrt{\sum_{i=1}^{n} w_i w_j Cov(R_i, R_j)} \leq 4.5\%, \sum_{i=1}^{n} w_i = 1 \tag{9.3}$$

Table 9.1: Characteristics of the Stocks in the Sample Portfolio

Ticker	Returns	STDEV	Weights	Ticker	Returns	STDEV	Weights	Ticker	Returns	STDEV	Weights
ABBV	1.32%	7.98%	2.84%	RCII	0.97%	16.26%	0.50%	SBNY	-0.37%	12.32%	1.35%
HD	1.19%	6.63%	2.18%	MSI	1.58%	7.08%	3.40%	HBI	-1.70%	12.32%	0.20%
WMT	1.00%	5.76%	1.90%	IP	-0.52%	7.69%	0.25%	NVR	1.41%	8.09%	1.94%
CAT	1.32%	8.49%	1.63%	D	-0.31%	5.12%	0.40%	IVZ	-0.73%	11.63%	0.20%
AAPL	2.09%	8.73%	6.99%	GWW	1.21%	8.68%	6.55%	TSLA	3.00%	18.19%	2.31%
DAL	-0.56%	11.25%	1.54%	ET	-0.68%	15.09%	0.07%	MPC	1.16%	13.55%	0.50%
BKNG	0.44%	8.93%	2.52%	KFRC	1.20%	9.79%	0.86%	LYB	-0.05%	9.49%	0.61%
CG	0.93%	10.82%	1.62%	TSN	0.01%	7.45%	0.86%	PII	0.28%	12.20%	1.32%
CVX	0.59%	8.68%	3.08%	MAR	0.82%	11.01%	1.40%	CNC	1.48%	8.37%	1.08%
CSCO	0.63%	7.36%	2.49%	DLB	0.62%	7.01%	0.73%	RMD	1.68%	7.44%	3.04%
CVS	0.23%	7.58%	1.76%	DVA	0.21%	9.15%	0.77%	JNPR	0.17%	7.21%	0.40%
DD	-0.24%	9.71%	1.59%	ALG	0.86%	7.61%	0.64%	SUN	0.66%	10.98%	0.20%
JPM	0.61%	7.51%	3.12%	PAYC	2.67%	12.29%	3.28%	TOL	0.66%	12.23%	0.68%
META	0.06%	10.86%	4.41%	KMI	-0.19%	7.60%	0.15%	VFC	-0.83%	9.67%	0.29%
PFE	0.71%	6.85%	1.55%	CMS	0.58%	4.98%	0.29%	STE	1.40%	6.70%	1.25%
SWK	-0.59%	8.94%	2.48%	WM	1.10%	5.21%	1.89%	HAS	-0.34%	8.10%	0.96%
UNH	1.66%	6.14%	1.98%	BXP	-0.86%	8.19%	0.72%	ALLY	0.35%	10.94%	0.54%
VTRS	-1.71%	11.27%	0.36%	GEN	-0.15%	10.78%	0.12%	KO	0.59%	5.12%	0.46%
FDP	-1.17%	9.76%	0.49%	ALK	-1.01%	11.76%	0.26%	CPT	0.40%	6.08%	1.52%
CMI	0.80%	7.23%	5.73%	CCI	0.62%	6.07%	2.28%	DG	1.67%	5.77%	2.13%
FE	0.42%	6.55%	0.32%	VNO	-1.94%	9.37%	0.49%	TSCO	1.51%	7.51%	2.52%

Notice that while the objective function for the problem is linear, the risk constraint is not. Hence, this problem is inherently a nonlinear optimization problem. The problem data that we will need for our nonlinear optimization problem includes the vector of the returns of the current component stocks of the portfolio (shown in Table 9.1) and the covariance matrix of the returns. The SAS data sets named PORTFOLIO_RETURNS.SAS7BDAT and PORTFOLIO_COVARIANCES. SAS7BDAT (located on the book's GitHub page) contain the monthly average returns and covariances for the current 63 stocks in the portfolio. The average returns and covariances were calculated using monthly returns from January 2016 to December 2021.

First, use the %DATAPULL macro to download both SAS data files into your WORK folder. In Program 9.1A, we demonstrate the SAS code to invoke the optimization of the portfolio returns, subject to the risk constraint. Be aware that we will be comparing several portfolio optimization methods that use other objective functions. To ensure that we can meaningfully perform an apples-to-apples comparison, we have included the code (along with comments to mark where they are included) for calculating these measures in all of the portfolio optimization problems we examine.

Program 9.1A: Maximizing Portfolio Returns (MVO Approach) Using PROC OPTMODEL

```
/*Maximizing Portfolio Return in the Mean-Variance Optimization using PROC OPTMODEL*/
%datapull(portret,portfolio_returns.sas7bdat);
%datapull(portvcv,portfolio_covariances.sas7bdat);
%let max_risk = 0.045;
%let alpha=0.99;
%let rfr=0.00178;

proc optmodel;
        /* declare sets and parameters */
        set <str> ASSETS;
        num returns {ASSETS};
        num covariance {ASSETS, ASSETS};

        /* read portfolio data from SAS data sets */
        read data Portfolio_Returns into ASSETS=[Ticker] returns;

        *print returns;
        read data Portfolio_Covariances into [Ticker]
                {j in ASSETS} <covariance[Ticker,j]=col(j)>;

        *print covariance;
        /* declare variables */
        var Weights {ASSETS} >= 0;

        /*Calculate Portfolio Risk Measures*/
        impvar Portfolio_Variance=sum {i in ASSETS, j in
         ASSETS}covariance[i,j]*Weights[i]*Weights[j];
        impvar Portfolio_Risk = sqrt(Portfolio_Variance);

        /*Included Code: Value at Risk and Expected Shortfall*/
        impvar zes =(((2*constant("pi"))**(0.5))*(exp(((2**-
        0.5)*quantile('normal',&alpha))**2))*(1-&alpha))**-1;
        impvar VaR=sum {j in ASSETS}
                -returns[j]*Weights[j]+quantile("normal",&alpha)*sqrt(Portfolio_Variance);
        impvar Expected_Shortfall=sum {j in ASSETS}
                -returns[j]*Weights[j]+zes*sqrt(Portfolio_Variance);

        /*Calculate portfolio return*/
        impvar Expected_Return=sum {j in ASSETS}
                returns[j] * Weights[j];

        /* declare constraints */
        con Portfolio_Weights: sum {j in ASSETS} Weights[j] = 1;
        con Variance: Portfolio_Variance <= &max_risk**2;

        /* declare objective */
        max Portfolio_Return = Expected_Return;
        solve ;

        /*Portfolio Sharpe Ratio*/
        Impvar Sharpe_Ratio = (Expected_Return-&rfr)/Portfolio_Risk;
```

```
          /*Print Optimization Outputs*/
          print   Portfolio_Return percent8.2 Portfolio_Risk percent8.2 Sharpe_Ratio best8.5
          VaR percent8.2 Expected_Shortfall percent8.2;
          print Variance.ub Variance.dual;
          print {j in ASSETS: Weights[j]>1e-4} Weights percent8.2
                  {j in ASSETS: Weights[j]>1e-4} returns percent8.2;

          /* write data to SAS data sets */
          create data mvmax from [Ticker]={j in ASSETS: Weights[j]>1e-4}
                  Weights=Weights;
quit;
```

The SAS code in Program 9.1A starts with the %DATAPULL macro to download the portfolio data from the book's GitHub page. We then create three macrovariables. &MAX_RISK=0.045 sets the maximum tolerable risk (standard deviation) for the portfolio to 4.5%. %ALPHA denotes a 99% value-at-risk threshold for the portfolio. %RFR sets the average monthly risk-free rate to 0.178%. Note that the only constraint in the MV maximization problem is not exceeding a specified portfolio risk. Next, the PROC OPTMODEL statement is used to invoke the procedure, while the SET <str> ASSETS statement was used to declare the index set named ASSETS. We declare the two required parameter arrays (vector of returns and covariance matrix) using the NUM statements. We then proceed to read the returns data for each stock in the Portfolio_Returns data set into the RETURN array and from the Portfolio_Covariance data set into the COVARIANCE array. We also declare the decision variable (Weights).

Notice that we impose nonnegative bounds on the weights. This is generally known as the no short-selling constraint. We generously use implicit variables in our SAS program to highlight measures that readers might be more familiar with throughout the code to facilitate code readability. The first group of implicit variables is used to calculate the portfolio variance and portfolio standard deviation, which is our main measure of risk in this optimization. The next set of implicit variables, which are not required but added for comparison purposes, calculates the 99%-VaR and expected shortfall (using the normal distribution) for the optimized portfolio. The next group of implicit variables calculates the expected return of the portfolio, which is the objective we will maximize subject to our risk constraint. Notice that it is currently specified as an implicit variable. We followed this approach to ensure consistency in the code for all the portfolio optimizations we will explore. In some of these problems, the portfolio return will not be the objective we will optimize. As you will notice shortly, the implicit variable is eventually called up in the declaration of the objective function for the problem.

In the next set of codes, we declare the formal constraints, which are the full investment constraint (in other words, portfolio weights must sum to 1) and the maximum tolerable portfolio risk using the &MAX_RISK macrovariable. The objective function (PORTFOLIO_RETURN) is then declared using the implicit variable (EXPECTED_RETURN) and the solver invoked. Notice that we did not request a specific solver for the problem. In this case, the procedure will automatically determine the best solver for the problem type. You can specify your preferred solver, using the WITH clause. The subsequent sets of code include implicit variables to calculate the portfolio Sharpe ratio as well as SAS statements to invoke the printing of the optimization results and create a SAS data set named MVMAX, which will be used to store the optimal portfolio weights, which are then plotted on a pie chart using the SGPIE procedure as shown in Program 9.1B.

Program 9.1B: Graphing Optimized Portfolio Allocations Using PROC SGPIE

```
/*Graphing Portfolio Allocations Using PROC SGPIE*/
proc sgpie data=mvmax;
      title1 font=swissb height=2 'Asset Allocations Using Mean-Variance Portfolio
Optimization';
      title2 font=swissb height=2 '(Return Maximization)';
      pie  Ticker / response=Weights otherpercent=1  statfmt=percent8.2
datalabelloc=callout;
run;

title1;
title2;
quit;
```

Output 9.1A: Portfolio Statistics Obtained from Return Maximization Optimization (MVO)

The OPTMODEL Procedure

Problem Summary

Objective Sense	Maximization
Objective Function	Portfolio_Return
Objective Type	Linear
Number of Variables	63
Bounded Above	0
Bounded Below	63
Bounded Below and Above	0
Free	0
Fixed	0
Number of Constraints	2
Linear LE (<=)	0
Linear EQ (=)	1
Linear GE (>=)	0
Linear Range	0
Nonlinear LE (<=)	1
Nonlinear EQ (=)	0
Nonlinear GE (>=)	0
Nonlinear Range	0

The OPTMODEL Procedure

Solution Summary

Solver	NLP
Algorithm	Interior Point Direct
Objective Function	Portfolio_Return
Solution Status	Optimal
Objective Value	0.0178826278
Optimality Error	2.1972396E-7
Infeasibility	4.662937E-15
Iterations	14
Presolve Time	0.00
Solution Time	0.02

[1]	Weights	returns
AAPL	15.31%	2.09%
ABBV	0.08%	1.32%
CAT	2.73%	1.32%
CNC	2.52%	1.48%
DG	38.55%	1.67%
MSI	0.02%	1.58%
NVR	0.07%	1.41%
PAYC	5.52%	2.67%
RMD	18.27%	1.68%
STE	0.03%	1.40%
TSLA	1.12%	3.00%
UNH	15.73%	1.66%

Portfolio_Return	Portfolio_Risk	Sharpe_Ratio	VaR	Expected_Shortfall
1.79%	4.50%	0.36	8.68%	10.21%

Output 9.1A shows the results from the optimization of the portfolio weights for the component stocks that were derived from solving the problem. Remember that the initial portfolio contains 63 stocks. The optimized portfolio, however, contains only 12 stocks and has a monthly expected return of 1.79% and a standard deviation of 4.5%. Annualized, the expected return is approximately 24.7% with a standard deviation of about 15.6%. Although the optimized portfolio

slightly underperformed the full portfolio of assets using the 2021 results,[2] in reality, the long-term performance of the optimized portfolio is significantly better than the full portfolio over the six years. The average monthly return for the full portfolio over the same period was 1.09% with a standard deviation of 4.75%. The economic value of optimizing the portfolio weights is evident in this example. By optimizing the portfolio, we have increased the expected average monthly return by about 70 basis points, without incurring any sacrifice in terms of bearing a higher amount of risk. The Sharpe ratio of the optimized portfolio (0.36) is also higher than the Sharpe ratio of the full portfolio (0.19). From a modern portfolio theory perspective, we will deem the optimized portfolio as more efficient than the full portfolio. Whether this portfolio will be more efficient than any other portfolio we can construct from the universe of 63 stocks in the full portfolio remains to be determined. However, it is evident that we have now moved from a well-diversified portfolio of 63 stocks to a highly concentrated portfolio that might be exposed to significant event risk. 93.3% of the value of our optimized portfolio is concentrated in just five stocks (Dollar General (DG), RESMED Inc (RMD), United Health (UNH), Apple Inc (AAPL), and Paycom Software (PAYC)), which might not be very appealing for many investors, regardless of the theoretical construct of how the modern portfolio theory proposes that investor should behave.

Output 9.1B graphically depicts the concentration in the optimal portfolio allocations derived from the return maximization on a pie chart. On the chart, more than 99% of the portfolio weights were allocated to just eight stocks. The remaining four stocks from the total of 12 were allocated an insignificant 0.19% of the total portfolio capital.

Output 9.1B: Optimal Portfolio Allocations for Return Maximization Optimization (MVO)

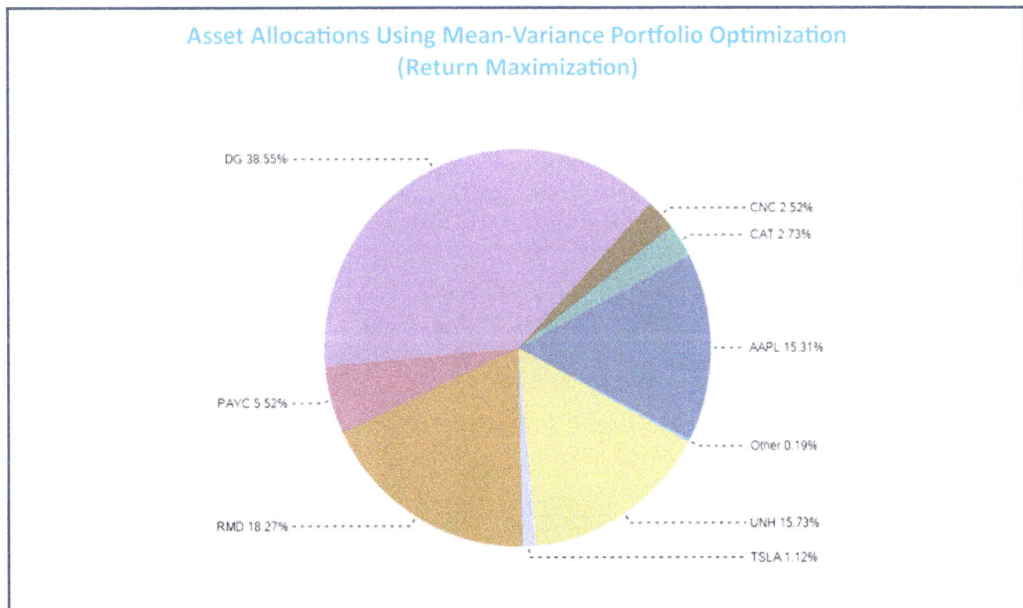

Asset Allocations Using Mean-Variance Portfolio Optimization (Return Maximization)

DG 38.55%
CNC 2.52%
CAT 2.73%
AAPL 15.31%
Other 0.19%
UNH 15.73%
TSLA 1.12%
RMD 18.27%
PAYC 5.52%

---

[2] See result table in Chapter 2.

Risk Minimization

Perhaps, we could obtain a different outcome if we optimized the risk of the portfolio at a given level of return. In this case, our objective function will be nonlinear in the form of a quadratic expression, while our return constraint will be linear. We will be searching for the set of portfolio weights that will yield a minimum risk at the desired minimum level of return (let's say 1.79% per month). The mathematical expression of our portfolio optimization problem is shown as follows:

$$\min_{w} \sigma_p = \sqrt{\sum_{i=1}^{n} w_i w_j Cov\left(R_i, R_j\right)}$$

(9.4)

$$\text{s.t.} \quad \mathrm{E}\left(R_p\right) = \sum_{i=1}^{n} w_i \mathrm{E}\left(R_i\right) \geq 1.79\%, \sum_{i=1}^{n} w_i = 1$$

In Program 9.2, we show the SAS code that can be invoked to optimize the portfolio risk, subject to the return constraint. Most of the code in the program is similar to what is in Program 9.1, so we removed it. We will only need to modify the constraints and objective function of Program 9.1 to implement the code for risk minimization.[3] The use of implicit variables for calculations that are similar across the different optimization methods is one way to bring some efficiency to your programming task. Notice that our objective function is specified as the square root of the portfolio variance, which we had calculated earlier using the implicit variable.

Program 9.2: Minimizing Portfolio Risk (MVO Approach) Using PROC OPTMODEL

```
/*Minimizing Portfolio Risk in the Mean-Variance Optimization using PROC OPTMODEL*/
%let minimum_return = 0.0179;
%let beta=0.99;
%let rfr=0.00178;

proc optmodel;

/********************************************/
/*         Same as Program 9.1          */
/********************************************/

    /* declare constraints */
    con Portfolio_Weights: sum {j in ASSETS} Weights[j] = 1;
    con Minimum_return: Expected_Return >= &minimum_return;

    /* declare objective */
    min Portfolio_Risk = sqrt(Portfolio_Variance);
    solve with qp;

/********************************************/
/*         Same as Program 9.1          */
/********************************************/
```

---

[3] The full code can be found on the book's GitHub page.

Let's review our output from the optimization, which is shown in Output 9.2. You will notice in the Problem Summary that the solver correctly determined that the objective function is nonlinear because it was written as the square root of a quadratic expression. In view of this, the solver selected by the procedure to optimize the objective function was the direct IPM solver. If preferred, you could respecify the objective function using the variance term.[4] This will cause the procedure to classify the problem as a quadratic optimization problem and to select the primal-dual IPM solver for the optimization task. However, you should note that it is more common to present portfolio risk using standard deviation than variance. Interestingly, optimizing the portfolio risk resulted in a smaller number of stocks (10) in the optimized portfolio than the number that we obtained from the return maximization optimization.

Output 9.2: Portfolio Statistics Obtained from Risk Minimization Optimization (MVO)

The OPTMODEL Procedure

Problem Summary

Objective Sense	Minimization
Objective Function	Portfolio_Risk
Objective Type	Nonlinear
Number of Variables	63
Bounded Above	0
Bounded Below	63
Bounded Below and Above	0
Free	0
Fixed	0
Number of Constraints	2
Linear LE (<=)	0
Linear EQ (=)	1
Linear GE (>=)	1
Linear Range	0

The OPTMODEL Procedure

Solution Summary

Solver	NLP
Algorithm	Interior Point Direct
Objective Function	Portfolio_Risk
Solution Status	Optimal
Objective Value	0.0450479652
Optimality Error	1.3529111E-7
Infeasibility	9.769963E-15
Iterations	16
Presolve Time	0.00
Solution Time	0.02

[1]	Weights	returns
AAPL	15.33%	2.09%
ABBV	0.02%	1.32%
CAT	2.74%	1.32%
CNC	2.48%	1.48%
DG	38.57%	1.67%
NVR	0.02%	1.41%
PAYC	5.58%	2.67%
RMD	18.29%	1.68%
TSLA	1.13%	3.00%
UNH	15.81%	1.66%

Portfolio_Return	Portfolio_Risk	Sharpe_Ratio	VaR	Expected_Shortfall
1.79%	4.50%	0.36	8.69%	10.22%

[4] If you change the portfolio risk measure to variance, remember to also change the Sharpe ratio formula to compute the square root of the optimal value of the portfolio risk.

Output 9.2: Portfolio Statistics Obtained from Risk Minimization Optimization (MVO) (continue)

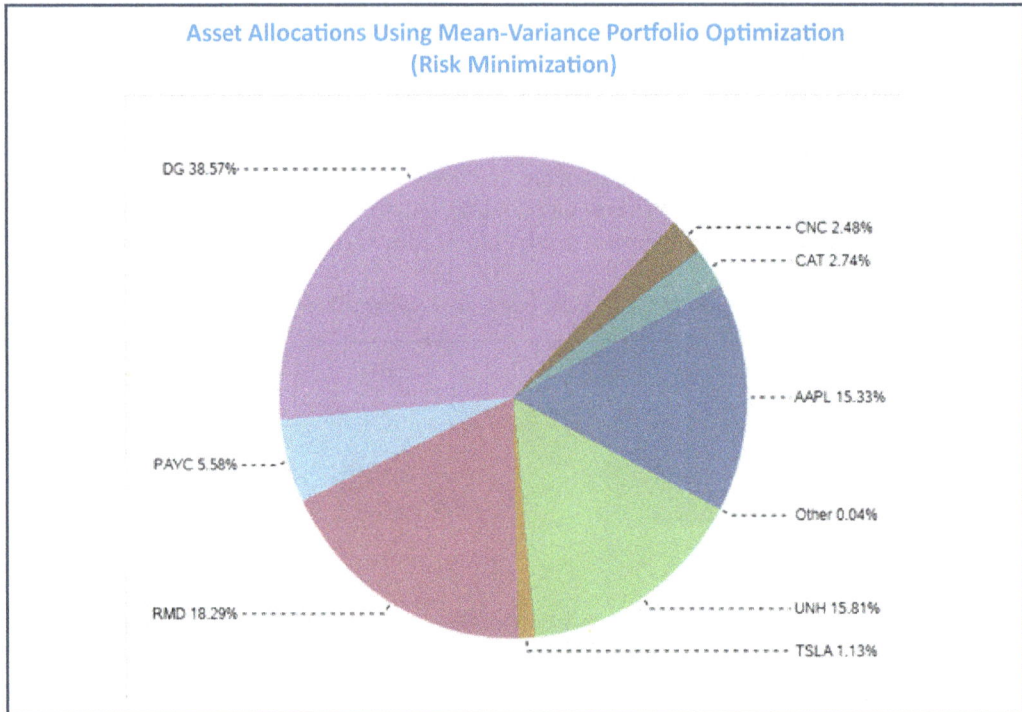

Asset Allocations Using Mean-Variance Portfolio Optimization (Risk Minimization)

DG 38.57%
CNC 2.48%
CAT 2.74%
AAPL 15.33%
PAYC 5.58%
Other 0.04%
RMD 18.29%
UNH 15.81%
TSLA 1.13%

You will also notice that the portfolio we obtained in the risk minimization optimization is quite similar to the return maximization in terms of its component stocks and the weights assigned to them. Dollar General Inc. continues to be the largest optimal holding in the portfolio, followed by ResMed Inc., Apple Inc., and United Health Inc., in decreasing order. The portfolio risk, Sharpe ratio, 99-VaR, and expected shortfall are approximately the same as in the previous optimization. The concentration of holdings in a small number of stocks is also evident in the optimal portfolio weights. 93.3% of the portfolio capital was assigned to the same five stocks shown in the return maximizing optimization. Although both portfolios show significant improvement in risk-return trade-off when compared to the initial portfolio, it is probably not realistic to expect risk-averse investors to hold such a highly concentrated portfolio, despite its optimality in terms of risk minimization.

Using PROC IML for Optimization Problems

If you have previously read Chapters Four and Five of the book, you would have come across examples of how PROC IML can be invoked for various simulation and estimation problems. It turns out that PROC IML can also be used to solve a wide variety of optimization problems. These include linear programming, mixed integer programming, and non-linear optimizations.

Matrix operation is a native feature of PROC IML, and the procedure supports a wide range of matrix operations, which enables you to implement them in your optimization routine very quickly. In contrast, a matrix operation can only be implemented in PROC OPTMODEL by calling up the function, which must have been precompiled using PROC FCMP (function compiler). Be aware that you most likely would have to write the code for the precompiled function or operation. Remember that PROC OPTMODEL was purpose-built for solving a wide range of optimization problems. Therefore, SAS code for optimization problems is much easier to write using PROC OPTMODEL than PROC IML. The results obtained from PROC OPTMODEL are also more comprehensive than those from PROC IML.

Optimization subroutines in PROC IML include Conjugate Gradient (NLPCG), Nelder-Mead Simplex (NLPNMS), Newton-Raphson (NLPNRA), Dual Quasi-Newton (NLPQN), and Quadratic Optimization (NLPQUA) methods. The Nelder-Mead is a variant of the simplex method, while the interior point and active-set methods are variants of the Newton-Raphson method. The great thing about solving optimization problems in SAS is that you can get the best features of both procedures by combining them in a single set of SAS code (as needed) to solve your optimization problem as you will see shortly.

Sharpe Ratio Maximization

It might be worthwhile to jointly optimize for higher returns and lower risk in a single model. The maximum Sharpe ratio optimization aims to achieve this objective. In the Sharpe ratio optimization, we will search for the portfolio allocations that yield the highest Sharpe ratio. Remember that portfolio variance is a quadratic function; therefore, Sharpe ratio optimization is also a convex optimization since it is a ratio of excess portfolio return to the standard deviation of excess portfolio returns. Since the Sharpe ratio combines both risk and return into a single expression, the only constraints we will impose on the model are the full investment and the no short selling constraints which we impose via the bounds on the decision variables. The mathematical formulation for the Sharpe ratio maximization problem is:

$$\max_{w} S_p = \frac{\mathrm{E}(R_p) - R_f}{\sigma_p} \text{ s.t. } \sum_{i=1}^{n} w_i = 1 \tag{9.5}$$

where S_p represents the Sharpe ratio of the portfolio, R_f the risk-free rate, and $\mathrm{E}(R_p)$ and σ_p are the expected return and risk of the portfolio.

To give you a short flavor of how to implement optimization in SAS/IML, we will use PROC IML for this example. You will get an opportunity to solve the same optimization problem using PROC OPTMODEL in the end-of-chapter exercises. Program 9.3 shows the SAS program to implement the maximization of the Sharpe ratio using PROC IML.

First, we use a macro variable to denote the number of assets in our portfolio universe. The IML procedure is then invoked, and the SAS data sets that contain the returns and covariance matrix of the assets are loaded into the procedure. Next, our objective function, which is to maximize the Sharpe ratio is computed as a user-function using the IML module. You will notice within the function that portfolio returns, portfolio risk, and subsequently the Sharpe ratio are computed, but only the Sharpe ratio is returned. To access the remaining computation outside the module, the GLOBAL statement is invoked.

Next, we specify the constraints. It is easier to specify constraints in the OPTMODEL procedure than in the IML procedure. We avoid the need to manually type into the program the upper and lower bounds for each weight element and the full investment constraint for all weight elements, by using a matrix form of constraint specification. First, we create the vector $P = \{0,1,1\}$ in which the elements of the first two rows of P impose a 0 lower bound and a 1 upper bound on the portfolio allocation for each stock. This is then duplicated across the 63 stocks using the REPEAT function and &N=63 macro variable. Using the same REPEAT function, we then use the last element of P and the matrix $\{. ., . ., 0\ 1\}$ to compute the collective sum of the weights, which is bounded by 0 and 1.

Next, we specify the optimization options. The value of the first element of OPTN specifies the type of optimization (0 = 'minimize' and 1 = 'maximize'), while the values of the second element specify the level of output (0 = 'No output', 1 = 'initial and final iteration summary'). We then used the CALL statement to invoke the non-linear Quasi-Newton solver. Remember that the interior point algorithm also uses the Newton method for solving optimization problems. The next set of codes is then used to format the results and to store the optimal portfolio weights in a SAS data set, which we then present in a pie chart using the SGPIE procedure.

Program 9.3: Maximizing Portfolio Sharpe Ratio (MVO Approach) Using PROC IML

```
/* Use PROC IML to implement Maximum Sharpe ratio optimization*/
%let n=63;

proc iml;
        /* Read asset returns and covariances into Returns and Sigma*/
        use Portfolio_Returns;
        read all var _num_ into returns[colname=NumerNames];
        read all var _char_ into assets[colname=CharNames];
        use Portfolio_Covariances;
        read all var _num_ into sigma[colname=NumerNames rowname=Ticker];
        rfr=0.00178;/*Monthly Risk-free rate*/
        start max_sharpe(w) global(rfr,sigma,returns,portfolio_return, portfolio_risk,
        sharpe);
                portfolio_return=W*returns;
                portfolio_risk=sqrt(w*sigma*t(w));
                sharpe=(portfolio_return-rfr)/portfolio_risk;
                return (sharpe);
        finish;

        /*Constraint: lower bound, upper bound, sum weights equals 1)*/
        p={0,1,1};
        con=repeat(p,1,&n)||{. .,. .,0 1};
```

```
        /* Setting the optimization to maximize the objective function and print
        optimization summary*/
        optn={1 1};

        /*Invoke non-linear Quasi Newton for the linearly constrained problem. Set initial
        value set to equal Weights*/
        w=j(1,&n,1/&n);
        call NLPQN(rc,OptW,"max_sharpe",w,optn,con);

        /* Print Optimization Output*/
        print portfolio_return[format=percent8.2] portfolio_risk[format=percent8.2]
        sharpe[format=best4.2];
        TOptW=t(OptW);
        ind = loc(TOptw>0);

        If ncol(ind)>0 then
                rn=NumerNames[ind];
        Weights=TOptW[ind];
        print Weights[format=percent8.2 l='Portfolio Allocations' colname='Ticker'
        rowname=rn ];
        cnames='Ticker'||'Weights';
        create Sharpemax from rn Weights[colname=cnames];
        append from rn Weights;
        close sharpemax;
proc sgpie data=sharpemax;
        title1 font=swissb height=2 'Asset Allocations from Mean-Variance Portfolio
        Optimization';
        title2 font=swissb height=2 '(Sharpe Ratio  Maximization)';
        pie  ticker / response=Weights otherpercent=1  statfmt=percent8.2
        datalabelloc=callout;
run;
```

Output 9.3A shows the summary of the pre-iteration conditions for the optimization. Notice that we have 63 lower and upper bounds, and 1 linear constraint, which is the full investment constraint. The initial objective function value is the Sharpe ratio resulting from equally weighting all 63 stocks as specified in our initial values. Output 9.3B shows the summary of the optimization results. The value shown in the objective function row is 0.36. This is the maximum Sharpe ratio obtained from the optimization. The value is also approximately the same as the Sharpe ratios we obtained from the return maximization and the risk minimization optimizations. However, the portfolio return and standard deviation are not the same. This is because we rounded up the values of the Sharpe ratios that were computed from the return maximization and the risk minimization problems. In reality, the Sharpe ratios from both optimizations are slightly lower than the value from the direct Sharpe ratio maximization problem. Remember that in the former optimization, the optimal value is constrained to lie in the feasible region of the maximum risk (for return maximization) and minimum return (for risk minimization), whereas, no such constraint was imposed in the direct Sharpe ratio optimization. Therefore, the solver can determine whatever combination of risk and return yields the highest Sharpe ratio.

Output 9.3A: Optimization Statistics Maximum Sharpe Ratio Optimization Using PROC IML

Asset Allocations from Mean Variance Portfolio Optimization

(Sharpe Ratio Maximization)

Dual Quasi-Newton Optimization

Dual Broyden - Fletcher - Goldfarb - Shanno Update (DBFGS)

Gradient Computed by Finite Differences

Parameter Estimates	63
Lower Bounds	63
Upper Bounds	63
Linear Constraints	1

Optimization Start			
Active Constraints	1	Objective Function	0.049813789
Max Abs Gradient Element	0.4491177164		

Notice on the Portfolio Allocations table that the stocks selected for inclusion in the Sharpe-optimized portfolio and their assigned weights are similar to the ones selected for both the return and risk optimizations. Comparatively, there were 13 stocks selected for the Sharpe-optimized portfolio, compared to the 12 and 10 stocks for the return-, and risk-optimized portfolios, respectively.

Output 9.3B: Portfolio Statistics from Maximum Sharpe Ratio Optimization Using PROC IML

Optimization Results					Portfolio Allocations	
						Ticker
					ABBV	0.91%
					CAT	4.01%
					AAPL	14.17%
Iterations	64	Function Calls	125		UNH	14.33%
Gradient Calls	117	Active Constraints	53		MSI	0.01%
Objective Function	0.3598308199	Max Abs Gradient Element	0.000017004		GWW	0.00%
Slope of Search Direction	-2.864817E-9				PAYC	2.30%
					NVR	1.70%
					MPC	0.00%
GCONV convergence criterion satisfied					CNC	3.69%
					RMD	18.89%
portfolio_return	portfolio_risk	sharpe			STE	1.43%
1.72%	4.28%	0.36			DG	38.55%

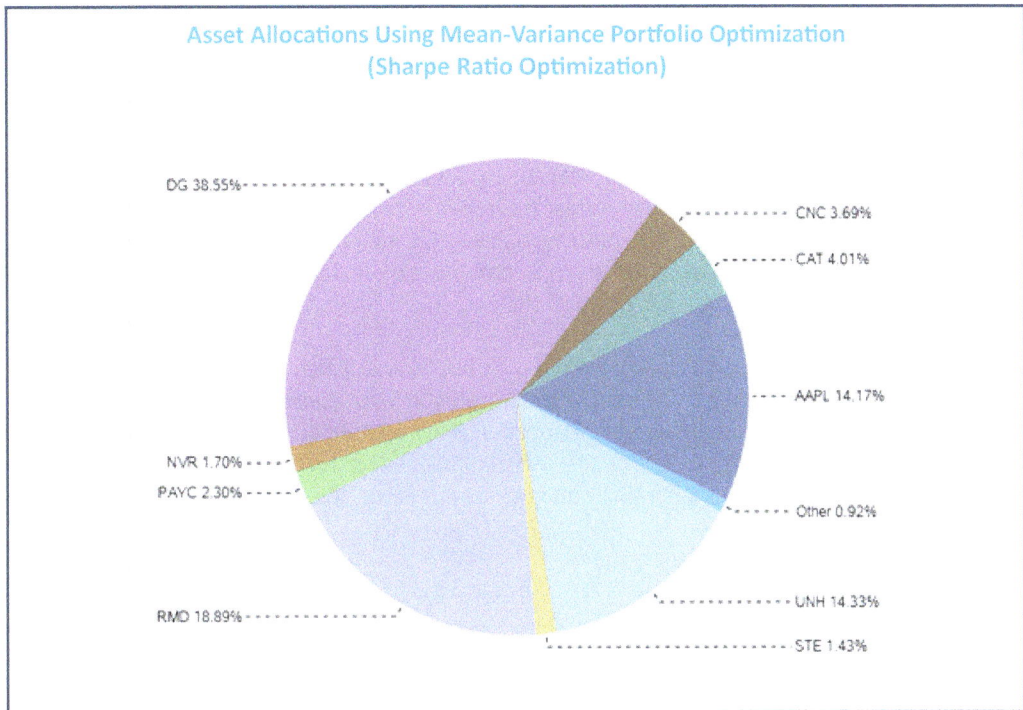

Asset Allocations Using Mean-Variance Portfolio Optimization
(Sharpe Ratio Optimization)

DG 38.55%
CNC 3.69%
CAT 4.01%
AAPL 14.17%
Other 0.92%
UNH 14.33%
STE 1.43%
RMD 18.89%
PAYC 2.30%
NVR 1.70%

Using SAS to Create the Efficient Frontier and Capital Allocation Line

Let us now extend the application of the SAS code we wrote for the MVO to a demonstration of how to construct the efficient frontier and capital allocation line for portfolios of large assets. Remember that efficient portfolios provide the highest return at a given level of risk or the lowest risk at a given level of return. More generally, efficient portfolios provide the highest Sharpe ratio at every level of risk. Most implementations of efficient frontiers tend to restrict the demonstrations to two to three assets because it is computationally demanding to implement them for portfolios of large assets. It turns out that we can use the OPTMODEL procedure, some basic SAS macro, and IML programming to generate the efficient frontier and capital allocation line for our portfolio of stocks. Before we go over the program, you should note that it will require a fair amount of programming and computational resources to achieve our desired output.

The first step will be to recursively re-optimize our portfolio to derive the highest returns for a range of maximum risk, starting from 3.34% to 11.24%. We will do this by embedding the code for the OPTMODEL procedure in a SAS DO loop macro. The portfolio returns and risks we will derive from the series of optimizations will be saved in a SAS data set. Next, we will use the IML procedure to simulate random weights for the portfolio and compute their associated portfolio returns and risks. Be aware that the simulated portfolios are just a collection of unoptimized portfolios, so they will have significantly lower Sharpe ratios. We will also include the plot of the risk and return for the initial portfolio allocation shown in Table 9.1 in our analysis.

We know from the previous optimization that the maximum Sharpe ratio we can derive from our portfolio is 0.36 and the average monthly risk-free rate over our study period is 0.178%. We will use these inputs to create two macrovariables that will be used for plotting the capital allocation line (CAL). We will use a DATA step to combine the previous three data sets into one and subsequently invoke the SGPLOT to graph the variables in the combined data set.

Before we proceed, you should note that while the unoptimized portfolios contain all 63 stocks with randomly generated weights, the set of optimized portfolios contains only the stocks with positive nonzero weights, while the CAL portfolios are created by combining the tangency portfolio (which contains 13 stocks) with the risk-free asset using a range of asset allocations between the two categories of asset (risky and risk-free). Hence, the CAL portfolio is a portfolio of portfolios.

Program 9.4A: Creating an Efficient Frontier Using SAS Macro and PROC OPTMODEL

```
/*Creating Efficient Frontier and Capital Allocation Line in SAS*/
%let rfr=0.00178; /*Risk-free rate*/
%let Max_Sharpe=0.36; /*Sharpe ratio*/
%let m =100;/*Number of portfolio to optimized and simulate*/
%let r =63;/*Number of current stocks in portfolio*/
%macro EFsim(nrep); /*specify number of reps*/
      proc datasets nodetails nolist;
            delete simfrontier;
      run;

      %local i nrep; /*local macro variable*/

      %do i=1 %to &nrep;

      proc optmodel printlevel=1;
            /* declare sets and parameters */
            set <str> ASSETS;
            num returns {ASSETS};
            num covariance {ASSETS, ASSETS};

            /* read portfolio data from SAS  data sets */
            read data Portfolio_Returns into ASSETS=[Ticker] returns;
            read data Portfolio_Covariances into [Ticker]
                  {j in ASSETS} <covariance[Ticker,j]=col(j)>;

            /* declare variables */
            var Weights {ASSETS} >= 0;
            impvar max_risk=&i*.001+.033;
```

```
                /*Calculate Portfolio Risk Measures*/
                impvar Portfolio_Variance=sum {i in ASSETS, j in
                        ASSETS}covariance[i,j]*Weights[i]*Weights[j];
                impvar Portfolio_Risk = sqrt(Portfolio_Variance);

                /*Calculate portfolio return*/
                impvar Expected_Return=sum {j in ASSETS}
                        returns[j] * Weights[j];

                /* declare constraints */
                con Portfolio_Weights:sum{j in ASSETS}Weights[j]=1;
                con Variance: Portfolio_Variance = max_risk**2;

                /* declare objective */
                max Portfolio_Return = Expected_Return;
                solve;

                /*Portfolio Sharpe Ratio*/
                Impvar Sharpe_Ratio = (Expected_Return-&rfr)/Portfolio_Risk;

                /*Print Optimization Outputs*/
                print  Portfolio_Return percent8.2 Portfolio_Risk percent8.2
                    Sharpe_Ratio best4.2;
                print {j in ASSETS: Weights[j]>1e-4} Weights percent8.2  {j in
                        ASSETS: Weights[j]>1e-4} returns percent8.2;

                /* write data to SAS  data sets */
                create data smvmax from index=&i Returns=Portfolio_return
                        Risks=Portfolio_Risk Sharpe=Sharpe_Ratio;
        quit;

        /*updated table with results from new iteration*/
        proc append base=simfrontier data=smvmax force;
        run;

        %end;
%mend;

%efsim(&m);
```

Program 9.4A shows the SAS code to implement the DO loop macro that was used to derive the efficient frontier. Most of the code we used in this step is in Program 9.1; therefore we will only discuss areas where new code is included.

We start by introducing a set of global macrovariables that will be needed throughout the program (%RFR, which is the risk-free rate; %MAX_SHARPE, which is the previously obtained maximum Sharpe Ratio; %M, which is the number of portfolio combinations to simulate; and %R, which is the number of stocks in our initial portfolio). We aim to derive 80 combinations of efficient portfolios (therefore, we set $\%M = 80$).

We then invoked the MACRO statement for the EFSIM macro, which employs NREP (number of repetitions) as the only macro input. You should note that %NREP and %i are local variables, which are only available during the execution of the macro. The PROC DATASET statement is included at the beginning of the macro. This will delete the current version of the SIMFRONTIER data set and replace it with a new version every time the macro is invoked. Notice how the optimization was recursively implemented using the IMPVAR statement (IMPVAR MAX_RISK=&I*.001+.0324). For each iteration, the maximum portfolio risk constraint is increased by 0.1% (from 3.34% to 11.24%), and the maximum return achievable at that threshold is then obtained by optimizing the return objective. The APPEND procedure is then used to append the portfolio statistics from each iteration to the SIMFRONTIER data set.

You might wonder why we started our recursive optimization from an initial risk level of 3.34%. That is because 3.34% is the standard deviation of the global minimum variance portfolio. You should note that efficient portfolio combinations must plot above the minimum variance portfolio because no further improvement in returns can be obtained from these portfolios without a commensurate increase in risk appetite.

Program 9.4B: Simulating Random Portfolios Using PROC IML

```
/*Simulating random portfolio weights using PROC IML*/
proc iml;
      use Portfolio_Returns;
      read all var _num_ into returns[colname=NumerNames];
      read all var _char_ into assets[colname=CharNames];
      use Portfolio_Covariances;
      read all var _num_ into sigma[colname=NumerNames rowname=Ticker];

      /*Simulate portfolio weights*/
      x=j(&m,&r);
      call randseed(12348);
      call randgen(x,'exp');
      W=x/x[,+];

      /*Create column names*/
      pnames ='Index'||'RReturns'||'RRisks';

      /*Create vector and calculate portfolio risk and returns*/
      portplot=j(&m,3);
      do i = 1 to &m;
            portplot[i,1]=i;
            portplot[i,2]=w[i,]*returns;
            portplot[i,3]=sqrt((w[i,])*(sigma*t(w[i,])));
      end;

      create Portplot from Portplot [colname=pnames];
      append from Portplot;
      close Portplot;
```

Let us also show the improvement in portfolio statistics that can be obtained from the efficient portfolios, relative to a collection of randomly constructed unoptimized portfolios. Program 9.4B shows the SAS code for the IML procedure that was used to simulate the 100 unoptimized portfolios. You might have seen some of the code we used here in the Sharpe ratio optimization, so we will only focus on the new code we used in this step. After importing the asset returns and covariance into the procedure, we created a 100 (rows) by 63 (columns) x matrix to collect randomly generated values from the exponential distribution. We then created a matrix of weights w with the same dimension as x to collect the weights. The weights are computed from the x matrix by dividing the row element of x by the total sum of row elements in each row. Next, we used the DO loop to compute the portfolio returns and portfolio variances for each simulated vector of weights. The data is then stored in the SAS data set PORTPLOT using the CREATE statement.

Program 9.4C: Plotting the Efficient Frontier and Capital Allocation Line (CAL) Using PROC SGPLOT

```
/*Creating the Efficient frontier and Capital Allocation Line using PROC SGPLOT*/
data EFrontier;
        merge Simfrontier Portplot;
        by index;
        if index=100 then do;
        Creturns=0.0109523; CRiskS =0.0474768;
        end;
run;

proc sgplot data=Efrontier;
        title "Optimal Portfolio Allocations With Six-Three Assets Portfolio";
        lineparm x=0 y=&rfr slope=&max_sharpe /lineattrs=graphdata6(thickness=4)
        legendlabel='Capital Allocation Line';
        series x=Risks Y=Returns/ legendlabel='Efficient Frontier'
        lineattrs=graphdata1(thickness=3 color=bippk );
        scatter x=RRisks Y=RReturns/legendlabel='Unoptimized Random Portfolios'
        markerattrs=(color=bipb symbol=circlefilled size=3 pt);
        scatter x=CRisks Y=CReturns/legendlabel='Initial Portfolio' markerattrs=(color=viypk
        symbol=starfilled size=6 pt);
        inset "Risk Free Rate = 1.78%" "Maximum Sharpe Ratio =0.36" /  border
        title="Portfolio Statistics" position=topleft;;
        xaxis label='Portfolio Standard Deviation' valuesformat=percent8.2 values=(0 to 0.11
        by 0.02);
        yaxis label='Portfolio Returns' valuesformat=percent8.2 values=(0 to 0.04 by 0.005);
run;
title;
```

Program 9.4C shows the SAS program that was used to complete the final step in creating the frontier and the Capital Allocation Line (CAL). First, we use the DATA step to create a new SAS data set (EFRONTIER), which merges the SIMFRONTIER and PORTPLOT data. We also include the risk (CRISK) and return (CRETURNS) statistics from the initial portfolio in the EFRONTIER data set using the IF statement. We then use the SGPLOT procedure to generate the plots. The efficient frontier is plotted using the RISKS and RETURNS variables that we created from the OPTMODEL estimation using a series plot.

We also create a scatter plot of the risks (RRISK) and returns (RRETURNS) variables for the unoptimized portfolios that we obtained from the IML procedure, and the CRISK and CRETURN variables, which are the risk and return coordinates of the initial portfolio. Because the Sharpe ratio is a constant slope throughout the CAL, we can use the LINEPARM statement to generate the plot of the CAL by specifying X=0, Y=&RFR (risk-free rate macrovariable), and SLOPE=&MAX_SHARPE (the macrovariable for storing the value of the maximum Sharpe ratio).

Output 9.4 shows the value of optimizing our portfolio. Notice how the efficient frontier that was created from our portfolio universe significantly improved upon it. On average, the Sharpe ratio of the portfolios that are plotted on the frontier appears to be at least twice those of the randomly weighted portfolio. Also notice on the CAL that by combining our highest Sharpe ratio portfolio with a risk-free asset, we can theoretically earn this superior reward-to-risk at all risk levels, a benefit that the efficient frontier does not provide.

Output 9.4: Efficient Frontier and Capital Allocation Line (CAL)

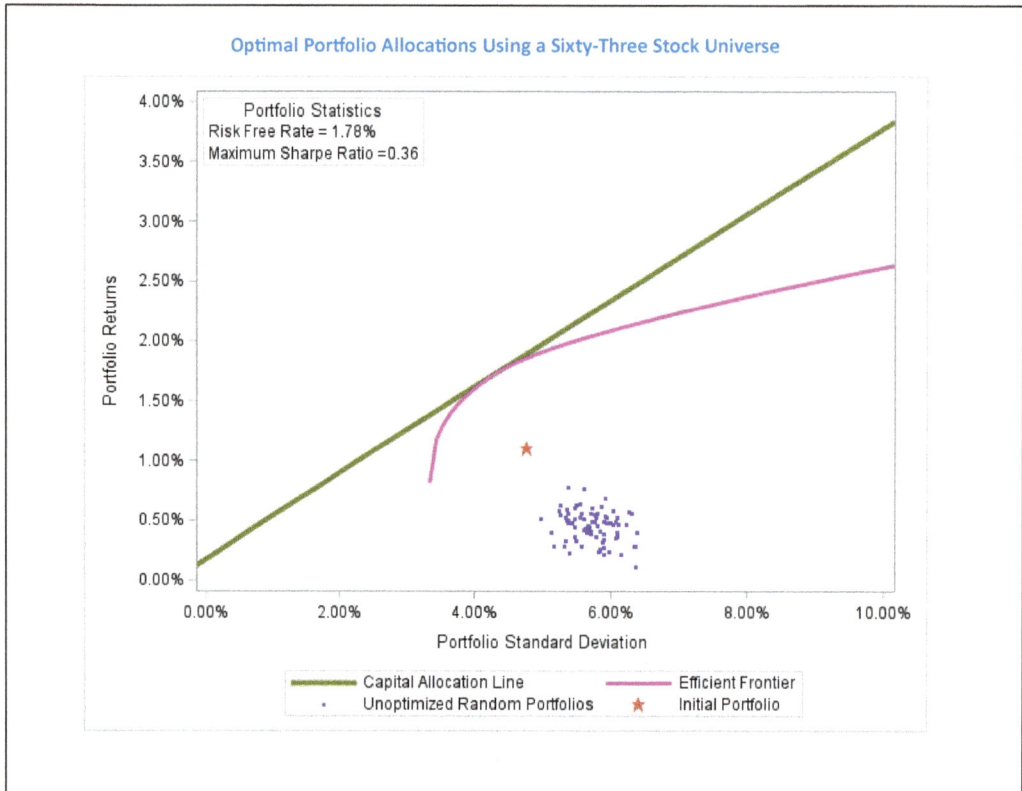

Optimal Portfolio Allocations Using a Sixty-Three Stock Universe

Portfolio Statistics
Risk Free Rate = 1.78%
Maximum Sharpe Ratio =0.36

Alternatives to the Mean-Variance Optimization

The concentration in portfolio holdings is an often-cited criticism of the mean-variance optimization (MVO) approach. However, the MVO suffers from other limitations besides portfolio concentration, including some of its basic assumptions, which are unrealistic in real-world settings. For example, the MVO assumes investors care about all volatility, when in reality most investors only care about volatility in the loss domain. The MVO also does not allow for the subjective views of investors to be incorporated into the portfolio decision. Furthermore, it assumes that all investors have a single holding period. Allocations from the MVO are extremely sensitive to the values of the input variables, which makes it inherently unstable when there are uncertainties in the input variables. All these shortcomings have led to the development of other portfolio optimization approaches such as the Black-Litterman, Risk-Parity, Mean-CVaR, and the robust portfolio optimization approach. The Black-Litterman and Risk-Parity are based on non-linear deterministic programming, so we will examine these approaches first, followed by the Mean-CVaR approach, which is based on stochastic programming, and lastly, the Robust Portfolio optimization, which is based on robust optimization.

Black-Litterman Portfolio Optimization

To overcome some of the weaknesses of the MVO, the Black-Litterman model was proposed by Fisher Black and Robert Litterman in a series of publications (1990–1992),[5] as a way to incorporate the portfolio manager's views into market equilibrium estimates of returns before optimizing the portfolio.

As we always do, let's focus on explaining the conceptual framework of this approach without delving too much into the mathematical framework. The main difference between the MVO and the Black-Litterman (BL) approach is the input that goes into the optimization problem. While the MVO applies raw historical returns and covariance data, the BL uses blended returns and covariance data in the optimization. The blended returns are estimated from the portfolio manager's view (absolute and relative) of the performance of the assets in the portfolio relative to their equilibrium returns. The equilibrium returns are calculated from the CAPM market portfolio using reverse optimization, where the market weights of each asset are used as the input to the reverse optimization.[6] Because the views are probabilistic by nature, they introduce uncertainty into the covariance matrix, which is then adjusted accordingly to reflect the views. Consequently, we can think of the BL approach as a Bayesian-based MVO approach, where the blended returns are the posterior means estimated from its priors and the views, which are future expectations that are conditional on the priors.

---

[5] The series of papers include Black, F. and Litterman, R. (1990, 1991, and 1992). See References for full citation.

[6] Think of the reverse optimization as deriving the vector of portfolio returns that yields the current market portfolio weights of the assets, given the covariance of their excess returns with the excess returns of other assets, and the average risk aversion of investors.

Let's denote the vector of equilibrium returns with a multivariate normal probability distribution as $R_E \sim N(\mu, \Sigma)$ and our views as $v \sim N(P\mu, \Omega)$. The views are stored in a P matrix of assets for which we hold views. The information contained in the views which might be the absolute or relative performance of the assets in the universe is stored in the Q matrix. The uncertainty of our views is expressed in the Ω matrix. We know from Bayes' rule that the equilibrium returns will influence our views of the posterior probability of returns as shown in Equation (9.6).

$$p(\mu|v) \ \alpha \ p(v|\mu) \cdot p(\mu) \tag{9.6}$$

We can also denote the posterior probability distribution of μ as a multivariate normal distribution.

$$p(\mu|v) = N\left(\mu_{BL}, \Sigma_{BL}\right) \tag{9.7}$$

From the above, the formula for the vector of blended return and its revised covariance matrix are then calculated as follows.

$$E(R_P) = \mu_{BL} = \left[(\tau\Sigma)^{-1} + P'\Omega^{-1}P \right]^{-1} \left[(\tau\Sigma)^{-1}\mu + P'\Omega^{-1}Q \right] \tag{9.8}$$
$$\Sigma_P = \Sigma_{BL} = \left[(\tau\Sigma)^{-1} + P'\Omega^{-1}P \right]^{-1}$$

Before proceeding further, let's summarize the pertinent information we will need to implement our BL optimization.

- μ is a $(n \times 1)$ vector of equilibrium returns for the assets in our universe.
- Σ is a $(n \times n)$ covariance matrix of excess returns of the assets in our universe.
- P is a $(k \times n)$ matrix of assets in which we hold views. In the elements of P, the value of 1 is recorded for assets that we hold absolute views on. For example, if our k^{th} view is that the nth asset will earn a monthly return of 2%, we will record the value of 1 for the (k, n) element of the matrix. The value of 0 is recorded for all other assets on the kth row. If we hold the $(k^{th} +1)$ view that the $(n^{th} +1)$ asset will outperform the $(n^{th} +2)$ asset by 1%, then we will enter the value of 1 for $(k+1, n+1)$ element and -1 for the $(k+1, n+2)$ element of the matrix. The value of 0 is recorded for all other assets on the $(k+1)$ row. This process continues until all views are recorded in P as shown below.

$$P = \begin{pmatrix} 1 & 0 & 0 & 0 & \cdots & 0 \\ 0 & 1 & -1 & 0 & \cdots & 0 \end{pmatrix} \tag{9.9}$$

- Q is a $(k \times 1)$ vector of views information held by the portfolio manager. For example, we can record the views held by the portfolio manager in the Q vector as shown below.

$$Q = \begin{pmatrix} 2\% \\ 1\% \end{pmatrix} \tag{9.10}$$

Table 9.2: Using Manager's Views as Input in Black-Litterman Portfolio Optimization

Views	Type	Return	Uncertainty
V1	Absolute	ABBV's monthly return will be 3%	0.0064
V2	Absolute	HD's monthly return will be 3%	0.0064
V3	Relative	DG will underperform TSCO by 20%	0.00625

- Ω is a $(k \times k)$ matrix of uncertainty about the views the manager holds. For $K = 2$ number of views in which the manager is 85% confident about both views, Ω is written in the form of:

$$\begin{pmatrix} 0.85 & 0 \\ 0 & 0.85 \end{pmatrix} \qquad (9.11)$$

- τ is the scalar parameter representing the degree of confidence in the equilibrium expected returns. Higher values of τ imply more weight is given to active views than passively holding the market portfolio. There are many perspectives in the literature on what the values of the parameter should be. However, in general, it tends to range from 0.025 to 0.05. High values imply large confidence intervals from the equilibrium expected return, which can then be exploited through active investing.

Implementing the Black-Litterman Model in SAS

Remember that the Black-Litterman optimization (BLO) is the same as the MVO. The only differences are the inputs, which in the BLO are the blended expected returns and covariances. This means that you can implement the blending outside the OPTMODEL procedure and then feed the blended data set into the same SAS code we used for the MVO optimization. Since the blending process involves matrix algebra, we can use the IML procedure to construct our blended returns and covariances.[7] Let's assume that we would like to maximize the return of the sample portfolio and now hold the following views about the assets in it.

All views are expected to be held over the next holding period. The degree of confidence in active investing τ is 0.05. We also assume that the average monthly returns that we calculated for the assets in our sample portfolio are the same as their equilibrium expected returns, although that might not be the case. But for our demonstration purpose, this assumption will suffice. In Table 9.2, the first two views the manager holds are that the absolute returns on ABBV and HD will be 2% and 3%, respectively, over the next one-month holding period. These values are greater than their equilibrium return of 1.31% and 1.19%, respectively. So, it is clearly a favorable

---

[7] PROC IML also has a solver for nonlinear optimization problems, so you can choose to implement all steps using the IML procedure. Visit https://documentation.sas.com/doc/en/imlcdc/14.2/imlug/imlug_nonlinearoptexpls_toc.htm to learn more about nonlinear optimization using the IML procedure.

view of both assets. The third view is a relative one, which is that DG will underperform TSCO by about 20% (in proportional terms) over the same single holding period. This view is unfavorable toward DG and favorable toward TSCO. Furthermore, the manager is 8% uncertain about the first two views, but extremely confident about the third view, hence the 2.5% uncertainty.[8]

Program 9.5A shows the SAS program that was used to blend equilibrium returns with the manager's views that we presented in Table 6.11. The SAS program to implement the BLO starts with using the %DATAPULL macro to download the PMATRIX SAS data set, which contains the universe of assets and the indicator showing those in which the manager holds views; the QRET data set, which contains the views information (the absolute and relative returns); and the OMEGA data set, which contains the uncertainty associated with each view. You should also download the PORTFOLIO_RETURNS and PORTFOLIO_COVARIANCES SAS data sets if you have not previously done so. Next, we introduce our macrovariables, which are the risk-free rate (%RFR), VaR threshold (%BETA), confidence in active management (%TAU), and the maximum tolerable risk (%MAX_RISK). Next, we invoked the IML procedure and employed the USE and READ statements to read all the required data sets into corresponding matrices.

Program 9.5A: Blending Manager's Views into Asset Returns and Covariance Using PROC IML

```
/* Using PROC IML to obtain Blended Expected Returns and Covariances */
%datapull(pmatrix,pmatrix.sas7bdat);
%datapull(omega,omega.sas7bdat);
%datapull(qret,qret.sas7bdat);
%let rfr=0.00178;/*Risk-Free Rate*/
%let alpha=0.99;/*VaR Threshold*/
%let tau=0.05;/*Weight of active risk*/
%let max_risk = 0.045;
/* Use PROC IML to set reverse optimization obtain Revised Expected Returns and
Covariances Forecast*/
proc iml;
      /*read subjective views (asset and returns) into vectors*/
      use PMatrix; /*asset with subjective views*/
      read  all var _NUM_ into p [colname=NumerNames rowname=Views];
      use qret; /*subjective performances*/
      read all var _all_ into q[colname=NumerNames rowname=Views];
      use omega; /*Confidence level of views*/
      read all var _all_ into omega[colname=NumerNames rowname=Views];

      *print p q;
      /* Read equilibrium returns and covariances into EQRET and SIGMA*/
      use Portfolio_Returns;
      read all var _num_ into eqret[colname=NumerNames rowname=Ticker];
      read all var _char_ into assets[colname=CharNames];/*Asset names*/
```

---

[8] Uncertainty is expressed here as the square root of the values in Table 9.2.

```
*print eqret;
use Portfolio_Covariances;
read all var _num_ into sigma[colname=NumerNames rowname=Ticker];

*print sigma;
/*Compute revised expected returns and covariances*/
RReturns=inv(inv(&tau*sigma)+t(p)*(inv(omega))*p)*(inv(&tau*sigma)*eqret+t(p)*(inv(
omega))*q);
RCovariances=sigma+inv(inv(&tau*sigma)+t(p)*(inv(omega))*p);
*print RReturns[colname='Returns'];

*print RCovariances[colname=Name rowname=Name];
/*Export revised expected returns into SAS data sets*/
Anames ='Ticker'||'Returns'||'EQReturns'; /*Variable names setup*/
create Revised_Portfolio_Returns from Assets rreturns Eqret[colname=Anames];
append from Assets RReturns Eqret;
close Revised_Portfolio_Returns;

/*Export revised covariance into SAS data sets*/
sname ={'Assets'};/*Variable names setup*/
cnames ='Ticker'||Numernames;

*print cnames;
create Revised_Porfolio_Covariances from Assets RCovariances[colname= cnames ];
append from Assets RCovariances;
close Revised_Porfolio_Covariances;
```

Notice that the actual portfolio returns and covariances were read into the EQRET and SIGMA matrices, respectively. That is because we will be replacing both data sets with the blended returns and the revised covariance matrix and implementing the computation in the IML procedure. The computed revised returns (RRETURNs) and covariances (RCOVARIANCES) are derived using the formula shown in Equation (9.8). The revised returns and covariances are then exported into SAS data sets using the CREATE statement. They are then used as input into the slightly modified version of the SAS code for the MVO as shown in Program 9.1. To ensure that we can easily reuse Program 9.1 for our BL optimization, we renamed the blended returns variable as RETURNS and equilibrium returns as EQRETURNS. Both variables are exported into the REVISED_PORTFOLIO_RETURNS data set.

The revised covariance matrix is also exported into the REVISED_PORTFOLIO_COVARIANCE data set. Both data sets are then read into their respective index sets in Program 9.5B, which is a revised version of Program 9.1. Since Program 9.5B is essentially the same as Program 9.1 which was used for the MVO for both risk minimization and return maximization, we will only highlight the portions of the code that are different from the previous programs. As in all cases, the full code is available on the book's GitHub page.

In the declaration statement, we add the actual (equilibrium) returns (EQRETURNS) to the ASSETS index set. We then read the blended return (RETURNS) also into the ASSETS index set. We retain the actual returns in the same index set so that we can compare the two values in the optimization results. We also use the READ statement to read the revised covariance matrix into the COVARIANCE index set. Since both inputs now retain the same variable names as used in Program 9.1, the rest of the code to implement the optimization in Program 9.5B is essentially the same as Program 9.1, except the additional PRINT statement to print the equilibrium returns and the CREATE statement, which is used to export the results of the optimization into a SAS data set named BLMAX.

Program 9.5B: Black-Litterman Portfolio Optimization Using PROC OPTMODEL

```
/*Black-Litterman Portfolio optimization using PROC OPTMODEL*/
proc optmodel;
       /* declare sets and parameters */
       set <str> ASSETS;
       num returns {ASSETS};
       num eqreturns {ASSETS};
       num covariance {ASSETS, ASSETS};

       /* read revised portfolio data from SAS  data sets */
       read data Revised_Portfolio_Returns into ASSETS=[Ticker] returns=returns eqreturns;
       read data Revised_Porfolio_Covariances into [Ticker]
              {j in ASSETS} <covariance[Ticker,j]=col(j)>;

       /*****************************************/
       /*           Same as Program 9.1                */
       /*****************************************/
       print Variance.ub Variance.dual;
       print {j in ASSETS: Weights[j]>1e-4} Weights percent8.2
              {j in ASSETS: Weights[j]>1e-4} returns percent8.2
              {j in ASSETS: Weights[j]>1e-4} eqreturns percent8.2;

       /* write data to SAS data sets */
       create data blmax from [Name]={j in ASSETS: Weights[j]>1e-4}
              Weights=Weights;
quit;

proc sgpie data=blmax;
       title1 font=swissb height=2 'Asset Allocations from Black-Litterman Portfolio
       Optimization';
       title2 font=swissb height=2 '(Return Maximization)';
       pie  Name / response=Weights otherpercent=1  statfmt=percent8.2
       datalabelloc=callout;
 run;

title1;
title2;
```

Output 9.5: Portfolio Statistics from Black-Litterman Optimization (BLO) Using PROC OPTMODEL

The OPTMODEL Procedure

Solution Summary	
Solver	NLP
Algorithm	Interior Point Direct
Objective Function	Portfolio_Return
Solution Status	Optimal
Objective Value	0.0183723229
Optimality Error	2.8354918E-7
Infeasibility	1.2428649E-9
Iterations	13
Presolve Time	0.00
Solution Time	0.03

[1]	Weights	Returns	EQReturns
AAPL	14.45%	2.35%	2.09%
ABBV	2.59%	1.54%	1.32%
CAT	4.82%	1.68%	1.32%
CNC	4.06%	1.68%	1.48%
DG	22.10%	1.45%	1.67%
MSI	1.10%	1.75%	1.58%
NVR	1.86%	1.53%	1.41%
PAYC	2.08%	2.84%	2.67%
RMD	18.25%	1.78%	1.68%
STE	1.27%	1.49%	1.40%
TSCO	12.78%	2.13%	1.51%
TSLA	0.09%	3.29%	3.00%
UNH	14.48%	1.80%	1.66%

Portfolio_Return	Portfolio_Risk	Sharpe_Ratio	VaR	Expected_Shortfall
1.84%	4.50%	0.37	8.63%	10.16%

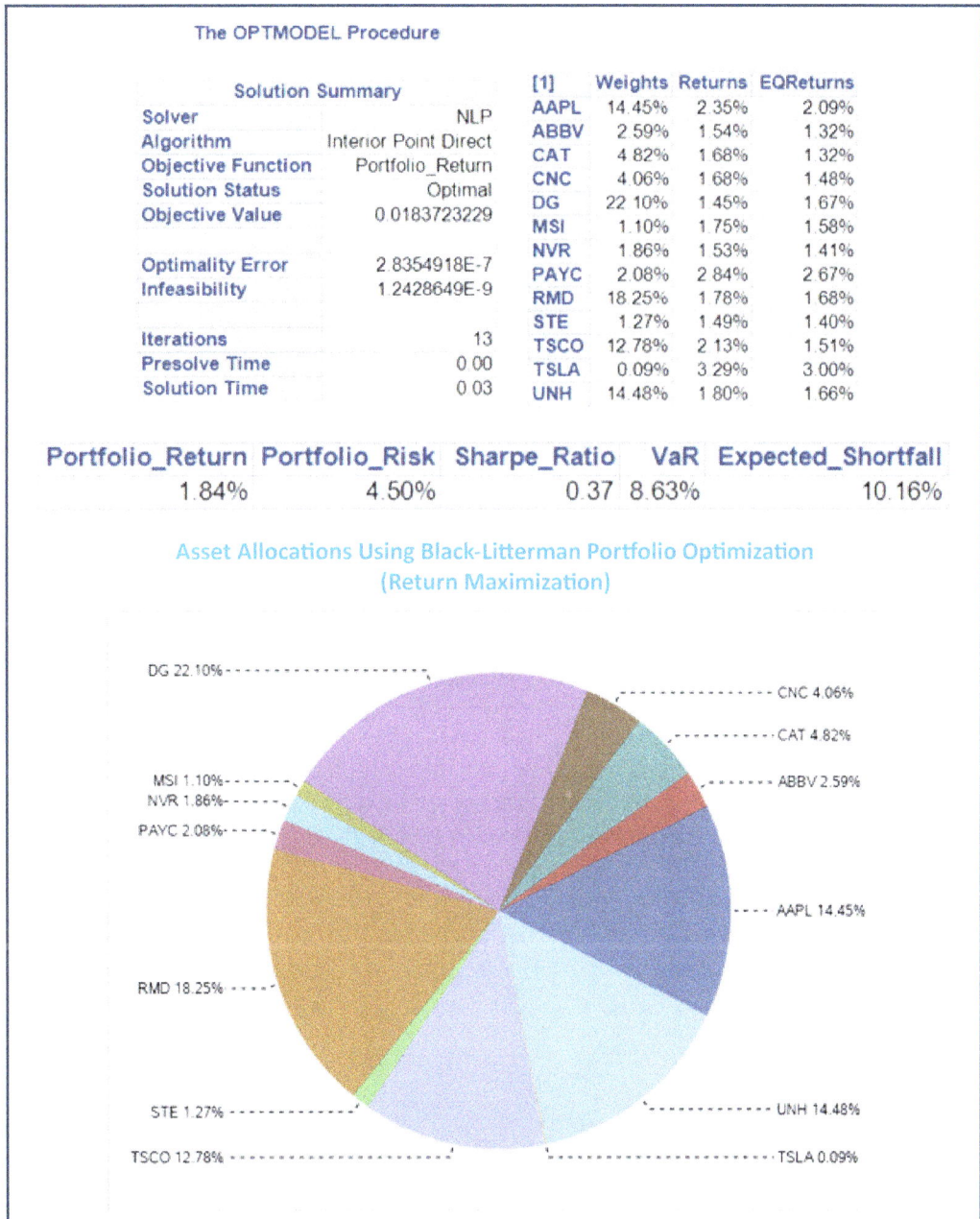

Asset Allocations Using Black-Litterman Portfolio Optimization (Return Maximization)

The impact of blending the manager's view into the equilibrium returns is non-trivial. In Output 9.5, we observe that portfolio allocation to ABBV increased from 0.02% in the MVO to 2.59% in the BLO, while the allocation to DG reduced from 38.57% to 22.10%. Furthermore, TSCO, which was not previously included in the optimal allocation obtained in the MVO now has a portfolio allocation of 12.78%. Notice the difference between the blended returns (RETURNS) and the equilibrium returns (EQReturns). Because most of our views are positive, except for DG, the overall impact on blended returns was positive. In terms of diversification, we have also gone from 12 to 13 stocks, with no assets controlling more than 23% of the capital that will be invested in the portfolio. The main benefit of the BLO is evident in the marginal improvement in the expected return and diversification of the portfolio. By employing the BLO, we have gained about 5 basis points per month, which translates into approximately 60 basis points improvement per year. Although the percentage amount might not appear to be a significant improvement, if you consider that the 60-basis point improvement for a $100 million portfolio equals $600 thousand of additional potential gains, plus improvements in diversification, then the value of the BLO approach becomes more compelling.

Risk Parity Optimization

The risk parity approach to portfolio optimization (RPO) differs from the MVO approach in the sense that while MVO focuses on the allocation of capital, risk parity focuses on the allocation of risk. Hence, the main aim of this approach is to determine the capital allocations amongst a universe of assets that achieve the desired risk budget that is assigned to each asset. Although we will use equal risk allocation in the demonstration we will provide, it is not necessary to do so in practice. Also, risk allocation can be performed in either absolute or relative terms. We will use relative risk allocation in our example.

Before we proceed to the example, let us begin with the conceptual framework of the RPO. From the MVO approach, we know that portfolio risk can be written as the weighted sum of the marginal contribution of each asset or the sum of the contribution of each asset to the total risk of the portfolio as shown below:

$$\sigma_p = \sqrt{w'\Sigma w} = \sum_{i=1}^{N} w_i MRC_i = \sum_{i=1}^{N} RC_i \tag{9.12}$$

where the marginal contribution of the ith asset to the overall risk of the portfolio can be written as

$$MRC_i = \frac{\partial \sigma}{\partial w_i} = \frac{(\Sigma w)_i}{\sqrt{w'\Sigma w}} \tag{9.13}$$

From this, we can calculate the relative contribution RRC_i of each asset to the overall risk of the portfolio as the ratio of the risk contribution of each asset to the total risk of the portfolio.

$$RRC_i = \frac{RC_i}{\sigma_p(w)} = \frac{w_i(\Sigma w)_i}{w'\Sigma w} \tag{9.14}$$

Following a similar framework as the MVO, the next item is to set up the desired risk budget for each asset in the portfolio. However, unlike the scalar values used in the return and risk constraint for the MVO, the risk budget in the RPO is a vector RB of risk allocation to each asset. As highlighted before, you can allocate varying risk budgets to each asset depending on the portfolio objectives. However, we will assume equal risk allocation across all 63 stocks in our portfolio. Remember RPO involves finding the optimal values of the portfolio weight that results in the desired risk budget for each asset in the portfolio. Therefore, the optimization problem involves finding the portfolio weights that result in the lowest deviation between the vectors of relative risk contribution RRC_i and risk budget RB_i subject to minimum total return and/or maximum total risk constraint, which can be expressed as follows.

$$\min_{w_i} \sum_{i=1}^{N} \left(RRC_i - RB_i \right)^2$$

$$\text{s.t.} \quad \mathrm{E}\left(R_p\right) = \sum_{i=1}^{n} w_i \mathrm{E}\left(R_i\right) \geq 1.79\%,$$

(9.15)

$$\sigma_p = \sqrt{\sum_{i=1}^{n} w_i w_j Cov\left(R_i, R_j\right)} \leq 4.5\%, \sum_{i=1}^{n} w_i = 1$$

Implementing Risk Parity Optimization in SAS

Our sample portfolio is comprised only of stocks, and it has a fairly large number of securities in it, so it is not necessarily the ideal portfolio on which to deploy the RPO approach. It is more common to use RPO to implement risk allocation in portfolios that combine low-risk assets such as bonds with relatively higher-risk assets such as stocks. In those cases, the asset allocation from the optimized portfolio will be significantly skewed toward the low-risk assets to equalize its risk contribution to the higher-risk asset. Leverage is then used to tilt the portfolio further toward the desired overall risk position. Nevertheless, we will use the portfolio to demonstrate the SAS program and leave the implementation of the SAS code for a more realistic scenario for you to explore on your own.

Program 9.6A: Implementing Risk Parity Optimization Using PROC OPTMODEL

```
/*Risk-Parity Portfolio optimization using PROC OPTMODEL*/
%let rfr=0.00178; /*Risk-Free Rate*/
%let beta=0.99; /*VaR Threshold*/
%let minimum_return = 0.01787;/*Minimum Portfolio Return*/
%let maximum_risk=0.045; /*Maximum Standard Deviation*/

proc optmodel;
        /*******************************************/
        /*          Same as Program 9.1          */
        /*******************************************/
        /*Count the number of securities in the portfolio*/
        impvar N=card(ASSETS);
```

```
        /*Calculate risk budget, currently equal risk contribution*/
        impvar rb{i in ASSETS}=1/N;

        /*Calculate relative risk contribution rrc*/
        impvar rrc{i in ASSETS} = ((sum{j in ASSETS}
               covariance[i,j] *Weights[j])* Weights[i])/(Portfolio_Variance);

        /*****************************************/
        /*         Same as Program 9.1           */
        /*****************************************/
        /* declare constraints */
        con Portfolio_Weights: sum {j in ASSETS} Weights[j] = 1;
        con Minimum_return: Portfolio_Return >= &minimum_return;
        con Maximum_Risk: Portfolio_Risk<=&maximum_risk;

        /* declare objective */
        min RiskDeviation =sum{i in Assets} (rrc[i] - rb[i])**2;
        solve;

        /*****************************************/
        /*         Same as Program 9.1           */
        /*****************************************/
        create data rpmin from [Ticker]={j in ASSETS: Weights[j]>1e-4}
               Weights=Weights;
quit;
```

Program 9.6A shows the SAS program that was used to implement the RPO for our sample portfolio of 63 stocks. Again, the SAS code for the RPO shares many steps with the code that we used for the previous optimizations. So, we will only highlight where there are differences between them. The complete code for the optimization is available on the book's GitHub page.

First, we include all of the constraint macrovariables in the code to give us the flexibility to impose any combination of the constraints (minimum returns and/or maximum risk). The code for reading the SAS data set into the problem and the decision variables that are portfolio weights are the same as in the MVO problem, so they are not included in the code excerpt shown in Program 9.6A. Next, we use an implicit variable and CARD statements to count the number of stocks (N) in our portfolio universe, which we then used to create our risk budget implicit variable (RB). RB is a $(N \times 1)$ vector of risk allocations. In the RB vector, each stock is assigned a risk relative budget of $\left(\dfrac{1}{N}\right) = \dfrac{1}{63} = 1.59\%$ of the total risk of the portfolio.[9]

The next set of codes is used to calculate the relative risk contribution RRC_i of each stock. Notice that RRC_i of each stock is calculated as the ratio of the weighted sum of the covariances of each stock with every other stock in the portfolio to the total risk of the portfolio. We then declare the constraints by including both the minimum returns and/or maximum risk constraints in the

---

[9] Remember that you can specify the alternative risk budget by manipulating the values of the elements of RB.

code to provide us the flexibility to deploy whichever combinations of constraints of our choice in each run of the code. Next, we declare the objective function, which is to minimize the sum of squared deviations between relative risk contribution RRC_i and risk budget RB_i. In the first run of the optimization, we did not impose the minimum return and maximum risk constraints. The aim of this run of the optimization is to reveal the portfolio allocations that will result in equal risk contribution from each of the 63 stocks in the portfolio, without limiting the feasible region for the search. We will impose both constraints in subsequent optimizations.

Output 9.6A shows the results from optimizing the portfolio without imposing both the risk and return constraints. Notice that the objective value shown in the Solution Summary is approximately 0. You can also verify that the optimization did achieve the minimum deviation by reviewing the values of relative risk contribution RRC_i and risk budget RB_i derived from the optimization. The expected portfolio returns (0.58%) and risk (4.80%), as well as the Sharpe ratio (0.08) of the optimal allocation under this scenario, are clearly subpar to the results obtained from the previous optimizations. The abbreviated list of portfolio weights assigned to each stock to achieve these values is also shown in the next table and on the pie chart shown in Output 9.6B.

Output 9.6A: Optimal Portfolio Allocation for Unconstrained Risk-Parity Optimization

The OPTMODEL Procedure

Solution Summary

Solver	NLP
Algorithm	Interior Point Direct
Objective Function	RiskDeviation
Solution Status	Optimal
Objective Value	7.258385E-11
Optimality Error	2.2476742E-7
Infeasibility	1.076916E-14
Iterations	9
Presolve Time	0.00
Solution Time	0.05

[1]	rrc	rb
AAPL	1.59%	1.59%
ABBV	1.59%	1.59%
ALG	1.59%	1.59%
ALK	1.59%	1.59%
ALLY	1.59%	1.59%
BKNG	1.59%	1.59%
BXP	1.59%	1.59%
CAT	1.59%	1.59%
CCI	1.59%	1.59%
CG	1.59%	1.59%

[1]	Weights	returns
AAPL	1.52%	2.09%
ABBV	2.15%	1.32%
ALG	1.48%	0.86%
ALK	0.87%	(1.01%)
ALLY	0.96%	0.35%
BKNG	1.21%	0.44%
BXP	1.29%	(0.86%)
CAT	1.43%	1.32%
CCI	2.41%	0.62%
CG	0.95%	0.93%

Portfolio_Return	Portfolio_Risk	Sharpe_Ratio	VaR	Expected_Shortfall
0.58%	4.80%	0.08	10.60%	12.22%

Output 9.6B: Portfolio Allocations from Unconstrained Risk Parity Optimization

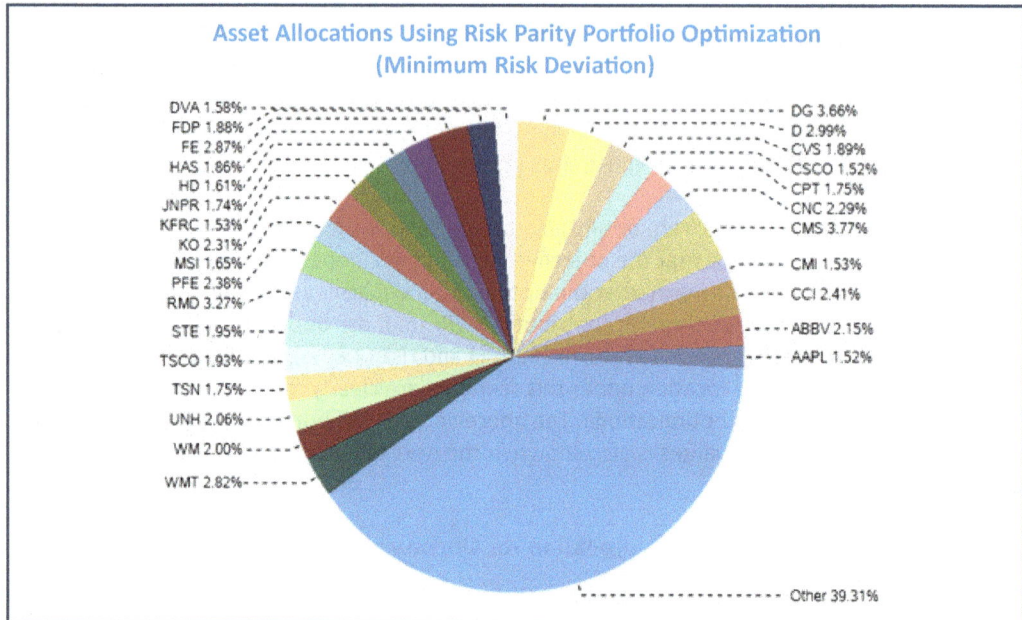

Asset Allocations Using Risk Parity Portfolio Optimization (Minimum Risk Deviation)

You will notice in the results that although the relative risk contribution and the risk budget for each stock are the same, the portfolio allocations to the stocks are not the same. That's because stocks with potentially higher risk contributions in the covariance matrix are assigned lower portfolio weights to equalize their relative risk contributions to the stocks with potentially lower risk contributions to the portfolio risk. If we assume that all stocks have equal weights in the portfolio, we can compute the potential contributions of each stock to the overall portfolio risk using Equations (9.12) and (9.13). To obtain the values of the risk contribution (assuming equal weights) for each stock to the portfolio in the OPTMODEL procedure, add the code excerpt shown in Program 9.6B to Program 9.6A.[10]

Program 9.6B: Implementing Risk Parity Optimization Using PROC OPTMODEL

```
/*Calculate risk contribution rc assuming equal weights*/

    impvar EQWeights{j in Assets}=1/N;

    impvar EQPortRisk=sqrt(sum {i in ASSETS, j in ASSETS}covariance[i,j] *
    EQWeights[i] * EQWeights[j]);

    impvar rc{i in ASSETS}=(((sum{j in
    ASSETS}covariance[i,j]*EQWeights[j])*EQWeights[i])/EQPortrisk);

    impvar SEQPortRisk =sum{j in ASSETS}rc[j];

    print rc percent8.2 SEQPortRisk percent8.2 EQPortRisk percent8.2;
```

---

[10] Program 9.6 on the book's GitHub page combines both Program 9.6A and 9.6B into one program.

Now that we have explored the unconstrained risk parity optimization, let's rerun the optimization after imposing the minimum return and maximum risk constraints on the problem. You may wonder why the minimum return constraint we imposed (1.787%) is slightly lower than the 1.79% we have used in the past. This is because values of portfolio return above 1.787% are not feasible given the other constraints that we have imposed on the problem.

Output 9.6C: Optimal Portfolio Allocation for Constrained Risk-Parity Optimization

The OPTMODEL Procedure

Solution Summary

Solver	NLP
Algorithm	Interior Point Direct
Objective Function	RiskDeviation
Solution Status	Optimal
Objective Value	0.1755047445
Optimality Error	9.0948163E-8
Infeasibility	7.327472E-15
Iterations	29
Presolve Time	0.00
Solution Time	0.16

[1]	rrc	rb
AAPL	17.60%	1.59%
ABBV	0.26%	1.59%
ALG	0.00%	1.59%
ALK	(0.00%)	1.59%
ALLY	0.00%	1.59%
BKNG	0.00%	1.59%
BXP	(0.00%)	1.59%
CAT	2.54%	1.59%
CCI	0.00%	1.59%
CG	0.00%	1.59%

[1]	Weights	returns
AAPL	14.22%	2.09%
ABBV	0.38%	1.32%
CAT	3.74%	1.32%
CNC	3.91%	1.48%
DG	36.02%	1.67%
NVR	0.73%	1.41%
PAYC	5.86%	2.67%
RMD	18.18%	1.68%
TSLA	1.73%	3.00%
UNH	15.24%	1.66%

Portfolio_Return	Portfolio_Risk	Sharpe_Ratio	VaR	Expected_Shortfall
1.787%	4.50%	0.36	8.68%	10.21%

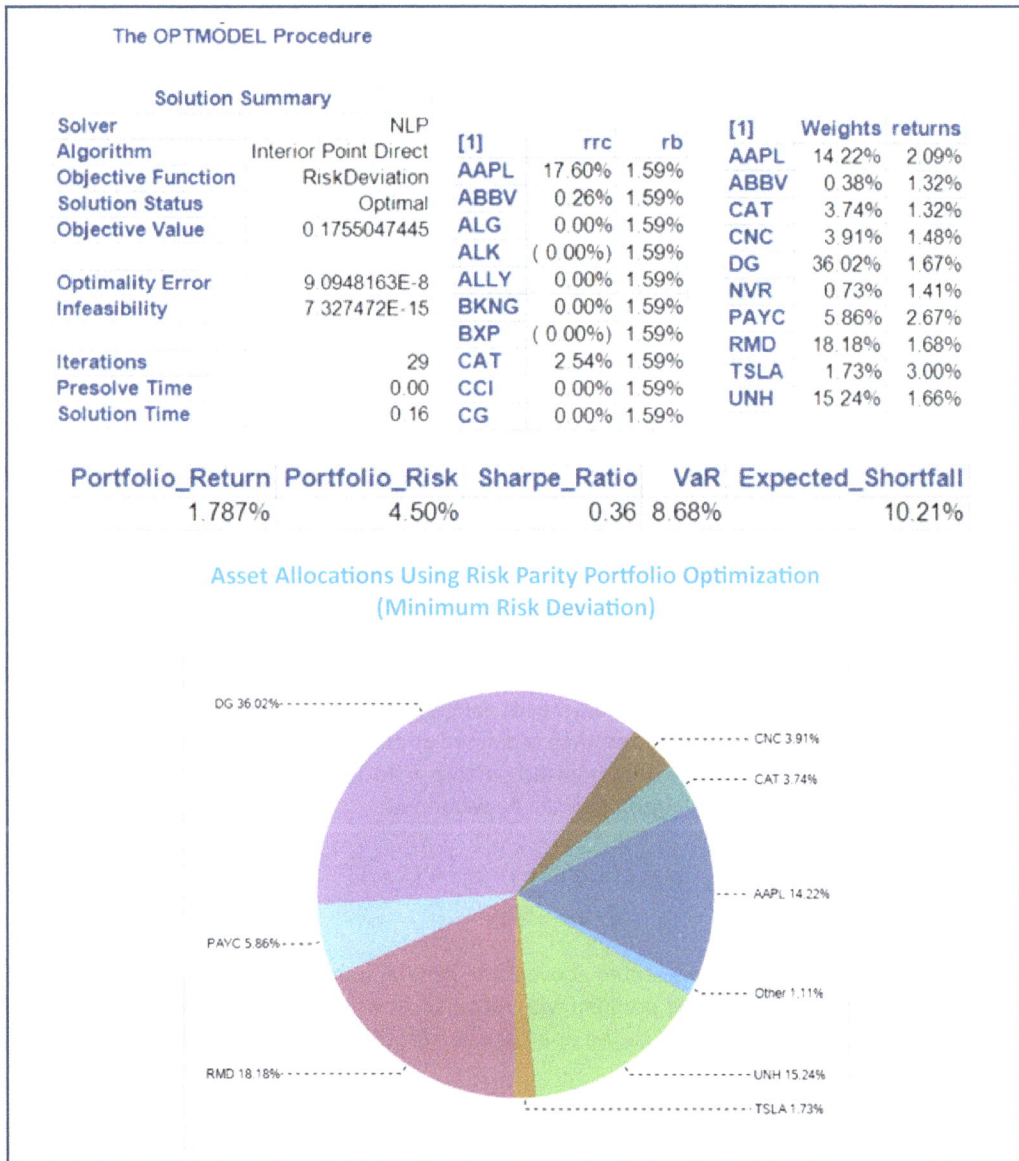

Asset Allocations Using Risk Parity Portfolio Optimization
(Minimum Risk Deviation)

You will notice in Output 9.6C that the same set of stocks that were selected for the MVO were also selected in the risk parity optimization given the minimum return and maximum risk constraint, albeit with slightly different allocations. You will also notice that imposing these constraints on the problem resulted in a significant deviation in the relative risk contribution RRC_i of the stocks from the specified risk budget RB_i.

Stochastic Optimization

All the optimization problems we have examined up to this point involve scenarios where the values of the problem data are known with certainty. The optimization of these types of problems is often described as deterministic programming. However, there are many instances where we are uncertain about the values of one or some of the problem data. In these instances, stochastic programming is often used to optimize the objective function. The main goal of stochastic programming is to determine the optimal course of action with the deterministic component of the problem, given the expected value of the random component of the problem. The three types of frameworks for solving stochastic programming problems are:

- **Anticipative model:** In this approach, the problem consists of deterministic objective functions and probabilistic constraints. Since the future realization of the constraints is uncertain, the aim of the optimization is then to select the optimal course of action that satisfies all possible scenarios of the constraint.
- **Adaptive model:** In this approach, the problem consists of both probabilistic objective functions and constraints. However, some information about the random variable is revealed before the model is fully optimized. Hence, the optimal decision will in part depend on the known information. Adaptive optimization is often described as optimization in a learning environment.
- **Recourse model:** This type of model combines both anticipative models and adaptive models, thereby creating optimization problems with objective functions that contain both deterministic and stochastic components. Mathematically, a stochastic programming problem with recourse is defined as one in which the objective function $f(x,\omega)$ is a function of a deterministic variable x and a random variable ω with a known probability distribution and can be written as:

$$\min f(x,\omega) = c'x + E_\omega \left[\Phi(x,\omega) \right]$$
$$\text{s.t.} \quad Ax = b, x \geq 0$$

(9.16)

The mathematical formulation presented above is the general framework of the classic two-stage stochastic programming problem with recourse, in which $c'x$ represents the first-stage optimization and $\Phi(x,\omega)$ is the optimal value for the second-stage optimization expressed below.

$$\Phi(x,\omega) = \min Q(\omega)' y(\omega)$$
$$\text{s.t.} \quad D(\omega)x + L(\omega)y(\omega) = h(\omega), y(\omega) \geq 0$$

(9.17)

The general idea behind the two-stage stochastic optimization is to first optimize the first-stage problem to determine the optimal values of the first-stage decision variable x for all the possible scenarios set Ω that the second-stage problem can take. Next, the expected value of the random variable is determined. This is then followed by optimizing the second-stage problem to determine the optimal values of the second-stage decision variable $y(\omega)$.

One issue that arises in stochastic programming is how to deal with the distribution of the random variable. As we all know, the possible values of a continuous random variable are infinite, which means we might need to perform an infinite number of first-stage optimizations. This is obviously not practical; therefore, it is common to reformulate the two-stage optimization problem shown in Equation (9.17) into its deterministic equivalent as shown below.

$$\min f(x,\omega) = c'x + G(x)$$
$$\text{s.t.} \quad Ax = b, x \geq 0 \tag{9.18}$$
$$D(\omega)x + W(\omega)y(\omega) = h(\omega), \text{ for } \omega \in \Omega,$$
$$y(\omega) \geq 0$$

where $G(x) = \mathrm{E}_\omega \left[\Phi(x,\omega) \right]$ is some function that approximates the second stage optimization problem. As you will see shortly, this approach allows us to solve a variety of financial optimization problems involving events with uncertain outcomes.

> The deterministic equivalent simplifies the two-stage stochastic programming into a one-stage problem, in which a function that can approximate the distribution of the random variable and model the optimal values of the second-stage decision variable is used. The ensuing model must also satisfy both the first-stage and second-stage constraints as shown in Equation (9.16).

Many of the financial optimization problems that we have examined so far such as liability funding, capital project selection, and portfolio optimization assume we know with certainty what the future values of every parameter of the problem will be, which is unrealistic. Stochastic optimization provides us the flexibility to now incorporate more realistic features of the problem into the model, and still be able to solve them to derive the optimal course of action.

Stochastic Portfolio Optimization

This approach reexamines the classic portfolio allocation problems from the perspective of how we select the optimal allocation of portfolio resources when the value of one or more input variables is uncertain. In the risk parity portfolio allocation problem, we optimized the portfolio to achieve a specific risk exposure. There are instances where we are uncertain about risk exposure itself, and we must optimize the portfolio to reduce our exposure to the risk. For example, for pension funds and insurance companies, the true extent of the future liabilities is unknown. Likewise, the degree of fluctuation in the future cash flows to be received or made in foreign currencies if such exposure is to be hedged using deterministic programming. Since we have been exploring various portfolio allocation problems using optimization, let's examine another case of portfolio optimization in which there is uncertainty about the future outcomes of the portfolio. Specifically, we would like to optimize the portfolio to reduce the risk of extreme losses in the values of the portfolio over a period of time. This is popularly regarded as a Mean-Value-at-risk (Mean-VaR) portfolio optimization approach.

Mean-CVaR Portfolio Optimization

Unlike the Mean-Variance optimization, which seeks the portfolio allocations that achieve the optimal trade-off between total risk and expected return, the Mean-VaR optimization is focused on optimizing the portfolio allocation concerning the portfolio risk in the loss domain. This proposition is anecdotally more realistic, in the sense that most investors care only about underperformance and in particular extreme underperformance rather than overperformance. Therefore, optimizing the portfolio to reduce the risk of catastrophic losses, while leaving room for the so-called 'good' volatility,[11] is worth exploring.

We know that the Value-at-Risk of a portfolio is the maximum amount of market-related losses the portfolio (under normal market conditions) can incur within a window of time with α level of confidence. It can also be specified as the minimum market-related loss a portfolio can incur within the same time frame with $(1-\alpha)$ level of confidence. In Chapter Five, we examined various VaR specifications. However, we did not discuss some of the challenges of modeling VaRs in the context of portfolios. These challenges include the fact that the VaRs of portfolios are not coherent in the sense that it is possible for the VaR of a combination of assets to be greater than the sum of the VaRs of the individual assets in the portfolio. The possible lack of subadditivity in portfolio VaR is inconsistent with the diversification principle of portfolio risk, which states that the risk of a portfolio cannot be greater than the sum of the independent risk of each asset in the portfolio. Hence, optimizing a portfolio by purely conditioning the risk on the VaR specification might actually lead to more concentrated portfolios. Furthermore, VaRs in general are nonsmooth and nonconvex functions, which makes them difficult to optimize, because they are discontinuous functions that can generate multiple local minima. Lastly, VaR does not inform us of the magnitude of losses that might occur if indeed the VaR of the portfolio is exceeded.

A coherent risk measure that was developed to address the shortcomings of VaR is the conditional value-at-risk (CVaR), which calculates the average loss that can occur beyond a confidence level over a specified period of time. For example, the 99%-CVaR calculates the average of the market-related losses in the portfolio value that could occur in the outcomes with the 1% lowest probabilities, within a specified period. It is also commonly called expected shortfall (ES), mean shortfall (MS), or conditional tail risk.

---

[11] Good volatility is regarded as the volatility that leads to upward movement in prices. In a study by Bollerslev et al. (2019), they found that stocks with more positive high frequency price movement outperformed stocks with more negative high frequency price movement, by about 15% a year.

Before we delve deeper into the mathematical framework of CVaR, let us begin with some steps toward formulating our portfolio optimization problem. First, we are dealing with market-related risks, which are random events, so let us use a vector y to denote the collection of these random events. Let us also denote a vector of portfolio choices or allocations that an investor can make by the vector W. Since we are only interested in the loss domain, we can also denote a loss function $f(w, y)$ that reflects the combined effect of our portfolio choice and the random event. It is important to note here that the values of our loss function are positive in the loss domain and negative in the gains domain of portfolio performance.[12] If we assume that y has a known probability distribution, then the cumulative distribution function of the loss function at a fixed portfolio choice w can be written as:

$$\Psi(w, \gamma) := P\left[f(w, y) \le \gamma \right] = \int_{f(w,y) \le \gamma} p(y) dy \qquad (9.19)$$

Notice that Equation (9.19) is the probability that portfolio loss does not exceed some real value γ. Having set up Equation (9.19), we can then define our VaR for a given confidence level $\alpha \in [0,1]$ as:

$$VaR_\alpha(w) := \min\left\{ \gamma \in \mathbb{R} : \Psi(w, \gamma) \ge \alpha \right\} \qquad (9.20)$$

Equation (9.20) can be described as the minimum loss a portfolio choice w can incur such that the cumulative distribution $\Psi(w, \gamma)$ is at least as great as the threshold α. From Equation (9.20), we then describe the CvaR for a given confidence level $\alpha \in [0,1]$ as:

$$CVaR_\alpha(w) = \frac{1}{(1-\alpha)} \int_{f(w,y) \ge \gamma} f(w, y) p(y) dy$$

$$= \frac{1}{(1-\alpha)} \int_{f(w,y) \ge VaR_\alpha(w)} f(w, y) p(y) dy \qquad (9.21)$$

We can deduce from Equation (9.21) that $CVaR_\alpha(w)$ cannot be lower than $VaR_\alpha(w)$ since $VaR_\alpha(w)$ is the lower support of the integral expression. Furthermore, we can see from Equation (9.21) that $CVaR_\alpha(w)$ can be described as the average or the integral of the loss distribution $f(w, y) \ge VaR_\alpha(w)$. Together these features imply that $CVaR_\alpha(w)$ is continuous with respect to α and jointly convex with respect to the collections of portfolio choices W and α. Equation (9.21) also implies that the α cumulative distribution of the loss function is continuous and has a minimum. If we assume that y follows a multivariate normal distribution, it is possible to write $VaR_\alpha(w)$ and $CVaR_\alpha(w)$ as a function of the portfolio return and variance. This method is commonly known as the delta-normal method.

---

[12] The function is positive when portfolio returns is negative, and negative when portfolio returns is positive.

$$VaR_{\alpha}(w) = -\mu(w) + \Pi_1(\alpha)\sqrt{w'\Sigma w}$$

$$\text{where } \Pi_1(\alpha) = \Phi^{-1}(\alpha)$$

(9.22)

$$CVaR_{\alpha}(w) = -\mu(w) + \Pi_2(\alpha)\sqrt{w'\Sigma w}$$

$$\text{where } \Pi_2(\alpha) = \frac{1}{(1-\alpha)\sqrt{2\pi}} \exp - \left[\frac{\left(\Phi^{-1}(\alpha)\right)^2}{\sqrt{2}} \right]$$

(9.23)

Where $\mu(w) = E(R_p)$ and $\sqrt{w'\Sigma w} = \sigma_p$. $\Phi^{-1}(\alpha)$ is the inverse cumulative distribution function of α. You may have noticed the code for computing these two values in the SAS code that we have used for all of our previous portfolio optimization problems. It turns out that you can also minimize either of these expressions subject to some constraints placed on some function of the portfolio weights such as the minimum return constraint. The resultant portfolio allocation would be the same as those obtained from the risk minimization problem in MVO as shown in Figure 9.1. We will let you create the SAS program to implement the optimization as one of the end-of-chapter exercises.

Figure 9.1: Optimal Portfolio from Mean-Expected Shortfall Optimization

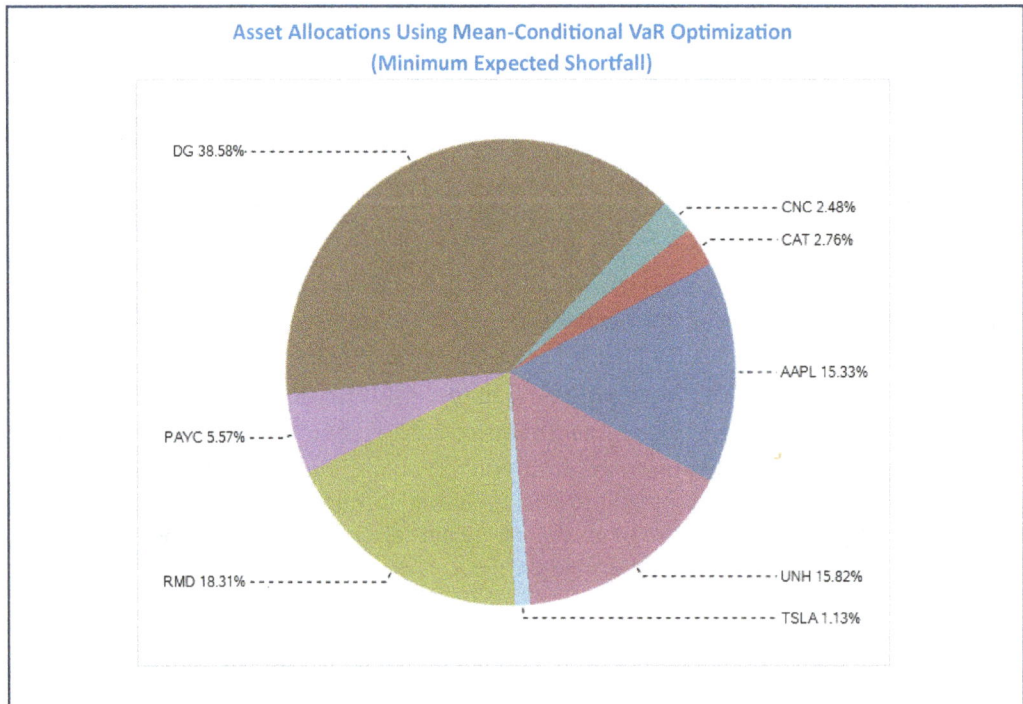

So far, we have assumed that y is continuous. When y follows a discrete probability distribution, $CVaR_\alpha(w)$ can be shown to be of the form:

$$CVaR_\alpha(w) = \frac{1}{(1-\alpha)} \sum_{f(w,y) \geq VaR_\alpha(w)} f(w,y) p_j(y) dy, \; j = 1,...,n \qquad (9.24)$$

Optimizing with Conditional Value-at-Risk

Now that we have developed the mathematical model for $CVaR_\alpha(w)$, let us proceed with developing the framework for optimizing our portfolio with it. Before we proceed, you will notice that the $CVaR_\alpha(w)$ function contains $VaR_\alpha(w)$, which we have described earlier as problematic to deal with. This problem is avoided by employing an auxiliary function $F_\alpha(w,\gamma)$ instead of Equation (9.21) to compute $CVaR_\alpha(w)$ as shown below.

$$F_\alpha(w,\gamma) = \gamma + \frac{1}{1-\alpha} \int_{f(w,y) \geq VaR_\alpha(w)} (f(w,y) - \gamma) p(y) dy$$
$$= \gamma + \frac{1}{1-\alpha} \int_{y \in \mathbb{R}} (f(w,y) - \gamma)^+ p(y) dy \qquad (9.25)$$

where the $(f(w,y) - \gamma)^+ = \max(f(w,y) - \gamma, 0)$. $F_\alpha(w,\gamma)$ has all the desired features for optimization problems in the sense that it is convex and continuously differentiable. This implies that we can then derive $CVaR_\alpha(w)$ as the minimum of $F_\alpha(w,\gamma)$, which is also a function of γ as shown below:

$$CVaR_\alpha(w) = \min_{w,\gamma} F_\alpha(w,\gamma) \qquad (9.26)$$

From the formula above, we observe that it is possible to calculate $CVaR_\alpha(w)$ without first calculating the $VaR_\alpha(w)$ of the portfolio. In reality, the $VaR_\alpha(w)$ is obtained as a by-product of the optimization, since γ is a support point, which at the minimum will be analogous to the $VaR_\alpha(w)$ of the portfolio loss. To approximate the integral, we can use discrete sampling of a finite number of portfolio scenarios using Monte Carlo simulation, where each scenario represents the realization of the random vector y of returns that is drawn from its probability distribution $p(y)$. The approximation of the $F_\alpha(w,\gamma)$, which we denote by $\tilde{F}_\alpha(w,\gamma)$ can then be written as:

$$\tilde{F}_\alpha(w,\gamma) = \gamma + \frac{1}{S(1-\alpha)} \sum_{s=1}^{S} [f(w,y) - \gamma]^+ \qquad (9.27)$$

In theory, each scenario should be weighted by its joint density function, $p(y_s)$. However, for a sufficiently large number of scenarios S, it is more practical to assume that each scenario has an equal probability of occurring. Hence, the expression is divided by S.

The last step before we present the optimization problem is to specify an expression for $f(w, y)$. From our portfolio point of view, the random vector y is the vector of randomly generated returns for the universe of assets and the portfolio choice w_j is the weight assigned to the assets in y such that $f(w, y) = w'y$. Replacing y with R results in $f(w, R) = -w'R$ the portfolio return formula, we have used in previous optimizations. Such that:[13]

$$\tilde{F}_\alpha(w, \gamma) = \gamma + \frac{1}{S(1-\alpha)} \sum_{s=1}^{S} \left[-w'R_s - \gamma\right]^+ \tag{9.28}$$

Drawing from Equation (9.22), we now know that to minimize $CVaR_\alpha(w)$, we will need to minimize $\tilde{F}_\alpha(w, \gamma)$ subject to some constraints that will ensure that the function is well-behaved and remains in the feasible region.

$$\min_{w, \gamma} CVaR_\alpha(w) = \gamma + \frac{1}{S(1-\alpha)} \sum_{s=1}^{S} \left[-w'R_s - \gamma\right]^+$$

$$\text{s.t. } E(R_p) = \sum_{i=1}^{N} w_i E(R_i) \geq \bar{R}, \sum_{i=1}^{N} w_i = 1 \tag{9.29}$$

The last issue will need to deal with is the piecewise linearity created by the $\left[-w'R_j - \gamma\right]^+$ expression in the objective function. Let us replace the expression with an auxiliary variable z_j and by doing this impose an additional constraint on $z_j + w'R_j + \gamma \geq 0$ as shown in the optimization problem. The resulting optimization problem, which is to minimize the Conditional Value-at-Risk (CVaR) subject to a minimum return constraint, can now be written as.

$$\min_{w, \gamma, z_s} CVaR_\alpha(w) = \gamma + \frac{1}{S(1-\alpha)} \sum_{s=1}^{S} z_s, (s = 1, ..., S)$$

$$\text{s.t. } z_s \geq 0, \quad (s = 1, ..., S)$$

$$z_s + w'R_s + \gamma \geq 0, \quad (s = 1, ..., S) \tag{9.30}$$

$$E(R_p) = \sum_{i=1}^{N} w_i E(R_i) \geq \bar{R}, \sum_{i=1}^{N} w_i = 1.$$

We can also write the mathematical expression for maximizing the portfolio return, subject to a maximum Conditional Value-at-Risk constraint as:

---

[13] Notice the negative sign in front of the portfolio return formula. That is because our loss function is positive in the loss domain, and negative in the gains domain of portfolio performance.

$$\max_{w,\gamma,z_i} E\left(R_p\right) = \sum_{i=1}^{N} w_i E\left(R_i\right)$$

$$\text{s.t.} \quad CVaR_\alpha\left(w\right) = \gamma + \frac{1}{S\left(1-\alpha\right)} \sum_{s=1}^{S} z_s \leq u_{\alpha_j}, \left(s=1,...,S\right)$$

$$z_s \geq 0, \quad \left(s=1,...,S\right)$$

$$z_s + w'R_s + \gamma \geq 0, \quad \left(s=1,...,S\right) \qquad (9.31)$$

$$\sum_{i=1}^{N} w_i = 1.$$

Although the mathematical derivation of the optimization problem is quite intense, conceptually it might be easier to consider the optimization problem as follows.

Minimization:

For a given confidence level α, the optimization involves the search for the portfolio allocations w_j, the minimum value at risk γ, and the scenario deviation z_s that results in the lowest average portfolio loss $CVaR_\alpha\left(w\right)$, when the VaR of the portfolio is exceeded without reducing portfolio returns below a specified level.

Maximization:

For a given confidence level α, the optimization involves the search for the portfolio allocations w_j, the value at risk γ, and the scenario deviation z_s that results in the maximum return attainable, without exceeding a specified average portfolio loss $CVaR_\alpha\left(w\right)$, when the VaR of the portfolio is exceeded.

You will notice that while Equations (9.30 and 9.31) include the stochastic elements of our optimization problem, they are essentially a one-stage optimization problem. This means that all of the decision variables in both problems will be optimized simultaneously and not as a two-stage stochastic programming problem with recourse. Furthermore, both objective functions are linear functions for all values of w in the feasible region defined by $z_j + w'R_j + \gamma \geq 0$. Therefore, both optimization problems are linear programming problems that can be solved using any of the popular solvers such as simplex, interior point, and active set.

Implementing Mean-CVaR Optimization in SAS

Implementing Mean-CVaR optimization in SAS involves a two-step process. First, we will generate the *S*-number of portfolio scenarios using Monte Carlo simulation. Second, we will then read the simulated returns into the optimization problem to optimize the objective function and consequently derive values of the decision variables at the optimal value of the objective function.

Our first step will be performed using the IML procedure. We will then invoke the OPTMODEL procedure in the second step. We assume that the probability distributions of the returns of the 63 stocks in the portfolio are multivariate normal. Therefore, we can simulate their joint returns from the return vector, which is stored in the SAS data set named PORTFOLIO_RETURNS, and their covariance matrix, which is stored in the SAS data set named PORTFOLIO_COVARIANCES. Program 9.7A shows the SAS code used in the IML procedure to simulate 1,000 portfolio scenarios. After invoking the IML procedure, the historical portfolio returns and covariances are read into the RETURNS vector and SIGMA matrix. We then simulate 1,000 portfolio scenarios. We also create a scenario index for each vector of simulated returns. We then save the scenario indices and the simulated return in the SAS data set named SIMULATED_RETURNS.

Program 9.7A: Simulating 1,000 Portfolio Scenarios for CVaR Optimization Using PROC IML

```
/* Use PROC IML to Simulate 1,000 Portfolio Scenarios*/
%let j =1000;

proc iml;
     /* Read returns and covariances into EQRET and SIGMA*/
     use Portfolio_Returns;
     read all var _num_ into returns [colname=NumerNames];
     read all var _char_ into assets[colname=CharNames];
     use Portfolio_Covariances;
     read all var _num_ into sigma[colname=NumerNames rowname=Ticker];
     call randseed (7564321);       /*Random Seed*/
     %let r =nrow(eqret);
     SRet =RandNormal(&j,returns,sigma);/*Simulate 1000x N-Assets*/
     SMean =mean(SRet); /*calculate sample mean*/
     SCOV = cov(SRet); /*calculate sample covariance*/

     /*Index of Scenarios*/
     SNum = t("SC1":"SC&j");

     /*Export revised expected returns into SAS  data sets*/
     Anames ='Scenario'||NumerNames; /*Variable names setup*/
     create Simulated_Returns from SNum SRet [colname=Anames];
     append from SNum SRet;
     close Simulated_Returns;
```

Program 9.7B shows the SAS program for implementing the 95% CVaR minimization model using the vectors of returns that were simulated from the IML procedure. First, we use macrovariables (&ALPHA=0.95, &RFR=0.00178, and &MINIMUM_RETURN=0.0179) to specify the confidence level for our CVaR, risk-free rate, and minimum return constraints, respectively. The OPTMODEL procedure is then invoked. Using the SET statements, we create two index sets (ASSETS and SCENARIOS). The parameter array RETURNS{ASSET} contains the actual returns, while the SRETURN{ASSET,SCENARIOS} contains the simulated returns for the 1,000 scenarios. The COVARIANCE{ASSETS,ASSETS} contains the covariances of the 63 stocks in our universe. The READ statement is then used to read the data sets into the respective arrays. Notice that the simulated returns are read into an $S \times N$ array, where $S = 1,000$ is the number of portfolio scenarios and $N = 63$ is the number of stocks in our universe. Next, we declare our three decision variables, WEIGHT{ASSETS}, which is equivalent to w; OPT_VAR, which is equivalent to γ; and Z{SCENARIOS}, which is equivalent to z_s. We then use implicit variables to compute the portfolio variance and standard deviation, as well as the value-at-risk and the expected shortfall of the portfolio using the analytical method. Next, we use another set of implicit variables to compute our substitute function FWVaR, which is equivalent to $-w'R_j - \gamma$.

Notice that for each scenario, we take the sum of the products of the weights and the simulated returns for the stocks in the universe. Just like in the past examples, we also use implicit variables to calculate expected returns and portfolio returns to enable us to compare the performances of the various optimization methods that we examine.

Program 9.7B: CVaR Minimization Using PROC OPTMODEL

```
/*Implementing Conditional Value-at-Risk Optimization using PROC OPTMODEL*/
%let alpha=0.95;
%let rfr=0.00178;
%let minimum_return = 0.0179;

proc optmodel;
        /* declare sets and parameters */
        set <str> ASSETS;
        set <str> SCENARIOS;
        num returns{ASSETS};
        num sreturns {ASSETS,SCENARIOS};
        num covariance {ASSETS, ASSETS};

        /* read portfolio data from SAS  data sets */
        read data Portfolio_Returns into ASSETS=[Ticker] returns;
        read data simulated_Returns into SCENARIOS=[Scenario]
          {i in ASSETS} <sreturns[i,Scenario]=col(i)>;
        read data Portfolio_Covariances into [Ticker]
          {i in ASSETS} <covariance[Ticker,i]=col(i)>;

        /* declare decision variables */
        var Weights {ASSETS} >= 0;
        Var Opt_VaR>=0;
        Var Z{SCENARIOS}>=0;

        /*Calculate Portfolio Risk Measures*/
        impvar Portfolio_Variance=sum {i in ASSETS, j in ASSETS}covariance[i,j] *
        Weights[i] * Weights[j];
        impvar Portfolio_Risk = sqrt(Portfolio_Variance);

        /*Value at Risk and Expected Shortfall*/
        impvar zes =(((2*constant("pi"))**(0.5))*(exp(((2**-
        0.5)*quantile('normal',&alpha))**2))*(1-&alpha))**-1;
        impvar VaR=sum {i in ASSETS}
                -returns[i] * Weights[i]+quantile("normal",&alpha)*sqrt(Portfolio_Variance);
```

```
        impvar Expected_Shortfall=sum {i in ASSETS}
              -returns[i] * Weights[i]+zes*sqrt(Portfolio_Variance);

        /*Functions of Scenario Portfolios and Optimized VaR*/
        impvar FWVaR{s in SCENARIOS}=sum{i in ASSETS}(-Weights[i]*sreturns[i,s])-Opt_VaR;

        /*Calculate portfolio return*/
        impvar Expected_Return=sum {i in ASSETS}
              returns[i] * Weights[i];
        impvar Portfolio_Return = Expected_Return;

        /* declare constraints */
        con CZ{s in SCENARIOS} : Z[s]+sum {i in ASSETS}
        Weights[i]*sreturns[i,s]+Opt_VaR>=0;
        con SZ{s in SCENARIOS} : Z[s]>=0;
        con Minimum_Return: Expected_Return>=&minimum_return;
        con Portfolio_Weights: sum {i in ASSETS} Weights[i] = 1;

        /* declare objective */
        min CVAR =Opt_VaR+1/(&j*(1-&alpha))*(sum{s in SCENARIOS}Z[s]);
        solve;

        /*Portfolio Sharpe Ratio*/
        Impvar Sharpe_Ratio = (Expected_Return-&rfr)/Portfolio_Risk;

        /*Print Optimization Outputs*/
        print  Portfolio_Return percent8.2 Portfolio_Risk percent8.2 Sharpe_Ratio best4.2
        CVAR percent8.2 Opt_VaR percent8.2 VaR percent8.2  Expected_Shortfall percent8.2;
        print {i in ASSETS: Weights[i]>1e-4} Weights percent8.2
          {i in ASSETS: Weights[i]>1e-4} returns percent8.2;
quit;
```

Next, we declare the four constraints shown in Equation (9.26) using the CON statement. Besides the constraint specification for the surplus variable, we also impose a 1.79% minimum return constraint on the optimization to ensure that the result is comparable with those obtained from the previous optimization. We declare the objective function, which is

$$\min CVaR_\alpha(w) = \gamma + \frac{1}{S(1-\alpha)} \sum_{s=1}^{S} z_s$$. You will also notice here that the sum is also over the S number of scenarios.

Output 9.7: Optimal Portfolio Allocation from CVaR Optimization Using PROC OPTMODEL

The OPTMODEL Procedure

Problem Summary	
Objective Sense	Minimization
Objective Function	CVAR
Objective Type	Linear
Number of Variables	1064
Bounded Above	0
Bounded Below	1064
Bounded Below and Above	0
Free	0
Fixed	0
Number of Constraints	2002
Linear LE (<=)	0
Linear EQ (=)	1
Linear GE (>=)	2001
Linear Range	0

The OPTMODEL Procedure

Solution Summary	
Solver	LP
Algorithm	Dual Simplex
Objective Function	CVAR
Solution Status	Optimal
Objective Value	0.0740337707
Primal Infeasibility	2.220446E-16
Dual Infeasibility	5.551115E-17
Bound Infeasibility	0
Iterations	259
Presolve Time	0.03
Solution Time	0.05

[1]	Weights	returns
AAPL	9.37%	2.09%
DG	38.39%	1.67%
NVR	0.69%	1.41%
PAYC	8.76%	2.67%
RMD	19.55%	1.68%
STE	1.71%	1.40%
UNH	21.53%	1.66%

Portfolio_Return	Portfolio_Risk	Sharpe_Ratio	CVAR	Opt_VaR	VaR	Expected_Shortfall
1.79%	4.56%	0.35	7.40%	5.50%	5.71%	7.62%

Asset Allocations Using Mean-CVaR Portfolio Optimization (CVaR Minimization)

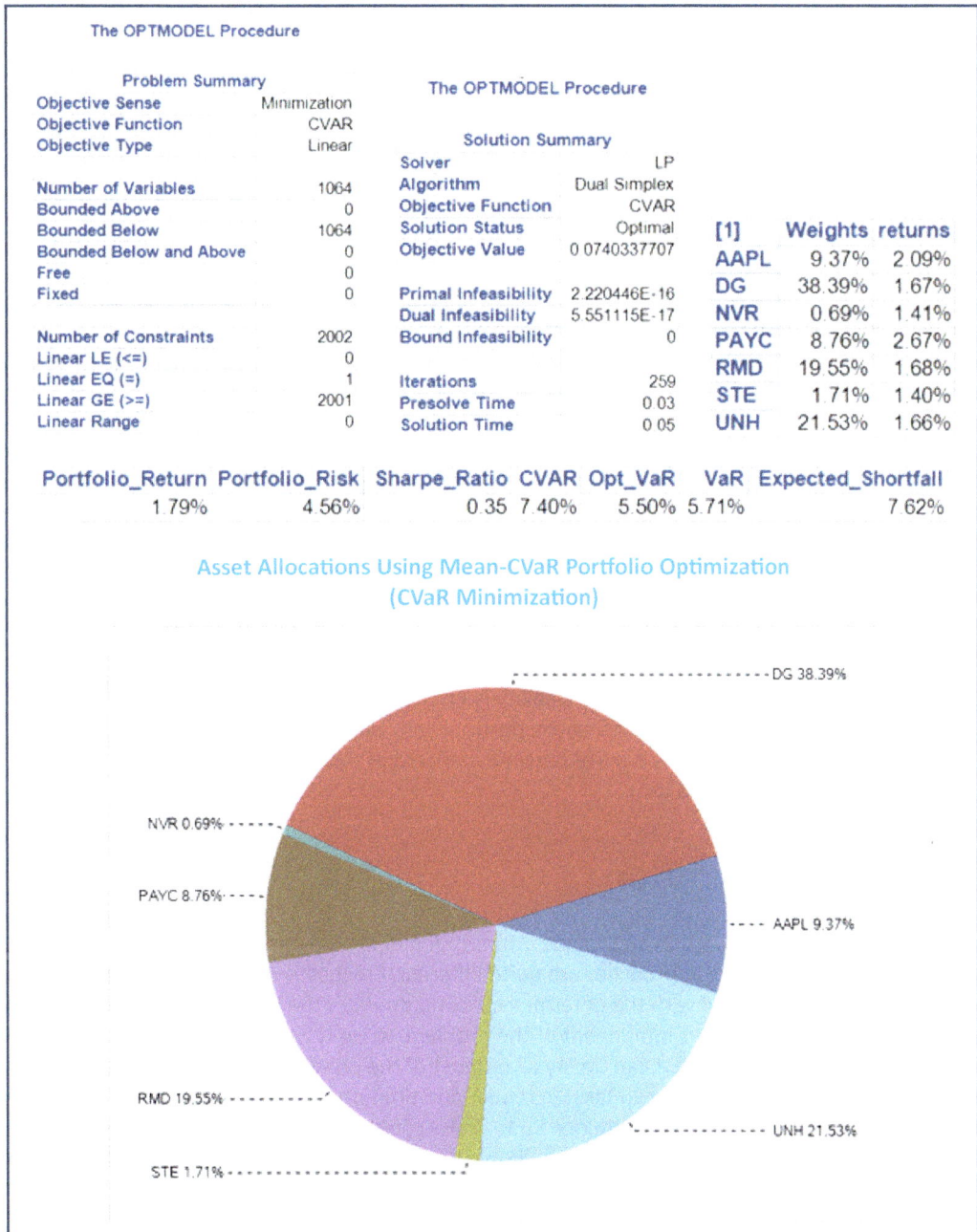

DG 38.39%
NVR 0.69%
PAYC 8.76%
AAPL 9.37%
RMD 19.55%
UNH 21.53%
STE 1.71%

Output 9.7 shows the results from minimizing the objective function specified in Equation (9.28). You will notice in the Problem Summary the large number of variables (1064) and constraints (2002). The problem variables include the 1,000 elements of the vector of auxiliary variables

$Z = \left[z_1, ..., z_{S=1,000} \right]$, the 63 elements of the vector of portfolio weights, and our optimized VaR

Y. The 2,002 constraints include 1,000 elements each of the $z_j + w'R_j + \gamma \geq 0$ and $z_s \geq 0$ constraints, the minimum portfolio return constraint, and the full investment constraint. You will notice that the objective value of our optimized CVaR and VaR, as well as the VaR and expected shortfall that were calculated using the delta-normal methods are much lower than any of the values we have obtained in previous portfolio optimization. More so, we were able to achieve this improvement in the tail risk without incurring significant sacrifice in the other measures of portfolio performance such as returns, risk, and Sharpe ratio. However, we can see that the resulting portfolio is significantly concentrated. Indeed, it is the most concentrated portfolio we have obtained amongst the various optimization approaches that we have used up to this point. Just six stocks account for 97.6% of the portfolio weights.

A more interesting feature of the optimization result is how the portfolio allocations were made. Notice the increase in portfolio allocation to United Health Inc., ResMed Inc., and Paycom Inc., and significantly lower allocation to Apple Inc. The former groups of companies operate in industries that are less susceptible to the economy and consequently have lower tail risk, while Apple Inc. sells mostly discretionary products, which makes it more susceptible to the economy. In line with our portfolio objective, the optimization algorithm created a safety-first type of portfolio where the value-at-risk is the safety threshold. In the safety-first portfolio optimization, we aim to minimize the probability that the portfolio return will fall below the safety threshold. For the case of our optimization, that probability is $(1 - \alpha) = 5\%$. This means that in any given month there is a five percent chance that the portfolio loss will exceed 5.0%. Furthermore, such losses when they do occur, there is a five percent chance that the average of losses will exceed 7.4% of the value of the portfolio.

Robust Optimization

Although stochastic optimization and robust optimization deal with uncertainty in the optimization problem, their approaches are quite different. Stochastic optimizations determine the optimal course of action with the deterministic component of the problem, given the expected value of the random component of the problem, while robust optimization determines the optimal course of action that can satisfy all or most of the possible scenarios in which the uncertain aspect of the problem can take. In robust optimizations, robustness might be required in the objective function or the constraints. Robustness could also be relative or absolute concerning some parameters of the problem. Robust optimizations are particularly useful for optimization problems in which the problem data consists of estimates, the constraints are uncertain, or the objective function is extremely sensitive to certain parameters or variables, which is one of the main criticisms of the MVO approach.

The main distinguishing feature of the various types of robust optimizations is how each approach deals with the uncertainty set in the problem. In some approaches, the uncertainty set represents a finite number of scenarios that are associated with possible outcomes for the parameters of the model. In other specifications, uncertainty could represent a range of values for the parameters of the model, or a specified confidence interval around a reference value of the parameter. In general, the types of uncertainty we encounter are determined by the problem, while the size of the uncertainty set is typically influenced by the degree of robustness we would like to see in the model. For example, for a problem with interval-based uncertainty, one might desire an optimal course of action that is robust to up to 99% of the possible range of values that a parameter of interest might take.

Constraint Robustness

The idea of ensuring that our optimal solution is robust to uncertainty in the constraint is relatively straightforward. In this framework, the solution to the problem must be feasible for possible values of the parameter with uncertainty in the constraint. For example, a portfolio manager with an uncertain liquidity constraint might be required to hold some portion of the portfolio capital in cash. Since the cash amount is unknown at the time of modeling, the optimal solution must be robust to a range of possible cash outflows during the holding period. Mathematically, optimization with constraint robustness can be written as:

$$\min_{x} f(x)$$
$$\text{s.t.} \quad G(x,u) \in H.$$

(9.32)

In the equation above, $f(x)$ is the objective function that contains no uncertainty, x is the decision variables, while $u \in U$ is the parameters, which is an element of a bounded uncertainty set U. $G(x,u)$ and H are structural elements of the constraint equation.

Objective Robustness

Robustness in the objective function is usually needed when some features of the function we are trying to optimize are uncertain. Therefore, we will need the optimal solution to be insensitive to the uncertain parameters in the objective function. For example, it is generally accepted that the optimal solutions from the mean-variance optimization (MVO) are extremely sensitive to the expected return of the assets in our selection universe. However, our estimates of the expected returns of the assets in our universe are also prone to statistical errors. Hence, the results of the MVO are not particularly reliable or even practical from a real-world perspective, given the significant amount of capital that could be at risk. Remember that in the MVO framework for portfolio return maximization, the expected return appears in the objective function. Therefore, the return maximization problem in the MVO will be analogous to an objective robustness problem in robust optimizations. Mathematically, optimization with objective robustness can be written as:

$$\min_x f(x,u)$$
$$\text{s.t.} \quad G(x) \in H. \tag{9.33}$$

where $f(x,u)$ is the objective function that includes the uncertainty parameter u. While we will not present the mathematical formula below, you should note that uncertainty can also simultaneously exist in both the objective function and constraint of a problem. In reality, you can respecify many problems with uncertainty in the objective function as a certain objective problem with uncertain constraints. For example, we can reformulate Equation (9.33) as:

$$\min_{x,z} \quad z$$
$$\text{s.t.} \quad z - f(x,u) \geq 0, \tag{9.34}$$
$$G(x) \in H.$$

Uncertainty Set

So far, we have provided a general description of the uncertainty set and how uncertainty enters into our optimization. Let's now consider the heterogeneity in the collections of the element of uncertainty sets. Our description of the uncertainty will assume that in all cases, the uncertainty is in the constraint and not the objective function. In all cases, we present the uncertainty model, followed by its robust counterpart formulation. The robust counterpart (RC) of the optimization problem is the deterministic equivalent of the optimization problem.

1. **Scenario uncertainty set:** In this specification, the uncertainty set is defined as a finite collection of discrete realizations of the uncertainty parameter. The mathematical expression for the scenario uncertainty set can be written as:

$$U = \{a_1, ..., a_S\}, \; RC : \hat{a}'x \leq b \; \text{for all} \; a \in U$$

2. **Box (interval) uncertainty set:** In this specification, the uncertainty set is defined by an interval or box in which a single nominal value $\hat{a}$ of the uncertainty parameter is assumed to lie within. The size of the interval is controlled by the parameter ρ, while u describes a constant disturbance term. If $\delta = \rho u$, then the mathematical expression for the box uncertainty set can be written as:

$$U = \{a = \hat{a} + \rho u, \|u\|_\alpha \leq 1\} \{a : |a - \hat{a}| \leq \rho\}, \; RC : \hat{a}'x + \delta \|x\|_1 \leq b$$

3. **Ellipsoidal uncertainty set:** This specification assumes that the uncertainty set is defined by an ellipse around some nominal value $\hat{a}$ of the uncertain parameter. Statistically, it can be described as a confidence region around the normal value of the uncertain parameter. The shape and size of the region is determined by the matrix $P = P' = R'R$. The mathematical expression for the ellipsoidal uncertainty set can be written as:

$$U = \{a = \hat{a} + \rho Ru, \|u\|_2 \leq 1\}, \; RC : \hat{a}'x + \delta \|R'x\|_2 \leq b.$$

$$U = \{a : (a - \hat{a})' P^{-1} (a - \hat{a}) \leq \rho^2\}$$

4. **Polyhedral uncertainty set:** In this specification, the uncertainty set consists of a system of linear inequalities. The size of the uncertainty set is controlled by an adjustable parameter Γ. The mathematical expression for the polyhedral uncertainty set can be written as:

$$U = \left\{ a : \sum_{j \in J}^{J} \|a_j\| \le \Gamma \right\}, \quad RC : a'x + \delta\|x\|_1 \le b \text{ for all } a \in U$$

Robust Portfolio Optimization

Having laid a rigorous foundation for robust optimization, let us now explore its application to portfolio optimization. In general, robust portfolio optimization aims to obtain portfolio allocations that are less sensitive to statistical errors in the estimation of the input parameters of the model, which are the expected returns of the component assets and their covariance matrix. In the ensuing examples, we will focus mainly on uncertainty in the expected returns of the component assets, because they are generally accepted to have a higher impact on the portfolio performance than uncertainty in the covariance matrix. We will denote the vector of expected returns of the component asset as μ and the covariance matrix of the same as Σ.

Remember that there is more than one approach to dealing with uncertainty in the optimization problem; therefore you should not be surprised to find out that there is more than one approach to implementing robust portfolio optimization. The common theme you will find amongst the various approaches is the emphasis on prudence, which we defined as optimizing for the worst-case scenario. In the context of input parameters, this means that the portfolio will be optimized for the worst-case mean scenario or worst-case variance scenario. As you may have noticed, the mathematical framework of robust optimization, in general, is a bit challenging, so we will focus on the easier of the two cases, which is the worst-case mean robust optimization.

Worst-case Mean Robust Optimization

From a worst-case mean portfolio return perspective, our optimization aims to maximize the lowest return portfolio possible, given the uncertainty that we face. Therefore, the solution we will seek is the portfolio allocation that provides the highest return in the worst possible case of expected returns in the component assets. Succinctly, our portfolio aim is to maximize the minimum portfolio returns possible as shown in Equation (9.35).

$$\max_{w} \left(\min_{\mu \in U\mu} w'\mu \right)$$

$$\text{s.t.} \quad w'1_N = 1$$

(9.35)

You will notice that in Equation (9.35), the uncertainty is in the objective function. This is generally not a concern as long as we can create a robust counterpart for the problem. In some cases, this might involve reformulating the problem with the uncertainty set as the bounds of the feasible region in the constraint. Nevertheless, let us formulate the types of uncertainty sets, which can be used for our robust portfolio optimization and their robust counterpart problem. We will then use some of the uncertainty sets to derive the optimal solutions to the problem.

1. **Scenario uncertainty set:** $U_\mu^S = \{\mu_1, ..., \mu_S\}$ consists of a finite number of the vectors of asset returns that can be simulated from their joint distribution. If we assume that our universe of asset returns is multivariate normal, then we can use the IML procedure to simulate 1,000 scenarios of asset returns. We will then feed those returns along with the covariance matrix into the optimization problem. We can also reformulate our objective function by moving the uncertainty to the constraint as shown in the robust counterpart formulation of the problem in Equation (9.36).

$$\max_{x,t} \quad z$$
$$\text{s.t.} \quad z - w'\hat{\mu} \le 0, \qquad \text{for all } \hat{\mu} \in U \tag{9.36}$$
$$w'1_N = 1, w \ge 0.$$

By including the auxiliary variable in the formulation, we sidestep the need to optimize the objective function over a large number of scenarios. It is helpful to note that the new specification retains all of the desired structural properties of the original problem such as linearity and convexity. However, we now have a much larger set of constraints to meet. You will also notice that the problem is similar to the stochastic optimization problem for CVaR that we examined earlier.

2. **Box uncertainty set:** $U_\mu^b = \{\mu \mid \delta \le \mu - \hat{\mu} \le \delta\}$ is an interval around the norm of the vector of asset returns. Let $\delta = \rho u$ and Σ_μ be the diagonal covariance matrix of errors, which is proportional to the variance of the assets in the portfolio universe, then the robust counterpart formulation of our objective function becomes:

$$\max_w \quad w'\hat{\mu} - \rho\sqrt{\Sigma_\mu}|w|'$$
$$\text{s.t.} \quad w'1_N = 1, \tag{9.37}$$
$$w \ge 0.$$

In estimating Σ_μ, we assume that the errors are uncorrelated amongst the assets. ρ is the uncertainty parameter that defines the maximum acceptable bounds of divergence between the estimated mean and true vector of means of the asset return. Smaller ρ implies a lower confidence interval around the mean. You should note that box uncertainty sets are less commonly used because they tend to yield extreme portfolio allocation if no other constraint is placed on the problem. We will leave the implementation of the robust portfolio optimization using the box uncertainty set for you to explore as an end-of-chapter exercise.

3. **Ellipsoidal uncertainty set:** $U_\mu^E = \{\mu = \hat{\mu} + \rho\Sigma_\mu u, \|u\|_2 \le 1\}$ is the uncertainty set formed by an ellipsoid around the nominal value $\hat{\mu}$. The boundary of the ellipsoid is defined by

$$U = \left\{\mu : (\mu - \hat{\mu})' \Sigma_\mu (\mu - \hat{\mu}) \le \rho^2\right\}$$

$$\max_w \quad w'\hat{\mu} - \rho\sqrt{w'\Sigma_\mu w}$$
$$\text{s.t.} \quad w'1_N = 1, \tag{9.38}$$
$$w \ge 0.$$

The ellipsoid uncertainty set allows for errors to be correlated among the asset returns. Therefore, the matrix of covariance error $\Sigma_\mu = R'R$ is estimated using the Cholesky decomposition of the covariance matrix Σ. ρ is the uncertainty parameter that defines the maximum acceptable bounds of divergence between the estimated mean and true vector of means of the asset return.

Implementing Robust Portfolio Optimization in SAS

Implementing robust portfolio optimization in SAS also involves a two-step process. For the scenario uncertainty set, we will first generate the *S*-number of portfolio scenarios using the IML procedure, before reading the simulated returns into the optimization problem. The model is then optimized to be robust to the worst case of the simulated scenario. For the box and ellipsoidal uncertainty set, we will first estimate the covariances of the errors using the IML procedure before importing the data into the OPTMODEL procedure to subsequently optimize the objective function to be robust to the worst boundary of the uncertainty set of each model. For all three examples, we will reuse our PORTFOLIO_RETURNS and PORTFOLIO_COVARIANCES SAS data sets.

Robust Portfolio Optimization with Scenario Uncertainty Set

Program 9.8 shows the SAS program for implementing the scenario-uncertainty set robust optimization. Just like in the past examples, the code used in this program is similar to the code you have seen in the previous programs. Therefore, we will only highlight areas where significant differences exist between this code and previous optimization code.

First, we simulate 1,000 asset returns scenarios using the IML procedure. The SAS code for this step is the same as the CVaR model. So, it is not presented in this section. We then import the simulated returns along with the estimated covariances into the OPTMODEL procedure. Our decision variables are portfolio weights (WEIGHTS) and the auxiliary variable T. For each scenario, we calculate the portfolio return using the FSRET implicit variable. We then declare the maximum constraint $\{CT[s]: T - FSRET[s] \le 0\}$ for all $s = \{1, ..., S = 1,000\}$. The aim of our objective function is to find the portfolio allocation and lowest value of T such that the maximum constraint is not violated. Think of this problem as selecting the optimal allocation in the worst-case return scenario that will result in a portfolio that can perform no worse than T. We also calculate the expected return on the portfolio using the actual return for each of the stocks that are selected for the optimized portfolio.

Program 9.8: Solving Robust Portfolio Optimization Problem with Scenario Uncertainty Set in PROC OPTMODEL

```
/*Robust Portfolio Optimization using Scenario Uncertainty Set*/
%let rfr=0.00178;
%let minimum_return = 0.0179;
%let max_risk = 0.045;

proc optmodel;
      /* declare sets and parameters */
      set <str> ASSETS;
      set <str> SCENARIOS;
      num returns{ASSETS};
      num sreturns {ASSETS,SCENARIOS};
      num covariance {ASSETS, ASSETS};

      /* read portfolio data from SAS  data sets */
      read data Portfolio_Returns into ASSETS=[Ticker] returns;
      read data simulated_Returns into SCENARIOS=[Scenario]
            {I in ASSETS} <sreturns[i,Scenario]=col(i)>;
      read data Portfolio_Covariances into [Ticker]
            {i in ASSETS} <covariance[Ticker,i]=col(i)>;

      /* declare decision variables */
      var Weights {ASSETS}>=0;
      Var T;

      /*******************************************/
      /*           Same as Program 9.1         */
      /*******************************************/

/*Functions of Scenario Portfolios*/
      impvar FSRet{s in SCENARIOS}=sum{i in ASSETS}(Weights[i]*sreturns[i,s]);

      /* declare constraints */
      con CT{s in SCENARIOS} : T-FSRet[s]<=0;
      con Maximum_Risk: Portfolio_Risk<=&max_risk;
      con Portfolio_Weights: sum {i in ASSETS} Weights[i] = 1;

      /* declare objective */
      max Z=T;
      solve;

      /*******************************************/
      /*           Same as Program 9.1         */
      /*******************************************/
```

Output 9.8A: Optimal Portfolio Allocation from Robust Portfolio Optimization (Scenario Uncertainty Set)

The OPTMODEL Procedure

Problem Summary

Objective Sense	Maximization
Objective Function	Z
Objective Type	Linear
Number of Variables	64
Bounded Above	0
Bounded Below	63
Bounded Below and Above	0
Free	1
Fixed	0
Number of Constraints	1002
Linear LE (<=)	1000
Linear EQ (=)	1
Linear GE (>=)	0
Linear Range	0
Nonlinear LE (<=)	1
Nonlinear EQ (=)	0
Nonlinear GE (>=)	0
Nonlinear Range	0

The OPTMODEL Procedure

Solution Summary

Solver	NLP
Algorithm	Interior Point Direct
Objective Function	Z
Solution Status	Optimal
Objective Value	-0.079879854
Optimality Error	1.1138928E-7
Infeasibility	1.376677E-14
Iterations	30
Presolve Time	0.01
Solution Time	0.47

[1]	Weights	returns
DG	23.50%	1.67%
FE	9.49%	0.42%
HD	0.65%	1.19%
KMI	18.53%	(0.19%)
KO	27.43%	0.59%
RMD	8.46%	1.68%
TSCO	1.37%	1.51%
WMT	10.54%	1.00%

Portfolio_Return	Portfolio_Risk	Sharpe_Ratio	VaR	Expected_Shortfall
0.84%	3.85%	0.17	8.13%	9.44%

In Output 9.8A, the Problem Statement table shows that our problem consists of 64 decision variables, which include 1 auxiliary variable Z and the 63 elements of the vector of portfolio weights. The 1,002 constraints include 1,000 scenario constraints, the maximum risk constraint, and the full investment constraint. From the Problem Summary table, we see that the worst-case return is about -7.99% with approximately an 8.13% VaR estimate. Using our estimated asset return and covariance to calculate the expected portfolio return yields a portfolio with a significantly lower return but better risk performance than our previous models. Although it is a significantly concentrated portfolio, you will notice that the optimal portfolio is comprised mostly of defensive stocks such as Dollar General (DG), Kinder Morgan (KMI), First Energy (FE), Coca-Cola (KO), ResMed Inc (RMD), and Walmart (WMT) to name a few.

Output 9.8B: Optimal Portfolio Allocation from Robust Portfolio Optimization (Scenario Uncertainty Set)

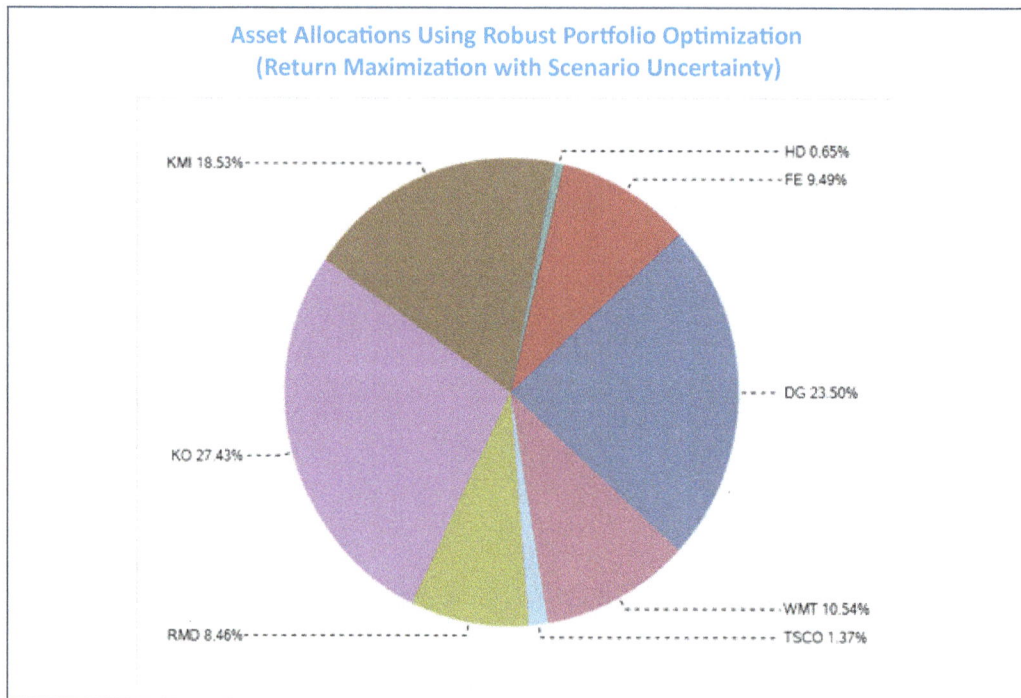

Robust Portfolio Optimization with Ellipsoidal Uncertainty Set

Programs 9.9A and 9.9B show the SAS code used in optimizing our portfolio using an ellipsoidal uncertainty set. Just like in the previous example, we will only highlight areas with significant differences in the code that we used in comparison to the previous optimization code. In Program 9.9A, we invoke the IML procedure to estimate the covariance matrix of the errors from the 1,000 asset returns we previously simulated. We then calculate the Cholesky decomposition of the matrix using the ROOT function in IML.

Program 9.9A: Computing Covariance Errors for Ellipsoidal Uncertainty Set Using PROC IML

```
/* Use PROC IML to Simulate 1,000 Portfolio Scenarios and calculate covariance
errors matrix*/
%let n =1000;
proc iml;
    use Portfolio_Returns;
    read all var _num_ into returns[colname=NumerNames rowname=Ticker];
    read all var _char_ into assets[colname=CharNames];/*Asset names*/
```

```
    use Portfolio_Covariances;
    read all var _num_ into sigma[colname=NumerNames rowname=Ticker];

    call randseed (7564321);
    SRet =RandNormal(&n,returns,sigma); /*Simulate 1000x2 vector*/

    SMReturns=t(mean(SRet)); /*calculate sample mean*/
    SSigma = cov(SRet); /*calculate sample covariance*/

    /*Compute Cholesky decompositions*/
    SigmaD=root((SSigma));

    /*Export covariance of error into SAS data sets*/
    sname ={'Assets'};/*Variable names setup*/
    cnames ='Ticker'||Numernames;

    create Portfolio_SigmaD from Assets SigmaD[colname= cnames ];
    append from Assets SigmaD;
    close Portfolio_SigmaD;
```

The estimated diagonal covariance matrix of errors along with the estimated returns and covariances are then imported into the OPTMODEL procedure as shown in Program 9.9B. We set ρ our certainty parameter to 0.2, which implies that we are willing to accept no more than 20% deviation from the true value of our vector of mean returns. We then declare our decision variables, which are the vector of portfolio weights (WEIGHTS). We also use implicit variables to calculate our asset-weighted covariance error $\left(w'\Sigma_\mu w\right)$. Next, we declare our objective function, which is to maximize our penalized portfolio return. The penalty term in the objective function is the product of the uncertainty parameter and norm (square root) of the weighted covariance error matrix $\left(\rho\sqrt{w'\Sigma_\mu w}\right)$.

Program 9.9B: Solving Robust Portfolio Optimization Problem with Ellipsoidal Uncertainty Set in PROC OPTMODEL

```
/* Implementing Robust Portfolio Optimization using Ellipsoidal Uncertainty Set
in PROC OPTMODEL*/
%let rfr=0.00178;
%let alpha=0.99;
%let max_risk = 0.045;
%let rho=0.2;

/*Portfolio optimization*/
 proc optmodel;
    /* declare sets and parameters */
    set <str> ASSETS;
    num returns {ASSETS};
    num sigmaD{ASSETS, ASSETS};
    num covariance{ASSETS, ASSETS};

    /*******************************************/
    /*          Same as Program 9.1          */
    /*******************************************/
```

```
read data Portfolio_SigmaD into [Ticker]
  {j in ASSETS} <sigmaD[Ticker,j]=col(j)>;

/* declare variables */
var Weights {ASSETS} >= 0;

/*Calculate Portfolio Risk Measures*/
impvar Robust_Sigma =sum{i in ASSETS, j in ASSETS}
(Weights[i]*sigmaD[i,j]*Weights[j]);

impvar Portfolio_Variance=sum {i in ASSETS, j in ASSETS}covariance[i,j] *
Weights[i] * Weights[j];
impvar Portfolio_Risk = sqrt(Portfolio_Variance);

   /*****************************************/
/*           Same as Program 9.1          */
   /*****************************************/

/* declare constraints */
con Portfolio_Weights: sum {j in ASSETS} Weights[j] = 1;

*con Maximum_Risk: Portfolio_Risk<=&max_risk;
/* declare objective */
max WRet=(Expected_Return-&rho*robust_sigma**0.5);
solve;

   /*****************************************/
/*           Same as Program 9.1          */
   /*****************************************/
```

Output 9.9A: Optimal Portfolio Allocation from Robust Portfolio Optimization (Ellipsoidal Uncertainty Set)

The OPTMODEL Procedure

Problem Summary	
Objective Sense	Maximization
Objective Function	WRet
Objective Type	Nonlinear
Number of Variables	63
Bounded Above	0
Bounded Below	63
Bounded Below and Above	0
Free	0
Fixed	0
Number of Constraints	2
Linear LE (<=)	0
Linear EQ (=)	1
Linear GE (>=)	0
Linear Range	0
Nonlinear LE (<=)	1
Nonlinear EQ (=)	0
Nonlinear GE (>=)	0
Nonlinear Range	0

The OPTMODEL Procedure

Solution Summary	
Solver	NLP
Algorithm	Interior Point Direct
Objective Function	WRet
Solution Status	Optimal
Objective Value	0.0058909014
Optimality Error	2.2521198E-7
Infeasibility	1.776357E-15
Iterations	13
Presolve Time	0.00
Solution Time	0.04

[1]	Weights	returns
CAT	4.19%	1.32%
CNC	10.38%	1.48%
CVS	0.36%	0.23%
DG	18.65%	1.67%
FE	0.02%	0.42%
GWW	0.78%	1.21%
KFRC	1.49%	1.20%
KO	3.84%	0.59%
MPC	0.83%	1.16%
NVR	11.21%	1.41%
PAYC	4.49%	2.67%
RMD	8.59%	1.68%
STE	12.67%	1.40%
TSCO	7.02%	1.51%
TSLA	6.05%	3.00%
WM	9.37%	1.10%

Portfolio_Return	Portfolio_Risk	Sharpe_Ratio	VaR	Expected_Shortfall
1.57%	4.50%	0.31	8.90%	10.42%

From the results shown in Output 9.9A, we observe that our ellipsoidal uncertainty set model consists of 63 decision variables, which are the 63 elements of the vector of portfolio weights. Unlike the scenario uncertainty set model, which had over 1,000 constraints, the number of constraints in the ellipsoidal uncertainty set model is just 2, which are the maximum risk and full investment constraints.

From the problem summary table, we see that the worst-case return (0.059%) in the ellipsoidal uncertainty set model is much higher than in the scenario uncertainty model. The same improvement can be seen in the expected portfolio return (1.57%), which we calculated using the vector of mean asset returns. To achieve these improvements, the optimization sacrificed in the risk domain, with higher portfolio standard deviation and VaR estimates. However, the trade-off between these two components is clearly higher using the ellipsoidal uncertainty set than the scenario uncertainty set.

The main benefit of the ellipsoidal uncertainty set model is the significant improvement in diversification without a proportional loss in portfolio return. Just like the case of scenario uncertainty, the optimized portfolio is comprised mostly of defensive stocks but with a more diffuse allocation. In all of the optimization methods we examined, the solution we obtained from the ellipsoidal uncertainty set model is the least concentrated. The scenario uncertainty set model appears to be more conservative.

Output 9.9B: Optimal Portfolio Allocation from Robust Portfolio Optimization (Ellipsoidal Uncertainty)

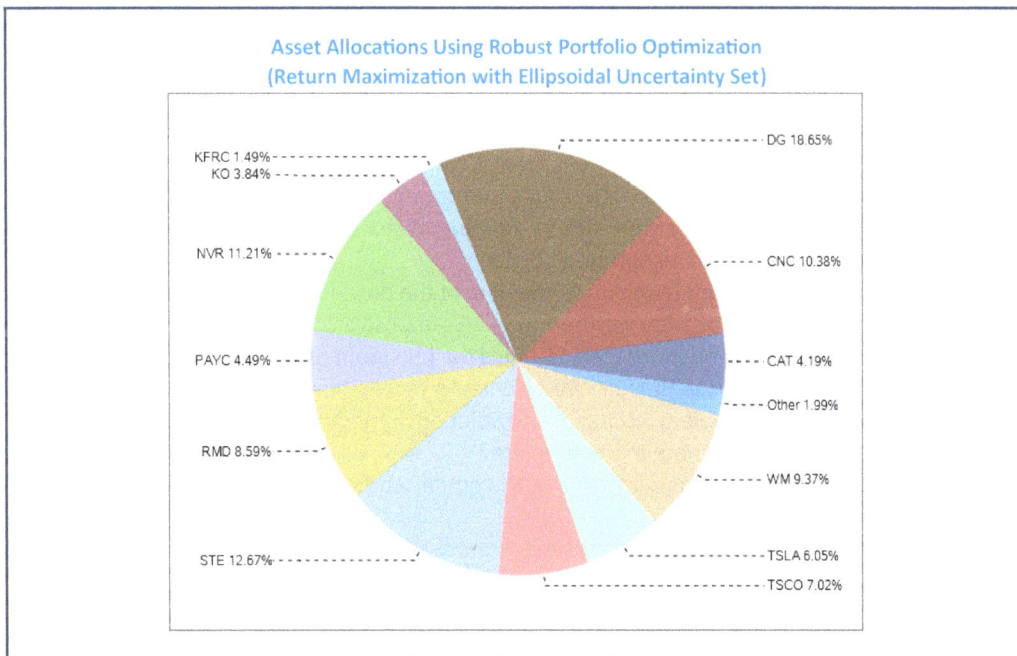

Asset Allocations Using Robust Portfolio Optimization
(Return Maximization with Ellipsoidal Uncertainty Set)

DG 18.65%
KFRC 1.49%
KO 3.84%
NVR 11.21%
CNC 10.38%
PAYC 4.49%
CAT 4.19%
Other 1.99%
RMD 8.59%
WM 9.37%
STE 12.67%
TSLA 6.05%
TSCO 7.02%

Machine Learning and Other Innovations in Portfolio Optimization

As we bring this chapter to a close, you should note that future updates to the OPTMODEL procedure will include support for conic optimization. This will allow us to solve benchmark-related optimizations such as maximizing portfolio alpha relative to the benchmark or minimizing tracking error relative to the same benchmark.

Another innovation in the portfolio optimization domain is the use of machine learning approaches such as regularized performance-based objective functions or constructing optimal portfolio weights using deep learning algorithms such as recurrent neural networks. In the regularized performance base optimization, the objective function is respecified to include a penalty function to account for utility loss from error in the estimation of the optimal portfolio weights. Examples of this approach include the least absolute shrinkage and selection operator (LASSO) method, in which the objective function of the mean-variance optimization is reformulated to include a penalty term that is specified as the L_1 norm of the vector of portfolio weights.[14] In the recurrent neural network approach to portfolio optimization, the algorithm attempts to learn the optimal portfolio weights that maximize the desired portfolio characteristics such as the Sharpe ratio in the next period. Starting from an initial guess of randomly selected weights, the algorithm iteratively optimizes the portfolio Sharpe ratio using the gradient descent method until a stopping criterion is met. The SAS program for these exciting innovations will be added to the book's GitHub page in a future update to the site.

Exercises

1. A portfolio manager would like to construct a minimum factor risk equity portfolio subject to a minimum return requirement. The factor risk of the portfolio is measured by beta. The SAS data set (STOCK_DATA) that contains the problem data for the portfolio optimization includes the stock tickers, number of shares, share prices, and the betas of the nine stocks in the concentrated portfolio.
   a. Write a SAS program to minimize the beta of the portfolio subject to a minimum return constraint of 1.5%. Furthermore, let's impose a constraint that the maximum allocation cannot be more than 11 times the minimum portfolio allocation. Also, remember to impose the full investment and short-selling constraints.
      i. Review the Problem Summary and Solution Summary tables. How many constraints are there in the problem?
      ii. What was the minimum value of the optimized function (lowest portfolio beta possible)?
      iii. Are the portfolio allocations typical or unusual?

---

[14] The L_1 norm of the vector portfolio weight w is calculated as the sum of the absolute values of the elements of the vector $\|w\| = \sum_{i=1}^{N} |w_i|$.

b. Let's modify the program to implement a risk parity optimization, where the risk budget is to allocate an equal amount of relative systematic risk to the nine stocks in the portfolio (that is, $\left(RB_i = \dfrac{1}{N} \right)$ where N=9). Because we are utilizing systematic risk, our relative systematic risk contribution is now a function of beta and should be calculated as: $RRC_i = \dfrac{w_i \beta_i}{\sum\limits_{i=1}^{N=9} w_i \beta_i}$.

   i. Compare the portfolio allocation to the allocations we obtained from the previous problem. Are the return and risk performance better?
   iii. Is the portfolio allocation more diversified or less diversified? Is the change in the portfolio beta consistent with better diversification or otherwise? What could be the reason for the inconsistency?

2. Let's revisit the mean-variance optimization (MVO) shown in Program 9.1. Write a SAS program to maximize the Sharpe ratio of our sample portfolio, subject to the full investment constraint and nonnegative bounds using the OPTMODEL procedure.
   a. Compare the portfolio allocation to the allocations obtained from the PROC IML version of the same optimization.
   b. Compare the portfolio allocation to the allocations we obtained from the return maximization and risk minimization problem.
   c. Remove the short-selling constraint, then reoptimize the portfolio.
      i. Did you obtain a better Sharpe ratio in terms of risk and return?
      ii. Did the portfolio allocation change significantly?
      iii. What could explain the change in the result between the optimization with the short-selling constraint and optimization with no short-selling constraint?

3. Modify the SAS code for the mean-variance optimization (MVO) shown in Program 9.1 from minimizing risk using portfolio standard deviation to minimizing risk using expected shortfall.
   a. Compare the portfolio allocation to the allocations we obtained from the return maximization and risk minimization problem.
   b. Compare the portfolio allocation to the allocations we obtained from the CVaR minimization problem.
   c. Now, modify the SAS code shown in Program 9.B. Change the objective function from minimizing CVaR to maximizing the portfolio return subject to the constraint that CVaR should not exceed 7.5%. Then compare the portfolio allocation to the allocations we obtained from the CVaR minimization problem.

4. Modify the SAS code for the robust mean-variance optimization (RMVO) shown in Program 9.9 from minimizing risk using an ellipsoidal uncertainty set to using a box uncertainty set. Set the uncertainty parameter to $\rho = 0.2$.

a. Compare the portfolio allocation to the allocations we obtained from the scenario uncertainty and ellipsoidal uncertainty set.
   i. Did the box uncertainty set improve on the return, risk, and diversification performance relative to the other approaches?
b. Change the uncertainty parameter to $\rho = 1$. Then reoptimize the problem.
   i. Did narrowing the range of uncertainty improve the performance of the optimization?
   ii. Why did narrowing the range change the performance of the model?

References

Amaro, S. (2018, December 5). Sell-offs could be down to machines that control 80% of the US stock market, fund manager says. CNBC.com. https://www.cnbc.com/2018/12/05/sell-offs-could-be-down-to-machines-that-control-80percent-of-us-stocks-fund-manager-says.html Retrieved: 08/09/2022.

Bacon, C.R, & Wright, M.A. (2019). Return Attribution, 2019 CIPM Program: Level 1 Volume 1. CFA Institute.

Balduzzi, Pierluigi, and Cesare Robotti. "Mimicking Portfolios, Economic Risk Premia, and Tests of Multi-Beta Models." Journal of Business & Economic Statistics 26, no. 3 (2008): 354–68. http://www.jstor.org/stable/27638994.

Barro, D., Consigli, G., & Varun, V. (2022). A stochastic programming model for dynamic portfolio management with financial derivatives. Journal of Banking & Finance, 140, 106445. doi:10.1016/j.jbankfin.2022.106445

Bartlett, R., Morse, A., Stanton, R., & Wallace, N. (2022). Consumer-lending discrimination in the FinTech era. Journal of Financial Economics, 143(1), 30-56. doi:10.1016/j.jfineco.2021.05.047

Bertsimas, D. & Sim, M. (2004). Robust discrete optimization under ellipsoidal uncertainty sets.

Bertsimas, D., & Brown, D. B. (2009). Constructing Uncertainty Sets for Robust Linear Optimization. Operations Research, 57(6), 1483–1495. http://www.jstor.org/stable/25614858

Bertsimas, D., Brown, D. B., & Caramanis, C. (2011). Theory and Applications of Robust Optimization. SIAM Review, 53(3), 464–501. http://www.jstor.org/stable/23070141

Black, F. (1989b). "Universal Hedging: Optimizing Currency Risk and Reward in International Equity Portfolios." Financial Analysts Journal, July/August,16-22.

Black, F. and Litterman, R. (1990). "Asset Allocation: Combining Investors Views with Market Equilibrium." Fixed Income Research, Goldman, Sachs & Company, September.

Black, F. and Litterman, R. (1991). "Global Asset Allocation with Equities, Bonds, and Currencies." Fixed Income Research, Goldman, Sachs & Company, October.

Bollerslev, T., Li, S., & Zhao, B. (2020). Good Volatility, Bad Volatility, and the Cross Section of Stock Returns. Journal of Financial and Quantitative Analysis, 55(3), 751-781. doi:10.1017/S0022109019000097

Brinson, G. P., & Fachler, N. (1985). Measuring non-US. equity portfolio performance. The Journal of Portfolio Management, 11(3), 73–76. https://doi.org/10.3905/jpm.1985.409005

Brinson, G. P., Hood, L. R., & Beebower, G. L. (1986). Determinants of portfolio performance. Financial Analysts Journal, 42(4), 39–44. https://doi.org/10.2469/faj.v42.n4.39

Butler, M. & Kazakov, D. (2011). The effects of variable stationarity in a financial time-series on Artificial Neural Networks. 1-8. 10.1109/CIFER.2011.5953557.

Clarke, R. De Silva, H., & Thorley, S. (2013). Risk Parity, Maximum Diversification, and Minimum Variance: An Analytic Perspective. The Journal of Portfolio Management, 39(3),39-53

Cochrane, J. H. (2010). Asset pricing. New Age International (P) Limited.

Cornuejols, G., Peña, J. F., & Tütüncü, R. (2018). Optimization methods in finance. Cambridge University Press.

Dixon, M.F, Halperin, I., & Bilokon P. (2000). Machine Learning in Finance. Springer Nature

Engle, Robert. (2001). GARCH 101: The Use of ARCH/GARCH Models in Applied Econometrics." Journal of Economic Perspectives, 15 (4): 157-168. DOI: 10.1257/jep.15.4.157

Freund, R. M. (2004). Duality Theory of Constrained Optimization. Massachusetts Institute of Technology.

Gearhart, J. (2020). End-to-End Data Science with SAS®: A Hands-On Programming Guide. Cary, NC. SAS Institute Inc.

Gerard, C. Goldfarb, D., & Iyengar, G.. (2003). Robust Portfolio Selection Problems. Mathematics of Operations Research, 28(1), 1–38. http://www.jstor.org/stable/4126989

Ghosh, S., & Resnick, S. (2010). A discussion on mean excess plots. Stochastic Processes and their Applications, 120(8), 1492-1517. doi:10.1016/j.spa.2010.04.002

Goldstein, M., & Flitter, E. (2023, March 13). Risky bet on crypto and a run on deposits tank Signature Bank. The New York Times. https://www.nytimes.com/2023/03/12/business/signature-bank-collapse.html

Gordon, S. (1997). Stochastic Trends, Deterministic Trends, and Business Cycle Turning Points. Journal of Applied Econometrics, 12(4), 411–434. http://www.jstor.org/stable/2284961

Gorissen, B. L., Yanıkoğlu, İ., & den Hertog, D. (2015). A practical guide to robust optimization. Omega, 53, 124-137. doi:10.1016/j.omega.2014.12.006

Hamilton, W. F., & Moses, M. A. (1973). An Optimization Model for Corporate Financial Planning. Operations Research, 21(3), 677–692. http://www.jstor.org/stable/169378

Hansen, B. E. (2017). Time series econometrics for the 21st Century. The Journal of Economic Education, 48(3), 137–145. https://doi.org/10.1080/00220485.2017.1320610

Harwell, D. (2018, February 18). A down day on the markets? Analysts say blame the machines. The Washington Post. https://www.washingtonpost.com/news/the-switch/wp/2018/02/06/algorithms-just-made-a-couple-crazy-trading-days-that-much-crazier/

Haugh, M. (2016). An Introduction to Copulas. In IEOR E4602: Quantitative Risk Management. Lecture Notes. New York: Columbia University.

Hayashi, F. (2000). Econometrics. Princeton University Press. Princeton, NJ

Heeler, R. M., Whipple, T. W., & Hustad, T. P. (1977). Maximum Likelihood Factor Analysis of Attitude Data. Journal of Marketing Research, 14(1), 42–51. https://doi.org/10.2307/3151053

Hosking, J. R. M., & Wallis, J. R. (1987). Parameter and Quantile Estimation for the Generalized Pareto Distribution. Technometrics, 29(3), 339–349. https://doi.org/10.2307/1269343

Huberman, G., Kandel, S., & Stambaugh, R. F. (1987). Mimicking Portfolios and Exact Arbitrage Pricing. The Journal of Finance, 42(1), 1–9. https://doi.org/10.2307/2328415

Hull, J. (2022). Options, futures, and other derivatives. Pearson.

Khokhlov, V. (2018). Conditional Value-at-Risk for Uncommon Distributions. Available at SSRN: https://ssrn.com/abstract=3200629 or http://dx.doi.org/10.2139/ssrn.3200629

Kim, W. C., Kim, J. H., & Fabozzi, F. J. (2014). Deciphering robust portfolios. Journal of Banking & Finance,

Levene, H. (1960). Robust Tests for the Equality of Variance. In Contributions to Probability and Statistics: Essays in Honor of Harold Hotelling, edited by I. Olkin, S. G. Ghurye, W. Hoeffding, W. G. Madow, and H. B. Mann, 278–292. Palo Alto, CA: Stanford University Press.

Li, A.X. (2013). Essentials of the Program Data Vector (PDV): Directing the Aim to Understanding the DATA Step! SAS Global Forum, 2013. SAS Institute Inc. Retrieved February 1, 2023, from https://support.sas.com/resources/papers/proceedings13/125-2013.pdf

Lopez de Prado, M. (2018). Advances in financial machine learning. John Wiley & Sons.

Malik, M., & Thomas, L. C. (2010). Modelling Credit Risk of Portfolio of Consumer Loans. The Journal of the Operational Research Society, 61(3), 411–420. http://www.jstor.org/stable/40540268

Nehemya, E., Mathov, Y., Shabtai, A., & Elovici, Y. (2020). Taking Over the Stock Market: Adversarial Perturbations Against Algorithmic Traders. ArXiv. /abs/2010.09246 .

Odening, M. & Hinrichs, J. (2003). Using extreme value theory to estimate Value-at-Risk. Agricultural Finance Review. 63. 55-73. 10.1108/00215000380001141.

Odusami, B. O (2022). The Relative Performance of Machine Learning and Predictive Algorithms in Equity Portfolio Strategies. Working Paper

Odusami, B. O. (2021). Forecasting the value-at-risk of REITs using realized volatility jump models. The North American Journal of Economics and Finance, 58, 101426. doi:10.1016/j.najef.2021.101426

Pisani, B. (2015, September 25). What happened during the Aug 24 'flash crash'. CNBC.COM. https://www.cnbc.com/2015/09/25/what-happened-during-the-aug-24-flash-crash.html

Pukthuanthong, K., Roll, R., Wang, J., & Zhang, T. (2019). A Toolkit for Factor-Mimicking Portfolios. SSRN Electronic Journal.

Romero-Ávila, D., & Usabiaga, C. (2007). Unit Root Tests, Persistence, and the Unemployment Rate of the U.S. States. Southern Economic Journal, 73(3), 698–716. http://www.jstor.org/stable/20111919

Sarykalin, S., Serraino, G., & Uryasev, S. (2008). Value-at-risk vs. conditional value-at-risk in risk management and optimization. State-of-the-art decision-making tools in the information-intensive age (pp. 270-294) INFORMS. doi:10.1287/educ.1080.0052 Retrieved from https://doi.org/10.1287/educ.1080.0052

SAS Institute Inc. (2016). Building and Solving Optimization Models with SAS® /OR Course Notes. Cary, NC: SAS Institute Inc.

SAS Institute Inc. (2016). Building and Solving Optimization Models with SAS® /OR Course Notes. Cary, NC: SAS Institute Inc.

SAS Institute Inc. (2016). SAS/GRAPH® 9.4: Reference, Fifth Edition. Cary, NC: SAS Institute Inc. Retrieved February 1, 2023, from https://documentation.sas.com/doc/en/pgmsascdc/9.4_3.5/graphref/titlepage.htm

SAS Institute Inc. (2016, June 16). "Estimating GARCH Model" SAS/ETS User Guide. Retrieved February 1, 2023, from https://support.sas.com/rnd/app/ets/examples/garchex/index.html

SAS Institute Inc. (2016, June 16). "The Copula Procedure" SAS/ETS® 15.1 User's Guide. Cary, NC: SAS Institute Inc. Retrieved February 1, 2023, from https://support.sas.com/rnd/app/ets/examples/garchex/index.html

SAS Institute Inc. (2016, June 16). "The Severity Procedure" SAS/ETS® 15.1 User's Guide. Cary, NC: SAS Institute Inc. Retrieved February 1, 2023, from https://support.sas.com/rnd/app/ets/examples/garchex/index.html

SAS Institute Inc. (2017). SAS/STAT® 14.3 User's Guide. Cary, NC: SAS Institute Inc. Retrieved February 1, 2023, from https://documentation.sas.com/doc/en/statcdc/14.3/statug/titlepage.htm

SAS Institute Inc. (2023). SAS® 9.4 SQL Procedure User's Guide, Fourth Edition. Cary, NC: SAS Institute Inc. Retrieved January 3, 2024, from https://documentation.sas.com/doc/en/pgmsascdc/9.4_3.5/sqlproc/titlepage.htm

SAS Institute Inc. (2023). SAS® Optimization: Mathematical Optimization Procedures. Cary, NC: SAS Institute Inc.

SAS Institute Inc.(2017). SAS Enterprise Miner 14.3: High-Performance Procedures. Cary, NC: SAS Institute Inc. Retrieved July 1, 2023, from https://documentation.sas.com/doc/en/pgmsascdc/9.4_3.3/emhpprcref/titlepage.htm

SAS Institute Inc.(2017). SAS/ETS® 15.1 User's Guide. Cary, NC: SAS Institute Inc. Retrieved July 1, 2023, from https://documentation.sas.com/doc/en/pgmsascdc/9.4_3.4/etsug/titlepage.htm

SAS Institute Inc.(2017). SAS/STAT 14.3 User's Guide: High-Performance Procedures. Cary, NC: SAS Institute Inc. Retrieved February 1, 2023, from https://documentation.sas.com/doc/en/pgmsascdc/9.4_3.3/stathpug/titlepage.htm

Sharma, P & Keighley, J. (2018). Application of heavy-tailed distribution using PROC IML, NLMIXED, and Severity. MWSUG. Conference Proceeding.

Sharpe, W. F. (1992). Asset Allocation: Management Style and Performance Measurement. Journal of Portfolio Management, 18, 7-19.http://dx.doi.org/10.3905/jpm.1992.409394

Stock, James, H., and Mark W. Watson. 2001. "Vector Autoregressions." Journal of Economic Perspectives, 15 (4): 101-115.

Sun, F.K., Lang, C.I., & Boning (2021). Adjusting for Autocorrelated Errors in Neural Networks for Time Series. Massachusetts Institute of Technology (MIT) Working Paper.

Sutradhar, B. C. (1986). On the Characteristic Function of Multivariate Student t-Distribution. The Canadian Journal of Statistics / La Revue Canadienne de Statistique, 14(4), 329–337. https://doi.org/10.2307/3315191

Walters, J. (2014). The Black-Litterman Model in Detail Available at SSRN: https://ssrn.com/abstract=1314585 or http://dx.doi.org/10.2139/ssrn.1314585

Welch, B. L. (1951). On the Comparison of Several Mean Values: An Alternative Approach. Biometrika 38:330–336.

Wicklin, R. (2013). Simulating Data with SAS. Cary, NC: SAS Institute Inc.

Wicklin, R. (2018, December 12). The essential guide to bootstrapping in SAS [web log]. Retrieved April 7, 2023, from https://blogs.sas.com/content/iml/2018/12/12/essential-guide-bootstrapping-sas.html.

Wicklin, R. (2018, November 14). Create and compare ROC curves for any predictive model [web log]. Retrieved July 17, 2023, from https://blogs.sas.com/content/iml/2018/11/14/compare-roc-curves-sas.html.

Wicklin, R. (2021, July 7). Simulate multivariate correlated data by using PROC COPULA in SAS [web log]. Retrieved April 7, 2023, from https://blogs.sas.com/content/iml/2021/07/07/proc-copula-sas.html.

Wigglesworth, R. (2019, January 9). Volatility: how 'algos' changed the rhythm of the market. Financial Times. https://www.ft.com/content/fdc1c064-1142-11e9-a581-4ff78404524e

Wooldridge, J.M. (2021). Introductory Econometrics: A Modern Approach. Cengage.

Wright, R. (2018). Interpreting Black-Box Machine Learning Models Using Partial Dependence and Individual Conditional Expectation Plots. 2018 SAS Global Forum. SAS Institute Inc.

Xia, K. Eberhardt, P., & Kastin, M. (2017). Get the Tangency Portfolio Using SAS/IML. SAS Global Forum Proceedings. Cary, NC: SAS Institute Inc.

Yadav, Y. (2015). How Algorithmic Trading Undermines Efficiency in Capital Markets. Vanderbilt Law Review, 68, 1607.

Yamani, E. and Rakowski, D. (2019), The Endogeneity of Trading Volume in Stock and Bond Returns: An Instrumental Variable Approach. Financial Review, 54: 303-344. https://doi.org/10.1111/fire.12182

Young, Z., & Steele, R. (2022). Empirical evaluation of performance degradation of machine learning-based predictive models – A case study in healthcare information systems. International Journal of Information Management Data Insights, 2(1), 100070. doi: https://doi.org/10.1016/j.jjimei.2022.100070

Zajko, M. (2022). Artificial intelligence, algorithms, and social inequality: Sociological contributions to contemporary debates. Sociology Compass, 16(3), e12962. https://doi.org/10.1111/soc4.12962

Zviot, E., (2011). Factor Models for Asset Returns. Lecture Handout. The University of Washington. Retrieved from https://faculty.washington.edu/ezivot/research/factormodellecture_handout.pdf